Insurance Statistics Yearbook

1992-1999

Annuaire des statistiques d'assurance

2001

ORGANISATION FOR ECONOMIC CO-OPERATION AND DEVELOPMENT

Pursuant to Article 1 of the Convention signed in Paris on 14th December 1960, and which came into force on 30th September 1961, the Organisation for Economic Co-operation and Development (OECD) shall promote policies designed:

- to achieve the highest sustainable economic growth and employment and a rising standard of living in Member countries, while maintaining financial stability, and thus to contribute to the development of the world economy;
- to contribute to sound economic expansion in Member as well as non-member countries in the process of economic development; and
- to contribute to the expansion of world trade on a multilateral, non-discriminatory basis in accordance with international obligations.

The original Member countries of the OECD are Austria, Belgium, Canada, Denmark, France, Germany, Greece, Iceland, Ireland, Italy, Luxembourg, the Netherlands, Norway, Portugal, Spain, Sweden, Switzerland, Turkey, the United Kingdom and the United States. The following countries became Members subsequently through accession at the dates indicated hereafter: Japan (28th April 1964), Finland (28th January 1969), Australia (7th June 1971), New Zealand (29th May 1973), Mexico (18th May 1994), the Czech Republic (21st December 1995), Hungary (7th May 1996), Poland (22nd November 1996), Korea (12th December 1996) and the Slovak Republic (14th December 2000). The Commission of the European Communities takes part in the work of the OECD (Article 13 of the OECD Convention).

ORGANISATION DE COOPÉRATION ET DE DÉVELOPPEMENT ÉCONOMIQUES

En vertu de l'article 1er de la Convention signée le 14 décembre 1960, à Paris, et entrée en vigueur le 30 septembre 1961, l'Organisation de Coopération et de Développement Économiques (OCDE) a pour objectif de promouvoir des politiques visant :

- à réaliser la plus forte expansion de l'économie et de l'emploi et une progression du niveau de vie dans les pays Membres, tout en maintenant la stabilité financière, et à contribuer ainsi au développement de l'économie mondiale ;
- à contribuer à une saine expansion économique dans les pays Membres, ainsi que les pays non membres, en voie de développement économique ;
- à contribuer à l'expansion du commerce mondial sur une base multilatérale et non discriminatoire conformément aux obligations internationales.

Les pays Membres originaires de l'OCDE sont : l'Allemagne, l'Autriche, la Belgique, le Canada, le Danemark, l'Espagne, les États-Unis, la France, la Grèce, l'Irlande, l'Islande, l'Italie, le Luxembourg, la Norvège, les Pays-Bas, le Portugal, le Royaume-Uni, la Suède, la Suisse et la Turquie. Les pays suivants sont ultérieurement devenus Membres par adhésion aux dates indiquées ci-après : le Japon (28 avril 1964), la Finlande (28 janvier 1969), l'Australie (7 juin 1971), la Nouvelle-Zélande (29 mai 1973), le Mexique (18 mai 1994), la République tchèque (21 décembre 1995), la Hongrie (7 mai 1996), la Pologne (22 novembre 1996), la Corée (12 décembre 1996) et la République slovaque (14 décembre 2000). La Commission des Communautés européennes participe aux travaux de l'OCDE (article 13 de la Convention de l'OCDE).

FOREWORD

This publication, the tenth in a series which is updated annually, contains time series of insurance statistics. It was compiled as part of the work by the OECD Insurance Committee and, more particularly, its Task Force on Insurance Statistics. It contains data collected from official bodies in OECD Member countries as well as Singapore which has an observer status at the OECD Insurance Committee, on the number of insurance companies and employees, insurance premiums and investments by insurance companies. Meanwhile, the scope of data collection has been expanded to include gross claims payments, gross operating expenses and commissions. The data relate to the period 1992-1999 and are broken down under numerous sub-headings.

This compilation has been prepared by the Directorate for Financial, Fiscal and Enterprise Affairs. However, it was made possible only by the close co-operation between the OECD and the various national bodies which collect data on insurance, and the work of the Task Force on Insurance Statistics. This work is published under the responsibility of the Secretary General of the OECD.

AVANT PROPOS

Cette publication, la dixième d'une série qui est mise à jour annuellement, contient des données chronologiques sur les statistiques d'assurance. Elle s'inscrit dans le cadre des travaux du Comité des assurances de l'OCDE, et plus particulièrement de son Groupe de réflexion sur les statistiques d'assurance. Elle contient des données collectées auprès des organismes officiels des pays Membres de l'OCDE ainsi que de Singapour qui a le statut d'observateur auprès du Comité des assurances de l'OCDE, sur le nombre de compagnies d'assurance et d'employés, les primes d'assurance et les investissements des compagnies d'assurance. Entre-temps, le champ de la collecte de données a été étendu et couvre les paiements bruts de sinistres, les dépenses brutes d'exploitation et les commissions. Ces données portent sur la période 1992-1999 et sont détaillées en nombreuses sous-rubriques.

Cette publication a été préparée par la Direction des affaires financières, fiscales et des entreprises. Cependant elle n'a pu être réalisée que grâce à une étroite coopération entre l'OCDE et les diverses administrations nationales chargées de la collecte des données statistiques en matière d'assurance, ainsi que grâce aux travaux du Groupe de réflexion sur les statistiques d'assurance. Elle est publiée sous la responsabilité du Secrétaire Général de l'OCDE.

TABLE OF CONTENTS

TABLE DES MATIÈRES

PARTIE III : DÉFINITIONS ET NOTES 253

INTRODUCTION

In November 1982, the OECD Insurance Committee constituted the Working Group on insurance statistics. Since then, the Working Group, which has been transformed in 1999 into the Task Force, has collected and analysed data on various insurance statistics, as well as discussed relevant methodologies.

As the qualitative and quantitative content of the statistical database has improved considerably over time, the Committee decided in November 1992 to issue a publication that would make the considerable body of information already collected available to the public at large. This publication is the ninth in a series which is updated annually.

This publication has the following three characteristics;

1. It covers major official insurance data from 1992 to 1999, obtained from all the governments of OECD countries as well as Singapore which has an observer status at the OECD Insurance Committee. (Exceptionally, data for the Czech Republic, Korea, Mexico, the Slovak Republic and Poland are available respectively since 1993, 1994, 1992, 1997 and 1993 only). The publication contains not only general information on insurance activities (number of companies, number of employees, gross premiums, net premiums etc.) but also data related to major trends of the international insurance industry such as the market share by foreign companies in each country, business written abroad, premiums in terms of risk destination (foreign or domestic risks), foreign and domestic investments. Meanwhile, the scope of data collection has been expanded to include gross claims payments, gross operating expenses and commissions.

2. In order to contribute to a better understanding of the insurance market, important insurance activity indicators (OECD market share, penetration, density, premiums per employee...) are included in the comparative tables. Some of these indicators are also shown in the graphs. With these indicators, the characteristics of insurance market can be more clearly perceived, in particular, in relation to national economic conditions.

3. In the comparative tables, a significant effort has been made to achieve comparability among OECD countries. Definitions, classifications, calculation methods, and units have been standardised as far as possible.

The publication has been prepared by the Directorate for Financial, Fiscal and Enterprises Affairs and is issued under the responsibility of the Secretary General of the Organisation. However, the collaboration with national administrations was essential to its achievement.

THE CONTENTS OF THE PUBLICATION

This publication consists of three main parts; comparative tables by indicators, statistical tables by country and notes and definitions relating to these tables.

Part I: Comparative Tables by Indicators

This part consists of tables by indicators, which reflect the most significant characteristics of the OECD insurance market. In most cases, the tables contain data of all OECD countries as well as aggregated "OECD", "EU15" (the 15 member countries of the European Union in 1995) and "NAFTA" data from 1992 to 1999, for the following categories: life insurance, non-life insurance and total. The premiums amounts are converted from national currencies into US dollar. Exchange rates used are an average for the reference year. Some of these indicators are also shown in the graphs.

1. Total Gross Premiums

    Gross premium, which represents total insurance premium written in the reporting country, is a major indicator of the importance of insurance industry in the economy of each country.

2. Market Share in the OECD (Direct Gross Premiums Basis)

    This indicator measures the importance of national insurance market of each OECD country as compared to the whole OECD insurance market.

3. Density of Insurance Industry

    This indicator is calculated by dividing direct gross premiums by the population and represents the average insurance spending per capita in a given country.

4. Penetration of Insurance Industry

    This is the ratio of direct gross premiums to Gross Domestic Product (GDP), which represents the relative importance of the insurance industry in the domestic economy.

5. Life Insurance Share

    This is the ratio of gross life insurance premium to total gross premium, which measures the relative importance of life insurance as compared to non-life insurance.

6. Premiums per Employee

    This indicator of the relative efficiency of a national insurance industry is calculated by dividing the direct gross premiums by the number of employees in insurance companies.

7. Retention Ratio

This is the ratio of net written premiums to total gross premiums. This ratio represents the proportion of retained business and thus, indirectly, the importance of reinsurance for domestic insurance companies.

8. Ratio of Reinsurance Accepted

This is calculated by dividing reinsurance accepted by total gross premiums and provides an indication of the significance of reinsurance accepted in the national insurance market.

9. Foreign Companies' Market Share in the Domestic Market

This figure describes the importance of foreign companies in the domestic insurance market and is measured through the following indicators :
a) Market share of "foreign-controlled companies" and "branches and agencies of foreign companies" in "total gross premiums".
b) Market share of "branches and agencies of foreign companies" in "total gross premiums".

Part II: Statistical tables by country

In this part, the main insurance statistics are presented through separate tables for each country following the order mentioned in the "complete list of items" reproduced in Part III. The premiums and the investment amounts are described in millions of the national currency unit. Figures refer to the calendar year. If all data concerning one line are not available, the line is deleted. The line is also deleted if all data are equal to "0" and if this is made obvious by reading other lines of the tables.

The tables of each country contain the following six parts;

(A and B)   General information on number of insurance companies and employees within the sector.

(C)   Business written in the reporting country on a gross and net premium basis. It contains a breakdown between domestic companies, foreign-controlled companies and branches and agencies of foreign companies.

(D)   Breakdown of net premiums written in the reporting country in terms of domestic risks and foreign risks, thus providing an indicator of direct cross-border operations of insurance business.

(E)   Premiums written abroad classified by subsidiaries, branches and agencies of domestic companies.

(F)   Outstanding investment by direct insurance companies, classified by investment category, by the companies' nationality and by its destination (domestic or foreign).

(G)   Breakdown of non-life insurance premiums by main non-life classification.

(H-J)   Gross claims payments, gross operating expenses and commissions in the reporting country, containing a breakdown between domestic companies, foreign-controlled companies and branches and agencies of foreign companies.

Part III: Definitions and Notes

This part covers the definitions of the main items used in the publication and the explanatory notes relating to the statistical tables.

1. Common Definitions and Notes

    This part includes definitions and notes that are common to all statistical tables.

2. Complete List of Items Contained in Tables by Country

    This list covers all items in tables by country and helps to understand which items are deleted in the tables of each country.

3. Definitions and Notes by Country

    This part is made of definitions and notes related only to the tables by country. After a paragraph on possible "General Remarks" and a paragraph on "Definition of Foreign Controlled Companies" this part follows the order of the sections of tables by country.

4. Definitions of Classes of Non-life Insurance

    This includes definitions of categories of non-life insurance, which detail the content of classes listed in section G "Others: breakdown of non-life premiums" of the tables by country.

DATA SOURCE

All the data in the statistical tables of each country have been reported by the relevant national insurance authorities. Regarding comparative tables of indicators, the data are mainly drawn from the tables by country mentioned above. The economic data on exchange rates, population and GDP are from the OECD MAIN ECONOMIC INDICATORS publication.

ABBREVIATIONS

The following abbreviations are used:

" - - ": not available.

INTRODUCTION

En novembre 1982, le Comité des assurances de l'OCDE a constitué un Groupe de Travail sur les statistiques. Depuis, le Groupe de travail, qui a été transformé en 1999 en groupe de réflexion, s'est consacré à la collecte et à l'analyse de données statistiques sur différents aspects de l'assurance, et à la discussion des méthodologies à adopter.

Face aux considérables améliorations, d'ordre tant qualitatif que quantitatif de la base de données statistiques, le Comité a décidé en novembre 1992 de diffuser une publication qui mettrait les très nombreuses informations déjà rassemblées à la disposition du grand public. Cette publication est la neuvième d'une nouvelle série qui sera mise à jour annuellement.

Cette publication possède les trois caractères suivants ;

1. Elle contient des données officielles majeures des assurances de 1992 à 1999, transmises par tous les gouvernements des pays de l'OCDE ainsi que par Singapour qui a le statut d'observateur auprès du Comité des assurances de l'OCDE. (Exceptionnellement, les données de la Corée, du Mexique, de la Pologne, de la République slovaque, de la République tchèque ne sont respectivement disponibles que depuis 1994, 1992, 1993, 1997 et 1993). La publication n'inclut pas seulement les informations générales sur les activités des assurances (nombre d'entreprises, effectifs, primes brutes, primes nettes...), mais également des indicateurs des grandes tendances du marché international de l'assurance comme les parts de marché des entreprises étrangères dans chacun des pays de l'OCDE, les opérations à l'étranger, la ventilation des primes en fonction de la destination des risques (risques dans le pays ou risques à l'étranger), les investissements dans le pays et à l'étranger. Entre-temps, le champ de la collecte de données a été étendu et couvre les paiements bruts de sinistres, les dépenses brutes d'exploitation et les commissions.

2. Pour contribuer à une meilleure compréhension du marché de l'assurance, les indicateurs importants des activités d'assurances (parts de marché dans les pays de l'OCDE, pénétration, densité, primes par employé ...) sont inclus dans les tableaux comparatifs. Certains de ces indicateurs sont également représentés par des graphiques. Grâce à ces indicateurs, les caractéristiques du marché de l'assurance peuvent être plus clairement perçues, en particulier par rapport aux conditions économiques nationales.

3. Dans les tableaux comparatifs, un effort important a été réalisé pour assurer la comparabilité des données entre les pays de l'OCDE. Définitions, classifications, modes de calcul et unités ont été standardisés autant que possible.

La publication a été préparée par la Direction des affaires financières, fiscales et des entreprises, et est diffusée sous la responsabilité du Secrétaire général de l'OCDE. Cependant, la collaboration avec les administrations nationales a été essentielle pour la réaliser.

LE CONTENU DE LA PUBLICATION

Cette publication se compose de trois parties principales ; tableaux comparatifs par indicateurs, tableaux statistiques par pays et notes et définitions relatives à ces tableaux.

Partie I : Tableaux comparatifs par indicateurs

Cette partie se compose de tableaux d'indicateurs qui reflètent les caractéristiques les plus significatives du marché de l'assurance de l'OCDE. Le plus souvent, les tableaux contiennent les données de tous les pays de l'OCDE, ainsi que les données "OCDE", "UE15" (les 15 pays membres de l'Union Européenne en 1995) et "ALENA" de 1992 à 1999, pour les catégories suivantes : assurance-vie, assurance non-vie et total des assurances. Les montants des primes sont convertis à partir de la monnaie nationale en dollar US. Les taux de change utilisés sont une moyenne sur l'année à laquelle il est fait référence. Certains de ces indicateurs sont également représentés par des graphiques.

1.   Total des primes brutes

Les primes brutes, qui représentent les primes totales des assurances émises dans le pays déclarant, sont un indicateur essentiel de l'importance de l'industrie de l'assurance dans chaque pays.

2.   Part de marché dans l'OCDE (sur la base des primes brutes directes)

Cet indicateur représente l'importance relative de l'assurance de chacun des pays de l'OCDE par rapport au marché de l'assurance dans l'ensemble de la zone de l'OCDE.

3.   Densité de l'industrie de l'assurance

Cet indicateur est calculé en divisant les primes brutes directes par la population nationale ; il représente les dépenses moyennes d'assurance par tête dans le pays considéré.

4.   Pénétration de l'industrie de l'assurance

C'est le rapport des primes brutes directes d'assurances sur le Produit Intérieur Brut (PIB) ; il représente l'importance de l'industrie de l'assurance dans l'économie nationale.

5.   Parts de l'assurance-vie

C'est le rapport des primes brutes d'assurance-vie sur les primes brutes totales ; il mesure l'importance relative de l'assurance-vie par rapport à l'assurance non-vie et vice-versa.

6.   Primes par employé

Cet indicateur de l'efficacité des effectifs dans l'industrie de l'assurance est calculé en faisant le rapport des primes brutes directes sur le nombre d'employés des entreprises d'assurances.

7. Taux de rétention

C'est le rapport entre les primes nettes émises et le total des primes brutes. Il représente la proportion des affaires retenues, et donc indirectement, l'importance de la réassurance pour les entreprises d'assurances nationales.

8. Taux de réassurance acceptée

C'est le rapport des réassurances acceptées sur les primes brutes totales ; il rend compte de l'importance de la réassurance acceptée dans le marché national des assurances.

9. Part du marché national détenue par les entreprises étrangères.

Elle mesure l'importance des entreprises étrangères dans le marché national des assureurs en fonction des indicateurs suivants :
a) Part de marché des "entreprises sous contrôle étranger" et "succursales et agences d'entreprises étrangères" dans le "total des primes brutes".
b) Part de marché des "succursales et agences d'entreprises étrangères" dans le "total des primes brutes".

Partie II: Tableaux statistiques par pays

Dans cette partie, les principales statistiques d'assurances sont présentées dans des tableaux séparés pour chaque pays suivant l'ordre indiqué dans la "liste complète de points" reproduite dans la partie III. Le montant des primes et des placements est inscrit en millions dans la monnaie nationale. Les chiffres correspondent à l'année civile. Si toutes les données d'une ligne sont "non disponibles", la ligne est supprimée. Elle l'est également si toutes les données sont égales à "0" et que ce résultat apparaît clairement à la lecture d'autres lignes.

Les tableaux par pays contiennent les six parties suivantes :

(A et B) Informations générales sur le nombre de compagnies d'assurances et le nombre d'employés.

(C) Chiffres concernant les opérations conclues dans le pays déclarant, sur la base des primes brutes et nettes. On distingue les entreprises nationales, les entreprises sous contrôle étranger et les agences et succursales d'entreprises étrangères.

(D) Ventilation des primes nettes émises dans le pays déclarant : risques nationaux et étrangers, fournissant un indicateur des opérations transfrontières des compagnies d'assurances.

(E) Primes émises à l'étranger par des filiales, succursales et agences d'entreprises nationales.

(F) Encours des placements des entreprises d'assurances directes dans le pays déclarant, classés par catégorie de placements, par nationalité des entreprises, ainsi que par destination des placements (dans le pays ou à l'étranger).

(G) Ventilation des primes d'assurances non-vie par catégories principales d'assurances non-vie.

(H-J) Paiements bruts des sinistres, dépenses brutes d'exploitation et commissions dans le pays déclarant, avec une ventilation entre les entreprises nationales, les entreprises sous contrôle étranger et les succursales et agences d'entreprises étrangères.

Partie III: Définitions et notes

Cette partie contient les définitions des points principaux utilisés dans la publication et les notes relatives aux tableaux statistiques.

1.   Définitions et notes communes

Cette partie inclut les définitions et notes communes à tous les tableaux statistiques.

2.   Liste complète des points contenus dans les tableaux par pays

Cette liste couvre tous les points des tableaux par pays et permet d'identifier ceux qui ont été supprimés dans les tableaux de chaque pays.

3.   Définitions et notes par pays

Cette partie se compose des définitions qui se rapportent uniquement aux tableaux par pays. Après un paragraphe contenant d'éventuelles "Remarques générales" et un paragraphe relatif à la "Définition d'entreprises sous contrôle étranger", cette partie suit l'ordre des sections des tableaux par pays.

4.   Définitions relatives aux branches des assurances non-vie

Cette partie inclut les définitions des catégories d'assurance non-vie qui détaillent le contenu des branches dans la section G : "Autres : ventilation des primes non vie" des tableaux par pays.

SOURCES DES DONNÉES

Toutes les données des tableaux chronologiques statistiques par pays ont été fournies par les autorités d'assurances nationales compétentes.

Concernant les tableaux comparatifs chronologiques d'indicateurs, les données sont, en principe, extraites des tableaux par pays mentionnés ci-dessus. Les données économiques utilisées (taux de change, population et PIB) sont extraites de la publication de l'OCDE : PRINCIPAUX INDICATEURS ÉCONOMIQUES.

ABRÉVIATIONS

L'abréviation suivante a été utilisée :

" - -" : non-disponible.

PART I

PARTIE I

COMPARATIVE TABLES

TABLEAUX COMPARATIFS

Market share in OECD - Total / Part de marché dans l'OCDE - Total

1999

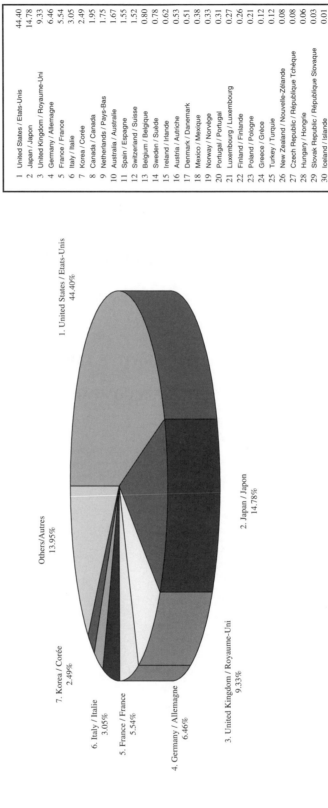

1	United States / États-Unis	44.40
2	Japan / Japon	14.78
3	United Kingdom / Royaume-Uni	9.33
4	Germany / Allemagne	6.46
5	France / France	5.54
6	Italy / Italie	3.05
7	Korea / Corée	2.49
8	Canada / Canada	1.95
9	Netherlands / Pays-Bas	1.75
10	Australia / Australie	1.67
11	Spain / Espagne	1.55
12	Switzerland / Suisse	1.52
13	Belgium / Belgique	0.80
14	Sweden / Suède	0.78
15	Ireland / Irlande	0.62
16	Austria / Autriche	0.53
17	Denmark / Danemark	0.51
18	Mexico / Mexique	0.38
19	Norway / Norvège	0.33
20	Portugal / Portugal	0.31
21	Luxembourg / Luxembourg	0.27
22	Finland / Finlande	0.26
23	Poland / Pologne	0.21
24	Greece / Grèce	0.12
25	Turkey / Turquie	0.12
26	New Zealand / Nouvelle-Zélande	0.08
27	Czech Republic / République Tchèque	0.08
28	Hungary / Hongrie	0.06
29	Slovak Republic / République Slovaque	0.03
30	Iceland / Islande	0.01

Market share in OECD - Life / Part de marché dans l'OCDE - Vie

1999

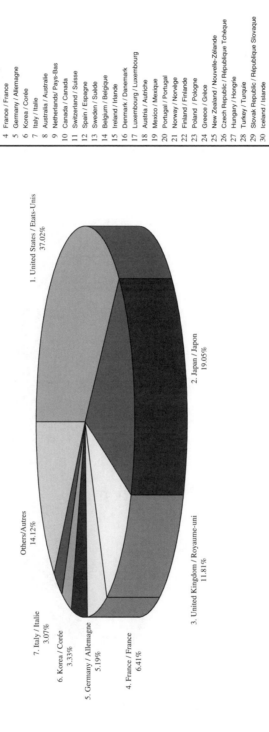

1	United States / Etats-Unis	37.02
2	Japan / Japon	19.05
3	United kingdom / Royaume-Uni	11.81
4	France / France	6.41
5	Germany / Allemagne	5.19
6	Korea / Corée	3.33
7	Italy / Italie	3.07
8	Australia / Australie	1.99
9	Netherlands/ Pays-Bas	1.77
10	Canada / Canada	1.69
11	Switzerland / Suisse	1.67
12	Spain / Espagne	1.43
13	Sweden / Suède	0.92
14	Belgium / Belgique	0.86
15	Ireland / Irlande	0.80
16	Denmark / Danemark	0.57
17	Luxembourg / Luxembourg	0.41
18	Austria / Autriche	0.41
19	Mexico / Mexique	0.32
20	Portugal / Portugal	0.31
21	Norway / Norvège	0.27
22	Finland / Finlande	0.27
23	Poland / Pologne	0.12
24	Greece / Grèce	0.12
25	New Zealand / Nouvelle-Zélande	0.06
26	Czech Republic / République Tchèque	0.05
27	Hungary / Hongrie	0.04
28	Turkey / Turquie	0.03
29	Slovak Republic / République Slovaque	0.02
30	Iceland / Islande	0.00

Market share in OECD - Non-Life / Part de marché dans l'OCDE - Non-Vie

1999

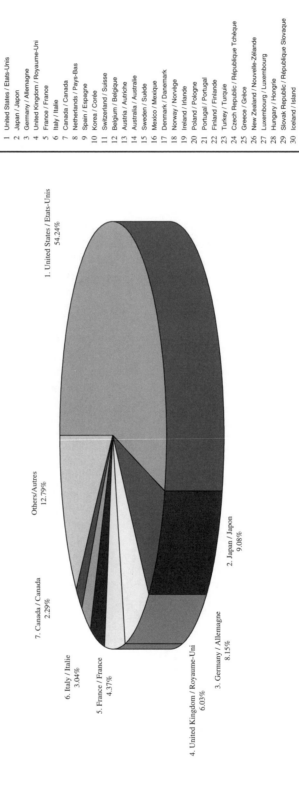

1	United States / Etats-Unis	54.24
2	Japan / Japon	9.08
3	Germany / Allemagne	8.15
4	United Kingdom / Royaume-Uni	6.03
5	France / France	4.37
6	Italy / Italie	3.04
7	Canada / Canada	2.29
8	Netherlands / Pays-Bas	1.73
9	Spain / Espagne	1.71
10	Korea / Corée	1.37
11	Switzerland / Suisse	1.32
12	Belgium / Belgique	0.74
13	Austria / Autriche	0.69
14	Australia / Australie	0.69
15	Sweden / Suède	0.60
16	Mexico / Mexique	0.45
17	Denmark / Danemark	0.44
18	Norway / Norvège	0.41
19	Ireland / Irlande	0.38
20	Poland / Pologne	0.33
21	Portugal / Portugal	0.31
22	Finland / Finlande	0.26
23	Turkey / Turquie	0.23
24	Czech Republic / République Tchèque	0.13
25	Greece / Grèce	0.13
26	New Zealand / Nouvelle-Zélande	0.10
27	Luxembourg / Luxembourg	0.08
28	Hungary / Hongrie	0.08
29	Slovak Republic / République Slovaque	0.04
30	Iceland / Island	0.02

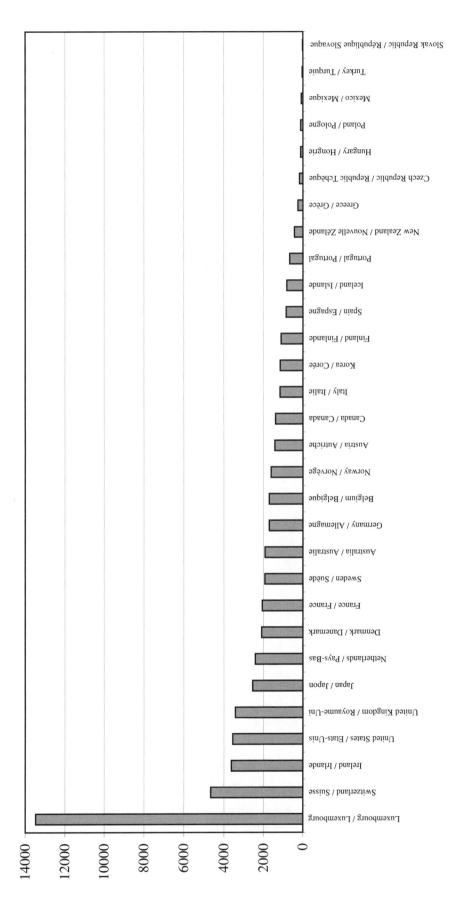

Premiums per capita - Total / Primes par tête - Total (1999)

Luxembourg / Luxembourg	
Switzerland / Suisse	
Ireland / Irlande	
United States / Etats-Unis	
United Kingdom / Royaume-Uni	
Japan / Japon	
Netherlands / Pays-Bas	
Denmark / Danemark	
France / France	
Sweden / Suède	
Australia / Australie	
Germany / Allemagne	
Belgium / Belgique	
Norway / Norvège	
Austria / Autriche	
Canada / Canada	
Italy / Italie	
Korea / Corée	
Finland / Finlande	
Spain / Espagne	
Iceland / Islande	
Portugal / Portugal	
New Zealand / Nouvelle Zélande	
Greece / Grèce	
Czech Republic / République Tchèque	
Hungary / Hongrie	
Poland / Pologne	
Mexico / Mexique	
Turkey / Turquie	
Slovak Republic / République Slovaque	

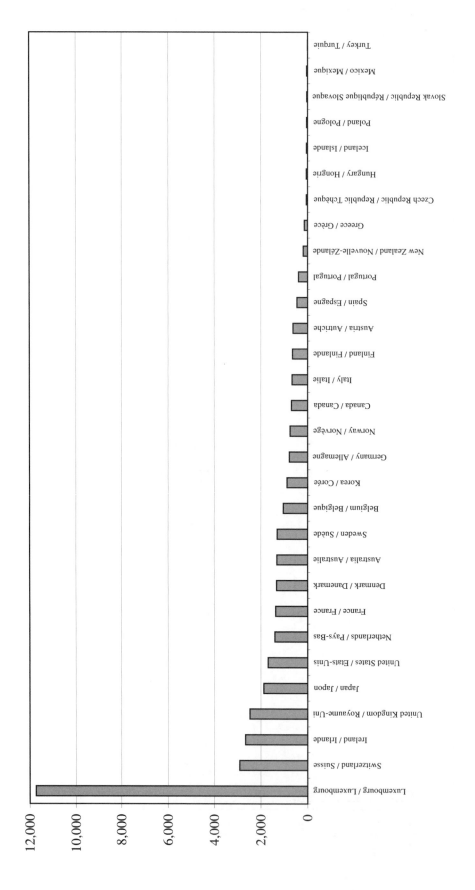

Premiums per capita - Life / Primes par tête - Vie (1999)

Turkey / Turquie
Mexico / Mexique
Slovak Republic / République Slovaque
Poland / Pologne
Iceland / Islande
Hungary / Hongrie
Czech Republic / Republic Tchèque
Greece / Grèce
New Zealand / Nouvelle-Zélande
Portugal / Portugal
Spain / Espagne
Austria / Autriche
Finland / Finlande
Italy / Italie
Canada / Canada
Norway / Norvège
Germany / Allemagne
Korea / Corée
Belgium / Belgique
Sweden / Suède
Australia / Australie
Denmark / Danemark
France / France
Netherlands / Pays-Bas
United States / Etats-Unis
Japan / Japon
United Kingdom / Royaume-Uni
Ireland / Irlande
Switzerland / Suisse
Luxembourg / Luxembourg

0
2,000
4,000
6,000
8,000
10,000
12,000

Premiums per capita - Non-Life / Primes par tete - Non-Vie (1999)

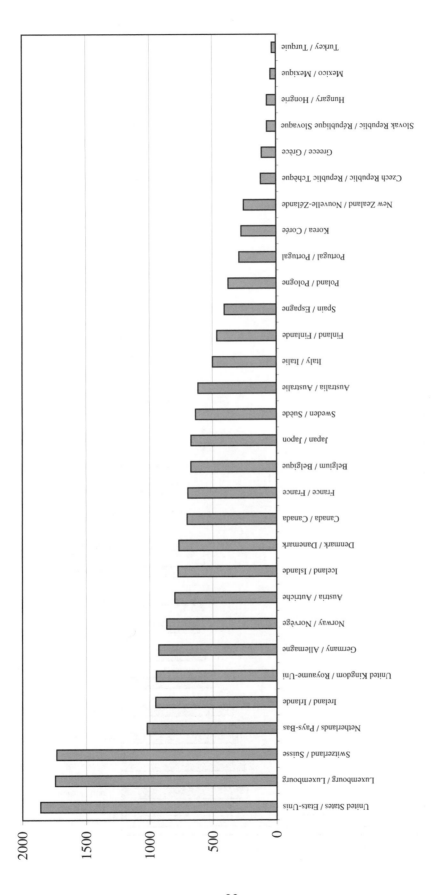

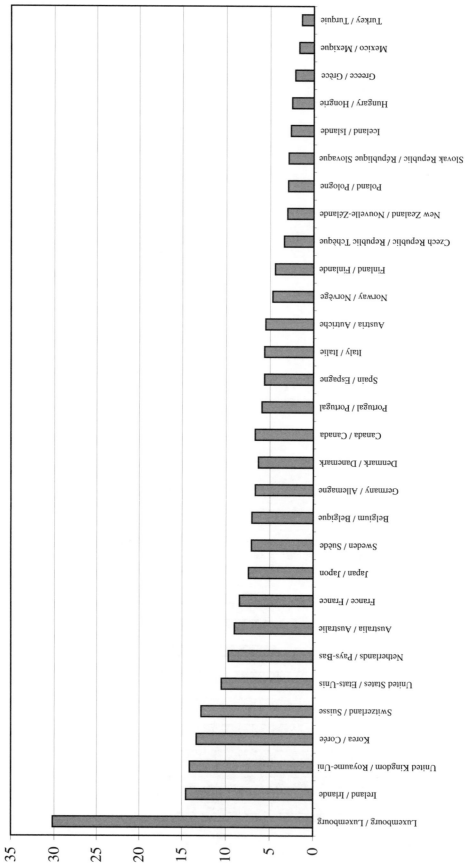

Premiums/GDP - Total/Primes/PIB - Total (1999)

% (per cent / pourcent)

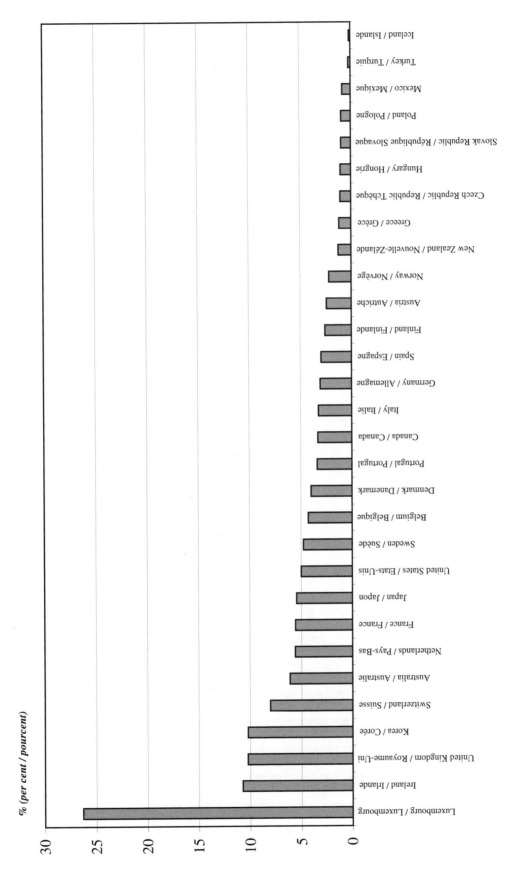

Premiums/GDP - Total/Primes/PIB - Vie (1999)

Premiums/GDP - Total/Primes/PIB - Non-Vie (1999)

% (per cent / pourcent)

United States / Etats-Unis	
Switzerland / Suisse	
Netherlands / Pays-Bas	
United Kingdom / Royaume-Uni	
Luxembourg / Luxembourg	
Ireland / Irlande	
Germany / Allemagne	
Canada / Canada	
Korea / Corée	
Austria / Autriche	
Australia / Australie	
France / France	
Belgium / Belgique	
Spain / Espagne	
Portugal / Portugal	
Norway / Norvège	
Iceland / Islande	
Italy / Italie	
Czech Republic / Republic Tchèque	
Sweden / Suède	
Denmark / Danemark	
Poland / Pologne	
Japan / Japon	
Slovak Republic / République Slovaque	
Finland / Finlande	
New Zealand / Nouvelle-Zélande	
Hungary / Hongrie	
Turkey / Turquie	
Greece / Grèce	
Mexico / Mexique	

Life and non-life insurance / Part de l'assurance-vie et non-vie (1999)

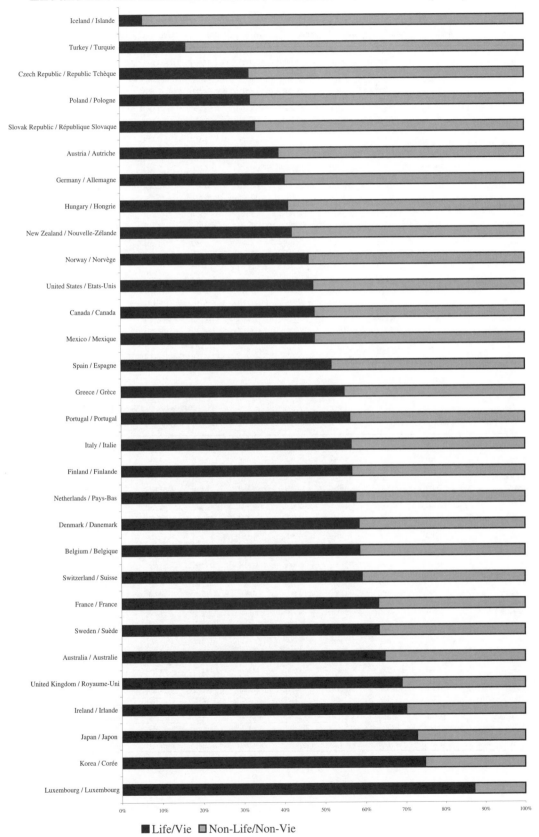

■ Life/Vie ■ Non-Life/Non-Vie

I. Total Gross premiums / Primes brutes totales

I.1 Total /Total

Million U.S. $ / Millions de $ U.S.

COUNTRY	1992	1993	1994	1995	1996	1997	1998	1999	PAYS
Australia[1]	19 254	27 187	30 604	29 449	32 659	37 302	34 569	39 497	Australie[1]
Austria	10 341	11 024	12 120	14 240	16 013	12 844	12 860	13 229	Autriche
Belgium	11 594	11 378	12 349	15 458	15 813	14 743	16 861	18 329	Belgique
Canada	31 940	28 033	28 758	30 083	30 232	29 914	28 100	47 157	Canada
Czech Republic	..	788	1 031	1 273	1 515	1 513	1 724	1 815	République Tchèque
Denmark	8 317	8 109	9 758	11 376	12 332	11 700	12 961	12 099	Danemark
Finland	7 414	2 665	3 115	4 474	5 319	4 658	5 242	5 924	Finlande
France	99 451	107 304	119 249	142 123	149 294	139 333	122 619	129 163	France
Germany	144 623	151 150	168 412	200 200	196 995	177 621	177 416	181 376	Allemagne
Greece	1 429	1 525	1 655	1 925	2 194	2 143	2 270	2 720	Grèce
Hungary	748	812	895	947	1 008	1 066	1 154	1 214	Hongrie
Iceland	275	230	228	237	234	217	226	244	Islande
Ireland	4 741	4 685	4 984	5 680	6 825	8 269	10 735	14 386	Irlande
Italy	43 426	37 095	38 943	42 654	48 245	52 001	61 943	71 204	Italie
Japan	316 151	372 829	406 604	448 384	376 514	344 074	300 649	328 617	Japon
Korea	..	..	44 450	58 488	63 815	61 705	48 580	55 694	Corée
Luxembourg[2]	562	528	1 582	4 156	3 631	4 811	5 505	5 841	Luxembourg[2]
Mexico	5 127	6 027	6 307	3 882	4 217	5 195	6 473	8 414	Mexique
Netherlands	26 789	26 647	29 911	36 502	37 118	34 654	37 970	39 154	Pays-Bas
New Zealand	1 603	1 489	1 688	1 854	2 528	2 611	2 040	1 667	Nouvelle Zélande
Norway[3]	6 659	5 996	6 388	6 850	6 979	7 255	7 227	7 264	Norvège[3]
Poland	..	1 707	1 824	2 302	3 038	3 757	4 464	4 663	Pologne
Portugal	3 242	3 322	3 632	4 856	5 585	5 100	6 003	6 927	Portugal
Slovak Republic	..	..	..	..	..	508	608	574	République Slovaque
Spain	24 671	21 640	25 703	27 971	30 378	28 527	29 698	35 324	Espagne
Sweden[4]	16 404	12 329	13 064	14 386	15 667	14 638	15 111	18 295	Suède[4]
Switzerland	32 658	33 723	37 985	45 444	38 963	34 713	36 491	35 680	Suisse
Turkey	1 216	1 564	1 084	1 394	1 591	1 883	2 142	2 632	Turquie
United Kingdom[5]	148 254	138 604	138 100	140 298	148 610	165 969	191 170	215 195	Royaume-Uni[5]
United States	654 071	705 008	731 673	763 639	795 115	891 694	994 961	1 055 045	Etats-Unis
N.A.F.T.A.[6]	691 138	739 067	766 738	797 605	829 564	926 804	1 029 534	1 110 616	N.A.F.T.A.[6]
EU15[6]	551 260	538 005	582 578	666 299	694 017	677 010	708 365	769 166	UE15[6]
O.E.C.D.[6]	1 620 960	1 723 397	1 882 097	2 060 526	2 052 423	2 100 417	2 177 772	2 359 343	O.C.D.E.[6]

I.2 Life / Vie

Million U.S. $ / Millions de $ U.S.

COUNTRY	1992	1993	1994	1995	1996	1997	1998	1999	PAYS
Australia[1]	13 202	16 063	16 727	15 328	16 087	21 651	22 457	25 530	Australie[1]
Austria	2 879	3 480	3 592	4 655	6 315	4 217	4 595	5 142	Autriche
Belgium	3 809	3 965	4 838	6 250	6 920	7 113	9 304	10 737	Belgique
Canada	14 217	10 776	15 686	16 799	11 239	10 872	9 999	22 454	Canada
Czech Republic	..	203	259	352	403	393	467	572	République Tchèque
Denmark	3 199	3 640	4 629	5 785	6 744	6 620	7 660	7 068	Danemark
Finland	4 539	490	742	1 643	2 587	2 196	2 579	3 359	Finlande
France	51 646	59 246	71 505	86 344	93 229	90 346	74 104	81 460	France
Germany	51 585	53 599	59 918	71 564	72 231	66 137	68 201	73 224	Allemagne
Greece	689	706	786	921	1 032	1 050	1 144	1 493	Grèce
Hungary	133	172	229	282	321	351	429	500	Hongrie
Iceland	7	7	8	9	8	9	10	13	Islande
Ireland	2 599	2 651	2 666	2 977	3 850	4 976	7 083	10 066	Irlande
Italy	12 436	11 336	12 995	15 699	18 639	23 526	31 656	40 272	Italie
Japan	233 121	273 375	298 246	327 029	269 751	250 922	220 314	238 798	Japon
Korea	..	..	33 436	43 723	46 353	44 146	36 755	41 563	Corée
Luxembourg[2]	181	169	1 150	3 649	3 083	4 348	4 751	5 083	Luxembourg[2]
Mexico	1 695	1 965	2 137	1 269	1 419	1 854	2 880	4 010	Mexique
Netherlands	14 393	13 754	15 213	19 445	20 040	19 239	21 930	22 584	Pays-Bas
New Zealand	628	639	735	659	869	932	698	702	Nouvelle Zélande
Norway	2 557	2 236	2 729	2 981	3 065	3 565	3 522	3 360	Norvège
Poland	..	489	565	634	869	1 040	1 297	1 484	Pologne
Portugal	930	1 032	1 251	2 092	2 604	2 317	3 006	3 896	Portugal
Slovak Republic	..	..	..	..	..	137	179	190	République Slovaque
Spain	7 976	6 950	10 809	11 080	12 968	13 121	13 718	18 264	Espagne
Sweden	7 713	5 758	7 047	7 899	8 963	8 502	9 478	11 559	Suède
Switzerland	13 328	14 098	16 641	21 981	22 826	21 671	24 520	21 087	Suisse
Turkey	229	226	130	178	232	297	362	423	Turquie
United Kingdom[5]	76 721	74 823	74 527	75 753	86 908	101 279	123 328	148 219	Royaume-Uni[5]
United States	240 904	267 026	277 744	294 353	315 538	338 343	400 688	499 628	Etats-Unis
N.A.F.T.A.[6]	256 816	279 767	295 567	312 420	328 197	351 069	413 567	526 092	N.A.F.T.A.[6]
EU15[6]	241 293	241 598	271 667	315 757	346 112	354 986	382 538	442 427	UE15[6]
O.E.C.D.[6]	761 315	828 873	936 938	1 041 333	1 035 093	1 051 168	1 107 115	1 302 741	O.C.D.E.[6]

I. Total Gross premiums / Primes brutes totales

I.3 Non-Life / Non-Vie									
								Million U.S. $ / Millions de $ U.S.	
COUNTRY	1992	1993	1994	1995	1996	1997	1998	1999	PAYS
Australia	6 052	11 123	13 877	14 121	16 572	15 651	12 112	13 967	Australie
Austria	7 462	7 544	8 528	9 585	9 698	8 627	8 265	8 087	Autriche
Belgium	7 785	7 413	7 511	9 208	8 893	7 631	7 557	7 592	Belgique
Canada	17 723	17 257	13 072	13 285	18 993	19 042	18 101	24 703	Canada
Czech Republic	..	585	772	921	1 112	1 120	1 256	1 243	République Tchèque
Denmark	5 118	4 469	5 128	5 591	5 588	5 080	5 301	5 031	Danemark
Finland	2 875	2 175	2 373	2 832	2 732	2 462	2 662	2 564	Finlande
France	47 805	48 058	47 744	55 778	56 064	48 987	48 516	47 703	France
Germany	93 039	97 550	108 495	128 636	124 764	111 485	109 216	108 152	Allemagne
Greece	740	819	870	1 004	1 161	1 093	1 127	1 226	Grèce
Hongary	614	640	666	665	687	715	726	714	Hongrie
Iceland	267	223	220	228	225	208	215	230	Islande
Ireland	2 141	2 034	2 319	2 703	2 974	3 293	3 653	4 320	Irlande
Italy	30 990	25 759	25 948	26 955	29 606	28 475	30 287	30 932	Italie
Japan	83 031	99 454	108 358	121 355	106 763	93 152	80 335	89 818	Japon
Korea	..	..	11 014	14 765	17 462	17 560	11 825	14 132	Corée
Luxembourg[2]	381	359	432	507	548	463	754	758	Luxembourg[2]
Mexico	3 432	4 061	4 170	2 614	2 797	3 342	3 593	4 404	Mexique
Netherlands	12 396	12 893	14 698	17 057	17 078	15 415	16 040	16 570	Pays-Bas
New Zealand	975	850	953	1 196	1 659	1 679	1 342	966	Nouvelle Zélande
Norway[3]	4 102	3 760	3 659	3 868	3 914	3 690	3 704	3 905	Norvège[3]
Poland	..	1 218	1 259	1 668	2 169	2 717	3 167	3 179	Pologne
Portugal	2 313	2 290	2 381	2 764	2 981	2 783	2 997	3 031	Portugal
Slovak Republic	..	..	..	..	..	371	429	384	Republique Slovaque
Spain	16 695	14 690	14 894	16 891	17 410	15 406	15 980	17 060	Espagne
Sweden[4]	8 692	6 571	6 017	6 487	6 704	6 136	5 632	6 736	Suède[4]
Switzerland	19 330	19 625	21 344	23 463	16 137	13 041	11 971	14 593	Suisse
Turkey	987	1 338	954	1 216	1 358	1 586	1 780	2 210	Turquie
United Kingdom	71 534	63 782	63 573	64 545	61 702	64 689	67 841	66 976	Royaume-Uni
United States	413 167	437 982	453 929	469 286	479 577	553 351	594 274	555 417	Etats-Unis
N.A.F.T.A.[6]	434 322	459 300	471 171	485 184	501 367	575 735	615 968	584 524	N.A.F.T.A.[6]
EU15[6]	309 967	296 407	310 911	350 542	347 905	322 024	325 827	326 739	UE15[6]
O.E.C.D.[9]	859 645	894 524	945 159	1 019 193	1 017 330	1 049 249	1 070 657	1 056 602	O.C.D.E.[9]

1. Net written premiums basis for life for 1994 and 1995 / Sur la base des primes nettes émises pour l'assurance vie pour 1994 et 1995

2. Direct gross premiums basis until 1993 / Sur la base des primes brutes directes jusqu'à 1993

3. Without branches of foreign insurers for non-life for 1994 and 1995 / Sans les succursales des assureurs étrangers pour l'assurance non-vie pour les années 1994 et 1995.

4. Without branches of foreign insurers for non-life until 1996 and for 1999/ Sans les succursales des assureurs étrangers pour l'assurance non-vie jusqu'à 1996 et pour 1999.

5. Net written premiums basis for life until 1992/ Sur la base des primes nettes émises pour l'assurance-vie jusqu'à 1992.

6. For available data only / Uniquement pour les données disponibles

II. Market share in O.E.C.D. (Direct gross premiums basis) / Part de marché dans l'O.C.D.E. (Sur la base des primes brutes directes)

II.1 Total / Total

COUNTRY	1992	1993	1994	1995	1996	1997	1998	1999	PAYS
Australia[1]	1.24	1.65	1.64	1.46	1.61	1.84	1.65	1.67	Australie[1]
Austria	0.64	0.64	0.61	0.68	0.75	0.57	0.57	0.53	Autriche
Belgium	0.75	0.70	0.70	0.77	0.79	0.72	0.81	0.80	Belgique
Canada	1.91	1.57	1.46	1.42	1.40	1.34	1.22	1.95	Canada
Czech Republic	..	0.05	0.06	0.07	0.08	0.08	0.09	0.08	République Tchèque
Denmark	0.47	0.46	0.49	0.55	0.60	0.56	0.60	0.51	Danemark
Finland	0.48	0.15	0.17	0.22	0.27	0.23	0.25	0.26	Finlande
France	6.00	6.10	6.39	6.99	7.39	6.71	5.73	5.54	France
Germany	7.82	7.65	7.67	8.39	8.24	7.10	6.95	6.46	Allemagne
Greece	0.10	0.09	0.09	0.10	0.11	0.11	0.11	0.12	Grèce
Hungary	0.05	0.05	0.05	0.05	0.05	0.05	0.06	0.06	Hongrie
Iceland	0.02	0.01	0.01	0.01	0.01	0.01	0.01	0.01	Islande
Ireland	0.29	0.28	0.28	0.29	0.35	0.39	0.51	0.62	Irlande
Italy	2.50	2.04	2.00	2.02	2.29	2.41	2.86	3.05	Italie
Japan	20.95	23.26	23.08	23.26	19.55	17.31	14.75	14.78	Japon
Korea	..	..	2.51	3.03	3.29	3.09	2.38	2.49	Corée
Luxembourg	0.04	0.03	0.09	0.22	0.19	0.25	0.27	0.27	Luxembourg
Mexico	0.33	0.37	0.35	0.20	0.21	0.26	0.32	0.38	Mexique
Netherlands[2]	1.74	1.59	1.63	1.87	1.91	1.74	1.86	1.75	Pays-Bas[2]
New Zealand[3,4]	0.11	0.09	0.09	0.09	0.13	0.13	0.10	0.08	Nouvelle Zélande[3,4]
Norway[5,6]	0.43	0.36	0.36	0.36	0.37	0.37	0.36	0.33	Norvège[5,6]
Poland[7,8]	..	0.08	0.08	0.12	0.16	0.19	0.22	0.21	Pologne[7,8]
Portugal	0.22	0.21	0.21	0.25	0.29	0.26	0.29	0.31	Portugal
Slovak Republic	..	..	..	..	..	0.03	0.03	0.03	Republique Slovaque
Spain	1.61	1.32	1.43	1.43	1.55	1.41	1.44	1.55	Espagne
Sweden	0.93	0.73	0.67	0.67	0.75	0.68	0.70	0.78	Suède
Switzerland	1.42	1.37	1.46	1.69	1.74	1.56	1.66	1.52	Suisse
Turkey	0.08	0.10	0.06	0.07	0.08	0.10	0.11	0.12	Turquie
United Kingdom[9]	9.11	7.92	7.10	6.80	7.36	8.04	8.96	9.33	Royaume-Uni[9]
United States	40.79	41.12	39.26	36.93	38.47	42.49	45.14	44.40	Etats-Unis
NAFTA[10]	43.03	43.05	41.07	38.55	40.09	44.09	46.68	46.72	ALENA[10]
EU-15[10]	32.68	29.92	29.53	31.26	32.84	31.16	31.91	31.91	UE-15[10]

II.2 Life / Vie

COUNTRY	1992	1993	1994	1995	1996	1997	1998	1999	PAYS
Australia[1]	2.47	2.02	1.85	1.53	1.61	2.10	2.11	1.99	Australie[1]
Austria	0.39	0.44	0.39	0.46	0.63	0.41	0.43	0.41	Autriche
Belgium	0.51	0.50	0.53	0.62	0.69	0.69	0.88	0.86	Belgique
Canada	1.86	1.32	1.64	1.58	1.05	0.98	0.86	1.69	Canada
Czech Republic	..	0.03	0.03	0.04	0.04	0.04	0.04	0.05	République Tchèque
Denmark	0.43	0.46	0.51	0.58	0.68	0.65	0.73	0.57	Danemark
Finland	0.62	0.06	0.08	0.16	0.26	0.21	0.24	0.27	Finlande
France	6.77	7.25	7.70	8.39	9.19	8.72	6.92	6.41	France
Germany	6.34	6.12	5.96	6.43	6.51	5.78	5.77	5.19	Allemagne
Greece	0.09	0.09	0.09	0.09	0.10	0.10	0.11	0.12	Grèce
Hungary	0.02	0.02	0.03	0.03	0.03	0.03	0.04	0.04	Hongrie
Iceland	0.00	0.00	0.00	0.00	0.00	0.00	0.00	0.00	Islande
Ireland	0.30	0.30	0.29	0.30	0.38	0.48	0.67	0.80	Irlande
Italy	1.38	1.22	1.28	1.41	1.68	2.11	2.83	3.07	Italie
Japan	31.66	34.48	32.97	32.61	27.04	24.56	20.89	19.05	Japon
Korea	..	..	3.70	4.37	4.65	4.33	3.50	3.33	Corée
Luxembourg	0.02	0.02	0.13	0.36	0.00	0.43	0.45	0.41	Luxembourg
Mexico	0.23	0.25	0.23	0.13	0.14	0.18	0.27	0.32	Mexique
Netherlands[2]	1.86	1.57	1.53	1.87	1.98	1.86	2.05	1.77	Pays-Bas[2]
New Zealand[3]	0.09	0.08	0.08	0.07	0.09	0.09	0.07	0.06	Nouvelle Zélande[3]
Norway[5]	0.35	0.28	0.30	0.30	0.31	0.35	0.34	0.27	Norvège[5]
Poland[7]	..	0.06	0.06	0.06	0.09	0.10	0.12	0.12	Pologne[7]
Portugal	0.13	0.13	0.14	0.21	0.26	0.23	0.29	0.31	Portugal
Slovak Republic	..	..	..	..	..	0.01	0.02	0.02	Republique Slovaque
Spain	1.08	0.87	1.19	1.10	1.30	1.28	1.30	1.43	Espagne
Sweden	0.98	0.69	0.76	0.76	0.90	0.83	0.90	0.92	Suède
Switzerland	1.64	1.62	1.71	2.04	2.21	2.09	2.30	1.67	Suisse
Turkey	0.03	0.03	0.01	0.02	0.02	0.03	0.03	0.03	Turquie
United Kingdom[9]	10.43	9.01	7.49	7.26	8.66	9.86	11.64	11.81	Royaume-Uni[9]
United States	30.33	31.08	29.31	27.24	29.52	31.47	34.20	37.02	Etats-Unis
NAFTA[10]	32.41	32.65	31.19	28.95	30.71	32.63	35.33	39.03	ALENA[10]
EU-15[10]	31.34	28.73	28.07	30.00	33.21	33.64	35.21	34.34	UE-15[10]

II.3 Non-Life / Non-Vie

% (per cent / pourcentage)

COUNTRY	1992	1993	1994	1995	1996	1997	1998	1999	PAYS
Australia	0.67	1.27	1.41	1.37	1.60	1.55	1.14	1.24	Australie
Austria	0.88	0.85	0.86	0.93	0.89	0.74	0.71	0.69	Autriche
Belgium	0.98	0.91	0.88	0.95	0.91	0.75	0.74	0.74	Belgique
Canada	1.94	1.82	1.26	1.24	1.80	1.73	1.63	2.29	Canada
Czech Republic	..	0.08	0.09	0.10	0.12	0.12	0.13	0.13	République Tchèque
Denmark	0.50	0.46	0.47	0.52	0.52	0.46	0.46	0.44	Danemark
Finland	0.34	0.25	0.26	0.29	0.28	0.24	0.26	0.26	Finlande
France	5.20	4.92	4.95	5.40	5.40	4.51	4.42	4.37	France
Germany	9.24	9.21	9.55	10.62	10.19	8.55	8.25	8.15	Allemagne
Greece	0.10	0.10	0.10	0.11	0.12	0.11	0.11	0.13	Grèce
Hungary	0.08	0.08	0.08	0.07	0.08	0.08	0.08	0.08	Hongrie
Iceland	0.03	0.02	0.02	0.02	0.02	0.02	0.02	0.02	Islande
Ireland	0.28	0.25	0.27	0.28	0.31	0.29	0.33	0.38	Irlande
Italy	3.60	2.89	2.79	2.70	2.97	2.74	2.89	3.04	Italie
Japan	10.17	11.79	12.17	12.63	11.24	9.39	7.97	9.08	Japon
Korea	..	..	1.20	1.51	1.79	1.74	1.14	1.37	Corée
Luxembourg	0.05	0.05	0.05	0.06	0.06	0.05	0.08	0.08	Luxembourg
Mexico	0.44	0.50	0.48	0.28	0.30	0.34	0.36	0.45	Mexique
Netherlands	1.61	1.61	1.74	1.87	1.85	1.60	1.64	1.73	Pays-Bas
New Zealand[4]	0.13	0.09	0.10	0.11	0.18	0.18	0.14	0.10	Nouvelle Zélande[4]
Norway[6]	0.50	0.45	0.43	0.43	0.43	0.39	0.39	0.41	Norvège[6]
Poland[8]	..	0.10	0.09	0.19	0.24	0.29	0.33	0.33	Pologne[8]
Portugal	0.31	0.29	0.29	0.31	0.33	0.29	0.30	0.31	Portugal
Slovak Republic	..	..	..	..	..	0.04	0.04	0.04	Republique Slovaque
Spain	2.12	1.77	1.70	1.80	1.84	1.55	1.58	1.71	Espagne
Sweden	0.86	0.77	0.57	0.58	0.59	0.51	0.48	0.60	Suède
Switzerland	1.19	1.12	1.18	1.29	1.24	0.99	0.96	1.32	Suisse
Turkey	0.13	0.17	0.11	0.14	0.15	0.17	0.19	0.23	Turquie
United Kingdom	7.73	6.81	6.67	6.27	5.93	6.05	6.00	6.03	Royaume-Uni
United States	50.92	51.38	50.24	47.93	48.62	54.53	57.23	54.24	Etats-Unis
NAFTA[10]	53.30	53.70	51.98	49.45	50.71	56.60	59.22	56.99	ALENA[10]
EU-15[10]	33.80	31.14	31.14	32.68	32.19	28.45	28.26	28.65	UE-15[10]

1. Net written premiums basis for life for 1994 and 1995 / Sur la base des primes nettes émises pour l'assurance vie pour 1994 et 1995

2. Net written premiums basis for life until 1994 / Sur la base des primes nettes émises pour l'assurance vie jusqu'à 1994

3. Total gross premiums basis for life since 1996 / Sur la base des primes brutes totales pour l'assurance vie depuis 1996

4. Net written premiums basis for 1992-1995 and total gross premiums basis for 1999 for non-life/ Sur la base des primes nettes émises
non-vie pour les années 1992 á 1995 et primes brutes totales pour 1999 pour l'assurance non-vie

5. Net written premiums basis for life for 1992 / Sur la base des primes nettes émises pour l'assurance vie pour 1992

6. Without branches of foreign insurers for non-life for 1994 and 1995 / Sans les succursales des assureurs étrangers pour l'assurance non-vie pour 1994 et 1995

7. Net written premiums basis for life until 1995 / Sur la base des primes nettes émises pour l'assurance vie jusqu'à 1995

8. Net written premiums basis for non-life until 1994 / Sur la base des primes nettes émises pour l'assurance non-vie jusqu'à 1994

9. Net written premiums basis for life until 1995 / Sur la base des primes nettes émises pour l'assurance vie jusqu'à 1995

10. For available data only / Uniquement pour les données disponibles

III. Density (Direct gross premiums/Population) / Densité (Primes brutes directes/Population)

III.1 Total / Total

COUNTRY	U.S. $ per inhabitant / $ US par habitant								PAYS
	1992	1993	1994	1995	1996	1997	1998	1999	
Australia[1]	1 039	1 462	1 584	1 517	1 657	1 937	1 757	1 926	Australie[1]
Austria	1 187	1 257	1 317	1 593	1 762	1 373	1 401	1 433	Autriche
Belgium	1 100	1 091	1 186	1 436	1 473	1 376	1 590	1 715	Belgique
Canada	982	847	859	903	882	865	807	1 395	Canada
Czech Republic	..	76	100	121	147	145	166	176	République Tchèque
Denmark	1 327	1 384	1 617	1 980	2 157	2 057	2 262	2 094	Danemark
Finland	1 399	474	570	824	985	866	978	1 111	Finlande
France	1 538	1 657	1 902	2 264	2 393	2 236	1 949	2 062	France
Germany	1 427	1 475	1 621	1 935	1 902	1 691	1 695	1 718	Allemagne
Greece	138	141	153	180	204	200	212	255	Grèce
Hungary	71	78	87	92	98	104	114	120	Hongrie
Iceland	880	733	737	784	770	717	751	824	Islande
Ireland	1 203	1 214	1 362	1 508	1 804	2 099	2 746	3 625	Irlande
Italy	647	560	601	662	752	819	1 004	1 168	Italie
Japan	2 476	2 919	3 179	3 488	2 936	2 680	2 334	2 547	Japon
Korea	..	..	969	1 266	1 368	1 313	1 026	1 160	Corée
Luxembourg	1 422	1 316	3 874	10 060	8 662	11 331	12 908	13 480	Luxembourg
Mexico[2]	58	67	68	41	44	53	66	84	Mexique
Netherlands[2]	1 685	1 629	1 820	2 283	2 334	2 224	2 366	2 419	Pays-Bas[2]
New Zealand[3,4]	456	391	431	445	674	688	534	438	Nouvelle Zélande[3,4]
Norway[5,6]	1 463	1 318	1 438	1 551	1 588	1 643	1 626	1 618	Norvège[5,6]
Poland[7,8]	..	32	34	59	78	96	114	118	Pologne[7,8]
Portugal	325	332	363	484	555	504	583	678	Portugal
Slovak Republic	..	..	..	..	..	18	22	23	Republique Slovaque
Spain	605	527	630	686	747	700	729	860	Espagne
Sweden	1 565	1 304	1 303	1 432	1 606	1 496	1 581	1 934	Suède
Switzerland	3 039	3 098	3 573	4 510	4 665	4 305	4 672	4 651	Suisse
Turkey	20	26	18	22	25	29	33	39	Turquie
United Kingdom[9]	2 308	2 128	2 093	2 184	2 366	2 661	3 028	3 424	Royaume-Uni[9]
United States	2 348	2 494	2 593	2 643	2 739	3 111	3 357	3 551	Etats-Unis
NAFTA[10]	1 715	1 804	1 869	1 895	1 955	2 202	2 364	2 544	N.A.F.T.A.[10]
EU-15[10]	1 306	1 267	1 370	1 582	1 664	1 628	1 705	1 858	UE15[10]
OECD[10]	1 393	1 471	1 605	1 742	1 737	1 775	1 807	1 957	O.C.D.E.[10]

III.2 Life / Vie

COUNTRY	U.S. $ per inhabitant / $ US par habitant								PAYS
	1992	1993	1994	1995	1996	1997	1998	1999	
Australia[1]	755	907	938	848	879	1 154	1 179	1 313	Australie[1]
Austria	362	432	444	574	778	517	563	631	Autriche
Belgium	375	389	472	607	671	690	903	1 043	Belgique
Canada	479	360	507	533	348	330	297	692	Canada
Czech Republic	..	20	25	34	39	38	45	56	République Tchèque
Denmark	616	700	885	1 104	1 278	1 250	1 442	1 326	Danemark
Finland	907	97	146	321	504	423	498	647	Finlande
France	867	996	1 202	1 445	1 569	1 517	1 235	1 365	France
Germany	579	597	662	788	792	719	739	789	Allemagne
Greece	67	68	75	88	98	100	109	142	Grèce
Hungary	13	16	22	28	31	34	42	50	Hongrie
Iceland	28	26	26	29	31	28	37	48	Islande
Ireland	622	674	743	823	1 052	1 348	1 900	2 672	Irlande
Italy	179	169	202	247	291	374	521	670	Italie
Japan	1 871	2 188	2 382	2 601	2 140	1 986	1 735	1 876	Japon
Korea	..	..	749	970	1 017	960	792	887	Corée
Luxembourg	457	420	2 819	8 834	7 355	10 241	11 151	11 738	Luxembourg
Mexico[2]	20	22	24	14	15	19	30	41	Mexique
Netherlands[2]	902	815	897	1 214	1 270	1 244	1 371	1 398	Pays-Bas[2]
New Zealand[3]	182	184	208	180	234	248	184	184	Nouvelle Zélande[3]
Norway[5]	596	519	629	686	701	812	797	753	Norvège[5]
Poland[7]	..	13	15	16	22	27	34	38	Pologne[7]
Portugal	94	104	126	211	262	232	301	388	Portugal
Slovak Republic	..	..	..	..	..	25	33	35	République Slovaque
Spain	203	177	275	281	329	331	347	454	Espagne
Sweden	830	623	776	856	1 012	958	1 068	1 300	Suède
Switzerland	1 759	1 848	2 198	2 896	3 107	3 004	3 394	2 919	Suisse
Turkey	4	4	2	3	4	5	6	6	Turquie
United Kingdom[9]	1 323	1 224	1 158	1 241	1 467	1 704	2 065	2 475	Royaume-Uni[9]
United States	873	954	1 016	1 037	1 107	1 203	1 335	1 692	Etats-Unis[9]
NAFTA[10]	646	692	745	757	789	851	939	1 214	ALENA[10]
EU-15[10]	626	615	683	807	895	918	988	1 143	UE-15[10]
OECD[10]	692	744	843	927	918	928	949	1 119	OCDE[10]

III. Density (Direct gross premiums/Population) / Densité (Primes brutes directes/Population)

III.3 Non-Life / Non-Vie

COUNTRY	1992	1993	1994	1995	1996	1997	1998	1999	PAYS
Australia	284	555	646	669	779	783	578	613	Australie
Austria	825	825	873	1 019	984	855	837	802	Autriche
Belgium	724	702	714	829	802	686	687	672	Belgique
Canada	504	487	352	370	534	535	510	703	Canada
Czech Republic	..	57	75	87	107	107	120	120	République Tchèque
Denmark	711	684	731	876	878	808	820	768	Danemark
Finland	492	377	424	503	481	442	480	464	Finlande
France	671	661	700	818	824	719	713	697	France
Germany	848	878	959	1 147	1 109	972	956	929	Allemagne
Greece	72	73	78	92	105	100	103	113	Grèce
Hungary	58	61	64	64	67	70	71	71	Hongrie
Iceland	853	707	711	754	739	689	714	776	Islande
Ireland	580	540	619	685	752	751	846	953	Irlande
Italy	469	392	399	415	461	445	483	498	Italie
Japan	605	731	796	887	796	695	599	671	Japon
Korea	..	..	220	296	351	353	234	273	Corée
Luxembourg	965	895	1 055	1 226	1 307	1 090	1 758	1 743	Luxembourg
Mexico	38	44	45	27	29	34	36	43	Mexique
Netherlands	783	814	923	1 069	1 064	979	995	1 021	Pays-Bas
New Zealand[4]	273	207	222	265	440	440	350	253	Nouvelle Zélande[4]
Norway[6]	867	799	808	865	887	831	828	865	Norvège[b]
Poland[8]	..	48	62	162	222	294	350	375	Pologne[8]
Portugal	230	227	236	273	293	271	283	290	Portugal
Slovak Republic	..	..	..	..	..	68	79	71	République Slovaque
Spain	402	350	356	405	418	369	382	406	Espagne
Sweden	734	681	526	576	593	538	513	634	Suède
Switzerland	1 279	1 250	1 376	1 614	1 558	1 301	1 278	1 732	Suisse
Turkey	16	22	16	19	21	25	27	32	Turquie
United Kingdom[9]	986	904	934	943	899	957	963	948	Royaume-Uni[9]
United States	1 475	1 541	1 577	1 606	1 632	1 908	2 022	1 859	Etats-Unis
NAFTA[10]	1 069	1 112	1 124	1 138	1 166	1 351	1 425	1 330	N.A.F.T.A.[10]
EU-15[10]	680	652	687	774	769	710	717	715	UE15[10]
OECD[10]	700	726	763	815	818	848	858	837	O.C.D.E.[10]

1. Net written premiums basis for life for 1994 and 1995 / Sur la base des primes nettes émises pour l'assurance vie pour 1994 et 1995

2. Net written premiums basis for life until 1994 / Sur la base des primes nettes émises pour l'assurance vie jusqu'à 1994

3. Total gross premiums basis for life since 1996 / Sur la base des primes brutes totales pour l'assurance vie depuis 1996

4. Net written premiums basis for 1992-1995 and total gross premiums for 1999 for non-life/ Sur la base des primes nettes émises
pour les années 1992 á 1995 et primes brutes totales pour 1999 pour lássurance non-vie

5. Net written premiums basis for life for 1992 / Sur la base des primes nettes émises pour l'assurance vie pour 1992

6. Without branches of foreign insurers for non-life for 1994 and 1995 / Sans les succursales des assureurs étrangers pour l'assurance non-vie pour 1994 et 1995

7. Net written premiums basis for life until 1995 / Sur la base des primes nettes émises pour l'assurance vie jusqu'à 1995

8. Net written premiums basis for non-life until 1994 / Sur la base des primes nettes émises pour l'assurance non-vie jusqu'à 1994

9. Net written premiums basis for life until 1995 / Sur la base des primes nettes émises pour l'assurance vie jusqu'à 1995

10. For available data only / Uniquement pour les données disponibles

IV. Penetration (Direct gross premiums/GDP) / Pénétration (Primes brutes directes/PIB)

IV.1 Total / Total

COUNTRY	% (per cent / pourcentage)								PAYS
	1992	1993	1994	1995	1996	1997	1998	1999	
Australia[1]	6.21	9.04	8.64	7.76	7.68	9.14	9.36	9.02	Australie[1]
Austria	5.00	5.50	5.40	5.54	6.23	5.38	5.33	5.52	Autriche
Belgium	4.91	5.14	5.17	5.33	5.58	5.77	6.47	7.06	Belgique
Canada	4.93	4.43	4.57	4.66	4.46	4.31	4.20	6.70	Canada
Czech Republic	..	2.29	2.58	2.47	2.68	2.88	3.10	3.41	République Tchèque
Denmark	4.67	5.17	5.54	5.72	6.17	6.39	6.86	6.32	Danemark
Finland	6.62	2.84	2.96	3.34	4.04	3.71	4.04	4.44	Finlande
France	6.68	7.64	8.27	8.57	9.08	9.40	8.00	8.44	France
Germany	5.84	6.26	6.45	6.55	6.65	6.64	6.51	6.68	Allemagne
Greece	1.45	1.59	1.61	1.62	1.73	1.76	1.85	2.15	Grèce
Hungary	1.98	2.08	2.14	2.13	2.25	2.35	2.43	2.51	Hongrie
Iceland	3.33	3.18	3.15	3.00	2.85	2.62	2.51	2.65	Islande
Ireland	8.15	8.79	8.95	8.28	9.08	9.96	12.23	14.53	Irlande
Italy	3.02	3.25	3.38	3.49	3.56	4.12	4.88	5.65	Italie
Japan	8.28	8.52	8.48	8.52	8.03	8.06	7.79	7.42	Japon
Korea	..	..	11.36	12.50	12.85	13.64	15.99	13.36	Corée
Luxembourg	4.45	4.11	10.81	24.02	21.35	30.46	32.93	30.20	Luxembourg
Mexico	1.35	1.43	1.44	1.30	1.23	1.25	1.52	1.70	Mexique
Netherlands[2]	7.95	7.96	8.30	8.86	9.11	9.35	9.84	9.71	Pays-Bas[2]
New Zealand[3,4]	3.92	3.11	2.96	2.71	3.82	3.98	3.81	3.04	Nouvelle Zélande[3,4]
Norway[5,6]	4.97	4.89	5.07	4.60	4.39	4.71	4.91	4.72	Norvège[5,6]
Poland[7,8]	..	1.45	1.43	1.92	2.25	2.74	2.94	2.95	Pologne[7,8]
Portugal	3.39	3.92	4.08	4.59	5.06	4.95	5.50	5.93	Portugal
Slovak Republic	..	..	..	..	..	2.48	2.85	2.90	République Slovaque
Spain	4.09	4.30	5.11	4.81	5.04	5.18	5.19	5.65	Espagne
Sweden	5.49	6.14	5.79	5.47	5.64	5.81	6.17	7.10	Suède
Switzerland	8.58	9.08	9.60	10.33	11.14	11.92	12.55	12.83	Suisse
Turkey[9]	0.75	0.85	0.82	0.81	0.87	0.98	1.07	1.38	Turquie
United Kingdom[9]	12.78	13.16	11.98	11.56	12.06	12.24	13.22	14.13	Royaume-Uni[9]
United States	9.95	10.15	10.05	9.89	9.84	10.61	10.97	10.49	Etats-Unis
NAFTA[10]	9.59	9.24	9.19	9.20	9.12	9.75	10.12	9.85	ALENA[10]
EU-15[10]	6.30	6.76	6.90	6.97	7.22	7.53	7.65	8.18	UE-15[10]
OECD[10]	7.48	7.88	8.12	8.11	8.09	8.53	8.71	8.73	OCDE[10]

IV.2 Life / Vie

COUNTRY	% (per cent / pourcentage)								PAYS
	1992	1993	1994	1995	1996	1997	1998	1999	
Australia[1]	4.51	5.61	5.12	4.34	4.07	5.44	6.28	6.15	Australie[1]
Austria	1.52	1.89	1.82	2.00	2.75	2.03	2.14	2.43	Autriche
Belgium	1.68	1.83	2.06	2.25	2.55	2.90	3.68	4.29	Belgique
Canada	2.40	1.88	2.70	2.76	1.76	1.64	1.55	3.32	Canada
Czech Republic	..	0.59	0.65	0.69	0.71	0.76	0.85	1.08	République Tchèque
Denmark	2.17	2.62	3.04	3.19	3.66	3.88	4.37	4.00	Danemark
Finland	4.30	0.58	0.76	1.30	2.07	1.81	2.06	2.59	Finlande
France	3.76	4.59	5.23	5.47	5.95	6.38	5.07	5.59	France
Germany	2.37	2.53	2.63	2.67	2.77	2.82	2.84	3.07	Allemagne
Greece	0.70	0.76	0.79	0.79	0.84	0.88	0.95	1.19	Grèce
Hungary	0.36	0.44	0.55	0.64	0.72	0.77	0.90	1.04	Hongrie
Iceland	0.10	0.11	0.11	0.11	0.11	0.10	0.12	0.15	Islande
Ireland	4.22	4.88	4.88	4.52	5.30	6.40	8.46	10.71	Irlande
Italy	0.83	0.98	1.14	1.30	1.38	1.88	2.53	3.24	Italie
Japan	6.26	6.39	6.35	6.36	5.86	5.97	5.79	5.47	Japon
Korea	..	..	8.78	9.58	9.55	9.98	12.34	10.21	Corée
Luxembourg	1.43	1.31	7.86	21.09	18.13	27.53	28.44	26.30	Luxembourg
Mexico	0.46	0.48	0.50	0.44	0.43	0.46	0.69	0.82	Mexique
Netherlands[2]	4.26	3.98	4.09	4.71	4.96	5.23	5.70	5.61	Pays-Bas[2]
New Zealand[3]	1.57	1.46	1.43	1.10	1.33	1.44	1.31	1.28	Nouvelle Zélande[3]
Norway[5]	2.02	1.93	2.22	2.03	1.94	2.32	2.41	2.20	Norvège[5]
Poland[7]	..	0.57	0.61	0.53	0.65	0.77	0.86	0.96	Pologne[7]
Portugal	0.98	1.23	1.42	2.00	2.39	2.28	2.83	3.40	Portugal
Slovak Republic	..	..	..	..	..	0.67	0.84	0.96	République Slovaque
Spain	1.37	1.44	2.23	1.97	2.22	2.45	2.47	2.98	Espagne
Sweden	2.92	2.93	3.45	3.27	3.56	3.72	4.17	4.77	Suède
Switzerland	4.97	5.41	5.90	6.63	7.42	8.32	9.11	8.05	Suisse
Turkey	0.14	0.13	0.10	0.10	0.13	0.16	0.18	0.23	Turquie
United Kingdom[9]	7.32	7.57	6.63	6.57	7.48	7.84	9.01	10.22	Royaume-Uni[9]
United States	3.70	3.88	3.94	3.88	3.98	4.10	4.36	5.00	Etats-Unis
NAFTA[10]	3.61	3.54	3.66	3.67	3.68	3.77	4.02	4.70	ALENA[10]
EU-15[10]	3.02	3.28	3.44	3.56	3.88	4.24	4.43	5.03	UE-15[10]
OECD[10]	3.72	3.99	4.26	4.32	4.28	4.46	4.57	5.00	OCDE[10]

IV.3 Non-Life / Non-Vie

% (per cent / pourcentage)

COUNTRY	1992	1993	1994	1995	1996	1997	1998	1999	PAYS
Australia	1.70	3.43	3.53	3.42	3.61	3.69	3.08	2.87	Australie
Austria	3.48	3.61	3.58	3.54	3.48	3.35	3.19	3.09	Autriche
Belgium	3.24	3.31	3.11	3.08	3.04	2.88	2.80	2.76	Belgique
Canada	2.53	2.55	1.87	1.91	2.70	2.66	2.66	3.38	Canada
Czech Republic	..	1.70	1.93	1.77	1.96	2.12	2.25	2.33	République Tchèque
Denmark	2.50	2.56	2.51	2.53	2.51	2.51	2.48	2.32	Danemark
Finland	2.33	2.26	2.21	2.04	1.97	1.90	1.98	1.86	Finlande
France	2.91	3.05	3.04	3.10	3.13	3.02	2.93	2.85	France
Germany	3.47	3.73	3.82	3.88	3.88	3.82	3.67	3.61	Allemagne
Greece	0.75	0.82	0.82	0.83	0.89	0.88	0.90	0.96	Grèce
Hungary	1.62	1.64	1.59	1.49	1.53	1.57	1.52	1.48	Hongrie
Iceland	3.22	3.06	3.04	2.89	2.73	2.52	2.38	2.50	Islande
Ireland	3.93	3.91	4.07	3.76	3.79	3.56	3.77	3.82	Irlande
Italy	2.19	2.27	2.25	2.19	2.18	2.24	2.35	2.41	Italie
Japan	2.02	2.13	2.12	2.17	2.18	2.09	2.00	1.95	Japon
Korea	..	..	2.58	2.92	3.30	3.67	3.65	3.15	Corée
Luxembourg	3.02	2.80	2.94	2.93	3.22	2.93	4.48	3.90	Luxembourg
Mexico	0.89	0.95	0.94	0.86	0.81	0.80	0.83	0.88	Mexique
Netherlands	3.69	3.98	4.21	4.15	4.15	4.12	4.14	4.10	Pays-Bas
New Zealand[4]	2.35	1.65	1.53	1.61	2.50	2.55	2.50	1.76	Nouvelle Zélande[4]
Norway[6]	2.94	2.97	2.85	2.57	2.45	2.38	2.50	2.52	Norvège[6]
Poland[8]	..	0.88	0.82	1.39	1.60	1.97	2.08	1.99	Pologne[8]
Portugal	2.40	2.68	2.66	2.59	2.67	2.67	2.67	2.53	Portugal
Slovak Republic	..	..	..	..	..	1.81	2.01	1.94	République Slovaque
Spain	2.72	2.86	2.88	2.84	2.82	2.73	2.72	2.67	Espagne
Sweden	2.58	3.21	2.34	2.20	2.08	2.09	2.00	2.33	Suède
Switzerland	3.61	3.66	3.69	3.70	3.72	3.60	3.43	4.78	Suisse
Turkey	0.60	0.73	0.72	0.71	0.74	0.83	0.89	1.15	Turquie
United Kingdom	5.46	5.59	5.35	4.99	4.58	4.40	4.20	3.91	Royaume-Uni
United States	6.25	6.27	6.12	6.01	5.86	6.51	6.61	5.49	Etats-Unis
NAFTA[10]	5.98	5.69	5.53	5.52	5.44	5.98	6.10	5.15	ALENA[10]
EU-15[10]	3.28	3.48	3.46	3.41	3.33	3.28	3.22	3.15	UE-15[10]
OECD[10]	3.76	3.89	3.86	3.80	3.81	4.07	4.13	3.74	OCDE[10]

1. Net written premiums basis for life for 1994 and 1995 / Sur la base des primes nettes émises pour l'assurance vie pour 1994 et 1995

2. Net written premiums basis for life until 1994 / Sur la base des primes nettes émises pour l'assurance vie jusqu'à 1994

3. Total gross premiums basis for life since 1996 / Sur la base des primes brutes totales pour l'assurance vie depuis 1996

4. Net written premiums basis for non-life for 1992-1995 and total gross premiums for 1999/ Sur la base des primes nettes émises pour l'assurance
non-vie pour les années 1992 á 1995 et primes brutes totales pour 1999

5. Net written premiums basis for life for 1992 / Sur la base des primes nettes émises pour l'assurance vie pour 1992

6. Without branches of foreign insurers for non-life for 1994 and 1995 / Sans les succursales des assureurs étrangers pour l'assurance non-vie pour 1994 et 1995

7. Net written premiums basis for life until 1995 / Sur la base des primes nettes émises pour l'assurance vie jusqu'à 1995

8. Net written premiums basis for non-life until 1994 / Sur la base des primes nettes émises pour l'assurance non-vie jusqu'à 1994

9. Net written premiums basis for life until 1995 / Sur la base des primes nettes émises pour l'assurance vie jusqu'à 1995

10. For available data only / Uniquement pour les données disponibles

V. Life Insurance share / Part de l'assurance-vie

COUNTRY	1992	1993	1994	1995	1996	1997	1998	1999	PAYS
							% (per cent / pourcentage)		
Australia[1]	68.57	59.09	59.81	56.71	49.26	58.04	64.96	64.64	Australie[1]
Austria	27.84	31.57	29.64	32.69	39.44	32.83	35.73	38.87	Autriche
Belgium	32.85	34.85	39.18	40.43	43.76	48.24	55.18	58.58	Belgique
Canada	44.51	38.44	54.55	55.84	37.18	36.34	35.58	47.62	Canada
Czech Republic	..	25.77	25.10	27.64	26.60	25.98	27.12	31.53	République Tchèque
Denmark	38.46	44.89	47.44	50.86	54.69	56.58	59.10	58.42	Danemark
Finland	61.22	18.37	23.82	36.71	48.63	47.15	49.21	56.71	Finlande
France	51.93	55.21	59.96	60.75	62.45	64.84	60.43	63.07	France
Germany	35.67	35.46	35.58	35.75	36.67	37.23	38.44	40.37	Allemagne
Greece	48.19	46.30	47.46	47.85	47.05	48.99	50.37	54.91	Grèce
Hungary	17.83	21.18	25.59	29.80	31.87	32.91	37.14	41.19	Hongrie
Iceland	2.71	3.05	3.51	3.96	3.55	4.22	4.52	5.48	Islande
Ireland	54.83	56.58	53.48	52.41	56.42	60.17	65.97	69.97	Irlande
Italy	28.64	30.56	33.37	36.81	38.63	45.24	51.10	56.56	Italie
Japan	73.74	73.32	73.35	72.93	71.64	72.93	73.28	72.67	Japon
Korea	..	..	75.22	74.76	72.64	71.54	75.66	74.63	Corée
Luxembourg[2]	32.13	31.95	72.70	87.80	84.91	90.38	86.31	87.02	Luxembourg[2]
Mexico	33.06	32.61	33.88	32.67	33.66	35.68	44.49	47.66	Mexique
Netherlands	53.73	51.62	50.86	53.27	53.99	55.52	57.76	57.68	Pays-Bas
New Zealand	39.18	42.89	43.54	35.53	34.38	35.70	34.21	42.07	Nouvelle Zélande
Norway[3]	38.40	37.29	42.72	43.53	43.92	49.14	48.74	46.25	Norvège[3]
Poland	..	28.65	30.98	27.54	28.60	27.67	29.06	31.83	Pologne
Portugal	28.68	31.06	34.44	43.07	46.62	45.43	50.08	56.25	Portugal
Slovak Republic	..	..	..	..	..	26.94	29.39	33.12	République Slovaque
Spain	32.33	32.12	42.05	39.61	42.69	45.99	46.19	51.70	Espagne
Sweden[4]	47.02	46.70	53.94	54.90	57.21	58.08	62.73	63.18	Suède[4]
Switzerland	40.81	41.81	43.81	48.37	58.58	62.43	67.20	59.10	Suisse
Turkey	18.84	14.45	11.97	12.79	14.61	15.75	16.88	16.05	Turquie
United Kingdom[5]	58.14	53.98	53.97	53.99	58.48	61.02	64.51	68.88	Royaume-Uni[5]
United States	36.83	37.88	37.96	38.55	39.68	37.94	40.27	47.36	Etats-Unis
N.A.F.T.A.[6]	37.16	37.85	38.55	39.17	39.56	37.88	39.82	47.62	ALENA[6]
EU15[6]	45.10	44.91	46.63	47.39	49.87	52.43	54.00	58.92	UE-15[6]
O.E.C.D.[6]	47.44	48.10	49.85	50.60	50.43	50.05	50.63	55.79	OCDE[6]

1. Net written premiums basis for 1994 and 1995 / Sur la base des primes nettes émises pour les années 1994 et 1995
2. Direct gross premiums basis until 1993 / Sur la base des primes brutes directes jusqu'à 1993
3. Without branches of foreign insurers for non-life for 1994 and 1995 / Sans les succursales des assureurs étrangers pour l'assurance non-vie pour 1994 et 1995
4. Without branches of foreign insurers for non-life until 1996 and for 1999/ Sans les succursales des assureurs étrangers pour l'assurance jusqu'à 1996 et pour 1999
5. Net written premiums basis until 1992 / Sur la base des primes nettes émises jusqu'à 1992
6. For available data only / Uniquement pour les données disponibles

VI. Direct total gross premiums / Number of employees of the insurance companies
Total des primes brutes directes / Nombre d'employés des entreprises d'assurances

COUNTRY	1992	1993	1994	1995	1996	1997	1998	1999	PAYS
						U.S. $ per employee / $ U.S. par employé			
Australia	..	..	..	..	..	..	..	..	Australie
Austria	285 804	304 575	326 102	396 267	437 246	344 835	365 035	372 111	Autriche
Belgium	395 605	407 221	462 149	571 916	597 558	554 060	640 756	695 206	Belgique
Canada						269 495	252 167	467 384	Canada
Czech Republic	..	70 966	79 111	93 348	99 436	92 315	103 902	109 967	République Tchèque
Denmark	..	..	..	719 215	..	714 800	794 963	724 506	Danemark
Finland	575 147	203 407	322 169	454 289	534 190	468 488	530 225	697 973	Finlande
France	712 996	782 934	902 495	1 078 813	1 031 945	984 698	868 468	913 817	France
Germany	450 703	470 660	526 868	673 398	697 723	644 662	644 346	619 651	Allemagne
Greece	142 872	172 292	166 245	196 308			..	..	Grèce
Hungary	55 185	51 316	54 277	54 997	38 509	36 192	40 300	38 844	Hongrie
Iceland	529 696	449 906	452 788	476 155	470 086	418 818	423 266	451 312	Islande
Ireland	421 816	429 049	469 078	522 847	639 228	765 918	970 943	1 199 171	Irlande
Italy	762 896	664 587	733 794	815 784	954 898	1 069 121	1 338 896	1 516 087	Italie
Japan	475 468	560 665	631 423	703 861	618 696	620 805	559 611	625 376	Japon
Korea	..	..	579 550	713 783	714 123	714 842	733 860	880 539	Corée
Luxembourg	472 082	436 684	1 233 489	3 184 741	2 275 972	2 791 343	3 124 437	3 035 353	Luxembourg
Mexico	237 579	287 717	297 701	191 130	206 567	244 642	282 637	374 949	Mexique
Netherlands	..	..	..	736 747	..	686 241	678 955	798 216	Pays-Bas
New Zealand	..	..	..	..	..	..	..	..	Nouvelle Zélande
Norway	..	488 078	..	..	744 648	790 206	672 671	703 098	Norvège
Poland	..	..	..	..	117 413	143 299	151 111	150 545	Pologne
Portugal	214 245	224 721	256 388	341 979	402 571	343 922	407 932	521 303	Portugal
Slovak Republic	..	..	..	..	..	78 825	71 012	73 472	République Slovaque
Spain	504 531	462 058	538 337	562 955	607 679	673 923	667 804	800 009	Espagne
Sweden	339 190	285 183	604 393	674 777	767 539	801 410	848 131	1 038 322	Suède
Switzerland	559 852	577 135	686 973	867 197	..	..	792 516	815 933	Suisse
Turkey	228 406	259 836	190 915	209 424	210 972	230 782	257 901	262 790	Turquie
United Kingdom	..	..	..	..	694 089	687 257	764 581	913 489	Royaume-Uni
United States	405 235	423 981	435 884	451 264	..	..	..	..	Etats-Unis
N.A.F.T.A.[1]	402 924	422 204	434 095	448 031	206 567	265 159	257 870	449 443	N.A.F.T.A.[1]
EU15[1]	504 120	507 541	595 925	726 081	748 105	725 441	751 320	826 054	UE15[1]
O.E.C.D.[1]	441 552	469 618	511 125	568 428	653 146	622 200	618 497	697 694	O.C.D.E.[1]

1. For available data only / Uniquement pour les données disponibles

VII. Retention ratio (= Net written premiums / Total gross premiums) / Taux de rétention (= Primes nettes émises / Total des primes brutes)

VII.1 Total / Total

COUNTRY	1992	1993	1994	1995	1996	1997	1998	1999	PAYS
					% (per cent / pourcentage)				
Australia	93.39	87.69	..	..	91.67	92.95	90.97	90.60	Australie
Austria	83.37	83.73	78.45	80.79	80.86	78.58	80.46	80.94	Autriche
Belgium	85.00	86.04	87.36	90.06	91.24	92.60	94.02	95.19	Belgique
Canada	86.31	84.66	84.72	85.78	84.45	84.30	84.80	87.65	Canada
Czech Republic	..	93.41	91.05	88.12	86.71	85.85	84.59	85.06	République Tchèque
Denmark	..	..	..	..	94.07	..	..	..	Danemark
Finland	95.08	90.38	89.91	92.05	94.17	94.17	94.97	95.60	Finlande
France	90.44	91.52	91.60	91.57	92.50	93.03	92.57	92.66	France
Germany	80.46	80.92	81.65	82.43	82.65	82.98	83.84	82.87	Allemagne
Greece	100.00	78.41	78.55	78.90	81.09	84.13	..	86.77	Grèce
Hungary	84.42	80.99	79.64	78.99	81.48	86.66	83.53	83.12	Hongrie
Iceland	65.39	66.45	66.53	68.47	70.61	71.42	73.54	77.45	Islande
Ireland	82.09	84.36	89.03	87.91	88.82	91.81	92.63	90.52	Irlande
Italy	79.26	81.36	84.95	86.06	86.94	88.28	90.34	91.73	Italie
Japan	95.44	95.78	95.79	95.68	95.68	..	95.76	..	Japon
Korea	..	..	96.27	96.53	96.69	96.80	97.01	96.46	Corée
Luxembourg	..	..	86.54	94.61	86.03	92.16	94.33	95.47	Luxembourg
Mexico	80.73	79.80	80.57	77.91	77.50	79.46	83.13	84.83	Mexique
Netherlands	90.66	88.27	88.37	90.28	91.40	91.79	91.51	92.80	Pays-Bas
New Zealand	97.87	91.36	89.96	87.72	..	..	..	..	Nouvelle Zélande
Norway	85.95	84.46	..	..	90.58	91.04	89.62	89.00	Norvège
Poland	..	73.06	72.68	75.22	75.22	75.13	81.48	79.83	Pologne
Portugal	89.40	89.90	91.01	91.61	91.20	90.78	90.49	91.69	Portugal
Slovak Republic	..	..	..	..	..	81.58	81.02	84.57	République Slovaque
Spain	87.00	86.90	89.54	90.11	90.73	91.70	91.98	92.90	Espagne
Sweden	..	..	..	..	..	90.76	91.57	..	Suède
Switzerland	86.95	86.63	..	..	87.15	91.02	88.29	93.10	Suisse
Turkey	61.27	85.78	79.87	80.43	81.36	81.00	65.50	86.73	Turquie
United Kingdom	..	87.75	84.95	87.64	89.30	90.33	90.92	91.30	Royaume-Uni
United States	90.02	89.90	90.47	88.95	89.85	92.10	90.12	89.89	Etats-Unis
N.A.F.T.A.[1]	89.78	89.62	90.17	88.78	89.59	91.78	89.93	89.75	N.A.F.T.A.[1]
EU15[1]	84.78	85.91	85.77	87.02	88.02	88.78	89.40	89.62	UE15[1]
O.E.C.D.[1]	89.57	89.61	90.10	89.90	90.30	90.75	89.84	89.91	O.C.D.E.[1]

VII.2 Life / Vie

COUNTRY	1992	1993	1994	1995	1996	1997	1998	1999	PAYS
					% (per cent / pourcentage)				
Australia	100.00	90.44	..	..	100.00	100.00	98.47	97.89	Australie
Austria	88.82	90.51	89.50	91.67	92.60	91.70	92.13	92.81	Autriche
Belgium	94.29	95.33	96.34	99.93	99.93	99.96	99.96	99.98	Belgique
Canada	94.95	92.56	91.63	91.29	88.88	87.78	89.36	92.11	Canada
Czech Republic	..	100.00	100.00	99.02	98.91	98.84	99.04	99.02	République Tchèque
Denmark	98.75	99.41	98.40	98.56	98.60	98.70	98.78	98.58	Danemark
Finland	99.20	95.47	95.28	98.48	99.12	99.01	99.27	99.29	Finlande
France	96.24	96.93	97.16	96.80	97.74	97.58	97.14	97.18	France
Germany	91.18	91.87	92.13	92.31	91.95	92.05	92.50	90.96	Allemagne
Greece	100.00	84.06	84.44	85.01	87.70	91.67	..	94.30	Grèce
Hungary	74.34	62.98	64.25	66.02	67.13	91.40	83.07	85.50	Hongrie
Iceland	64.02	66.03	71.71	72.58	66.18	72.20	69.79	76.81	Islande
Ireland	82.41	86.56	96.98	95.91	95.93	97.38	97.23	95.48	Irlande
Italy	81.46	83.08	89.68	90.68	90.95	92.24	94.29	95.35	Italie
Japan	99.86	99.85	99.84	99.83	99.81	99.50	99.14	99.25	Japon
Korea	..	..	99.72	99.73	99.69	99.50	99.71	99.55	Corée
Luxembourg	..	..	95.50	98.20	88.00	94.17	97.46	98.48	Luxembourg
Mexico	94.43	94.49	93.61	93.28	92.58	92.59	93.67	94.97	Mexique
Netherlands	95.21	90.64	90.67	92.90	94.44	94.37	94.27	96.22	Pays-Bas
New Zealand	100.00	100.00	100.00	100.00	..	..	..	..	Nouvelle Zélande
Norway	99.91	100.00	100.00	100.00	98.76	98.92	96.75	96.44	Norvège
Poland	..	100.00	99.93	99.87	99.70	98.85	97.71	97.48	Pologne
Portugal	97.39	97.66	97.91	97.74	98.11	98.26	98.35	98.28	Portugal
Slovak Republic	..	..	..	..	..	99.14	99.43	99.24	République Slovaque
Spain	96.91	96.76	97.86	97.36	97.68	98.25	98.30	98.73	Espagne
Sweden	99.05	96.92	98.67	97.80	98.98	98.88	98.97	99.57	Suède
Switzerland	96.71	96.74	96.71	97.15	98.14	98.65	97.89	98.20	Suisse
Turkey	96.21	98.58	98.39	97.48	97.52	97.76	95.43	99.17	Turquie
United Kingdom	..	95.35	90.76	96.00	96.96	97.70	97.26	96.48	Royaume-Uni
United States	92.88	92.31	94.78	91.27	92.55	95.56	91.42	91.33	Etats-Unis
N.A.F.T.A.[1]	93.00	92.33	94.61	91.27	92.42	95.30	91.38	91.39	N.A.F.T.A.[1]
EU15[1]	93.37	94.07	93.50	95.10	95.65	96.06	95.82	95.86	UE15[1]
O.E.C.D.[1]	95.66	95.38	96.22	95.70	96.02	96.92	95.05	94.87	O.C.D.E.[1]

VII. Retention ratio (= Net written premiums / Total gross premiums) / Taux de rétention (= Primes nettes émises / Total des primes brutes)

VII.3 Non-Life / Non-Vie

% (per cent / pourcentage)

COUNTRY	1992	1993	1994	1995	1996	1997	1998	1999	PAYS
Australia	78.98	83.72	80.99	82.88	83.59	83.19	77.07	77.29	Australie
Austria	81.27	80.60	73.79	75.51	73.22	72.16	73.97	73.39	Autriche
Belgium	80.44	81.08	81.57	83.35	84.48	85.74	86.71	88.42	Belgique
Canada	79.38	79.73	76.44	78.81	81.83	82.32	82.28	83.59	Canada
Czech Republic	..	91.13	88.06	83.96	82.29	81.29	79.22	78.64	République Tchèque
Denmark	..	..	..	..	88.60	..	..	..	Danemark
Finland	88.56	89.23	88.23	88.31	89.47	89.85	90.81	90.77	Finlande
France	84.18	84.85	83.28	83.46	83.78	84.65	85.59	84.95	France
Germany	74.51	74.90	75.87	76.94	77.27	77.60	78.43	77.38	Allemagne
Greece	100.00	73.53	73.23	73.29	75.22	76.89	..	77.61	Grèce
Hungary	86.61	85.83	84.94	84.50	88.19	84.33	83.81	81.45	Hongrie
Iceland	65.42	66.46	66.34	68.30	70.78	71.38	73.72	77.48	Islande
Ireland	81.70	81.49	79.90	79.09	79.62	83.40	83.72	78.95	Irlande
Italy	78.38	80.60	82.58	83.36	84.41	85.01	86.20	87.01	Italie
Japan	78.99	80.69	81.17	81.01	81.82	..	86.48	..	Japon
Korea	..	..	85.78	87.05	88.70	89.99	88.61	87.35	Corée
Luxembourg	..	..	62.66	68.79	74.91	73.36	74.63	75.35	Luxembourg
Mexico	73.97	72.69	73.89	70.46	69.86	72.18	74.68	75.60	Mexique
Netherlands	85.38	85.74	85.99	87.29	87.84	88.56	87.75	88.15	Pays-Bas
New Zealand	96.50	84.88	82.21	80.95	86.82	87.96	89.09	..	Nouvelle Zélande
Norway	77.24	75.21	..	..	84.18	83.42	82.84	82.60	Norvège
Poland	..	62.25	60.45	65.86	65.42	66.06	74.83	71.58	Pologne
Portugal	86.19	86.40	87.38	86.98	85.16	84.55	82.61	83.21	Portugal
Slovak Republic	..	..	..	..	..	75.11	73.36	77.30	République Slovaque
Spain	82.26	82.23	83.50	85.35	85.55	86.13	86.56	86.66	Espagne
Sweden	..	..	..	..	..	79.51	79.11	..	Suède
Switzerland	80.22	79.36	..	..	71.59	78.35	68.62	85.73	Suisse
Turkey	53.16	83.62	77.35	77.93	78.60	77.86	59.42	84.35	Turquie
United Kingdom	77.21	78.84	78.15	77.82	78.51	78.79	79.38	79.85	Royaume-Uni
United States	88.36	88.43	87.82	87.50	88.07	89.99	89.25	88.59	Etats-Unis
N.A.F.T.A.[1]	87.88	87.97	87.38	87.17	87.73	89.63	88.96	88.28	N.A.F.T.A.[1]
EU15[1]	78.70	79.40	79.27	79.94	80.57	80.84	81.62	81.41	UE15[1]
O.E.C.D.[1]	83.58	84.13	83.87	83.87	84.38	86.31	86.03	85.67	O.C.D.E.[1]

1. For available data only / Uniquement pour les données disponibles

VIII. Ratio of reinsurance accepted (= Reinsurance accepted / Total gross premiums) / Taux de réassurance acceptée (= Réassurance acceptée / Total des primes brutes)

VIII.1 Total / Total

COUNTRY	\% (per cent / pourcentage)								PAYS
	1992	1993	1994	1995	1996	1997	1998	1999	
Australia	..	5.02	..	..	7.08	3.76	4.67	7.64	Australie
Austria	9.50	8.87	12.72	9.99	11.31	13.74	12.01	12.32	Autriche
Belgium	4.74	3.34	2.81	5.65	5.26	5.06	3.81	4.21	Belgique
Canada	12.21	12.55	12.66	11.08	12.57	12.45	13.00	9.79	Canada
Czech Republic	..	0.00	0.00	1.60	0.29	1.10	1.11	0.33	République Tchèque
Denmark	17.48	11.46	13.77	9.01	7.98	7.09	7.50	7.94	Danemark
Finland	4.89	9.93	6.91	5.88	5.06	4.48	3.90	3.03	Finlande
France	11.24	10.98	7.67	7.39	6.41	5.93	6.47	6.40	France
Germany	20.49	20.76	21.61	21.07	20.95	21.87	21.62	22.26	Allemagne
Greece	..	3.95	3.62	2.11	2.74	1.84	1.97	1.32	Grèce
Hungary	1.47	1.22	0.58	0.44	0.33	0.28	0.32	0.13	Hongrie
Iceland	16.25	15.79	14.19	11.67	10.94	10.82	8.82	6.03	Islande
Ireland	9.97	7.64	2.11	4.40	4.17	7.09	5.23	5.64	Irlande
Italy	15.23	13.80	11.76	11.04	10.44	9.31	7.67	6.35	Italie
Japan	2.55	2.30	2.25	2.33	1.85	1.71	1.81	1.81	Japon
Korea	..	..	2.69	2.43	2.40	2.17	1.97	2.38	Corée
Luxembourg	..	..	0.43	0.08	0.21	0.21	0.11	0.07	Luxembourg
Mexico	4.13	4.20	3.95	4.50	3.69	3.29	2.51	2.32	Mexique
Netherlands	..	..	..	3.32	2.58	1.98	2.19	2.35	Pays-Bas
New Zealand	..	..	..	..	..	..	..	..	Nouvelle Zélande
Norway	..	5.25	..	..	0.56	0.54	0.62	0.62	Norvège
Poland	..	..	..	..	0.44	1.19	1.01	1.86	Pologne
Portugal	1.28	1.30	1.11	1.15	1.41	1.70	3.02	2.25	Portugal
Slovak Republic	..	..	..	..	..	0.56	0.30	0.26	République Slovaque
Spain	4.29	4.83	3.97	3.85	3.44	3.49	3.29	4.02	Espagne
Sweden	..	..	..	..	..	..	9.56	7.39	Suède
Switzerland	36.03	36.27	33.97	30.12	15.33	12.11	9.02	6.87	Suisse
Turkey	2.05	1.47	1.39	1.21	1.15	1.00	0.80	3.01	Turquie
United Kingdom	..	..	..	..	6.40	5.38	6.18	5.34	Royaume-Uni
United States	8.31	8.69	7.62	8.92	8.51	6.91	9.22	8.14	Etats-Unis
N.A.F.T.A.[1]	8.45	8.80	7.78	8.98	8.63	7.07	9.28	8.17	N.A.F.T.A.[1]
EU15[1]	14.19	14.31	13.22	12.20	10.35	9.83	9.66	9.51	UE15[1]
O.E.C.D.[1]	9.19	8.97	7.55	7.99	7.79	6.89	8.05	7.43	O.C.D.E.[1]

VIII.2 Life / Vie

COUNTRY	\% (per cent / pourcentage)								PAYS
	1992	1993	1994	1995	1996	1997	1998	1999	
Australia	..	0.30	..	..	0.00	1.24	1.52	2.59	Australie
Austria	0.97	0.79	0.71	0.71	0.71	0.98	0.96	0.69	Autriche
Belgium	1.02	1.11	1.24	1.35	1.33	1.28	0.98	0.56	Belgique
Canada	3.93	3.31	5.44	5.95	7.28	8.06	9.99	6.03	Canada
Czech Republic	..	0.00	0.00	0.00	0.00	0.00	0.00	0.00	République Tchèque
Denmark	0.38	0.27	0.46	0.25	0.25	0.26	0.21	0.21	Danemark
Finland	-0.73	0.04	0.10	0.08	0.14	0.97	0.54	0.44	Finlande
France	3.64	3.09	2.68	2.67	1.74	1.57	1.89	1.76	France
Germany	9.60	9.54	10.06	10.04	10.17	10.83	11.11	11.56	Allemagne
Greece	..	0.14	0.11	0.06	0.16	0.09	0.11	0.13	Grèce
Hungary	0.73	1.61	0.00	0.00	0.00	0.00	0.00	0.00	Hongrie
Iceland	2.34	2.11	14.77	16.91	0.36	17.51	0.41	0.00	Islande
Ireland	15.05	9.38	0.18	0.43	0.96	0.82	0.62	0.59	Irlande
Italy	18.36	15.00	11.12	9.85	10.23	8.43	6.25	5.01	Italie
Japan	0.12	0.12	0.13	0.14	0.15	0.15	0.41	0.46	Japon
Korea	..	..	0.00	0.01	0.12	0.00	0.00	0.01	Corée
Luxembourg	..	..	0.34	0.06	0.20	0.20	0.03	0.00	Luxembourg
Mexico	1.00	1.13	1.13	1.14	1.07	1.32	0.94	0.75	Mexique
Netherlands	..	..	..	3.48	1.79	1.19	1.89	2.15	Pays-Bas
New Zealand	..	..	..	..	..	..	..	..	Nouvelle Zélande
Norway	..	0.00	0.00	0.00	0.00	0.00	0.00	0.00	Norvège
Poland	..	..	..	..	0.00	0.00	0.00	0.00	Pologne
Portugal	0.11	0.08	0.01	0.02	0.15	0.20	0.23	0.46	Portugal
Slovak Republic	..	..	..	..	..	0.00	0.00	0.00	République Slovaque
Spain	0.61	0.68	0.44	0.65	0.44	0.68	0.27	2.05	Espagne
Sweden	6.42	5.39	2.90	4.26	0.13	0.31	0.24	0.39	Suède
Switzerland	9.25	9.07	7.30	7.24	3.75	1.77	1.65	1.10	Suisse
Turkey	0.02	0.02	0.03	0.57	0.54	0.55	0.01	0.00	Turquie
United Kingdom	..	..	..	..	0.76	0.71	0.83	0.63	Royaume-Uni
United States	7.40	7.82	4.66	7.31	6.79	5.12	10.34	7.57	Etats-Unis
N.A.F.T.A.[1]	7.17	7.60	4.67	7.21	6.79	5.19	10.27	7.45	N.A.F.T.A.[1]
EU15[1]	6.76	6.11	5.37	5.11	3.52	3.34	3.31	3.15	UE15[1]
O.E.C.D.[1]	4.60	4.37	3.04	3.88	3.46	2.96	5.13	4.24	O.C.D.E.[1]

40

VIII. Ratio of reinsurance accepted (= Reinsurance accepted / Total gross premiums) / Taux de réassurance acceptée (= Réassurance acceptée / Total des primes brutes)

VIII.3 Non-Life / Non-Vie									
								% (per cent / pourcentage)	
COUNTRY	1992	1993	1994	1995	1996	1997	1998	1999	PAYS
Australia	17.94	11.84	16.97	14.40	13.95	7.25	10.51	16.89	Australie
Austria	12.79	12.60	17.78	14.49	18.21	19.98	18.16	19.71	Autriche
Belgium	6.55	4.53	3.83	8.57	8.32	8.59	7.29	9.36	Belgique
Canada	18.84	18.32	21.33	17.57	15.71	14.95	14.66	13.21	Canada
Czech Republic	..	0.00	0.00	2.21	0.40	1.48	1.53	0.48	République Tchèque
Denmark	28.17	20.59	25.79	18.07	17.31	15.99	18.02	18.78	Danemark
Finland	13.76	12.15	9.04	9.24	9.71	7.61	7.16	6.41	Finlande
France	19.46	20.71	15.13	14.70	14.17	13.98	13.47	14.33	France
Germany	26.52	26.92	27.99	27.21	27.19	28.42	28.17	29.50	Allemagne
Greece		7.23	6.80	3.99	5.03	3.52	3.85	2.78	Grèce
Hungary	1.63	1.12	0.77	0.63	0.49	0.42	0.51	0.23	Hongrie
Iceland	16.64	16.22	14.17	11.45	11.33	10.53	9.22	6.38	Islande
Ireland	3.81	5.39	4.33	8.77	8.33	16.55	14.17	17.41	Irlande
Italy	13.97	13.28	12.07	11.73	10.57	10.04	9.16	8.10	Italie
Japan	9.37	8.30	8.10	8.24	6.14	5.92	5.66	5.43	Japon
Korea	..	..	10.86	9.62	8.46	7.60	8.08	9.35	Corée
Luxembourg	..	..	0.66	0.19	0.21	0.26	0.66	0.48	Luxembourg
Mexico	5.68	5.68	5.39	6.14	5.01	4.38	3.78	3.75	Mexique
Netherlands	4.09	3.48	3.35	3.14	3.50	2.96	2.59	2.61	Pays-Bas
New Zealand			..	..	1.53	1.43	1.08	..	Nouvelle Zélande
Norway	9.39	8.37	..	..	1.00	1.06	1.21	1.15	Norvège
Poland	..	..	..	0.63	0.61	1.65	1.42	2.73	Pologne
Portugal	1.74	1.85	1.68	1.99	2.52	2.95	5.81	4.55	Portugal
Slovak Republic	..	..	..	..	..	0.76	0.42	0.39	République Slovaque
Spain	6.05	6.80	6.53	5.95	5.68	5.88	5.88	6.12	Espagne
Sweden	..	..	..	..	..	22.37	19.42	..	Suède
Switzerland	54.50	55.80	54.76	51.56	31.72	29.29	24.11	15.22	Suisse
Turkey	2.52	1.71	1.58	1.30	1.25	1.08	0.96	3.58	Turquie
United Kingdom	20.06	17.35	14.17	14.37	14.34	12.70	15.90	15.76	Royaume-Uni
United States	8.83	9.21	9.43	9.94	9.64	8.00	8.46	8.65	Etats-Unis
N.A.F.T.A.[1]	9.22	9.52	9.73	10.13	9.84	8.21	8.61	8.81	N.A.F.T.A.[1]
EU15[1]	18.60	19.28	17.98	17.25	17.02	16.90	17.00	17.60	UE15[1]
O.E.C.D.[1]	13.60	13.29	12.10	12.34	12.14	10.79	11.05	11.33	O.C.D.E.[1]

1. For available data only / Uniquement pour les données disponibles

IX.1 Foreign companies' market share in the domestic market (Gross premiums basis) / Life
Part du marché national détenue par les entreprises étrangères (Sur la base des primes brutes) / Vie

IX.1.1 Market share of (foreign controlled undertakings) and (branches/agencies of foreign undertakings) in total domestic business (Gross premium basis)/Part du marché des (entreprises sous contrôle étranger) et (succursales et agences d'entreprises étrangères dans le marché national (Sur la base des primes brutes)

% (per cent \ pourcentage)

COUNTRY	1992	1993	1994	1995	1996	1997	1998	1999	PAYS
Australia	26.17	..	..	..	30.32	45.50	31.24	30.53	Australie
Austria	36.49	33.82	37.51	34.74	34.36	35.03	32.49	30.28	Autriche
Belgium	..						..	..	Belgique
Canada	35.81	28.72	33.17	38.19	37.25			31.02	Canada
Czech Republic	..	6.88	14.96	20.85	24.34	28.23	32.03	32.54	République Tchèque
Denmark	9.55	7.65	8.67	7.54	7.48	6.88	6.25	17.92	Danemark
Finland	0.00	..	0.00	..	..	0.00	0.00	0.00	Finlande
France	6.66	..						..	France
Germany	11.43	11.33	9.80	9.14	8.48	8.58	7.68	17.21	Allemagne
Greece	..						..	..	Grèce
Hungary	99.66	99.78	99.62	98.63	97.07	94.86	88.62	84.77	Hongrie
Iceland	1.64	3.38	4.09	4.76	4.88	0.00	0.00	0.00	Islande
Ireland	..	..	..	..	..	..	..	..	Irlande
Italy	..	..	..	..	..	..	..	..	Italie
Japan	2.48	2.66	3.07	3.40	3.81	3.77	4.96	8.90	Japon
Korea			0.38	0.34	0.36	0.38	0.90	5.95	Corée
Luxembourg	..	..	..	..	91.70	82.96	84.85	70.97	Luxembourg
Mexico	0.00	0.00	0.00	1.13	2.04	9.85	9.72	6.60	Mexique
Netherlands	23.30	22.85	22.36	22.22	20.77	34.23	34.31	32.08	Pays-Bas
New Zealand	..	..	..	..	..	..		..	Nouvelle Zélande
Norway	2.18	1.77	..	2.48	2.80	2.82	3.63	4.00	Norvège
Poland	..	..	..	..	..	33.07	38.31	45.60	Pologne
Portugal	27.86	28.78	29.35	12.15	12.11	13.16	15.22	12.03	Portugal
Slovak Republic	..	..	..	..	..	25.14	33.48	46.27	République Slovaque
Spain	..	27.13	19.43	26.69	21.56	20.41	28.74	15.75	Espagne
Sweden	0.00	0.00	0.00	0.00	0.00	0.00	0.00	..	Suède
Switzerland	2.35	2.78	..	7.35	..	..	..	..	Suisse
Turkey	..	4.88	5.80	6.60	8.96	6.76	7.08	10.40	Turquie
United Kingdom	..	..	..	..	21.50	19.94	26.31	26.06	Royaume-Uni
United States	12.14	15.15	13.41	12.65	14.34	12.97	17.23	19.79	Etats-Unis

IX.1.2 Market share of (branches/agencies of foreign undertakings) in total domestic business (Gross premium basis)
Part du marché des (succursales et agences d'entreprises étrangères) dans le marché national (Sur la base des primes brutes)

% (per cent \ pourcentage)

COUNTRY	1992	1993	1994	1995	1996	1997	1998	1999	PAYS
Australia	8.17	..	..	..	0.09	0.00	0.04	0.00	Australie
Austria	0.37	0.52	0.07	0.12	0.00	0.00	0.00	0.00	Autriche
Belgium	7.09	8.40	8.19	4.16	3.56	3.50	3.11	2.79	Belgique
Canada	19.39	8.73	20.99	21.54	18.57	16.78	12.34	7.84	Canada
Czech Republic	..	5.43	9.70	14.09	15.49	17.30	18.89	17.86	République Tchèque
Denmark	2.37	1.70	0.68	0.58	0.48	0.40	0.33	0.31	Danemark
Finland	0.00	..	0.00	..	0.00	0.00	0.00	0.00	Finlande
France	1.94	1.65	1.07	1.00	1.03	0.95	1.00	1.04	France
Germany	2.99	3.00	2.65	2.09	2.10	2.10	2.18	2.14	Allemagne
Greece	23.04	23.50	24.16	25.25	25.97	10.20	9.73	7.95	Grèce
Hungary	0.00	0.00	0.00	0.00	0.00	0.00	0.00	0.00	Hongrie
Iceland	0.00	0.00	0.00	0.00	0.00	0.00	0.00	0.00	Islande
Ireland	24.75	21.95	23.69	22.43	22.59	19.45	17.19	10.95	Irlande
Italy	1.42	1.57	1.80	2.18	2.49	2.41	2.32	2.27	Italie
Japan	1.94	2.10	2.38	2.31	2.66	2.77	3.22	3.81	Japon
Korea	..		0.13	0.11	0.10	0.10	0.08	0.13	Corée
Luxembourg	..	..	4.05	2.26	2.28	2.82	4.47	7.83	Luxembourg
Mexico	0.00	0.00	0.00	0.00	0.00	0.00	0.00	0.00	Mexique
Netherlands	5.82	6.51	5.68	5.64	5.50	5.14	4.27	4.77	Pays-Bas
New Zealand	..	..	..	..	..	..		..	Nouvelle Zélande
Norway	0.00	0.00	..	0.00	0.02	0.01	0.20	0.45	Norvège
Poland	..	..	..	..	..	0.00	0.00	0.00	Pologne
Portugal	18.73	12.91	5.89	2.22	1.93	2.33	2.23	1.66	Portugal
Slovak Republic	..	..	..	..	..	0.00	0.00	0.00	République Slovaque
Spain	6.30	5.51	7.11	3.67	3.94	3.63	0.96	0.75	Espagne
Sweden	0.00	0.00	0.00	0.00	0.00	0.00	0.00	..	Suède
Switzerland	0.00	0.00	..	0.00	0.00	..	0.00	0.02	Suisse
Turkey	..	0.00	0.00	0.00	0.00	0.00	0.00	0.00	Turquie
United Kingdom	..	2.27	2.12	2.68	3.06	2.51	4.81	4.05	Royaume-Uni
United States	2.44	2.15	1.14	1.19	1.04	0.59	0.51	0.00	Etats-Unis

IX.2 Foreign companies' market share in the domestic market (Gross premiums basis) / Non-Life
   Part du marché national détenue par les entreprises étrangères (Sur la base des primes brutes) / Non-Vie

IX.2.1 Market share of (foreign controlled undertakings) and (branches/agencies of foreign undertakings) in total domestic
business (Gross premium basis). Part du marché des (entreprises sous contrôle étranger) et (succursales et agences d'entreprises
étrangères) dans le marché national (Sur la base des primes brutes)   % (per cent \ pourcentage)

COUNTRY	1992	1993	1994	1995	1996	1997	1998	1999	PAYS
Australia	58.08	38.91	37.05	38.13	36.89	32.87	53.23	47.98	Australie
Austria	48.18	48.78	49.25	47.60	49.34	49.16	50.85	48.83	Autriche
Belgium	..	..	..	..	..	..	..	..	Belgique
Canada	64.37	61.58	70.50	72.06	63.68	..	..	22.61	Canada
Czech Republic	..	9.64	20.66	25.63	30.03	28.43	28.09	28.78	République Tchèque
Denmark	34.48	36.74	22.15	32.84	30.86	28.64	30.17	43.67	Danemark
Finland	0.23	..	..	..	..	0.13	0.13	0.24	Finlande
France	18.29	..	..	..	..	..	..	..	France
Germany	14.26	16.29	7.83	7.30	13.08	12.70	12.20	13.60	Allemagne
Greece	..	..	..	..	..	..	..	..	Grèce
Hungary	95.20	95.69	93.96	92.30	91.01	90.93	91.79	90.68	Hongrie
Iceland	3.92	4.11	0.68	3.63	3.57	0.00	0.00	0.00	Islande
Ireland	..	..	..	..	..	..	..	..	Irlande
Italy	..	..	..	..	..	..	..	..	Italie
Japan	3.17	3.16	3.29	3.33	3.33	3.59	3.68	3.95	Japon
Korea	..	..	0.24	0.59	0.41	0.36	0.34	0.37	Corée
Luxembourg	..	..	..	..	36.03	31.74	25.56	23.94	Luxembourg
Mexico	0.00	0.00	0.05	3.87	6.99	10.98	10.33	13.81	Mexique
Netherlands	29.05	25.85	23.51	22.29	20.96	36.63	36.69	35.81	Pays-Bas
New Zealand	..	..	..	..	..	..	..	..	Nouvelle Zélande
Norway	15.72	16.60	..	..	19.25	21.02	22.88	21.07	Norvège
Poland	..	..	..	..	..	..	12.06	16.25	Pologne
Portugal	25.72	12.76	9.12	15.35	14.94	15.03	26.43	26.71	Portugal
Slovak Republic	..	..	..	..	..	31.36	26.78	..	République Slovaque
Spain	..	41.29	32.10	33.09	29.32	27.29	26.65	25.18	Espagne
Sweden	..	..	..	..	..	..	..	..	Suède
Switzerland	9.79	12.22	10.89	7.81	..	..	..	..	Suisse
Turkey	12.30	11.47	10.01	9.82	10.18	8.74	7.77	3.44	Turquie
United Kingdom	..	..	..	..	..	37.34	39.91	44.45	Royaume-Uni
United States	10.04	10.39	9.81	10.00	10.73	8.75	8.67	10.38	Etats-Unis

IX.2.2 Market share of (branches/agencies of foreign undertakings) in total domestic business (Gross premium basis)
   Part du marché des (succursales et agences d'entreprises étrangères) dans le marché national (Sur la base des primes brutes)   % (per cent \ pourcentage)

COUNTRY	1992	1993	1994	1995	1996	1997	1998	1999	PAYS
Australia	6.96	5.86	4.68	5.12	4.88	5.00	6.76	6.41	Australie
Austria	0.89	0.85	0.16	0.17	0.16	0.17	0.13	0.16	Autriche
Belgium	7.25	6.84	2.92	2.34	2.57	2.46	2.57	2.58	Belgique
Canada	25.04	24.59	26.96	26.62	26.80	25.17	23.51	19.00	Canada
Czech Republic	..	0.32	0.87	0.68	1.10	1.44	1.07	1.38	République Tchèque
Denmark	5.09	6.24	3.42	2.43	1.80	1.73	1.81	1.62	Danemark
Finland	0.23	0.32	0.44	0.12	0.12	0.13	0.13	0.24	Finlande
France	2.75	2.73	1.35	1.25	1.25	1.24	1.23	1.04	France
Germany	2.27	2.21	1.53	1.11	0.70	0.66	0.67	0.67	Allemagne
Greece	13.99	12.32	10.91	10.67	10.13	10.25	9.82	8.26	Grèce
Hungary	0.00	0.00	0.00	0.00	0.00	0.00	0.00	0.00	Hongrie
Iceland	0.00	0.00	0.00	0.00	0.00	0.00	0.00	0.00	Islande
Ireland	34.36	27.80	24.86	18.07	19.68	16.05	16.74	16.54	Irlande
Italy	3.74	3.67	2.80	3.67	3.86	4.53	4.83	5.57	Italie
Japan	2.88	2.86	2.96	3.00	2.59	2.74	2.98	3.22	Japon
Korea	..	..	0.24	0.59	0.41	0.36	0.34	0.37	Corée
Luxembourg	..	..	18.70	15.91	15.78	14.94	12.34	10.01	Luxembourg
Mexico	0.00	0.00	0.00	0.00	0.00	0.00	0.00	0.00	Mexique
Netherlands	6.27	5.80	5.11	3.06	2.55	2.50	2.41	2.12	Pays-Bas
New Zealand	..	..	..	..	..	..	..	..	Nouvelle Zélande
Norway	1.37	1.45	..	..	1.76	2.84	2.77	2.82	Norvège
Poland	..	..	..	..	..	..	0.00	0.00	Pologne
Portugal	7.37	7.65	3.67	0.70	0.71	0.74	0.78	0.05	Portugal
Slovak Republic	..	..	..	..	..	0.00	0.00	..	République Slovaque
Spain	7.69	6.32	6.67	3.77	3.19	3.38	0.05	0.06	Espagne
Sweden	..	..	..	..	..	..	..	..	Suède
Switzerland	1.09	1.07	1.07	0.97	1.60	1.81	1.95	1.78	Suisse
Turkey	0.12	0.30	0.20	0.10	0.00	0.00	0.00	0.00	Turquie
United Kingdom	5.24	6.25	6.35	6.25	6.60	7.40	10.90	9.93	Royaume-Uni
United States	0.87	1.00	0.84	1.06	0.95	0.65	0.55	0.59	Etats-Unis

PART II

PARTIE II

TABLES BY COUNTRY

TABLEAUX PAR PAYS

AUSTRALIA

Monetary Unit: million Australian dollars

AUSTRALIE

Unité monétaire : million de dollars australiens

		1992	1993	1994	1995	1996	1997	1998	1999
A. NUMBER OF COMPANIES IN THE REPORTING COUNTRY	**A. NOMBRE D'ENTREPRISES DANS LE PAYS DECLARANT**								
A.1. Life	**A.1. Vie**								
A.1.1. Domestic Companies	A.1.1. Entreprises Nationales	46	37	41	42	42	40	43	43
A.1.2. (Foreign Controlled Companies)	A.1.2. (Entreprises Sous Contrôle Etranger)	19	13	18	18	19	21	20	23
A.1.3. Branches & Agencies of Foreign Cies	A.1.3. Succursales et Agences d'Ent. Etrangères	2	7	2	1	1	0	1	0
A.1. All Companies	A.1. Ensemble des Entreprises	48	44	43	43	43	40	44	43
A.2. Non-Life	**A.2. Non-Vie**								
A.2.1. Domestic Companies	A.2.1. Entreprises Nationales	108	108	119	124	126	129	115	111
A.2.2. (Foreign Controlled Companies)	A.2.2. (Entreprises Sous Contrôle Etranger)	45	44	53	51	45	39	38	36
A.2.3. Branches & Agencies of Foreign Cies	A.2.3. Succursales et Agences d'Ent. Etrangères	21	21	17	17	17	15	16	17
A.2. All Companies	A.2. Ensemble des Entreprises	129	129	136	141	143	144	131	128
A.3. Composite	**A.3. Mixte**								
A.3.1. Domestic Companies	A.3.1. Entreprises Nationales	0	2	0	0	0	0	0	0
A.3.2. (Foreign Controlled Companies)	A.3.2. (Entreprises Sous Contrôle Etranger)	0	1	0	0	0	0	0	0
A.3. All Companies	A.3. Ensemble des Entreprises	0	2	0	0	0	0	0	0
A.4. Reinsurance	**A.4. Réassurance**								
A.4.1. Domestic Companies	A.4.1. Entreprises Nationales	17	12	18	18	19	20	23	28
A.4.2. (Foreign Controlled Companies)	A.4.2. (Entreprises Sous Contrôle Etranger)	14	9	13	15	15	17	18	19
A.4.3. Branches & Agencies of Foreign Cies	A.4.3. Succursales et Agences d'Ent. Etrangères	15	15	13	14	14	12	15	13
A.4. All Companies	A.4. Ensemble des Entreprises	32	27	31	32	33	32	38	41
A.5. Total	**A.5. Total**								
A.5.1. Domestic Companies	A.5.1. Entreprises Nationales	171	159	178	184	187	189	181	182
A.5.2. (Foreign Controlled Companies)	A.5.2. (Entreprises Sous Contrôle Etranger)	78	67	84	84	79	77	76	78
A.5.3. Branches & Agencies of Foreign Cies	A.5.3. Succursales et Agences d'Ent. Etrangères	38	43	32	32	32	27	32	30
A.5. All Insurance Companies	A.5. Ensemble des Entreprises d'Assurances	209	202	210	216	219	216	213	212
C. BUSINESS WRITTEN IN THE REPORTING COUNTRY	**C. OPERATIONS CONCLUES DANS LE PAYS DECLARANT**								
C.1. Life	**C.1. Vie**								
C.1.1. Gross Premiums	C.1.1. Primes Brutes								
C.1.1.1. Direct Business	C.1.1.1. Assurances Directes								
C.1.1.1.1. Domestic Companies	C.1.1.1.1. Entreprises Nationales	16 514	23 591	:	:	20 522	28 824	35 199	38 537
C.1.1.1.2. (Foreign Controlled Companies)	C.1.1.1.2. (Entreprises Sous Contrôle Etranger)	3 236	6 492	:	:	6 208	12 919	10 611	11 052
C.1.1.1.3. Branches & Agencies of Foreign Cies	C.1.1.1.3. Succursales et Agences d'Ent. Etrangères	1 470	..	:	:	19	0	15	0
C.1.1.1. Total	C.1.1.1. Total	17 985	23 591	:	:	20 541	28 824	35 214	38 537
C.1.1.2. Reinsurance Accepted	C.1.1.2. Réassurance Acceptée								
C.1.1.2.1. Domestic Companies	C.1.1.2.1. Entreprises Nationales	..	71	:	:	0	362	545	1 024
C.1.1.2.2. (Foreign Controlled Companies)	C.1.1.2.2. (Entreprises Sous Contrôle Etranger)	..	68	:	:	0	362	545	1 024
C.1.1.2. Total	C.1.1.2. Total	..	71	:	:	0	362	545	1 024
C.1.1.3. Total	C.1.1.3. Total								
C.1.1.3.1. Domestic Companies	C.1.1.3.1. Entreprises Nationales	16 514	23 662	:	:	20 522	29 186	35 744	39 561
C.1.1.3.2. (Foreign Controlled Companies)	C.1.1.3.2. (Entreprises Sous Contrôle Etranger)	3 236	6 560	:	:	6 208	13 281	11 156	12 076
C.1.1.3.3. Branches & Agencies of Foreign Cies	C.1.1.3.3. Succursales et Agences d'Ent. Etrangères	1 470	..	:	:	19	0	15	0
C.1.1.3. Total Gross Premiums	C.1.1.3. Total des Primes Brutes	17 985	23 662	:	:	20 541	29 186	35 759	39 561
C.1.2. Ceded Premiums	C.1.2. Primes Cédées								
C.1.2.1. Domestic Companies	C.1.2.1. Entreprises Nationales	..	2 263	..	..	0	..	546	836
C.1.2.2. (Foreign Controlled Companies)	C.1.2.2. (Entreprises Sous Contrôle Etranger)	..	621	..	..	0	..	325	500
C.1.2. Total	C.1.2. Total	..	2 263	..	..	0	..	546	836
C.1.3. Net Written Premiums	C.1.3. Primes Nettes Emises								
C.1.3.1. Domestic Companies	C.1.3.1. Entreprises Nationales	16 514	21 399	21 434	20 667	20 522	29 186	35 198	38 725
C.1.3.2. (Foreign Controlled Companies)	C.1.3.2. (Entreprises Sous Contrôle Etranger)	3 236	5 939	4 475	5 646	6 208	13 281	10 831	11 575
C.1.3.3. Branches & Agencies of Foreign Cies	C.1.3.3. Succursales et Agences d'Ent. Etrangères	1 470	..	1 466	19	19	0	15	0
C.1.3. Total	C.1.3. Total	17 985	21 399	22 900	20 686	20 541	29 186	35 213	38 725

Monetary Unit: million Australian dollars   Unité monétaire : million de dollars australiens

C.2. Non-Life — C.2. Non-Vie

Label (English)	Label (Français)	1992	1993	1994	1995	1996	1997	1998	1999
C.2.1. Gross premiums	**C.2.1. Primes Brutes**								
C.2.1.1. Direct Business	C.2.1.1. Assurances Directes								
C.2.1.1.1. Domestic Companies	C.2.1.1.1. Entreprises Nationales	6 525	13 971	15 399	15 874	17 769	19 159	16 063	16 892
C.2.1.1.2. (Foreign Controlled Companies)	C.2.1.1.2. (Entreprises Sous Contrôle Etranger)	3 314	4 554	5 328	5 221	5 576	5 200	7 238	7 280
C.2.1.1.3. Branches & Agencies of Foreign Cies	C.2.1.1.3. Succursales et Agences d'Ent. Etrangères	240	474	376	438	439	409	1 197	1 096
C.2.1.1. Total	C.2.1.1. Total	6 765	14 445	15 775	16 312	18 208	19 568	17 260	17 988
C.2.1.2. Reinsurance Accepted	C.2.1.2. Réassurance Acceptée								
C.2.1.2.1. Domestic Companies	C.2.1.2.1. Entreprises Nationales	926	1 454	2 711	2 207	2 359	884	1 919	3 364
C.2.1.2.2. (Foreign Controlled Companies)	C.2.1.2.2. (Entreprises Sous Contrôle Etranger)	900	962	822	1 070	1 197	680	1 724	1 718
C.2.1.2.3. Branches & Agencies of Foreign Cies	C.2.1.2.3. Succursales et Agences d'Ent. Etrangères	334	486	513	538	594	646	107	291
C.2.1.2. Total	C.2.1.2. Total	1 479	1 940	3 224	2 745	2 953	1 530	2 026	3 655
C.2.1.3. Total	C.2.1.3. Total								
C.2.1.3.1. Domestic Companies	C.2.1.3.1. Entreprises Nationales	7 451	15 425	18 110	18 081	20 128	20 043	17 982	20 256
C.2.1.3.2. (Foreign Controlled Companies)	C.2.1.3.2. (Entreprises Sous Contrôle Etranger)	4 214	5 416	6 150	6 291	6 773	5 880	8 962	8 998
C.2.1.3.3. Branches & Agencies of Foreign Cies	C.2.1.3.3. Succursales et Agences d'Ent. Etrangères	574	960	889	976	1 033	1 055	1 304	1 387
C.2.1.3. Total Gross Premiums	C.2.1.3. Total des Primes Brutes	8 244	16 385	18 999	19 057	21 161	21 098	19 286	21 643
C.2.2. Ceded Premiums	**C.2.2. Primes Cédées**								
C.2.2.1. Domestic Companies	C.2.2.1. Entreprises Nationales	1 569	2 342	3 312	3 020	3 266	2 977	3 684	4 126
C.2.2.2. (Foreign Controlled Companies)	C.2.2.2. (Entreprises Sous Contrôle Etranger)	1 009	1 491	1 362	1 595	1 861	1 835	6 933	..
C.2.2.3. Branches & Agencies of Foreign Cies	C.2.2.3. Succursales et Agences d'Ent. Etrangères	164	324	300	243	206	569	738	790
C.2.2. Total	C.2.2. Total	1 733	2 667	3 612	3 263	3 472	3 546	4 422	4 916
C.2.3. Net Written Premiums	**C.2.3. Primes Nettes Emises**								
C.2.3.1. Domestic Companies	C.2.3.1. Entreprises Nationales	5 918	13 083	14 798	15 061	16 862	17 066	14 298	16 130
C.2.3.2. (Foreign Controlled Companies)	C.2.3.2. (Entreprises Sous Contrôle Etranger)	3 205	3 925	4 788	4 696	4 912	4 045	2 029	..
C.2.3.3. Branches & Agencies of Foreign Cies	C.2.3.3. Succursales et Agences d'Ent. Etrangères	410	636	589	733	827	486	566	597
C.2.3. Total	C.2.3. Total	6 511	13 718	15 387	15 794	17 689	17 552	14 864	16 727

C.3. Total

Label (English)	Label (Français)	1992	1993	1994	1995	1996	1997	1998	1999
C.3.1. Gross Premiums	**C.3.1. Primes Brutes**								
C.3.1.1. Direct Business	C.3.1.1. Assurances Directes								
C.3.1.1.1. Domestic Companies	C.3.1.1.1. Entreprises Nationales	23 039	37 562	..	..	38 291	47 983	51 262	55 429
C.3.1.1.2. (Foreign Controlled Companies)	C.3.1.1.2. (Entreprises Sous Contrôle Etranger)	6 550	11 046	..	..	11 784	18 119	17 849	18 332
C.3.1.1.3. Branches & Agencies of Foreign Cies	C.3.1.1.3. Succursales et Agences d'Ent. Etrangères	1 710	..	..	..	458	409	1 212	1 096
C.3.1.1. Total	C.3.1.1. Total	24 750	38 036	..	..	38 749	48 392	52 474	56 525
C.3.1.2. Reinsurance Accepted	C.3.1.2. Réassurance Acceptée								
C.3.1.2.1. Domestic Companies	C.3.1.2.1. Entreprises Nationales	..	1 525	..	..	2 359	1 246	2 464	4 388
C.3.1.2.2. (Foreign Controlled Companies)	C.3.1.2.2. (Entreprises Sous Contrôle Etranger)	..	1 030	..	..	1 197	1 042	2 269	2 742
C.3.1.2.3. Branches & Agencies of Foreign Cies	C.3.1.2.3. Succursales et Agences d'Ent. Etrangères	..	..	..	..	594	646	107	291
C.3.1.2. Total	C.3.1.2. Total	..	2 011	..	..	2 953	1 892	2 571	4 679
C.3.1.3. Total	C.3.1.3. Total								
C.3.1.3.1. Domestic Companies	C.3.1.3.1. Entreprises Nationales	23 965	39 087	..	..	40 650	49 229	53 726	59 817
C.3.1.3.2. (Foreign Controlled Companies)	C.3.1.3.2. (Entreprises Sous Contrôle Etranger)	7 450	11 976	..	..	12 981	19 161	20 118	21 074
C.3.1.3.3. Branches & Agencies of Foreign Cies	C.3.1.3.3. Succursales et Agences d'Ent. Etrangères	2 044	..	..	..	1 052	1 055	1 319	1 387
C.3.1.3. Total Gross Premiums	C.3.1.3. Total des Primes Brutes	26 229	40 047	..	..	41 702	50 284	55 045	61 204
C.3.2. Ceded Premiums	**C.3.2. Primes Cédées**								
C.3.2.1. Domestic Companies	C.3.2.1. Entreprises Nationales	..	4 605	..	..	3 266	..	4 230	4 962
C.3.2.2. (Foreign Controlled Companies)	C.3.2.2. (Entreprises Sous Contrôle Etranger)	..	2 112	..	..	1 861	..	7 258	..
C.3.2.3. Branches & Agencies of Foreign Cies	C.3.2.3. Succursales et Agences d'Ent. Etrangères	..	..	..	..	206	569	738	790
C.3.2. Total	C.3.2. Total	..	4 930	..	..	3 472	..	4 968	5 752
C.3.3. Net Written Premiums	**C.3.3. Primes Nettes Emises**								
C.3.3.1. Domestic Companies	C.3.3.1. Entreprises Nationales	22 432	34 482	36 232	35 728	37 384	46 252	49 496	54 855
C.3.3.2. (Foreign Controlled Companies)	C.3.3.2. (Entreprises Sous Contrôle Etranger)	6 441	9 864	9 263	10 342	11 120	17 326	12 860	..
C.3.3.3. Branches & Agencies of Foreign Cies	C.3.3.3. Succursales et Agences d'Ent. Etrangères	1 880	..	2 055	752	846	486	581	597
C.3.3. Total	C.3.3. Total	24 496	35 117	38 287	36 480	38 230	46 738	50 077	55 452

47

Monetary Unit: million Australian dollars · Unité monétaire : million de dollars australiens

D. NET WRITTEN PREMIUMS IN THE REPORTING COUNTRY IN TERMS OF DOMESTIC AND FOREIGN RISKS
D. PRIMES NETTES EMISES DANS LE PAYS DECLARANT EN RISQUES NATIONAUX ET ETRANGERS

D.1. Life / D.1. Vie

	1992	1993	1994	1995	1996	1997	1998	1999
D.1.1. Domestic Risks / D.1.1. Risques Nationaux								
D.1.1.1. Domestic Companies / Entreprises Nationales	:	:	:	:	:	27 899	34 592	38 160
D.1.1.2. (Foreign Controlled Companies) / (Entreprises Sous Contrôle Etranger)	:	:	:	:	:	12 695	10 544	11 304
D.1.1.3. Branches & Agencies of Foreign Cies / Succursales et Agences d'Ent. Etrangères	:	:	:	:	:	0	15	0
D.1.1. Total / Total des Primes Nettes Vie	:	:	:	:	:	27 899	34 607	38 160
D.1.2. Foreign Risks / D.1.2. Risques Etrangers								
D.1.2.1. Domestic Companies / Entreprises Nationales	:	:	:	:	:	1 287	606	565
D.1.2.2. (Foreign Controlled Companies) / (Entreprises Sous Contrôle Etranger)	:	:	:	:	:	586	287	271
D.1.2. Total / Total des Primes Nettes Vie	:	:	:	:	:	1 287	606	565
D.1.3. Total								
D.1.3.1. Domestic Companies / Entreprises Nationales	:	21 399	21 434	20 667	20 522	29 186	35 198	38 725
D.1.3.2. (Foreign Controlled Companies) / (Entreprises Sous Contrôle Etranger)	:	5 939	4 425	5 646	6 208	13 281	10 831	11 575
D.1.3.3. Branches & Agencies of Foreign Cies / Succursales et Agences d'Ent. Etrangères	:	:	1 466	19	19	0	15	0
D.1.3. Total of Life Net Premiums / Total des Primes Nettes Vie	:	:	22 900	20 686	20 541	29 186	35 213	38 725

D.2. Non-Life / D.2. Non-Vie

	1992	1993	1994	1995	1996	1997	1998	1999
D.2.1. Domestic Risks / D.2.1. Risques Nationaux								
D.2.1.1. Domestic Companies / Entreprises Nationales	2 713	11 360	13 769	13 927	15 619	15 712	12 631	13 410
D.2.1.2. (Foreign Controlled Companies) / (Entreprises Sous Contrôle Etranger)	3 205	3 790	4 698	4 563	4 760	3 912	1 863	
D.2.1.3. Branches & Agencies of Foreign Cies / Succursales et Agences d'Ent. Etrangères	410	623	589	733	826	483	566	597
D.2.1. Total / Total des Primes Nettes Vie	6 511	11 983	14 358	14 660	16 445	16 195	13 197	14 007
D.2.2. Foreign Risks / D.2.2. Risques Etrangers								
D.2.2.1. Domestic Companies / Entreprises Nationales	:	1 723	1 029	1 134	1 243	1 354	1 667	2 720
D.2.2.2. (Foreign Controlled Companies) / (Entreprises Sous Contrôle Etranger)	:	135	90	133	152	133	166	
D.2.2.3. Branches & Agencies of Foreign Cies / Succursales et Agences d'Ent. Etrangères	:	13	0	0	1	3	0	0
D.2.2. Total / Total des Primes Nettes Vie	:	1 736	1 029	1 134	1 244	1 357	1 667	2 720
D.2.3. Total								
D.2.3.1. Domestic Companies / Entreprises Nationales	2 713	13 083	14 798	15 061	16 862	17 066	14 298	16 130
D.2.3.2. (Foreign Controlled Companies) / (Entreprises Sous Contrôle Etranger)	3 205	3 925	4 788	4 696	4 912	4 045	2 029	
D.2.3.3. Branches & Agencies of Foreign Cies / Succursales et Agences d'Ent. Etrangères	410	636	589	733	827	486	566	597
D.2.3. Total / Total des Primes Nettes Vie	6 511	13 719	15 387	15 794	17 689	17 552	14 864	16 727

E. BUSINESS WRITTEN ABROAD
E. OPERATIONS A L'ETRANGER

E.1. Life / E.1. Vie

	1992	1993	1994	1995	1996	1997	1998	1999
E.1.1. Gross Premiums / E.1.1. Primes Brutes								
E.1.1.1. Direct Business / E.1.1.1. Assurance Directe								
E.1.1.1. Total	1 378	:	:	:	1 150	:	:	:
E.1.1.3. Total								
E.1.1.3. Total Gross Premiums / Total des Primes Brutes	1 378	:	:	:	1 150	:	:	:
E.1.3. Net Written Premiums / E.1.3. Primes Nettes Emises								
E.1.3. Total	1 378	:	1 397	1 189	1 150	:	:	:

AUSTRALIA / AUSTRALIE

Monetary Unit: million Australian dollars — Unité monétaire : million de dollars australiens

E.2. Non-Life / E.2. Non-Vie

Item	1992	1993	1994	1995	1996	1997	1998	1999
E.2.1. Gross Premiums / Primes Brutes								
E.2.1.1. Direct Business / Assurance Directe								
E.2.1.1.1. Branches & Agencies / Succursales & Agences	83	..	..					
E.2.1.1. Total	83	..	..	146	245	295	681	
E.2.1.2. Reinsurance Accepted / Réassurance Acceptée								
E.2.1.2.1. Branches & Agencies / Succursales & Agences	65	..	..					
E.2.1.2. Total	65	..	..	1 194	1 215	1 463	2 200	
E.2.1.3. Total								
E.2.1.3.1. Branches & Agencies / Succursales & Agences	148	..	..					
E.2.1.3. Total Gross Premiums / Total des Primes Brutes	148	..	..	1 340	1 460	1 758	2 881	
E.2.2. Ceded Premiums / Primes Cédées								
E.2.2.1. Branches & Agencies / Succursales & Agences	12	..	..					
E.2.2. Total	12	..	..	246	216	401	1 214	
E.2.3. Net Written Premiums / Primes Nettes Emises								
E.2.3.1. Branches & Agencies / Succursales & Agences	136	..	..					
E.2.3. Total	136	..	..	1 267	1 244	1 357	1 667	

F. OUTSTANDING INVESTMENT BY DIRECT INSURANCE COMPANIES / F. ENCOURS DES PLACEMENTS DES ENTREPRISES D'ASSURANCES DIRECTES

F.1. Life / F.1. Vie

Item	1992	1993	1994	1995	1996	1997	1998	1999
F.1.1. Real Estate / Immobilier								
F.1.1.1. Domestic Companies / Entreprises Nationales	9 093	8 221	8 363	8 160	8 131	13 745	16 104	16 586
F.1.1.2. (Foreign Controlled Companies) / (Entreprises Sous Contrôle Etranger)	317	836	989	933	938	5 395	3 301	3 020
F.1.1.3. Branches & Agencies of Foreign Cies / Succursales et Agences d'Ent. Etrangères	636	..	509	1	1	0	0	0
F.1.1.4. Domestic Investment / Placement dans le Pays	10 046	8 221	..	7 111	7 081	13 519	15 848	16 329
F.1.1.5. Foreign Investment / Placement à l'Etranger	1 358	..	..	1 050	1 051	226	256	257
F.1.1. Total	11 404	..	8 872	8 161	8 131	13 745	16 104	16 586
F.1.2. Mortgage Loans / Prêts Hypothécaires								
F.1.2.1. Domestic Companies / Entreprises Nationales	..	2 223	..	..	0	..	..	..
F.1.2.2. (Foreign Controlled Companies) / (Entreprises Sous Contrôle Etranger)	..	1 217	..	..	0	..	..	..
F.1.2.4. Domestic Investment / Placement dans le Pays	..	2 223	..	..	0	..	..	..
F.1.3. Shares / Actions								
F.1.3.1. Domestic Companies / Entreprises Nationales	20 943	31 703	28 970	46 578	45 415	57 449	58 733	72 476
F.1.3.2. (Foreign Controlled Companies) / (Entreprises Sous Contrôle Etranger)	3 556	6 493	4 512	7 168	7 593	25 508	13 749	17 318
F.1.3.3. Branches & Agencies of Foreign Cies / Succursales et Agences d'Ent. Etrangères	1 280	..	1 589	0	0	0	2	0
F.1.3.4. Domestic Investment / Placement dans le Pays	25 778	31 703	..	31 211	30 285	41 284	42 330	53 099
F.1.3.5. Foreign Investment / Placement à l'Etranger	9 796	..	..	15 367	15 130	16 165	16 405	19 377
F.1.3. Total	35 574	..	30 559	46 578	45 415	57 449	58 735	72 476
F.1.4. Bonds with Fixed Revenue / Obligations								
F.1.4.1. Domestic Companies / Entreprises Nationales	15 383	31 100	22 734	29 517	29 835	60 303	65 542	64 147
F.1.4.2. (Foreign Controlled Companies) / (Entreprises Sous Contrôle Etranger)	3 924	7 703	4 997	6 405	6 900	27 102	19 556	19 040
F.1.4.3. Branches & Agencies of Foreign Cies / Succursales et Agences d'Ent. Etrangères	1 273	..	2 139	4	4	0	14	0
F.1.4.4. Domestic Investment / Placement dans le Pays	20 581	31 100	..	23 742	23 986	56 350	59 696	58 609
F.1.4.5. Foreign Investment / Placement à l'Etranger	4 932	..	..	5 779	5 853	3 953	5 860	5 538
F.1.4. Total	25 513	..	24 873	29 521	29 839	60 303	65 556	64 147
F.1.5. Loans other than Mortgage Loans / Prêts Autres qu'Hypothécaires								
F.1.5.1. Domestic Companies / Entreprises Nationales	3 062	4 845	5 814	9 270	9 094	9 394	10 095	9 976
F.1.5.2. (Foreign Controlled Companies) / (Entreprises Sous Contrôle Etranger)	1 416	1 640	1 911	4 622	4 741	6 185	4 306	4 325
F.1.5.3. Branches & Agencies of Foreign Cies / Succursales et Agences d'Ent. Etrangères	1 030	..	1 214	1	1	0	0	0
F.1.5.4. Domestic Investment / Placement dans le Pays	5 508	4 845	..	8 647	8 468	8 579	10 095	9 623
F.1.5.5. Foreign Investment / Placement à l'Etranger	520	..	..	624	626	815	0	353
F.1.5. Total	6 028	..	7 028	9 271	9 094	9 394	10 095	9 976

AUSTRALIA

AUSTRALIE

Monetary Unit: million Australian dollars

Unité monétaire : million de dollars australiens

Label (EN)	1992	1993	1994	1995	1996	1997	1998	1999	Label (FR)
F.1.6. Other Investments									F.1.6. Autres Placements
F.1.6.1. Domestic Companies	22 109	21 878	28 659	41 223	47 291	9 533	10 047	10 805	F.1.6.1. Entreprises Nationales
F.1.6.2. (Foreign Controlled Companies)	5 088	4 649	4 299	8 087	8 846	4 145	2 629	3 180	F.1.6.2. (Entreprises Sous Contrôle Etranger)
F.1.6.3. Branches & Agencies of Foreign Cies	777	..	655	2	2	0	4	4	F.1.6.3. Succursales et Agences d'Ent. Etrangères
F.1.6.4. Domestic Investment	27 974	21 878	..	34 128	39 143	8 138	9 127	9 870	F.1.6.4. Placement dans le Pays
F.1.6.5. Foreign Investment	6 018	..	..	7 097	8 151	1 395	924	935	F.1.6.5. Placement à l' Etranger
F.1.6. Total	33 992	..	29 314	41 225	47 293	9 533	10 051	10 805	F.1.6. Total
F.1.7. Total									F.1.7. Total
F.1.7.1. Domestic Companies	70 590	99 970	94 540	134 748	139 767	150 424	160 521	173 990	F.1.7.1. Entreprises Nationales
F.1.7.2. (Foreign Controlled Companies)	14 301	22 539	16 708	27 215	29 018	68 335	43 541	46 883	F.1.7.2. (Entreprises Sous Contrôle Etranger)
F.1.7.3. Branches & Agencies of Foreign Cies	4 996	..	6 106	7	7	0	20	0	F.1.7.3. Succursales et Agences d'Ent. Etrangères
F.1.7.4. Domestic Investment	89 888	99 970	..	104 839	108 963	127 870	137 096	147 530	F.1.7.4. Placement dans le Pays
F.1.7.5. Foreign Investment	22 623	16 457	..	29 917	30 811	22 554	23 445	26 460	F.1.7.5. Placement à l' Etranger
F.1.7. Total of Life Investments	112 511	116 647	100 646	134 756	139 774	150 424	160 541	173 990	F.1.7. Total des Placements Vie
F.2. Non-Life									F.2. Non-Vie
F.2.1. Real Estate									F.2.1. Immobilier
F.2.1.1. Domestic Companies	534	1 045	1 038	2 317	1 881	3 497	748	707	F.2.1.1. Entreprises Nationales
F.2.1.2. (Foreign Controlled Companies)	385	362	387	375	345	412	150	328	F.2.1.2. (Entreprises Sous Contrôle Etranger)
F.2.1.3. Branches & Agencies of Foreign Cies	43	36	47	46	49	54	55	59	F.2.1.3. Succursales et Agences d'Ent. Etrangères
F.2.1.4. Domestic Investment	961	1 081	..	2 363	1 929	3 550	802	765	F.2.1.4. Placement dans le Pays
F.2.1.5. Foreign Investment	1	0	..	0	1	1	1	1	F.2.1.5. Placement à l' Etranger
F.2.1. Total	962	1 081	1 085	2 363	1 930	3 551	803	766	F.2.1. Total
F.2.2. Mortgage Loans									F.2.2. Prêts Hypothécaires
F.2.2.1. Domestic Companies	..	710	794	794	895	856	..	..	F.2.2.1. Entreprises Nationales
F.2.2.2. (Foreign Controlled Companies)	..	271	210	155	143	173	..	..	F.2.2.2. (Entreprises Sous Contrôle Etranger)
F.2.2.3. Branches & Agencies of Foreign Cies	..	4	3	3	2	2	..	..	F.2.2.3. Succursales et Agences d'Ent. Etrangères
F.2.2.4. Domestic Investment	..	714	797	797	896	858	..	..	F.2.2.4. Placement dans le Pays
F.2.2. Total	..	714	797	797	896	858	..	..	F.2.2. Total
F.2.3. Shares									F.2.3. Actions
F.2.3.1. Domestic Companies	2 637	5 059	5 025	10 663	10 742	11 522	7 471	8 199	F.2.3.1. Entreprises Nationales
F.2.3.2. (Foreign Controlled Companies)	1 423	1 792	1 343	1 706	2 124	2 155	1 561	2 280	F.2.3.2. (Entreprises Sous Contrôle Etranger)
F.2.3.3. Branches & Agencies of Foreign Cies	234	268	279	385	439	483	53	55	F.2.3.3. Succursales et Agences d'Ent. Etrangères
F.2.3.4. Domestic Investment	4 089	5 327	..	9 728	10 609	11 245	7 183	5 919	F.2.3.4. Placement dans le Pays
F.2.3.5. Foreign Investment	205	247	..	1 320	571	760	341	2 335	F.2.3.5. Placement à l' Etranger
F.2.3. Total	4 294	5 571	5 304	11 048	11 181	12 005	7 524	8 254	F.2.3. Total
F.2.4. Bonds with Fixed Revenue									F.2.4. Obligations
F.2.4.1. Domestic Companies	3 598	9 500	10 104	19 063	20 327	22 173	11 963	14 052	F.2.4.1. Entreprises Nationales
F.2.4.2. (Foreign Controlled Companies)	3 684	4 588	4 078	4 961	5 472	5 730	4 150	4 815	F.2.4.2. (Entreprises Sous Contrôle Etranger)
F.2.4.3. Branches & Agencies of Foreign Cies	1 060	1 414	1 048	1 211	1 381	1 518	483	472	F.2.4.3. Succursales et Agences d'Ent. Etrangères
F.2.4.4. Domestic Investment	7 995	10 914	..	19 147	20 627	22 420	11 080	11 662	F.2.4.4. Placement dans le Pays
F.2.4.5. Foreign Investment	347	671	..	1 127	1 081	1 271	1 366	2 863	F.2.4.5. Placement à l' Etranger
F.2.4. Total	8 342	11 585	11 152	20 274	21 708	23 691	12 446	14 525	F.2.4. Total
F.2.5. Loans other than Mortgage Loans									F.2.5. Prêts Autres qu'Hypothécaires
F.2.5.1. Domestic Companies	1 462	1 108	1 102	1 558	1 480	1 915	1 846	2 540	F.2.5.1. Entreprises Nationales
F.2.5.2. (Foreign Controlled Companies)	500	160	185	211	263	312	165	727	F.2.5.2. (Entreprises Sous Contrôle Etranger)
F.2.5.3. Branches & Agencies of Foreign Cies	4	4	2	1	1	1	..	..	F.2.5.3. Succursales et Agences d'Ent. Etrangères
F.2.5.4. Domestic Investment	1 965	1 112	..	1 549	1 469	1 732	1 825	2 517	F.2.5.4. Placement dans le Pays
F.2.5.5. Foreign Investment	1	4	..	11	13	184	22	24	F.2.5.5. Placement à l' Etranger
F.2.5. Total	1 966	1 116	1 104	1 560	1 482	1 916	1 847	2 541	F.2.5. Total
F.2.6. Other Investments									F.2.6. Autres Placements
F.2.6.1. Domestic Companies	971	10 810	11 992	20 994	24 766	23 526	5 162	6 021	F.2.6.1. Entreprises Nationales
F.2.6.2. (Foreign Controlled Companies)	818	5 650	5 987	6 801	8 182	10 251	1 366	2 524	F.2.6.2. (Entreprises Sous Contrôle Etranger)
F.2.6.3. Branches & Agencies of Foreign Cies	134	1 265	1 043	1 182	1 224	1 345	221	268	F.2.6.3. Succursales et Agences d'Ent. Etrangères
F.2.6.4. Domestic Investment	1 712	12 075	..	19 721	23 618	23 918	4 966	5 920	F.2.6.4. Placement dans le Pays
F.2.6.5. Foreign Investment	211	1 032	..	2 455	2 372	953	417	369	F.2.6.5. Placement à l' Etranger
F.2.6. Total	1 923	13 107	13 035	22 176	25 990	24 871	5 383	6 289	F.2.6. Total

Monetary Unit: million Australian dollars

	1992	1993	1994	1995	1996	1997	1998	1999
F.2.7. Total								
F.2.7.1. Domestic Companies — F.2.7.1. Entreprises Nationales	9 202	28 232	30 055	55 389	60 091	63 489	27 190	31 519
F.2.7.2. (Foreign Controlled Companies) — F.2.7.2. (Entreprises Sous Contrôle Etranger)	6 810	12 823	12 190	14 209	16 530	19 033	7 392	10 674
F.2.7.3. Branches & Agencies of Foreign Cies — F.2.7.3. Succursales et Agences d'Ent. Etrangères	1 475	2 991	2 422	2 829	3 096	3 403	813	855
F.2.7.4. Domestic Investment — F.2.7.4. Placement dans le Pays	16 722	31 223	:	53 305	59 148	63 723	25 856	28 548
F.2.7.5. Foreign Investment — F.2.7.5. Placement à l'Etranger	764	1 954	:	4 913	4 038	3 169	2 147	3 827
F.2.7. Total of Non-Life Investments — F.2.7. Total des Placements Non-Vie	17 486	33 177	32 477	58 218	63 186	66 892	28 003	32 375

G. BREAKDOWN OF NON-LIFE PREMIUMS — G. VENTILATIONS DES PRIMES NON-VIE

	1992	1993	1994	1995	1996	1997	1998	1999
G.1. Motor vehicle — G.1. Assurance Automobile								
G.1.1. Direct Business — G.1.1. Assurances Directes								
G.1.1.1. Gross Premiums — G.1.1.1. Primes Brutes	2 991	5 578	5 746	6 238	6 698	7 003	7 558	7 681
G.1.1.2. Ceded Premiums — G.1.1.2. Primes Cédées	:	:	:	:	616	641	790	1 383
G.1.1.3. Net Written Premiums — G.1.1.3. Primes Nettes Emises	:	:	:	:	6 082	6 362	6 768	6 298
G.1.2. Reinsurance Accepted — G.1.2. Réassurance Acceptée								
G.1.2.1. Gross Premiums — G.1.2.1. Primes Brutes	407	:	:	:	:	:	:	:
G.1.3. Total — G.1.3. Total								
G.1.3.1. Gross Premiums — G.1.3.1. Primes Brutes	3 398	:	:	:	:	:	:	:
G.1.3.2. Ceded Premiums — G.1.3.2. Primes Cédées	472	:	:	:	:	:	:	:
G.1.3.3. Net Written Premiums — G.1.3.3. Primes Nettes Emises	2 926	:	:	:	:	:	:	:
G.2. Marine, Aviation — G.2. Marine, Aviation								
G.2.1. Direct Business — G.2.1. Assurances Directes								
G.2.1.1. Gross Premiums — G.2.1.1. Primes Brutes	184	178	406	273	244	247	358	630
G.2.1.2. Ceded Premiums — G.2.1.2. Primes Cédées	:	:	:	:	72	57	196	113
G.2.1.3. Net Written Premiums — G.2.1.3. Primes Nettes Emises	:	:	:	:	172	190	162	517
G.2.2. Reinsurance Accepted — G.2.2. Réassurance Acceptée								
G.2.2.1. Gross Premiums — G.2.2.1. Primes Brutes	79	:	:	:	:	:	:	:
G.2.3. Total — G.2.3. Total								
G.2.3.1. Gross Premiums — G.2.3.1. Primes Brutes	263	:	:	:	:	:	:	:
G.2.3.2. Ceded Premiums — G.2.3.2. Primes Cédées	73	:	:	:	:	:	:	:
G.2.3.3. Net Written Premiums — G.2.3.3. Primes Nettes Emises	190	:	:	:	:	:	:	:
G.3. Freight — G.3. Fret								
G.3.1. Direct Business — G.3.1. Assurances Directes								
G.3.1.1. Gross Premiums — G.3.1.1. Primes Brutes	165	163	163	180	179	161	:	:
G.3.1.2. Ceded Premiums — G.3.1.2. Primes Cédées	:	:	:	:	42	37	:	:
G.3.1.3. Net Written Premiums — G.3.1.3. Primes Nettes Emises	:	:	:	:	137	134	:	:
G.3.2. Reinsurance Accepted — G.3.2. Réassurance Acceptée								
G.3.2.1. Gross Premiums — G.3.2.1. Primes Brutes	34	:	:	:	:	:	:	:
G.3.3. Total — G.3.3. Total								
G.3.3.1. Gross Premiums — G.3.3.1. Primes Brutes	139	:	:	:	:	:	:	:
G.3.3.2. Ceded Premiums — G.3.3.2. Primes Cédées	35	:	:	:	:	:	:	:
G.3.3.3. Net Written Premiums — G.3.3.3. Primes Nettes Emises	104	:	:	:	:	:	:	:
G.4. Fire, Property Damages — G.4. Incendie, Dommages aux Biens								
G.4.1. Direct Business — G.4.1. Assurances Directes								
G.4.1.1. Gross Premiums — G.4.1.1. Primes Brutes	1 863	3 076	3 590	3 556	3 735	3 587	3 256	4 277
G.4.1.2. Ceded Premiums — G.4.1.2. Primes Cédées	:	:	:	:	912	833	690	761
G.4.1.3. Net Written Premiums — G.4.1.3. Primes Nettes Emises	:	:	:	:	2 823	2 754	2 566	3 466
G.4.2. Reinsurance Accepted — G.4.2. Réassurance Acceptée								
G.4.2.1. Gross Premiums — G.4.2.1. Primes Brutes	639	:	:	:	:	:	:	:
G.4.3. Total — G.4.3. Total								
G.4.3.1. Gross Premiums — G.4.3.1. Primes Brutes	2 502	:	:	:	:	:	:	:
G.4.3.2. Ceded Premiums — G.4.3.2. Primes Cédées	740	:	:	:	:	:	:	:
G.4.3.3. Net Written Premiums — G.4.3.3. Primes Nettes Emises	1 762	:	:	:	:	:	:	:

Monetary Unit: million Australian dollars · Unité monétaire : million de dollars australiens

		1992	1993	1994	1995	1996	1997	1998	1999
G.5. Pecuniary Losses	G.5. Pertes Pécuniaires								
G.5.1. Direct Business	G.5.1. Assurances Directes								
G.5.1.1. Gross Premiums	G.5.1.1. Primes Brutes	192	295	375	326	333	240	1 352	1 637
G.5.1.2. Ceded Premiums	G.5.1.2. Primes Cédées	..	..	..	..	49	32	126	295
G.5.1.3. Net Written Premiums	G.5.1.3. Primes Nettes Emises					284	208	1 226	1 342
G.5.2. Reinsurance Accepted	G.5.2. Réassurance Acceptée								
G.5.2.1. Gross Premiums	G.5.2.1. Primes Brutes	29	..			..	..	..	..
G.5.3. Total	G.5.3. Total								
G.5.3.1. Gross Premiums	G.5.3.1. Primes Brutes	221	..			..	..	..	..
G.5.3.2. Ceded Premiums	G.5.3.2. Primes Cédées	50	..			..	..	..	..
G.5.3.3. Net Written Premiums	G.5.3.3. Primes Nettes Emises	171	..			..	..	..	..
G.6. General Liability	G.6. Responsabilité Générale								
G.6.1. Direct Business	G.6.1. Assurances Directes								
G.6.1.1. Gross Premiums	G.6.1.1. Primes Brutes	902	4 524	4 518	4 606	5 248	6 237	3 311	1 889
G.6.1.2. Ceded Premiums	G.6.1.2. Primes Cédées	..	..	..	..	1 238	1 147	1 072	340
G.6.1.3. Net Written Premiums	G.6.1.3. Primes Nettes Emises	..	..	..	..	4 010	5 090	2 239	1 549
G.6.2. Reinsurance Accepted	G.6.2. Réassurance Acceptée								
G.6.2.1. Gross Premiums	G.6.2.1. Primes Brutes	167	..			..	..	..	..
G.6.3. Total	G.6.3. Total								
G.6.3.1. Gross Premiums	G.6.3.1. Primes Brutes	1 069	..			..	..	..	..
G.6.3.2. Ceded Premiums	G.6.3.2. Primes Cédées	217	..			..	..	..	..
G.6.3.3. Net Written Premiums	G.6.3.3. Primes Nettes Emises	852	..			..	..	..	..
G.7. Accident, Health	G.7. Accident, Santé								
G.7.1. Direct Business	G.7.1. Assurances Directes								
G.7.1.1. Gross Premiums	G.7.1.1. Primes Brutes	173	193	216	233	1 101	1 301	528	845
G.7.1.2. Ceded Premiums	G.7.1.2. Primes Cédées	..	..	..	..	19	36	96	152
G.7.1.3. Net Written Premiums	G.7.1.3. Primes Nettes Emises	..	..	..	..	1 082	1 265	432	693
G.7.2. Reinsurance Accepted	G.7.2. Réassurance Acceptée								
G.7.2.1. Gross Premiums	G.7.2.1. Primes Brutes	17	..			..	..	..	..
G.7.3. Total	G.7.3. Total								
G.7.3.1. Gross Premiums	G.7.3.1. Primes Brutes	190	..			..	..	..	..
G.7.3.2. Ceded Premiums	G.7.3.2. Primes Cédées	25	..			..	..	..	..
G.7.3.3. Net Written Premiums	G.7.3.3. Primes Nettes Emises	165	..			..	..	..	..
G.8. Others	G.8. Autres								
G.8.1. Direct Business	G.8.1. Assurances Directes								
G.8.1.1. Gross Premiums	G.8.1.1. Primes Brutes	355	856	760	900	670	792	897	1 079
G.8.1.2. Ceded Premiums	G.8.1.2. Primes Cédées	..	..	..	..	152	287	168	194
G.8.1.3. Net Written Premiums	G.8.1.3. Primes Nettes Emises	..	..	..	..	518	505	729	885
G.8.2. Reinsurance Accepted	G.8.2. Réassurance Acceptée								
G.8.2.1. Gross Premiums	G.8.2.1. Primes Brutes	106	..			..	..	..	..
G.8.3. Total	G.8.3. Total								
G.8.3.1. Gross Premiums	G.8.3.1. Primes Brutes	461	..			..	..	..	..
G.8.3.2. Ceded Premiums	G.8.3.2. Primes Cédées	119	..			..	..	..	..
G.8.3.3. Net Written Premiums	G.8.3.3. Primes Nettes Emises	342	..			..	..	..	..
G.10. Total	G.10. Total								
G.10.1. Direct Business	G.10.1. Assurances Directes								
G.10.1.1. Gross Premiums	G.10.1.1. Primes Brutes	6 765	14 763	15 775	16 312	18 208	19 568	17 260	17 988
G.10.1.2. Ceded Premiums	G.10.1.2. Primes Cédées	..	..	..	..	3 100	3 070	3 138	3 238
G.10.1.3. Net Written Premiums	G.10.1.3. Primes Nettes Emises	..	..	..	..	15 108	16 498	14 122	14 750
G.10.2. Reinsurance Accepted	G.10.2. Réassurance Acceptée								
G.10.2.1. Gross Premiums	G.10.2.1. Primes Brutes	1 478	2 005	3 224	2 745	2 953	1 530	2 026	3 655
G.10.2.2. Ceded Premiums	G.10.2.2. Primes Cédées	..	..	..	..	372	476	1 284	1 678
G.10.2.3. Net Written Premiums	G.10.2.3. Primes Nettes Emises	..	..	..	..	2 581	1 054	742	1 977
G.10.3. Total	G.10.3. Total								
G.10.3.1. Gross Premiums	G.10.3.1. Primes Brutes	8 243	16 768	18 999	19 057	21 161	21 098	19 286	21 643
G.10.3.2. Ceded Premiums	G.10.3.2. Primes Cédées	1 733	..	3 612	3 263	3 472	3 546	4 422	4 916
G.10.3.3. Net Written Premiums	G.10.3.3. Primes Nettes Emises	6 510	..	15 387	15 794	17 689	17 552	14 864	16 727

Monetary Unit: million Australian dollars   Unité monétaire : million de dollars australiens

		1992	1993	1994	1995	1996	1997	1998	1999
H. GROSS CLAIMS PAYMENTS	**H. PAIEMENTS BRUTS DES SINISTRES**								
H.1. Life	**H.1. Vie**								
H.1.1. Domestic Companies	H.1.1. Entreprises Nationales					3 929	25 166	29 949	31 671
H.1.2. (Foreign Controlled Companies)	H.1.2. (Entreprises Sous Contrôle Etranger)					867	13 927	8 828	8 694
H.1.3. Branches & Agencies of Foreign Cies	H.1.3. Succursales et Agences d'Ent. Etrangères					12	0	7	0
H.1. Total	H.1. Total					3 941	25 166	29 956	31 671
H.2. Non-Life	**H.2. Non-Vie**								
H.2.1. Domestic Companies	H.2.1. Entreprises Nationales					13 867	12 860	12 482	15 587
H.2.2. (Foreign Controlled Companies)	H.2.2. (Entreprises Sous Contrôle Etranger)					3 786	4 946	5 281	7 552
H.2.3. Branches & Agencies of Foreign Cies	H.2.3. Succursales et Agences d'Ent. Etrangères					440	714	2 633	358
H.2. Total	H.2. Total					14 307	13 574	15 115	15 945
I. GROSS OPERATING EXPENSES	**I. DEPENSES BRUTES D'EXPLOITATION**								
I.1. Life	**I.1. Vie**								
I.1.1. Domestic Companies	I.1.1. Entreprises Nationales					2 248	3 584	3 652	3 678
I.1.2. (Foreign Controlled Companies)	I.1.2. (Entreprises Sous Contrôle Etranger)					583	1 912	1 434	1 602
I.1.3. Branches & Agencies of Foreign Cies	I.1.3. Succursales et Agences d'Ent. Etrangères					2	0	3	0
I.1. Total	I.1. Total des Primes Nettes Vie					2 250	3 584	3 655	3 678
I.2. Non-Life	**I.2. Non-Vie**								
I.2.1. Domestic Companies	I.2.1. Entreprises Nationales					2 480	3 360	2 615	2 711
I.2.2. (Foreign Controlled Companies)	I.2.2. (Entreprises Sous Contrôle Etranger)					941	1 357	756	899
I.2.3. Branches & Agencies of Foreign Cies	I.2.3. Succursales et Agences d'Ent. Etrangères					118	255	762	792
I.2. Total	I.2. Total					2 598	3 615	3 377	3 503
J. COMMISSIONS	**J. COMMISSIONS**								
J.1. Life	**J.1. Vie**								
J.1.1. Direct Business	J.1.1. Assurance directe								
J.1.1.1. Domestic Companies	J.1.1.1. Entreprises Nationales					818	822	939	976
J.1.1.2. (Foreign Controlled Companies)	J.1.1.2. (Entreprises Sous Contrôle Etranger)					358	400	431	461
J.1.1.3. Branches & Agencies of Foreign Cies	J.1.1.3. Succursales et Agences d'Ent. Etrangères					2	0	0	0
J.1.1. Total	J.1.1. Total					820	822	939	976
J.1.2. Reinsurance Accepted	J.1.2. Réassurances acceptées								
J.1.2.1. Domestic Companies	J.1.2.1. Entreprises Nationales					0	83	102	148
J.1.2.2. (Foreign Controlled Companies)	J.1.2.2. (Entreprises Sous Contrôle Etranger)					0	83	102	148
J.1.2. Total	J.1.2. Total					0	83	102	148
J.1.3. Total	J.1.3. Total								
J.1.3.1. Domestic Companies	J.1.3.1. Entreprises Nationales					818	905	1 041	1 124
J.1.3.2. (Foreign Controlled Companies)	J.1.3.2. (Entreprises Sous Contrôle Etranger)					358	483	533	609
J.1.3.3. Branches & Agencies of Foreign Cies	J.1.3.3. Succursales et Agences d'Ent. Etrangères					2	0	0	0
J.1.3. Total of Life Net Premiums	J.1.3. Total					820	905	1 041	1 124

Monetary Unit: million Australian dollars

Unité monétaire : million de dollars australiens

J.2. Non-Life

J.2. Non-Vie

	1992	1993	1994	1995	1996	1997	1998	1999	
J.2.1. Direct Business									J.2.1. Assurance directe
J.2.1.1. Domestic Companies					1 175	1 144	1 041	1 307	J.2.1.1. Entreprises Nationales
J.2.1.2. (Foreign Controlled Companies)					595	584	552	882	J.2.1.2. (Entreprises Sous Contrôle Etranger)
J.2.1.3. Branches & Agencies of Foreign Cies					53	52	49	54	J.2.1.3. Succursales et Agences d'Ent. Etrangères
J.2.1. Total					1 228	1 196	1 090	1 361	J.2.1. Total des Primes Nettes Vie
J.2.2. Reinsurance Accepted									J.2.2. Réassurances acceptées
J.2.2.1. Domestic Companies					181	161	133	138	J.2.2.1. Entreprises Nationales
J.2.2.2. (Foreign Controlled Companies)					152	135	113	116	J.2.2.2. (Entreprises Sous Contrôle Etranger)
J.2.2.3. Branches & Agencies of Foreign Cies					140	125	144	4	J.2.2.3. Succursales et Agences d'Ent. Etrangères
J.2.2. Total					321	286	277	142	J.2.2. Total
J.2.3. Total									J.2.3. Total
J.2.3.1. Domestic Companies					1 356	1 305	1 174	1 445	J.2.3.1. Entreprises Nationales
J.2.3.2. (Foreign Controlled Companies)					747	719	665	998	J.2.3.2. (Entreprises Sous Contrôle Etranger)
J.2.3.3. Branches & Agencies of Foreign Cies					193	177	193	58	J.2.3.3. Succursales et Agences d'Ent. Etrangères
J.2.3. Total					1 549	1 482	1 367	1 503	J.2.3. Total

AUTRICHE

Monetary Unit: million schillings

Unité monétaire : million de schillings

A. NUMBER OF COMPANIES IN THE REPORTING COUNTRY / **A. NOMBRE D'ENTREPRISES DANS LE PAYS DECLARANT**

English Label	1992	1993	1994	1995	1996	1997	1998	1999	French Label
A.1. Life									**A.1. Vie**
A.1.1. Domestic Companies	5	5	5	6	7	7	6	5	A.1.1. Entreprises Nationales
A.1.2. (Foreign Controlled Companies)	2	2	3	3	4	4	3	2	A.1.2. (Entreprises Sous Contrôle Etranger)
A.1.3. Branches & Agencies of Foreign Cies	1	1	1	1	0	0	0	0	A.1.3. Succursales et Agences d'Ent. Etrangères
A.1. All Companies	6	6	6	7	7	7	6	5	A.1. Ensemble des Entreprises
A.2. Non-Life									**A.2. Non-Vie**
A.2.1. Domestic Companies	19	19	19	18	17	16	17	15	A.2.1. Entreprises Nationales
A.2.2. (Foreign Controlled Companies)	6	6	8	7	7	6	6	8	A.2.2. (Entreprises Sous Contrôle Etranger)
A.2.3. Branches & Agencies of Foreign Cies	10	9	3	3	3	2	2	2	A.2.3. Succursales et Agences d'Ent. Etrangères
A.2. All Companies	29	28	22	21	20	18	19	17	A.2. Ensemble des Entreprises
A.3. Composite									**A.3. Mixte**
A.3.1. Domestic Companies	32	32	34	34	35	34	33	33	A.3.1. Entreprises Nationales
A.3.2. (Foreign Controlled Companies)	12	12	12	12	12	11	10	11	A.3.2. (Entreprises Sous Contrôle Etranger)
A.3. All Companies	32	32	34	34	35	34	33	33	A.3. Ensemble des Entreprises
A.4. Reinsurance									**A.4. Réassurance**
A.4.1. Domestic Companies	3	3	4	4	5	5	3	4	A.4.1. Entreprises Nationales
A.4.2. (Foreign Controlled Companies)	2	2	3	3	3	3	3	3	A.4.2. (Entreprises Sous Contrôle Etranger)
A.4. All Companies	3	3	4	4	5	5	3	4	A.4. Ensemble des Entreprises
A.5. Total									**A.5. Total**
A.5.1. Domestic Companies	59	59	62	62	64	62	59	57	A.5.1. Entreprises Nationales
A.5.2. (Foreign Controlled Companies)	22	22	26	25	26	24	22	24	A.5.2. (Entreprises Sous Contrôle Etranger)
A.5.3. Branches & Agencies of Foreign Cies	11	10	4	4	3	2	2	2	A.5.3. Succursales et Agences d'Ent. Etrangères
A.5. All Insurance Companies	70	69	66	66	67	64	61	59	A.5. Ensemble des Entreprises d'Assurances

B. NUMBER OF EMPLOYEES / **B. NOMBRE D'EMPLOYES**

English Label	1992	1993	1994	1995	1996	1997	1998	1999	French Label
B.1. Insurance Companies	32 744	32 985	32 440	32 346	32 481	32 128	30 998	31 171	B.1. Entreprises d'Assurances

C. BUSINESS WRITTEN IN THE REPORTING COUNTRY / **C. OPERATIONS CONCLUES DANS LE PAYS DECLARANT**

C.1. Life / **C.1. Vie**

English Label	1992	1993	1994	1995	1996	1997	1998	1999	French Label
C.1.1. Gross Premiums									**C.1.1. Primes Brutes**
C.1.1.1. Direct Business									C.1.1.1. Assurances Directes
C.1.1.1.1. Domestic Companies	31 213	39 957	40 703	46 545	66 335	50 930	56 321	65 940	C.1.1.1.1. Entreprises Nationales
C.1.1.1.2. (Foreign Controlled Companies)	11 373	13 426	15 299	16 180	22 889	17 946	18 403	20 027	C.1.1.1.2. (Entreprises Sous Contrôle Etranger)
C.1.1.1.3. Branches & Agencies of Foreign Cies	117	209	27	55	0	0	0	0	C.1.1.1.3. Succursales et Agences d'Ent. Etrangères
C.1.1.1. Total	31 330	40 166	40 730	46 600	66 335	50 930	56 321	65 940	C.1.1.1. Total
C.1.1.2. Reinsurance Accepted									C.1.1.2. Réassurance Acceptée
C.1.1.2.1. Domestic Companies	308	320	293	335	472	503	547	455	C.1.1.2.1. Entreprises Nationales
C.1.1.2.2. (Foreign Controlled Companies)	56	58	63	68	67	70	75	80	C.1.1.2.2. (Entreprises Sous Contrôle Etranger)
C.1.1.2. Total	308	320	293	335	472	503	547	455	C.1.1.2. Total
C.1.1.3. Total									C.1.1.3. Total
C.1.1.3.1. Domestic Companies	31 521	40 277	40 996	46 880	66 807	51 433	56 868	66 395	C.1.1.3.1. Entreprises Nationales
C.1.1.3.2. (Foreign Controlled Companies)	11 429	13 484	15 362	16 248	22 956	18 016	18 478	20 107	C.1.1.3.2. (Entreprises Sous Contrôle Etranger)
C.1.1.3.3. Branches & Agencies of Foreign Cies	117	209	27	55	0	0	0	0	C.1.1.3.3. Succursales et Agences d'Ent. Etrangères
C.1.1.3. Total Gross Premiums	31 638	40 486	41 023	46 935	66 807	51 433	56 868	66 395	C.1.1.3. Total des Primes Brutes
C.1.2. Ceded Premiums									**C.1.2. Primes Cédées**
C.1.2.1. Domestic Companies	3 480	3 770	4 308	3 912	4 944	4 268	4 475	4 771	C.1.2.1. Entreprises Nationales
C.1.2.2. (Foreign Controlled Companies)	2 634	2 861	3 365	2 901	3 874	3 163	3 247	3 340	C.1.2.2. (Entreprises Sous Contrôle Etranger)
C.1.2.3. Branches & Agencies of Foreign Cies	57	72	0	0	0	0	0	0	C.1.2.3. Succursales et Agences d'Ent. Etrangères
C.1.2. Total	3 537	3 842	4 308	3 912	4 944	4 268	4 475	4 771	C.1.2. Total
C.1.3. Net Written Premiums									**C.1.3. Primes Nettes Emises**
C.1.3.1. Domestic Companies	28 041	36 507	36 688	42 968	61 863	47 165	52 393	61 624	C.1.3.1. Entreprises Nationales
C.1.3.2. (Foreign Controlled Companies)	8 795	10 623	11 997	13 347	19 082	14 853	15 231	16 767	C.1.3.2. (Entreprises Sous Contrôle Etranger)
C.1.3.3. Branches & Agencies of Foreign Cies	60	137	27	55	0	0	0	0	C.1.3.3. Succursales et Agences d'Ent. Etrangères
C.1.3. Total	28 101	36 644	36 715	43 023	61 863	47 165	52 393	61 624	C.1.3. Total

Monetary Unit: million schillings   Unité monétaire : million de schillings

C.2. Non-Life / C.2. Non-Vie

	1992	1993	1994	1995	1996	1997	1998	1999
C.2.1. Gross premiums / C.2.1. Primes Brutes								
C.2.1.1. Direct Business / C.2.1.1. Assurances Directes								
C.2.1.1.1. Domestic Companies / Entreprises Nationales	70 823	75 976	79 913	82 478	83 746	84 040	83 618	83 727
C.2.1.1.2. (Foreign Controlled Companies) / (Entreprises Sous Contrôle Etranger)	31 678	34 023	35 831	36 806	37 290	37 157	37 585	37 506
C.2.1.1.3. Branches & Agencies of Foreign Cies / Succursales et Agences d'Ent. Etrangères	703	726	160	161	161	161	100	112
C.2.1.1. Total / Total	71 526	76 702	80 073	82 639	83 907	84 201	83 718	83 839
C.2.1.2. Reinsurance Accepted / C.2.1.2. Réassurance Acceptée								
C.2.1.2.1. Domestic Companies / Entreprises Nationales	10 461	11 029	17 312	14 004	18 675	21 008	18 535	20 530
C.2.1.2.2. (Foreign Controlled Companies) / (Entreprises Sous Contrôle Etranger)	7 108	8 030	11 974	9 039	13 159	14 391	14 290	13 313
C.2.1.2.3. Branches & Agencies of Foreign Cies / Succursales et Agences d'Ent. Etrangères	28	24	0	0	6	17	38	56
C.2.1.2. Total / Total	10 489	11 053	17 312	14 004	18 681	21 025	18 573	20 586
C.2.1.3. Total								
C.2.1.3.1. Domestic Companies / Entreprises Nationales	81 284	87 005	97 225	96 482	102 421	105 048	102 153	104 257
C.2.1.3.2. (Foreign Controlled Companies) / (Entreprises Sous Contrôle Etranger)	38 786	42 053	47 805	45 845	50 449	51 548	51 875	50 819
C.2.1.3.3. Branches & Agencies of Foreign Cies / Succursales et Agences d'Ent. Etrangères	731	750	160	161	167	178	138	168
C.2.1.3. Total Gross Premiums / Total des Primes Brutes	82 015	87 755	97 385	96 643	102 588	105 226	102 291	104 425
C.2.2. Ceded Premiums / C.2.2. Primes Cédées								
C.2.2.1. Domestic Companies / Entreprises Nationales	15 003	16 673	25 507	23 655	27 451	29 282	26 614	27 777
C.2.2.2. (Foreign Controlled Companies) / (Entreprises Sous Contrôle Etranger)	9 107	10 629	15 886	13 605	15 842	16 794	17 486	15 321
C.2.2.3. Branches & Agencies of Foreign Cies / Succursales et Agences d'Ent. Etrangères	360	355	16	16	19	9	8	8
C.2.2. Total / Total	15 363	17 028	25 523	23 671	27 470	29 291	26 622	27 785
C.2.3. Net Written Premiums / C.2.3. Primes Nettes Emises								
C.2.3.1. Domestic Companies / Entreprises Nationales	66 281	70 332	71 718	72 827	74 970	75 766	75 539	76 480
C.2.3.2. (Foreign Controlled Companies) / (Entreprises Sous Contrôle Etranger)	29 679	31 424	31 919	32 240	34 607	34 754	34 389	35 498
C.2.3.3. Branches & Agencies of Foreign Cies / Succursales et Agences d'Ent. Etrangères	371	395	144	145	148	169	130	160
C.2.3. Total / Total	66 652	70 727	71 862	72 972	75 118	75 935	75 669	76 640

C.3. Total / C.3. Total

	1992	1993	1994	1995	1996	1997	1998	1999
C.3.1. Gross Premiums / C.3.1. Primes Brutes								
C.3.1.1. Direct Business / C.3.1.1. Assurances Directes								
C.3.1.1.1. Domestic Companies / Entreprises Nationales	102 036	115 933	120 616	129 023	150 081	134 970	139 939	149 667
C.3.1.1.2. (Foreign Controlled Companies) / (Entreprises Sous Contrôle Etranger)	43 051	47 449	51 130	52 986	60 179	55 103	55 988	57 533
C.3.1.1.3. Branches & Agencies of Foreign Cies / Succursales et Agences d'Ent. Etrangères	820	935	187	216	161	161	100	112
C.3.1.1. Total / Total	102 856	116 868	120 803	129 239	150 242	135 131	140 039	149 779
C.3.1.2. Reinsurance Accepted / C.3.1.2. Réassurance Acceptée								
C.3.1.2.1. Domestic Companies / Entreprises Nationales	10 769	11 349	17 605	14 339	19 147	21 511	19 082	20 985
C.3.1.2.2. (Foreign Controlled Companies) / (Entreprises Sous Contrôle Etranger)	7 164	8 088	12 037	9 107	13 226	14 461	14 365	13 393
C.3.1.2.3. Branches & Agencies of Foreign Cies / Succursales et Agences d'Ent. Etrangères	28	24	0	0	6	17	38	56
C.3.1.2. Total / Total	10 797	11 373	17 605	14 339	19 153	21 528	19 120	21 041
C.3.1.3. Total								
C.3.1.3.1. Domestic Companies / Entreprises Nationales	112 805	127 282	138 221	143 362	169 228	156 481	158 321	170 652
C.3.1.3.2. (Foreign Controlled Companies) / (Entreprises Sous Contrôle Etranger)	50 215	55 537	63 167	62 093	73 405	69 564	66 353	70 926
C.3.1.3.3. Branches & Agencies of Foreign Cies / Succursales et Agences d'Ent. Etrangères	848	959	187	216	167	178	138	168
C.3.1.3. Total Gross Premiums / Total des Primes Brutes	113 653	128 241	138 408	143 578	169 395	156 659	159 159	170 820
C.3.2. Ceded Premiums / C.3.2. Primes Cédées								
C.3.2.1. Domestic Companies / Entreprises Nationales	18 483	20 443	29 815	27 567	32 395	33 550	31 089	32 548
C.3.2.2. (Foreign Controlled Companies) / (Entreprises Sous Contrôle Etranger)	11 741	13 490	19 251	16 506	19 716	19 957	20 733	18 661
C.3.2.3. Branches & Agencies of Foreign Cies / Succursales et Agences d'Ent. Etrangères	417	427	16	16	19	9	8	8
C.3.2. Total / Total	18 900	20 870	29 831	27 583	32 414	33 559	31 097	32 556
C.3.3. Net Written Premiums / C.3.3. Primes Nettes Emises								
C.3.3.1. Domestic Companies / Entreprises Nationales	94 322	106 839	108 406	115 795	136 833	122 931	127 932	138 104
C.3.3.2. (Foreign Controlled Companies) / (Entreprises Sous Contrôle Etranger)	38 474	42 047	43 916	45 587	53 689	49 607	49 620	52 265
C.3.3.3. Branches & Agencies of Foreign Cies / Succursales et Agences d'Ent. Etrangères	431	532	171	200	148	169	130	160
C.3.3. Total / Total	94 753	107 371	108 577	115 995	136 981	123 100	128 062	138 264

Monetary Unit: million schillings   Unité monétaire : million de schillings

D. NET WRITTEN PREMIUMS IN THE REPORTING COUNTRY IN TERMS OF DOMESTIC AND FOREIGN RISKS
D. PRIMES NETTES EMISES DANS LE PAYS DECLARANT EN RISQUES NATIONAUX ET ETRANGERS

D.1. Life / D.1. Vie

Code	Label (English / Français)	1992	1993	1994	1995	1996	1997	1998	1999
D.1.1.	Domestic Risks / Risques Nationaux								
D.1.1.1.	Domestic Companies / Entreprises Nationales	..	..	..	42 964	..	..	52 357	61 479
D.1.1.2.	(Foreign Controlled Companies) / (Entreprises Sous Contrôle Etranger)	..	..	..	13 344	..	..	15 209	16 727
D.1.1.3.	Branches & Agencies of Foreign Cies / Succursales et Agences d'Ent. Etrangeres	..	..	..	55	..	..	0	0
D.1.1.	Total / Total des Primes Nettes Vie	..	..	..	43 019	..	..	52 357	61 479
D.1.2.	Foreign Risks / Risques Etrangers								
D.1.2.1.	Domestic Companies / Entreprises Nationales	..	..	..	4	..	..	36	145
D.1.2.2.	(Foreign Controlled Companies) / (Entreprises Sous Contrôle Etranger)	..	..	..	3	..	..	22	39
D.1.2.	Total / Total des Primes Nettes Vie	..	..	..	4	..	..	36	145
D.1.3.	Total								
D.1.3.1.	Domestic Companies / Entreprises Nationales	..	36 507	..	42 968	61 863	47 165	52 393	61 624
D.1.3.2.	(Foreign Controlled Companies) / (Entreprises Sous Contrôle Etranger)	..	10 623	..	13 347	19 082	14 853	15 231	16 766
D.1.3.3.	Branches & Agencies of Foreign Cies / Succursales et Agences d'Ent. Etrangeres	..	137	..	55	0	0	0	0
D.1.3.	Total of Life Net Premiums / Total des Primes Nettes Vie	..	36 644	..	43 023	61 863	47 165	52 393	61 624

D.2. Non-Life / D.2. Non-Vie

Code	Label (English / Français)	1992	1993	1994	1995	1996	1997	1998	1999
D.2.1.	Domestic Risks / Risques Nationaux								
D.2.1.1.	Domestic Companies / Entreprises Nationales	..	..	..	72 802	..	..	75 042	69 815
D.2.1.2.	(Foreign Controlled Companies) / (Entreprises Sous Contrôle Etranger)	..	..	..	32 224	..	..	34 244	30 528
D.2.1.3.	Branches & Agencies of Foreign Cies / Succursales et Agences d'Ent. Etrangeres	..	..	..	145	..	..	130	160
D.2.1.	Total / Total des Primes Nettes Vie	..	..	..	72 947	..	..	75 172	69 975
D.2.2.	Foreign Risks / Risques Etrangers								
D.2.2.1.	Domestic Companies / Entreprises Nationales	..	..	..	25	..	..	497	6 665
D.2.2.2.	(Foreign Controlled Companies) / (Entreprises Sous Contrôle Etranger)	..	..	..	16	..	..	145	4 970
D.2.2.	Total / Total des Primes Nettes Vie	..	..	..	25	..	..	497	6 665
D.2.3.	Total								
D.2.3.1.	Domestic Companies / Entreprises Nationales	..	70 332	..	72 827	74 970	75 766	75 539	76 480
D.2.3.2.	(Foreign Controlled Companies) / (Entreprises Sous Contrôle Etranger)	..	31 424	..	32 240	34 607	34 754	34 389	35 498
D.2.3.3.	Branches & Agencies of Foreign Cies / Succursales et Agences d'Ent. Etrangeres	..	395	..	145	148	169	130	160
D.2.3.	Total / Total des Primes Nettes Vie	..	70 727	..	72 972	75 118	75 935	75 669	76 640

E. BUSINESS WRITTEN ABROAD / E. OPERATIONS A L'ETRANGER

E.1. Life / E.1. Vie

Code	Label (English / Français)	1992	1993	1994	1995	1996	1997	1998	1999
E.1.1.	Gross Premiums / Primes Brutes								
E.1.1.1.	Direct Business / Assurance Directe								
E.1.1.1.1.	Branches & Agencies / Succursales & Agences	..	..	1	1	1	1	0	0
E.1.1.1.	Total	..	..	1	1	..	1	..	..
E.1.1.3.	Total								
E.1.1.3.1.	Branches & Agencies / Succursales & Agences	..	..	1	1	..	1	..	..
E.1.1.3.	Total Gross Premiums / Total des Primes Brutes	..	..	1	..	..	1	..	..
E.1.2.	Ceded Premiums / Primes Cédées								
E.1.2.1.	Branches & Agencies / Succursales & Agences	..	..	1	1	0	0	0	0
E.1.2.	Total	..	..	..	..	0	0	..	..
E.1.3.	Net Written Premiums / Primes Nettes Emises								
E.1.3.1.	Branches & Agencies / Succursales & Agences	..	..	1	0	1	1	0	0
E.1.3.	Total	..	..	1	..	..	1	..	..

Monetary Unit: million schillings — Unité monétaire : million de schillings

E.2. Non-Life / E.2. Non-Vie

Code — Label (EN)	Libellé (FR)	1992	1993	1994	1995	1996	1997	1998	1999
E.2.1. Gross Premiums	E.2.1. Primes Brutes								
E.2.1.1. Direct Business	E.2.1.1. Assurance Directe								
E.2.1.1.1. Branches & Agencies	E.2.1.1.1. Succursales & Agences	83	67	21	1	1	1	0	0
E.2.1.1. Total	E.2.1.1. Total	83	67	21	..	..	1	..	:
E.2.1.2. Reinsurance Accepted	E.2.1.2. Réassurance Acceptée								
E.2.1.2.1. Branches & Agencies	E.2.1.2.1. Succursales & Agences	2 235	2 444	0	2 920	..	0	0	0
E.2.1.2. Total	E.2.1.2. Total	2 235	2 444	0	..	..	0	0	:
E.2.1.3. Total	E.2.1.3. Total								
E.2.1.3.1. Branches & Agencies	E.2.1.3.1. Succursales & Agences	2 317	2 511	21	2 921	..	1	1	:
E.2.1.3. Total Gross Premiums	E.2.1.3. Total des Primes Brutes	2 317	2 511	21	..	..	1	1	:
E.2.2. Ceded Premiums	E.2.2. Primes Cédées								
E.2.2.1. Branches & Agencies	E.2.2.1. Succursales & Agences	1 464	1 657	7	1 841	1	1	1	0
E.2.2. Total	E.2.2. Total	1 464	1 657	7	..	..	1	1	:
E.2.3. Net Written Premiums	E.2.3. Primes Nettes Emises								
E.2.3.1. Branches & Agencies	E.2.3.1. Succursales & Agences	853	854	15	1 080	0	0	0	0
E.2.3. Total	E.2.3. Total	853	854	15	..	..	0	..	:

F. OUTSTANDING INVESTMENT BY DIRECT INSURANCE COMPANIES / F. ENCOURS DES PLACEMENTS DES ENTREPRISES D'ASSURANCES DIRECTES

F.1. Life / F.1. Vie

Code — Label (EN)	Libellé (FR)	1992	1993	1994	1995	1996	1997	1998	1999
F.1.1. Real Estate	F.1.1. Immobilier								
F.1.1.1. Domestic Companies	F.1.1.1. Entreprises Nationales	6 773	13 521	16 045	17 218	17 683	16 411	17 495	19 263
F.1.1.2. (Foreign Controlled Companies)	F.1.1.2. (Entreprises Sous Contrôle Etranger)	4 339	4 997	6 113	5 928	6 130	5 781	5 727	6 113
F.1.1.4. Domestic Investment	F.1.1.4. Placement dans le Pays	11 112	13 521	16 045	..	0	0	0	0
F.1.1. Total	F.1.1. Total	11 112	13 521	16 045	..	17 683	..	..	..
F.1.2. Mortgage Loans	F.1.2. Prêts Hypothécaires								
F.1.2.1. Domestic Companies	F.1.2.1. Entreprises Nationales	4 719	5 047	6 084	6 587	6 533	6 611	5 864	5 632
F.1.2.2. (Foreign Controlled Companies)	F.1.2.2. (Entreprises Sous Contrôle Etranger)	117	113	234	302	337	619	201	152
F.1.2.3. Branches & Agencies of Foreign Cies	F.1.2.3. Succursales et Agences d'Ent. Etrangères	11	12	0	0	0	0	0	0
F.1.2.4. Domestic Investment	F.1.2.4. Placement dans le Pays	4 847	5 059	6 084	..	..	..	..	..
F.1.2.5. Foreign Investment	F.1.2.5. Placement à l' Etranger	0	..	..	..	..	..	..	..
F.1.2. Total	F.1.2. Total	4 847	5 059	6 084	..	6 533	..	..	..
F.1.3. Shares	F.1.3. Actions								
F.1.3.1. Domestic Companies	F.1.3.1. Entreprises Nationales	13 420	25 747	29 117	32 746	39 998	52 032	80 221	106 666
F.1.3.2. (Foreign Controlled Companies)	F.1.3.2. (Entreprises Sous Contrôle Etranger)	5 576	7 162	9 147	10 061	11 824	15 423	23 671	32 250
F.1.3.3. Branches & Agencies of Foreign Cies	F.1.3.3. Succursales et Agences d'Ent. Etrangères	8	194	0	0	0	..	0	0
F.1.3.4. Domestic Investment	F.1.3.4. Placement dans le Pays	19 004	25 941	29 117	..	..	..	..	..
F.1.3. Total	F.1.3. Total	19 004	25 941	29 117	..	39 998	..	..	..
F.1.4. Bonds with Fixed Revenue	F.1.4. Obligations								
F.1.4.1. Domestic Companies	F.1.4.1. Entreprises Nationales	45 935	75 037	83 387	99 628	118 281	133 613	144 882	167 780
F.1.4.2. (Foreign Controlled Companies)	F.1.4.2. (Entreprises Sous Contrôle Etranger)	33 093	25 142	27 744	39 508	47 222	52 762	52 258	53 587
F.1.4.3. Branches & Agencies of Foreign Cies	F.1.4.3. Succursales et Agences d'Ent. Etrangères	300	262	35	30	0	0	0	0
F.1.4.4. Domestic Investment	F.1.4.4. Placement dans le Pays	79 329	75 299	83 422	..	..	..	..	..
F.1.4.5. Foreign Investment	F.1.4.5. Placement à l' Etranger	0	..	..	..	..	..	..	..
F.1.4. Total	F.1.4. Total	79 329	75 299	83 422	..	118 281	..	..	..
F.1.5. Loans other than Mortgage Loans	F.1.5. Prêts Autres qu'Hypothécaires								
F.1.5.1. Domestic Companies	F.1.5.1. Entreprises Nationales	57 990	102 151	112 045	131 182	144 883	139 150	131 232	121 165
F.1.5.2. (Foreign Controlled Companies)	F.1.5.2. (Entreprises Sous Contrôle Etranger)	33 954	38 207	41 737	50 315	55 762	54 984	51 570	48 087
F.1.5.3. Branches & Agencies of Foreign Cies	F.1.5.3. Succursales et Agences d'Ent. Etrangères	22	21	0	0	0	0	0	0
F.1.5.4. Domestic Investment	F.1.5.4. Placement dans le Pays	91 967	102 172	112 045	..	..	..	..	..
F.1.5.5. Foreign Investment	F.1.5.5. Placement à l' Etranger	0	..	..	..	..	..	..	..
F.1.5. Total	F.1.5. Total	91 967	102 172	112 045	..	144 883	..	..	..

Monetary Unit: million schillings / Unité monétaire : million de schillings

	1992	1993	1994	1995	1996	1997	1998	1999
F.1.6. Other Investments / F.1.6. Autres Placements								
F.1.6.1. Domestic Companies / Entreprises Nationales	4 331	23 372	26 814	16 558	19 508	26 801	25 903	19 702
F.1.6.2. (Foreign Controlled Companies) / (Entreprises Sous Contrôle Etranger)	1 545	12 690	14 008	2 103	3 374	10 223	4 062	3 235
F.1.6.3. Branches & Agencies of Foreign Cies / Succursales et Agences d'Ent. Etrangères	1	0	0	0	0	0	0	0
F.1.6.4. Domestic Investment / Placement dans le Pays	5 876	:	:	:	:	:	:	:
F.1.6.5. Foreign Investment / Placement à l' Etranger	0	:	:	:	:	:	:	:
F.1.6. Total	5 876	23 372	26 814	16 558	19 508	:	:	:
F.1.7. Total								
F.1.7.1. Domestic Companies / Entreprises Nationales	133 168	244 875	273 492	303 919	346 886	374 618	405 597	440 208
F.1.7.2. (Foreign Controlled Companies) / (Entreprises Sous Contrôle Etranger)	78 624	88 311	98 983	108 217	124 649	139 792	137 489	143 424
F.1.7.3. Branches & Agencies of Foreign Cies / Succursales et Agences d'Ent. Etrangères	342	489	35	30	0	0	0	0
F.1.7.4. Domestic Investment / Placement dans le Pays	212 135	:	:	:	:	:	:	:
F.1.7.5. Foreign Investment / Placement à l' Etranger		:	:	:	:	:	:	:
F.1.7. Total of Life Investments / Total des Placements Vie	212 135	245 364	273 527	:	346 886	:	:	:
F.2. Non-Life / F.2. Non-Vie								
F.2.1. Real Estate / F.2.1. Immobilier								
F.2.1.1. Domestic Companies / Entreprises Nationales	10 984	23 158	22 359	22 699	24 176	26 004	28 459	27 320
F.2.1.2. (Foreign Controlled Companies) / (Entreprises Sous Contrôle Etranger)	9 835	10 839	9 965	10 311	10 415	10 460	11 147	10 874
F.2.1.3. Branches & Agencies of Foreign Cies / Succursales et Agences d'Ent. Etrangères	120	117	38	37	36	2	2	2
F.2.1.4. Domestic Investment / Placement dans le Pays	20 939	:	:	:	:	:	:	:
F.2.1.5. Foreign Investment / Placement à l' Etranger	0	:	:	:	:	:	:	:
F.2.1. Total	20 939	23 275	22 397	:	24 212	:	:	:
F.2.2. Mortgage Loans / F.2.2. Prêts Hypothécaires								
F.2.2.1. Domestic Companies / Entreprises Nationales	2 457	4 465	5 191	5 384	6 252	6 164	6 568	5 869
F.2.2.2. (Foreign Controlled Companies) / (Entreprises Sous Contrôle Etranger)	1 804	1 630	1 839	1 962	1 924	1 960	2 008	1 938
F.2.2.3. Branches & Agencies of Foreign Cies / Succursales et Agences d'Ent. Etrangères	1	1	0	0	0	0	0	0
F.2.2.4. Domestic Investment / Placement dans le Pays	4 175	:	:	:	:	:	:	:
F.2.2.5. Foreign Investment / Placement à l' Etranger	86	:	:	:	:	:	:	:
F.2.2. Total	4 261	4 466	5 191	:	6 252	:	:	:
F.2.3. Shares / F.2.3. Actions								
F.2.3.1. Domestic Companies / Entreprises Nationales	9 144	19 215	20 450	21 943	24 802	27 767	38 421	41 121
F.2.3.2. (Foreign Controlled Companies) / (Entreprises Sous Contrôle Etranger)	6 363	7 134	6 927	7 629	9 117	11 096	13 878	18 367
F.2.3.3. Branches & Agencies of Foreign Cies / Succursales et Agences d'Ent. Etrangères	2	2	0	0	0	0	0	0
F.2.3.4. Domestic Investment / Placement dans le Pays	15 321	:	:	:	:	:	:	:
F.2.3.5. Foreign Investment / Placement à l' Etranger	190	:	:	:	:	:	:	:
F.2.3. Total	15 511	19 217	20 450	:	24 802	:	:	:
F.2.4. Bonds with Fixed Revenue / F.2.4. Obligations								
F.2.4.1. Domestic Companies / Entreprises Nationales	13 976	28 735	30 414	32 802	34 429	35 539	33 988	33 860
F.2.4.2. (Foreign Controlled Companies) / (Entreprises Sous Contrôle Etranger)	13 456	14 684	14 258	15 256	15 550	16 251	17 873	15 571
F.2.4.3. Branches & Agencies of Foreign Cies / Succursales et Agences d'Ent. Etrangères	517	490	197	228	292	262	284	300
F.2.4.4. Domestic Investment / Placement dans le Pays	27 839	:	:	:	:	:	:	:
F.2.4.5. Foreign Investment / Placement à l' Etranger	109	:	:	:	:	:	:	:
F.2.4. Total	27 948	29 225	30 611	:	34 721	:	:	:
F.2.5. Loans other than Mortgage Loans / F.2.5. Prêts Autres qu'Hypothécaires								
F.2.5.1. Domestic Companies / Entreprises Nationales	12 950	25 540	27 477	33 612	34 748	33 928	31 956	29 556
F.2.5.2. (Foreign Controlled Companies) / (Entreprises Sous Contrôle Etranger)	10 623	12 361	13 840	16 117	17 925	16 939	15 840	14 852
F.2.5.3. Branches & Agencies of Foreign Cies / Succursales et Agences d'Ent. Etrangères	81	88	19	19	25	32	32	31
F.2.5.4. Domestic Investment / Placement dans le Pays	23 299	:	:	:	:	:	:	:
F.2.5.5. Foreign Investment / Placement à l' Etranger	355	:	:	:	:	:	:	:
F.2.5. Total	23 654	25 628	27 496	:	34 773	:	:	:
F.2.6. Other Investments / F.2.6. Autres Placements								
F.2.6.1. Domestic Companies / Entreprises Nationales	8 252	36 056	30 308	16 518	18 221	38 176	58 498	64 146
F.2.6.2. (Foreign Controlled Companies) / (Entreprises Sous Contrôle Etranger)	7 454	21 973	4 167	3 395	2 877	14 333	35 013	37 786
F.2.6.3. Branches & Agencies of Foreign Cies / Succursales et Agences d'Ent. Etrangères	190	341	55	50	14	61	9	10
F.2.6.4. Domestic Investment / Placement dans le Pays	14 696	:	:	:	:	:	:	:
F.2.6.5. Foreign Investment / Placement à l' Etranger	1 199	:	:	:	:	:	:	:
F.2.6. Total	15 895	36 397	30 363	:	18 235	:	:	:

Monetary Unit: million schillings

Unité monétaire : million de schillings

	1992	1993	1994	1995	1996	1997	1998	1999
F.2.7. Total / F.2.7. Total								
F.2.7.1. Domestic Companies / F.2.7.1. Entreprises Nationales	57 763	137 169	136 199	132 958	142 628	167 578	197 890	201 872
F.2.7.2. (Foreign Controlled Companies) / F.2.7.2. (Entreprises Sous Contrôle Etranger)	49 535	68 621	50 996	54 670	57 808	71 039	95 759	99 388
F.2.7.3. Branches & Agencies of Foreign Cies / F.2.7.3. Succursales et Agences d'Ent. Etrangères	911	1 039	309	334	367	357	327	343
F.2.7.4. Domestic Investment / F.2.7.4. Placement dans le Pays	106 269	:	:	:	:	:	:	:
F.2.7.5. Foreign Investment / F.2.7.5. Placement à l'Etranger	1 939	:	:	:	:	:	:	:
F.2.7. Total of Non-Life Investments / F.2.7. Total des Placements Non-Vie	108 208	138 208	136 508	:	142 995	:	:	:
G. BREAKDOWN OF NON-LIFE PREMIUMS / **G. VENTILATIONS DES PRIMES NON-VIE**								
G.1. Motor vehicle / G.1. Assurance Automobile								
G.1.1. Direct Business / G.1.1. Assurances Directes								
G.1.1.1. Gross Premiums / G.1.1.1. Primes Brutes	26 924	28 411	30 013	30 377	30 360	29 590	28 185	27 387
G.1.1.2. Ceded Premiums / G.1.1.2. Primes Cédées	3 020	3 350	4 568	4 615	4 995	5 238	4 385	5 349
G.1.1.3. Net Written Premiums / G.1.1.3. Primes Nettes Emises	23 904	25 061	25 445	25 762	25 365	24 352	23 800	22 038
G.2. Marine, Aviation / G.2. Marine, Aviation								
G.2.1. Direct Business / G.2.1. Assurances Directes								
G.2.1.1. Gross Premiums / G.2.1.1. Primes Brutes	129	160	146	81	83	92	98	121
G.2.1.2. Ceded Premiums / G.2.1.2. Primes Cédées	108	139	134	25	28	34	32	33
G.2.1.3. Net Written Premiums / G.2.1.3. Primes Nettes Emises	21	21	12	56	55	58	66	88
G.3. Freight / G.3. Fret								
G.3.1. Direct Business / G.3.1. Assurances Directes								
G.3.1.1. Gross Premiums / G.3.1.1. Primes Brutes	1 139	1 174	1 116	1 020	984	1 016	1 032	948
G.3.1.2. Ceded Premiums / G.3.1.2. Primes Cédées	446	446	449	411	422	421	424	405
G.3.1.3. Net Written Premiums / G.3.1.3. Primes Nettes Emises	693	728	667	609	562	595	608	543
G.4. Fire, Property Damages / G.4. Incendie, Dommages aux Biens								
G.4.1. Direct Business / G.4.1. Assurances Directes								
G.4.1.1. Gross Premiums / G.4.1.1. Primes Brutes	15 550	17 734	18 486	19 415	20 083	20 444	20 791	20 849
G.4.1.2. Ceded Premiums / G.4.1.2. Primes Cédées	4 692	5 408	6 974	7 425	8 002	7 706	7 409	7 659
G.4.1.3. Net Written Premiums / G.4.1.3. Primes Nettes Emises	10 858	12 326	11 512	11 990	12 081	12 738	13 382	13 190
G.5. Pecuniary Losses / G.5. Pertes Pécuniaires								
G.5.1. Direct Business / G.5.1. Assurances Directes								
G.5.1.1. Gross Premiums / G.5.1.1. Primes Brutes	497	484	537	594	690	763	816	807
G.5.1.2. Ceded Premiums / G.5.1.2. Primes Cédées	407	437	474	519	588	638	662	624
G.5.1.3. Net Written Premiums / G.5.1.3. Primes Nettes Emises	90	47	63	75	102	125	154	183
G.6. General Liability / G.6. Responsabilité Générale								
G.6.1. Direct Business / G.6.1. Assurances Directes								
G.6.1.1. Gross Premiums / G.6.1.1. Primes Brutes	4 165	4 602	4 736	5 010	5 224	5 421	5 629	5 763
G.6.1.2. Ceded Premiums / G.6.1.2. Primes Cédées	677	743	988	1 027	1 094	1 330	1 311	1 953
G.6.1.3. Net Written Premiums / G.6.1.3. Primes Nettes Emises	3 488	3 859	3 748	3 983	4 130	4 091	4 318	3 810
G.7. Accident, Health / G.7. Accident, Santé								
G.7.1. Direct Business / G.7.1. Assurances Directes								
G.7.1.1. Gross Premiums / G.7.1.1. Primes Brutes	18 660	20 621	21 475	22 293	22 339	22 425	7 414	7 696
G.7.1.2. Ceded Premiums / G.7.1.2. Primes Cédées	781	983	1 174	1 039	1 089	1 189	1 170	1 673
G.7.1.3. Net Written Premiums / G.7.1.3. Primes Nettes Emises	17 879	19 638	20 301	21 254	21 250	21 236	6 244	6 023
G.8. Others / G.8. Autres								
G.8.1. Direct Business / G.8.1. Assurances Directes								
G.8.1.1. Gross Premiums / G.8.1.1. Primes Brutes	4 106	3 346	3 564	3 849	4 144	4 450	19 753	20 268
G.8.1.2. Ceded Premiums / G.8.1.2. Primes Cédées	993	537	680	808	780	882	922	979
G.8.1.3. Net Written Premiums / G.8.1.3. Primes Nettes Emises	3 113	2 809	2 884	3 041	3 364	3 568	18 831	19 289

Monetary Unit: million schillings   Unité monétaire : million de schillings

	1992	1993	1994	1995	1996	1997	1998	1999
G.10. Total								
G.10.1. Direct Business — Assurances Directes								
G.10.1.1. Gross Premiums — Primes Brutes	71 170	76 532	80 073	82 639	83 907	84 201	83 718	83 839
G.10.1.2. Ceded Premiums — Primes Cédées	11 124	12 043	15 441	15 869	16 998	17 438	16 315	18 675
G.10.1.3. Net Written Premiums — Primes Nettes Emises	60 046	64 489	64 632	66 770	66 909	66 763	67 403	65 164
G.10.2. Reinsurance Accepted — Réassurance Acceptée								
G.10.2.1. Gross Premiums — Primes Brutes	10 334	11 139	17 312	14 004	18 681	21 025	18 573	20 585
G.10.2.2. Ceded Premiums — Primes Cédées	4 169	4 967	10 082	7 802	10 472	11 853	10 307	9 110
G.10.2.3. Net Written Premiums — Primes Nettes Emises	6 165	6 172	7 230	6 202	8 209	9 172	8 266	11 475
G.10.3. Total								
G.10.3.1. Gross Premiums — Primes Brutes	81 504	87 671	97 385	96 643	102 588	105 226	102 291	104 424
G.10.3.2. Ceded Premiums — Primes Cédées	15 293	17 010	25 523	23 671	27 470	29 291	26 622	27 785
G.10.3.3. Net Written Premiums — Primes Nettes Emises	66 211	70 661	71 862	72 972	75 118	75 935	75 669	76 639
H. GROSS CLAIMS PAYMENTS — PAIEMENTS BRUTS DES SINISTRES								
H.1. Life — Vie								
H.1.1. Domestic Companies — Entreprises Nationales					29 930	38 743	38 706	40 905
H.1.2. (Foreign Controlled Companies) — (Entreprises Sous Contrôle Etranger)					11 218	14 607	14 820	15 285
H.1. Total					29 930	38 743	38 706	40 905
H.2. Non-Life — Non-Vie								
H.2.1. Domestic Companies — Entreprises Nationales					65 520	67 558	70 288	74 043
H.2.2. (Foreign Controlled Companies) — (Entreprises Sous Contrôle Etranger)					32 616	33 700	36 750	38 074
H.2.3. Branches & Agencies of Foreign Cies — Succursales et Agences d'Ent. Etrangères					98	71	81	95
H.2. Total					65 618	67 629	70 369	74 138
I. GROSS OPERATING EXPENSES — DEPENSES BRUTES D'EXPLOITATION								
I.1. Life — Vie								
I.1.1. Domestic Companies — Entreprises Nationales					9 152	9 016	10 031	11 013
I.1.2. (Foreign Controlled Companies) — (Entreprises Sous Contrôle Etranger)					3 388	3 104	3 341	3 733
I.1. Total — Total des Primes Nettes Vie					9 152	9 016	10 031	11 013
I.2. Non-Life — Non-Vie								
I.2.1. Domestic Companies — Entreprises Nationales					28 656	30 478	30 680	31 799
I.2.2. (Foreign Controlled Companies) — (Entreprises Sous Contrôle Etranger)					14 927	15 924	16 341	16 397
I.2.3. Branches & Agencies of Foreign Cies — Succursales et Agences d'Ent. Etrangères					58	55	61	65
I.2. Total					28 714	30 533	30 741	31 864
J. COMMISSIONS								
J.1. Life — Vie								
J.1.1. Direct Business — Assurance directe								
J.1.1.1. Domestic Companies — Entreprises Nationales					3 910	3 483	4 091	4 741
J.1.1.2. (Foreign Controlled Companies) — (Entreprises Sous Contrôle Etranger)					1 166	923	1 021	1 232
J.1.1. Total					3 910	3 483	4 091	4 741
J.1.2. Reinsurance Accepted — Réassurances acceptées								
J.1.2.1. Domestic Companies — Entreprises Nationales					137	105	135	102
J.1.2.2. (Foreign Controlled Companies) — (Entreprises Sous Contrôle Etranger)					13	9	10	10
J.1.2. Total					137	105	135	102
J.1.3. Total								
J.1.3.1. Domestic Companies — Entreprises Nationales					4 047	3 588	4 226	4 843
J.1.3.2. (Foreign Controlled Companies) — (Entreprises Sous Contrôle Etranger)					1 179	932	1 031	1 242
J.1.3. Total of Life Net Premiums					4 047	3 588	4 226	4 843

AUSTRIA

AUTRICHE

Monetary Unit: million schillings

Unité monétaire : million de schillings

J.2. Non-Life

J.2. Non-Vie

	1992	1993	1994	1995	1996	1997	1998	1999	
J.2.1. Direct Business									J.2.1. Assurance directe
J.2.1.1. Domestic Companies					7 250	7 472	7 877	8 056	J.2.1.1. Entreprises Nationales
J.2.1.2. (Foreign Controlled Companies)					3 768	3 833	4 117	4 252	J.2.1.2. (Entreprises Sous Contrôle Etranger)
J.2.1.3. Branches & Agencies of Foreign Cies					28	26	26	27	J.2.1.3. Succursales et Agences d'Ent. Etrangères
J.2.1. Total					7 278	7 498	7 903	8 083	J.2.1. Total des Primes Nettes Vie
J.2.2. Reinsurance Accepted									J.2.2. Réassurances acceptées
J.2.2.1. Domestic Companies					2 339	2 760	2 725	3 238	J.2.2.1. Entreprises Nationales
J.2.2.2. (Foreign Controlled Companies)					900	968	1 429	1 100	J.2.2.2. (Entreprises Sous Contrôle Etranger)
J.2.2.3. Branches & Agencies of Foreign Cies					1	1	2	1	J.2.2.3. Succursales et Agences d'Ent. Etrangères
J.2.2. Total					2 340	2 761	2 727	3 239	J.2.2. Total
J.2.3. Total									J.2.3. Total
J.2.3.1. Domestic Companies					9 589	10 232	10 602	11 294	J.2.3.1. Entreprises Nationales
J.2.3.2. (Foreign Controlled Companies)					4 668	4 801	5 546	5 352	J.2.3.2. (Entreprises Sous Contrôle Etranger)
J.2.3.3. Branches & Agencies of Foreign Cies					29	27	28	28	J.2.3.3. Succursales et Agences d'Ent. Etrangères
J.2.3. Total					9 618	10 259	10 630	11 322	J.2.3. Total

BELGIUM

Monetary Unit: million Belgian francs

Unité monétaire : million de francs belges

	1992	1993	1994	1995	1996	1997	1998	1999
A. NUMBER OF COMPANIES IN THE REPORTING COUNTRY — **A. NOMBRE D'ENTREPRISES DANS LE PAYS DECLARANT**								
A.1. Life — **A.1. Vie**								
A.1.1. Domestic Companies — A.1.1. Entreprises Nationales	32	31	30	30	27	27	25	23
A.1.3. Branches & Agencies of Foreign Cies — A.1.3. Succursales et Agences d'Ent. Etrangères	11	11	1	0	0	0	0	0
A.1. All Companies — A.1. Ensemble des Entreprises	43	42	31	30	27	27	25	23
A.2. Non-Life — **A.2. Non-Vie**								
A.2.1. Domestic Companies — A.2.1. Entreprises Nationales	86	85	84	82	84	87	84	74
A.2.3. Branches & Agencies of Foreign Cies — A.2.3. Succursales et Agences d'Ent. Etrangères	83	78	9	8	8	6	4	4
A.2. All Companies — A.2. Ensemble des Entreprises	169	163	93	90	92	93	88	78
A.3. Composite — **A.3. Mixte**								
A.3.1. Domestic Companies — A.3.1. Entreprises Nationales	51	47	44	41	44	40	39	36
A.3.3. Branches & Agencies of Foreign Cies — A.3.3. Succursales et Agences d'Ent. Etrangères	3	3	3	2	2	2	2	2
A.3. All Companies — A.3. Ensemble des Entreprises	54	50	47	43	46	42	41	38
A.5. Total — **A.5. Total**								
A.5.1. Domestic Companies — A.5.1. Entreprises Nationales	169	163	158	153	155	154	148	133
A.5.3. Branches & Agencies of Foreign Cies — A.5.3. Succursales et Agences d'Ent. Etrangères	97	92	13	10	10	8	6	6
A.5. All Insurance Companies — A.5. Ensemble des Entreprises d'Assurances	266	255	171	163	165	162	154	139
B. NUMBER OF EMPLOYEES — **B. NOMBRE D'EMPLOYES**								
B.1. Insurance Companies — B.1. Entreprises d'Assurances	27 920	27 007	25 969	25 501	25 070	25 262	25 313	25 256
B.2. Intermediaries — B.2. Intermediaires	24 000	24 000	24 000	28 750	28 085	28 642	28 866	28 524
B. Total — B. Total	51 920	51 007	49 969	54 251	53 155	53 904	54 179	53 780
C. BUSINESS WRITTEN IN THE REPORTING COUNTRY — **C. OPERATIONS CONCLUES DANS LE PAYS DECLARANT**								
C.1. Life — **C.1. Vie**								
C.1.1. Gross Premiums — C.1.1. Primes Brutes								
C.1.1.1. Direct Business — C.1.1.1. Assurances Directes								
C.1.1.1.1. Domestic Companies — C.1.1.1.1. Entreprises Nationales	112 562	124 087	146 610	174 220	203 871	242 192	323 932	392 831
C.1.1.1.3. Branches & Agencies of Foreign Cies — C.1.1.1.3. Succursales et Agences d'Ent. Etrangères	8 638	11 361	13 260	7 661	7 619	8 894	10 492	11 354
C.1.1.1. Total — C.1.1.1. Total	121 200	135 448	159 870	181 881	211 490	251 086	334 425	404 185
C.1.1.2. Reinsurance Accepted — C.1.1.2. Réassurance Acceptée								
C.1.1.2.1. Domestic Companies — C.1.1.2.1. Entreprises Nationales	1 203	1 384	2 000	2 482	2 847	3 252	3 304	2 277
C.1.1.2.3. Branches & Agencies of Foreign Cies — C.1.1.2.3. Succursales et Agences d'Ent. Etrangères	48	140	4	3	3	3	3	3
C.1.1.2. Total — C.1.1.2. Total	1 252	1 523	2 004	2 485	2 850	3 254	3 306	2 280
C.1.1.3. Total — C.1.1.3. Total								
C.1.1.3.1. Domestic Companies — C.1.1.3.1. Entreprises Nationales	113 765	125 470	148 610	176 702	206 718	245 444	327 236	395 108
C.1.1.3.3. Branches & Agencies of Foreign Cies — C.1.1.3.3. Succursales et Agences d'Ent. Etrangères	8 686	11 501	13 264	7 664	7 622	8 896	10 495	11 357
C.1.1.3. Total Gross Premiums — C.1.1.3. Total des Primes Brutes	122 451	136 971	161 874	184 367	214 340	254 340	337 731	406 465
C.1.2. Ceded Premiums — C.1.2. Primes Cédées								
C.1.2.1. Domestic Companies — C.1.2.1. Entreprises Nationales	6 180	5 672	5 790	0	0	0	0	0
C.1.2.3. Branches & Agencies of Foreign Cies — C.1.2.3. Succursales et Agences d'Ent. Etrangères	806	718	132	131	160	92	132	90
C.1.2. Total — C.1.2. Total	6 986	6 390	5 922	131	160	92	132	90
C.1.3. Net Written Premiums — C.1.3. Primes Nettes Emises								
C.1.3.1. Domestic Companies — C.1.3.1. Entreprises Nationales	107 585	119 798	142 820	176 702	206 718	245 444	327 236	395 108
C.1.3.3. Branches & Agencies of Foreign Cies — C.1.3.3. Succursales et Agences d'Ent. Etrangères	7 880	10 783	13 132	7 533	7 462	8 804	10 363	11 267
C.1.3. Total — C.1.3. Total	115 465	130 581	155 952	184 236	214 180	254 248	337 599	406 374

Monetary Unit: million Belgian francs

Unité monétaire : million de francs belges

C.2. Non-Life / C.2. Non-Vie

Code	Label	1992	1993	1994	1995	1996	1997	1998	1999
C.2.1.	Gross premiums / Primes Brutes								
C.2.1.1.	Direct Business / Assurances Directes								
C.2.1.1.1.	Domestic Companies / Entreprises Nationales	217 617	227 735	234 503	242 070	245 673	242 896	247 409	253 242
C.2.1.1.3.	Branches & Agencies of Foreign Cies / Succursales et Agences d'Ent. Etrangères	16 247	16 778	7 206	6 249	6 874	6 516	6 884	7 256
C.2.1.1.	Total	233 864	244 513	241 709	248 319	252 547	249 412	254 302	260 498
C.2.1.2.	Reinsurance Accepted / Réassurance Acceptée								
C.2.1.2.1.	Domestic Companies / Entreprises Nationales	14 494	10 848	9 496	23 183	22 700	23 255	19 833	26 730
C.2.1.2.3.	Branches & Agencies of Foreign Cies / Succursales et Agences d'Ent. Etrangères	1 904	747	126	95	217	188	161	172
C.2.1.2.	Total	16 398	11 595	9 622	23 278	22 917	23 443	19 994	26 903
C.2.1.3.	Total								
C.2.1.3.1.	Domestic Companies / Entreprises Nationales	232 112	238 583	243 999	265 253	268 373	266 152	267 242	279 973
C.2.1.3.3.	Branches & Agencies of Foreign Cies / Succursales et Agences d'Ent. Etrangères	18 151	17 526	7 332	6 345	7 091	6 704	7 054	7 428
C.2.1.3.	Total Gross Premiums / Total des Primes Brutes	250 263	256 109	251 331	271 598	275 464	272 856	274 296	287 401
C.2.2.	Ceded Premiums / Primes Cédées								
C.2.2.1.	Domestic Companies / Entreprises Nationales	43 336	43 370	45 245	44 403	41 909	38 143	35 630	32 277
C.2.2.3.	Branches & Agencies of Foreign Cies / Succursales et Agences d'Ent. Etrangères	5 602	5 095	1 069	807	855	775	811	1 002
C.2.2.	Total	48 938	48 465	46 314	45 210	42 764	38 917	36 442	33 279
C.2.3.	Net Written Premiums / Primes Nettes Emises								
C.2.3.1.	Domestic Companies / Entreprises Nationales	188 775	195 213	198 754	220 850	226 464	228 009	231 611	247 696
C.2.3.3.	Branches & Agencies of Foreign Cies / Succursales et Agences d'Ent. Etrangères	12 549	12 430	6 263	5 537	6 236	5 929	6 243	6 426
C.2.3.	Total	201 324	207 643	205 017	226 387	232 700	233 938	237 854	254 121

C.3. Total / C.3. Total

Code	Label	1992	1993	1994	1995	1996	1997	1998	1999
C.3.1.	Gross Premiums / Primes Brutes								
C.3.1.1.	Direct Business / Assurances Directes								
C.3.1.1.1.	Domestic Companies / Entreprises Nationales	330 179	351 822	381 113	416 290	449 544	485 088	571 341	646 073
C.3.1.1.3.	Branches & Agencies of Foreign Cies / Succursales et Agences d'Ent. Etrangères	24 885	28 139	20 466	13 910	14 493	15 410	17 386	18 610
C.3.1.1.	Total	355 064	379 961	401 579	430 200	464 037	500 498	588 727	664 683
C.3.1.2.	Reinsurance Accepted / Réassurance Acceptée								
C.3.1.2.1.	Domestic Companies / Entreprises Nationales	15 697	12 232	11 496	25 665	25 547	26 507	23 137	29 007
C.3.1.2.3.	Branches & Agencies of Foreign Cies / Succursales et Agences d'Ent. Etrangères	1 952	887	130	98	220	191	164	175
C.3.1.2.	Total	17 650	13 118	11 626	25 763	25 767	26 697	23 300	29 182
C.3.1.3.	Total								
C.3.1.3.1.	Domestic Companies / Entreprises Nationales	345 877	364 053	392 609	441 955	475 091	511 596	594 478	675 081
C.3.1.3.3.	Branches & Agencies of Foreign Cies / Succursales et Agences d'Ent. Etrangères	26 837	29 027	20 596	14 009	14 713	15 600	17 549	18 785
C.3.1.3.	Total Gross Premiums / Total des Primes Brutes	372 714	393 080	413 205	455 965	489 804	527 196	612 027	693 865
C.3.2.	Ceded Premiums / Primes Cédées								
C.3.2.1.	Domestic Companies / Entreprises Nationales	49 516	49 042	51 035	44 403	41 909	38 143	35 630	32 277
C.3.2.3.	Branches & Agencies of Foreign Cies / Succursales et Agences d'Ent. Etrangères	6 408	5 813	1 201	938	1 015	867	943	1 093
C.3.2.	Total	55 924	54 855	52 236	45 341	42 924	39 009	36 574	33 370
C.3.3.	Net Written Premiums / Primes Nettes Emises								
C.3.3.1.	Domestic Companies / Entreprises Nationales	296 360	315 011	341 574	397 552	433 182	473 453	558 847	642 804
C.3.3.3.	Branches & Agencies of Foreign Cies / Succursales et Agences d'Ent. Etrangères	20 429	23 213	19 395	13 070	13 698	14 733	16 606	17 692
C.3.3.	Total	316 789	338 224	360 969	410 623	446 880	488 186	575 453	660 496

E. BUSINESS WRITTEN ABROAD / E. OPERATIONS A L'ETRANGER

E.1. Life / E.1. Vie

Code	Label	1992	1993	1994	1995	1996	1997	1998	1999
E.1.1.	Gross Premiums / Primes Brutes								
E.1.1.1.	Direct Business / Assurance Directe								
E.1.1.1.1.	Branches & Agencies / Succursales & Agences	:	:	:	1 194	1 749	2 715	2 338	2 424
E.1.1.1.	Total	:	:	:				2 338	2 424
E.1.1.3.	Total	3 309	2 648	2 253	:	:	:	:	:
E.1.1.3.1.	Branches & Agencies / Succursales & Agences								

Monetary Unit: million Belgian francs

Unité monétaire : million de francs belges

	1992	1993	1994	1995	1996	1997	1998	1999	
E.1.2. Ceded Premiums									E.1.2. Primes Cédées
E.1.2.1. Branches & Agencies	517	637	349	..	..	..	..	..	E.1.2.1. Succursales & Agences
E.1.3. Net Written Premiums									E.1.3. Primes Nettes Emises
E.1.3.1. Branches & Agencies	2 793	2 012	1 904	..	..	..	..	..	E.1.3.1. Succursales & Agences
E.2. Non-Life									**E.2. Non-Vie**
E.2.1. Gross Premiums									E.2.1. Primes Brutes
E.2.1.1. Direct Business									E.2.1.1. Assurance Directe
E.2.1.1.1. Branches & Agencies	..	..	..	38 373	43 296	49 338	57 292	67 802	E.2.1.1.1. Succursales & Agences
E.2.1.1. Total	..	..	..		43 296	49 338	57 292	67 802	E.2.1.1. Total
E.2.1.3. Total									E.2.1.3. Total
E.2.1.3.1. Branches & Agencies	37 368	48 768	49 816	..	..	..	..	..	E.2.1.3.1. Succursales & Agences
E.2.2. Ceded Premiums									E.2.2. Primes Cédées
E.2.2.1. Branches & Agencies	14 714	18 469	18 031	..	..	..	..	..	E.2.2.1. Succursales & Agences
E.2.3. Net Written Premiums									E.2.3. Primes Nettes Emises
E.2.3.1. Branches & Agencies	22 654	30 298	31 785	..	..	..	..	..	E.2.3.1. Succursales & Agences
F. OUTSTANDING INVESTMENT BY DIRECT INSURANCE COMPANIES									**F. ENCOURS DES PLACEMENTS DES ENTREPRISES D'ASSURANCES DIRECTES**
F.1. Life									**F.1. Vie**
F.1.1. Real Estate									F.1.1. Immobilier
F.1.1.1. Domestic Companies	71 183	43 864	49 665	51 214	50 725	57 541	55 490	50 312	F.1.1.1. Entreprises Nationales
F.1.1.3. Branches & Agencies of Foreign Cies	8 029	9 266	7 081	7 081	7 081	6 327	6 271	6 203	F.1.1.3. Succursales et Agences d'Ent. Etrangères
F.1.2. Mortgage Loans									F.1.2. Prêts Hypothécaires
F.1.2.1. Domestic Companies	195 088	197 161	203 194	199 834	189 813	174 906	169 272	165 510	F.1.2.1. Entreprises Nationales
F.1.2.3. Branches & Agencies of Foreign Cies	7 445	7 143	2 384	2 347	2 348	2 343	2 154	1 814	F.1.2.3. Succursales et Agences d'Ent. Etrangères
F.1.3. Shares									F.1.3. Actions
F.1.3.1. Domestic Companies	118 545	136 977	175 551	219 970	258 710	369 108	534 905	827 826	F.1.3.1. Entreprises Nationales
F.1.3.3. Branches & Agencies of Foreign Cies	4 356	7 153	3 511	5 460	9 182	11 636	17 923	20 896	F.1.3.3. Succursales et Agences d'Ent. Etrangères
F.1.4. Bonds with Fixed Revenue									F.1.4. Obligations
F.1.4.1. Domestic Companies	481 363	560 343	624 764	731 850	824 227	952 202	1 093 675	1 278 030	F.1.4.1. Entreprises Nationales
F.1.4.3. Branches & Agencies of Foreign Cies	44 765	50 426	36 150	41 891	44 250	45 457	52 304	54 403	F.1.4.3. Succursales et Agences d'Ent. Etrangères
F.1.5. Loans other than Mortgage Loans									F.1.5. Prêts Autres qu'Hypothécaires
F.1.5.1. Domestic Companies	19 815	26 745	20 617	19 467	20 240	19 702	12 578	11 927	F.1.5.1. Entreprises Nationales
F.1.5.3. Branches & Agencies of Foreign Cies	42	34	11	10	8	6	5	465	F.1.5.3. Succursales et Agences d'Ent. Etrangères
F.1.6. Other Investments									F.1.6. Autres Placements
F.1.6.1. Domestic Companies	64 903	70 254	68 132	91 355	110 031	133 904	147 014	171 791	F.1.6.1. Entreprises Nationales
F.1.6.3. Branches & Agencies of Foreign Cies	5 765	7 081	4 023	3 790	4 613	6 574	4 877	4 909	F.1.6.3. Succursales et Agences d'Ent. Etrangères
F.1.7. Total									F.1.7. Total
F.1.7.1. Domestic Companies	950 897	1 035 345	1 141 923	1 313 689	1 453 746	1 707 363	2 012 935	2 505 398	F.1.7.1. Entreprises Nationales
F.1.7.3. Branches & Agencies of Foreign Cies	70 402	81 104	53 160	60 579	67 482	72 344	83 534	88 689	F.1.7.3. Succursales et Agences d'Ent. Etrangères
F.2. Non-Life									**F.2. Non-Vie**
F.2.1. Real Estate									F.2.1. Immobilier
F.2.1.1. Domestic Companies	35 371	55 809	54 436	51 047	49 266	51 333	49 952	45 793	F.2.1.1. Entreprises Nationales
F.2.1.3. Branches & Agencies of Foreign Cies	4 090	4 028	2 564	2 554	2 312	1 966	1 947	1 550	F.2.1.3. Succursales et Agences d'Ent. Etrangères
F.2.2. Mortgage Loans									F.2.2. Prêts Hypothécaires
F.2.2.1. Domestic Companies	31 936	20 533	22 361	22 224	21 166	18 547	14 921	12 205	F.2.2.1. Entreprises Nationales
F.2.2.3. Branches & Agencies of Foreign Cies	56	46	0	8	8	8	8	6	F.2.2.3. Succursales et Agences d'Ent. Etrangères
F.2.3. Shares									F.2.3. Actions
F.2.3.1. Domestic Companies	54 114	63 082	77 447	89 780	109 371	152 948	191 018	220 858	F.2.3.1. Entreprises Nationales
F.2.3.3. Branches & Agencies of Foreign Cies	690	542	0	997	1 621	2 421	3 757	4 615	F.2.3.3. Succursales et Agences d'Ent. Etrangères
F.2.4. Bonds with Fixed Revenue									F.2.4. Obligations
F.2.4.1. Domestic Companies	206 941	225 835	258 946	280 475	307 088	308 656	327 664	344 920	F.2.4.1. Entreprises Nationales
F.2.4.3. Branches & Agencies of Foreign Cies	11 752	13 309	5 665	6 335	7 505	7 749	6 930	5 831	F.2.4.3. Succursales et Agences d'Ent. Etrangères

Monetary Unit: million Belgian francs   Unité monétaire : million de francs belges

	1992	1993	1994	1995	1996	1997	1998	1999	
F.2.5. Loans other than Mortgage Loans									F.2.5. Prêts Autres qu'Hypothécaires
F.2.5.1. Domestic Companies	1 435	1 942	713	712	790	1 121	954	789	F.2.5.1. Entreprises Nationales
F.2.5.3. Branches & Agencies of Foreign Cies	409	81	0	62	57	51	48	347	F.2.5.3. Succursales et Agences d'Ent. Etrangères
F.2.6. Other Investments									F.2.6. Autres Placements
F.2.6.1. Domestic Companies	56 625	51 557	73 901	111 841	127 149	136 143	127 974	143 341	F.2.6.1. Entreprises Nationales
F.2.6.3. Branches & Agencies of Foreign Cies	5 604	6 147	1 210	655	623	663	704	1 009	F.2.6.3. Succursales et Agences d'Ent. Etrangères
F.2.7. Total									F.2.7. Total
F.2.7.1. Domestic Companies	386 422	418 759	487 804	556 079	614 830	668 748	712 482	767 906	F.2.7.1. Entreprises Nationales
F.2.7.3. Branches & Agencies of Foreign Cies	22 601	24 153	9 439	10 611	12 126	12 858	13 393	13 357	F.2.7.3. Succursales et Agences d'Ent. Etrangères
G. BREAKDOWN OF NON-LIFE PREMIUMS									**G. VENTILATIONS DES PRIMES NON-VIE**
G.1. Motor vehicle									G.1. Assurance Automobile
G.1.1. Direct Business									G.1.1. Assurances Directes
G.1.1.1. Gross Premiums	91 899	91 615	92 122	95 987	95 257	94 081	95 194	97 775	G.1.1.1. Primes Brutes
G.2. Marine, Aviation									G.2. Marine, Aviation
G.2.1. Direct Business									G.2.1. Assurances Directes
G.2.1.1. Gross Premiums	6 663	5 629	5 112	5 301	5 402	5 186	4 924	4 553	G.2.1.1. Primes Brutes
G.4. Fire, Property Damages									G.4. Incendie, Dommages aux Biens
G.4.1. Direct Business									G.4.1. Assurances Directes
G.4.1.1. Gross Premiums	50 564	50 499	50 724	53 018	54 552	52 588	52 605	53 620	G.4.1.1. Primes Brutes
G.5. Pecuniary Losses									G.5. Pertes Pécunières
G.5.1. Direct Business									G.5.1. Assurances Directes
G.5.1.1. Gross Premiums	7 568	9 759	10 522	10 241	9 755	9 216	8 890	9 035	G.5.1.1. Primes Brutes
G.6. General Liability									G.6. Responsabilité Générale
G.6.1. Direct Business									G.6.1. Assurances Directes
G.6.1.1. Gross Premiums	16 245	16 280	16 779	17 636	18 402	18 571	19 202	19 323	G.6.1.1. Primes Brutes
G.7. Accident, Health									G.7. Accident, Santé
G.7.1. Direct Business									G.7.1. Assurances Directes
G.7.1.1. Gross Premiums	49 184	52 410	53 854	54 271	58 242	58 238	60 667	63 813	G.7.1.1. Primes Brutes
G.8. Others									G.8. Autres
G.8.1. Direct Business									G.8.1. Assurances Directes
G.8.1.1. Gross Premiums	10 180	16 324	11 356	9 126	10 937	11 532	12 823	12 380	G.8.1.1. Primes Brutes
G.10. Total									G.10. Total
G.10.1. Direct Business									G.10.1. Assurances Directes
G.10.1.1. Gross Premiums	232 304	242 516	240 469	245 580	252 547	249 412	254 304	260 499	G.10.1.1. Primes Brutes
H. GROSS CLAIMS PAYMENTS									**H. PAIEMENTS BRUTS DES SINISTRES**
H.1. Life									H.1. Vie
H.1.1. Domestic Companies		90 067	92 209	97 986	109 891	124 542	142 473	158 698	H.1.1. Entreprises Nationales
H.1.3. Branches & Agencies of Foreign Cies		6 558	6 046	7 336	5 481	8 285	6 631	9 351	H.1.3. Succursales et Agences d'Ent. Etrangères
H.1. Total		96 625	98 255	105 322	115 372	132 827	149 104	168 049	H.1. Total
H.2. Non-Life									H.2. Non-Vie
H.2.1. Domestic Companies		141 866	144 291	142 553	142 351	146 883	150 581	160 753	H.2.1. Entreprises Nationales
H.2.3. Branches & Agencies of Foreign Cies		9 712	3 787	3 188	3 722	3 576	4 393	4 644	H.2.3. Succursales et Agences d'Ent. Etrangères
H.2. Total		151 577	148 078	145 741	146 073	150 459	154 974	165 397	H.2. Total

Monetary Unit: million Belgian francs   Unité monétaire : million de francs belges

I. GROSS OPERATING EXPENSES / I. DEPENSES BRUITES D'EXPLOITATION

	1992	1993	1994	1995	1996	1997	1998	1999	
I.1. Life									**I.1. Vie**
I.1.1. Domestic Companies		24 708	24 768	21 169	21 924	23 218	25 704	26 839	I.1.1. Entreprises Nationales
I.1.3. Branches & Agencies of Foreign Cies		2 326	1 755	1 304	1 462	1 505	1 646	1 788	I.1.3. Succursales et Agences d'Ent. Etrangères
I.1. Total		27 034	26 522	22 473	23 386	24 723	27 350	28 627	I.1. Total des Primes Nettes Vie
I.2. Non-Life									**I.2. Non-Vie**
I.2.1. Domestic Companies		63 655	64 820	58 132	58 371	60 493	62 364	65 088	I.2.1. Entreprises Nationales
I.2.3. Branches & Agencies of Foreign Cies		3 858	1 683	1 240	1 473	1 441	1 469	1 410	I.2.3. Succursales et Agences d'Ent. Etrangères
I.2. Total		67 513	66 503	59 372	59 844	61 934	63 833	66 498	I.2. Total

J. COMMISSIONS / J. COMMISSIONS

	1992	1993	1994	1995	1996	1997	1998	1999	
J.1. Life									**J.1. Vie**
J.1.1. Direct Business									**J.1.1. Assurance directe**
J.1.1.1. Domestic Companies		6 301	7 609	8 813	9 621	11 119	13 739	16 295	J.1.1.1. Entreprises Nationales
J.1.1.3. Branches & Agencies of Foreign Cies		590	332	229	230	261	329	436	J.1.1.3. Succursales et Agences d'Ent. Etrangères
J.1.1. Total		6 892	7 942	9 041	9 851	11 379	14 068	16 731	J.1.1. Total
J.1.2. Reinsurance Accepted									**J.1.2. Réassurances acceptées**
J.1.2.1. Domestic Companies		0	0	318	469	327	185	221	J.1.2.1. Entreprises Nationales
J.1.2. Total		0	0	318	469	327	185	221	J.1.2. Total
J.1.3. Total									**J.1.3. Total**
J.1.3.1. Domestic Companies		6 301	7 609	9 131	10 090	11 446	13 924	16 516	J.1.3.1. Entreprises Nationales
J.1.3.3. Branches & Agencies of Foreign Cies		590	332	229	230	261	329	436	J.1.3.3. Succursales et Agences d'Ent. Etrangères
J.1.3. Total of Life Net Premiums		6 892	7 942	9 360	10 320	11 707	14 253	16 952	J.1.3. Total
J.2. Non-Life									**J.2. Non-Vie**
J.2.1. Direct Business									**J.2.1. Assurance directe**
J.2.1.1. Domestic Companies		32 982	33 246	34 794	35 303	34 813	35 519	36 687	J.2.1.1. Entreprises Nationales
J.2.1.3. Branches & Agencies of Foreign Cies		2 490	871	841	907	957	1 001	1 024	J.2.1.3. Succursales et Agences d'Ent. Etrangères
J.2.1. Total		35 472	34 117	35 635	36 210	35 771	36 520	37 711	J.2.1. Total des Primes Nettes Vie
J.2.2. Reinsurance Accepted									**J.2.2. Réassurances acceptées**
J.2.2.1. Domestic Companies		169	68	4 558	4 667	4 663	4 316	5 341	J.2.2.1. Entreprises Nationales
J.2.2.3. Branches & Agencies of Foreign Cies		27	9	13	21	21	14	4	J.2.2.3. Succursales et Agences d'Ent. Etrangères
J.2.2. Total		196	77	4 571	4 688	4 684	4 330	5 345	J.2.2. Total
J.2.3. Total									**J.2.3. Total**
J.2.3.1. Domestic Companies		33 150	33 314	39 352	39 970	39 476	39 835	42 028	J.2.3.1. Entreprises Nationales
J.2.3.3. Branches & Agencies of Foreign Cies		2 517	880	854	928	978	1 015	1 028	J.2.3.3. Succursales et Agences d'Ent. Etrangères
J.2.3. Total		35 667	34 194	40 206	40 898	40 454	40 850	43 056	J.2.3. Total

Monetary Unit: million Ca..dian dollars

A. NUMBER OF COMPANIES IN THE REPORTING COUNTRY
A. NOMBRE D'ENTREPRISES DANS LE PAYS DECLARANT

	1992	1993	1994	1995	1996	1997	1998	1999
A.1. Life / A.1. Vie								
A.1.1. Domestic Companies	63	60	63	70	59	52	51	99
A.1.2. (Foreign Controlled Companies)	27	26	22	27	23	:	:	22
A.1.3. Branches & Agencies of Foreign Cies	79	74	74	89	65	58	59	52
A.1. All Companies	142	134	137	159	124	110	110	151
A.2. Non-Life / A.2. Non-Vie								
A.2.1. Domestic Companies	92	92	89	90	91	90	90	104
A.2.2. (Foreign Controlled Companies)	42	38	38	43	45	:	:	0
A.2.3. Branches & Agencies of Foreign Cies	103	98	94	100	88	98	84	114
A.2. All Companies	195	190	183	190	179	188	174	218
A.3. Composite / A.3. Mixte								
A.3.1. Domestic Companies	1	1	0	0	0	0	0	0
A.3.2. (Foreign Controlled Companies)	1	1	0	0	0	0	:	:
A.3.3. Branches & Agencies of Foreign Cies	8	6	1	0	0	0	3	:
A.3. All Companies	9	7	1	0	0	0	3	6
A.4. Reinsurance / A.4. Réassurance								
A.4.1. Domestic Companies	11	11	10	10	11	9	11	12
A.4.2. (Foreign Controlled Companies)	9	9	10	10	9	:	:	2
A.4.3. Branches & Agencies of Foreign Cies	42	39	43	44	55	30	39	43
A.4. All Companies	53	50	53	54	66	39	50	55
A.5. Total								
A.5.1. Domestic Companies	167	164	162	170	161	151	152	:
A.5.2. (Foreign Controlled Companies)	79	74	70	80	77	:	:	:
A.5.3. Branches & Agencies of Foreign Cies	232	217	212	233	208	186	185	185
A.5. All Insurance Companies	399	381	374	403	369	337	337	430

B. NUMBER OF EMPLOYEES
B. NOMBRE D'EMPLOYES

	1992	1993	1994	1995	1996	1997	1998	1999
B.1. Insurance Companies / Entreprises d'Assurances	:	:	:	:	:	97 184	96 953	91 017
B.2. Intermediaries / Intermédiaires	:	:	:	:	:	107 574	109 334	116 282
B. Total	172 520	:	:	:	:	204 758	206 287	207 299

C. BUSINESS WRITTEN IN THE REPORTING COUNTRY
C. OPERATIONS CONCLUES DANS LE PAYS DECLARANT

C.1. Life / C.1. Vie

	1992	1993	1994	1995	1996	1997	1998	1999
C.1.1. Gross Premiums / Primes Brutes								
C.1.1.1. Direct Business / Assurances Directes								
C.1.1.1.1. Domestic Companies / Entreprises Nationales	13 504	12 357	16 410	17 428	11 917	11 880	12 013	29 470
C.1.1.1.2. (Foreign Controlled Companies / Entreprises Sous Contrôle Etranger)	2 558	2 545	2 255	3 433	2 486	1 964	1 339	6 879
C.1.1.1.3. Branches & Agencies of Foreign Cies / Succursales et Agences d'Ent. Etrangères	3 007	1 086	3 851	4 257	2 295	:	:	1 875
C.1.1.1. Total	16 511	13 443	20 261	21 685	14 212	13 845	13 352	31 345
C.1.1.2. Reinsurance Accepted / Réassurance Acceptée								
C.1.1.2.1. Domestic Companies / Entreprises Nationales	350	332	519	661	564	651	990	1 270
C.1.1.2.2. (Foreign Controlled Companies / Entreprises Sous Contrôle Etranger)	264	234	354	405	377	:	:	852
C.1.1.2.3. Branches & Agencies of Foreign Cies / Succursales et Agences d'Ent. Etrangères	326	128	646	710	552	563	492	740
C.1.1.2. Total	676	460	1 165	1 371	1 116	1 214	1 482	2 010
C.1.1.3. Total								
C.1.1.3.1. Domestic Companies / Entreprises Nationales	13 854	12 689	16 929	18 089	12 481	12 531	13 003	30 740
C.1.1.3.2. (Foreign Controlled Companies / Entreprises Sous Contrôle Etranger)	2 822	2 779	2 609	3 838	2 863	:	:	7 731
C.1.1.3.3. Branches & Agencies of Foreign Cies / Succursales et Agences d'Ent. Etrangères	3 333	1 214	4 497	4 967	2 847	2 527	1 831	2 615
C.1.1.3. Total Gross Premiums / Total des Primes Brutes	17 187	13 903	21 426	23 056	15 328	15 058	14 834	33 355
C.1.2. Ceded Premiums / Primes Cédées								
C.1.2.1. Domestic Companies / Entreprises Nationales	708	975	1 362	1 555	1 323	1 506	1 459	2 211
C.1.2.2. (Foreign Controlled Companies / Entreprises Sous Contrôle Etranger)	358	427	523	666	582	:	:	1 146
C.1.2.3. Branches & Agencies of Foreign Cies / Succursales et Agences d'Ent. Etrangères	160	59	432	454	382	335	120	420
C.1.2. Total	868	1 034	1 794	2 009	1 705	1 841	1 578	2 631

Monetary Unit: million Ca..dian dollars · Unité monétaire : million de dollars ca..diens

	1992	1993	1994	1995	1996	1997	1998	1999
C.1.3. Net Written Premiums / C.1.3. Primes Nettes Emises								
C.1.3.1. Domestic Companies / C.1.3.1. Entreprises Nationales	13 146	11 714	15 567	16 534	11 158	11 025	11 544	28 529
C.1.3.2. (Foreign Controlled Companies) / C.1.3.2. (Entreprises Sous Contrôle Etranger)	2 464	2 352	2 086	3 172	2 281	..	..	6 585
C.1.3.3. Branches & Agencies of Foreign Cies / C.1.3.3. Succursales et Agences d'Ent. Etrangères	3 173	1 155	4 065	4 513	2 465	2 193	1 711	2 195
C.1.3. Total	16 319	12 869	19 632	21 047	13 623	13 218	13 256	30 724
C.2. Non-Life / C.2. Non-Vie								
C.2.1. Gross premiums / C.2.1. Primes Brutes								
C.2.1.1. Direct Business / C.2.1.1. Assurances Directes								
C.2.1.1.1. Domestic Companies / C.2.1.1.1. Entreprises Nationales	13 779	14 229	10 741	11 584	16 694	17 498	18 234	26 754
C.2.1.1.2. (Foreign Controlled Companies) / C.2.1.1.2. (Entreprises Sous Contrôle Etranger)	6 510	6 198	5 715	6 660	7 418	..	..	1 085
C.2.1.1.3. Branches & Agencies of Foreign Cies / C.2.1.1.3. Succursales et Agences d'Ent. Etrangères	3 609	3 957	3 306	3 445	5 140	4 931	4 683	5 094
C.2.1.1. Total	17 388	18 186	14 047	15 029	21 834	22 429	22 917	31 848
C.2.1.2. Reinsurance Accepted / C.2.1.2. Réassurance Acceptée								
C.2.1.2.1. Domestic Companies / C.2.1.2.1. Entreprises Nationales	2 282	2 562	2 301	1 795	2 267	2 237	2 305	2 971
C.2.1.2.2. (Foreign Controlled Companies) / C.2.1.2.2. (Entreprises Sous Contrôle Etranger)	1 917	2 039	2 060	1 625	2 135	..	..	242
C.2.1.2.3. Branches & Agencies of Foreign Cies / C.2.1.2.3. Succursales et Agences d'Ent. Etrangères	1 755	1 517	1 507	1 409	1 801	1 707	1 631	1 877
C.2.1.2. Total	4 037	4 079	3 808	3 204	4 068	3 944	3 936	4 848
C.2.1.3. Total								
C.2.1.3.1. Domestic Companies / C.2.1.3.1. Entreprises Nationales	16 061	16 791	13 042	13 379	18 961	19 735	20 539	29 725
C.2.1.3.2. (Foreign Controlled Companies) / C.2.1.3.2. (Entreprises Sous Contrôle Etranger)	8 427	8 237	7 775	8 285	9 553	..	..	1 327
C.2.1.3.3. Branches & Agencies of Foreign Cies / C.2.1.3.3. Succursales et Agences d'Ent. Etrangères	5 364	5 474	4 813	4 854	6 941	6 638	6 314	6 971
C.2.1.3. Total Gross Premiums / C.2.1.3. Total des Primes Brutes	21 425	22 265	17 855	18 233	25 902	26 373	26 853	36 696
C.2.2. Ceded Premiums / C.2.2. Primes Cédées								
C.2.2.1. Domestic Companies / C.2.2.1. Entreprises Nationales	3 257	3 426	3 051	2 803	3 410	3 394	3 553	4 658
C.2.2.2. (Foreign Controlled Companies) / C.2.2.2. (Entreprises Sous Contrôle Etranger)	2 362	2 130	2 050	1 901	2 251	..	..	257
C.2.2.3. Branches & Agencies of Foreign Cies / C.2.2.3. Succursales et Agences d'Ent. Etrangères	1 161	1 088	1 156	1 061	1 297	1 270	1 206	1 362
C.2.2. Total	4 418	4 514	4 207	3 864	4 707	4 663	4 758	6 020
C.2.3. Net Written Premiums / C.2.3. Primes Nettes Emises								
C.2.3.1. Domestic Companies / C.2.3.1. Entreprises Nationales	12 804	13 365	9 991	10 576	15 551	16 341	16 987	25 067
C.2.3.2. (Foreign Controlled Companies) / C.2.3.2. (Entreprises Sous Contrôle Etranger)	6 065	6 107	5 725	6 384	7 302	..	..	1 070
C.2.3.3. Branches & Agencies of Foreign Cies / C.2.3.3. Succursales et Agences d'Ent. Etrangères	4 203	4 386	3 657	3 793	5 644	5 368	5 108	5 609
C.2.3. Total	17 007	17 751	13 648	14 369	21 195	21 710	22 095	30 676
C.3. Total								
C.3.1. Gross Premiums / C.3.1. Primes Brutes								
C.3.1.1. Direct Business / C.3.1.1. Assurances Directes								
C.3.1.1.1. Domestic Companies / C.3.1.1.1. Entreprises Nationales	27 283	26 586	27 151	29 012	28 611	29 378	30 248	56 224
C.3.1.1.2. (Foreign Controlled Companies) / C.3.1.1.2. (Entreprises Sous Contrôle Etranger)	9 068	8 743	7 970	10 093	9 904	..	..	7 964
C.3.1.1.3. Branches & Agencies of Foreign Cies / C.3.1.1.3. Succursales et Agences d'Ent. Etrangères	6 616	5 043	7 157	7 702	7 435	6 895	6 022	6 969
C.3.1.1. Total	33 899	31 629	34 308	36 714	36 046	36 274	36 269	63 193
C.3.1.2. Reinsurance Accepted / C.3.1.2. Réassurance Acceptée								
C.3.1.2.1. Domestic Companies / C.3.1.2.1. Entreprises Nationales	2 632	2 894	2 820	2 456	2 831	2 888	3 295	4 241
C.3.1.2.2. (Foreign Controlled Companies) / C.3.1.2.2. (Entreprises Sous Contrôle Etranger)	2 181	2 273	2 414	2 030	2 512	..	..	1 094
C.3.1.2.3. Branches & Agencies of Foreign Cies / C.3.1.2.3. Succursales et Agences d'Ent. Etrangères	2 081	1 645	2 153	2 119	2 353	2 270	2 123	2 617
C.3.1.2. Total	4 713	4 539	4 973	4 575	5 184	5 158	5 418	6 858
C.3.1.3. Total								
C.3.1.3.1. Domestic Companies / C.3.1.3.1. Entreprises Nationales	29 915	29 480	29 971	31 468	31 442	32 266	33 542	60 465
C.3.1.3.2. (Foreign Controlled Companies) / C.3.1.3.2. (Entreprises Sous Contrôle Etranger)	11 249	11 016	10 384	12 123	12 416	..	..	9 058
C.3.1.3.3. Branches & Agencies of Foreign Cies / C.3.1.3.3. Succursales et Agences d'Ent. Etrangères	8 697	6 688	9 310	9 821	9 788	9 165	8 145	9 586
C.3.1.3. Total Gross Premiums / C.3.1.3. Total des Primes Brutes	38 612	36 168	39 281	41 289	41 230	41 431	41 687	70 051
C.3.2. Ceded Premiums / C.3.2. Primes Cédées								
C.3.2.1. Domestic Companies / C.3.2.1. Entreprises Nationales	3 965	4 401	4 413	4 358	4 733	4 900	5 011	6 869
C.3.2.2. (Foreign Controlled Companies) / C.3.2.2. (Entreprises Sous Contrôle Etranger)	2 720	2 557	2 573	2 567	2 833	..	..	1 403
C.3.2.3. Branches & Agencies of Foreign Cies / C.3.2.3. Succursales et Agences d'Ent. Etrangères	1 321	1 147	1 588	1 515	1 679	1 605	1 325	1 782
C.3.2. Total	5 286	5 548	6 001	5 873	6 412	6 504	6 337	8 651

CANADA

Monetary Unit: million Canadian dollars / Unité monétaire : million de dollars ca..diens

D. NET WRITTEN PREMIUMS IN THE REPORTING COUNTRY IN TERMS OF DOMESTIC AND FOREIGN RISKS
D. PRIMES NETTES EMISES DANS LE PAYS DECLARANT EN RISQUES NATIONAUX ET ETRANGERS

Label	1992	1993	1994	1995	1996	1997	1998	1999
C.3.3. Net Written Premiums / Primes Nettes Emises								
C.3.3.1. Domestic Companies / Entreprises Nationales	25 950	25 079	25 558	27 110	26 709	27 366	28 531	53 596
C.3.3.2. (Foreign Controlled Companies) / (Entreprises Sous Contrôle Etranger)	8 529	8 459	7 811	9 556	9 583			7 655
C.3.3.3. Branches & Agencies of Foreign Cies / Succursales et Agences d'Ent. Etrangeres	7 376	5 541	7 722	8 306	8 109	7 561	6 819	7 804
C.3.3. Total	33 326	30 620	33 280	35 416	34 818	34 928	35 350	61 400
D.1. Life / Vie								
D.1.1. Domestic Risks / Risques Nationaux								
D.1.1.1. Domestic Companies / Entreprises Nationales	13 146	11 714	15 567	16 534	11 158	11 025	11 544	11 544
D.1.1.2. (Foreign Controlled Companies) / (Entreprises Sous Contrôle Etranger)	2 464	2 352	2 086	3 172	2 281	:	:	:
D.1.1.3. Branches & Agencies of Foreign Cies / Succursales et Agences d'Ent. Etrangeres	3 173	1 155	4 065	4 513	2 465	2 193	1 711	1 711
D.1.1. Total / Total des Primes Nettes Vie	16 319	12 869	19 632	21 047	13 623	13 218	13 256	13 256
D.1.3. Total								
D.1.3.1. Domestic Companies / Entreprises Nationales	13 146	11 714	15 567	16 534	11 158	11 025	11 544	11 544
D.1.3.2. (Foreign Controlled Companies) / (Entreprises Sous Contrôle Etranger)	2 464	2 352	2 086	3 172	2 281	:	:	:
D.1.3.3. Branches & Agencies of Foreign Cies / Succursales et Agences d'Ent. Etrangeres	3 173	1 155	4 065	4 513	2 465	2 193	1 711	1 711
D.1.3. Total of Life Net Premiums / Total des Primes Nettes Vie	16 319	12 869	19 632	21 047	13 623	13 218	13 256	13 256
D.2. Non-Life / Non-Vie								
D.2.1. Domestic Risks / Risques Nationaux								
D.2.1.1. Domestic Companies / Entreprises Nationales	12 804	13 365	9 991	10 576	15 551	16 341	16 987	16 987
D.2.1.2. (Foreign Controlled Companies) / (Entreprises Sous Contrôle Etranger)	6 065	6 107	5 725	6 384	7 302	:	:	:
D.2.1.3. Branches & Agencies of Foreign Cies / Succursales et Agences d'Ent. Etrangeres	4 203	4 386	3 657	3 793	5 644	5 368	5 108	5 108
D.2.1. Total / Total des Primes Nettes Vie	17 007	17 751	13 648	14 369	21 195	21 710	22 095	22 095
D.2.3. Total								
D.2.3.1. Domestic Companies / Entreprises Nationales	12 804	13 365	9 991	10 576	15 551	16 341	16 987	16 987
D.2.3.2. (Foreign Controlled Companies) / (Entreprises Sous Contrôle Etranger)	6 065	6 107	5 725	6 384	7 302	:	:	:
D.2.3.3. Branches & Agencies of Foreign Cies / Succursales et Agences d'Ent. Etrangeres	4 203	4 386	3 657	3 793	5 644	5 368	5 108	5 108
D.2.3. Total / Total des Primes Nettes Vie	17 007	17 751	13 648	14 369	21 195	21 710	22 095	22 095

E. BUSINESS WRITTEN ABROAD / E. OPERATIONS A L'ETRANGER

E.1. Life / E.1. Vie

Label	1992	1993	1994	1995	1996	1997	1998	1999
E.1.1. Gross Premiums / Primes Brutes								
E.1.1.1. Direct Business / Assurance Directe								
E.1.1.1.1. Branches & Agencies / Succursales & Agences	8 222	8 176	9 771	10 829	10 022	4 389	:	5 516
E.1.1.1.2. Subsidiaries / Filiales								28 952
E.1.1.1. Total	8 222	8 176						34 468
E.1.1.2. Reinsurance Accepted / Réassurance Acceptée								
E.1.1.2.1. Branches & Agencies / Succursales & Agences	843	493	1 654	1 857	779	450	:	1 017
E.1.1.2.2. Subsidiaries / Filiales								1 889
E.1.1.2. Total	843	493						2 906
E.1.1.3.1. Branches & Agencies / Succursales & Agences	9 065	8 669	11 425	12 686	10 801	4 839	:	6 533
E.1.1.3.2. Subsidiaries / Filiales								30 841
E.1.1.3. Total Gross Premiums / Total des Primes Brutes	9 065	8 669						37 374
E.1.2. Ceded Premiums / Primes Cédées								
E.1.2.1. Branches & Agencies / Succursales & Agences	880	835	1 805	1 198	894	681	:	767
E.1.2.2. Subsidiaries / Filiales								2 389
E.1.2. Total	880	835						3 156
E.1.3. Net Written Premiums / Primes Nettes Emises								
E.1.3.1. Branches & Agencies / Succursales & Agences	8 185	7 834	9 620	11 488	9 907	4 159	:	5 766
E.1.3.2. Subsidiaries / Filiales								28 452
E.1.3. Total	8 185	7 834						34 218

70

Monetary Unit: million Canadian dollars

Unité monétaire : million de dollars canadiens

E.2. Non-Life / E.2. Non-Vie

	1992	1993	1994	1995	1996	1997	1998	1999
E.2.1. Gross Premiums / Primes Brutes								
E.2.1.1. Direct Business / Assurance Directe								
E.2.1.1.1. Branches & Agencies / Succursales & Agences	763	1 194	279	334	877	883	:	919
E.2.1.1.2. Subsidiaries / Filiales							:	6 001
E.2.1.1. Total	763	1 194	:	:	:	:	:	6 920
E.2.1.2. Reinsurance Accepted / Réassurance Acceptée								
E.2.1.2.1. Branches & Agencies / Succursales & Agences	1 272	1 006	244	231	1 413	1 099	:	338
E.2.1.2.2. Subsidiaries / Filiales							:	315
E.2.1.2. Total	1 272	1 006	:	:	:	:	:	653
E.2.1.3. Total								
E.2.1.3.1. Branches & Agencies / Succursales & Agences	2 035	2 200	523	565	2 290	1 982	:	1 257
E.2.1.3.2. Subsidiaries / Filiales							:	6 316
E.2.1.3. Total Gross Premiums / Total des Primes Brutes	2 035	2 200	:	:	:	:	:	7 573
E.2.2. Ceded Premiums / Primes Cédées								
E.2.2.1. Branches & Agencies / Succursales & Agences	377	540	172	224	628	499	:	240
E.2.2.2. Subsidiaries / Filiales							:	240
E.2.2. Total	377	540	:	:	:	:	:	480
E.2.3. Net Written Premiums / Primes Nettes Emises								
E.2.3.1. Branches & Agencies / Succursales & Agences	1 658	1 660	351	341	1 662	1 483	:	1 017
E.2.3.2. Subsidiaries / Filiales							:	6 076
E.2.3. Total	1 658	1 660	:	:	:	:	:	7 093

F. OUTSTANDING INVESTMENT BY DIRECT INSURANCE COMPANIES / F. ENCOURS DES PLACEMENTS DES ENTREPRISES D'ASSURANCES DIRECTES

F.1. Life / F.1. Vie

	1992	1993	1994	1995	1996	1997	1998	1999
F.1.1. Real Estate / Immobilier								
F.1.1.1. Domestic Companies / Entreprises Nationales	9 819	9 455	8 956	7 881	7 701	6 308	6 188	6 597
F.1.1.2. (Foreign Controlled Companies) / (Entreprises Sous Contrôle Etranger)	260	236	283	251	235	:	:	213
F.1.1.3. Branches & Agencies of Foreign Cies / Succursales et Agences d'Ent. Etrangères	1 237	1 345	1 704	839	1 787	1 503	1 035	1 034
F.1.1.4. Domestic Investment / Placement dans le Pays	:	:	:	:	:	6 208	5 435	7 631
F.1.1.5. Foreign Investment / Placement à l'Etranger	:	:	:	:	:	1 603	1 788	0
F.1.1. Total	:	:	10 660	:	:	7 810	7 223	7 631
F.1.2. Mortgage Loans / Prêts Hypothécaires								
F.1.2.1. Domestic Companies / Entreprises Nationales	46 668	43 613	41 474	41 000	7 099	39 044	38 608	6 145
F.1.2.2. (Foreign Controlled Companies) / (Entreprises Sous Contrôle Etranger)	5 016	4 418	3 522	3 656	335	:	:	388
F.1.2.3. Branches & Agencies of Foreign Cies / Succursales et Agences d'Ent. Etrangères	7 204	8 014	9 606	3 710	7 314	6 719	5 291	46
F.1.2.4. Domestic Investment / Placement dans le Pays	:	:	:	:	:	40 566	38 499	6 191
F.1.2.5. Foreign Investment / Placement à l'Etranger	:	:	:	:	:	5 197	5 399	0
F.1.2. Total	:	:	51 080	:	:	45 763	43 899	6 191
F.1.3. Shares / Actions								
F.1.3.1. Domestic Companies / Entreprises Nationales	11 152	10 185	11 950	10 590	11 827	10 535	11 396	34 482
F.1.3.2. (Foreign Controlled Companies) / (Entreprises Sous Contrôle Etranger)	2 217	549	673	677	589	:	:	5 493
F.1.3.3. Branches & Agencies of Foreign Cies / Succursales et Agences d'Ent. Etrangères	1 201	701	882	747	585	560	552	1 684
F.1.3.4. Domestic Investment / Placement dans le Pays	:	:	:	:	:	5 929	6 561	30 223
F.1.3.5. Foreign Investment / Placement à l'Etranger	:	:	:	:	:	5 166	5 387	5 943
F.1.3. Total	:	:	12 832	:	:	11 096	11 949	36 166
F.1.4. Bonds with Fixed Revenue / Obligations								
F.1.4.1. Domestic Companies / Entreprises Nationales	54 569	52 607	62 981	70 640	74 621	76 188	82 220	92 283
F.1.4.2. (Foreign Controlled Companies) / (Entreprises Sous Contrôle Etranger)	12 619	7 554	7 301	9 158	8 605	:	:	12 949
F.1.4.3. Branches & Agencies of Foreign Cies / Succursales et Agences d'Ent. Etrangères	14 661	9 663	12 718	12 802	11 603	12 708	11 011	12 886
F.1.4.4. Domestic Investment / Placement dans le Pays	:	:	:	:	:	73 812	77 128	102 353
F.1.4.5. Foreign Investment / Placement à l'Etranger	:	:	:	:	:	15 084	16 103	2 816
F.1.4. Total	:	:	75 699	:	:	88 895	93 231	105 169
F.1.5. Loans other than Mortgage Loans / Prêts Autres qu'Hypothécaires								
F.1.5.1. Domestic Companies / Entreprises Nationales	9 435	5 702	5 633	6 090	37 757	4 750	4 997	3 703
F.1.5.2. (Foreign Controlled Companies) / (Entreprises Sous Contrôle Etranger)	175	168	150	351	3 485	:	:	232
F.1.5.3. Branches & Agencies of Foreign Cies / Succursales et Agences d'Ent. Etrangères	810	460	622	672	345	409	247	178
F.1.5.4. Domestic Investment / Placement dans le Pays	:	:	:	:	:	3 814	3 954	3 881
F.1.5.5. Foreign Investment / Placement à l'Etranger	:	:	:	:	:	1 346	1 289	0
F.1.5. Total	:	:	6 255	:	:	5 160	5 243	3 881

Monetary Unit: million Ca..dian dollars

Unité monétaire : million de dollars ca..diens

	1992	1993	1994	1995	1996	1997	1998	1999	
F.1.6. Other Investments									F.1.6. Autres Placements
F.1.6.1. Domestic Companies	8 158	8 737	8 534	16 006	6 089	6 024	7 153	81 007	F.1.6.1. Entreprises Nationales
F.1.6.2. (Foreign Controlled Companies)	117	62	194	883	495	..	..	12 054	F.1.6.2. (Entreprises Sous Contrôle Etranger)
F.1.6.3. Branches & Agencies of Foreign Cies	489	306	685	1 550	1 819	624	642	7 172	F.1.6.3. Succursales et Agences d'Ent. Etrangères
F.1.6.4. Domestic Investment	..	..	..	..	..	5 282	6 042	84 812	F.1.6.4. Placement dans le Pays
F.1.6.5. Foreign Investment	..	..	..	..	..	1 366	1 752	3 367	F.1.6.5. Placement à l' Etranger
F.1.6. Total	..	..	9 219	..	..	6 648	7 794	88 179	F.1.6. Total
F.1.7. Total									F.1.7. Total
F.1.7.1. Domestic Companies	139 801	130 299	139 528	152 207	145 094	142 848	150 561	224 217	F.1.7.1. Entreprises Nationales
F.1.7.2. (Foreign Controlled Companies)	20 403	12 987	12 123	14 976	13 744	..	..	31 329	F.1.7.2. (Entreprises Sous Contrôle Etranger)
F.1.7.3. Branches & Agencies of Foreign Cies	25 602	20 488	26 217	20 320	23 453	22 523	18 778	23 000	F.1.7.3. Succursales et Agences d'Ent. Etrangères
F.1.7.4. Domestic Investment	..	..	..	..	..	135 610	137 620	235 091	F.1.7.4. Placement dans le Pays
F.1.7.5. Foreign Investment	..	..	..	..	..	29 761	31 719	12 126	F.1.7.5. Placement à l' Etranger
F.1.7. Total of Life Investments	..	..	165 745	..	..	165 371	169 339	247 217	F.1.7. Total des Placements Vie
F.2. Non-Life									**F.2. Non-Vie**
F.2.1. Real Estate									F.2.1. Immobilier
F.2.1.1. Domestic Companies	175	180	239	226	218	186	187	175	F.2.1.1. Entreprises Nationales
F.2.1.2. (Foreign Controlled Companies)	37	34	76	81	71	..	..	..	F.2.1.2. (Entreprises Sous Contrôle Etranger)
F.2.1.3. Branches & Agencies of Foreign Cies	24	24	29	30	52	29	28	28	F.2.1.3. Succursales et Agences d'Ent. Etrangères
F.2.1.4. Domestic Investment	..	..	..	..	..	214	215	203	F.2.1.4. Placement dans le Pays
F.2.1.5. Foreign Investment	..	..	..	..	..	..	0	0	F.2.1.5. Placement à l' Etranger
F.2.1. Total	..	..	268	..	..	214	215	203	F.2.1. Total
F.2.2. Mortgage Loans									F.2.2. Prêts Hypothécaires
F.2.2.1. Domestic Companies	283	212	529	367	352	334	667	802	F.2.2.1. Entreprises Nationales
F.2.2.2. (Foreign Controlled Companies)	212	191	306	226	212	..	..	..	F.2.2.2. (Entreprises Sous Contrôle Etranger)
F.2.2.3. Branches & Agencies of Foreign Cies	55	52	52	49	46	42	33	17	F.2.2.3. Succursales et Agences d'Ent. Etrangères
F.2.2.4. Domestic Investment	..	..	..	..	..	374	696	819	F.2.2.4. Placement dans le Pays
F.2.2.5. Foreign Investment	..	..	..	..	..	3	3	0	F.2.2.5. Placement à l' Etranger
F.2.2. Total	..	..	581	..	..	376	700	819	F.2.2. Total
F.2.3. Shares									F.2.3. Actions
F.2.3.1. Domestic Companies	1 779	1 977	3 705	4 065	4 414	5 427	5 817	5 909	F.2.3.1. Entreprises Nationales
F.2.3.2. (Foreign Controlled Companies)	1 664	1 700	1 844	2 328	2 178	..	..	..	F.2.3.2. (Entreprises Sous Contrôle Etranger)
F.2.3.3. Branches & Agencies of Foreign Cies	448	457	557	758	771	868	895	830	F.2.3.3. Succursales et Agences d'Ent. Etrangères
F.2.3.4. Domestic Investment	..	..	..	..	..	6 295	6 712	6 055	F.2.3.4. Placement dans le Pays
F.2.3.5. Foreign Investment	..	..	..	..	..	..	0	684	F.2.3.5. Placement à l' Etranger
F.2.3. Total	..	..	4 262	..	..	6 295	6 712	6 739	F.2.3. Total
F.2.4. Bonds with Fixed Revenue									F.2.4. Obligations
F.2.4.1. Domestic Companies	3 545	3 888	10 049	11 727	12 975	13 460	14 009	14 476	F.2.4.1. Entreprises Nationales
F.2.4.2. (Foreign Controlled Companies)	5 271	5 129	5 974	7 661	8 400	..	..	..	F.2.4.2. (Entreprises Sous Contrôle Etranger)
F.2.4.3. Branches & Agencies of Foreign Cies	5 309	5 598	7 544	7 430	8 451	9 138	9 448	10 154	F.2.4.3. Succursales et Agences d'Ent. Etrangères
F.2.4.4. Domestic Investment	..	..	..	..	..	22 308	23 141	24 146	F.2.4.4. Placement dans le Pays
F.2.4.5. Foreign Investment	..	..	..	..	..	290	316	484	F.2.4.5. Placement à l' Etranger
F.2.4. Total	..	..	17 593	..	..	22 598	23 457	24 630	F.2.4. Total
F.2.6. Other Investments									F.2.6. Autres Placements
F.2.6.1. Domestic Companies	47	22	537	643	664	163	200	2 382	F.2.6.1. Entreprises Nationales
F.2.6.2. (Foreign Controlled Companies)	20	17	358	309	278	..	..	..	F.2.6.2. (Entreprises Sous Contrôle Etranger)
F.2.6.3. Branches & Agencies of Foreign Cies	..	4	4	357	0	28	11	1 526	F.2.6.3. Succursales et Agences d'Ent. Etrangères
F.2.6.4. Domestic Investment	..	..	..	..	..	154	185	3 908	F.2.6.4. Placement dans le Pays
F.2.6.5. Foreign Investment	..	..	..	..	..	37	27	0	F.2.6.5. Placement à l' Etranger
F.2.6. Total	..	..	541	..	..	191	212	3 908	F.2.6. Total
F.2.7. Total									F.2.7. Total
F.2.7.1. Domestic Companies	5 830	6 275	15 059	17 028	18 623	19 570	20 881	23 744	F.2.7.1. Entreprises Nationales
F.2.7.2. (Foreign Controlled Companies)	7 204	7 071	8 558	10 605	11 139	..	..	..	F.2.7.2. (Entreprises Sous Contrôle Etranger)
F.2.7.3. Branches & Agencies of Foreign Cies	5 835	6 134	8 186	8 624	9 320	10 104	10 415	12 555	F.2.7.3. Succursales et Agences d'Ent. Etrangères
F.2.7.4. Domestic Investment	..	..	..	..	..	29 345	30 950	35 131	F.2.7.4. Placement dans le Pays
F.2.7.5. Foreign Investment	..	..	..	..	..	330	346	1 168	F.2.7.5. Placement à l' Etranger
F.2.7. Total of Non-Life Investments	..	..	23 245	..	..	29 674	31 295	36 299	F.2.7. Total des Placements Non-Vie

G. BREAKDOWN OF NON-LIFE PREMIUMS
G. VENTILATIONS DES PRIMES NON-VIE

	1992	1993	1994	1995	1996	1997	1998	1999
G.1. Motor vehicle / G.1. Assurance Automobile								
G.1.1. Direct Business / G.1.1. Assurances Directes								
G.1.1.1. Gross Premiums / G.1.1.1. Primes Brutes	6 575	6 642	6 988	7 489	7 721	7 859	8 041	8 199
G.1.1.2. Ceded Premiums / G.1.1.2. Primes Cédées	1 525	1 398	1 435	1 282	1 334	:	:	:
G.1.1.3. Net Written Premiums / G.1.1.3. Primes Nettes Emises	5 050	5 244	5 553	6 207	6 387	:	:	:
G.1.2. Reinsurance Accepted / G.1.2. Réassurance Acceptée								
G.1.2.1. Gross Premiums / G.1.2.1. Primes Brutes	1 497	1 415	1 405	1 111	1 248	1 238	1 326	1 621
G.1.2.3. Net Written Premiums / G.1.2.3. Primes Nettes Emises	1 497	1 415	1 405	1 111	1 248	:	:	:
G.1.3. Total								
G.1.3.1. Gross Premiums / G.1.3.1. Primes Brutes	8 072	8 057	8 393	8 600	8 969	9 097	9 367	9 820
G.1.3.2. Ceded Premiums / G.1.3.2. Primes Cédées	1 525	1 398	1 435	1 282	1 334	1 381	1 431	1 675
G.1.3.3. Net Written Premiums / G.1.3.3. Primes Nettes Emises	6 547	6 659	6 958	7 318	7 635	7 716	7 937	8 145
G.2. Marine, Aviation								
G.2.1. Direct Business / G.2.1. Assurances Directes								
G.2.1.1. Gross Premiums / G.2.1.1. Primes Brutes	215	252	270	218	308	325	255	283
G.2.1.2. Ceded Premiums / G.2.1.2. Primes Cédées	179	210	228	152	195	:	:	:
G.2.1.3. Net Written Premiums / G.2.1.3. Primes Nettes Emises	36	42	42	66	113	:	:	:
G.2.2. Reinsurance Accepted / G.2.2. Réassurance Acceptée								
G.2.2.1. Gross Premiums / G.2.2.1. Primes Brutes	116	132	173	84	112	87	77	89
G.2.2.3. Net Written Premiums / G.2.2.3. Primes Nettes Emises	116	132	173	84	112	:	:	:
G.2.3. Total								
G.2.3.1. Gross Premiums / G.2.3.1. Primes Brutes	331	384	443	302	420	412	332	372
G.2.3.2. Ceded Premiums / G.2.3.2. Primes Cédées	179	210	228	152	195	154	135	164
G.2.3.3. Net Written Premiums / G.2.3.3. Primes Nettes Emises	152	174	215	150	225	258	197	208
G.4. Fire, Property Damages / G.4. Incendie, Dommages aux Biens								
G.4.1. Direct Business / G.4.1. Assurances Directes								
G.4.1.1. Gross Premiums / G.4.1.1. Primes Brutes	4 197	4 420	4 850	5 065	5 290	5 132	5 151	5 210
G.4.1.2. Ceded Premiums / G.4.1.2. Primes Cédées	1 712	1 748	1 845	1 874	1 951	:	:	:
G.4.1.3. Net Written Premiums / G.4.1.3. Primes Nettes Emises	2 485	2 672	3 005	3 191	3 339	:	:	:
G.4.2. Reinsurance Accepted / G.4.2. Réassurance Acceptée								
G.4.2.1. Gross Premiums / G.4.2.1. Primes Brutes	1 572	1 608	1 663	1 517	1 690	1 473	1 415	1 523
G.4.2.3. Net Written Premiums / G.4.2.3. Primes Nettes Emises	1 572	1 608	1 663	1 517	1 690	:	:	:
G.4.3. Total								
G.4.3.1. Gross Premiums / G.4.3.1. Primes Brutes	5 769	6 028	6 513	6 582	6 980	6 605	6 565	6 733
G.4.3.2. Ceded Premiums / G.4.3.2. Primes Cédées	1 712	1 748	1 845	1 874	1 951	1 699	1 729	1 970
G.4.3.3. Net Written Premiums / G.4.3.3. Primes Nettes Emises	4 057	4 280	4 668	4 708	5 029	4 906	4 837	4 763
G.5. Pecuniary Losses / G.5. Pertes Pécunières								
G.5.1. Direct Business / G.5.1. Assurances Directes								
G.5.1.1. Gross Premiums / G.5.1.1. Primes Brutes	219	225	233	209	270	234	287	287
G.5.1.2. Ceded Premiums / G.5.1.2. Primes Cédées	121	110	114	91	102	:	:	:
G.5.1.3. Net Written Premiums / G.5.1.3. Primes Nettes Emises	98	115	119	118	168	:	:	:
G.5.2. Reinsurance Accepted / G.5.2. Réassurance Acceptée								
G.5.2.1. Gross Premiums / G.5.2.1. Primes Brutes	89	77	73	66	67	90	96	110
G.5.2.3. Net Written Premiums / G.5.2.3. Primes Nettes Emises	89	77	73	66	67	:	:	:
G.5.3. Total								
G.5.3.1. Gross Premiums / G.5.3.1. Primes Brutes	308	302	306	275	337	324	384	397
G.5.3.2. Ceded Premiums / G.5.3.2. Primes Cédées	121	110	114	91	102	94	103	120
G.5.3.3. Net Written Premiums / G.5.3.3. Primes Nettes Emises	187	192	192	184	235	230	281	277

Monetary Unit: million Ca..dian dollars — **Unité monétaire : million de dollars ca..diens**

Code / Label (EN / FR)	1992	1993	1994	1995	1996	1997	1998	1999
G.6. General Liability / Responsabilité Générale								
G.6.1. Direct Business / Assurances Directes								
G.6.1.1. Gross Premiums / Primes Brutes	1 172	225	1 359	1 438	1 604	1 640	1 672	1 758
G.6.1.2. Ceded Premiums / Primes Cédées	454	110	510	407	493	:	:	:
G.6.1.3. Net Written Premiums / Primes Nettes Emises	718	115	849	1 031	1 111	:	:	:
G.6.2. Reinsurance Accepted / Réassurance Acceptée								
G.6.2.1. Gross Premiums / Primes Brutes	403	77	424	356	428	401	382	430
G.6.2.3. Net Written Premiums / Primes Nettes Emises	403	77	424	356	428	401	382	430
G.6.3. Total								
G.6.3.1. Gross Premiums / Primes Brutes	1 575	302	1 783	1 794	2 032	2 041	2 054	2 188
G.6.3.2. Ceded Premiums / Primes Cédées	454	110	510	407	493	488	520	581
G.6.3.3. Net Written Premiums / Primes Nettes Emises	1 121	192	1 273	1 387	1 539	1 553	1 534	1 607
G.7. Accident, Health / Accident, Santé								
G.7.1. Direct Business / Assurances Directes								
G.7.1.1. Gross Premiums / Primes Brutes	4 833	1 226	346	606	6 634	6 911	7 186	15 695
G.7.1.2. Ceded Premiums / Primes Cédées	360	470	75	57	632	:	:	:
G.7.1.3. Net Written Premiums / Primes Nettes Emises	4 473	756	271	549	6 002	:	:	:
G.7.2. Reinsurance Accepted / Réassurance Acceptée								
G.7.2.1. Gross Premiums / Primes Brutes	304	390	70	70	523	575	590	983
G.7.2.3. Net Written Premiums / Primes Nettes Emises	304	390	70	70	523	575	590	983
G.7.3. Total								
G.7.3.1. Gross Premiums / Primes Brutes	5 137	1 616	416	676	7 157	7 486	7 776	16 678
G.7.3.2. Ceded Premiums / Primes Cédées	360	470	75	57	632	715	713	1 325
G.7.3.3. Net Written Premiums / Primes Nettes Emises	4 777	1 146	341	619	6 525	6 772	7 063	15 353
G.8. Others / Autres								
G.8.1. Direct Business / Assurances Directes								
G.8.1.1. Gross Premiums / Primes Brutes	178	5 273	1	4	7	329	325	416
G.8.1.2. Ceded Premiums / Primes Cédées	68	501	0	0	0	:	:	:
G.8.1.3. Net Written Premiums / Primes Nettes Emises	110	4 773	1	4	7	:	:	:
G.8.2. Reinsurance Accepted / Réassurance Acceptée								
G.8.2.1. Gross Premiums / Primes Brutes	55	399	0	0	0	79	50	92
G.8.2.3. Net Written Premiums / Primes Nettes Emises	55	399	0	0	0	79	50	92
G.8.3. Total								
G.8.3.1. Gross Premiums / Primes Brutes	233	5 672	1	4	7	408	374	508
G.8.3.2. Ceded Premiums / Primes Cédées	68	501	0	0	0	133	128	185
G.8.3.3. Net Written Premiums / Primes Nettes Emises	165	5 171	1	4	7	275	246	323
G.10. Total								
G.10.1. Direct Business / Assurances Directes								
G.10.1.1. Gross Premiums / Primes Brutes	17 389	18 185	14 047	15 029	21 834	22 429	22 917	31 848
G.10.1.2. Ceded Premiums / Primes Cédées	4 419	4 514	4 207	3 863	4 707	:	:	:
G.10.1.3. Net Written Premiums / Primes Nettes Emises	12 970	13 671	9 840	11 166	17 127	:	:	:
G.10.2. Reinsurance Accepted / Réassurance Acceptée								
G.10.2.1. Gross Premiums / Primes Brutes	4 036	4 079	3 808	3 204	4 068	3 944	3 936	4 848
G.10.2.3. Net Written Premiums / Primes Nettes Emises	4 036	4 079	3 808	3 204	4 068	3 944	3 936	4 848
G.10.3. Total								
G.10.3.1. Gross Premiums / Primes Brutes	21 425	22 264	17 855	18 233	25 902	26 373	26 853	36 696
G.10.3.2. Ceded Premiums / Primes Cédées	4 419	4 514	4 207	3 863	4 707	4 663	4 758	6 020
G.10.3.3. Net Written Premiums / Primes Nettes Emises	17 006	17 750	13 648	14 370	21 195	21 710	22 095	30 676

H. GROSS CLAIMS PAYMENTS / H. PAIEMENTS BRUTS DES SINISTRES

H.1. Life / H.1. Vie

Code / Label (EN / FR)	1992	1993	1994	1995	1996	1997	1998	1999
H.1.1. Domestic Companies / Entreprises Nationales					14 255	15 051	14 047	26 339
H.1.2. (Foreign Controlled Companies) / (Entreprises Sous Contrôle Etranger)					2 555			3 212
H.1.3. Branches & Agencies of Foreign Cies / Succursales et Agences d'Ent. Etrangères					2 942	2 546	2 171	2 213
H.1. Total					17 197	17 597	16 218	28 552

CANADA

Monetary Unit: million Canadian dollars / Unité monétaire : million de dollars canadiens

H.2. Non-Life / H.2. Non-Vie

Code	Description	1992	1993	1994	1995	1996	1997	1998	1999
H.2.1.	Domestic Companies / Entreprises Nationales					16 888	14 296	15 697	21 869
H.2.2.	(Foreign Controlled Companies) / (Entreprises Sous Contrôle Etranger)					6 832	..	..	1 430
H.2.3.	Branches & Agencies of Foreign Cies / Succursales et Agences d'Ent. Etrangères					5 552	4 671	5 157	4 168
H.2.	Total					22 440	18 966	20 854	26 037

I. GROSS OPERATING EXPENSES / DEPENSES BRUTES D'EXPLOITATION

I.1. Life / I.1. Vie

Code	Description	1992	1993	1994	1995	1996	1997	1998	1999
I.1.1.	Domestic Companies / Entreprises Nationales					3 309	5 220	5 373	4 830
I.1.2.	(Foreign Controlled Companies) / (Entreprises Sous Contrôle Etranger)					543	..	..	694
I.1.3.	Branches & Agencies of Foreign Cies / Succursales et Agences d'Ent. Etrangères					666	952	718	361
I.1.	Total / Total des Primes Nettes Vie					3 975	6 172	6 092	5 191

I.2. Non-Life / I.2. Non-Vie

Code	Description	1992	1993	1994	1995	1996	1997	1998	1999
I.2.1.	Domestic Companies / Entreprises Nationales					782	3 677	3 902	2 262
I.2.2.	(Foreign Controlled Companies) / (Entreprises Sous Contrôle Etranger)					407	..	..	176
I.2.3.	Branches & Agencies of Foreign Cies / Succursales et Agences d'Ent. Etrangères					321	1 288	1 324	450
I.2.	Total					1 103	4 965	5 226	2 712

J. COMMISSIONS

J.1. Life / J.1. Vie

Code	Description	1992	1993	1994	1995	1996	1997	1998	1999
J.1.1.	Direct Business / Assurance directe								
J.1.1.1.	Domestic Companies / Entreprises Nationales					1 038	1 164	1 259	1 638
J.1.1.2.	(Foreign Controlled Companies) / (Entreprises Sous Contrôle Etranger)					214	..	..	469
J.1.1.3.	Branches & Agencies of Foreign Cies / Succursales et Agences d'Ent. Etrangères					159	138	110	116
J.1.1.	Total					1 197	1 302	1 368	1 754
J.1.2.	Reinsurance Accepted / Réassurances acceptées								
J.1.2.1.	Domestic Companies / Entreprises Nationales					74	148	44	199
J.1.2.2.	(Foreign Controlled Companies) / (Entreprises Sous Contrôle Etranger)					61	..	..	58
J.1.2.3.	Branches & Agencies of Foreign Cies / Succursales et Agences d'Ent. Etrangères					93	171	120	128
J.1.2.	Total					167	319	163	327
J.1.3.	Total								
J.1.3.1.	Domestic Companies / Entreprises Nationales					1 112	1 313	1 302	1 837
J.1.3.2.	(Foreign Controlled Companies) / (Entreprises Sous Contrôle Etranger)					275	..	..	527
J.1.3.3.	Branches & Agencies of Foreign Cies / Succursales et Agences d'Ent. Etrangères					252	309	230	244
J.1.3.	Total of Life Net Premiums					1 364	1 622	1 532	2 081

J.2. Non-Life / J.2. Non-Vie

Code	Description	1992	1993	1994	1995	1996	1997	1998	1999
J.2.1.	Direct Business / Assurance directe								
J.2.1.1.	Domestic Companies / Entreprises Nationales					1 744	1 787	1 849	
J.2.1.2.	(Foreign Controlled Companies) / (Entreprises Sous Contrôle Etranger)					1 012	..	..	140
J.2.1.3.	Branches & Agencies of Foreign Cies / Succursales et Agences d'Ent. Etrangères					431	431	447	
J.2.1.	Total					2 175	2 218	2 296	
J.2.2.	Reinsurance Accepted / Réassurances acceptées								
J.2.2.1.	Domestic Companies / Entreprises Nationales					445	469	466	
J.2.2.2.	(Foreign Controlled Companies) / (Entreprises Sous Contrôle Etranger)					404	..	..	30
J.2.2.3.	Branches & Agencies of Foreign Cies / Succursales et Agences d'Ent. Etrangères					309	287	287	
J.2.2.	Total					754	756	754	
J.2.3.	Total								
J.2.3.1.	Domestic Companies / Entreprises Nationales					2 189	2 256	2 316	2 441
J.2.3.2.	(Foreign Controlled Companies) / (Entreprises Sous Contrôle Etranger)					1 416	..	..	170
J.2.3.3.	Branches & Agencies of Foreign Cies / Succursales et Agences d'Ent. Etrangères					740	718	734	868
J.2.3.	Total					2 929	2 974	3 050	3 309

Monetary Unit: million Czech koruna

Unité monétaire : million de couronnes tchèques

	1992	1993	1994	1995	1996	1997	1998	1999
A. NUMBER OF COMPANIES IN THE REPORTING COUNTRY / **A. NOMBRE D'ENTREPRISES DANS LE PAYS DECLARANT**								
A.1. Life / **A.1. Vie**								
A.1.1. Domestic Companies / A.1.1. Entreprises Nationales	..	1	1	2	0	2	3	2
A.1.2. (Foreign Controlled Companies) / A.1.2. (Entreprises Sous Contrôle Etranger)	..	0	1	0	0	2	3	2
A.1.3. Branches & Agencies of Foreign Cies / A.1.3. Succursales et Agences d'Ent. Etrangères	..	4	3	3	2	2	3	1
A.1. All Companies / A.1. Ensemble des Entreprises	..	5	4	5	2	4	5	3
A.2. Non-Life / **A.2. Non-Vie**								
A.2.1. Domestic Companies / A.2.1. Entreprises Nationales	..	6	7	11	10	14	15	16
A.2.2. (Foreign Controlled Companies) / A.2.2. (Entreprises Sous Contrôle Etranger)	..	2	2	3	3	3	4	4
A.2.3. Branches & Agencies of Foreign Cies / A.2.3. Succursales et Agences d'Ent. Etrangères	..	1	3	4	4	4	4	5
A.2. All Companies / A.2. Ensemble des Entreprises	..	7	10	15	14	18	19	21
A.3. Composite / **A.3. Mixte**								
A.3.1. Domestic Companies / A.3.1. Entreprises Nationales	..	7	12	14	17	17	16	17
A.3.2. (Foreign Controlled Companies) / A.3.2. (Entreprises Sous Contrôle Etranger)	..	6	1	9	9	8	8	8
A.3.3. Branches & Agencies of Foreign Cies / A.3.3. Succursales et Agences d'Ent. Etrangères	..	1	1	1	2	1	1	1
A.3. All Companies / A.3. Ensemble des Entreprises	..	8	13	15	19	18	17	18
A.5. Total / **A.5. Total**								
A.5.1. Domestic Companies / A.5.1. Entreprises Nationales	..	14	20	27	27	33	34	35
A.5.2. (Foreign Controlled Companies) / A.5.2. (Entreprises Sous Contrôle Etranger)	..	8	10	12	12	13	15	14
A.5.3. Branches & Agencies of Foreign Cies / A.5.3. Succursales et Agences d'Ent. Etrangères	..	6	7	8	8	7	7	7
A.5. All Insurance Companies / A.5. Ensemble des Entreprises d'Assurances	..	20	27	35	35	40	41	42
B. NUMBER OF EMPLOYEES / **B. NOMBRE D'EMPLOYES**								
B.1. Insurance Companies / B.1. Entreprises d'Assurances	..	11 097	13 029	13 423	15 189	16 215	16 404	16 451
B.2. Intermediaries / B.2. Intermediaires	..	2 000	3 000	35 000	35 000	35 500	35 000	42 000
B. Total / B. Total	..	13 097	16 029	48 423	50 189	51 715	51 404	58 451
C. BUSINESS WRITTEN IN THE REPORTING COUNTRY / **C. OPERATIONS CONCLUES DANS LE PAYS DECLARANT**								
C.1. Life / **C.1. Vie**								
C.1.1. Gross Premiums / C.1.1. Primes Brutes								
C.1.1.1. Direct Business / C.1.1.1. Assurances Directes								
C.1.1.1.1. Domestic Companies / C.1.1.1.1. Entreprises Nationales	..	5 596	6 725	8 026	9 243	10 310	12 239	16 258
C.1.1.1.2. (Foreign Controlled Companies) / C.1.1.1.2. (Entreprises Sous Contrôle Etranger)	..	86	392	632	968	1 363	1 982	2 906
C.1.1.1.3. Branches & Agencies of Foreign Cies / C.1.1.1.3. Succursales et Agences d'Ent. Etrangères	..	321	722	1 316	1 694	2 157	2 851	3 535
C.1.1.1. Total / C.1.1.1. Total	..	5 917	7 447	9 342	10 937	12 467	15 089	19 793
C.1.1.3. Total								
C.1.1.3.1. Domestic Companies / C.1.1.3.1. Entreprises Nationales	..	5 596	6 725	8 026	9 243	10 310	12 239	16 258
C.1.1.3.2. (Foreign Controlled Companies) / C.1.1.3.2. (Entreprises Sous Contrôle Etranger)	..	86	392	632	968	1 363	1 982	2 906
C.1.1.3.3. Branches & Agencies of Foreign Cies / C.1.1.3.3. Succursales et Agences d'Ent. Etrangères	..	321	722	1 316	1 694	2 157	2 851	3 535
C.1.1.3. Total Gross Premiums / C.1.1.3. Total des Primes Brutes	..	5 917	7 447	9 342	10 937	12 467	15 089	19 793
C.1.2. Ceded Premiums / C.1.2. Primes Cédées								
C.1.2.1. Domestic Companies / C.1.2.1. Entreprises Nationales	..	0	0	90	116	139	134	186
C.1.2.2. (Foreign Controlled Companies) / C.1.2.2. (Entreprises Sous Contrôle Etranger)	..	0	0	89	114	135	127	170
C.1.2.3. Branches & Agencies of Foreign Cies / C.1.2.3. Succursales et Agences d'Ent. Etrangères	..	0	0	2	3	6	11	9
C.1.2. Total / C.1.2. Total	..	0	0	92	119	145	145	195
C.1.3. Net Written Premiums / C.1.3. Primes Nettes Emises								
C.1.3.1. Domestic Companies / C.1.3.1. Entreprises Nationales	..	5 596	6 725	7 936	9 127	10 171	12 105	16 072
C.1.3.2. (Foreign Controlled Companies) / C.1.3.2. (Entreprises Sous Contrôle Etranger)	..	86	392	543	854	1 228	1 855	2 736
C.1.3.3. Branches & Agencies of Foreign Cies / C.1.3.3. Succursales et Agences d'Ent. Etrangères	..	321	722	1 314	1 691	2 151	2 840	3 527
C.1.3. Total / C.1.3. Total	..	5 917	7 447	9 250	10 818	12 322	14 945	19 599

Monetary Unit: million Czech koruna   Unité monétaire : million de couronnes tchèques

C.2. Non-Life — C.2. Non-Vie

	1992	1993	1994	1995	1996	1997	1998	1999
C.2.1. Gross premiums — C.2.1. Primes Brutes								
C.2.1.1. Direct Business — C.2.1.1. Assurances Directes								
C.2.1.1.1. Domestic Companies — C.2.1.1.1. Entreprises Nationales	..	16 988	22 030	23 746	29 734	34 478	39 495	42 190
C.2.1.1.2. (Foreign Controlled Companies) — C.2.1.1.2. (Entreprises Sous Contrôle Etranger)	..	1 589	4 398	6 101	8 731	9 586	10 958	11 773
C.2.1.1.3. Branches & Agencies of Foreign Cies — C.2.1.1.3. Succursales et Agences d'Ent. Etrangères	..	54	193	167	333	513	434	592
C.2.1.1. Total — C.2.1.1. Total	..	17 042	22 223	23 913	30 067	34 991	39 929	42 782
C.2.1.2. Reinsurance Accepted — C.2.1.2. Réassurance Acceptée								
C.2.1.2.1. Domestic Companies — C.2.1.2.1. Entreprises Nationales	..	0	0	541	120	526	619	208
C.2.1.2.1 (Foreign Controlled Companies) — C.2.1.2.2 (Entreprises sous Contrôle Etranger)	..					..	..	9
C.2.1.2. Total — C.2.1.2. Total	..	0	0	541	120	526	619	208
C.2.1.3. Total — C.2.1.3. Total								
C.2.1.3.1. Domestic Companies — C.2.1.3.1. Entreprises Nationales	..	16 988	22 030	24 287	29 854	35 004	40 114	42 399
C.2.1.3.2. (Foreign Controlled Companies) — C.2.1.3.2. (Entreprises Sous Contrôle Etranger)	..	1 589	4 398	6 101	8 731	9 586	10 958	11 782
C.2.1.3.3. Branches & Agencies of Foreign Cies — C.2.1.3.3. Succursales et Agences d'Ent. Etrangères	..	54	193	167	333	513	434	592
C.2.1.3. Total Gross Premiums — C.2.1.3. Total des Primes Brutes	..	17 042	22 223	24 454	30 187	35 517	40 548	42 991
C.2.2. Ceded Premiums — C.2.2. Primes Cédées								
C.2.2.1. Domestic Companies — C.2.2.1. Entreprises Nationales	..	1 478	2 542	3 819	5 219	6 404	8 087	8 753
C.2.2.2. (Foreign Controlled Companies) — C.2.2.2. (Entreprises Sous Contrôle Etranger)	..	716	2 430	2 264	3 043	3 519	4 361	4 983
C.2.2.3. Branches & Agencies of Foreign Cies — C.2.2.3. Succursales et Agences d'Ent. Etrangères	..	34	112	104	128	241	341	431
C.2.2. Total — C.2.2. Total	..	1 512	2 654	3 923	5 347	6 645	8 428	9 184
C.2.3. Net Written Premiums — C.2.3. Primes Nettes Emises								
C.2.3.1. Domestic Companies — C.2.3.1. Entreprises Nationales	..	15 510	19 488	20 468	24 635	28 600	32 028	33 646
C.2.3.2. (Foreign Controlled Companies) — C.2.3.2. (Entreprises Sous Contrôle Etranger)	..	873	1 968	3 837	5 688	6 067	6 597	6 799
C.2.3.3. Branches & Agencies of Foreign Cies — C.2.3.3. Succursales et Agences d'Ent. Etrangères	..	20	81	63	205	272	93	161
C.2.3. Total — C.2.3. Total	..	15 530	19 569	20 531	24 840	28 872	32 120	33 807

C.3. Total — C.3. Total

	1992	1993	1994	1995	1996	1997	1998	1999
C.3.1. Gross Premiums — C.3.1. Primes Brutes								
C.3.1.1. Direct Business — C.3.1.1. Assurances Directes								
C.3.1.1.1. Domestic Companies — C.3.1.1.1. Entreprises Nationales	..	22 584	28 755	31 772	38 977	44 788	51 734	58 448
C.3.1.1.2. (Foreign Controlled Companies) — C.3.1.1.2. (Entreprises Sous Contrôle Etranger)	..	1 675	4 790	6 733	9 699	10 949	12 940	14 679
C.3.1.1.3. Branches & Agencies of Foreign Cies — C.3.1.1.3. Succursales et Agences d'Ent. Etrangères	..	375	915	1 483	2 027	2 670	3 284	4 128
C.3.1.1. Total — C.3.1.1. Total	..	22 959	29 670	33 255	41 004	47 458	55 018	62 576
C.3.1.2. Reinsurance Accepted — C.3.1.2. Réassurance Acceptée								
C.3.1.2.1. Domestic Companies — C.3.1.2.1. Entreprises Nationales	..	0	0	541	120	526	619	208
C.3.1.2.2. (Foreign Controlled Companies) — C.3.1.2.2. (Entreprises Sous Contrôle Etranger)	..					..	..	9
C.3.1.2. Total — C.3.1.2. Total	..	0	0	541	120	526	619	208
C.3.1.3. Total — C.3.1.3. Total								
C.3.1.3.1. Domestic Companies — C.3.1.3.1. Entreprises Nationales	..	22 584	28 755	32 313	39 097	45 314	52 353	58 657
C.3.1.3.2. (Foreign Controlled Companies) — C.3.1.3.2. (Entreprises Sous Contrôle Etranger)	..	1 675	4 790	6 733	9 699	10 949	12 940	14 688
C.3.1.3.3. Branches & Agencies of Foreign Cies — C.3.1.3.3. Succursales et Agences d'Ent. Etrangères	..	375	915	1 483	2 027	2 670	3 284	4 128
C.3.1.3. Total Gross Premiums — C.3.1.3. Total des Primes Brutes	..	22 959	29 670	33 796	41 124	47 984	55 637	62 784
C.3.2. Ceded Premiums — C.3.2. Primes Cédées								
C.3.2.1. Domestic Companies — C.3.2.1. Entreprises Nationales	..	1 478	2 542	3 909	5 335	6 543	8 220	8 938
C.3.2.2. (Foreign Controlled Companies) — C.3.2.2. (Entreprises Sous Contrôle Etranger)	..	716	2 430	2 353	3 157	3 654	4 488	5 153
C.3.2.3. Branches & Agencies of Foreign Cies — C.3.2.3. Succursales et Agences d'Ent. Etrangères	..	34	112	106	131	247	352	440
C.3.2. Total — C.3.2. Total	..	1 512	2 654	4 015	5 466	6 790	8 572	9 378
C.3.3. Net Written Premiums — C.3.3. Primes Nettes Emises								
C.3.3.1. Domestic Companies — C.3.3.1. Entreprises Nationales	..	21 106	26 213	28 404	33 762	38 771	44 132	49 718
C.3.3.2. (Foreign Controlled Companies) — C.3.3.2. (Entreprises Sous Contrôle Etranger)	..	959	2 360	4 380	6 542	7 295	8 452	9 536
C.3.3.3. Branches & Agencies of Foreign Cies — C.3.3.3. Succursales et Agences d'Ent. Etrangères	..	341	803	1 377	1 896	2 423	2 933	3 688
C.3.3. Total — C.3.3. Total	..	21 447	27 016	29 781	35 658	41 194	47 065	53 406

CZECH REPUBLIC — REPUBLIQUE TCHEQUE

Monetary Unit: million Czech koruna — Unité monétaire : million de couronnes tchèques

D. NET WRITTEN PREMIUMS IN THE REPORTING COUNTRY IN TERMS OF DOMESTIC AND FOREIGN RISKS
D. PRIMES NETTES EMISES DANS LE PAYS DECLARANT EN RISQUES NATIONAUX ET ETRANGERS

D.1. Life — D.1. Vie

	1992	1993	1994	1995	1996	1997	1998	1999
D.1.1. Domestic Risks — Risques Nationaux								
D.1.1.1. Domestic Companies — Entreprises Nationales	..	5 596	6 725	7 936	9 127	10 171	12 105	16 072
D.1.1.2. (Foreign Controlled Companies) — (Entreprises Sous Contrôle Etranger)	..	86	392	543	854	1 228	1 855	2 736
D.1.1.3. Branches & Agencies of Foreign Cies — Succursales et Agences d'Ent. Etrangères	..	321	722	1 314	1 691	2 151	2 840	3 527
D.1.1. Total — Total des Primes Nettes Vie	..	5 917	7 447	9 250	10 818	12 322	14 945	19 599
D.1.3. Total								
D.1.3.1. Domestic Companies — Entreprises Nationales	..	5 596	6 725	7 936	9 127	10 171	12 105	16 072
D.1.3.2. (Foreign Controlled Companies) — (Entreprises Sous Contrôle Etranger)	..	86	392	543	854	1 228	1 855	2 736
D.1.3.3. Branches & Agencies of Foreign Cies — Succursales et Agences d'Ent. Etrangères	..	321	722	1 314	1 691	2 151	2 840	3 527
D.1.3. Total of Life Net Premiums — Total des Primes Nettes Vie	..	5 917	7 447	9 250	10 818	12 322	14 945	19 599

D.2. Non-Life — D.2. Non-Vie

	1992	1993	1994	1995	1996	1997	1998	1999
D.2.1. Domestic Risks — Risques Nationaux								
D.2.1.1. Domestic Companies — Entreprises Nationales	..	14 543	18 511	20 096	24 202	28 176	31 360	32 929
D.2.1.2. (Foreign Controlled Companies) — (Entreprises Sous Contrôle Etranger)	..	873	1 968	3 775	5 538	5 900	6 379	6 557
D.2.1.3. Branches & Agencies of Foreign Cies — Succursales et Agences d'Ent. Etrangères	..	20	81	63	205	272	93	161
D.2.1. Total — Total des Primes Nettes Vie	..	14 563	18 592	20 159	24 407	28 448	31 452	33 090
D.2.2. Foreign Risks — Risques Etrangers								
D.2.2.1. Domestic Companies — Entreprises Nationales	..	967	977	372	433	424	668	718
D.2.2.2. (Foreign Controlled Companies) — (Entreprises Sous Contrôle Etranger)	..	..	..	62	150	167	217	242
D.2.2. Total — Total des Primes Nettes Vie	..	967	977	372	433	424	668	718
D.2.3. Total								
D.2.3.1. Domestic Companies — Entreprises Nationales	..	15 510	19 488	20 468	24 635	28 600	32 028	33 646
D.2.3.2. (Foreign Controlled Companies) — (Entreprises Sous Contrôle Etranger)	..	873	1 968	3 837	5 688	6 067	6 597	6 799
D.2.3.3. Branches & Agencies of Foreign Cies — Succursales et Agences d'Ent. Etrangères	..	20	81	63	205	272	93	161
D.2.3. Total — Total des Primes Nettes Vie	..	15 530	19 569	20 531	24 840	28 872	32 120	33 807

F. OUTSTANDING INVESTMENT BY DIRECT INSURANCE COMPANIES
F. ENCOURS DES PLACEMENTS DES ENTREPRISES D'ASSURANCES DIRECTES

F.1. Life — F.1. Vie

	1992	1993	1994	1995	1996	1997	1998	1999
F.1.1. Real Estate — Immobilier								
F.1.1.1. Domestic Companies — Entreprises Nationales		2 175	3 420	4 603	4 995	5 922	6 245	9 850
F.1.1.2. (Foreign Controlled Companies) — (Entreprises Sous Contrôle Etranger)		0	4	4	13	36	37	90
F.1.1.4. Domestic Investment — Placement dans le Pays		2 175	3 420	4 603	4 995	5 922	6 245	9 850
F.1.1.5. Foreign Investment — Placement à l'Etranger		0	4	0	0	0	0	0
F.1.1. Total		2 175	3 420	4 603	4 995	5 922	6 245	9 850
F.1.2. Mortgage Loans — Prêts Hypothécaires								
F.1.2.1. Domestic Companies — Entreprises Nationales							1	0
F.1.2.4. Domestic Investment — Placement dans le Pays							1	0
F.1.2. Total							1	0
F.1.3. Shares — Actions								
F.1.3.1. Domestic Companies — Entreprises Nationales		5 806	8 816	7 801	11 810	12 032	10 353	11 435
F.1.3.2. (Foreign Controlled Companies) — (Entreprises Sous Contrôle Etranger)		..	1	2	3	7	15	36
F.1.3.3. Branches & Agencies of Foreign Cies — Succursales et Agences d'Ent. Etrangères		0	0	0	0	18	31	54
F.1.3.4. Domestic Investment — Placement dans le Pays		5 806	8 816	7 801	11 810	12 050	10 384	11 489
F.1.3.5. Foreign Investment — Placement à l'Etranger		0	1	0	0	0	0	0
F.1.3. Total		5 806	8 816	7 801	11 810	12 050	10 384	11 489

Monetary Unit: million Czech koruna — Unité monétaire : million de couronnes tchèques

Item (EN)	Item (FR)	1992	1993	1994	1995	1996	1997	1998	1999
F.1.4. Bonds with Fixed Revenue	F.1.4. Obligations								
F.1.4.1. Domestic Companies	F.1.4.1. Entreprises Nationales		36 938	1 738	7 889	15 862	20 309	22 807	33 097
F.1.4.2. (Foreign Controlled Companies)	F.1.4.2. (Entreprises Sous Contrôle Etranger)		65	7	411	545	819	1 836	2 909
F.1.4.3. Branches & Agencies of Foreign Cies	F.1.4.3. Succursales et Agences d'Ent. Etrangères		266	234	1 128	1 790	2 700	3 326	4 925
F.1.4.4. Domestic Investment	F.1.4.4. Placement dans le Pays		37 204	1 972	9 017	17 652	23 009	26 133	38 022
F.1.4.5. Foreign Investment	F.1.4.5. Placement à l' Etranger		331	7	0	0	0	0	0
F.1.4. Total	F.1.4. Total		37 204	1 972	9 017	17 652	23 009	26 133	38 022
F.1.5. Loans other than Mortgage Loans	F.1.5. Prêts Autres qu'Hypothécaires								
F.1.5.1. Domestic Companies	F.1.5.1. Entreprises Nationales		899	1 753	1 694	5 753	5 411	4 346	7 695
F.1.5.3. Branches & Agencies of Foreign Cies	F.1.5.3. Succursales et Agences d'Ent. Etrangères		..	0	0	246	0	0	0
F.1.5.4. Domestic Investment	F.1.5.4. Placement dans le Pays		899	1 753	1 694	5 999	5 411	4 346	7 695
F.1.5. Total	F.1.5. Total		899	1 753	1 694	5 999	5 411	4 346	7 695
F.1.6. Other Investments	F.1.6. Autres Placements								
F.1.6.1. Domestic Companies	F.1.6.1. Entreprises Nationales		..	3 357	31 733	16 869	13 388	16 675	15 615
F.1.6.2. (Foreign Controlled Companies)	F.1.6.2. (Entreprises Sous Contrôle Etranger)		..	13	59	375	583	545	983
F.1.6.3. Branches & Agencies of Foreign Cies	F.1.6.3. Succursales et Agences d'Ent. Etrangères		..	80	0	677	728	1 596	1 955
F.1.6.4. Domestic Investment	F.1.6.4. Placement dans le Pays		..	3 437	31 733	17 546	14 116	18 271	17 570
F.1.6.5. Foreign Investment	F.1.6.5. Placement à l' Etranger		..	13	0	0	0	0	0
F.1.6. Total	F.1.6. Total		..	3 437	31 733	17 546	14 116	18 271	17 570
F.1.7. Total	F.1.7. Total								
F.1.7.1. Domestic Companies	F.1.7.1. Entreprises Nationales		45 818	19 084	53 720	55 289	57 062	60 427	77 691
F.1.7.2. (Foreign Controlled Companies)	F.1.7.2. (Entreprises Sous Contrôle Etranger)		65	25	476	936	1 445	2 433	4 018
F.1.7.3. Branches & Agencies of Foreign Cies	F.1.7.3. Succursales et Agences d'Ent. Etrangères		266	314	1 128	2 713	3 446	4 953	6 934
F.1.7.4. Domestic Investment	F.1.7.4. Placement dans le Pays		46 084	19 398	54 848	58 002	60 508	65 380	84 625
F.1.7.5. Foreign Investment	F.1.7.5. Placement à l' Etranger		331	25	0	0	0	0	0
F.1.7. Total of Life Investments	F.1.7. Total des Placements Vie		46 084	19 398	54 848	58 002	60 508	65 380	84 625
F.2. Non-Life	**F.2. Non-Vie**								
F.2.1. Real Estate	F.2.1. Immobilier								
F.2.1.1. Domestic Companies	F.2.1.1. Entreprises Nationales		66	406	592	652	873	817	492
F.2.1.2. (Foreign Controlled Companies)	F.2.1.2. (Entreprises Sous Contrôle Etranger)		40	368	534	597	740	758	371
F.2.1.3. Branches & Agencies of Foreign Cies	F.2.1.3. Succursales et Agences d'Ent. Etrangères		..	2	0	0	0	0	0
F.2.1.4. Domestic Investment	F.2.1.4. Placement dans le Pays		66	408	592	652	873	817	492
F.2.1.5. Foreign Investment	F.2.1.5. Placement à l' Etranger		40	408	0	0	0	0	0
F.2.1. Total	F.2.1. Total		66	774	592	652	873	817	492
F.2.2. Mortgage Loans	F.2.2. Prêts Hypothécaires								
F.2.2.1. Domestic Companies	F.2.2.1. Entreprises Nationales		0	0	1	1	0	12	13
F.2.2.2. (Foreign Controlled Companies)	F.2.2.2. (Entreprises Sous Contrôle Etranger)		0	0	1	1	0	0	0
F.2.2.4. Domestic Investment	F.2.2.4. Placement dans le Pays		..	0	1	1	0	12	13
F.2.2. Total	F.2.2. Total		..	0	1	1	0	12	13
F.2.3. Shares	F.2.3. Actions								
F.2.3.1. Domestic Companies	F.2.3.1. Entreprises Nationales		39	245	200	4 312	2 887	4 155	1 028
F.2.3.2. (Foreign Controlled Companies)	F.2.3.2. (Entreprises Sous Contrôle Etranger)		29	82	200	238	163	173	190
F.2.3.3. Branches & Agencies of Foreign Cies	F.2.3.3. Succursales et Agences d'Ent. Etrangères		..	0	0	0	3	5	9
F.2.3.4. Domestic Investment	F.2.3.4. Placement dans le Pays		39	245	200	4 312	2 890	4 161	1 037
F.2.3.5. Foreign Investment	F.2.3.5. Placement à l' Etranger		29	82	0	0	0	0	0
F.2.3. Total	F.2.3. Total		39	245	200	4 312	2 890	4 161	1 037
F.2.4. Bonds with Fixed Revenue	F.2.4. Obligations								
F.2.4.1. Domestic Companies	F.2.4.1. Entreprises Nationales		1 341	465	322	7 011	5 066	8 369	8 039
F.2.4.2. (Foreign Controlled Companies)	F.2.4.2. (Entreprises Sous Contrôle Etranger)		627	262	147	822	1 445	1 860	2 586
F.2.4.3. Branches & Agencies of Foreign Cies	F.2.4.3. Succursales et Agences d'Ent. Etrangères		21	0	0	0	508	656	861
F.2.4.4. Domestic Investment	F.2.4.4. Placement dans le Pays		1 989	465	322	7 011	5 574	9 025	8 900
F.2.4.5. Foreign Investment	F.2.4.5. Placement à l' Etranger		648	262	0	0	0	0	0
F.2.4. Total	F.2.4. Total		1 989	465	322	7 011	5 574	9 025	8 900
F.2.5. Loans other than Mortgage Loans	F.2.5. Prêts Autres qu'Hypothécaires								
F.2.5.1. Domestic Companies	F.2.5.1. Entreprises Nationales		35	146	51	3 533	4 906	2 817	2 501
F.2.5.2. (Foreign Controlled Companies)	F.2.5.2. (Entreprises Sous Contrôle Etranger)		35	146	51	840	13	439	0
F.2.5.4. Domestic Investment	F.2.5.4. Placement dans le Pays		35	146	51	3 533	4 906	2 817	2 501
F.2.5.5. Foreign Investment	F.2.5.5. Placement à l' Etranger		35	146	0	0	0	0	0
F.2.5. Total	F.2.5. Total		35	146	51	3 533	4 906	2 817	2 501

CZECH REPUBLIC **REPUBLIQUE TCHEQUE**

Monetary Unit: million Czech koruna — Unité monétaire : million de couronnes tchèques

	1992	1993	1994	1995	1996	1997	1998	1999
F.2.6. Other Investments / Autres Placements								
F.2.6.1. Domestic Companies / Entreprises Nationales		..	649	12 160	12 123	17 739	14 109	27 065
F.2.6.2. (Foreign Controlled Companies) / (Entreprises Sous Contrôle Etranger)		..	422	577	2 345	2 222	2 165	2 281
F.2.6.3. Branches & Agencies of Foreign Cies / Succursales et Agences d'Ent. Etrangères		..	0	57	85	265	344	592
F.2.6.4. Domestic Investment / Placement dans le Pays		..	649	12 217	12 208	18 004	14 453	27 656
F.2.6.5. Foreign Investment / Placement à l'Etranger		..	422	0	0	0	0	0
F.2.6. Total		..	649	12 217	12 208	18 004	14 453	27 656
F.2.7. Total								
F.2.7.1. Domestic Companies / Entreprises Nationales		2 108	1 911	13 326	27 632	31 471	30 278	39 136
F.2.7.2. (Foreign Controlled Companies) / (Entreprises Sous Contrôle Etranger)		731	1 280	1 510	4 843	4 583	5 395	5 429
F.2.7.3. Branches & Agencies of Foreign Cies / Succursales et Agences d'Ent. Etrangères		21	2	57	85	776	1 006	1 462
F.2.7.4. Domestic Investment / Placement dans le Pays		2 129	1 913	13 383	27 717	32 247	31 284	40 599
F.2.7.5. Foreign Investment / Placement à l'Etranger		752	1 280	0	0	0	0	0
F.2.7. Total of Non-Life Investments / Total des Placements Non-Vie		2 129	1 913	13 383	27 717	32 247	31 284	40 599
G. BREAKDOWN OF NON-LIFE PREMIUMS / VENTILATIONS DES PRIMES NON-VIE								
G.1. Motor vehicle / Assurance Automobile								
G.1.1. Direct Business / Assurances Directes								
G.1.1.1. Gross Premiums / Primes Brutes		4 886	4 519	5 057	8 620	15 355	19 875	21 428
G.1.1.2. Ceded Premiums / Primes Cédées		..	..	..	..	1 528	2 236	2 726
G.1.1.3. Net Written Premiums / Primes Nettes Emises		..	..	..	..	13 827	17 639	18 702
G.1.3. Total								
G.1.3.1. Gross Premiums / Primes Brutes		4 886	4 519	5 057	8 620	15 355	19 875	21 428
G.1.3.2. Ceded Premiums / Primes Cédées		..	0	..	..	1 528	2 236	2 726
G.1.3.3. Net Written Premiums / Primes Nettes Emises		..	0	..	..	13 827	17 639	18 702
G.2. Marine, Aviation								
G.2.1. Direct Business / Assurances Directes								
G.2.1.1. Gross Premiums / Primes Brutes		686	1 029	972	1 014	239	217	177
G.2.1.2. Ceded Premiums / Primes Cédées		..	..	..	..	175	145	108
G.2.1.3. Net Written Premiums / Primes Nettes Emises		..	..	..	..	64	72	68
G.2.2. Reinsurance Accepted / Réassurance Acceptée								
G.2.2.1. Gross Premiums / Primes Brutes		..	..	170	120	0	0	..
G.2.3. Total								
G.2.3.1. Gross Premiums / Primes Brutes		686	1 029	1 142	1 134	239	217	177
G.2.3.2. Ceded Premiums / Primes Cédées		..	..	..	..	175	145	108
G.2.3.3. Net Written Premiums / Primes Nettes Emises		..	..	..	..	64	72	68
G.3. Freight / Fret								
G.3.1. Direct Business / Assurances Directes								
G.3.1.1. Gross Premiums / Primes Brutes		284	426	268	268	278	348	303
G.3.1.2. Ceded Premiums / Primes Cédées		..	..	..	..	167	150	155
G.3.1.3. Net Written Premiums / Primes Nettes Emises		..	..	..	..	111	198	148
G.3.2. Reinsurance Accepted / Réassurance Acceptée								
G.3.2.1. Gross Premiums / Primes Brutes		..	..	170	0	0	0	..
G.3.3. Total								
G.3.3.1. Gross Premiums / Primes Brutes		284	426	438	268	278	348	303
G.3.3.2. Ceded Premiums / Primes Cédées		..	..	..	..	167	150	155
G.3.3.3. Net Written Premiums / Primes Nettes Emises		..	..	..	..	111	198	148
G.4. Fire, Property Damages / Incendie, Dommages aux Biens								
G.4.1. Direct Business / Assurances Directes								
G.4.1.1. Gross Premiums / Primes Brutes		2 302	5 844	7 261	7 420	7 869	7 150	9 885
G.4.1.2. Ceded Premiums / Primes Cédées		..	..	..	..	2 604	2 528	4 209
G.4.1.3. Net Written Premiums / Primes Nettes Emises		..	..	..	..	5 265	4 622	5 676
G.4.2. Reinsurance Accepted / Réassurance Acceptée								
G.4.2.1. Gross Premiums / Primes Brutes		..	..	190	0	526	619	205
G.4.2.3. Net Written Premiums / Primes Nettes Emises		..	..	..	..	526	619	205
G.4.3. Total								
G.4.3.1. Gross Premiums / Primes Brutes		2 302	5 844	7 451	7 420	8 395	7 769	10 090
G.4.3.2. Ceded Premiums / Primes Cédées		..	..	..	..	2 604	2 528	4 209
G.4.3.3. Net Written Premiums / Primes Nettes Emises		..	..	..	..	5 791	5 241	5 881

Monetary Unit: million Czech koruna   Unité monétaire : million de couronnes tchèques

		1992	1993	1994	1995	1996	1997	1998	1999
G.5. Pecuniary Losses	G.5. Pertes Pécuniaires								
G.5.1. Direct Business	G.5.1. Assurances Directes								
G.5.1.1. Gross Premiums	G.5.1.1. Primes Brutes		200	625	650	720	49	661	110
G.5.1.2. Ceded Premiums	G.5.1.2. Primes Cédées			..	..	..	34	26	39
G.5.1.3. Net Written Premiums	G.5.1.3. Primes Nettes Emises			..	..	..	15	635	70
G.5.3. Total	G.5.3. Total								
G.5.3.1. Gross Premiums	G.5.3.1. Primes Brutes		200	625	650	720	49	661	110
G.5.3.2. Ceded Premiums	G.5.3.2. Primes Cédées			..	..	..	34	26	39
G.5.3.3. Net Written Premiums	G.5.3.3. Primes Nettes Emises			..	..	..	15	635	70
G.6. General Liability	G.6. Responsabilité Générale								
G.6.1. Direct Business	G.6.1. Assurances Directes								
G.6.1.1. Gross Premiums	G.6.1.1. Primes Brutes		3 198	3 872	4 299	6 220	1 809	2 045	3 087
G.6.1.2. Ceded Premiums	G.6.1.2. Primes Cédées						500	586	832
G.6.1.3. Net Written Premiums	G.6.1.3. Primes Nettes Emises						1 309	1 459	2 255
G.6.2. Reinsurance Accepted	G.6.2. Réassurance Acceptée								
G.6.2.1. Gross Premiums	G.6.2.1. Primes Brutes				11	0	0	0	4
G.6.2.3. Net Written Premiums	G.6.2.3. Primes Nettes Emises								4
G.6.3. Total	G.6.3. Total								
G.6.3.1. Gross Premiums	G.6.3.1. Primes Brutes		3 198	3 872	4 310	6 220	1 809	2 045	3 091
G.6.3.2. Ceded Premiums	G.6.3.2. Primes Cédées						500	586	832
G.6.3.3. Net Written Premiums	G.6.3.3. Primes Nettes Emises						1 309	1 459	2 258
G.7. Accident, Health	G.7. Accident, Santé								
G.7.1. Direct Business	G.7.1. Assurances Directes								
G.7.1.1. Gross Premiums	G.7.1.1. Primes Brutes		1 499	1 730	1 981	2 254	3 714	3 755	3 314
G.7.1.2. Ceded Premiums	G.7.1.2. Primes Cédées						805	408	399
G.7.1.3. Net Written Premiums	G.7.1.3. Primes Nettes Emises						2 909	3 347	2 915
G.7.3. Total	G.7.3. Total								
G.7.3.1. Gross Premiums	G.7.3.1. Primes Brutes		1 499	1 730	1 981	2 254	3 714	3 755	3 314
G.7.3.2. Ceded Premiums	G.7.3.2. Primes Cédées						805	408	399
G.7.3.3. Net Written Premiums	G.7.3.3. Primes Nettes Emises						2 909	3 347	2 915
G.8. Others	G.8. Autres								
G.8.1. Direct Business	G.8.1. Assurances Directes								
G.8.1.1. Gross Premiums	G.8.1.1. Primes Brutes		3 987	4 178	3 425	3 551	5 678	5 878	4 479
G.8.1.2. Ceded Premiums	G.8.1.2. Primes Cédées						832	2 349	714
G.8.1.3. Net Written Premiums	G.8.1.3. Primes Nettes Emises						4 846	3 529	3 765
G.8.3. Total	G.8.3. Total								
G.8.3.1. Gross Premiums	G.8.3.1. Primes Brutes		3 987	4 178	3 425	3 551	5 678	5 878	4 479
G.8.3.2. Ceded Premiums	G.8.3.2. Primes Cédées			0			832	2 349	714
G.8.3.3. Net Written Premiums	G.8.3.3. Primes Nettes Emises			0			4 846	3 529	3 765
G.10. Total	G.10. Total								
G.10.1. Direct Business	G.10.1. Assurances Directes								
G.10.1.1. Gross Premiums	G.10.1.1. Primes Brutes		17 042	22 223	23 913	30 067	34 991	39 929	42 782
G.10.1.2. Ceded Premiums	G.10.1.2. Primes Cédées		1 512	2 654			6 645	8 428	9 184
G.10.1.3. Net Written Premiums	G.10.1.3. Primes Nettes Emises		15 530	19 569			28 346	31 501	33 599
G.10.2. Reinsurance Accepted	G.10.2. Réassurance Acceptée								
G.10.2.1. Gross Premiums	G.10.2.1. Primes Brutes				541	120	526	619	208
G.10.2.3. Net Written Premiums	G.10.2.3. Primes Nettes Emises						526	619	208
G.10.3. Total	G.10.3. Total								
G.10.3.1. Gross Premiums	G.10.3.1. Primes Brutes		17 042	22 223	24 454	30 187	35 517	40 548	42 991
G.10.3.2. Ceded Premiums	G.10.3.2. Primes Cédées		1 512	2 654	3 923	5 347	6 645	8 428	9 184
G.10.3.3. Net Written Premiums	G.10.3.3. Primes Nettes Emises		15 530	19 569	20 531	24 840	28 872	32 120	33 807

Monetary Unit: million Czech koruna — Unité monétaire : million de couronnes tchèques

	1992	1993	1994	1995	1996	1997	1998	1999	
H. GROSS CLAIMS PAYMENTS									**H. PAIEMENTS BRUTS DES SINISTRES**
H.1. Life									**H.1. Vie**
H.1.1. Domestic Companies					6 901	7 976	8 775	9 389	H.1.1. Entreprises Nationales
H.1.2. (Foreign Controlled Companies)					41	75	125	251	H.1.2. (Entreprises Sous Contrôle Etranger)
H.1.3. Branches & Agencies of Foreign Cies					90	184	330	460	H.1.3. Succursales et Agences d'Ent. Etrangères
H.1. Total					6 991	8 160	9 105	9 850	H.1. Total
H.2. Non-Life									**H.2. Non-Vie**
H.2.1. Domestic Companies					14 659	24 790	23 847	25 383	H.2.1. Entreprises Nationales
H.2.2. (Foreign Controlled Companies)					3 207	5 865	6 509	6 528	H.2.2. (Entreprises Sous Contrôle Etranger)
H.2.3. Branches & Agencies of Foreign Cies					43	72	118	290	H.2.3. Succursales et Agences d'Ent. Etrangères
H.2. Total					14 702	24 862	23 965	25 673	H.2. Total
I. GROSS OPERATING EXPENSES									**I. DEPENSES BRUITES D'EXPLOITATION**
I.1. Life									**I.1. Vie**
I.1.1. Domestic Companies					2 117	2 735	3 341	4 599	I.1.1. Entreprises Nationales
I.1.2. (Foreign Controlled Companies)					625	804	1 116	1 488	I.1.2. (Entreprises Sous Contrôle Etranger)
I.1.3. Branches & Agencies of Foreign Cies					361	449	481	493	I.1.3. Succursales et Agences d'Ent. Etrangères
I.1. Total					2 478	3 184	3 822	5 092	I.1. Total des Primes Nettes Vie .
I.2. Non-Life									**I.2. Non-Vie**
I.2.1. Domestic Companies					6 157	7 959	9 826	11 050	I.2.1. Entreprises Nationales
I.2.2. (Foreign Controlled Companies)					1 916	2 645	3 651	4 746	I.2.2. (Entreprises Sous Contrôle Etranger)
I.2.3. Branches & Agencies of Foreign Cies					120	136	201	243	I.2.3. Succursales et Agences d'Ent. Etrangères
I.2. Total					6 277	8 095	10 027	11 293	I.2. Total
J. COMMISSIONS									**J. COMMISSIONS**
J.1. Life									**J.1. Vie**
J.1.1. Direct Business									J.1.1. Assurance directe
J.1.1.1. Domestic Companies					373	75	99	152	J.1.1.1. Entreprises Nationales
J.1.1.2. (Foreign Controlled Companies)					156	75	99	150	J.1.1.2. (Entreprises Sous Contrôle Etranger)
J.1.1. Total					373	75	99	152	J.1.1. Total
J.1.3. Total									J.1.3. Total
J.1.3.1. Domestic Companies					373	75	99	152	J.1.3.1. Entreprises Nationales
J.1.3.2. (Foreign Controlled Companies)					156	75	99	150	J.1.3.2. (Entreprises Sous Contrôle Etranger)
J.1.3. Total of Life Net Premiums					373	75	99	152	J.1.3. Total
J.2. Non-Life									**J.2. Non-Vie**
J.2.1. Direct Business									J.2.1. Assurance directe
J.2.1.1. Domestic Companies					2 873	1 940	2 417	2 727	J.2.1.1. Entreprises Nationales
J.2.1.2. (Foreign Controlled Companies)					1 106	1 193	1 488	1 697	J.2.1.2. (Entreprises Sous Contrôle Etranger)
J.2.1.3. Branches & Agencies of Foreign Cies					33	54	73	99	J.2.1.3. Succursales et Agences d'Ent. Etrangères
J.2.1. Total					2 906	1 994	2 490	2 827	J.2.1. Total des Primes Nettes Vie
J.2.2. Reinsurance Accepted									J.2.2. Réassurances acceptées
J.2.3. Total									J.2.3. Total
J.2.3.1. Domestic Companies					2 873	1 940	2 417	2 727	J.2.3.1. Entreprises Nationales
J.2.3.2. (Foreign Controlled Companies)					1 106	1 193	1 488	1 697	J.2.3.2. (Entreprises Sous Contrôle Etranger)
J.2.3.3. Branches & Agencies of Foreign Cies					33	54	73	99	J.2.3.3. Succursales et Agences d'Ent. Etrangères
J.2.3. Total					2 906	1 994	2 490	2 827	J.2.3. Total

Monetary Unit: million Danish kroner   Unité monétaire : million de couronnes danoises

Code (EN) / (FR)	Label (EN) / (FR)	1992	1993	1994	1995	1996	1997	1998	1999
A.	**NUMBER OF COMPANIES IN THE REPORTING COUNTRY** / **NOMBRE D'ENTREPRISES DANS LE PAYS DECLARANT**								
A.1.	**Life** / **Vie**								
A.1.1.	Domestic Companies / Entreprises Nationales	39	48	84	83	88	85	88	90
A.1.2.	(Foreign Controlled Companies) / (Entreprises Sous Contrôle Etranger)	6	6	8	7	7	10	12	21
A.1.3.	Branches & Agencies of Foreign Cies / Succursales et Agences d'Ent. Etrangères	2	2	1	1	1	1	1	1
A.1.	All Companies / Ensemble des Entreprises	41	50	85	84	89	86	89	91
A.2.	**Non-Life** / **Non-Vie**								
A.2.1.	Domestic Companies / Entreprises Nationales	148	156	151	149	156	139	137	130
A.2.2.	(Foreign Controlled Companies) / (Entreprises Sous Contrôle Etranger)	15	15	11	12	12	11	11	11
A.2.3.	Branches & Agencies of Foreign Cies / Succursales et Agences d'Ent. Etrangères	27	33	8	3	5	2	2	1
A.2.	All Companies / Ensemble des Entreprises	175	189	159	152	161	141	139	131
A.4.	**Reinsurance** / **Réassurance**								
A.4.1.	Domestic Companies / Entreprises Nationales	9	4	8	5	5	9	10	9
A.4.2.	(Foreign Controlled Companies) / (Entreprises Sous Contrôle Etranger)	1	1	2	2	2	3	4	3
A.4.3.	Branches & Agencies of Foreign Cies / Succursales et Agences d'Ent. Etrangères	20	15	4	0	0	0	0	0
A.4.	All Companies / Ensemble des Entreprises	29	19	12	5	5	9	10	9
A.5.	**Total**								
A.5.1.	Domestic Companies / Entreprises Nationales	196	208	243	237	249	233	235	229
A.5.2.	(Foreign Controlled Companies) / (Entreprises Sous Contrôle Etranger)	22	22	21	21	21	24	27	35
A.5.3.	Branches & Agencies of Foreign Cies / Succursales et Agences d'Ent. Etrangères	49	50	13	4	6	3	3	2
A.5.	All Insurance Companies / Ensemble des Entreprises d'Assurances	245	258	256	241	255	236	238	231
B.	**NUMBER OF EMPLOYEES** / **NOMBRE D'EMPLOYES**								
B.1.	Insurance Companies / Entreprises d'Assurances	14 300	14 662	15 000	14 393	15 512	15 207	15 082	15 374
B.	Total	..	..	..	..	..	..	..	..
C.	**BUSINESS WRITTEN IN THE REPORTING COUNTRY** / **OPERATIONS CONCLUES DANS LE PAYS DECLARANT**								
C.1.	**Life** / **Vie**								
C.1.1.	Gross Premiums / Primes Brutes								
C.1.1.1.	Direct Business / Assurances Directes								
C.1.1.1.1.	Domestic Companies / Entreprises Nationales	18 784	23 132	29 109	32 151	38 817	43 428	51 017	49 072
C.1.1.1.2.	(Foreign Controlled Companies) / (Entreprises Sous Contrôle Etranger)	1 386	1 403	2 337	2 242	2 723	2 816	3 022	8 634
C.1.1.1.3.	Branches & Agencies of Foreign Cies / Succursales et Agences d'Ent. Etrangères	458	402	201	189	189	176	169	155
C.1.1.1.	Total	19 242	23 534	29 310	32 340	39 006	43 604	51 186	49 227
C.1.1.2.	Reinsurance Accepted / Réassurance Acceptée								
C.1.1.2.1.	Domestic Companies / Entreprises Nationales	74	63	134	80	97	115	110	106
C.1.1.2.2.	(Foreign Controlled Companies) / (Entreprises Sous Contrôle Etranger)	0	0	13	13	13	14	15	50
C.1.1.2.	Total	74	63	134	80	97	115	110	106
C.1.1.3.	Total								
C.1.1.3.1.	Domestic Companies / Entreprises Nationales	18 858	23 195	29 243	32 231	38 914	43 543	51 127	49 178
C.1.1.3.2.	(Foreign Controlled Companies) / (Entreprises Sous Contrôle Etranger)	1 386	1 403	2 351	2 255	2 736	2 830	3 037	8 684
C.1.1.3.3.	Branches & Agencies of Foreign Cies / Succursales et Agences d'Ent. Etrangères	458	402	201	189	189	176	169	155
C.1.1.3.	Total Gross Premiums / Total des Primes Brutes	19 316	23 597	29 444	32 420	39 103	43 719	51 296	49 333
C.1.2.	Ceded Premiums / Primes Cédées								
C.1.2.1.	Domestic Companies / Entreprises Nationales	222	205	471	465	547	569	623	699
C.1.2.2.	(Foreign Controlled Companies) / (Entreprises Sous Contrôle Etranger)	40	47	50	48	71	54	58	139
C.1.2.3.	Branches & Agencies of Foreign Cies / Succursales et Agences d'Ent. Etrangères	20	- 65	1	1	1	1	1	1
C.1.2.	Total	242	140	472	466	548	570	624	700
C.1.3.	Net Written Premiums / Primes Nettes Emises								
C.1.3.1.	Domestic Companies / Entreprises Nationales	18 636	22 990	28 772	31 766	38 367	42 974	50 504	48 479
C.1.3.2.	(Foreign Controlled Companies) / (Entreprises Sous Contrôle Etranger)	1 346	1 356	2 301	2 207	2 665	2 776	2 979	8 545
C.1.3.3.	Branches & Agencies of Foreign Cies / Succursales et Agences d'Ent. Etrangères	438	467	200	188	188	175	168	154
C.1.3.	Total	19 074	23 457	28 972	31 954	38 555	43 149	50 672	48 633

DENMARK   **DANEMARK**

Monetary Unit: million Danish kroner   Unité monétaire : million de couronnes danoises

C.2. Non-Life / C.2. Non-Vie

Label	1992	1993	1994	1995	1996	1997	1998	1999
C.2.1. Gross premiums / Primes Brutes								
C.2.1.1. Direct Business / Assurances Directes								
C.2.1.1.1. Domestic Companies / Entreprises Nationales	20 789	21 403	23 314	25 142	26 416	27 842	28 679	28 106
C.2.1.1.2. (Foreign Controlled Companies / Entreprises Sous Contrôle Etranger)	3 172	5 397	5 560	5 847	5 911	6 231	6 639	11 463
C.2.1.1.3. Branches & Agencies of Foreign Cies / Succursales et Agences d'Ent. Etrangères	1 411	1 600	892	526	375	340	420	413
C.2.1.1. Total	22 200	23 003	24 206	25 668	26 791	28 182	29 099	28 519
C.2.1.2. Reinsurance Accepted / Réassurance Acceptée								
C.2.1.2.1. Domestic Companies / Entreprises Nationales	8 544	5 756	8 189	5 427	5 402	5 123	6 173	6 439
C.2.1.2.2. (Foreign Controlled Companies / Entreprises Sous Contrôle Etranger)	5 911	3 438	550	3 682	3 506	2 797	3 426	3 302
C.2.1.2.3. Branches & Agencies of Foreign Cies / Succursales et Agences d'Ent. Etrangères	161	207	223	234	208	241	223	157
C.2.1.2. Total	8 705	5 963	8 412	5 661	5 610	5 364	6 396	6 596
C.2.1.3. Total								
C.2.1.3.1. Domestic Companies / Entreprises Nationales	29 333	27 159	31 503	30 569	31 818	32 965	34 852	34 545
C.2.1.3.2. (Foreign Controlled Companies / Entreprises Sous Contrôle Etranger)	9 083	8 835	6 110	9 529	9 417	9 028	10 065	14 765
C.2.1.3.3. Branches & Agencies of Foreign Cies / Succursales et Agences d'Ent. Etrangères	1 572	1 807	1 115	760	583	581	643	570
C.2.1.3. Total Gross Premiums / Total des Primes Brutes	30 905	28 966	32 618	31 329	32 401	33 546	35 495	35 115
C.2.2. Ceded Premiums / Primes Cédées								
C.2.2.1. Domestic Companies / Entreprises Nationales	4 517	4 389	4 372	4 235	3 693	3 865	4 237	4 173
C.2.2.2. (Foreign Controlled Companies / Entreprises Sous Contrôle Etranger)	1 170	1 730	1 381	1 598	1 313	1 534	1 765	1 535
C.2.2. Total	:	:	:	:	3 693	:	:	:
C.2.3. Net Written Premiums / Primes Nettes Emises								
C.2.3.1. Domestic Companies / Entreprises Nationales	24 816	22 770	27 131	26 334	28 125	29 100	30 615	30 372
C.2.3.2. (Foreign Controlled Companies / Entreprises Sous Contrôle Etranger)	7 913	7 105	4 729	7 931	8 104	7 494	8 300	13 230
C.2.3.3. Branches & Agencies of Foreign Cies / Succursales et Agences d'Ent. Etrangères	:	:	:	:	583	:	:	:
C.2.3. Total	:	:	:	:	28 708	:	:	:

C.3. Total

Label	1992	1993	1994	1995	1996	1997	1998	1999
C.3.1. Gross Premiums / Primes Brutes								
C.3.1.1. Direct Business / Assurances Directes								
C.3.1.1.1. Domestic Companies / Entreprises Nationales	39 573	44 535	52 423	57 293	65 233	71 270	79 696	77 178
C.3.1.1.2. (Foreign Controlled Companies / Entreprises Sous Contrôle Etranger)	4 558	6 800	7 897	8 089	8 634	9 047	9 661	20 097
C.3.1.1.3. Branches & Agencies of Foreign Cies / Succursales et Agences d'Ent. Etrangères	1 869	2 002	1 093	715	564	516	589	568
C.3.1.1. Total	41 442	46 537	53 516	58 008	65 797	71 786	80 285	77 746
C.3.1.2. Reinsurance Accepted / Réassurance Acceptée								
C.3.1.2.1. Domestic Companies / Entreprises Nationales	8 618	5 819	8 323	5 507	5 499	5 238	6 283	6 545
C.3.1.2.2. (Foreign Controlled Companies / Entreprises Sous Contrôle Etranger)	5 911	3 438	563	3 695	3 519	2 811	3 441	3 352
C.3.1.2.3. Branches & Agencies of Foreign Cies / Succursales et Agences d'Ent. Etrangères	161	207	223	234	208	241	223	157
C.3.1.2. Total	8 779	6 026	8 546	5 741	5 707	5 479	6 506	6 702
C.3.1.3. Total								
C.3.1.3.1. Domestic Companies / Entreprises Nationales	48 191	50 354	60 746	62 800	70 732	76 508	85 979	83 723
C.3.1.3.2. (Foreign Controlled Companies / Entreprises Sous Contrôle Etranger)	10 469	10 238	8 461	11 784	12 153	11 858	13 102	23 449
C.3.1.3.3. Branches & Agencies of Foreign Cies / Succursales et Agences d'Ent. Etrangères	2 030	2 209	1 316	949	772	757	812	725
C.3.1.3. Total Gross Premiums / Total des Primes Brutes	50 221	52 563	62 062	63 749	71 504	77 265	86 791	84 448
C.3.2. Ceded Premiums / Primes Cédées								
C.3.2.1. Domestic Companies / Entreprises Nationales	4 739	4 594	4 843	4 700	4 240	4 434	4 860	4 872
C.3.2.2. (Foreign Controlled Companies / Entreprises Sous Contrôle Etranger)	1 210	1 777	1 431	1 646	1 384	1 588	1 823	1 674
C.3.2. Total	:	:	:	:	4 241	:	:	:
C.3.3. Net Written Premiums / Primes Nettes Emises								
C.3.3.1. Domestic Companies / Entreprises Nationales	43 452	45 760	55 903	58 100	66 492	72 074	81 119	78 851
C.3.3.2. (Foreign Controlled Companies / Entreprises Sous Contrôle Etranger)	9 259	8 461	7 030	10 138	10 769	10 270	11 279	21 775
C.3.3.3. Branches & Agencies of Foreign Cies / Succursales et Agences d'Ent. Etrangères	:	:	:	:	771	:	:	:
C.3.3. Total	:	:	:	:	67 263	:	:	:

Monetary Unit: million Danish kroner

Unité monétaire : million de couronnes danoises

D. NET WRITTEN PREMIUMS IN THE REPORTING COUNTRY IN TERMS OF DOMESTIC AND FOREIGN RISKS
D. PRIMES NETTES EMISES DANS LE PAYS DECLARANT EN RISQUES NATIONAUX ET ETRANGERS

D.2. Non-Life / D.2. Non-Vie

Label	1992	1993	1994	1995	1996	1997	1998	1999
D.2.1. Domestic Risks / Risques Nationaux								
D.2.1.1. Domestic Companies / Entreprises Nationales	17 871	23 926	20 391	22 658	22 206	24 863	::	
D.2.1.2. (Foreign Controlled Companies) / (Entreprises Sous Contrôle Etranger)	3 009	4 927	4 537	5 587	7 039	5 381	::	
D.2.2. Foreign Risks / Risques Etrangers								
D.2.2.1. Domestic Companies / Entreprises Nationales	3 668	4 452	6 740	3 676	4 217	4 237	::	
D.2.2.2. (Foreign Controlled Companies) / (Entreprises Sous Contrôle Etranger)	1 831	2 033	192	2 344	2 649	2 113	::	
D.2.3. Total / Total								
D.2.3.1. Domestic Companies / Entreprises Nationales	21 540	28 378	27 131	26 334	26 423	29 100	30 615	
D.2.3.2. (Foreign Controlled Companies) / (Entreprises Sous Contrôle Etranger)	4 840	6 960	4 729	7 931	9 688	7 494	8 300	
D.2.3.3. Branches & Agencies of Foreign Cies / Succursales et Agences d'Ent. Etrangères	::	::	::	::	::	::	::	
D.2.3. Total / Total des Primes Nettes Vie	::	::	::	::	::	::	::	

E. BUSINESS WRITTEN ABROAD / E. OPERATIONS A L'ETRANGER

E.1. Life / E.1. Vie

Label	1992	1993	1994	1995	1996	1997	1998	1999
E.1.1. Gross Premiums / Primes Brutes								
E.1.1.1. Direct Business / Assurance Directe								
E.1.1.1.1. Branches & Agencies / Succursales & Agences	0	0	0	119	::	0	0	161
E.1.1.3. Total / Total								
E.1.1.3.1. Branches & Agencies / Succursales & Agences								161

E.2. Non-Life / E.2. Non-Vie

Label	1992	1993	1994	1995	1996	1997	1998	1999
E.2.1. Gross Premiums / Primes Brutes								
E.2.1.1. Direct Business / Assurance Directe								
E.2.1.1.1. Branches & Agencies / Succursales & Agences	349	361	375	399	75	85	99	159
E.2.1.2. Reinsurance Accepted / Réassurance Acceptée								
E.2.1.2.1. Branches & Agencies / Succursales & Agences	6 980	4 654	7 118	3 655	1 790	859	1 373	1 741
E.2.1.3. Total / Total								
E.2.1.3.1. Branches & Agencies / Succursales & Agences	7 329	5 015	7 493	4 054	1 865	944	1 472	1 900
E.2.2. Ceded Premiums / Primes Cédées								
E.2.2.1. Branches & Agencies / Succursales & Agences	::	::	::	::	84	11	::	::
E.2.3. Net Written Premiums / Primes Nettes Emises								
E.2.3.1. Branches & Agencies / Succursales & Agences	::	::	::	::	1 781	933	::	::

F. OUTSTANDING INVESTMENT BY DIRECT INSURANCE COMPANIES
F. ENCOURS DES PLACEMENTS DES ENTREPRISES D'ASSURANCES DIRECTES

F.1. Life / F.1. Vie

Label	1992	1993	1994	1995	1996	1997	1998	1999
F.1.1. Real Estate / Immobilier								
F.1.1.1. Domestic Companies / Entreprises Nationales	7 315	5 370	12 760	14 270	14 794	15 353	15 934	19 842
F.1.1.2. (Foreign Controlled Companies) / (Entreprises Sous Contrôle Etranger)	264	278	311	282	292	854	3 486	2 989
F.1.1.3. Branches & Agencies of Foreign Cies / Succursales et Agences d'Ent. Etrangères	2	2	0	0	0	0	0	0
F.1.1. Total / Total	7 317	5 372	12 760	14 270	14 794	15 353	::	::
F.1.2. Mortgage Loans / Prêts Hypothécaires								
F.1.2.1. Domestic Companies / Entreprises Nationales	4 105	4 357	5 833	5 026	4 230	3 506	3 067	3 058
F.1.2.2. (Foreign Controlled Companies) / (Entreprises Sous Contrôle Etranger)	6	5	3	1	0	1	1	104
F.1.2.3. Branches & Agencies of Foreign Cies / Succursales et Agences d'Ent. Etrangères	70	70	0	0	0	0	0	0
F.1.2. Total / Total	4 175	4 427	5 833	5 026	4 230	3 506	::	::

Monetary Unit: million Danish kroner

Unité monétaire : million de couronnes danoises

	1992	1993	1994	1995	1996	1997	1998	1999	
F.1.3. Shares									F.1.3. Actions
F.1.3.1. Domestic Companies	61 522	79 516	116 166	132 716	166 320	221 277	266 660	385 685	F.1.3.1. Entreprises Nationales
F.1.3.2. (Foreign Controlled Companies)	1 892	2 398	4 409	5 377	7 361	15 808	16 468	65 132	F.1.3.2. (Entreprises Sous Contrôle Etranger)
F.1.3.3. Branches & Agencies of Foreign Cies	120	171	154	170	219	..	334	450	F.1.3.3. Succursales et Agences d'Ent. Etrangères
F.1.3.4. Domestic Investment	51 873	66 387	93 899	105 410	127 376	162 109	..	..	F.1.3.4. Placement dans le Pays
F.1.3.5. Foreign Investment	9 769	13 067	22 421	27 476	39 163	59 168	..	..	F.1.3.5. Placement à l' Etranger
F.1.3. Total	61 642	79 454	116 320	132 886	166 539	221 277	..	..	F.1.3. Total
F.1.4. Bonds with Fixed Revenue									F.1.4. Obligations
F.1.4.1. Domestic Companies	169 669	195 410	298 231	320 575	352 732	378 721	404 282	420 755	F.1.4.1. Entreprises Nationales
F.1.4.2. (Foreign Controlled Companies)	10 572	11 873	17 686	16 127	17 219	34 477	34 332	2 173	F.1.4.2. (Entreprises Sous Contrôle Etranger)
F.1.4.3. Branches & Agencies of Foreign Cies	1 904	2 277	1 036	1 127	1 223	..	1 399	1 443	F.1.4.3. Succursales et Agences d'Ent. Etrangères
F.1.4.4. Domestic Investment	170 933	197 386	297 477	318 994	350 299	372 830	..	..	F.1.4.4. Placement dans le Pays
F.1.4.5. Foreign Investment	640	301	1 790	2 708	3 656	5 891	..	..	F.1.4.5. Placement à l' Etranger
F.1.4. Total	171 573	197 687	299 267	321 702	353 955	378 721	..	..	F.1.4. Total
F.1.5. Loans other than Mortgage Loans									F.1.5. Prêts Autres qu'Hypothécaires
F.1.5.1. Domestic Companies	3 120	3 009	2 896	2 370	2 227	1 814	1 601	1 384	F.1.5.1. Entreprises Nationales
F.1.5.2. (Foreign Controlled Companies)	65	60	54	43	39	71	26	116	F.1.5.2. (Entreprises Sous Contrôle Etranger)
F.1.5.3. Branches & Agencies of Foreign Cies	5	4	3	3	2	..	2	2	F.1.5.3. Succursales et Agences d'Ent. Etrangères
F.1.5. Total	3 125	3 013	2 899	2 373	2 229	1 814	..	..	F.1.5. Total
F.1.6. Other Investments									F.1.6. Autres Placements
F.1.6.1. Domestic Companies	16 479	17 205	25 254	2 609	2 310	2 285	1 517	1 377	F.1.6.1. Entreprises Nationales
F.1.6.2. (Foreign Controlled Companies)	1 089	862	912	28	506	404	24	0	F.1.6.2. (Entreprises Sous Contrôle Etranger)
F.1.6.3. Branches & Agencies of Foreign Cies	320	327	127	39	58	..	18	31	F.1.6.3. Succursales et Agences d'Ent. Etrangères
F.1.6. Total	16 799	17 532	25 381	2 648	2 368	2 285	..	..	F.1.6. Total
F.1.7. Total									F.1.7. Total
F.1.7.1. Domestic Companies	262 210	304 867	461 140	477 566	542 613	622 956	693 061	832 101	F.1.7.1. Entreprises Nationales
F.1.7.2. (Foreign Controlled Companies)	13 888	15 476	23 375	21 858	25 417	51 615	54 336	70 514	F.1.7.2. (Entreprises Sous Contrôle Etranger)
F.1.7.3. Branches & Agencies of Foreign Cies	2 421	2 851	1 320	1 339	1 502	..	1 753	1 926	F.1.7.3. Succursales et Agences d'Ent. Etrangères
F.1.7.4. Domestic Investment	..	66 387	..	..	..	..	..	..	F.1.7.4. Placement dans le Pays
F.1.7.5. Foreign Investment	..	13 067	..	..	..	..	..	..	F.1.7.5. Placement à l' Etranger
F.1.7. Total of Life Investments	264 631	307 485	462 460	478 905	544 115	622 956	..	..	F.1.7. Total des Placements Vie
F.2. Non-Life									F.2. Non-Vie
F.2.1. Real Estate									F.2.1. Immobilier
F.2.1.1. Domestic Companies	3 354	3 480	3 301	2 848	2 940	3 121	3 263	2 874	F.2.1.1. Entreprises Nationales
F.2.1.2. (Foreign Controlled Companies)	1 327	1 298	1 306	1 223	1 366	1 491	1 527	2 003	F.2.1.2. (Entreprises Sous Contrôle Etranger)
F.2.1. Total	3 354	3 480	3 301	2 848	2 940	3 121	..	..	F.2.1. Total
F.2.2. Mortgage Loans									F.2.2. Prêts Hypothécaires
F.2.2.1. Domestic Companies	2 036	1 758	1 345	1 087	852	612	562	568	F.2.2.1. Entreprises Nationales
F.2.2.2. (Foreign Controlled Companies)	229	416	137	74	37	24	12	219	F.2.2.2. (Entreprises Sous Contrôle Etranger)
F.2.2. Total	2 036	1 758	1 345	1 087	852	612	..	..	F.2.2. Total
F.2.3. Shares									F.2.3. Actions
F.2.3.1. Domestic Companies	21 529	22 707	23 922	23 331	28 311	32 748	37 835	37 442	F.2.3.1. Entreprises Nationales
F.2.3.2. (Foreign Controlled Companies)	2 698	6 197	6 803	5 393	6 129	8 563	8 779	14 632	F.2.3.2. (Entreprises Sous Contrôle Etranger)
F.2.3.4. Domestic Investment	20 428	21 515	..	..	26 183	29 994	..	..	F.2.3.4. Placement dans le Pays
F.2.3.5. Foreign Investment	1 101	1 193	..	..	2 128	2 754	..	..	F.2.3.5. Placement à l' Etranger
F.2.3. Total	21 529	22 709	..	..	28 311	32 748	..	..	F.2.3. Total
F.2.4. Bonds with Fixed Revenue									F.2.4. Obligations
F.2.4.1. Domestic Companies	37 208	39 254	43 010	39 449	51 956	49 274	50 177	43 357	F.2.4.1. Entreprises Nationales
F.2.4.2. (Foreign Controlled Companies)	8 192	8 139	4 475	5 088	13 205	11 212	12 380	16 233	F.2.4.2. (Entreprises Sous Contrôle Etranger)
F.2.4.4. Domestic Investment	32 059	34 439	..	..	43 419	43 165	..	..	F.2.4.4. Placement dans le Pays
F.2.4.5. Foreign Investment	5 149	4 816	..	..	8 537	6 109	..	..	F.2.4.5. Placement à l' Etranger
F.2.4. Total	37 208	39 255	..	..	51 956	49 274	..	..	F.2.4. Total
F.2.5. Loans other than Mortgage Loans									F.2.5. Prêts Autres qu'Hypothécaires
F.2.5.1. Domestic Companies	3 159	2 344	1 461	563	428	177	261	143	F.2.5.1. Entreprises Nationales
F.2.5.2. (Foreign Controlled Companies)	700	682	204	707	109	70	26	313	F.2.5.2. (Entreprises Sous Contrôle Etranger)
F.2.5. Total	3 159	2 344	..	..	428	177	..	..	F.2.5. Total

Monetary Unit: million Danish kroner
Unité monétaire : million de couronnes danoises

	1992	1993	1994	1995	1996	1997	1998	1999
F.2.6. Other Investments / Autres Placements								
F.2.6.1. Domestic Companies / Entreprises Nationales	18 024	17 451	15 509	3 762	3 246	3 519	1 833	2 401
F.2.6.2. (Foreign Controlled Companies) / (Entreprises Sous Contrôle Etranger)	7 943	8 348	2 029	267	1 432	1 262	316	10
F.2.6. Total	18 024	17 451	..	..	3 246	3 519	..	..
F.2.7. Total								
F.2.7.1. Domestic Companies / Entreprises Nationales	85 310	86 996	88 548	71 040	87 733	89 451	93 931	86 785
F.2.7.2. (Foreign Controlled Companies) / (Entreprises Sous Contrôle Etranger)	21 089	25 080	14 954	12 752	22 278	22 622	23 040	33 410
F.2.7.4. Domestic Investment / Placement dans le Pays	..	21 515	..	..	..	..	..	..
F.2.7.5. Foreign Investment / Placement à l'Etranger	..	1 193	..	..	..	..	..	..
F.2.7. Total of Non-Life Investments / Total des Placements Non-Vie	85 310	86 997	..	..	87 733	89 451	..	..
G. BREAKDOWN OF NON-LIFE PREMIUMS / VENTILATIONS DES PRIMES NON-VIE								
G.1. Motor vehicle / Assurance Automobile								
G.1.1. Direct Business / Assurances Directes								
G.1.1.1. Gross Premiums / Primes Brutes	5 774	5 881	6 339	7 016	7 390	8 162	8 556	8 755
G.1.1.2. Ceded Premiums / Primes Cédées							307	327
G.1.1.3. Net Written Premiums / Primes Nettes Emises							8 249	8 428
G.2. Marine, Aviation								
G.2.1. Direct Business / Assurances Directes								
G.2.1.1. Gross Premiums / Primes Brutes	1 364	1 297	1 295	987	1 010	944	871	813
G.2.1.2. Ceded Premiums / Primes Cédées							424	407
G.2.1.3. Net Written Premiums / Primes Nettes Emises							447	406
G.4. Fire, Property Damages / Incendie, Dommages aux Biens								
G.4.1. Direct Business / Assurances Directes								
G.4.1.1. Gross Premiums / Primes Brutes	8 764	8 862	9 191	9 510	9 874	11 380	11 741	11 497
G.4.1.2. Ceded Premiums / Primes Cédées							1 709	1 725
G.4.1.3. Net Written Premiums / Primes Nettes Emises							10 032	9 772
G.5. Pecuniary Losses / Pertes Pécunières								
G.5.1. Direct Business / Assurances Directes								
G.5.1.1. Gross Premiums / Primes Brutes	474	484	466	492	483	303	..	..
G.6. General Liability / Responsabilité Générale								
G.6.1. Direct Business / Assurances Directes								
G.6.1.1. Gross Premiums / Primes Brutes	770	867	815	885	930	960	989	979
G.6.1.2. Ceded Premiums / Primes Cédées							100	61
G.6.1.3. Net Written Premiums / Primes Nettes Emises							889	918
G.7. Accident, Health / Accident, Santé								
G.7.1. Direct Business / Assurances Directes								
G.7.1.1. Gross Premiums / Primes Brutes	3 788	4 253	4 679	5 621	5 960	6 432	6 224	6 206
G.7.1.2. Ceded Premiums / Primes Cédées							191	235
G.7.1.3. Net Written Premiums / Primes Nettes Emises							6 033	5 971
G.8. Others / Autres								
G.8.1. Direct Business / Assurances Directes								
G.8.1.1. Gross Premiums / Primes Brutes	915	997	1 046	1 156	1 144	1	299	269
G.8.1.2. Ceded Premiums / Primes Cédées							183	126
G.8.1.3. Net Written Premiums / Primes Nettes Emises							116	143
G.9. Treaty Reinsurance / Réassurance Obligatoire								
G.9.1. Direct Business / Assurances Directes								
G.9.1.1. Gross Premiums / Primes Brutes	21 849	22 641					..	..
G.9.2. Reinsurance Accepted / Réassurance Acceptée								
G.9.2.1. Gross Premiums / Primes Brutes			375	0	0		6 173	6 173
G.9.2.2. Ceded Premiums / Primes Cédées							1 324	1 324
G.9.2.3. Net Written Premiums / Primes Nettes Emises							4 849	4 849
G.10. Total								
G.10.1. Direct Business / Assurances Directes								
G.10.1.1. Gross Premiums / Primes Brutes	22 199	23 003	24 206	25 667	26 791	28 182	28 680	28 519
G.10.1.2. Ceded Premiums / Primes Cédées							2 914	2 881
G.10.1.3. Net Written Premiums / Primes Nettes Emises							25 766	25 638

Monetary Unit: million Danish kroner — Unité monétaire : million de couronnes danoises

	1992	1993	1994	1995	1996	1997	1998	1999
G.10.2. Reinsurance Accepted / Réassurance Acceptée								
G.10.2.1. Gross Premiums / Primes Brutes	8 705	5 963	8 412	5 662	5 610	5 364	6 173	:
G.10.2.2. Ceded Premiums / Primes Cédées							1 324	:
G.10.2.3. Net Written Premiums / Primes Nettes Emises							4 849	:
G.10.3. Total / Total								
G.10.3.1. Gross Premiums / Primes Brutes	30 905	28 966	32 618	31 329	32 401	33 546	:	:
G.10.3.2. Ceded Premiums / Primes Cédées	:			:	3 693	:	:	:
G.10.3.3. Net Written Premiums / Primes Nettes Emises	:			:	28 708	:	:	:
H. GROSS CLAIMS PAYMENTS / PAIEMENTS BRUTS DES SINISTRES								
H.1. Life / Vie								
H.1.1. Domestic Companies / Entreprises Nationales					24 797	25 808	28 583	31 080
H.1.2. (Foreign Controlled Companies) / (Entreprises Sous Contrôle Etranger)					1 275	3 146	3 093	6 815
H.1.3. Branches & Agencies of Foreign Cies / Succursales et Agences d'Ent. Etrangères					112	139	133	126
H.1. Total / Total					24 909	25 947	28 716	31 206
H.2. Non-Life / Non-Vie								
H.2.1. Domestic Companies / Entreprises Nationales					25 755	20 294	24 407	26 233
H.2.2. (Foreign Controlled Companies) / (Entreprises Sous Contrôle Etranger)					9 476	9 639	6 701	11 397
H.2.3. Branches & Agencies of Foreign Cies / Succursales et Agences d'Ent. Etrangères					532	463	353	526
H.2. Total / Total					26 287	20 757	24 760	26 759
I. GROSS OPERATING EXPENSES / DEPENSES BRUTES D'EXPLOITATION								
I.1. Life / Vie								
I.1.1. Domestic Companies / Entreprises Nationales					2 064	2 867	2 746	3 729
I.1.2. (Foreign Controlled Companies) / (Entreprises Sous Contrôle Etranger)					123	330	353	96
I.1.3. Branches & Agencies of Foreign Cies / Succursales et Agences d'Ent. Etrangères					17	22	16	17
I.1. Total / Total des Primes Nettes Vie					2 081	2 889	2 762	3 746
I.2. Non-Life / Non-Vie								
I.2.1. Domestic Companies / Entreprises Nationales					4 862	8 355	5 748	9 218
I.2.2. (Foreign Controlled Companies) / (Entreprises Sous Contrôle Etranger)					1 382	2 736	1 728	4 369
I.2. Total / Total					4 862	:	:	:
J. COMMISSIONS								
J.1. Life / Vie								
J.1.1. Direct Business / Assurance directe								
J.1.1.1. Domestic Companies / Entreprises Nationales							251	266
J.1.1.2. (Foreign Controlled Companies) / (Entreprises Sous Contrôle Etranger)							89	124
J.1.1.3. Branches & Agencies of Foreign Cies / Succursales et Agences d'Ent. Etrangères							2	2
J.1.1. Total / Total							253	268
J.1.3. Total / Total								
J.1.3.1. Domestic Companies / Entreprises Nationales					305	382	:	:
J.1.3.2. (Foreign Controlled Companies) / (Entreprises Sous Contrôle Etranger)					69	76	:	:
J.1.3.3. Branches & Agencies of Foreign Cies / Succursales et Agences d'Ent. Etrangères					2	3	:	:
J.1.3. Total of Life Net Premiums / Total					307	385	:	:

Monetary Unit: million Danish kroner Unité monétaire : million de couronnes danoises

J.2. Non-Life J.2. Non-Vie

	1992	1993	1994	1995	1996	1997	1998	1999
J.2.1. Direct Business — J.2.1. Assurance directe								
J.2.1.1. Domestic Companies — J.2.1.1. Entreprises Nationales							2 913	2 997
J.2.1.2. (Foreign Controlled Companies) — J.2.1.2. (Entreprises Sous Contrôle Etranger)							1 363	1 594
J.2.3. Total — J.2.3. Total								
J.2.3.1. Domestic Companies — J.2.3.1. Entreprises Nationales					2 220	2 387	:	:
J.2.3.2. (Foreign Controlled Companies) — J.2.3.2. (Entreprises Sous Contrôle Etranger)					1 235	1 244	:	:
J.2.3. Total — J.2.3. Total					2 220	2 387		

FINLAND — FINLANDE

Monetary Unit: million markka — Unité monétaire : million de markkas

	1992	1993	1994	1995	1996	1997	1998	1999	
A. NUMBER OF COMPANIES IN THE REPORTING COUNTRY									**A. NOMBRE D'ENTREPRISES DANS LE PAYS DECLARANT**
A.1. Life									**A.1. Vie**
A.1.1. Domestic Companies	17	12	12	11	14	14	14	14	A.1.1. Entreprises Nationales
A.1. All Companies	17	12	12	11	14	14	14	14	A.1. Ensemble des Entreprises
A.2. Non-Life									**A.2. Non-Vie**
A.2.1. Domestic Companies	29	28	146	145	145	147	152	150	A.2.1. Entreprises Nationales
A.2.3. Branches & Agencies of Foreign Cies	2	2	2	2	2	2	2	2	A.2.3. Succursales et Agences d'Ent. Etrangères
A.2. All Companies	31	30	148	147	147	149	154	152	A.2. Ensemble des Entreprises
A.4. Reinsurance									**A.4. Réassurance**
A.4.1. Domestic Companies	9	11	12	9	8	6	5	5	A.4.1. Entreprises Nationales
A.4. All Companies	9	11	12	9	8	6	5	5	A.4. Ensemble des Entreprises
A.5. Total									**A.5. Total**
A.5.1. Domestic Companies	55	51	170	165	167	167	171	169	A.5.1. Entreprises Nationales
A.5.3. Branches & Agencies of Foreign Cies	2	2	2	2	2	2	2	2	A.5.3. Succursales et Agences d'Ent. Etrangères
A.5. All Insurance Companies	57	53	172	167	169	169	173	171	A.5. Ensemble des Entreprises d'Assurances
B. NUMBER OF EMPLOYEES									**B. NOMBRE D'EMPLOYES**
B.1. Insurance Companies	12 260	11 800	9 000	9 270	9 454	9 497	9 500	8 230	B.1. Entreprises d'Assurances
B.2. Intermediaries	..	..	..	100	93	119	38	270	B.2. Intermediaires
B. Total	..	..	..	9 370	9 547	..	9 538	8 500	B. Total
C. BUSINESS WRITTEN IN THE REPORTING COUNTRY									**C. OPERATIONS CONCLUES DANS LE PAYS DECLARANT**
C.1. Life									**C.1. Vie**
C.1.1. Gross Premiums									C.1.1. Primes Brutes
C.1.1.1. Direct Business									C.1.1.1. Assurances Directes
C.1.1.1.1. Domestic Companies	20 509	2 800	3 871	7 168	11 862	11 281	13 713	18 661	C.1.1.1.1. Entreprises Nationales
C.1.1.1. Total	20 509	2 800	3 871	7 168	11 862	11 281	13 713	18 661	C.1.1.1. Total
C.1.1.2. Reinsurance Accepted									C.1.1.2. Réassurance Acceptée
C.1.1.2.1. Domestic Companies	- 148	1	4	6	17	111	75	83	C.1.1.2.1. Entreprises Nationales
C.1.1.2. Total	- 148	1	4	6	17	111	75	83	C.1.1.2. Total
C.1.1.3. Total									C.1.1.3. Total
C.1.1.3.1. Domestic Companies	20 361	2 801	3 875	7 174	11 879	11 392	13 788	18 744	C.1.1.3.1. Entreprises Nationales
C.1.1.3. Total Gross Premiums	20 361	2 801	3 875	7 174	11 879	11 392	13 788	18 744	C.1.1.3. Total des Primes Brutes
C.1.2. Ceded Premiums									C.1.2. Primes Cédées
C.1.2.1. Domestic Companies	162	127	183	109	104	113	101	133	C.1.2.1. Entreprises Nationales
C.1.2. Total	162	127	183	109	104	113	101	133	C.1.2. Total
C.1.3. Net Written Premiums									C.1.3. Primes Nettes Emises
C.1.3.1. Domestic Companies	20 199	2 674	3 692	7 065	11 775	11 279	13 687	18 611	C.1.3.1. Entreprises Nationales
C.1.3. Total	20 199	2 674	3 692	7 065	11 775	11 279	13 687	18 611	C.1.3. Total
C.2. Non-Life									**C.2. Non-Vie**
C.2.1. Gross premiums									C.2.1. Primes Brutes
C.2.1.1. Direct Business									C.2.1.1. Assurances Directes
C.2.1.1.1. Domestic Companies	11 111	10 911	11 249	11 212	11 319	11 786	13 197	13 363	C.2.1.1.1. Entreprises Nationales
C.2.1.1.3. Branches & Agencies of Foreign Cies	11	20	24	11	11	12	15	27	C.2.1.1.3. Succursales et Agences d'Ent. Etrangères
C.2.1.1. Total	11 122	10 931	11 273	11 223	11 330	11 798	13 212	13 390	C.2.1.1. Total
C.2.1.2. Reinsurance Accepted									C.2.1.2. Réassurance Acceptée
C.2.1.2.1. Domestic Companies	1 756	1 492	1 089	1 139	1 214	968	1 015	910	C.2.1.2.1. Entreprises Nationales
C.2.1.2.3. Branches & Agencies of Foreign Cies	19	20	31	4	4	4	4	7	C.2.1.2.3. Succursales et Agences d'Ent. Etrangères
C.2.1.2. Total	1 775	1 512	1 120	1 143	1 218	972	1 019	917	C.2.1.2. Total
C.2.1.3. Total									C.2.1.3. Total
C.2.1.3.1. Domestic Companies	12 867	12 403	12 338	12 351	12 533	12 754	14 212	14 273	C.2.1.3.1. Entreprises Nationales
C.2.1.3.3. Branches & Agencies of Foreign Cies	30	40	55	15	15	16	19	34	C.2.1.3.3. Succursales et Agences d'Ent. Etrangères
C.2.1.3. Total Gross Premiums	12 897	12 443	12 393	12 366	12 548	12 770	14 231	14 307	C.2.1.3. Total des Primes Brutes

Monetary Unit: million markka   Unité monétaire : million de markkas

Label (English / Français)	1992	1993	1994	1995	1996	1997	1998	1999
C.2.2. Ceded Premiums / C.2.2. Primes Cédées								
C.2.2.1. Domestic Companies / C.2.2.1. Entreprises Nationales	1 456	1 315	1 423	1 435	1 314	1 292	1 302	1 294
C.2.2.3. Branches & Agencies of Foreign Cies / C.2.2.3. Succursales et Agences d'Ent. Etrangères	19	25	37	10	7	7	6	27
C.2.2. Total / C.2.2. Total	1 475	1 340	1 460	1 445	1 321	1 296	1 308	1 321
C.2.3. Net Written Premiums / C.2.3. Primes Nettes Emises								
C.2.3.1. Domestic Companies / C.2.3.1. Entreprises Nationales	11 411	11 088	10 915	10 916	11 219	11 462	12 910	12 979
C.2.3.3. Branches & Agencies of Foreign Cies / C.2.3.3. Succursales et Agences d'Ent. Etrangères	11	15	19	5	8	12	13	7
C.2.3. Total / C.2.3. Total	11 422	11 103	10 934	10 921	11 227	11 474	12 923	12 986
C.3. Total / C.3. Total								
C.3.1. Gross Premiums / C.3.1. Primes Brutes								
C.3.1.1. Direct Business / C.3.1.1. Assurances Directes								
C.3.1.1.1. Domestic Companies / C.3.1.1.1. Entreprises Nationales	31 620	13 711	15 120	18 380	23 181	23 067	26 910	32 024
C.3.1.1.3. Branches & Agencies of Foreign Cies / C.3.1.1.3. Succursales et Agences d'Ent. Etrangères	11	..	24	..	11	12	15	27
C.3.1.1. Total / C.3.1.1. Total	31 631	13 731	15 144	18 391	23 192	23 079	26 925	32 051
C.3.1.2. Reinsurance Accepted / C.3.1.2. Réassurance Acceptée								
C.3.1.2.1. Domestic Companies / C.3.1.2.1. Entreprises Nationales	1 608	1 493	1 093	1 145	1 231	1 079	1 090	993
C.3.1.2.3. Branches & Agencies of Foreign Cies / C.3.1.2.3. Succursales et Agences d'Ent. Etrangères	19	..	31	4	4	4	4	34
C.3.1.2. Total / C.3.1.2. Total	1 627	1 513	1 124	1 149	1 235	1 083	1 094	997
C.3.1.3. Total / C.3.1.3. Total								
C.3.1.3.1. Domestic Companies / C.3.1.3.1. Entreprises Nationales	33 228	15 204	16 213	19 525	24 412	24 146	28 000	33 017
C.3.1.3.3. Branches & Agencies of Foreign Cies / C.3.1.3.3. Succursales et Agences d'Ent. Etrangères	30	..	55	15	15	16	19	68
C.3.1.3. Total Gross Premiums / C.3.1.3. Total des Primes Brutes	33 258	15 244	16 268	19 540	24 427	24 162	28 019	33 051
C.3.2. Ceded Premiums / C.3.2. Primes Cédées								
C.3.2.1. Domestic Companies / C.3.2.1. Entreprises Nationales	1 618	1 442	1 606	1 544	1 418	1 405	1 403	1 427
C.3.2.3. Branches & Agencies of Foreign Cies / C.3.2.3. Succursales et Agences d'Ent. Etrangères	19	..	37	..	7	4	6	27
C.3.2. Total / C.3.2. Total	1 637	1 467	1 643	1 554	1 425	1 409	1 409	1 454
C.3.3. Net Written Premiums / C.3.3. Primes Nettes Emises								
C.3.3.1. Domestic Companies / C.3.3.1. Entreprises Nationales	31 610	13 762	14 607	17 981	22 994	22 741	26 597	31 590
C.3.3.3. Branches & Agencies of Foreign Cies / C.3.3.3. Succursales et Agences d'Ent. Etrangères	11	19	19	5	8	12	13	7
C.3.3. Total / C.3.3. Total	31 621	13 777	14 626	17 986	23 002	22 753	26 610	31 597

D. NET WRITTEN PREMIUMS IN THE REPORTING COUNTRY IN TERMS OF DOMESTIC AND FOREIGN RISKS / D. PRIMES NETTES EMISES DANS LE PAYS DECLARANT EN RISQUES NATIONAUX ET ETRANGERS

Label (English / Français)	1992	1993	1994	1995	1996	1997	1998	1999
D.1. Life / D.1. Vie								
D.1.1. Domestic Risks / D.1.1. Risques Nationaux								
D.1.1.1. Domestic Companies / D.1.1.1. Entreprises Nationales	20 199	2 674	..	7 064	11 775	11 279	12 945	16 181
D.1.1. Total / D.1.1. Total des Primes Nettes Vie	20 199	2 674	..	7 064	11 775	11 279	12 945	16 181
D.1.2. Foreign Risks / D.1.2. Risques Etrangers								
D.1.2.1. Domestic Companies / D.1.2.1. Entreprises Nationales	0	..	..	1	0	0	742	2 430
D.1.2. Total / D.1.2. Total des Primes Nettes Vie	0	..	..	1	0	0	742	2 430
D.1.3. Total / D.1.3. Total								
D.1.3.1. Domestic Companies / D.1.3.1. Entreprises Nationales	20 199	2 674	3 692	7 065	11 775	11 279	13 687	18 611
D.1.3. Total of Life Net Premiums / D.1.3. Total des Primes Nettes Vie	20 199	2 674	3 692	7 065	11 775	11 279	13 687	18 611
D.2. Non-Life / D.2. Non-Vie								
D.2.1. Domestic Risks / D.2.1. Risques Nationaux								
D.2.1.1. Domestic Companies / D.2.1.1. Entreprises Nationales	10 384	11 088	..	10 791	11 187	11 428	12 818	12 930
D.2.1.3. Branches & Agencies of Foreign Cies / D.2.1.3. Succursales et Agences d'Ent. Etrangères	11	15	19	5	8	12	13	7
D.2.1. Total / D.2.1. Total des Primes Nettes Vie	10 395	11 103	..	10 796	11 195	11 440	12 831	12 937
D.2.2. Foreign Risks / D.2.2. Risques Etrangers								
D.2.2.1. Domestic Companies / D.2.2.1. Entreprises Nationales	1 027	..	..	125	32	34	92	49
D.2.2. Total / D.2.2. Total des Primes Nettes Vie	1 027	..	..	125	32	34	92	49

FINLANDE

Monetary Unit: million markka

	1992	1993	1994	1995	1996	1997	1998	1999	
D.2.3. Total									D.2.3. Total
D.2.3.1. Domestic Companies	11 411	11 088	10 915	10 916	11 219	11 462	12 910	12 979	D.2.3.1. Entreprises Nationales
D.2.3.3. Branches & Agencies of Foreign Cies	11	15	..	5	8	12	13	7	D.2.3.3. Succursales et Agences d'Ent. Etrangères
D.2.3. Total	11 422	11 103	10 934	10 921	11 227	11 474	12 923	12 986	D.2.3. Total des Primes Nettes Vie
E. BUSINESS WRITTEN ABROAD									**E. OPERATIONS A L'ETRANGER**
E.1. Life									**E.1. Vie**
E.1.1. Gross Premiums									E.1.1. Primes Brutes
E.1.1.1. Direct Business									E.1.1.1. Assurance Directe
E.1.1.1.1. Branches & Agencies	0	..	0	..	..	0	742	2 430	E.1.1.1.1. Succursales & Agences
E.1.1.1. Total	0	..	44	..	..	0	742	2 430	E.1.1.1. Total
E.2. Non-Life									**E.2. Non-Vie**
E.2.1. Gross Premiums									E.2.1. Primes Brutes
E.2.1.1. Direct Business									E.2.1.1. Assurance Directe
E.2.1.1.1. Branches & Agencies	0	167	44	- 2	41	14	25	31	E.2.1.1.1. Succursales & Agences
E.2.1.1. Total	0	167	..	- 2	..	14	25	31	E.2.1.1. Total
E.2.1.2. Reinsurance Accepted									E.2.1.2. Réassurance Acceptée
E.2.1.3. Total	0	..	44	- 2	..	0	..	..	E.2.1.3. Total
E.2.1.3.1. Branches & Agencies	0	..	44	- 2	..	0	..	..	E.2.1.3.1. Succursales & Agences
E.2.1.3. Total Gross Premiums	0	..	0	- 2	..	0	..	..	E.2.1.3. Total des Primes Brutes
F. OUTSTANDING INVESTMENT BY DIRECT INSURANCE COMPANIES									**F. ENCOURS DES PLACEMENTS DES ENTREPRISES D'ASSURANCES DIRECTES**
F.1. Life									**F.1. Vie**
F.1.1. Real Estate									F.1.1. Immobilier
F.1.1.1. Domestic Companies	13 087	4 975	3 366	7 609	7 589	7 535	7 818	7 800	F.1.1.1. Entreprises Nationales
F.1.1.4. Domestic Investment	..	4 975	3 366	7 609	7 589	7 535	..	..	F.1.1.4. Placement dans le Pays
F.1.1. Total	13 087	4 975	3 366	7 609	7 589	7 535	7 818	7 800	F.1.1. Total
F.1.2. Mortgage Loans									F.1.2. Prêts Hypothécaires
F.1.2.1. Domestic Companies	0	..	0	1 737	1 416	1 325	945	899	F.1.2.1. Entreprises Nationales
F.1.2.4. Domestic Investment	0	..	..	1 737	1 416	1 325	..	..	F.1.2.4. Placement dans le Pays
F.1.2. Total	0	..	..	1 737	..	1 325	945	899	F.1.2. Total
F.1.3. Shares									F.1.3. Actions
F.1.3.1. Domestic Companies	3 608	1 934	2 438	4 209	6 924	10 942	14 239	22 533	F.1.3.1. Entreprises Nationales
F.1.3.4. Domestic Investment	..	1 934	2 438	4 209	6 924	10 942	14 239	22 533	F.1.3.4. Placement dans le Pays
F.1.3. Total	3 608	1 934	2 438	4 209	6 924	10 942	14 239	22 533	F.1.3. Total
F.1.4. Bonds with Fixed Revenue									F.1.4. Obligations
F.1.4.1. Domestic Companies	10 023	6 006	..	..	..	..	0	0	F.1.4.1. Entreprises Nationales
F.1.4.4. Domestic Investment	..	6 006	..	..	..	..	0	0	F.1.4.4. Placement dans le Pays
F.1.4. Total	10 023	6 006	..	..	..	..	0	0	F.1.4. Total
F.1.5. Loans other than Mortgage Loans									F.1.5. Prêts Autres qu'Hypothécaires
F.1.5.1. Domestic Companies	77 535	3 584	14 266	17 987	23 960	32 015	40 753	46 268	F.1.5.1. Entreprises Nationales
F.1.5.4. Domestic Investment	..	3 584	14 266	17 987	23 960	32 015	..	..	F.1.5.4. Placement dans le Pays
F.1.5. Total	77 535	3 584	14 266	17 987	..	32 015	40 753	46 268	F.1.5. Total
F.1.6. Other Investments									F.1.6. Autres Placements
F.1.6.1. Domestic Companies	4 504	1 255	1 952	5	2 558	3 158	3 932	3 572	F.1.6.1. Entreprises Nationales
F.1.6.4. Domestic Investment	..	1 255	1 952	5	2 558	3 158	..	..	F.1.6.4. Placement dans le Pays
F.1.6. Total	4 504	1 255	1 952	5	..	3 158	3 932	3 572	F.1.6. Total

Monetary Unit: million markka — Unité monétaire : million de markkas

Label (EN) / Label (FR)	1992	1993	1994	1995	1996	1997	1998	1999
F.1.7. Total — F.1.7. Total								
F.1.7.1. Domestic Companies — F.1.7.1. Entreprises Nationales	108 757	17 754	22 022	31 547	42 447	54 975	67 687	81 072
F.1.7.4. Domestic Investment — F.1.7.4. Placement dans le Pays	108 757	17 754	22 022	31 547	42 447	54 975	67 687	81 072
F.1.7. Total of Life Investments — F.1.7. Total des Placements Vie	108 757	17 754	22 022	31 547	42 447	54 975	67 687	81 072
F.2. Non-Life — **F.2. Non-Vie**								
F.2.1. Real Estate — F.2.1. Immobilier								
F.2.1.1. Domestic Companies — F.2.1.1. Entreprises Nationales	5 997	6 376	4 517	8 299	7 214	8 103	7 371	6 937
F.2.1.3. Branches & Agencies of Foreign Cies — F.2.1.3. Succursales et Agences d'Ent. Etrangères	17	17	17	17	231	30	27	36
F.2.1.4. Domestic Investment — F.2.1.4. Placement dans le Pays	..	6 376	4 534	8 316	7 445	8 133	..	..
F.2.1.5. Foreign Investment — F.2.1.5. Placement à l' Etranger	17	17	..	..	..	..	..	..
F.2.1. Total — F.2.1. Total	6 014	6 393	4 534	8 316	..	..	7 398	6 973
F.2.2. Mortgage Loans — F.2.2. Prêts Hypothécaires								
F.2.2.1. Domestic Companies — F.2.2.1. Entreprises Nationales	0	..	0	1 221	1 019	983	485	531
F.2.2.3. Branches & Agencies of Foreign Cies — F.2.2.3. Succursales et Agences d'Ent. Etrangères	0	..	0	0	13	0	0	0
F.2.2.4. Domestic Investment — F.2.2.4. Placement dans le Pays	0	..	..	1 221	1 032	983	..	..
F.2.2. Total — F.2.2. Total	0	..	..	1 221	..	..	485	531
F.2.3. Shares — F.2.3. Actions								
F.2.3.1. Domestic Companies — F.2.3.1. Entreprises Nationales	3 396	4 401	5 506	8 177	9 460	13 201	15 379	27 228
F.2.3.3. Branches & Agencies of Foreign Cies — F.2.3.3. Succursales et Agences d'Ent. Etrangères	0	0	0	4	48	0	0	0
F.2.3.4. Domestic Investment — F.2.3.4. Placement dans le Pays	..	4 401	5 506	8 181	9 508	13 201	15 379	27 228
F.2.3. Total — F.2.3. Total	3 396	4 401	5 506	8 181	..	..	15 379	27 228
F.2.4. Bonds with Fixed Revenue — F.2.4. Obligations								
F.2.4.1. Domestic Companies — F.2.4.1. Entreprises Nationales	3 870	5 696	..	..	0	..	0	0
F.2.4.4. Domestic Investment — F.2.4.4. Placement dans le Pays	3 870	5 696	..	..	0	..	0	0
F.2.4. Total — F.2.4. Total	3 870	5 696	..	..	..	..	0	0
F.2.5. Loans other than Mortgage Loans — F.2.5. Prêts Autres qu'Hypothécaires								
F.2.5.1. Domestic Companies — F.2.5.1. Entreprises Nationales	7 847	6 072	14 890	13 663	11 293	13 757	15 623	21 552
F.2.5.3. Branches & Agencies of Foreign Cies — F.2.5.3. Succursales et Agences d'Ent. Etrangères	28	32	32	28	12	0	59	51
F.2.5.4. Domestic Investment — F.2.5.4. Placement dans le Pays	..	6 072	14 960	13 691	11 305	13 757	..	..
F.2.5.5. Foreign Investment — F.2.5.5. Placement à l' Etranger	..	32	0	..	..	..	..	..
F.2.5. Total — F.2.5. Total	7 875	6 104	14 922	13 691	..	..	15 682	21 603
F.2.6. Other Investments — F.2.6. Autres Placements								
F.2.6.1. Domestic Companies — F.2.6.1. Entreprises Nationales	1 713	1 298	1 204	338	6 420	1 580	1 979	3 349
F.2.6.3. Branches & Agencies of Foreign Cies — F.2.6.3. Succursales et Agences d'Ent. Etrangères	0	1	0	1	285	73	23	9
F.2.6.4. Domestic Investment — F.2.6.4. Placement dans le Pays	..	1 298	1 204	339	6 705	1 653	..	..
F.2.6.5. Foreign Investment — F.2.6.5. Placement à l' Etranger	..	1	..	..	..	..	..	..
F.2.6. Total — F.2.6. Total	1 713	1 299	1 204	339	..	..	2 002	3 358
F.2.7. Total — F.2.7. Total								
F.2.7.1. Domestic Companies — F.2.7.1. Entreprises Nationales	22 823	23 843	26 117	31 698	35 406	37 624	40 837	59 597
F.2.7.3. Branches & Agencies of Foreign Cies — F.2.7.3. Succursales et Agences d'Ent. Etrangères	45	50	49	50	589	103	109	96
F.2.7.4. Domestic Investment — F.2.7.4. Placement dans le Pays	..	23 843	26 166	31 748	35 995	37 727	..	..
F.2.7.5. Foreign Investment — F.2.7.5. Placement à l' Etranger	..	50	0	..	..	..	..	..
F.2.7. Total of Non-Life Investments — F.2.7. Total des Placements Non-Vie	22 868	23 893	26 166	31 748	35 995	..	40 946	59 693
G. BREAKDOWN OF NON-LIFE PREMIUMS — **G. VENTILATIONS DES PRIMES NON-VIE**								
G.1. Motor vehicle — G.1. Assurance Automobile								
G.1.1. Direct Business — G.1.1. Assurances Directes								
G.1.1.1. Gross Premiums — G.1.1.1. Primes Brutes	3 888	3 527	3 124	3 208	3 403	3 715	4 110	4 612
G.1.1.2. Ceded Premiums — G.1.1.2. Primes Cédées	..	..	0	56	60	65	65	76
G.1.1.3. Net Written Premiums — G.1.1.3. Primes Nettes Emises	..	..	0	3 152	3 343	3 650	4 045	4 536
G.1.3. Total — G.1.3. Total								
G.1.3.1. Gross Premiums — G.1.3.1. Primes Brutes	3 888	..	0	0	3 403	..	..	..
G.1.3.2. Ceded Premiums — G.1.3.2. Primes Cédées	..	..	0	0	60	..	..	..
G.1.3.3. Net Written Premiums — G.1.3.3. Primes Nettes Emises	..	..	0	0	3 343	..	..	..

Monetary Unit: million markka   Unité monétaire : million de markkas

	1992	1993	1994	1995	1996	1997	1998	1999
G.2. Marine, Aviation — G.2. Marine, Aviation								
G.2.1. Direct Business — G.2.1. Assurances Directes								
G.2.1.1. Gross Premiums — G.2.1.1. Primes Brutes	278	707	702	308	259	235	245	269
G.2.1.2. Ceded Premiums — G.2.1.2. Primes Cédées	..	..	..	109	172	1 226	61	137
G.2.1.3. Net Written Premiums — G.2.1.3. Primes Nettes Emises	..	..	..	199	87	109	184	132
G.2.3. Total — G.2.3. Total								
G.2.3.1. Gross Premiums — G.2.3.1. Primes Brutes	278	..	..	..	259	..	..	..
G.2.3.2. Ceded Premiums — G.2.3.2. Primes Cédées	..	..	..	..	172	..	..	..
G.2.3.3. Net Written Premiums — G.2.3.3. Primes Nettes Emises	..	..	..	..	87	..	..	..
G.3. Freight — G.3. Fret								
G.3.1. Direct Business — G.3.1. Assurances Directes								
G.3.1.1. Gross Premiums — G.3.1.1. Primes Brutes	323	..	..	372	355	365	355	343
G.3.1.2. Ceded Premiums — G.3.1.2. Primes Cédées	..	..	..	132	24	23	2	44
G.3.1.3. Net Written Premiums — G.3.1.3. Primes Nettes Emises	..	..	..	240	331	342	353	299
G.3.3. Total — G.3.3. Total								
G.3.3.1. Gross Premiums — G.3.3.1. Primes Brutes	323	..	..	..	355	..	..	..
G.3.3.2. Ceded Premiums — G.3.3.2. Primes Cédées	..	..	..	..	24	..	..	..
G.3.3.3. Net Written Premiums — G.3.3.3. Primes Nettes Emises	..	..	..	..	331	..	..	..
G.4. Fire, Property Damages — G.4. Incendie, Dommages aux Biens								
G.4.1. Direct Business — G.4.1. Assurances Directes								
G.4.1.1. Gross Premiums — G.4.1.1. Primes Brutes	2 698	3 025	2 959	2 968	2 902	2 943	3 016	3 073
G.4.1.2. Ceded Premiums — G.4.1.2. Primes Cédées	..	..	..	450	438	461	43	452
G.4.1.3. Net Written Premiums — G.4.1.3. Primes Nettes Emises	..	..	..	2 518	2 464	2 482	2 973	2 621
G.4.3. Total — G.4.3. Total								
G.4.3.1. Gross Premiums — G.4.3.1. Primes Brutes	2 698	..	..	..	2 902	..	..	..
G.4.3.2. Ceded Premiums — G.4.3.2. Primes Cédées	..	..	..	..	438	..	..	..
G.4.3.3. Net Written Premiums — G.4.3.3. Primes Nettes Emises	..	..	..	..	2 464	..	..	..
G.5. Pecuniary Losses — G.5. Pertes Pécunières								
G.5.1. Direct Business — G.5.1. Assurances Directes								
G.5.1.1. Gross Premiums — G.5.1.1. Primes Brutes	161	..	1 072	747	577	367	307	524
G.5.1.2. Ceded Premiums — G.5.1.2. Primes Cédées	..	..	..	54	44	41	173	195
G.5.1.3. Net Written Premiums — G.5.1.3. Primes Nettes Emises	..	..	..	693	533	326	134	329
G.5.3. Total — G.5.3. Total								
G.5.3.1. Gross Premiums — G.5.3.1. Primes Brutes	161	..	..	..	577	..	..	..
G.5.3.2. Ceded Premiums — G.5.3.2. Primes Cédées	..	..	..	..	44	..	..	..
G.5.3.3. Net Written Premiums — G.5.3.3. Primes Nettes Emises	..	..	..	..	533	..	..	..
G.6. General Liability — G.6. Responsabilité Générale								
G.6.1. Direct Business — G.6.1. Assurances Directes								
G.6.1.1. Gross Premiums — G.6.1.1. Primes Brutes	294	288	296	468	512	536	680	669
G.6.1.2. Ceded Premiums — G.6.1.2. Primes Cédées	..	..	..	93	89	98	41	129
G.6.1.3. Net Written Premiums — G.6.1.3. Primes Nettes Emises	..	..	..	375	423	438	639	540
G.6.3. Total — G.6.3. Total								
G.6.3.1. Gross Premiums — G.6.3.1. Primes Brutes	294	..	..	..	512	..	..	..
G.6.3.2. Ceded Premiums — G.6.3.2. Primes Cédées	..	..	..	..	89	..	..	..
G.6.3.3. Net Written Premiums — G.6.3.3. Primes Nettes Emises	..	..	..	..	423	..	..	..
G.7. Accident, Health — G.7. Accident, Santé								
G.7.1. Direct Business — G.7.1. Assurances Directes								
G.7.1.1. Gross Premiums — G.7.1.1. Primes Brutes	2 535	2 526	2 693	2 778	2 910	3 238	4 035	3 726
G.7.1.2. Ceded Premiums — G.7.1.2. Primes Cédées	..	..	..	101	98	85	12	15
G.7.1.3. Net Written Premiums — G.7.1.3. Primes Nettes Emises	..	..	..	2 677	2 812	3 153	4 023	3 711
G.7.3. Total — G.7.3. Total								
G.7.3.1. Gross Premiums — G.7.3.1. Primes Brutes	2 535	..	..	..	2 910	..	..	..
G.7.3.2. Ceded Premiums — G.7.3.2. Primes Cédées	..	..	..	..	98	..	..	..
G.7.3.3. Net Written Premiums — G.7.3.3. Primes Nettes Emises	..	..	..	..	2 812	..	..	..

Monetary Unit: million markka

Unité monétaire : million de markkas

	1992	1993	1994	1995	1996	1997	1998	1999
G.8. Others — G.8. Autres								
G.8.1. Direct Business — G.8.1. Assurances Directes								
G.8.1.1. Gross Premiums — G.8.1.1. Primes Brutes	766	1 385	427	374	412	395	464	174
G.8.1.2. Ceded Premiums — G.8.1.2. Primes Cédées				176	165	145	- 3	5
G.8.1.3. Net Written Premiums — G.8.1.3. Primes Nettes Emises				198	247	250	467	169
G.8.3. Total								
G.8.3.1. Gross Premiums — G.8.3.1. Primes Brutes	766				412	:	:	:
G.8.3.2. Ceded Premiums — G.8.3.2. Primes Cédées					165	:	:	:
G.8.3.3. Net Written Premiums — G.8.3.3. Primes Nettes Emises					247	:	:	:
G.9. Treaty Reinsurance — G.9. Réassurance Obligatoire								
G.9.1. Direct Business — G.9.1. Assurances Directes								
G.9.1.1. Gross Premiums — G.9.1.1. Primes Brutes	179				0	:	0	0
G.9.2. Reinsurance Accepted — G.9.2. Réassurance Acceptée								
G.9.2.1. Gross Premiums — G.9.2.1. Primes Brutes	1 775				1 216	971	1 019	917
G.9.2.2. Ceded Premiums — G.9.2.2. Primes Cédées					229	218	:	:
G.9.2.3. Net Written Premiums — G.9.2.3. Primes Nettes Emises					987	753	:	:
G.9.3. Total								
G.9.3.1. Gross Premiums — G.9.3.1. Primes Brutes	1 954				1 216	:	:	:
G.9.3.2. Ceded Premiums — G.9.3.2. Primes Cédées					229	:	:	:
G.9.3.3. Net Written Premiums — G.9.3.3. Primes Nettes Emises					987	:	:	:
G.10. Total								
G.10.1. Direct Business — G.10.1. Assurances Directes								
G.10.1.1. Gross Premiums — G.10.1.1. Primes Brutes	11 122	11 458	11 273	11 223	11 330	11 794	13 212	13 390
G.10.1.2. Ceded Premiums — G.10.1.2. Primes Cédées				1 171	1 090	1 044	394	1 053
G.10.1.3. Net Written Premiums — G.10.1.3. Primes Nettes Emises				10 052	10 240	10 750	12 818	12 337
G.10.2. Reinsurance Accepted — G.10.2. Réassurance Acceptée								
G.10.2.1. Gross Premiums — G.10.2.1. Primes Brutes	1 775				1 216	:	1 019	917
G.10.2.2. Ceded Premiums — G.10.2.2. Primes Cédées					229	:	:	:
G.10.2.3. Net Written Premiums — G.10.2.3. Primes Nettes Emises					987	:	:	:
G.10.3. Total								
G.10.3.1. Gross Premiums — G.10.3.1. Primes Brutes	12 897				12 546	:	:	:
G.10.3.2. Ceded Premiums — G.10.3.2. Primes Cédées	1 475				1 319	:	:	:
G.10.3.3. Net Written Premiums — G.10.3.3. Primes Nettes Emises	11 422				11 227	:	:	:
H. GROSS CLAIMS PAYMENTS — H. PAIEMENTS BRUTS DES SINISTRES								
H.1. Life — H.1. Vie								
H.1.1. Domestic Companies — H.1.1. Entreprises Nationales					2 661	3 260	4 197	5 500
H.1. Total — H.1. Total					2 661	3 260	4 197	5 500
H.2. Non-Life — H.2. Non-Vie								
H.2.1. Domestic Companies — H.2.1. Entreprises Nationales					10 260	10 828	10 500	10 787
H.2.3. Branches & Agencies of Foreign Cies — H.2.3. Succursales et Agences d'Ent. Etrangères					18	7	6	8
H.2. Total — H.2. Total					10 278	10 835	10 506	10 795
I. GROSS OPERATING EXPENSES — I. DEPENSES BRUITES D'EXPLOITATION								
I.1. Life — I.1. Vie								
I.1.1. Domestic Companies — I.1.1. Entreprises Nationales					766	844	795	908
I.1. Total — I.1. Total des Primes Nettes Vie					766	844	795	908
I.2. Non-Life — I.2. Non-Vie								
I.2.1. Domestic Companies — I.2.1. Entreprises Nationales					2 310	2 326	2 609	2 786
I.2.3. Branches & Agencies of Foreign Cies — I.2.3. Succursales et Agences d'Ent. Etrangères					4	6	12	15
I.2. Total — I.2. Total					2 314	2 332	2 621	2 801

Monetary Unit: million markka | Unité monétaire : million de markkas

J. COMMISSIONS / J. COMMISSIONS

J.1. Life / J.1. Vie

	1992	1993	1994	1995	1996	1997	1998	1999	
J.1.1. Direct Business									J.1.1. Assurance directe
J.1.1.1. Domestic Companies					158	177	131	180	J.1.1.1. Entreprises Nationales
J.1.1. Total					158	177	131	180	J.1.1. Total
J.1.2. Reinsurance Accepted									J.1.2. Réassurances acceptées
J.1.2.1. Domestic Companies					1	20	8	16	J.1.2.1. Entreprises Nationales
J.1.2. Total					1	20	8	16	J.1.2. Total
J.1.3. Total									J.1.3. Total
J.1.3.1. Domestic Companies					159	197	139	196	J.1.3.1. Entreprises Nationales
J.1.3. Total of Life Net Premiums					159	197	139	196	J.1.3. Total

J.2. Non-Life / J.2. Non-Vie

	1992	1993	1994	1995	1996	1997	1998	1999	
J.2.1. Direct Business									J.2.1. Assurance directe
J.2.1.1. Domestic Companies					170	111	106	388	J.2.1.1. Entreprises Nationales
J.2.1.3. Branches & Agencies of Foreign Cies					0	1	1	2	J.2.1.3. Succursales et Agences d'Ent. Etrangères
J.2.1. Total					170	112	107	390	J.2.1. Total des Primes Nettes Vie
J.2.2. Reinsurance Accepted									J.2.2. Réassurances acceptées
J.2.2.1. Domestic Companies					243	189	- 16	140	J.2.2.1. Entreprises Nationales
J.2.2.3. Branches & Agencies of Foreign Cies					1	1	- 0	- 3	J.2.2.3. Succursales et Agences d'Ent. Etrangères
J.2.2. Total					244	190	- 16	137	J.2.2. Total
J.2.3. Total									J.2.3. Total
J.2.3.1. Domestic Companies					413	300	90	528	J.2.3.1. Entreprises Nationales
J.2.3.3. Branches & Agencies of Foreign Cies					1	2	1	- 1	J.2.3.3. Succursales et Agences d'Ent. Etrangères
J.2.3. Total					414	302	91	527	J.2.3. Total

FRANCE

Monetary Unit: million French francs

Unité monétaire : million de francs français

	1992	1993	1994	1995	1996	1997	1998	1999
A. NUMBER OF COMPANIES IN THE REPORTING COUNTRY / **A. NOMBRE D'ENTREPRISES DANS LE PAYS DECLARANT**								
A.1. Life / **A.1. Vie**								
A.1.1. Domestic Companies / A.1.1. Entreprises Nationales	136	133	132	132	123	111	94	88
A.1.3. Branches & Agencies of Foreign Cies / A.1.3. Succursales et Agences d'Ent. Etrangères	11	10	6	5	5	5	4	4
A.1. All Companies / A.1. Ensemble des Entreprises	147	143	138	137	128	116	98	92
A.2. Non-Life / **A.2. Non-Vie**								
A.2.1. Domestic Companies / A.2.1. Entreprises Nationales	333	352	333	329	327	298	295	288
A.2.3. Branches & Agencies of Foreign Cies / A.2.3. Succursales et Agences d'Ent. Etrangères	134	114	23	16	16	14	12	12
A.2. All Companies / A.2. Ensemble des Entreprises	467	466	356	345	343	312	307	300
A.3. Composite / **A.3. Mixte**								
A.3.1. Domestic Companies / A.3.1. Entreprises Nationales	..	0	0	1	14	22	33	34
A.3. All Companies / A.3. Ensemble des Entreprises	..	..	0	1	14	22	33	34
A.4. Reinsurance / **A.4. Réassurance**								
A.4.1. Domestic Companies / A.4.1. Entreprises Nationales	20	21	20	21	22	26	28	33
A.4. All Companies / A.4. Ensemble des Entreprises	20	21	20	21	22	26	28	33
A.5. Total / **A.5. Total**								
A.5.1. Domestic Companies / A.5.1. Entreprises Nationales	489	506	485	483	486	457	450	443
A.5.3. Branches & Agencies of Foreign Cies / A.5.3. Succursales et Agences d'Ent. Etrangères	145	124	29	21	21	19	16	16
A.5. All Insurance Companies / A.5. Ensemble des Entreprises d'Assurances	634	630	514	504	507	476	466	459
B. NUMBER OF EMPLOYEES / **B. NOMBRE D'EMPLOYES**								
B.1. Insurance Companies / B.1. Entreprises d'Assurances	123 800	122 000	122 000	122 000	135 400	133 100	132 050	132 300
B.2. Intermediaries / B.2. Intermediaries	89 800	89 100	75 200	75 200	74 900	74 700	71 180	69 600
B. Total	213 600	211 100	197 200	197 200	210 300	207 800	203 230	201 900
C. BUSINESS WRITTEN IN THE REPORTING COUNTRY / **C. OPERATIONS CONCLUES DANS LE PAYS DECLARANT**								
C.1. Life / **C.1. Vie**								
C.1.1. Gross Premiums / C.1.1. Primes Brutes								
C.1.1.1. Direct Business / C.1.1.1. Assurances Directes								
C.1.1.1.1. Domestic Companies / C.1.1.1.1. Entreprises Nationales	258 148	319 769	382 305	415 105	463 734	514 104	424 553	487 493
C.1.1.1.3. Branches & Agencies of Foreign Cies / C.1.1.1.3. Succursales et Agences d'Ent. Etrangères	5 303	5 328	4 037	4 311	4 902	4 991	4 346	5 150
C.1.1.1. Total / C.1.1.1. Total	263 451	325 097	386 342	419 416	468 636	519 095	428 889	492 643
C.1.1.2. Reinsurance Accepted / C.1.1.2. Réassurance Acceptée								
C.1.1.2.1. Domestic Companies / C.1.1.2.1. Entreprises Nationales	9 940	10 175	10 445	11 513	8 290	8 239	8 264	8 758
C.1.1.2.3. Branches & Agencies of Foreign Cies / C.1.1.2.3. Succursales et Agences d'Ent. Etrangères	9	197	211	0	16	42	5	46
C.1.1.2. Total / C.1.1.2. Total	9 949	10 372	10 656	11 513	8 306	8 281	8 269	8 804
C.1.1.3. Total / C.1.1.3. Total								
C.1.1.3.1. Domestic Companies / C.1.1.3.1. Entreprises Nationales	268 088	329 944	392 750	426 618	472 024	522 343	432 817	496 251
C.1.1.3.2. (Foreign Controlled Companies) / C.1.1.3.2. (Entreprises Sous Contrôle Etranger)	12 890							
C.1.1.3.3. Branches & Agencies of Foreign Cies / C.1.1.3.3. Succursales et Agences d'Ent. Etrangères	5 312	5 525	4 248	4 311	4 918	5 033	4 351	5 196
C.1.1.3. Total Gross Premiums / C.1.1.3. Total des Primes Brutes	273 400	335 469	396 998	430 929	476 942	527 376	437 168	501 446
C.1.2. Ceded Premiums / C.1.2. Primes Cédées								
C.1.2.1. Domestic Companies / C.1.2.1. Entreprises Nationales	9 993	9 922	10 957	13 387	10 353	12 378	12 068	13 684
C.1.2.3. Branches & Agencies of Foreign Cies / C.1.2.3. Succursales et Agences d'Ent. Etrangères	295	389	327	388	406	392	444	446
C.1.2. Total / C.1.2. Total	10 288	10 311	11 284	13 775	10 759	12 770	12 512	14 130
C.1.3. Net Written Premiums / C.1.3. Primes Nettes Emises								
C.1.3.1. Domestic Companies / C.1.3.1. Entreprises Nationales	258 095	320 022	381 793	413 231	461 671	509 965	420 749	246 544
C.1.3.3. Branches & Agencies of Foreign Cies / C.1.3.3. Succursales et Agences d'Ent. Etrangères	5 017	5 136	3 921	3 923	4 512	4 641	3 907	4 749
C.1.3. Total / C.1.3. Total	263 112	325 158	385 714	417 154	466 183	514 606	424 656	487 316

FRANCE

Monetary Unit: million French francs

Unité monétaire : million de francs français

C.2. Non-Life — C.2. Non-Vie

	1992	1993	1994	1995	1996	1997	1998	1999
C.2.1. Gross premiums — Primes Brutes								
C.2.1.1. Direct Business — Assurances Directes								
C.2.1.1.1. Domestic Companies — Entreprises Nationales	197 163	208 698	221 450	234 048	242 630	242 440	244 158	248 526
C.2.1.1.3. Branches & Agencies of Foreign Cies — Succursales et Agences d'Ent. Etrangères	6 656	7 059	3 514	3 404	3 541	3 521	3 493	3 044
C.2.1.1. Total	203 819	215 757	224 964	237 452	246 171	245 961	247 651	251 569
C.2.1.2. Reinsurance Accepted — Réassurance Acceptée								
C.2.1.2.1. Domestic Companies — Entreprises Nationales	48 950	56 000	40 045	40 850	40 589	39 960	38 542	42 056
C.2.1.2.3. Branches & Agencies of Foreign Cies — Succursales et Agences d'Ent. Etrangères	298	365	70	77	54	29	20	20
C.2.1.2. Total	49 248	56 365	40 115	40 927	40 643	39 989	38 562	42 076
C.2.1.3. Total								
C.2.1.3.1. Domestic Companies — Entreprises Nationales	246 113	264 698	261 495	274 898	283 219	282 400	282 700	290 582
C.2.1.3.2. (Foreign Controlled Companies) — (Entreprises Sous Contrôle Etranger)	39 320							
C.2.1.3.3. Branches & Agencies of Foreign Cies — Succursales et Agences d'Ent. Etrangères	6 954	7 424	3 584	3 481	3 595	3 550	3 513	3 064
C.2.1.3. Total Gross Premiums — Total des Primes Brutes	253 067	272 122	265 079	278 379	286 814	285 950	286 213	293 645
C.2.2. Ceded Premiums — Primes Cédées								
C.2.2.1. Domestic Companies — Entreprises Nationales	38 050	38 910	43 683	45 600	46 036	43 392	40 486	44 037
C.2.2.3. Branches & Agencies of Foreign Cies — Succursales et Agences d'Ent. Etrangères	1 984	2 315	645	451	489	513	769	157
C.2.2. Total	40 034	41 225	44 328	46 051	46 525	43 905	41 255	44 195
C.2.3. Net Written Premiums — Primes Nettes Emises								
C.2.3.1. Domestic Companies — Entreprises Nationales	208 063	225 788	217 812	229 298	237 183	239 008	242 214	246 544
C.2.3.3. Branches & Agencies of Foreign Cies — Succursales et Agences d'Ent. Etrangères	4 970	5 109	2 939	3 030	3 106	3 037	2 744	2 906
C.2.3. Total	213 033	230 897	220 751	232 328	240 289	242 045	244 958	249 451

C.3. Total

	1992	1993	1994	1995	1996	1997	1998	1999
C.3.1. Gross Premiums — Primes Brutes								
C.3.1.1. Direct Business — Assurances Directes								
C.3.1.1.1. Domestic Companies — Entreprises Nationales	455 311	528 467	603 755	649 153	706 364	756 544	668 711	736 019
C.3.1.1.3. Branches & Agencies of Foreign Cies — Succursales et Agences d'Ent. Etrangères	11 959	12 387	7 551	7 715	8 443	8 512	7 839	8 193
C.3.1.1. Total	467 270	540 854	611 306	656 868	714 807	765 056	676 550	744 212
C.3.1.2. Reinsurance Accepted — Réassurance Acceptée								
C.3.1.2.1. Domestic Companies — Entreprises Nationales	58 890	66 175	50 490	52 363	48 879	48 199	46 806	50 814
C.3.1.2.3. Branches & Agencies of Foreign Cies — Succursales et Agences d'Ent. Etrangères	307	562	281	77	70	71	25	66
C.3.1.2. Total	59 197	66 737	50 771	52 440	48 949	48 270	46 831	50 879
C.3.1.3. Total								
C.3.1.3.1. Domestic Companies — Entreprises Nationales	514 201	594 642	654 245	701 516	755 243	804 743	715 517	786 833
C.3.1.3.2. (Foreign Controlled Companies) — (Entreprises Sous Contrôle Etranger)	52 210							
C.3.1.3.3. Branches & Agencies of Foreign Cies — Succursales et Agences d'Ent. Etrangères	12 266	12 949	7 832	7 792	8 513	8 583	7 864	8 259
C.3.1.3. Total Gross Premiums — Total des Primes Brutes	526 467	607 591	662 077	709 308	763 756	813 326	723 381	795 092
C.3.2. Ceded Premiums — Primes Cédées								
C.3.2.1. Domestic Companies — Entreprises Nationales	48 043	48 832	54 640	58 987	56 389	55 770	52 554	57 721
C.3.2.3. Branches & Agencies of Foreign Cies — Succursales et Agences d'Ent. Etrangères	2 279	2 704	972	839	895	905	1 213	604
C.3.2. Total	50 322	51 536	55 612	59 826	57 284	56 675	53 767	58 325
C.3.3. Net Written Premiums — Primes Nettes Emises								
C.3.3.1. Domestic Companies — Entreprises Nationales	466 158	545 810	599 605	642 529	698 854	748 973	662 963	493 089
C.3.3.3. Branches & Agencies of Foreign Cies — Succursales et Agences d'Ent. Etrangères	9 987	10 245	6 860	6 953	7 618	7 678	6 651	7 656
C.3.3. Total	476 145	556 055	606 465	649 482	706 472	756 651	669 614	736 767

E. BUSINESS WRITTEN ABROAD — E. OPERATIONS A L'ETRANGER

E.1. Life — E.1. Vie

	1992	1993	1994	1995	1996	1997	1998	1999
E.1.1. Gross Premiums — Primes Brutes								
E.1.1.1. Direct Business — Assurance Directe								
E.1.1.1.1. Branches & Agencies — Succursales & Agences	636	484	563	1 117	618	446	251	243
E.1.1.1.2. Subsidiaries — Filliales	70 719	104 976	102 556	:	:	:	:	:
E.1.1.1. Total	71 355	105 460	103 119	:	:	:	:	:

Monetary Unit: million French francs — Unité monétaire : million de francs français

	1992	1993	1994	1995	1996	1997	1998	1999	
E.1.1.2. Reinsurance Accepted									E.1.1.2. Réassurance Acceptée
E.1.1.2.1. Branches & Agencies	4	191	154	7	2	2	0	..	E.1.1.1.2. Succursales & Agences
E.1.1.3. Total									E.1.1.3. Total
E.1.1.3.1. Branches & Agencies	640	675	717	1 124	620	448	251	243	E.1.1.3.1. Succursales & Agences
E.1.2. Ceded Premiums									E.1.2. Primes Cédées
E.1.2.1. Branches & Agencies	56	46	32	37	43	12	3	..	E.1.2.1. Succursales & Agences
E.1.3. Net Written Premiums									E.1.3. Primes Nettes Emises
E.1.3.1. Branches & Agencies	584	629	685	1 087	577	436	248	243	E.1.3.1. Succursales & Agences
E.2. Non-Life									**E.2. Non-Vie**
E.2.1. Gross Premiums									E.2.1. Primes Brutes
E.2.1.1. Direct Business									E.2.1.1. Assurance Directe
E.2.1.1.1. Branches & Agencies	6 009	7 107	6 476	6 679	6 023	5 880	4 914	5 904	E.2.1.1.1. Succursales & Agences
E.2.1.1.2. Subsidiaries	71 572	76 305	74 732	..	..	..	..	..	E.2.1.1.2. Filliales
E.2.1.1. Total	77 581	83 412	81 208	..	..	..	..	..	E.2.1.1. Total
E.2.1.2. Reinsurance Accepted									E.2.1.2. Réassurance Acceptée
E.2.1.2.1. Branches & Agencies	1 773	1 848	1 781	428	894	865	1 220	958	E.2.1.2.1. Succursales & Agences
E.2.1.2.2. Subsidiaries	18 917	25 990	11 817	..	..	..	..	..	E.2.1.2.2. Filliales
E.2.1.2. Total	20 690	27 838	13 598	..	..	..	..	..	E.2.1.2. Total
E.2.1.3. Total									E.2.1.3. Total
E.2.1.3.1. Branches & Agencies	7 782	8 955	8 257	7 107	6 917	6 745	6 134	6 862	E.2.1.3.1. Succursales & Agences
E.2.1.3.2. Subsidiaries	90 489	102 295	86 549	..	..	..	..	..	E.2.1.3.2. Filliales
E.2.1.3. Total Gross Premiums	98 271	111 250	94 806	..	..	..	..	..	E.2.1.3. Total des Primes Brutes
E.2.2. Ceded Premiums									E.2.2. Primes Cédées
E.2.2.1. Branches & Agencies	3 428	3 782	3 596	3 527	3 653	3 777	3 623	4 080	E.2.2.1. Succursales & Agences
E.2.3. Net Written Premiums									E.2.3. Primes Nettes Emises
E.2.3.1. Branches & Agencies	4 354	5 173	4 661	3 580	3 264	2 968	2 511	2 781	E.2.3.1. Succursales & Agences
F. OUTSTANDING INVESTMENT BY DIRECT INSURANCE COMPANIES									**F. ENCOURS DES PLACEMENTS DES ENTREPRISES D'ASSURANCES DIRECTES**
F.1. Life									**F.1. Vie**
F.1.1. Real Estate									F.1.1. Immobilier
F.1.1.1. Domestic Companies	137 324	150 215	151 878	..	..	..	..	..	F.1.1.1. Entreprises Nationales
F.1.1.3. Branches & Agencies of Foreign Cies	3 930	4 081	2 332	..	..	..	..	..	F.1.1.3. Succursales et Agences d'Ent. Etrangères
F.1.1.4. Domestic Investment	141 254	154 296	154 210	..	..	..	..	..	F.1.1.4. Placement dans le Pays
F.1.1.5. Foreign Investment	276	279	269	..	..	..	..	..	F.1.1.5. Placement à l' Etranger
F.1.1. Total	141 530	154 575	154 479	142 933	142 338	128 580	137 677	141 880	F.1.1. Total
F.1.2. Mortgage Loans									F.1.2. Prêts Hypothécaires
F.1.2. Total	..	..	..	4 310	3 967	1 898	1 711	1 555	F.1.2. Total
F.1.3. Shares									F.1.3. Actions
F.1.3.1. Domestic Companies	264 585	307 198	366 170	..	..	..	..	..	F.1.3.1. Entreprises Nationales
F.1.3.3. Branches & Agencies of Foreign Cies	5 995	6 863	4 603	..	..	..	..	..	F.1.3.3. Succursales et Agences d'Ent. Etrangères
F.1.3.4. Domestic Investment	270 580	314 061	370 773	..	..	..	..	..	F.1.3.4. Placement dans le Pays
F.1.3.5. Foreign Investment	668	933	1 718	..	..	..	..	..	F.1.3.5. Placement à l' Etranger
F.1.3. Total	271 248	314 994	372 491	300 294	355 194	487 259	649 505	926 475	F.1.3. Total
F.1.4. Bonds with Fixed Revenue									F.1.4. Obligations
F.1.4.1. Domestic Companies	854 319	1 064 655	1 310 595	..	..	..	..	..	F.1.4.1. Entreprises Nationales
F.1.4.3. Branches & Agencies of Foreign Cies	15 774	17 619	16 695	..	..	..	..	..	F.1.4.3. Succursales et Agences d'Ent. Etrangères
F.1.4.4. Domestic Investment	870 093	1 082 274	1 327 290	..	..	..	..	..	F.1.4.4. Placement dans le Pays
F.1.4.5. Foreign Investment	1 616	3 195	6 486	..	..	..	..	..	F.1.4.5. Placement à l' Etranger
F.1.4. Total	871 709	1 085 469	1 333 776	1 681 078	2 107 976	2 469 365	2 679 397	2 894 167	F.1.4. Total
F.1.5. Loans other than Mortgage Loans									F.1.5. Prêts Autres qu'Hypothécaires
F.1.5.1. Domestic Companies	44 206	58 506	56 544	..	..	..	..	..	F.1.5.1. Entreprises Nationales
F.1.5.3. Branches & Agencies of Foreign Cies	689	629	331	..	..	..	..	..	F.1.5.3. Succursales et Agences d'Ent. Etrangères
F.1.5.4. Domestic Investment	44 895	59 135	56 875	..	..	..	..	..	F.1.5.4. Placement dans le Pays
F.1.5.5. Foreign Investment	180	73	47	..	..	..	..	..	F.1.5.5. Placement à l' Etranger
F.1.5. Total	45 075	59 208	56 922	44 153	57 472	66 552	61 299	54 848	F.1.5. Total

Monetary Unit: million French francs

Unité monétaire : million de francs français

English label	1992	1993	1994	1995	1996	1997	1998	1999	French label
F.1.6. Other Investments									**F.1.6. Autres Placements**
F.1.6.1. Domestic Companies	62 027	78 316	82 456	:	:	:	:	:	F.1.6.1. Entreprises Nationales
F.1.6.3. Branches & Agencies of Foreign Cies	1 156	918	1 097	:	:	:	:	:	F.1.6.3. Succursales et Agences d'Ent. Etrangères
F.1.6.4. Domestic Investment	63 183	79 234	83 553	:	:	:	:	:	F.1.6.4. Placement dans le Pays
F.1.6.5. Foreign Investment	1 785	1 849	988	:	:	:	:	:	F.1.6.5. Placement à l'Etranger
F.1.6. Total	64 968	81 083	84 541	52 305	55 935	54 582	56 793	57 780	F.1.6. Total
F.1.7. Total									**F.1.7. Total**
F.1.7.1. Domestic Companies	1 362 461	1 658 890	1 967 643	:	:	:	:	:	F.1.7.1. Entreprises Nationales
F.1.7.3. Branches & Agencies of Foreign Cies	27 544	30 110	25 058	:	:	:	:	:	F.1.7.3. Succursales et Agences d'Ent. Etrangères
F.1.7.4. Domestic Investment	1 390 005	1 689 000	1 992 700	:	:	:	:	:	F.1.7.4. Placement dans le Pays
F.1.7.5. Foreign Investment	4 525	6 309	9 508	:	:	:	:	:	F.1.7.5. Placement à l'Etranger
F.1.7. Total of Life Investments	1 394 530	1 695 329	2 002 208	2 225 073	2 722 882	3 208 236	3 586 382	4 076 705	F.1.7. Total des Placements Vie
F.2. Non-Life									**F.2. Non-Vie**
F.2.1. Real Estate									**F.2.1. Immobilier**
F.2.1.1. Domestic Companies	68 189	71 553	79 663	:	:	:	:	:	F.2.1.1. Entreprises Nationales
F.2.1.3. Branches & Agencies of Foreign Cies	1 772	1 811	1 348	:	:	:	:	:	F.2.1.3. Succursales et Agences d'Ent. Etrangères
F.2.1.4. Domestic Investment	69 961	73 364	81 011	:	:	:	:	:	F.2.1.4. Placement dans le Pays
F.2.1.5. Foreign Investment	709	689	528	:	:	:	:	:	F.2.1.5. Placement à l'Etranger
F.2.1. Total	70 670	74 053	81 539	66 133	65 221	64 317	61 529	62 582	F.2.1. Total
F.2.2. Mortgage Loans									**F.2.2. Prêts Hypothécaires**
F.2.2. Total	:	:	:	1 014	886	593	359	328	F.2.2. Total
F.2.3. Shares									**F.2.3. Actions**
F.2.3.1. Domestic Companies	128 681	137 029	147 578	:	:	:	:	:	F.2.3.1. Entreprises Nationales
F.2.3.3. Branches & Agencies of Foreign Cies	3 243	3 349	2 249	:	:	:	:	:	F.2.3.3. Succursales et Agences d'Ent. Etrangères
F.2.3.4. Domestic Investment	131 924	140 378	149 827	:	:	:	:	:	F.2.3.4. Placement dans le Pays
F.2.3.5. Foreign Investment	3 285	4 252	3 980	:	:	:	:	:	F.2.3.5. Placement à l'Etranger
F.2.3. Total	135 209	144 630	153 807	133 965	136 668	147 013	170 046	190 719	F.2.3. Total
F.2.4. Bonds with Fixed Revenue									**F.2.4. Obligations**
F.2.4.1. Domestic Companies	160 138	167 786	184 873	:	:	:	:	:	F.2.4.1. Entreprises Nationales
F.2.4.3. Branches & Agencies of Foreign Cies	5 843	6 385	3 144	:	:	:	:	:	F.2.4.3. Succursales et Agences d'Ent. Etrangères
F.2.4.4. Domestic Investment	165 981	174 171	188 017	:	:	:	:	:	F.2.4.4. Placement dans le Pays
F.2.4.5. Foreign Investment	3 373	3 908	3 934	:	:	:	:	:	F.2.4.5. Placement à l'Etranger
F.2.4. Total	169 354	178 079	191 951	198 125	230 279	267 595	280 010	297 680	F.2.4. Total
F.2.5. Loans other than Mortgage Loans									**F.2.5. Prêts Autres qu'Hypothécaires**
F.2.5.1. Domestic Companies	13 509	12 522	10 462	:	:	:	:	:	F.2.5.1. Entreprises Nationales
F.2.5.3. Branches & Agencies of Foreign Cies	356	291	100	:	:	:	:	:	F.2.5.3. Succursales et Agences d'Ent. Etrangères
F.2.5.4. Domestic Investment	13 865	12 813	10 562	:	:	:	:	:	F.2.5.4. Placement dans le Pays
F.2.5.5. Foreign Investment	335	334	303	:	:	:	:	:	F.2.5.5. Placement à l'Etranger
F.2.5. Total	14 200	13 147	10 865	9 671	11 418	12 486	11 567	13 678	F.2.5. Total
F.2.6. Other Investments									**F.2.6. Autres Placements**
F.2.6.1. Domestic Companies	44 778	50 476	51 088	:	:	:	:	:	F.2.6.1. Entreprises Nationales
F.2.6.3. Branches & Agencies of Foreign Cies	550	686	391	:	:	:	:	:	F.2.6.3. Succursales et Agences d'Ent. Etrangères
F.2.6.4. Domestic Investment	45 328	51 162	51 479	:	:	:	:	:	F.2.6.4. Placement dans le Pays
F.2.6.5. Foreign Investment	3 920	4 126	4 243	:	:	:	:	:	F.2.6.5. Placement à l'Etranger
F.2.6. Total	49 246	55 288	55 722	29 407	35 203	30 234	27 222	29 166	F.2.6. Total
F.2.7. Total									**F.2.7. Total**
F.2.7.1. Domestic Companies	415 295	439 366	473 664	:	:	:	:	:	F.2.7.1. Entreprises Nationales
F.2.7.3. Branches & Agencies of Foreign Cies	11 764	12 522	7 232	:	:	:	:	:	F.2.7.3. Succursales et Agences d'Ent. Etrangères
F.2.7.4. Domestic Investment	427 057	451 888	480 896	:	:	:	:	:	F.2.7.4. Placement dans le Pays
F.2.7.5. Foreign Investment	11 622	13 309	12 988	:	:	:	:	:	F.2.7.5. Placement à l'Etranger
F.2.7. Total of Non-Life Investments	438 679	465 197	493 884	438 315	479 675	522 238	550 733	594 152	F.2.7. Total des Placements Non-Vie
G. BREAKDOWN OF NON-LIFE PREMIUMS									**G. VENTILATIONS DES PRIMES NON-VIE**
G.1. Motor vehicle									**G.1. Assurance Automobile**
G.1.1. Direct Business									**G.1.1. Assurances Directes**
G.1.1.1. Gross Premiums	73 489	77 714	82 494	89 212	92 340	92 444	91 152	92 450	G.1.1.1. Primes Brutes
G.1.1.2. Ceded Premiums	4 110	4 522	5 021	7 220	7 444	7 018	6 625	6 973	G.1.1.2. Primes Cédées
G.1.1.3. Net Written Premiums	69 379	73 192	77 473	81 992	84 896	85 426	84 527	85 477	G.1.1.3. Primes Nettes Emises

Monetary Unit: million French francs — Unité monétaire : million de francs français

	1992	1993	1994	1995	1996	1997	1998	1999	
G.2. Marine, Aviation									G.2. Marine, Aviation
G.2.1. Direct Business									G.2.1. Assurances Directes
G.2.1.1. Gross Premiums	8 215	5 089	9 257	9 838	9 205	6 601	4 238	4 979	G.2.1.1. Primes Brutes
G.2.1.2. Ceded Premiums	4 152	4 353	4 538	4 926	4 628	3 499	2 046	2 604	G.2.1.2. Primes Cédées
G.2.1.3. Net Written Premiums	4 063	1 736	4 719	4 912	4 577	3 102	2 192	2 375	G.2.1.3. Primes Nettes Emises
G.3. Freight									G.3. Fret
G.3.1. Direct Business									G.3.1. Assurances Directes
G.3.1.1. Gross Premiums	..	3 142	..	..	..	2 227	2 431	2 257	G.3.1.1. Primes Brutes
G.3.1.2. Ceded Premiums	..		..	..	..	1 180	1 201	1 187	G.3.1.2. Primes Cédées
G.3.1.3. Net Written Premiums	..	3 142	..	..	..	1 047	1 230	1 069	G.3.1.3. Primes Nettes Emises
G.4. Fire, Property Damages									G.4. Incendie, Dommages aux Biens
G.4.1. Direct Business									G.4.1. Assurances Directes
G.4.1.1. Gross Premiums	53 076	56 480	57 568	61 995	65 040	65 337	64 515	64 649	G.4.1.1. Primes Brutes
G.4.1.2. Ceded Premiums	12 575	13 539	13 538	15 321	15 900	14 117	13 130	13 422	G.4.1.2. Primes Cédées
G.4.1.3. Net Written Premiums	40 501	42 941	44 030	46 674	49 140	51 220	51 385	51 227	G.4.1.3. Primes Nettes Emises
G.5. Pecuniary Losses									G.5. Pertes Pécunières
G.5.1. Direct Business									G.5.1. Assurances Directes
G.5.1.1. Gross Premiums	3 119	3 446	..	..	..	4 000	8 972	9 420	G.5.1.1. Primes Brutes
G.5.1.2. Ceded Premiums	..		..	..	..	1 836	1 888	1 889	G.5.1.2. Primes Cédées
G.5.1.3. Net Written Premiums	..	3 446	..	..	..	2 164	7 084	7 531	G.5.1.3. Primes Nettes Emises
G.6. General Liability									G.6. Responsabilité Générale
G.6.1. Direct Business									G.6.1. Assurances Directes
G.6.1.1. Gross Premiums	11 830	11 840	11 756	12 827	14 022	14 700	14 853	15 508	G.6.1.1. Primes Brutes
G.6.1.2. Ceded Premiums	1 657	1 947	1 795	2 137	2 409	2 586	2 640	2 591	G.6.1.2. Primes Cédées
G.6.1.3. Net Written Premiums	10 173	9 893	9 961	10 690	11 613	12 114	12 213	12 917	G.6.1.3. Primes Nettes Emises
G.7. Accident, Health									G.7. Accident, Santé
G.7.1. Direct Business									G.7.1. Assurances Directes
G.7.1.1. Gross Premiums	43 581	45 776	48 051	49 900	51 601	54 287	55 293	55 976	G.7.1.1. Primes Brutes
G.7.1.2. Ceded Premiums	4 877	5 416	6 092	7 120	7 362	7 155	7 485	8 088	G.7.1.2. Primes Cédées
G.7.1.3. Net Written Premiums	38 704	40 360	41 959	42 780	44 239	47 132	47 808	47 888	G.7.1.3. Primes Nettes Emises
G.8. Others									G.8. Autres
G.8.1. Direct Business									G.8.1. Assurances Directes
G.8.1.1. Gross Premiums	13 628	11 270	15 838	13 680	13 963	6 365	6 197	6 330	G.8.1.1. Primes Brutes
G.8.1.2. Ceded Premiums	3 210	3 179	3 204	2 735	2 541	924	1 177	1 207	G.8.1.2. Primes Cédées
G.8.1.3. Net Written Premiums	10 418	8 091	12 634	10 945	11 422	5 441	5 020	5 123	G.8.1.3. Primes Nettes Emises
G.10. Total									G.10. Total
G.10.1. Direct Business									G.10.1. Assurances Directes
G.10.1.1. Gross Premiums	203 819	215 757	224 964	237 452	246 171	245 961	247 651	251 569	G.10.1.1. Primes Brutes
G.10.1.2. Ceded Premiums	30 581	32 956	34 188	39 459	40 284	38 315	36 192	37 963	G.10.1.2. Primes Cédées
G.10.1.3. Net Written Premiums	173 238	182 801	190 776	197 993	205 887	207 646	211 459	213 607	G.10.1.3. Primes Nettes Emises
G.10.2. Reinsurance Accepted									G.10.2. Réassurance Acceptée
G.10.2.1. Gross Premiums	49 248	56 365	40 115	40 927	40 643	39 989	38 562	42 076	G.10.2.1. Primes Brutes
G.10.2.2. Ceded Premiums	9 453	8 269	10 140	6 592	6 241	5 590	5 063	6 232	G.10.2.2. Primes Cédées
G.10.2.3. Net Written Premiums	39 795	48 096	29 975	34 335	34 402	34 399	33 499	35 844	G.10.2.3. Primes Nettes Emises
G.10.3. Total									G.10.3. Total
G.10.3.1. Gross Premiums	253 067	272 122	265 079	278 379	286 814	385 950	286 213	293 645	G.10.3.1. Primes Brutes
G.10.3.2. Ceded Premiums	40 034	41 225	44 328	46 051	46 525	43 905	41 255	44 195	G.10.3.2. Primes Cédées
G.10.3.3. Net Written Premiums	213 033	230 897	220 751	232 328	240 289	242 045	244 958	249 451	G.10.3.3. Primes Nettes Emises

H. GROSS CLAIMS PAYMENTS — **H. PAIEMENTS BRUTS DES SINISTRES**

H.1. Life — **H.1. Vie**

	1992	1993	1994	1995	1996	1997	1998	1999	
H.1.1. Domestic Companies		137 381	162 694	191 744	193 424	206 066	245 202	269 222	H.1.1. Entreprises Nationales
H.1.3. Branches & Agencies of Foreign Cies		2 631	2 951	3 347	3 322	3 225	2 243	3 785	H.1.3. Succursales et Agences d'Ent. Etrangères
H.1. Total		140 012	165 645	195 091	196 746	209 291	247 445	273 008	H.1. Total

H.2. Non-Life — **H.2. Non-Vie**

	1992	1993	1994	1995	1996	1997	1998	1999	
H.2.1. Domestic Companies		184 368	187 835	193 781	196 692	206 832	210 268	205 426	H.2.1. Entreprises Nationales
H.2.3. Branches & Agencies of Foreign Cies		2 995	2 566	2 523	2 395	2 429	2 371	2 132	H.2.3. Succursales et Agences d'Ent. Etrangères
H.2. Total		187 363	190 401	196 304	199 087	209 261	212 639	207 558	H.2. Total

FRANCE

Monetary Unit: million French francs

Unité monétaire : million de francs français

I. GROSS OPERATING EXPENSES — I. DEPENSES BRUTES D'EXPLOITATION

	1992	1993	1994	1995	1996	1997	1998	1999	
I.1. Life									**I.1. Vie**
I.1.1. Domestic Companies		21 317	21 834	10 590	11 257	12 134	13 767	13 350	I.1.1. Entreprises Nationales
I.1.3. Branches & Agencies of Foreign Cies		560	464	254	254	255	243	302	I.1.3. Succursales et Agences d'Ent. Etrangères
I.1. Total		21 877	22 298	10 844	11 511	12 389	14 010	13 651	I.1. Total des Primes Nettes Vie
I.2. Non-Life									**I.2. Non-Vie**
I.2.1. Domestic Companies		38 179	41 033	23 619	24 209	24 347	25 902	24 666	I.2.1. Entreprises Nationales
I.2.3. Branches & Agencies of Foreign Cies		927	817	362	372	285	328	335	I.2.3. Succursales et Agences d'Ent. Etrangères
I.2. Total		39 106	41 850	23 981	24 581	24 632	26 230	25 000	I.2. Total
J. COMMISSIONS									**J. COMMISSIONS**
J.1. Life									**J.1. Vie**
J.1.1. Direct Business									J.1.1. Assurance directe
J.1.1.1. Domestic Companies		10 429	12 134	23 336	24 526	25 972	25 419	27 506	J.1.1.1. Entreprises Nationales
J.1.1.3. Branches & Agencies of Foreign Cies		119	264	358	340	363	315	289	J.1.1.3. Succursales et Agences d'Ent. Etrangères
J.1.1. Total		10 548	12 398	23 694	24 866	26 335	25 734	27 795	J.1.1. Total
J.1.2. Reinsurance Accepted									J.1.2. Réassurances acceptées
J.1.2.1. Domestic Companies		508	565	354	330	279	255	308	J.1.2.1. Entreprises Nationales
J.1.2.3. Branches & Agencies of Foreign Cies		35	32	..	..	..	0	0	J.1.2.3. Succursales et Agences d'Ent. Etrangères
J.1.2. Total		543	597	354	330	279	255	308	J.1.2. Total
J.1.3. Total									J.1.3. Total
J.1.3.1. Domestic Companies		10 937	12 699	23 690	24 856	26 251	25 674	27 814	J.1.3.1. Entreprises Nationales
J.1.3.3. Branches & Agencies of Foreign Cies		154	296	358	340	363	315	289	J.1.3.3. Succursales et Agences d'Ent. Etrangères
J.1.3. Total of Life Net Premiums		11 091	12 995	24 048	25 196	26 614	25 989	28 103	J.1.3. Total
J.2. Non-Life									**J.2. Non-Vie**
J.2.1. Direct Business									J.2.1. Assurance directe
J.2.1.1. Domestic Companies		25 506	26 395	29 441	31 180	32 559	33 411	34 617	J.2.1.1. Entreprises Nationales
J.2.1.3. Branches & Agencies of Foreign Cies		638	641	621	710	777	768	728	J.2.1.3. Succursales et Agences d'Ent. Etrangères
J.2.1. Total		26 144	27 036	30 062	31 890	33 336	34 179	35 345	J.2.1. Total des Primes Nettes Vie
J.2.2. Reinsurance accepted									J.2.2. Réassurances acceptées
J.2.2.1. Domestic Companies		4 453	4 934	4 074	4 385	4 121	4 302	4 959	J.2.2.1. Entreprises Nationales
J.2.2.3. Branches & Agencies of Foreign Cies		7	19	3	5	3	1	0	J.2.2.3. Succursales et Agences d'Ent. Etrangères
J.2.2. Total		4 460	4 953	4 077	4 390	4 124	4 303	4 959	J.2.2. Total
J.2.3. Total									J.2.3. Total
J.2.3.1. Domestic Companies		29 959	31 329	33 515	35 565	36 680	37 713	39 576	J.2.3.1. Entreprises Nationales
J.2.3.3. Branches & Agencies of Foreign Cies		645	660	624	715	780	769	728	J.2.3.3. Succursales et Agences d'Ent. Etrangères
J.2.3. Total		30 604	31 989	34 139	36 280	37 460	38 482	40 305	J.2.3. Total

Monetary Unit: million deutschmarks

Unité monétaire : million de deutschemarks

	1992	1993	1994	1995	1996	1997	1998	1999
A. NUMBER OF COMPANIES IN THE REPORTING COUNTRY / **A. NOMBRE D'ENTREPRISES DANS LE PAYS DECLARANT**								
A.1. Life / **A.1. Vie**								
A.1.1. Domestic Companies / A.1.1. Entreprises Nationales	321	321	315	319	316	315	314	310
A.1.2. (Foreign Controlled Companies) / A.1.2. (Entreprises Sous Contrôle Etranger)	20	19	16	16	16	16	19	19
A.1.3. Branches & Agencies of Foreign Cies / A.1.3. Succursales et Agences d'Ent. Etrangères	5	6	4	4	4	4	4	4
A.1. All Companies / A.1. Ensemble des Entreprises	326	327	319	323	320	319	318	314
A.2. Non-Life / **A.2. Non-Vie**								
A.2.1. Domestic Companies / A.2.1. Entreprises Nationales	333	332	324	327	325	323	320	319
A.2.2. (Foreign Controlled Companies) / A.2.2. (Entreprises Sous Contrôle Etranger)	38	39	29	29	29	29	28	24
A.2.3. Branches & Agencies of Foreign Cies / A.2.3. Succursales et Agences d'Ent. Etrangères	77	71	10	10	9	8	8	8
A.2. All Companies / A.2. Ensemble des Entreprises	410	403	334	337	334	331	328	327
A.4. Reinsurance / **A.4. Réassurance**								
A.4.1. Domestic Companies / A.4.1. Entreprises Nationales	31	32	32	36	36	36	38	42
A.4.2. (Foreign Controlled Companies) / A.4.2. (Entreprises Sous Contrôle Etranger)		5	5	5	8	8	8	7
A.4. All Companies / A.4. Ensemble des Entreprises	31	32	32	36	36	36	38	42
A.5. Total								
A.5.1. Domestic Companies / A.5.1. Entreprises Nationales	685	685	671	682	677	674	672	671
A.5.2. (Foreign Controlled Companies) / A.5.2. (Entreprises Sous Contrôle Etranger)	63	63	50	52	53	53	55	50
A.5.3. Branches & Agencies of Foreign Cies / A.5.3. Succursales et Agences d'Ent. Etrangères	82	77	14	14	13	12	12	12
A.5. All Insurance Companies / A.5. Ensemble des Entreprises d'Assurances	767	762	685	696	690	686	684	683
B. NUMBER OF EMPLOYEES / **B. NOMBRE D'EMPLOYES**								
B.1. Insurance Companies / B.1. Entreprises d'Assurances	255 149	254 484	250 561	234 653	223 199	215 273	215 827	227 556
C. BUSINESS WRITTEN IN THE REPORTING COUNTRY / **C. OPERATIONS CONCLUES DANS LE PAYS DECLARANT**								
C.1. Life / **C.1. Vie**								
C.1.1. Gross Premiums / C.1.1. Primes Brutes								
C.1.1.1. Direct Business / C.1.1.1. Assurances Directes								
C.1.1.1.1. Domestic Companies / C.1.1.1.1. Entreprises Nationales	70 429	77 499	84 882	90 106	95 344	99 864	104 048	115 972
C.1.1.1.3. Branches & Agencies of Foreign Cies / C.1.1.1.3. Succursales et Agences d'Ent. Etrangères	2 413	2 661	2 576	2 148	2 286	2 408	2 611	2 882
C.1.1.1. Total / C.1.1.1. Total	72 842	80 160	87 458	92 255	97 630	102 272	106 659	118 855
C.1.1.2. Reinsurance Accepted / C.1.1.2. Réassurance Acceptée								
C.1.1.2.1. Domestic Companies / C.1.1.2.1. Entreprises Nationales	7 731	8 456	9 784	10 297	11 054	12 418	13 333	15 541
C.1.1.2. Total / C.1.1.2. Total	7 731	8 456	9 784	10 297	11 054	12 418	13 333	15 541
C.1.1.3. Total								
C.1.1.3.1. Domestic Companies / C.1.1.3.1. Entreprises Nationales	78 160	85 955	94 666	100 403	106 398	112 283	117 381	131 514
C.1.1.3.2. (Foreign Controlled Companies) / C.1.1.3.2. (Entreprises Sous Contrôle Etranger)	6 794	7 383	6 957	7 227	6 931	7 428	6 600	20 241
C.1.1.3.3. Branches & Agencies of Foreign Cies / C.1.1.3.3. Succursales et Agences d'Ent. Etrangères	2 413	2 661	2 576	2 148	2 286	2 408	2 611	2 882
C.1.1.3. Total Gross Premiums / C.1.1.3. Total des Primes Brutes	80 573	88 616	97 242	102 552	108 684	114 690	119 992	134 396
C.1.2. Ceded Premiums / C.1.2. Primes Cédées								
C.1.2.1. Domestic Companies / C.1.2.1. Entreprises Nationales	7 074	7 167	7 611	7 720	8 563	8 930	8 801	11 885
C.1.2.2. (Foreign Controlled Companies) / C.1.2.2. (Entreprises Sous Contrôle Etranger)	::	::		556	558	591	495	1 829
C.1.2.3. Branches & Agencies of Foreign Cies / C.1.2.3. Succursales et Agences d'Ent. Etrangères	30	36	45	165	184	192	196	260
C.1.2. Total / C.1.2. Total	7 104	7 203	7 656	7 885	8 747	9 122	8 997	12 145
C.1.3. Net Written Premiums / C.1.3. Primes Nettes Emises								
C.1.3.1. Domestic Companies / C.1.3.1. Entreprises Nationales	71 086	78 788	87 055	92 683	97 835	103 352	108 580	119 629
C.1.3.2. (Foreign Controlled Companies) / C.1.3.2. (Entreprises Sous Contrôle Etranger)	::	::		6 672	6 373	6 837	6 105	18 412
C.1.3.3. Branches & Agencies of Foreign Cies / C.1.3.3. Succursales et Agences d'Ent. Etrangères	2 383	2 625	2 531	1 983	2 102	2 216	2 415	2 622
C.1.3. Total / C.1.3. Total	73 469	81 413	89 586	94 667	99 937	105 568	110 995	122 250

103

Monetary Unit: million deutschmarks — Unité monétaire : million de deutschmarks

C.2. Non-Life — C.2. Non-Vie

	1992	1993	1994	1995	1996	1997	1998	1999
C.2.1. Gross premiums — C.2.1. Primes Brutes								
C.2.1.1. Direct Business — C.2.1.1. Assurances Directes								
C.2.1.1.1. Domestic Companies — Entreprises Nationales	103 788	114 621	124 272	132 137	135 373	137 106	136 731	138 617
C.2.1.1.3. Branches & Agencies of Foreign Cies — Succursales et Agences d'Ent. Etrangères	2 990	3 245	2 517	2 045	1 321	1 284	1 285	1 330
C.2.1.1. Total	106 778	117 866	126 789	134 182	136 694	138 389	138 016	139 946
C.2.1.2. Reinsurance Accepted — Réassurance Acceptée								
C.2.1.2.1. Domestic Companies — Entreprises Nationales	38 241	43 094	49 113	50 154	51 035	54 941	54 138	58 556
C.2.1.2.3. Branches & Agencies of Foreign Cies — Succursales et Agences d'Ent. Etrangères	304	321	177	0	0	0	0	0
C.2.1.2. Total	38 545	43 415	49 290	50 154	51 035	54 941	54 138	58 556
C.2.1.3. Total								
C.2.1.3.1. Domestic Companies — Entreprises Nationales	142 029	157 715	173 385	182 291	186 408	192 046	190 869	197 173
C.2.1.3.2. (Foreign Controlled Companies) — (Entreprises Sous Contrôle Etranger)	17 431	22 701	11 087	11 418	23 235	23 276	22 167	25 670
C.2.1.3.3. Branches & Agencies of Foreign Cies — Succursales et Agences d'Ent. Etrangères	3 294	3 566	2 694	2 045	1 321	1 284	1 285	1 330
C.2.1.3. Total Gross Premiums — Total des Primes Brutes	145 323	161 281	176 079	184 336	187 729	193 330	192 154	198 502
C.2.2. Ceded Premiums — C.2.2. Primes Cédées								
C.2.2.1. Domestic Companies — Entreprises Nationales	36 239	39 664	42 212	42 040	42 377	43 022	41 162	44 593
C.2.2.2. (Foreign Controlled Companies) — (Entreprises Sous Contrôle Etranger)	..	..	..	2 633	5 282	5 214	4 780	5 806
C.2.2.3. Branches & Agencies of Foreign Cies — Succursales et Agences d'Ent. Etrangères	804	824	273	472	300	288	277	301
C.2.2. Total	37 043	40 488	42 485	42 512	42 677	43 310	41 439	44 894
C.2.3. Net Written Premiums — C.2.3. Primes Nettes Emises								
C.2.3.1. Domestic Companies — Entreprises Nationales	105 790	118 051	131 173	140 251	144 031	149 024	149 707	152 580
C.2.3.2. (Foreign Controlled Companies) — (Entreprises Sous Contrôle Etranger)	..	..	..	8 785	17 953	18 061	17 386	19 864
C.2.3.3. Branches & Agencies of Foreign Cies — Succursales et Agences d'Ent. Etrangères	2 490	2 742	2 421	1 574	1 020	996	1 008	1 029
C.2.3. Total	108 280	120 793	133 594	141 824	145 052	150 020	150 715	153 609

C.3. Total — C.3. Total

	1992	1993	1994	1995	1996	1997	1998	1999
C.3.1. Gross Premiums — C.3.1. Primes Brutes								
C.3.1.1. Direct Business — C.3.1.1. Assurances Directes								
C.3.1.1.1. Domestic Companies — Entreprises Nationales	174 217	192 120	209 154	222 243	230 717	236 970	240 779	254 589
C.3.1.1.3. Branches & Agencies of Foreign Cies — Succursales et Agences d'Ent. Etrangères	5 403	5 906	5 093	4 193	3 607	3 692	3 896	4 212
C.3.1.1. Total	179 620	198 026	214 247	226 437	234 324	240 661	244 675	258 801
C.3.1.2. Reinsurance Accepted — Réassurance Acceptée								
C.3.1.2.1. Domestic Companies — Entreprises Nationales	45 972	51 550	58 897	60 451	62 089	67 359	67 471	74 097
C.3.1.2.3. Branches & Agencies of Foreign Cies — Succursales et Agences d'Ent. Etrangères	304	321	177	0	0	0	0	0
C.3.1.2. Total	46 276	51 871	59 074	60 451	62 089	67 359	67 471	74 097
C.3.1.3. Total								
C.3.1.3.1. Domestic Companies — Entreprises Nationales	220 189	243 670	268 051	282 694	292 806	304 329	308 250	328 687
C.3.1.3.2. (Foreign Controlled Companies) — (Entreprises Sous Contrôle Etranger)	24 225	30 084	18 044	18 645	30 166	30 704	28 767	45 911
C.3.1.3.3. Branches & Agencies of Foreign Cies — Succursales et Agences d'Ent. Etrangères	5 707	6 227	5 270	4 193	3 607	3 692	3 896	4 212
C.3.1.3. Total Gross Premiums — Total des Primes Brutes	225 896	249 897	273 321	286 888	296 413	308 020	312 146	332 898
C.3.2. Ceded Premiums — C.3.2. Primes Cédées								
C.3.2.1. Domestic Companies — Entreprises Nationales	43 313	46 831	49 823	49 760	50 940	51 952	49 963	56 478
C.3.2.2. (Foreign Controlled Companies) — (Entreprises Sous Contrôle Etranger)	..	..	..	3 189	5 840	5 805	5 275	7 635
C.3.2.3. Branches & Agencies of Foreign Cies — Succursales et Agences d'Ent. Etrangères	834	860	318	637	484	480	473	561
C.3.2. Total	44 147	47 691	50 141	50 397	51 424	52 432	50 436	57 039
C.3.3. Net Written Premiums — C.3.3. Primes Nettes Emises								
C.3.3.1. Domestic Companies — Entreprises Nationales	176 876	196 839	218 228	232 934	241 866	252 376	258 287	272 209
C.3.3.2. (Foreign Controlled Companies) — (Entreprises Sous Contrôle Etranger)	..	..	..	15 457	24 326	24 898	23 491	38 276
C.3.3.3. Branches & Agencies of Foreign Cies — Succursales et Agences d'Ent. Etrangères	4 873	5 367	4 952	3 557	3 122	3 212	3 423	3 651
C.3.3. Total	181 749	202 206	223 180	236 491	244 989	255 588	261 710	275 859

Monetary Unit: million deutschmarks — Unité monétaire : million de deutschemarks

D. NET WRITTEN PREMIUMS IN THE REPORTING COUNTRY IN TERMS OF DOMESTIC AND FOREIGN RISKS
D. PRIMES NETTES EMISES DANS LE PAYS DECLARANT EN RISQUES NATIONAUX ET ETRANGERS

D.1. Life — D.1. Vie

Code / Description (EN)	Libellé (FR)	1992	1993	1994	1995	1996	1997	1998	1999
D.1.1. Domestic Risks	D.1.1. Risques Nationaux								
D.1.1.1. Domestic Companies	D.1.1.1. Entreprises Nationales		..	..	90 038	94 585	99 037	103 729	113 500
D.1.1.2. (Foreign Controlled Companies)	D.1.1.2. (Entreprises Sous Contrôle Etranger)		..	..	6 481	6 161	6 552	5 832	17 469
D.1.1.3. Branches & Agencies of Foreign Cies	D.1.1.3. Succursales et Agences d'Ent. Etrangères		..	..	1 983	2 102	2 216	2 415	2 622
D.1.1. Total	D.1.1. Total des Primes Nettes Vie		..	..	92 021	96 687	101 254	106 144	116 122
D.1.2. Foreign Risks	D.1.2. Risques Etrangers								
D.1.2.1. Domestic Companies	D.1.2.1. Entreprises Nationales		..	..	2 645	3 251	4 315	4 851	6 128
D.1.2.2. (Foreign Controlled Companies)	D.1.2.2. (Entreprises Sous Contrôle Etranger)		..	..	190	212	285	273	943
D.1.2. Total	D.1.2. Total des Primes Nettes Vie		..	..	2 645	3 251	4 315	4 851	6 128
D.1.3. Total	D.1.3. Total								
D.1.3.1. Domestic Companies	D.1.3.1. Entreprises Nationales		78 788	87 055	92 683	97 835	103 352	108 580	119 629
D.1.3.2. (Foreign Controlled Companies)	D.1.3.2. (Entreprises Sous Contrôle Etranger)		..	..	6 672	6 373	6 837	6 105	18 412
D.1.3.3. Branches & Agencies of Foreign Cies	D.1.3.3. Succursales et Agences d'Ent. Etrangères		2 625	2 531	1 983	2 102	2 216	2 415	2 622
D.1.3. Total of Life Net Premiums	D.1.3. Total des Primes Nettes Vie		81 413	89 586	94 667	99 937	105 568	110 995	122 250

D.2. Non-Life — D.2. Non-Vie

Code / Description (EN)	Libellé (FR)	1992	1993	1994	1995	1996	1997	1998	1999
D.2.1. Domestic Risks	D.2.1. Risques Nationaux								
D.2.1.1. Domestic Companies	D.2.1.1. Entreprises Nationales		..	..	126 235	129 647	131 553	132 375	131 697
D.2.1.2. (Foreign Controlled Companies)	D.2.1.2. (Entreprises Sous Contrôle Etranger)		..	..	7 907	16 160	15 944	15 373	17 146
D.2.1.3. Branches & Agencies of Foreign Cies	D.2.1.3. Succursales et Agences d'Ent. Etrangères		..	..	1 574	1 020	996	1 008	1 029
D.2.1. Total	D.2.1. Total des Primes Nettes Vie		..	..	127 808	130 667	132 550	133 383	132 726
D.2.2. Foreign Risks	D.2.2. Risques Etrangers								
D.2.2.1. Domestic Companies	D.2.2.1. Entreprises Nationales		..	..	14 016	14 384	17 470	17 332	20 883
D.2.2.2. (Foreign Controlled Companies)	D.2.2.2. (Entreprises Sous Contrôle Etranger)		..	..	878	1 793	2 117	2 013	2 719
D.2.2. Total	D.2.2. Total des Primes Nettes Vie		..	..	14 016	14 384	17 470	17 332	20 883
D.2.3. Total	D.2.3. Total								
D.2.3.1. Domestic Companies	D.2.3.1. Entreprises Nationales		118 051	131 173	140 251	144 031	149 024	149 707	152 580
D.2.3.2. (Foreign Controlled Companies)	D.2.3.2. (Entreprises Sous Contrôle Etranger)		..	..	8 785	17 953	18 061	17 386	19 864
D.2.3.3. Branches & Agencies of Foreign Cies	D.2.3.3. Succursales et Agences d'Ent. Etrangères		2 742	2 421	1 574	1 020	996	1 008	1 029
D.2.3. Total	D.2.3. Total des Primes Nettes Vie		120 793	133 594	141 824	145 052	150 020	150 715	153 609

E. BUSINESS WRITTEN ABROAD — E. OPERATIONS A L'ETRANGER

E.1. Life — E.1. Vie

Code / Description (EN)	Libellé (FR)	1992	1993	1994	1995	1996	1997	1998	1999
E.1.1. Gross Premiums	E.1.1. Primes Brutes								
E.1.1.1. Direct Business	E.1.1.1. Assurance Directe								
E.1.1.1.1. Branches & Agencies	E.1.1.1.1. Succursales & Agences	97	105	..	1	4	10	31	87
E.1.1.3. Total	E.1.1.3. Total	97	105	..	1	4	10	31	87
E.1.1.3.1. Branches & Agencies	E.1.1.3.1. Succursales & Agences								
E.1.2. Ceded Premiums	E.1.2. Primes Cédées								
E.1.2.1. Branches & Agencies	E.1.2.1. Succursales & Agences		..	..	0	0	1	2	8
E.1.3. Net Written Premiums	E.1.3. Primes Nettes Emises								
E.1.3.1. Branches & Agencies	E.1.3.1. Succursales & Agences		..	..	1	4	9	28	79

Monetary Unit: million deutschmarks

Unité monétaire : million de deutschemarks

E.2. Non-Life / E.2. Non-Vie

	1992	1993	1994	1995	1996	1997	1998	1999
E.2.1. Gross Premiums / E.2.1. Primes Brutes								
E.2.1.1. Direct Business / E.2.1.1. Assurance Directe								
E.2.1.1.1. Branches & Agencies / E.2.1.1.1. Succursales & Agences	894	1 022	1 148	1 042	1 168	1 367	1 464	1 356
E.2.1.2. Reinsurance Accepted / E.2.1.2. Réassurance Acceptée								
E.2.1.2.1. Branches & Agencies / E.2.1.2.1. Succursales & Agences	14 994	17 815	21 954	0	0	0	0	0
E.2.1.3. Total / E.2.1.3. Total								
E.2.1.3.1. Branches & Agencies / E.2.1.3.1. Succursales & Agences	15 888	18 837	23 102	1 042	1 168	1 367	1 464	1 356
E.2.2. Ceded Premiums / E.2.2. Primes Cédées								
E.2.2.1. Branches & Agencies / E.2.2.1. Succursales & Agences	..	..	..	240	266	306	316	307
E.2.3. Net Written Premiums / E.2.3. Primes Nettes Emises								
E.2.3.1. Branches & Agencies / E.2.3.1. Succursales & Agences	..	..	..	802	903	1 061	1 148	1 049

F. OUTSTANDING INVESTMENT BY DIRECT INSURANCE COMPANIES / F. ENCOURS DES PLACEMENTS DES ENTREPRISES D'ASSURANCES DIRECTES

F.1. Life / F.1. Vie

	1992	1993	1994	1995	1996	1997	1998	1999
F.1.1. Real Estate / F.1.1. Immobilier								
F.1.1.1. Domestic Companies / F.1.1.1. Entreprises Nationales	34 501	36 743	38 081	..	..	..	..	..
F.1.1.3. Branches & Agencies of Foreign Cies / F.1.1.3. Succursales et Agences d'Ent. Etrangères	789	808	795	..	..	..	..	..
F.1.1. Total / F.1.1. Total	35 290	37 551	38 876	38 792	37 476	37 773	38 227	37 271
F.1.2. Mortgage Loans / F.1.2. Prêts Hypothécaires								
F.1.2.1. Domestic Companies / F.1.2.1. Entreprises Nationales	91 541	97 093	105 809	..	..	..	..	..
F.1.2.3. Branches & Agencies of Foreign Cies / F.1.2.3. Succursales et Agences d'Ent. Etrangères	1 830	1 874	1 985	..	..	..	..	..
F.1.2. Total / F.1.2. Total	93 371	98 967	107 794	112 686	116 470	120 077	120 335	123 089
F.1.3. Shares / F.1.3. Actions								
F.1.3.1. Domestic Companies / F.1.3.1. Entreprises Nationales	27 123	29 399	33 832	..	..	..	..	..
F.1.3.3. Branches & Agencies of Foreign Cies / F.1.3.3. Succursales et Agences d'Ent. Etrangères	269	347	410	..	..	..	..	..
F.1.3. Total / F.1.3. Total	27 392	29 746	34 242	37 193	43 409	54 934	67 920	72 958
F.1.4. Bonds with Fixed Revenue / F.1.4. Obligations								
F.1.4.1. Domestic Companies / F.1.4.1. Entreprises Nationales	91 562	102 739	103 263	..	..	..	..	..
F.1.4.3. Branches & Agencies of Foreign Cies / F.1.4.3. Succursales et Agences d'Ent. Etrangères	3 114	3 436	2 839	..	..	..	..	..
F.1.4. Total / F.1.4. Total	94 676	106 175	106 102	112 074	112 540	114 141	114 332	100 693
F.1.5. Loans other than Mortgage Loans / F.1.5. Prêts Autres qu'Hypothécaires								
F.1.5.1. Domestic Companies / F.1.5.1. Entreprises Nationales	273 762	298 943	335 264	..	..	..	..	..
F.1.5.3. Branches & Agencies of Foreign Cies / F.1.5.3. Succursales et Agences d'Ent. Etrangères	8 701	9 706	10 938	..	..	..	..	..
F.1.5. Total / F.1.5. Total	282 463	308 649	346 202	399 001	441 220	464 652	485 813	531 380
F.1.6. Other Investments / F.1.6. Autres Placements								
F.1.6.1. Domestic Companies / F.1.6.1. Entreprises Nationales	84 131	96 277	103 036	..	..	..	..	..
F.1.6.3. Branches & Agencies of Foreign Cies / F.1.6.3. Succursales et Agences d'Ent. Etrangères	2 397	2 745	3 328	..	..	..	..	..
F.1.6. Total / F.1.6. Total	86 528	99 022	106 364	102 263	124 222	157 141	200 490	251 591
F.1.7. Total / F.1.7. Total								
F.1.7.1. Domestic Companies / F.1.7.1. Entreprises Nationales	602 620	661 794	719 285	..	..	..	..	..
F.1.7.3. Branches & Agencies of Foreign Cies / F.1.7.3. Succursales et Agences d'Ent. Etrangères	17 100	18 916	20 295	..	..	..	..	..
F.1.7. Total of Life Investments / F.1.7. Total des Placements Vie	619 720	680 100	739 580	802 009	875 337	948 718	1 027 117	1 116 982

106

F.2. Non-Life — F.2. Non-Vie

		1992	1993	1994	1995	1996	1997	1998	1999
F.2.1. Real Estate	F.2.1. Immobilier								
F.2.1.1. Domestic Companies	F.2.1.1. Entreprises Nationales	11 230	11 509	11 893	:	:	:	:	:
F.2.1.3. Branches & Agencies of Foreign Cies	F.2.1.3. Succursales et Agences d'Ent. Etrangères	550	539	553	:	:	:	:	:
F.2.1. Total	F.2.1. Total	11 780	12 048	12 446	12 325	12 462	12 838	12 804	12 691
F.2.2. Mortgage Loans	F.2.2. Prêts Hypothécaires								
F.2.2.1. Domestic Companies	F.2.2.1. Entreprises Nationales	5 115	5 508	5 915	:	:	:	:	:
F.2.2.3. Branches & Agencies of Foreign Cies	F.2.2.3. Succursales et Agences d'Ent. Etrangères	82	80	77	:	:	:	:	:
F.2.2. Total	F.2.2. Total	5 197	5 588	5 992	6 328	6 412	6 623	6 499	6 285
F.2.3. Shares	F.2.3. Actions								
F.2.3.1. Domestic Companies	F.2.3.1. Entreprises Nationales	15 790	17 219	20 256	:	:	:	:	:
F.2.3.3. Branches & Agencies of Foreign Cies	F.2.3.3. Succursales et Agences d'Ent. Etrangères	339	381	361	:	:	:	:	:
F.2.3. Total	F.2.3. Total	16 129	17 600	20 617	25 633	30 282	34 170	37 740	41 515
F.2.4. Bonds with Fixed Revenue	F.2.4. Obligations								
F.2.4.1. Domestic Companies	F.2.4.1. Entreprises Nationales	31 690	34 874	38 006	:	:	:	:	:
F.2.4.3. Branches & Agencies of Foreign Cies	F.2.4.3. Succursales et Agences d'Ent. Etrangères	1 210	1 375	884	:	:	:	:	:
F.2.4. Total	F.2.4. Total	32 900	36 249	38 890	41 084	41 690	41 546	41 931	36 714
F.2.5. Loans other than Mortgage Loans	F.2.5. Prêts Autres qu'Hypothécaires								
F.2.5.1. Domestic Companies	F.2.5.1. Entreprises Nationales	61 364	68 328	79 267	:	:	:	:	:
F.2.5.3. Branches & Agencies of Foreign Cies	F.2.5.3. Succursales et Agences d'Ent. Etrangères	1 180	1 165	1 366	:	:	:	:	:
F.2.5. Total	F.2.5. Total	62 544	69 493	80 633	96 456	110 619	120 330	129 577	141 158
F.2.6. Other Investments	F.2.6. Autres Placements								
F.2.6.1. Domestic Companies	F.2.6.1. Entreprises Nationales	24 325	28 110	31 534	:	:	:	:	:
F.2.6.3. Branches & Agencies of Foreign Cies	F.2.6.3. Succursales et Agences d'Ent. Etrangères	585	672	570	:	:	:	:	:
F.2.6. Total	F.2.6. Total	24 910	28 782	32 104	34 537	40 890	50 383	61 274	73 725
F.2.7. Total	F.2.7. Total								
F.2.7.1. Domestic Companies	F.2.7.1. Entreprises Nationales	149 514	165 548	186 871	:	:	:	:	:
F.2.7.3. Branches & Agencies of Foreign Cies	F.2.7.3. Succursales et Agences d'Ent. Etrangères	3 946	4 212	3 811	:	:	:	:	:
F.2.7. Total of Non-Life Investments	F.2.7. Total des Placements Non-Vie	153 460	169 760	190 682	216 363	242 355	265 890	289 825	312 088

G. BREAKDOWN OF NON-LIFE PREMIUMS — G. VENTILATIONS DES PRIMES NON-VIE

		1992	1993	1994	1995	1996	1997	1998	1999
G.1. Motor vehicle	G.1. Assurance Automobile								
G.1.1. Direct Business	G.1.1. Assurances Directes								
G.1.1.1. Gross Premiums	G.1.1.1. Primes Brutes	35 446	38 766	43 186	44 378	42 782	40 908	39 180	38 850
G.1.1.2. Ceded Premiums	G.1.1.2. Primes Cédées	9 468	10 468	11 289	11 503	10 909	10 247	9 594	9 432
G.1.1.3. Net Written Premiums	G.1.1.3. Primes Nettes Emises	25 978	28 298	31 897	32 875	31 873	30 661	29 585	29 418
G.1.2. Reinsurance Accepted	G.1.2. Réassurance Acceptée								
G.1.2.1. Gross Premiums	G.1.2.1. Primes Brutes	11 108	12 365	13 934	14 190	13 791	13 978	13 475	14 319
G.1.2.2. Ceded Premiums	G.1.2.2. Primes Cédées	3 337	3 536	3 904	3 818	4 024	4 050	3 892	3 987
G.1.2.3. Net Written Premiums	G.1.2.3. Primes Nettes Emises	7 771	8 829	10 030	10 372	9 767	9 928	9 583	10 332
G.1.3. Total	G.1.3. Total								
G.1.3.1. Gross Premiums	G.1.3.1. Primes Brutes	46 554	51 131	57 120	58 568	56 574	54 885	52 655	53 169
G.1.3.2. Ceded Premiums	G.1.3.2. Primes Cédées	12 805	14 004	15 193	15 321	14 934	14 297	13 487	13 419
G.1.3.3. Net Written Premiums	G.1.3.3. Primes Nettes Emises	33 749	37 127	41 927	43 246	41 640	40 589	39 168	39 751

107

Monetary Unit: million deutschmarks

Unité monétaire : million de deutschemarks

Item (EN) / Poste (FR)	1992	1993	1994	1995	1996	1997	1998	1999
G.2. Marine, Aviation / G.2. Marine, Aviation								
G.2.1. Direct Business / G.2.1. Assurances Directes								
G.2.1.1. Gross Premiums / G.2.1.1. Primes Brutes	2 734	2 984	2 882	2 827	2 904	2 980	2 901	2 841
G.2.1.2. Ceded Premiums / G.2.1.2. Primes Cédées	1 213	1 345	1 279	1 227	1 219	1 209	1 165	1 250
G.2.1.3. Net Written Premiums / G.2.1.3. Primes Nettes Emises	1 521	1 639	1 603	1 599	1 685	1 771	1 736	1 591
G.2.2. Reinsurance Accepted / G.2.2. Réassurance Acceptée								
G.2.2.1. Gross Premiums / G.2.2.1. Primes Brutes	2 140	2 971	3 612	3 674	3 767	4 643	4 637	5 231
G.2.2.2. Ceded Premiums / G.2.2.2. Primes Cédées	657	852	873	768	784	1 130	1 273	1 704
G.2.2.3. Net Written Premiums / G.2.2.3. Primes Nettes Emises	1 483	2 119	2 739	2 905	2 983	3 514	3 364	3 527
G.2.3. Total / G.2.3. Total								
G.2.3.1. Gross Premiums / G.2.3.1. Primes Brutes	4 874	5 955	6 494	6 500	6 672	7 623	7 538	8 071
G.2.3.2. Ceded Premiums / G.2.3.2. Primes Cédées	1 870	2 197	2 152	1 996	2 004	2 339	2 437	2 953
G.2.3.3. Net Written Premiums / G.2.3.3. Primes Nettes Emises	3 004	3 758	4 342	4 505	4 668	5 284	5 100	5 118
G.4. Fire, Property Damages / G.4. Incendie, Dommages aux Biens								
G.4.1. Direct Business / G.4.1. Assurances Directes								
G.4.1.1. Gross Premiums / G.4.1.1. Primes Brutes	23 745	26 579	27 486	26 479	27 155	27 519	26 784	27 237
G.4.1.2. Ceded Premiums / G.4.1.2. Primes Cédées	8 211	9 014	9 260	8 420	8 460	8 199	7 685	8 485
G.4.1.3. Net Written Premiums / G.4.1.3. Primes Nettes Emises	15 534	17 565	18 226	18 059	18 695	19 320	19 099	18 752
G.4.2. Reinsurance Accepted / G.4.2. Réassurance Acceptée								
G.4.2.1. Gross Premiums / G.4.2.1. Primes Brutes	16 116	18 107	20 798	19 381	20 167	21 322	20 621	22 011
G.4.2.2. Ceded Premiums / G.4.2.2. Primes Cédées	5 649	6 085	6 428	5 750	5 789	6 170	6 072	7 052
G.4.2.3. Net Written Premiums / G.4.2.3. Primes Nettes Emises	10 467	12 022	14 370	13 631	14 378	15 152	14 549	14 959
G.4.3. Total / G.4.3. Total								
G.4.3.1. Gross Premiums / G.4.3.1. Primes Brutes	39 861	44 686	48 284	45 860	47 323	48 841	47 405	49 248
G.4.3.2. Ceded Premiums / G.4.3.2. Primes Cédées	13 859	15 099	15 688	14 170	14 249	14 369	13 757	15 537
G.4.3.3. Net Written Premiums / G.4.3.3. Primes Nettes Emises	26 002	29 587	32 596	31 690	33 073	34 472	33 648	33 711
G.5. Pecuniary Losses / G.5. Pertes Pécuniières								
G.5.1. Direct Business / G.5.1. Assurances Directes								
G.5.1.1. Gross Premiums / G.5.1.1. Primes Brutes	1 211	1 306	1 322	2 854	2 934	2 972	2 944	2 782
G.5.1.2. Ceded Premiums / G.5.1.2. Primes Cédées	865	939	968	2 116	2 148	2 168	2 113	1 936
G.5.1.3. Net Written Premiums / G.5.1.3. Primes Nettes Emises	346	367	354	738	787	805	830	845
G.5.2. Reinsurance Accepted / G.5.2. Réassurance Acceptée								
G.5.2.1. Gross Premiums / G.5.2.1. Primes Brutes	1 230	1 380	1 505	2 760	2 895	3 196	3 307	3 328
G.5.2.2. Ceded Premiums / G.5.2.2. Primes Cédées	162	181	202	618	587	699	774	831
G.5.2.3. Net Written Premiums / G.5.2.3. Primes Nettes Emises	1 068	1 199	1 303	2 143	2 308	2 497	2 533	2 497
G.5.3. Total / G.5.3. Total								
G.5.3.1. Gross Premiums / G.5.3.1. Primes Brutes	2 441	2 686	2 827	5 615	5 830	6 168	6 251	6 109
G.5.3.2. Ceded Premiums / G.5.3.2. Primes Cédées	1 027	1 120	1 170	2 734	2 735	2 866	2 887	2 767
G.5.3.3. Net Written Premiums / G.5.3.3. Primes Nettes Emises	1 414	1 566	1 657	2 881	3 095	3 302	3 364	3 342
G.6. General Liability / G.6. Responsabilité Générale								
G.6.1. Direct Business / G.6.1. Assurances Directes								
G.6.1.1. Gross Premiums / G.6.1.1. Primes Brutes	9 221	10 124	10 901	11 416	11 862	12 280	12 280	12 701
G.6.1.2. Ceded Premiums / G.6.1.2. Primes Cédées	2 928	3 230	3 350	3 410	3 406	3 508	3 442	3 570
G.6.1.3. Net Written Premiums / G.6.1.3. Primes Nettes Emises	6 293	6 894	7 551	8 006	8 456	8 772	8 838	9 131
G.6.2. Reinsurance Accepted / G.6.2. Réassurance Acceptée								
G.6.2.1. Gross Premiums / G.6.2.1. Primes Brutes	4 557	4 954	5 550	5 845	5 642	6 039	6 136	6 525
G.6.2.2. Ceded Premiums / G.6.2.2. Primes Cédées	1 229	1 286	1 325	1 166	1 345	1 438	1 452	1 557
G.6.2.3. Net Written Premiums / G.6.2.3. Primes Nettes Emises	3 328	3 668	4 225	4 678	4 296	4 601	4 685	4 968
G.6.3. Total / G.6.3. Total								
G.6.3.1. Gross Premiums / G.6.3.1. Primes Brutes	13 778	15 078	16 451	17 260	17 504	18 319	18 416	19 226
G.6.3.2. Ceded Premiums / G.6.3.2. Primes Cédées	4 157	4 516	4 675	4 576	4 751	4 947	4 894	5 127
G.6.3.3. Net Written Premiums / G.6.3.3. Primes Nettes Emises	9 621	10 562	11 776	12 684	12 752	13 372	13 522	14 099

Monetary Unit: million deutschmarks — Unité monétaire : million de deutschemarks

	1992	1993	1994	1995	1996	1997	1998	1999
G.7. Accident, Health / G.7. Accident, Santé								
G.7.1. Direct Business / G.7.1. Assurances Directes								
G.7.1.1. Gross Premiums / G.7.1.1. Primes Brutes	30 594	34 039	36 759	41 287	43 833	46 223	48 078	49 552
G.7.1.2. Ceded Premiums / G.7.1.2. Primes Cédées	2 141	2 293	2 335	2 370	2 535	2 681	1 930	2 738
G.7.1.3. Net Written Premiums / G.7.1.3. Primes Nettes Emises	28 453	31 746	34 424	38 917	41 298	43 542	46 148	46 814
G.7.2. Reinsurance Accepted / G.7.2. Réassurance Acceptée								
G.7.2.1. Gross Premiums / G.7.2.1. Primes Brutes	2 842	3 067	3 287	3 546	3 954	4 863	5 007	6 174
G.7.2.2. Ceded Premiums / G.7.2.2. Primes Cédées	618	675	677	619	676	930	1 082	1 359
G.7.2.3. Net Written Premiums / G.7.2.3. Primes Nettes Emises	2 224	2 392	2 610	2 927	3 278	3 933	3 925	4 814
G.7.3. Total								
G.7.3.1. Gross Premiums / G.7.3.1. Primes Brutes	33 436	37 106	40 046	44 833	47 787	51 086	53 085	55 726
G.7.3.2. Ceded Premiums / G.7.3.2. Primes Cédées	2 759	2 968	3 012	2 989	3 211	3 611	3 012	4 097
G.7.3.3. Net Written Premiums / G.7.3.3. Primes Nettes Emises	30 677	34 138	37 034	41 844	44 576	47 475	50 072	51 628
G.8. Others / G.8. Autres								
G.8.1. Direct Business / G.8.1. Assurances Directes								
G.8.1.1. Gross Premiums / G.8.1.1. Primes Brutes	3 827	4 067	4 253	4 942	5 223	5 508	5 850	5 985
G.8.1.2. Ceded Premiums / G.8.1.2. Primes Cédées	499	519	525	623	657	688	773	791
G.8.1.3. Net Written Premiums / G.8.1.3. Primes Nettes Emises	3 328	3 550	3 728	4 319	4 566	4 819	5 076	5 194
G.8.2. Reinsurance Accepted / G.8.2. Réassurance Acceptée								
G.8.2.1. Gross Premiums / G.8.2.1. Primes Brutes	552	570	604	758	818	900	955	968
G.8.2.2. Ceded Premiums / G.8.2.2. Primes Cédées	65	65	71	102	136	193	191	203
G.8.2.3. Net Written Premiums / G.8.2.3. Primes Nettes Emises	487	505	533	657	681	707	764	765
G.8.3. Total								
G.8.3.1. Gross Premiums / G.8.3.1. Primes Brutes	4 379	4 637	4 857	5 700	6 041	6 408	6 805	6 953
G.8.3.2. Ceded Premiums / G.8.3.2. Primes Cédées	564	584	596	725	793	881	965	993
G.8.3.3. Net Written Premiums / G.8.3.3. Primes Nettes Emises	3 815	4 055	4 261	4 975	5 247	5 526	5 840	5 959
G.10. Total								
G.10.1. Direct Business / G.10.1. Assurances Directes								
G.10.1.1. Gross Premiums / G.10.1.1. Primes Brutes	106 778	117 866	126 789	134 182	136 694	138 389	138 016	139 946
G.10.1.2. Ceded Premiums / G.10.1.2. Primes Cédées	25 325	27 808	29 006	29 670	29 335	28 700	26 703	28 201
G.10.1.3. Net Written Premiums / G.10.1.3. Primes Nettes Emises	81 453	90 059	97 783	104 512	107 359	109 689	111 313	111 745
G.10.2. Reinsurance Accepted / G.10.2. Réassurance Acceptée								
G.10.2.1. Gross Premiums / G.10.2.1. Primes Brutes	38 545	43 415	49 290	50 154	51 035	54 941	54 138	58 556
G.10.2.2. Ceded Premiums / G.10.2.2. Primes Cédées	11 717	12 680	13 480	12 842	13 343	14 610	14 736	16 693
G.10.2.3. Net Written Premiums / G.10.2.3. Primes Nettes Emises	26 828	30 734	35 810	37 312	37 692	40 331	39 402	41 863
G.10.3. Total								
G.10.3.1. Gross Premiums / G.10.3.1. Primes Brutes	145 323	161 281	176 079	184 336	187 729	193 330	192 154	198 502
G.10.3.2. Ceded Premiums / G.10.3.2. Primes Cédées	37 043	40 488	42 485	42 512	42 677	43 310	41 439	44 894
G.10.3.3. Net Written Premiums / G.10.3.3. Primes Nettes Emises	108 281	120 793	133 594	141 824	145 052	150 020	150 715	153 609
H. GROSS CLAIMS PAYMENTS / H. PAIEMENTS BRUTS DES SINISTRES								
H.1. Life / H.1. Vie								
H.1.1. Domestic Companies / H.1.1. Entreprises Nationales		45 594	51 553	57 514	62 220	69 157	74 897	84 315
H.1.2. (Foreign Controlled Companies) / H.1.2. (Entreprises Sous Contrôle Etranger)		3 916	3 789	4 140	4 053	4 575	4 211	12 977
H.1.3. Branches & Agencies of Foreign Cies / H.1.3. Succursales et Agences d'Ent. Etrangères		1 412	1 403	1 230	1 337	1 483	1 666	1 848
H.1. Total / H.1. Total		47 006	52 956	58 744	63 557	70 640	76 564	86 163
H.2. Non-Life / H.2. Non-Vie								
H.2.1. Domestic Companies / H.2.1. Entreprises Nationales		121 109	124 121	125 594	131 883	136 338	135 063	151 116
H.2.2. (Foreign Controlled Companies) / H.2.2. (Entreprises Sous Contrôle Etranger)		17 432	7 937	7 867	16 439	16 524	15 686	19 674
H.2.3. Branches & Agencies of Foreign Cies / H.2.3. Succursales et Agences d'Ent. Etrangères		2 738	1 929	1 409	934	911	909	1 019
H.2. Total / H.2. Total		123 848	126 050	127 003	132 817	137 249	135 972	152 135

109

GERMANY — ALLEMAGNE

Monetary Unit: million deutschmarks — Unité monétaire : million de deutschemarks

I. GROSS OPERATING EXPENSES — I. DEPENSES BRUITES D'EXPLOITATION

	1992	1993	1994	1995	1996	1997	1998	1999
I.1. Life — I.1. Vie								
I.1.1. Domestic Companies — I.1.1. Entreprises Nationales		17 139	17 876	17 041	17 831	18 535	19 374	26 137
I.1.2. (Foreign Controlled Companies) — I.1.2. (Entreprises Sous Contrôle Etranger)		1 472	1 314	1 227	1 162	1 226	1 089	4 023
I.1.3. Branches & Agencies of Foreign Cies — I.1.3. Succursales et Agences d'Ent. Etrangères		531	486	365	383	397	431	573
I.1. Total — I.1. Total des Primes Nettes Vie		17 670	18 363	17 405	18 214	18 933	19 805	26 710
I.2. Non-Life — I.2. Non-Vie								
I.2.1. Domestic Companies — I.2.1. Entreprises Nationales		37 158	38 340	41 440	42 723	45 317	46 268	47 722
I.2.2. (Foreign Controlled Companies) — I.2.2. (Entreprises Sous Contrôle Etranger)		5 348	2 452	2 596	5 325	5 492	5 373	6 213
I.2.3. Branches & Agencies of Foreign Cies — I.2.3. Succursales et Agences d'Ent. Etrangères		840	596	465	303	303	311	322
I.2. Total — I.2. Total		37 998	38 936	41 905	43 026	45 620	46 580	48 043

J. COMMISSIONS — J. COMMISSIONS

	1992	1993	1994	1995	1996	1997	1998	1999
J.1. Life — J.1. Vie								
J.1.1. Direct Business — J.1.1. Assurance directe								
J.1.1.1. Domestic Companies — J.1.1.1. Entreprises Nationales		6 810	7 216	6 561	7 125	7 160	7 509	11 692
J.1.1.3. Branches & Agencies of Foreign Cies — J.1.1.3. Succursales et Agences d'Ent. Etrangères		234	219	225	171	173	188	291
J.1.1. Total — J.1.1. Total		7 044	7 435	6 786	7 296	7 333	7 698	11 982
J.1.2. Reinsurance Accepted — J.1.2. Réassurances acceptées								
J.1.2.1. Domestic Companies — J.1.2.1. Entreprises Nationales		2 673	2 940	2 390	2 634	3 257	3 735	4 866
J.1.2. Total — J.1.2. Total		2 673	2 940	2 390	2 634	3 257	3 735	4 866
J.1.3. Total — J.1.3. Total								
J.1.3.1. Domestic Companies — J.1.3.1. Entreprises Nationales		9 483	10 155	8 951	9 759	10 417	11 244	16 558
J.1.3.2. (Foreign Controlled Companies) — J.1.3.2. (Entreprises Sous Contrôle Etranger)		810	742	647	633	686	629	2 538
J.1.3.3. Branches & Agencies of Foreign Cies — J.1.3.3. Succursales et Agences d'Ent. Etrangères		234	219	225	171	173	188	291
J.1.3. Total of Life Net Premiums — J.1.3. Total		9 717	10 374	9 176	9 930	10 590	11 432	16 848
J.2. Non-Life — J.2. Non-Vie								
J.2.1. Direct Business — J.2.1. Assurance directe								
J.2.1.1. Domestic Companies — J.2.1.1. Entreprises Nationales		12 179	12 889	12 867	13 410	13 950	14 421	14 453
J.2.1.3. Branches & Agencies of Foreign Cies — J.2.1.3. Succursales et Agences d'Ent. Etrangères		345	261	364	131	131	136	139
J.2.1. Total — J.2.1. Total des Primes Nettes Vie		12 523	13 150	13 231	13 541	14 080	14 556	14 592
J.2.2. Reinsurance Accepted — J.2.2. Réassurances acceptées								
J.2.2.1. Domestic Companies — J.2.2.1. Entreprises Nationales		11 923	11 974	11 431	11 943	13 145	13 153	14 249
J.2.2.3. Branches & Agencies of Foreign Cies — J.2.2.3. Succursales et Agences d'Ent. Etrangères		89	43	85	0	0	0	0
J.2.2. Total — J.2.2. Total		12 012	12 017	11 516	11 943	13 145	13 153	14 249
J.2.3. Total — J.2.3. Total								
J.2.3.1. Domestic Companies — J.2.3.1. Entreprises Nationales		24 102	24 863	24 297	25 353	27 094	27 574	28 702
J.2.3.2. (Foreign Controlled Companies) — J.2.3.2. (Entreprises Sous Contrôle Etranger)		3 453	1 585	1 533	3 154	3 278	3 197	3 730
J.2.3.3. Branches & Agencies of Foreign Cies — J.2.3.3. Succursales et Agences d'Ent. Etrangères		434	304	449	131	131	136	139
J.2.3. Total — J.2.3. Total		24 536	25 167	24 747	25 484	27 225	27 709	28 840

GREECE

Monetary Unit: million drachmas   Unité monétaire : million de drachmes

	1992	1993	1994	1995	1996	1997	1998	1999	
A. NUMBER OF COMPANIES IN THE REPORTING COUNTRY									**A. NOMBRE D'ENTREPRISES DANS LE PAYS DECLARANT**
A.1. Life									**A.1. Vie**
A.1.1. Domestic Companies	21	23	18	25	24	22	20	18	A.1.1. Entreprises Nationales
A.1.3. Branches & Agencies of Foreign Cies	4	1	2	2	3	2	2	2	A.1.3. Succursales et Agences d'Ent. Etrangères
A.1. All Companies	25	24	20	27	27	24	22	20	A.1. Ensemble des Entreprises
A.2. Non-Life									**A.2. Non-Vie**
A.2.1. Domestic Companies	60	59	57	67	64	58	55	51	A.2.1. Entreprises Nationales
A.2.3. Branches & Agencies of Foreign Cies	61	51	45	49	45	42	38	35	A.2.3. Succursales et Agences d'Ent. Etrangères
A.2. All Companies	121	110	102	116	109	100	93	86	A.2. Ensemble des Entreprises
A.3. Composite									**A.3. Mixte**
A.3.1. Domestic Companies	31	20	25	13	15	16	16	13	A.3.1. Entreprises Nationales
A.3.3. Branches & Agencies of Foreign Cies	1	1	1	1	1	1	1	1	A.3.3. Succursales et Agences d'Ent. Etrangères
A.3. All Companies	32	21	26	14	16	17	17	14	A.3. Ensemble des Entreprises
A.4. Reinsurance									**A.4. Reassurance**
A.4.3. Branches & Agencies of Foreign Cies	..	..	1	0	0	0	..	..	A.4.3. Succursales et Agences d'Ent. Etrangères
A.4. All Companies	..	..	1	0	0	0	..	..	A.4. Ensemble des Entreprises
A.5. Total									**A.5. Total**
A.5.1. Domestic Companies	112	102	100	105	103	96	91	82	A.5.1. Entreprises Nationales
A.5.3. Branches & Agencies of Foreign Cies	66	54	49	52	49	45	41	38	A.5.3. Succursales et Agences d'Ent. Etrangères
A.5. All Insurance Companies	178	156	149	157	152	141	132	120	A.5. Ensemble des Entreprises d'Assurances
B. NUMBER OF EMPLOYEES									**B. NOMBRE D'EMPLOYES**
B.1. Insurance Companies	10 000	8 500	9 596	9 600	..	..	..	..	B.1. Entreprises d'Assurances
B.2. Intermediaries	30 000	..	..	..	..	..	..	..	B.2. Intermediaires
B. Total	40 000	..	..	..	..	..	..	..	B. Total
C. BUSINESS WRITTEN IN THE REPORTING COUNTRY									**C. OPERATIONS CONCLUES DANS LE PAYS DECLARANT**
C.1. Life									**C.1. Vie**
C.1.1. Gross Premiums									C.1.1. Primes Brutes
C.1.1.1. Direct Business									C.1.1.1. Assurances Directes
C.1.1.1.1. Domestic Companies	100 927	123 494	144 111	159 337	183 692	257 025	304 425	419 633	C.1.1.1.1. Entreprises Nationales
C.1.1.1.3. Branches & Agencies of Foreign Cies	30 220	37 996	45 967	53 854	64 318	29 230	32 863	36 286	C.1.1.1.3. Succursales et Agences d'Ent. Etrangères
C.1.1.1. Total	131 147	161 490	190 078	213 192	248 010	286 255	337 288	455 919	C.1.1.1. Total
C.1.1.2. Reinsurance Accepted									C.1.1.2. Réassurance Acceptée
C.1.1.2.1. Domestic Companies	..	229	209	132	205	269	377	551	C.1.1.2.1. Entreprises Nationales
C.1.1.2.3. Branches & Agencies of Foreign Cies	..	0	0	..	200	..	7	25	C.1.1.2.3. Succursales et Agences d'Ent. Etrangères
C.1.1.2. Total	..	229	209	132	405	269	384	576	C.1.1.2. Total
C.1.1.3. Total									C.1.1.3. Total
C.1.1.3.1. Domestic Companies	100 927	123 723	144 320	159 470	183 897	257 294	304 802	420 184	C.1.1.3.1. Entreprises Nationales
C.1.1.3.3. Branches & Agencies of Foreign Cies	30 220	37 996	45 967	53 854	64 518	29 230	32 870	36 311	C.1.1.3.3. Succursales et Agences d'Ent. Etrangères
C.1.1.3. Total Gross Premiums	131 147	161 719	190 287	213 325	248 415	286 524	337 672	456 495	C.1.1.3. Total des Primes Brutes
C.1.2. Ceded Premiums									C.1.2. Primes Cédées
C.1.2.1. Domestic Companies	..	25 264	29 168	31 407	29 763	23 070	..	25 029	C.1.2.1. Entreprises Nationales
C.1.2.3. Branches & Agencies of Foreign Cies	..	515	435	565	786	795	..	1 013	C.1.2.3. Succursales et Agences d'Ent. Etrangères
C.1.2. Total	..	25 779	29 603	31 972	30 549	23 865	..	26 042	C.1.2. Total
C.1.3. Net Written Premiums									C.1.3. Primes Nettes Emises
C.1.3.1. Domestic Companies	100 927	98 459	115 152	128 063	154 134	234 224	..	395 155	C.1.3.1. Entreprises Nationales
C.1.3.3. Branches & Agencies of Foreign Cies	30 220	37 481	45 532	53 289	63 732	28 435	..	35 298	C.1.3.3. Succursales et Agences d'Ent. Etrangères
C.1.3. Total	131 147	135 940	160 684	181 353	217 866	262 659	..	430 453	C.1.3. Total

111

C.2. Non-Life / C.2. Non-Vie

Label	1992	1993	1994	1995	1996	1997	1998	1999
C.2.1. Gross premiums / C.2.1. Primes Brutes								
C.2.1.1. Direct Business / C.2.1.1. Assurances Directes								
C.2.1.1.1. Domestic Companies / Entreprises Nationales	121 249	153 159	175 235	200 772	239 409	261 174	292 110	337 335
C.2.1.1.3. Branches & Agencies of Foreign Cies / Succursales et Agences d'Ent. Etrangères	19 729	20 820	21 134	22 459	26 035	26 677	27 760	27 107
C.2.1.1. Total	140 978	173 979	196 369	223 231	265 444	287 851	319 870	364 442
C.2.1.2. Reinsurance Accepted / Réassurance Acceptée								
C.2.1.2.1. Domestic Companies / Entreprises Nationales	..	11 270	12 471	6 923	11 782	6 608	7 905	6 559
C.2.1.2.3. Branches & Agencies of Foreign Cies / Succursales et Agences d'Ent. Etrangères	..	2 284	1 854	2 359	2 288	3 891	4 903	3 850
C.2.1.2. Total	..	13 554	14 325	9 283	14 070	10 499	12 808	10 409
C.2.1.3. Total								
C.2.1.3.1. Domestic Companies / Entreprises Nationales	121 249	164 429	187 706	207 695	251 191	267 782	300 015	343 894
C.2.1.3.3. Branches & Agencies of Foreign Cies / Succursales et Agences d'Ent. Etrangères	19 729	23 104	22 988	24 819	28 323	30 568	32 663	30 957
C.2.1.3. Total Gross Premiums / Total des Primes Brutes	140 978	187 533	210 694	232 515	279 514	298 350	332 678	374 851
C.2.2. Ceded Premiums / C.2.2. Primes Cédées								
C.2.2.1. Domestic Companies / Entreprises Nationales	..	42 378	49 259	56 522	61 326	59 973	..	73 299
C.2.2.3. Branches & Agencies of Foreign Cies / Succursales et Agences d'Ent. Etrangères	..	7 254	7 143	5 584	7 931	8 979	..	10 629
C.2.2. Total	..	49 632	56 402	62 106	69 257	68 952	..	83 928
C.2.3. Net Written Premiums / C.2.3. Primes Nettes Emises								
C.2.3.1. Domestic Companies / Entreprises Nationales	121 249	122 051	138 447	151 173	189 865	207 809	..	270 595
C.2.3.3. Branches & Agencies of Foreign Cies / Succursales et Agences d'Ent. Etrangères	19 729	15 850	15 845	19 235	20 392	21 589	..	20 328
C.2.3. Total	140 978	137 901	154 292	170 409	210 257	229 398	..	290 923

C.3. Total / C.3. Total

Label	1992	1993	1994	1995	1996	1997	1998	1999
C.3.1. Gross Premiums / C.3.1. Primes Brutes								
C.3.1.1. Direct Business / C.3.1.1. Assurances Directes								
C.3.1.1.1. Domestic Companies / Entreprises Nationales	222 177	276 653	319 346	360 109	423 101	518 199	596 535	756 968
C.3.1.1.3. Branches & Agencies of Foreign Cies / Succursales et Agences d'Ent. Etrangères	49 948	58 816	67 101	76 313	90 353	55 907	60 623	63 393
C.3.1.1. Total	272 125	335 469	386 447	436 423	513 454	574 106	657 158	820 361
C.3.1.2. Reinsurance Accepted / Réassurance Acceptée								
C.3.1.2.1. Domestic Companies / Entreprises Nationales	..	11 499	12 680	7 055	11 987	6 877	8 282	7 110
C.3.1.2.3. Branches & Agencies of Foreign Cies / Succursales et Agences d'Ent. Etrangères	..	2 284	1 854	..	2 488	..	4 910	3 875
C.3.1.2. Total	..	13 783	14 534	9 415	14 475	10 768	13 192	10 985
C.3.1.3. Total								
C.3.1.3.1. Domestic Companies / Entreprises Nationales	222 177	288 152	332 026	367 165	435 088	525 076	604 817	764 078
C.3.1.3.3. Branches & Agencies of Foreign Cies / Succursales et Agences d'Ent. Etrangères	49 948	61 100	68 955	78 673	92 841	59 798	65 533	67 268
C.3.1.3. Total Gross Premiums / Total des Primes Brutes	272 125	349 252	400 981	445 840	527 929	584 874	670 350	831 346
C.3.2. Ceded Premiums / C.3.2. Primes Cédées								
C.3.2.1. Domestic Companies / Entreprises Nationales	..	67 642	78 427	87 929	91 089	83 043	..	98 328
C.3.2.3. Branches & Agencies of Foreign Cies / Succursales et Agences d'Ent. Etrangères	..	7 769	7 578	6 149	8 717	9 774	..	21 528
C.3.2. Total	..	75 411	86 005	94 078	99 806	92 817	..	167 656
C.3.3. Net Written Premiums / C.3.3. Primes Nettes Emises								
C.3.3.1. Domestic Companies / Entreprises Nationales	222 177	220 510	253 599	279 236	343 999	442 033	..	665 750
C.3.3.3. Branches & Agencies of Foreign Cies / Succursales et Agences d'Ent. Etrangères	49 948	53 331	61 377	72 524	84 124	50 024	..	40 656
C.3.3. Total	272 125	273 841	314 976	351 762	428 123	492 057	..	721 376

D. NET WRITTEN PREMIUMS IN THE REPORTING COUNTRY IN TERMS OF DOMESTIC AND FOREIGN RISKS / D. PRIMES NETTES EMISES DANS LE PAYS DECLARANT EN RISQUES NATIONAUX ET ETRANGERS

D.1. Life / D.1. Vie

Label	1992	1993	1994	1995	1996	1997	1998	1999
D.1.1. Domestic Risks / D.1.1. Risques Nationaux								
D.1.1.1. Domestic Companies / Entreprises Nationales								
D.1.1.3. Branches & Agencies of Foreign Cies / Succursales et Agences d'Ent. Etrangères								
D.1.1. Total / Total des Primes Nettes Vie								
D.1.3. Total								
D.1.3.1. Domestic Companies / Entreprises Nationales	..	98 459	115 152	128 063	154 134	..	..	395 155
D.1.3.3. Branches & Agencies of Foreign Cies / Succursales et Agences d'Ent. Etrangères	..	37 481	45 532	53 289	63 732	..	..	35 298
D.1.3. Total of Life Net Premiums / Total des Primes Nettes Vie	..	135 940	160 684	181 353	217 866	..	..	430 453

Monetary Unit: million drachmas

D.2. Non-Life / D.2. Non-Vie

Item	1992	1993	1994	1995	1996	1997	1998	1999
D.2.1. Domestic Risks / **D.2.1. Risques Nationaux**								
D.2.1.1. Domestic Companies / D.2.1.1. Entreprises Nationales	..	..	..	..	189 865	..	..	
D.2.1.3. Branches & Agencies of Foreign Cies / D.2.1.3. Succursales et Agences d'Ent. Etrangères	..	..	..	..	20 392	..	..	
D.2.1. Total / D.2.1. Total des Primes Nettes Vie	..	..	..	..	210 257	..	..	
D.2.3. Total								
D.2.3.1. Domestic Companies / D.2.3.1. Entreprises Nationales	..	122 051	138 447	151 173	189 865	..	..	270 595
D.2.3.3. Branches & Agencies of Foreign Cies / D.2.3.3. Succursales et Agences d'Ent. Etrangères	..	15 850	15 845	19 235	20 392	..	..	20 328
D.2.3. Total / D.2.3. Total des Primes Nettes Vie	..	137 901	154 292	170 409	210 257	..	..	290 923

E. BUSINESS WRITTEN ABROAD / E. OPERATIONS A L'ETRANGER

E.1. Life / E.1. Vie

Item	1992	1993	1994	1995	1996	1997	1998	1999
E.1.1. Gross Premiums / **E.1.1. Primes Brutes**								
E.1.1.1. Direct Business / E.1.1.1. Assurance Directe								
E.1.1.1.1. Branches & Agencies / E.1.1.1.1. Succursales & Agences							2 391	
E.1.1.1. Total / E.1.1.1. Total							2 391	
E.1.1.3. Total / E.1.1.3 Total								
E.1.1.3.1. Branches & Agencies / E.1.1.3.1. Succursales & Agences								14 593
E.1.1.3. Total Gross Premiums / E.1.1.3.1. Total des Primes Brutes								14 593

F. OUTSTANDING INVESTMENT BY DIRECT INSURANCE COMPANIES / F. ENCOURS DES PLACEMENTS DES ENTREPRISES D'ASSURANCES DIRECTES

F.1. Life / F.1. Vie

Item	1992	1993	1994	1995	1996	1997	1998	1999
F.1.1. Real Estate / F.1.1. Immobilier								
F.1.1. Total / F.1.1. Total	..	..	..	..	..	38 275	..	
F.1.2. Mortgage Loans / F.1.2. Prêts Hypothécaires								
F.1.2. Total / F.1.2. Total	..	..	..	..	..	1 120	..	
F.1.3. Shares / F.1.3. Actions								
F.1.3. Total / F.1.3. Total	..	..	..	..	..	104 832	..	
F.1.4. Bonds with Fixed Revenue / F.1.4. Obligations								
F.1.4. Total / F.1.4. Total	..	..	..	..	..	261 280	..	
F.1.5. Loans other than Mortgage Loans / F.1.5. Prêts Autres qu'Hypothécaires								
F.1.5. Total / F.1.5. Total	..	..	..	..	..	10 447	..	
F.1.6. Other Investments / F.1.6. Autres Placements								
F.1.6. Total / F.1.6. Total	..	..	..	..	..	32 960	..	
F.1.7. Total / F.1.7. Total								
F.1.7. Total of Life Investments / F.1.7. Total des Placements Vie	..	..	..	..	..	448 914	..	

F.2. Non-Life / F.2. Non-Vie

Item	1992	1993	1994	1995	1996	1997	1998	1999
F.2.1. Real Estate / F.2.1. Immobilier								
F.2.1. Total / F.2.1. Total	..	..	..	..	..	59 188	..	
F.2.2. Mortgage Loans / F.2.2. Prêts Hypothécaires								
F.2.2. Total / F.2.2. Total	..	..	..	..	..	4 916	..	
F.2.3. Shares / F.2.3. Actions								
F.2.3. Total / F.2.3. Total	..	..	..	..	..	108 928	..	
F.2.4. Bonds with Fixed Revenue / F.2.4. Obligations								
F.2.4. Total / F.2.4. Total	..	..	..	..	..	340 580	..	
F.2.5. Loans other than Mortgage Loans / F.2.5. Prêts Autres qu'Hypothécaires								
F.2.5. Total / F.2.5. Total	..	..	..	..	..	5 379	..	
F.2.6. Other Investments / F.2.6. Autres Placements								
F.2.6. Total / F.2.6. Total	..	..	..	..	..	37 050	..	
F.2.7. Total / F.2.7. Total								
F.2.7. Total of Non-Life Investments / F.2.7. Total des Placements Non-Vie	..	..	..	..	..	556 041	..	

113

Monetary Unit: million drachmas — Unité monétaire : million de drachmes

G. BREAKDOWN OF NON-LIFE PREMIUMS — G. VENTILATIONS DES PRIMES NON-VIE

	1992	1993	1994	1995	1996	1997	1998	1999
G.1. Motor vehicle — G.1. Assurance Automobile								
G.1.1. Direct Business — G.1.1. Assurances Directes								
G.1.1.1. Gross Premiums — G.1.1.1. Primes Brutes	76 845	104 464	118 227	134 936	164 239	186 128	208 119	237 008
G.1.2. Reinsurance Accepted — G.1.2. Réassurance Acceptée								
G.1.2.1. Gross Premiums — G.1.2.1. Primes Brutes	:	1 517	1 365	1 065	1 092	635	1 083	893
G.1.3. Total								
G.1.3.1. Gross Premiums — G.1.3.1. Primes Brutes	:	105 981	119 592	136 001	165 331	186 763	209 202	237 901
G.1.3.2. Ceded Premiums — G.1.3.2. Primes Cédées								14 865
G.1.3.3. Net Written Premiums — G.1.3.3. Primes Nettes Emises								223 036
G.2. Marine, Aviation — G.2. Marine, Aviation								
G.2.1. Direct Business — G.2.1. Assurances Directes								
G.2.1.1. Gross Premiums — G.2.1.1. Primes Brutes	10 788	12 470	5 784	6 468	4 767	16 517	16 286	5 886
G.2.2. Reinsurance Accepted — G.2.2. Réassurance Acceptée								
G.2.2.1. Gross Premiums — G.2.2.1. Primes Brutes	:	1 089	684	674	424	619	2 770	815
G.2.3. Total								
G.2.3.1. Gross Premiums — G.2.3.1. Primes Brutes	:	13 559	6 468	7 142	5 191	17 136	19 056	6 701
G.2.3.2. Ceded Premiums — G.2.3.2. Primes Cédées								3 460
G.2.3.3. Net Written Premiums — G.2.3.3. Primes Nettes Emises								3 241
G.3. Freight — G.3. Fret								
G.3.1. Direct Business — G.3.1. Assurances Directes								
G.3.1.1. Gross Premiums — G.3.1.1. Primes Brutes	773	:	8 859	10 118	9 705	9 893	1 512	10 956
G.3.2. Reinsurance Accepted — G.3.2. Réassurance Acceptée								
G.3.2.1. Gross Premiums — G.3.2.1. Primes Brutes	:	:	535	603	480	687	15	435
G.3.3. Total								
G.3.3.1. Gross Premiums — G.3.3.1. Primes Brutes	:	:	9 394	10 721	10 185	10 580	1 527	11 391
G.3.3.2. Ceded Premiums — G.3.3.2. Primes Cédées								7 283
G.3.3.3. Net Written Premiums — G.3.3.3. Primes Nettes Emises								4 108
G.4. Fire, Property Damages — G.4. Incendie, Dommages aux Biens								
G.4.1. Direct Business — G.4.1. Assurances Directes								
G.4.1.1. Gross Premiums — G.4.1.1. Primes Brutes	32 122	33 570	36 268	38 190	53 066	41 482	60 576	70 900
G.4.2. Reinsurance Accepted — G.4.2. Réassurance Acceptée								
G.4.2.1. Gross Premiums — G.4.2.1. Primes Brutes	:	3 332	4 070	3 063	3 828	3 836	3 442	3 350
G.4.3. Total								
G.4.3.1. Gross Premiums — G.4.3.1. Primes Brutes	:	36 902	40 338	41 253	56 894	45 318	64 018	74 250
G.4.3.2. Ceded Premiums — G.4.3.2. Primes Cédées								43 267
G.4.3.3. Net Written Premiums — G.4.3.3. Primes Nettes Emises								30 983
G.5. Pecuniary Losses — G.5. Pertes Pécunières								
G.5.1. Direct Business — G.5.1. Assurances Directes								
G.5.1.1. Gross Premiums — G.5.1.1. Primes Brutes	72	:	:	:	1 980	1 475	1 764	5 212
G.5.2. Reinsurance Accepted — G.5.2. Réassurance Acceptée								
G.5.2.1. Gross Premiums — G.5.2.1. Primes Brutes	:	:	:	:	207	163	165	210
G.5.3. Total								
G.5.3.1. Gross Premiums — G.5.3.1. Primes Brutes	:	:	:	:	2 187	1 638	1 929	5 422
G.5.3.2. Ceded Premiums — G.5.3.2. Primes Cédées								2 800
G.5.3.3. Net Written Premiums — G.5.3.3. Primes Nettes Emises								2 622
G.6. General Liability — G.6. Responsabilité Générale								
G.6.1. Direct Business — G.6.1. Assurances Directes								
G.6.1.1. Gross Premiums — G.6.1.1. Primes Brutes	1 837	2 291	2 980	3 453	3 853	5 111	4 914	5 465
G.6.2. Reinsurance Accepted — G.6.2. Réassurance Acceptée								
G.6.2.1. Gross Premiums — G.6.2.1. Primes Brutes	:	126	177	134	218	313	282	213
G.6.3. Total								
G.6.3.1. Gross Premiums — G.6.3.1. Primes Brutes	:	2 417	3 157	3 587	4 071	5 424	5 196	5 678
G.6.3.2. Ceded Premiums — G.6.3.2. Primes Cédées								3 640
G.6.3.3. Net Written Premiums — G.6.3.3. Primes Nettes Emises								2 038
G.7. Accident, Health — G.7. Accident, Santé								
G.7.1. Direct Business — G.7.1. Assurances Directes								
G.7.1.1. Gross Premiums — G.7.1.1. Primes Brutes	7 032	8 653	9 932	11 245	11 962	13 439	15 058	15 995
G.7.2. Reinsurance Accepted — G.7.2. Réassurance Acceptée								
G.7.2.1. Gross Premiums — G.7.2.1. Primes Brutes	:	2 381	2 514	2 664	2 538	3 704	3 137	1 947
G.7.3. Total								
G.7.3.1. Gross Premiums — G.7.3.1. Primes Brutes	:	11 034	12 446	13 909	14 500	17 143	18 195	17 942
G.7.3.2. Ceded Premiums — G.7.3.2. Primes Cédées								5 646
G.7.3.3. Net Written Premiums — G.7.3.3. Primes Nettes Emises								12 296

114

Monetary Unit: million drachmas

	1992	1993	1994	1995	1996	1997	1998	1999
G.8. Others / G.8. Autres								
G.8.1. Direct Business / G.8.1. Assurances Directes								
G.8.1.1. Gross Premiums / G.8.1.1. Primes Brutes	::	12 531	14 319	18 821	15 872	13 806	11 641	13 020
G.8.2. Reinsurance Accepted / G.8.2. Réassurance Acceptée								
G.8.2.1. Gross Premiums / G.8.2.1. Primes Brutes	::	5 109	4 980	1 080	5 283	542	1 914	2 546
G.8.3. Total / G.8.3. Total								
G.8.3.1. Gross Premiums / G.8.3.1. Primes Brutes	::	17 640	19 299	19 901	21 155	14 348	13 555	15 566
G.8.3.2. Ceded Premiums / G.8.3.2. Primes Cédées								2 967
G.8.3.3. Net Written Premiums / G.8.3.3. Primes Nettes Emises								12 599
G.10. Total								
G.10.1. Direct Business / G.10.1. Assurances Directes								
G.10.1.1. Gross Premiums / G.10.1.1. Primes Brutes	129 469	173 979	196 369	223 231	265 444	287 851	319 870	364 442
G.10.2. Reinsurance Accepted / G.10.2. Réassurance Acceptée								
G.10.2.1. Gross Premiums / G.10.2.1. Primes Brutes	::	13 554	14 325	9 283	14 070	10 499	12 808	10 409
G.10.3. Total / G.10.3. Total								
G.10.3.1. Gross Premiums / G.10.3.1. Primes Brutes	::	187 533	210 694	232 514	279 514	298 350	332 678	374 851
G.10.3.2. Ceded Premiums / G.10.3.2. Primes Cédées	::	49 632	56 402	::	::	::	::	83 928
G.10.3.3. Net Written Premiums / G.10.3.3. Primes Nettes Emises	::	137 901	154 292	::	::	::	::	290 923
H. GROSS CLAIMS PAYMENTS / H. PAIEMENTS BRUTS DES SINISTRES								
H.1. Life / H.1. Vie								
H.1.1. Domestic Companies / H.1.1. Entreprises Nationales					69 784	101 852	128 282	199 419
H.1.3. Branches & Agencies of Foreign Cies / H.1.3. Succursales et Agences d'Ent. Etrangères					20 982	17 310	19 932	21 947
H.1. Total / H.1. Total					90 766	119 162	148 214	221 366
H.2. Non-Life / H.2. Non-Vie								
H.2.1. Domestic Companies / H.2.1. Entreprises Nationales					148 109	160 246	203 951	226 523
H.2.3. Branches & Agencies of Foreign Cies / H.2.3. Succursales et Agences d'Ent. Etrangères					13 667	16 240	23 147	23 984
H.2. Total / H.2. Total					161 776	176 486	227 098	250 507
I. GROSS OPERATING EXPENSES / I. DEPENSES BRUTES D'EXPLOITATION								
I.1. Life / I.1. Vie								
I.1.1. Domestic Companies / I.1.1. Entreprises Nationales					225 201	80 381	81 409	::
I.1.3. Branches & Agencies of Foreign Cies / I.1.3. Succursales et Agences d'Ent. Etrangères					80 433	3 019	4 329	::
I.1. Total / I.1. Total des Primes Nettes Vie					305 634	83 400	85 738	::
I.2. Non-Life / I.2. Non-Vie								
I.2.1. Domestic Companies / I.2.1. Entreprises Nationales					288 296	85 186	90 444	::
I.2.3. Branches & Agencies of Foreign Cies / I.2.3. Succursales et Agences d'Ent. Etrangères					32 391	6 325	4 929	::
I.2. Total / I.2. Total					320 687	91 511	95 373	::
J. COMMISSIONS / J. COMMISSIONS								
J.1. Life / J.1. Vie								
J.1.1. Direct Business / J.1.1. Assurance directe								
J.1.1.1. Domestic Companies / J.1.1.1. Entreprises Nationales					28 520	40 302	47 414	::
J.1.1.3. Branches & Agencies of Foreign Cies / J.1.1.3. Succursales et Agences d'Ent. Etrangères					7 550	2 073	2 286	::
J.1.1. Total / J.1.1. Total					36 070	42 375	49 700	::

GRECE

Monetary Unit: million drachmas

Unité monétaire : million de drachmes

	1992	1993	1994	1995	1996	1997	1998	1999	
J.1.2. Reinsurance Accepted									J.1.2. Réassurances acceptées
J.1.2.1. Domestic Companies					14	:	8 126	:	J.1.2.1. Entreprises Nationales
J.1.2.2. (Foreign Controlled Companies)							412	:	J.1.2.2. (Entreprises Sous Contrôle Etranger)
J.1.2. Total					14	:	8 538	:	J.1.2. Total
J.1.3. Total									J.1.3. Total
J.1.3.1. Domestic Companies					28 534	40 302	55 540	:	J.1.3.1. Entreprises Nationales
J.1.3.3. Branches & Agencies of Foreign Cies					7 550	2 073	2 698	:	J.1.3.3. Succursales et Agences d'Ent. Etrangères
J.1.3. Total of Life Net Premiums					36 084	42 375	58 238	:	J.1.3. Total
J.2. Non-Life									**J.2. Non-Vie**
J.2.1. Direct Business									J.2.1. Assurance directe
J.2.1.1. Domestic Companies					34 995	39 065	51 526	:	J.2.1.1. Entreprises Nationales
J.2.1.3. Branches & Agencies of Foreign Cies					5 590	5 905	6 400	:	J.2.1.3. Succursales et Agences d'Ent. Etrangères
J.2.1. Total					40 585	44 970	57 926	:	J.2.1. Total des Primes Nettes Vie
J.2.2. Reinsurance Accepted									J.2.2. Réassurances acceptées
J.2.2.1. Domestic Companies					3 106	:	15 417	:	J.2.2.1. Entreprises Nationales
J.2.2.3. Branches & Agencies of Foreign Cies					731	:	2 270	:	J.2.2.3. Succursales et Agences d'Ent. Etrangères
J.2.2. Total					3 837	:	17 687	:	J.2.2. Total
J.2.3. Total									J.2.3. Total
J.2.3.1. Domestic Companies					38 101	39 065	66 943	28 582	J.2.3.1. Entreprises Nationales
J.2.3.3. Branches & Agencies of Foreign Cies					6 321	5 905	8 670	6 920	J.2.3.3. Succursales et Agences d'Ent. Etrangères
J.2.3. Total					44 422	44 970	75 613	35 502	J.2.3. Total

Monetary Unit: million forints

Unité monétaire : million de forints

	1992	1993	1994	1995	1996	1997	1998	1999	
A. NUMBER OF COMPANIES IN THE REPORTING COUNTRY									**A. NOMBRE D'ENTREPRISES DANS LE PAYS DECLARANT**
A.1. Life									**A.1. Vie**
A.1.1. Domestic Companies	0	0	0	0	4	5	6	8	A.1.1. Entreprises Nationales
A.1.2. (Foreign Controlled Companies)	0	0	0	0	0	1	1	2	A.1.2. (Entreprises Sous Contrôle Etranger)
A.1. All Companies	0	0	0	0	4	5	6	8	A.1. Ensemble des Entreprises
A.2. Non-Life									**A.2. Non-Vie**
A.2.1. Domestic Companies	..	..	1	1	25	29	37	37	A.2.1. Entreprises Nationales
A.2.2. (Foreign Controlled Companies)	0	0	0	0	2	3	4	3	A.2.2. (Entreprises Sous Contrôle Etranger)
A.2. All Companies	..	..	1	1	25	29	37	37	A.2. Ensemble des Entreprises
A.3. Composite									**A.3. Mixte**
A.3.1. Domestic Companies	13	14	13	14	14	14	14	12	A.3.1. Entreprises Nationales
A.3.2. (Foreign Controlled Companies)	10	11	11	11	12	12	12	11	A.3.2. (Entreprises Sous Contrôle Etranger)
A.3. All Companies	13	14	13	14	14	14	14	12	A.3. Ensemble des Entreprises
A.5. Total									**A.5. Total**
A.5.1. Domestic Companies	13	14	14	15	43	48	57	57	A.5.1. Entreprises Nationales
A.5.2. (Foreign Controlled Companies)	10	11	11	11	15	16	17	16	A.5.2. (Entreprises Sous Contrôle Etranger)
A.5. All Insurance Companies	13	14	14	15	43	48	57	57	A.5. Ensemble des Entreprises d'Assurances
B. NUMBER OF EMPLOYEES									**B. NOMBRE D'EMPLOYES**
B.1. Insurance Companies	13 349	15 636	16 388	17 138	26 100	29 365	28 550	31 199	B.1. Entreprises d'Assurances
B.2. Intermediaries	..	755	642	..	..	..	..		B.2. Intermediaires
B. Total	..	16 391	17 030	..	..	..	..		B. Total
C. BUSINESS WRITTEN IN THE REPORTING COUNTRY									**C. OPERATIONS CONCLUES DANS LE PAYS DECLARANT**
C.1. Life									**C.1. Vie**
C.1.1. Gross Premiums									C.1.1. Primes Brutes
C.1.1.1. Direct Business									C.1.1.1. Assurances Directes
C.1.1.1.1. Domestic Companies	10 455	15 559	24 070	35 469	49 040	65 451	91 856	118 501	C.1.1.1.1. Entreprises Nationales
C.1.1.1.2. (Foreign Controlled Companies)	10 419	15 524	23 978	34 983	47 602	62 086	81 405	100 451	C.1.1.1.2. (Entreprises Sous Contrôle Etranger)
C.1.1.1. Total	10 455	15 559	24 070	35 469	49 040	65 451	91 856	118 501	C.1.1.1. Total
C.1.1.2. Reinsurance Accepted									C.1.1.2. Réassurance Acceptée
C.1.1.2.1. Domestic Companies	77	255	0	0	0	0	0	0	C.1.1.2.1. Entreprises Nationales
C.1.1.2.2. (Foreign Controlled Companies)	77	255	0	0	0	0	4	0	C.1.1.2.2. (Entreprises Sous Contrôle Etranger)
C.1.1.2. Total	77	255	0	0	0	0	4	0	C.1.1.2. Total
C.1.1.3. Total									C.1.1.3. Total
C.1.1.3.1. Domestic Companies	10 532	15 814	24 070	35 469	49 040	65 451	91 859	118 501	C.1.1.3.1. Entreprises Nationales
C.1.1.3.2. (Foreign Controlled Companies)	10 496	15 779	23 978	34 983	47 602	62 086	81 405	100 451	C.1.1.3.2. (Entreprises Sous Contrôle Etranger)
C.1.1.3. Total Gross Premiums	10 532	15 814	24 070	35 469	49 040	65 451	91 859	118 501	C.1.1.3. Total des Primes Brutes
C.1.2. Ceded Premiums									C.1.2. Primes Cédées
C.1.2.1. Domestic Companies	2 703	5 855	8 606	12 053	16 121	5 629	15 556	17 187	C.1.2.1. Entreprises Nationales
C.1.2.2. (Foreign Controlled Companies)	2 703	5 854	8 604	12 048	16 118	5 587	15 506	17 147	C.1.2.2. (Entreprises Sous Contrôle Etranger)
C.1.2. Total	2 703	5 855	8 606	12 053	16 121	5 629	15 556	17 187	C.1.2. Total
C.1.3. Net Written Premiums									C.1.3. Primes Nettes Emises
C.1.3.1. Domestic Companies	7 829	9 959	15 464	23 416	32 919	59 822	76 303	101 314	C.1.3.1. Entreprises Nationales
C.1.3.2. (Foreign Controlled Companies)	7 793	9 925	15 373	22 935	31 484	56 499	65 899	83 304	C.1.3.2. (Entreprises Sous Contrôle Etranger)
C.1.3. Total	7 829	9 959	15 464	23 416	32 919	59 822	76 303	101 314	C.1.3. Total

117

Monetary Unit: million forints

Unité monétaire : million de forints

C.2. Non-Life / C.2. Non-Vie

	1992	1993	1994	1995	1996	1997	1998	1999
C.2.1. Gross premiums / C.2.1. Primes Brutes								
C.2.1.1. Direct Business / C.2.1.1. Assurances Directes								
C.2.1.1.1.Domestic Companies / C.2.1.1.1. Entreprises Nationales	47 734	58 187	69 435	83 026	104 346	132 895	154 665	168 790
C.2.1.1.2. (Foreign Controlled Companies) / C.2.1.1.2. (Entreprises Sous Contrôle Etranger)	45 404	55 827	65 226	76 651	95 018	120 977	142 168	153 023
C.2.1.1. Total	47 734	58 187	69 435	83 026	104 346	132 895	154 665	168 790
C.2.1.2. Reinsurance Accepted / C.2.1.2. Réassurance Acceptée								
C.2.1.2.1. Domestic Companies / C.2.1.2.1. Entreprises Nationales	789	658	542	527	513	560	790	384
C.2.1.2.2. (Foreign Controlled Companies) / C.2.1.2.2. (Entreprises Sous Contrôle Etranger)	789	483	522	469	416	374	520	384
C.2.1.2. Total	789	658	542	527	513	560	790	384
C.2.1.3. Total	48 523	58 845	69 978	83 553	104 859	133 455	155 454	169 174
C.2.1.3.1. Domestic Companies / C.2.1.3.1. Entreprises Nationales	46 193	56 310	65 748	77 120	95 434	121 351	142 689	153 407
C.2.1.3.2. (Foreign Controlled Companies) / C.2.1.3.2. (Entreprises Sous Contrôle Etranger)								
C.2.1.3. Total Gross Premiums / C.2.1.3. Total des Primes Brutes	48 523	58 845	69 978	83 553	104 859	133 455	155 454	169 174
C.2.2. Ceded Premiums / C.2.2. Primes Cédées								
C.2.2.1. Domestic Companies / C.2.2.1. Entreprises Nationales	6 496	8 341	10 541	12 953	12 384	20 907	25 172	31 386
C.2.2.2. (Foreign Controlled Companies) / C.2.2.2. (Entreprises Sous Contrôle Etranger)	6 374	8 075	10 185	12 293	11 978	20 304	23 350	28 885
C.2.2. Total	6 496	8 341	10 541	12 953	12 384	20 907	25 172	31 386
C.2.3. Net Written Premiums / C.2.3. Primes Nettes Emises								
C.2.3.1. Domestic Companies / C.2.3.1. Entreprises Nationales	42 027	50 504	59 437	70 600	92 475	112 548	130 283	137 788
C.2.3.2. (Foreign Controlled Companies) / C.2.3.2. (Entreprises Sous Contrôle Etranger)	39 819	48 235	55 562	64 827	83 456	101 047	119 338	124 522
C.2.3. Total	42 027	50 504	59 437	70 600	92 475	112 548	130 283	137 788

C.3. Total / C.3. Total

	1992	1993	1994	1995	1996	1997	1998	1999
C.3.1. Gross Premiums / C.3.1. Primes Brutes								
C.3.1.1. Direct Business / C.3.1.1. Assurances Directes								
C.3.1.1.1. Domestic Companies / C.3.1.1.1. Entreprises Nationales	58 189	73 746	93 505	118 495	153 386	198 346	246 520	287 291
C.3.1.1.2. (Foreign Controlled Companies) / C.3.1.1.2. (Entreprises Sous Contrôle Etranger)	55 823	71 351	89 204	111 634	142 620	183 063	223 574	253 474
C.3.1.1. Total	58 189	73 746	93 505	118 495	153 386	198 346	246 520	287 291
C.3.1.2. Reinsurance Accepted / C.3.1.2. Réassurance Acceptée								
C.3.1.2.1. Domestic Companies / C.3.1.2.1. Entreprises Nationales	866	913	542	527	513	560	793	384
C.3.1.2.2. (Foreign Controlled Companies) / C.3.1.2.2. (Entreprises Sous Contrôle Etranger)	866	738	522	469	416	374	520	384
C.3.1.2. Total	866	913	542	527	513	560	793	384
C.3.1.3. Total	59 055	74 659	94 048	119 022	153 899	198 906	247 314	287 675
C.3.1.3.1. Domestic Companies / C.3.1.3.1. Entreprises Nationales	56 689	72 089	89 726	112 103	143 036	183 437	224 094	253 858
C.3.1.3.2. (Foreign Controlled Companies) / C.3.1.3.2. (Entreprises Sous Contrôle Etranger)								
C.3.1.3. Total Gross Premiums / C.3.1.3. Total des Primes Brutes	59 055	74 659	94 048	119 022	153 899	198 906	247 314	287 675
C.3.2. Ceded Premiums / C.3.2. Primes Cédées								
C.3.2.1. Domestic Companies / C.3.2.1. Entreprises Nationales	9 199	14 196	19 147	25 006	28 505	26 536	40 728	48 573
C.3.2.2. (Foreign Controlled Companies) / C.3.2.2. (Entreprises Sous Contrôle Etranger)	9 077	13 929	18 789	24 341	28 096	25 891	38 857	46 032
C.3.2. Total	9 199	14 196	19 147	25 006	28 505	26 536	40 728	48 573
C.3.3. Net Written Premiums / C.3.3. Primes Nettes Emises								
C.3.3.1. Domestic Companies / C.3.3.1. Entreprises Nationales	49 856	60 463	74 901	94 016	125 394	172 370	206 586	239 102
C.3.3.2. (Foreign Controlled Companies) / C.3.3.2. (Entreprises Sous Contrôle Etranger)	47 612	58 160	70 935	87 762	114 940	157 546	185 287	207 826
C.3.3. Total	49 856	60 463	74 901	94 016	125 394	172 370	206 586	239 102

Monetary Unit: million forints

D. NET WRITTEN PREMIUMS IN THE REPORTING COUNTRY IN TERMS OF DOMESTIC AND FOREIGN RISKS

D.1. Life

D.2. Non-Life

F. OUTSTANDING INVESTMENT BY DIRECT INSURANCE COMPANIES

F.1. Life

Label (EN)	1992	1993	1994	1995	1996	1997	1998	1999	Label (FR)
D. NET WRITTEN PREMIUMS IN THE REPORTING COUNTRY IN TERMS OF DOMESTIC AND FOREIGN RISKS									D. PRIMES NETTES EMISES DANS LE PAYS DECLARANT EN RISQUES NATIONAUX ET ETRANGERS
D.1. Life									D.1. Vie
D.1.1. Domestic Risks									D.1.1. Risques Nationaux
D.1.1.1. Domestic Companies	..	..	12 281	23 416	..	..	..	..	D.1.1.1. Entreprises Nationales
D.1.1.2. (Foreign Controlled Companies)	..	..	12 191	22 935	..	..	..	..	D.1.1.2. (Entreprises Sous Contrôle Etranger)
D.1.1. Total	..	..	12 281	23 416	..	..	..	..	D.1.1. Total des Primes Nettes Vie
D.1.2. Foreign Risks									D.1.2. Risques Etrangers
D.1.2.1. Domestic Companies	..	..	3 182	0	..	..	..	..	D.1.2.1. Entreprises Nationales
D.1.2.2. (Foreign Controlled Companies)	..	..	3 182	0	..	..	..	..	D.1.2.2. (Entreprises Sous Contrôle Etranger)
D.1.2. Total	..	..	3 182	0	..	..	..	..	D.1.2. Total des Primes Nettes Vie
D.1.3. Total									D.1.3. Total
D.1.3.1. Domestic Companies	..	9 959	15 464	23 416	32 919	59 822	76 303	101 314	D.1.3.1. Entreprises Nationales
D.1.3.2. (Foreign Controlled Companies)	..	9 925	15 373	22 935	31 484	56 499	65 899	83 304	D.1.3.2. (Entreprises Sous Contrôle Etranger)
D.1.3. Total of Life Net Premiums	..	9 959	15 464	23 416	32 919	59 822	76 303	101 314	D.1.3. Total des Primes Nettes Vie
D.2. Non-Life									D.2. Non-Vie
D.2.1. Domestic Risks									D.2.1. Risques Nationaux
D.2.1.1. Domestic Companies	..	..	57 308	69 721	..	..	..	..	D.2.1.1. Entreprises Nationales
D.2.1.2. (Foreign Controlled Companies)	..	..	54 216	64 754	..	..	..	..	D.2.1.2. (Entreprises Sous Contrôle Etranger)
D.2.1. Total	..	..	57 308	69 721	..	..	..	..	D.2.1. Total des Primes Nettes Vie
D.2.2. Foreign Risks									D.2.2. Risques Etrangers
D.2.2.1. Domestic Companies	..	..	2 129	879	..	..	..	..	D.2.2.1. Entreprises Nationales
D.2.2.2. (Foreign Controlled Companies)	..	..	1 346	73	..	..	..	..	D.2.2.2. (Entreprises Sous Contrôle Etranger)
D.2.2. Total	..	..	2 129	879	..	..	..	..	D.2.2. Total des Primes Nettes Vie
D.2.3. Total									D.2.3. Total
D.2.3.1. Domestic Companies	..	50 504	59 437	70 600	92 475	112 548	130 283	137 788	D.2.3.1. Entreprises Nationales
D.2.3.2. (Foreign Controlled Companies)	..	48 235	55 562	64 827	83 456	101 047	119 338	124 522	D.2.3.2. (Entreprises Sous Contrôle Etranger)
D.2.3. Total	..	50 504	59 437	70 600	92 475	112 548	130 283	137 788	D.2.3. Total des Primes Nettes Vie
F. OUTSTANDING INVESTMENT BY DIRECT INSURANCE COMPANIES									F. ENCOURS DES PLACEMENTS DES ENTREPRISES D'ASSURANCES DIRECTES
F.1. Life									F.1. Vie
F.1.1. Real Estate									F.1.1. Immobilier
F.1.1.1. Domestic Companies	3 872	4 105	3 270	2 156	2 141	375	3 276	2 259	F.1.1.1. Entreprises Nationales
F.1.1.2. (Foreign Controlled Companies)	3 872	4 105	3 270	2 010	2 062	124	2 536	1 828	F.1.1.2. (Entreprises Sous Contrôle Etranger)
F.1.1. Total	3 872	4 105	..	..	..	..	..	..	F.1.1. Total
F.1.2. Mortgage Loans									F.1.2. Prêts Hypothécaires
F.1.2.1. Domestic Companies							150	810	F.1.2.1. Entreprises Nationales
F.1.2.2. (Foreign Controlled Companies)							150	810	F.1.2.2. (Entreprises Sous Contrôle Etranger)
F.1.2. Total									F.1.2. Total
F.1.3. Shares									F.1.3. Actions
F.1.3.1. Domestic Companies	3 343	2 820	3 570	3 481	774	5 735	8 816	10 108	F.1.3.1. Entreprises Nationales
F.1.3.2. (Foreign Controlled Companies)	3 343	2 820	3 570	3 481	728	5 565	7 698	8 610	F.1.3.2. (Entreprises Sous Contrôle Etranger)
F.1.3. Total	3 343	2 820	..	..	..	..	..	..	F.1.3. Total
F.1.4. Bonds with Fixed Revenue									F.1.4. Obligations
F.1.4.1. Domestic Companies	24 533	37 803	44 997	57 711	110 394	114 871	199 019	280 439	F.1.4.1. Entreprises Nationales
F.1.4.2. (Foreign Controlled Companies)	24 323	37 590	44 755	57 501	107 638	114 228	193 130	262 607	F.1.4.2. (Entreprises Sous Contrôle Etranger)
F.1.4. Total	24 533	37 803	..	..	..	..	..	..	F.1.4. Total
F.1.5. Loans other than Mortgage Loans									F.1.5. Prêts Autres qu'Hypothécaires
F.1.5.1. Domestic Companies	3 909	3 692	3 678	3 986	2 434	1 805	1 354	3 106	F.1.5.1. Entreprises Nationales
F.1.5.2. (Foreign Controlled Companies)	3 909	3 692	3 678	3 986	2 334	1 760	1 312	3 050	F.1.5.2. (Entreprises Sous Contrôle Etranger)
F.1.5. Total	3 909	3 692	..	..	..	..	..	..	F.1.5. Total
F.1.6. Other Investments									F.1.6. Autres Placements
F.1.6.1. Domestic Companies	6 027	4 486	1 949	1 514	1 182	2 437	318	912	F.1.6.1. Entreprises Nationales
F.1.6.2. (Foreign Controlled Companies)	5 917	4 486	1 937	1 348	1 058	1 726	248	903	F.1.6.2. (Entreprises Sous Contrôle Etranger)
F.1.6. Total	6 027	4 486	..	..	..	..	..	..	F.1.6. Total

Monetary Unit: million forints — Unité monétaire : million de forints

	1992	1993	1994	1995	1996	1997	1998	1999	
F.1.7. Total									F.1.7. Total
F.1.7.1. Domestic Companies	41 684	52 906	57 464	68 848	116 925	125 223	212 933	297 634	F.1.7.1. Entreprises Nationales
F.1.7.2. (Foreign Controlled Companies)	41 364	52 693	57 210	68 326	113 820	123 403	205 074	277 808	F.1.7.2. (Entreprises Sous Contrôle Etranger)
F.1.7. Total of Life Investments	41 684	52 906	:	:	:	:	:	:	F.1.7. Total des Placements Vie
F.2. Non-Life									**F.2. Non-Vie**
F.2.1. Real Estate									F.2.1. Immobilier
F.2.1.1. Domestic Companies	1 384	2 143	2 328	2 668	2 476	5 055	957	1 291	F.2.1.1. Entreprises Nationales
F.2.1.2. (Foreign Controlled Companies)	1 384	2 143	2 328	2 175	2 428	3 938	517	140	F.2.1.2. (Entreprises Sous Contrôle Etranger)
F.2.1. Total	1 384	2 143	:	:	:	:	:	:	F.2.1. Total
F.2.2. Mortgage Loans							101	104	F.2.2. Prêts Hypothécaires
F.2.2.1. Domestic Companies							101	104	F.2.2.1. Entreprises Nationales
F.2.2.2. (Foreign Controlled Companies)									F.2.2.2. (Entreprises Sous Contrôle Etranger)
F.2.3. Shares									F.2.3. Actions
F.2.3.1. Domestic Companies	694	1 228	1 124	6 913	10 043	6 230	9 347	8 815	F.2.3.1. Entreprises Nationales
F.2.3.2. (Foreign Controlled Companies)	694	1 228	1 124	6 913	9 880	5 956	7 207	6 981	F.2.3.2. (Entreprises Sous Contrôle Etranger)
F.2.3. Total	694	1 228	:	:	:	:	:	:	F.2.3. Total
F.2.4. Bonds with Fixed Revenue									F.2.4. Obligations
F.2.4.1. Domestic Companies	2 574	18 246	26 984	47 127	56 884	71 903	94 638	106 060	F.2.4.1. Entreprises Nationales
F.2.4.2. (Foreign Controlled Companies)	2 281	17 269	25 545	46 074	55 680	70 433	93 409	104 389	F.2.4.2. (Entreprises Sous Contrôle Etranger)
F.2.4. Total	2 574	18 246	:	:	:	:	:	:	F.2.4. Total
F.2.5. Loans other than Mortgage Loans							24	19	F.2.5. Prêts Autres qu'Hypothécaires
F.2.5.1. Domestic Companies							24	19	F.2.5.1. Entreprises Nationales
F.2.5.2. (Foreign Controlled Companies)							0	0	F.2.5.2. (Entreprises Sous Contrôle Etranger)
F.2.6. Other Investments									F.2.6. Autres Placements
F.2.6.1. Domestic Companies	6 528	2 529	11 205	3 570	5 130	8 046	6 673	6 397	F.2.6.1. Entreprises Nationales
F.2.6.2. (Foreign Controlled Companies)	6 528	2 504	11 143	2 972	2 943	6 787	6 379	5 652	F.2.6.2. (Entreprises Sous Contrôle Etranger)
F.2.6. Total	6 528	2 529	:	:	:	:	:	:	F.2.6. Total
F.2.7. Total									F.2.7. Total
F.2.7.1. Domestic Companies	11 180	24 146	41 641	60 278	74 533	91 234	111 740	122 686	F.2.7.1. Entreprises Nationales
F.2.7.2. (Foreign Controlled Companies)	10 887	23 144	40 139	58 134	70 931	87 114	107 612	117 266	F.2.7.2. (Entreprises Sous Contrôle Etranger)
F.2.7. Total of Non-Life Investments	11 180	24 146	:	:	:	:	:	:	F.2.7. Total des Placements Non-Vie
G. BREAKDOWN OF NON-LIFE PREMIUMS									**G. VENTILATIONS DES PRIMES NON-VIE**
G.1. Motor vehicle									G.1. Assurance Automobile
G.1.1. Direct Business									G.1.1. Assurances Directes
G.1.1.1. Gross Premiums	25 698	32 441	41 541	49 216	63 375	78 514	91 354	97 488	G.1.1.1. Primes Brutes
G.1.2. Reinsurance Accepted									G.1.2. Réassurance Acceptée
G.1.2.1. Gross Premiums	:	:	269	428	416	454	130	64	G.1.2.1. Primes Brutes
G.1.3. Total									G.1.3. Total
G.1.3.1. Gross Premiums	:	:	41 810	49 644	63 791	78 968	91 484	97 552	G.1.3.1. Primes Brutes
G.1.3.2. Ceded Premiums	:	:	:	3 841	4 199	6 647	8 199	11 431	G.1.3.2. Primes Cédées
G.1.3.3. Net Written Premiums	:	:	:	45 803	59 592	72 321	83 285	86 121	G.1.3.3. Primes Nettes Emises
G.2. Marine, Aviation									G.2. Marine, Aviation
G.2.1. Direct Business									G.2.1. Assurances Directes
G.2.1.1. Gross Premiums								543	G.2.1.1. Primes Brutes
G.2.3. Total									G.2.3. Total
G.2.3.1. Gross Premiums								543	G.2.3.1. Primes Brutes
G.2.3.2. Ceded Premiums								251	G.2.3.2. Primes Cédées
G.2.3.3. Net Written Premiums								292	G.2.3.3. Primes Nettes Emises
G.3. Freight									G.3. Fret
G.3.1. Direct Business									G.3.1. Assurances Directes
G.3.1.1. Gross Premiums	954	596	845	1 215	1 480	2 026	2 298	2 137	G.3.1.1. Primes Brutes
G.3.2. Reinsurance Accepted									G.3.2. Réassurance Acceptée
G.3.2.1. Gross Premiums	:	:	2	0	0	0	18	4	G.3.2.1. Primes Brutes
G.3.3. Total									G.3.3. Total
G.3.3.1. Gross Premiums	:	:	847	1 215	1 480	2 026	2 317	2 141	G.3.3.1. Primes Brutes
G.3.3.2. Ceded Premiums	:	:	:	692	560	1 066	949	1 081	G.3.3.2. Primes Cédées
G.3.3.3. Net Written Premiums	:	:	:	523	920	960	1 367	1 060	G.3.3.3. Primes Nettes Emises
G.4. Fire, Property Damages									G.4. Incendie, Dommages aux Biens
G.4.1. Direct Business									G.4.1. Assurances Directes
G.4.1.1. Gross Premiums	16 117	17 331	18 747	8 724	14 013	11 632	19 618	24 243	G.4.1.1. Primes Brutes
G.4.2. Reinsurance Accepted									G.4.2. Réassurance Acceptée
G.4.2.1. Gross Premiums	:	:	185	5	5	7	168	30	G.4.2.1. Primes Brutes

Monetary Unit: million forints   Unité monétaire : million de forints

	1992	1993	1994	1995	1996	1997	1998	1999	
G.4.3. Total									G.4.3. Total
G.4.3.1. Gross Premiums	:	:	18 933	8 729	14 018	11 639	19 786	24 273	G.4.3.1. Primes Brutes
G.4.3.2. Ceded Premiums	:	:	:	5 202	5 380	6 117	7 317	9 922	G.4.3.2. Primes Cédées
G.4.3.3. Net Written Premiums	:	:	:	3 527	8 638	5 522	12 469	14 351	G.4.3.3. Primes Nettes Emises
G.5. Pecuniary Losses									G.5. Pertes Pécunières
G.5.1. Direct Business									G.5.1. Assurances Directes
G.5.1.1. Gross Premiums	232	489	79	239	644	901	1 455	1 753	G.5.1.1. Primes Brutes
G.5.2. Reinsurance Accepted									G.5.2. Réassurance Acceptée
G.5.2.1. Gross Premiums	:	:	2	1	0	0	0	0	G.5.2.1. Primes Brutes
G.5.3. Total									G.5.3. Total
G.5.3.1. Gross Premiums	:	:	81	240	644	901	1 455	1 753	G.5.3.1. Primes Brutes
G.5.3.2. Ceded Premiums	:	:	:	1	232	508	722	946	G.5.3.2. Primes Cédées
G.5.3.3. Net Written Premiums	:	:	:	239	412	393	732	807	G.5.3.3. Primes Nettes Emises
G.6. General Liability									G.6. Responsabilité Générale
G.6.1. Direct Business									G.6.1. Assurances Directes
G.6.1.1. Gross Premiums	940	1 667	1 855	2 732	4 108	5 125	5 810	6 546	G.6.1.1. Primes Brutes
G.6.2. Reinsurance Accepted									G.6.2. Réassurance Acceptée
G.6.2.1. Gross Premiums	:	:	:	:	:	:	132	29	G.6.2.1. Primes Brutes
G.6.3. Total									G.6.3. Total
G.6.3.1. Gross Premiums	:	:	1 855	2 732	4 108	5 125	5 942	6 575	G.6.3.1. Primes Brutes
G.6.3.2. Ceded Premiums	:	:	:	643	700	1 906	2 327	3 014	G.6.3.2. Primes Cédées
G.6.3.3. Net Written Premiums	:	:	:	2 089	3 408	3 219	3 615	3 561	G.6.3.3. Primes Nettes Emises
G.7. Accident, Health									G.7. Accident, Santé
G.7.1. Direct Business									G.7.1. Assurances Directes
G.7.1.1. Gross Premiums	3 246	3 330	1 981	2 652	2 928	5 248	5 100	6 475	G.7.1.1. Primes Brutes
G.7.2. Reinsurance Accepted									G.7.2. Réassurance Acceptée
G.7.2.1. Gross Premiums	:	:	20	58	56	62	160	119	G.7.2.1. Primes Brutes
G.7.3. Total									G.7.3. Total
G.7.3.1. Gross Premiums	:	:	2 001	2 710	2 984	5 310	5 259	6 594	G.7.3.1. Primes Brutes
G.7.3.2. Ceded Premiums	:	:	:	126	120	258	544	622	G.7.3.2. Primes Cédées
G.7.3.3. Net Written Premiums	:	:	:	2 584	2 864	5 052	4 716	5 972	G.7.3.3. Primes Nettes Emises
G.8. Others									G.8. Autres
G.8.1. Direct Business									G.8.1. Assurances Directes
G.8.1.1. Gross Premiums	547	2 333	4 387	18 248	17 798	29 449	29 029	29 605	G.8.1.1. Primes Brutes
G.8.2. Reinsurance Accepted									G.8.2. Réassurance Acceptée
G.8.2.1. Gross Premiums	:	:	64	35	36	37	182	138	G.8.2.1. Primes Brutes
G.8.3. Total									G.8.3. Total
G.8.3.1. Gross Premiums	:	:	4 451	18 283	17 834	29 486	29 211	29 743	G.8.3.1. Primes Brutes
G.8.3.2. Ceded Premiums	:	:	:	2 448	1 193	4 405	5 113	4 119	G.8.3.2. Primes Cédées
G.8.3.3. Net Written Premiums	:	:	:	15 835	16 641	25 081	24 098	25 624	G.8.3.3. Primes Nettes Emises
G.9.2. Reinsurance Accepted									G.9.2. Réassurance Acceptée
G.9.2.1. Gross Premiums	789	658	0	0	0	0	:	:	G.9.2.1. Primes Brutes
G.10. Total									G.10. Total
G.10.1. Direct Business									G.10.1. Assurances Directes
G.10.1.1. Gross Premiums	47 734	58 187	69 435	83 026	104 346	132 895	154 665	168 790	G.10.1.1. Primes Brutes
G.10.2. Reinsurance Accepted									G.10.2. Réassurance Acceptée
G.10.2.1. Gross Premiums	789	658	542	527	513	560	790	384	G.10.2.1. Primes Brutes
G.10.3. Total									G.10.3. Total
G.10.3.1. Gross Premiums	48 523	58 845	69 978	83 553	104 859	133 455	155 454	169 174	G.10.3.1. Primes Brutes
G.10.3.2. Ceded Premiums	6 496	8 341	:	12 953	12 384	20 907	25 172	31 386	G.10.3.2. Primes Cédées
G.10.3.3. Net Written Premiums	42 027	50 504	:	70 600	92 475	112 548	130 283	137 788	G.10.3.3. Primes Nettes Emises

H. GROSS CLAIMS PAYMENTS — **H. PAIEMENTS BRUTS DES SINISTRES**

H.1. Life — **H.1. Vie**

	1992	1993	1994	1995	1996	1997	1998	1999	
H.1.1. Domestic Companies					16 519	16 326	16 480	21 094	H.1.1. Entreprises Nationales
H.1.2. (Foreign Controlled Companies)					16 179	16 043	15 628	19 487	H.1.2. (Entreprises Sous Contrôle Etranger)
H.1. Total					16 519	16 326	16 480	21 094	H.1. Total

121

Monetary Unit: million forints

Unité monétaire : million de forints

	1992	1993	1994	1995	1996	1997	1998	1999
H.2. Non-Life / **H.2. Non-Vie**								
H.2.1. Domestic Companies / H.2.1. Entreprises Nationales					61 090	68 161	77 761	97 401
H.2.2. (Foreign Controlled Companies) / H.2.2. (Entreprises Sous Contrôle Etranger)					55 766	62 487	71 926	88 987
H.2. Total / H.2. Total					61 090	68 161	77 761	97 401
I. GROSS OPERATING EXPENSES / **I. DEPENSES BRUITES D'EXPLOITATION**								
I.1. Life / **I.1. Vie**								
I.1.1. Domestic Companies / I.1.1. Entreprises Nationales					9 426	10 836	14 743	15 473
I.1.2. (Foreign Controlled Companies) / I.1.2. (Entreprises Sous Contrôle Etranger)					9 077	9 924	13 179	13 157
I.1. Total / I.1. Total des Primes Nettes Vie					9 426	10 836	14 743	15 473
I.2. Non-Life / **I.2. Non-Vie**								
I.2.1. Domestic Companies / I.2.1. Entreprises Nationales					18 451	22 930	24 545	26 242
I.2.2. (Foreign Controlled Companies) / I.2.2. (Entreprises Sous Contrôle Etranger)					15 583	22 213	22 231	23 586
I.2. Total / I.2. Total					18 451	22 930	24 545	26 242
J. COMMISSIONS / **J. COMMISSIONS**								
J.1. Life / **J.1. Vie**								
J.1.1. Direct Business / J.1.1. Assurance directe								
J.1.1.1. Domestic Companies / J.1.1.1. Entreprises Nationales							20 304	:
J.1.1.3. Branches & Agencies of Foreign Cies / J.1.1.3. Succursales et Agences d'Ent. Etrangères							17 381	:
J.1.1. Total / J.1.1. Total							20 304	:
J.1.3. Total / J.1.3. Total								
J.1.3.1. Domestic Companies / J.1.3.1. Entreprises Nationales					9 448	13 533	:	25 233
J.1.3.2. (Foreign Controlled Companies) / J.1.3.2. (Entreprises Sous Contrôle Etranger)					9 204	12 995	:	21 033
J.1.3. Total of Life Net Premiums / J.1.3. Total					9 448	13 533	:	25 233
J.2. Non-Life / **J.2. Non-Vie**								
J.2.1. Direct Business / J.2.1. Assurance directe								
J.2.1.1. Domestic Companies / J.2.1.1. Entreprises Nationales							25 642	:
J.2.1.2. (Foreign Controlled Companies) / J.2.1.2. (Entreprises Sous Contrôle Etranger)							23 548	:
J.2.1. Total / J.2.1. Total des Primes Nettes Vie							25 642	:
J.2.3. Total / J.2.3. Total								
J.2.3.1. Domestic Companies / J.2.3.1. Entreprises Nationales					8 550	12 356	:	30 937
J.2.3.2. (Foreign Controlled Companies) / J.2.3.2. (Entreprises Sous Contrôle Etranger)					7 598	11 728	:	28 363
J.2.3. Total / J.2.3. Total					8 550	12 356	:	30 937

122

ICELAND

Monetary Unit: million Icelandic kronur

ISLANDE

Unité monétaire : million de couronnes islandaises

	1992	1993	1994	1995	1996	1997	1998	1999
A. NUMBER OF COMPANIES IN THE REPORTING COUNTRY / A. NOMBRE D'ENTREPRISES DANS LE PAYS DECLARANT								
A.1. Life / A.1. Vie								
A.1.1. Domestic Companies / A.1.1. Entreprises Nationales	5	5	5	4	4	3	3	3
A.1.2. (Foreign Controlled Companies) / A.1.2. (Entreprises Sous Contrôle Etranger)	1	1	1	1	1	0	0	0
A.1. All Companies / A.1. Ensemble des Entreprises	5	5	5	4	4	3	3	3
A.2. Non-Life / A.2. Non-Vie								
A.2.1. Domestic Companies / A.2.1. Entreprises Nationales	19	19	17	14	13	10	10	10
A.2.2. (Foreign Controlled Companies) / A.2.2. (Entreprises Sous Contrôle Etranger)	2	2	1	1	1	0	0	0
A.2. All Companies / A.2. Ensemble des Entreprises	19	19	17	14	13	10	10	10
A.4. Reinsurance / A.4. Réassurance								
A.4.1. Domestic Companies / A.4.1. Entreprises Nationales	2	2	1	1	1	1	1	1
A.4.2. (Foreign Controlled Companies) / A.4.2. (Entreprises Sous Contrôle Etranger)	1	1	0	0	0	0	0	0
A.4. All Companies / A.4. Ensemble des Entreprises	2	2	1	1	1	1	1	1
A.5. Total								
A.5.1. Domestic Companies / A.5.1. Entreprises Nationales	26	26	23	19	18	14	14	14
A.5.2. (Foreign Controlled Companies) / A.5.2. (Entreprises Sous Contrôle Etranger)	4	4	2	2	2	0	0	0
A.5. All Insurance Companies / A.5. Ensemble des Entreprises d'Assurances	26	26	23	19	18	14	14	14
B. NUMBER OF EMPLOYEES / B. NOMBRE D'EMPLOYES								
B.1. Insurance Companies / B.1. Entreprises d'Assurances	434	430	433	440	443	463	486	507
C. BUSINESS WRITTEN IN THE REPORTING COUNTRY / C. OPERATIONS CONCLUES DANS LE PAYS DECLARANT								
C.1. Life / C.1. Vie								
C.1.1. Gross Premiums / C.1.1. Primes Brutes								
C.1.1.1. Direct Business / C.1.1.1. Assurances Directes								
C.1.1.1.1. Domestic Companies / C.1.1.1.1. Entreprises Nationales	418	464	479	506	551	537	722	966
C.1.1.1.2. (Foreign Controlled Companies) / C.1.1.1.2. (Entreprises Sous Contrôle Etranger)	7	16	23	29	27	0	0	0
C.1.1.1. Total	418	464	479	506	551	537	722	966
C.1.1.2. Reinsurance Accepted / C.1.1.2. Réassurance Acceptée								
C.1.1.2.1. Domestic Companies / C.1.1.2.1. Entreprises Nationales	10	10	83	103	2	114	3	0
C.1.1.2. Total	10	10	83	103	2	114	3	0
C.1.1.3. Total								
C.1.1.3.1. Domestic Companies / C.1.1.3.1. Entreprises Nationales	428	474	562	609	553	651	725	966
C.1.1.3.2. (Foreign Controlled Companies) / C.1.1.3.2. (Entreprises Sous Contrôle Etranger)	7	16	23	29	27	0	0	0
C.1.1.3. Total Gross Premiums / C.1.1.3. Total des Primes Brutes	428	474	562	609	553	651	725	966
C.1.2. Ceded Premiums / C.1.2. Primes Cédées								
C.1.2.1. Domestic Companies / C.1.2.1. Entreprises Nationales	154	161	159	167	186	182	219	224
C.1.2.2. (Foreign Controlled Companies) / C.1.2.2. (Entreprises Sous Contrôle Etranger)	3	8	15	22	14	0	0	0
C.1.2. Total	154	161	159	167	186	182	219	224
C.1.3. Net Written Premiums / C.1.3. Primes Nettes Emises								
C.1.3.1. Domestic Companies / C.1.3.1. Entreprises Nationales	274	313	403	442	366	470	506	742
C.1.3.2. (Foreign Controlled Companies) / C.1.3.2. (Entreprises Sous Contrôle Etranger)	4	8	8	7	13	0	0	0
C.1.3. Total	274	313	403	442	366	470	506	742

123

Monetary Unit: million Icelandic kronur   Unité monétaire : million de couronnes islandaises

C.2. Non-Life / C.2. Non-Vie

Code	Label (EN) / Libellé (FR)	1992	1993	1994	1995	1996	1997	1998	1999
C.2.1.	Gross premiums / Primes Brutes								
C.2.1.1.	Direct Business / Assurances Directes								
C.2.1.1.1.	Domestic Companies / Entreprises Nationales	12 828	12 622	13 243	13 063	13 322	13 210	13 919	15 607
C.2.1.1.2.	(Foreign Controlled Companies) / (Entreprises Sous Contrôle Etranger)	604	619	370	535	536	0	0	0
C.2.1.1.	Total	12 828	12 622	13 243	13 063	13 322	13 210	13 919	15 607
C.2.1.2.	Reinsurance Accepted / Réassurance Acceptée								
C.2.1.2.1.	Domestic Companies / Entreprises Nationales	2 561	2 443	2 187	1 689	1 703	1 554	1 413	1 064
C.2.1.2.2.	(Foreign Controlled Companies) / (Entreprises Sous Contrôle Etranger)	0	0		0	0	0	0	0
C.2.1.2.	Total	2 561	2 443	2 187	1 689	1 703	1 554	1 413	1 064
C.2.1.3.	Total								
C.2.1.3.1.	Domestic Companies / Entreprises Nationales	15 389	15 065	15 430	14 752	15 025	14 764	15 332	16 672
C.2.1.3.2.	(Foreign Controlled Companies) / (Entreprises Sous Contrôle Etranger)	604	619	105	535	536	0	0	10
C.2.1.3.	Total Gross Premiums / Total des Primes Brutes	15 389	15 065	15 430	14 752	15 025	14 764	15 332	16 672
C.2.2.	Ceded Premiums / Primes Cédées								
C.2.2.1.	Domestic Companies / Entreprises Nationales	5 321	5 053	5 193	4 677	4 391	4 225	4 030	3 754
C.2.2.2.	(Foreign Controlled Companies) / (Entreprises Sous Contrôle Etranger)	206	206	185	270	268	0	0	0
C.2.2.	Total	5 321	5 053	5 193	4 677	4 391	4 225	4 030	3 754
C.2.3.	Net Written Premiums / Primes Nettes Emises								
C.2.3.1.	Domestic Companies / Entreprises Nationales	10 068	10 012	10 237	10 075	10 634	10 539	11 302	12 918
C.2.3.2.	(Foreign Controlled Companies) / (Entreprises Sous Contrôle Etranger)	398	413	185	265	268	0	0	0
C.2.3.	Total	10 068	10 012	10 237	10 075	10 634	10 539	11 302	12 918

C.3. Total

Code	Label (EN) / Libellé (FR)	1992	1993	1994	1995	1996	1997	1998	1999
C.3.1.	Gross Premiums / Primes Brutes								
C.3.1.1.	Direct Business / Assurances Directes								
C.3.1.1.1.	Domestic Companies / Entreprises Nationales	13 246	13 086	13 722	13 569	13 873	13 747	14 641	16 573
C.3.1.1.2.	(Foreign Controlled Companies) / (Entreprises Sous Contrôle Etranger)	611	635	393	564	563	0	0	0
C.3.1.1.	Total	13 246	13 086	13 722	13 569	13 873	13 747	14 641	16 573
C.3.1.2.	Reinsurance Accepted / Réassurance Acceptée								
C.3.1.2.1.	Domestic Companies / Entreprises Nationales	2 571	2 453	2 270	1 792	1 705	1 668	1 416	1 064
C.3.1.2.2.	(Foreign Controlled Companies) / (Entreprises Sous Contrôle Etranger)	0	0		0	0	0	0	0
C.3.1.2.	Total	2 571	2 453	2 270	1 792	1 705	1 668	1 416	1 064
C.3.1.3.	Total								
C.3.1.3.1.	Domestic Companies / Entreprises Nationales	15 817	15 539	15 992	15 361	15 578	15 415	16 057	17 638
C.3.1.3.2.	(Foreign Controlled Companies) / (Entreprises Sous Contrôle Etranger)	611	635	128	564	563	0	0	0
C.3.1.3.	Total Gross Premiums / Total des Primes Brutes	15 817	15 539	15 992	15 361	15 578	15 415	16 057	17 638
C.3.2.	Ceded Premiums / Primes Cédées								
C.3.2.1.	Domestic Companies / Entreprises Nationales	5 475	5 214	5 352	4 844	4 577	4 407	4 249	3 978
C.3.2.2.	(Foreign Controlled Companies) / (Entreprises Sous Contrôle Etranger)	209	214	200	292	282	0	0	0
C.3.2.	Total	5 475	5 214	5 352	4 844	4 577	4 407	4 259	3 978
C.3.3.	Net Written Premiums / Primes Nettes Emises								
C.3.3.1.	Domestic Companies / Entreprises Nationales	10 342	10 325	10 640	10 517	11 000	11 009	11 808	13 660
C.3.3.2.	(Foreign Controlled Companies) / (Entreprises Sous Contrôle Etranger)	402	421	193	272	281	0	0	0
C.3.3.	Total	10 342	10 325	10 640	10 517	11 000	11 009	11 808	13 660

D. NET WRITTEN PREMIUMS IN THE REPORTING COUNTRY IN TERMS OF DOMESTIC AND FOREIGN RISKS
D. PRIMES NETTES EMISES DANS LE PAYS DECLARANT EN RISQUES NATIONAUX ET ETRANGERS

D.1. Life / D.1. Vie

Code	Label (EN) / Libellé (FR)	1992	1993	1994	1995	1996	1997	1998	1999
D.1.1.	Domestic Risks / Risques Nationaux								
D.1.1.1.	Domestic Companies / Entreprises Nationales	274	475	403	...	366	470	506	742
D.1.1.2.	(Foreign Controlled Companies) / (Entreprises Sous Contrôle Etranger)	4	16	8	...	13	0	0	0
D.1.1.	Total	274	475	403	...	366	470	506	742
D.1.3.	Total								
D.1.3.1.	Domestic Companies / Entreprises Nationales	274	475	403	...	366	470	506	742
D.1.3.2.	(Foreign Controlled Companies) / (Entreprises Sous Contrôle Etranger)	4	16	8	...	13	0	0	0
D.1.3.	Total of Life Net Premiums / Total des Primes Nettes Vie	274	475	403	...	366	470	506	742

Monetary Unit: million Icelandic kronur   Unité monétaire : million de couronnes islandaises

D.2. Non-Life / D.2. Non-Vie

	1992	1993	1994	1995	1996	1997	1998	1999	
D.2.1. Domestic Risks									**D.2.1. Risques Nationaux**
D.2.1.1. Domestic Companies	10 061	15 065	10 237	..	10 614	10 494	11 267	12 900	D.2.1.1. Entreprises Nationales
D.2.1.2. (Foreign Controlled Companies)	398	619	185	..	268	..	0	0	D.2.1.2. (Entreprises Sous Contrôle Etranger)
D.2.1. Total	10 061	15 065	10 237	..	10 614	10 494	11 267	12 900	D.2.1. Total des Primes Nettes Vie
D.2.2. Foreign Risks									**D.2.2. Risques Etrangers**
D.2.2.1. Domestic Companies	7	- 1	0	..	20	45	35	18	D.2.2.1. Entreprises Nationales
D.2.2. Total	7	- 1	0	..	20	45	35	18	D.2.2. Total des Primes Nettes Vie
D.2.3. Total									**D.2.3. Total**
D.2.3.1. Domestic Companies	10 068	15 064	10 237	..	10 634	10 539	11 302	12 918	D.2.3.1. Entreprises Nationales
D.2.3.2. (Foreign Controlled Companies)	398	619	185	..	268	0	0	0	D.2.3.2. (Entreprises Sous Contrôle Etranger)
D.2.3. Total	10 068	15 064	10 237	..	10 634	10 539	11 302	12 918	D.2.3. Total des Primes Nettes Vie

F. OUTSTANDING INVESTMENT BY DIRECT INSURANCE COMPANIES / F. ENCOURS DES PLACEMENTS DES ENTREPRISES D'ASSURANCES DIRECTES

F.1. Life / F.1. Vie

	1992	1993	1994	1995	1996	1997	1998	1999	
F.1.1. Real Estate									**F.1.1. Immobilier**
F.1.1.1. Domestic Companies	13	15	..	..	..	52	45	204	F.1.1.1. Entreprises Nationales
F.1.1.4. Domestic Investment	13	15	..	..	..	..	45	204	F.1.1.4. Placement dans le Pays
F.1.1. Total	13	15	..	..	..	..	45	204	F.1.1. Total
F.1.2. Mortgage Loans									**F.1.2. Prêts Hypothécaires**
F.1.2.1. Domestic Companies	32	214	..	..	..	41	47	47	F.1.2.1. Entreprises Nationales
F.1.2.2. (Foreign Controlled Companies)	0	1	..	..	..	..	0	0	F.1.2.2. (Entreprises Sous Contrôle Etranger)
F.1.2.4. Domestic Investment	32	214	..	..	..	..	47	47	F.1.2.4. Placement dans le Pays
F.1.2. Total	32	214	..	..	..	..	47	47	F.1.2. Total
F.1.3. Shares									**F.1.3. Actions**
F.1.3.1. Domestic Companies	117	126	..	..	..	268	531	754	F.1.3.1. Entreprises Nationales
F.1.3.4. Domestic Investment	117	126	..	..	..	..	531	754	F.1.3.4. Placement dans le Pays
F.1.3. Total	117	126	..	..	..	..	531	754	F.1.3. Total
F.1.4. Bonds with Fixed Revenue									**F.1.4. Obligations**
F.1.4.1. Domestic Companies	353	461	..	..	..	1 096	872	920	F.1.4.1. Entreprises Nationales
F.1.4.2. (Foreign Controlled Companies)	1	1	..	..	..	..	0	0	F.1.4.2. (Entreprises Sous Contrôle Etranger)
F.1.4.4. Domestic Investment	353	461	..	..	..	..	872	920	F.1.4.4. Placement dans le Pays
F.1.4. Total	353	461	..	..	..	..	872	920	F.1.4. Total
F.1.5. Loans other than Mortgage Loans									**F.1.5. Prêts Autres qu'Hypothécaires**
F.1.5.1. Domestic Companies	250	155	..	..	..	..	0	0	F.1.5.1. Entreprises Nationales
F.1.5.2. (Foreign Controlled Companies)	1	0	..	..	..	..	0	0	F.1.5.2. (Entreprises Sous Contrôle Etranger)
F.1.5.4. Domestic Investment	250	155	..	..	..	..	0	0	F.1.5.4. Placement dans le Pays
F.1.5. Total	250	155	..	..	..	..	0	0	F.1.5. Total
F.1.6. Other Investments									**F.1.6. Autres Placements**
F.1.6.1. Domestic Companies	8	5	..	..	..	..	0	0	F.1.6.1. Entreprises Nationales
F.1.6.4. Domestic Investment	8	5	..	..	..	..	0	0	F.1.6.4. Placement dans le Pays
F.1.6. Total	8	5	..	..	..	..	0	0	F.1.6. Total
F.1.7. Total									**F.1.7. Total**
F.1.7.1. Domestic Companies	773	976	..	..	1 325	1 456	1 495	1 925	F.1.7.1. Entreprises Nationales
F.1.7.2. (Foreign Controlled Companies)	2	2	..	..	..	..	0	0	F.1.7.2. (Entreprises Sous Contrôle Etranger)
F.1.7.4. Domestic Investment	773	976	..	..	..	..	1 495	1 925	F.1.7.4. Placement dans le Pays
F.1.7. Total of Life Investments	773	976	..	..	..	..	1 495	1 925	F.1.7. Total des Placements Vie

F.2. Non-Life / F.2. Non-Vie

	1992	1993	1994	1995	1996	1997	1998	1999	
F.2.1. Real Estate									**F.2.1. Immobilier**
F.2.1.1. Domestic Companies	1 689	1 710	..	..	..	1 667	1 764	1 989	F.2.1.1. Entreprises Nationales
F.2.1.2. (Foreign Controlled Companies)	22	22	..	..	..	..	0	0	F.2.1.2. (Entreprises Sous Contrôle Etranger)
F.2.1.4. Domestic Investment	1 689	1 710	..	..	..	..	1 764	1 989	F.2.1.4. Placement dans le Pays
F.2.1. Total	1 689	1 710	..	..	..	..	1 764	1 989	F.2.1. Total

Monetary Unit: million Icelandic kronur

Unité monétaire : million de couronnes islandaises

Code / English label	1992	1993	1994	1995	1996	1997	1998	1999	French label
F.2.2. Mortgage Loans									F.2.2. Prêts Hypothécaires
F.2.2.1. Domestic Companies	575	3 733	:	:	:	10 919	12 515	14 065	F.2.2.1. Entreprises Nationales
F.2.2.2. (Foreign Controlled Companies)	12	70					0	0	F.2.2.2. (Entreprises Sous Contrôle Etranger)
F.2.2.4. Domestic Investment	575	3 733	:	:	:	:	12 515	14 065	F.2.2.4. Placement dans le Pays
F.2.2. Total	575	3 733	:	:	:	:	12 515	14 065	F.2.2. Total
F.2.3. Shares									F.2.3. Actions
F.2.3.1. Domestic Companies	2 694	3 151	:	:	:	6 996	10 185	12 080	F.2.3.1. Entreprises Nationales
F.2.3.2. (Foreign Controlled Companies)	21	24					0	0	F.2.3.2. (Entreprises Sous Contrôle Etranger)
F.2.3.4. Domestic Investment	2 694	3 151	:	:	:	:	10 185	12 080	F.2.3.4. Placement dans le Pays
F.2.3. Total	2 694	3 151	:	:	:	:	10 185	12 080	F.2.3. Total
F.2.4. Bonds with Fixed Revenue									F.2.4. Obligations
F.2.4.1. Domestic Companies	6 452	8 042	:	:	:	10 542	11 363	10 174	F.2.4.1. Entreprises Nationales
F.2.4.2. (Foreign Controlled Companies)	126	152					0	0	F.2.4.2. (Entreprises Sous Contrôle Etranger)
F.2.4.4. Domestic Investment	6 452	8 052	:	:	:	:	11 363	10 174	F.2.4.4. Placement dans le Pays
F.2.4. Total	6 452	8 052	:	:	:	:	11 363	10 174	F.2.4. Total
F.2.5. Loans other than Mortgage Loans									F.2.5. Prêts Autres qu'Hypothécaires
F.2.5.1. Domestic Companies	4 494	2 586	:	:	:	1 985	1 904	1 586	F.2.5.1. Entreprises Nationales
F.2.5.2. (Foreign Controlled Companies)	87	49					0	0	F.2.5.2. (Entreprises Sous Contrôle Etranger)
F.2.5.4. Domestic Investment	4 494	2 586	:	:	:	:	1 904	1 586	F.2.5.4. Placement dans le Pays
F.2.5. Total	4 494	2 586	:	:	:	:	1 904	1 586	F.2.5. Total
F.2.6. Other Investments									F.2.6. Autres Placements
F.2.6.1. Domestic Companies	375	315	:	:	:	97	0	0	F.2.6.1. Entreprises Nationales
F.2.6.2. (Foreign Controlled Companies)	38	37					0	0	F.2.6.2. (Entreprises Sous Contrôle Etranger)
F.2.6.4. Domestic Investment	0	315	:	:	:	:	0	0	F.2.6.4. Placement dans le Pays
F.2.6. Total	0	315	:	:	:	:	0	0	F.2.6. Total
F.2.7. Total									F.2.7. Total
F.2.7.1. Domestic Companies	16 279	19 537	:	:	31 932	32 205	37 731	39 894	F.2.7.1. Entreprises Nationales
F.2.7.2. (Foreign Controlled Companies)	306	354					0	0	F.2.7.2. (Entreprises Sous Contrôle Etranger)
F.2.7.4. Domestic Investment	16 279	19 537	:	:	:	:	37 731	39 894	F.2.7.4. Placement dans le Pays
F.2.7. Total of Non-Life Investments	16 279	19 537	:	:	:	:	37 731	39 894	F.2.7. Total des Placements Non-Vie
G. BREAKDOWN OF NON-LIFE PREMIUMS									**G. VENTILATIONS DES PRIMES NON-VIE**
G.1. Motor vehicle									G.1. Assurance Automobile
G.1.1. Direct Business									G.1.1. Assurances Directes
G.1.1.1. Gross Premiums	5 554	5 309	5 658	5 562	5 685	5 098	5 666	7 136	G.1.1.1. Primes Brutes
G.1.1.2. Ceded Premiums	220	223	292	330	328	83	83	154	G.1.1.2. Primes Cédées
G.1.1.3. Net Written Premiums	5 334	5 086	5 366	5 232	5 357	5 015	5 583	6 982	G.1.1.3. Primes Nettes Emises
G.1.2. Reinsurance Accepted									G.1.2. Réassurance Acceptée
G.1.2.1. Gross Premiums	19	32	35	36	46	23	32	17	G.1.2.1. Primes Brutes
G.1.2.2. Ceded Premiums	7	7	11	11	22	11	24	16	G.1.2.2. Primes Cédées
G.1.2.3. Net Written Premiums	12	25	24	25	24	12	8	1	G.1.2.3. Primes Nettes Emises
G.1.3. Total									G.1.3. Total
G.1.3.1. Gross Premiums	5 573	5 341	5 693	5 598	5 731	5 121	5 698	7 153	G.1.3.1. Primes Brutes
G.1.3.2. Ceded Premiums	227	230	303	341	350	94	107	170	G.1.3.2. Primes Cédées
G.1.3.3. Net Written Premiums	5 346	5 111	5 390	5 257	5 381	5 027	5 591	6 983	G.1.3.3. Primes Nettes Emises
G.2. Marine, Aviation									G.2. Marine, Aviation
G.2.1. Direct Business									G.2.1. Assurances Directes
G.2.1.1. Gross Premiums	1 912	1 913	1 918	1 780	1 695	1 757	1 628	1 589	G.2.1.1. Primes Brutes
G.2.1.2. Ceded Premiums	1 187	1 163	1 186	1 086	957	929	835	747	G.2.1.2. Primes Cédées
G.2.1.3. Net Written Premiums	725	750	732	694	738	829	793	842	G.2.1.3. Primes Nettes Emises
G.2.2. Reinsurance Accepted									G.2.2. Réassurance Acceptée
G.2.2.1. Gross Premiums	1 177	1 155	1 182	995	934	886	740	486	G.2.2.1. Primes Brutes
G.2.2.2. Ceded Premiums	684	648	713	629	563	510	409	223	G.2.2.2. Primes Cédées
G.2.2.3. Net Written Premiums	493	507	469	366	371	376	331	263	G.2.2.3. Primes Nettes Emises
G.2.3. Total									G.2.3. Total
G.2.3.1. Gross Premiums	3 089	3 068	3 100	2 775	2 629	2 643	2 368	2 075	G.2.3.1. Primes Brutes
G.2.3.2. Ceded Premiums	1 871	1 811	1 898	1 715	1 520	1 439	1 244	970	G.2.3.2. Primes Cédées
G.2.3.3. Net Written Premiums	1 218	1 257	1 202	1 060	1 109	1 204	1 124	1 105	G.2.3.3. Primes Nettes Emises

Monetary Unit: million Icelandic kronur Unité monétaire : million de couronnes islandaises

		1992	1993	1994	1995	1996	1997	1998	1999
G.3. Freight	**G.3. Fret**								
G.3.1. Direct Business	G.3.1. Assurances Directes								
G.3.1.1. Gross Premiums	G.3.1.1. Primes Brutes	407	374	365	374	434	458	436	405
G.3.1.2. Ceded Premiums	G.3.1.2. Primes Cédées	178	167	153	145	101	117	64	29
G.3.1.3. Net Written Premiums	G.3.1.3. Primes Nettes Emises	229	207	212	229	333	341	372	376
G.3.2. Reinsurance Accepted	G.3.2. Réassurance Acceptée								
G.3.2.1. Gross Premiums	G.3.2.1. Primes Brutes	20	21	12	10	0	0	0	0
G.3.2.2. Ceded Premiums	G.3.2.2. Primes Cédées	15	16	3	1	0	0	0	0
G.3.2.3. Net Written Premiums	G.3.2.3. Primes Nettes Emises	5	5	9	9	0	0	0	0
G.3.3. Total	G.3.3. Total								
G.3.3.1. Gross Premiums	G.3.3.1. Primes Brutes	427	395	377	384	434	458	436	405
G.3.3.2. Ceded Premiums	G.3.3.2. Primes Cédées	193	183	156	146	101	117	64	29
G.3.3.3. Net Written Premiums	G.3.3.3. Primes Nettes Emises	234	212	221	238	333	341	372	376
G.4. Fire, Property Damages	**G.4. Incendie, Dommages aux Biens**								
G.4.1. Direct Business	G.4.1. Assurances Directes								
G.4.1.1. Gross Premiums	G.4.1.1. Primes Brutes	3 150	3 236	3 373	3 400	3 549	3 766	3 894	4 020
G.4.1.2. Ceded Premiums	G.4.1.2. Primes Cédées	1 541	1 469	1 601	1 553	1 554	1 652	1 774	1 785
G.4.1.3. Net Written Premiums	G.4.1.3. Primes Nettes Emises	1 609	1 767	1 771	1 847	1 995	2 115	2 120	2 235
G.4.2. Reinsurance Accepted	G.4.2. Réassurance Acceptée								
G.4.2.1. Gross Premiums	G.4.2.1. Primes Brutes	686	576	327	112	127	99	112	60
G.4.2.2. Ceded Premiums	G.4.2.2. Primes Cédées	585	471	274	49	59	21	26	8
G.4.2.3. Net Written Premiums	G.4.2.3. Primes Nettes Emises	101	105	52	63	68	78	86	52
G.4.3. Total	G.4.3. Total								
G.4.3.1. Gross Premiums	G.4.3.1. Primes Brutes	3 836	3 812	3 699	3 512	3 676	3 865	4 006	4 080
G.4.3.2. Ceded Premiums	G.4.3.2. Primes Cédées	2 126	1 940	1 876	1 602	1 613	1 672	1 800	1 793
G.4.3.3. Net Written Premiums	G.4.3.3. Primes Nettes Emises	1 710	1 872	1 823	1 910	2 063	2 193	2 206	2 287
G.5. Pecuniary Losses	**G.5. Pertes Pécunières**								
G.5.1. Direct Business	G.5.1. Assurances Directes								
G.5.1.1. Gross Premiums	G.5.1.1. Primes Brutes	20	13	14	12	25	35	23	35
G.5.1.2. Ceded Premiums	G.5.1.2. Primes Cédées	16	9	9	8	18	27	16	25
G.5.1.3. Net Written Premiums	G.5.1.3. Primes Nettes Emises	4	4	4	4	7	9	7	10
G.5.3. Total	G.5.3. Total								
G.5.3.1. Gross Premiums	G.5.3.1. Primes Brutes	19	13	14	12	25	35	23	35
G.5.3.2. Ceded Premiums	G.5.3.2. Primes Cédées	16	9	9	8	18	27	16	25
G.5.3.3. Net Written Premiums	G.5.3.3. Primes Nettes Emises	3	4	4	4	7	9	7	10
G.6. General Liability	**G.6. Responsabilité Générale**								
G.6.1. Direct Business	G.6.1. Assurances Directes								
G.6.1.1. Gross Premiums	G.6.1.1. Primes Brutes	635	632	690	701	743	836	915	983
G.6.1.2. Ceded Premiums	G.6.1.2. Primes Cédées	213	203	214	190	196	222	185	256
G.6.1.3. Net Written Premiums	G.6.1.3. Primes Nettes Emises	422	429	476	511	547	614	730	727
G.6.2. Reinsurance Accepted	G.6.2. Réassurance Acceptée								
G.6.2.1. Gross Premiums	G.6.2.1. Primes Brutes	244	236	240	190	192	221	79	103
G.6.2.2. Ceded Premiums	G.6.2.2. Primes Cédées	109	104	103	79	73	79	9	13
G.6.2.3. Net Written Premiums	G.6.2.3. Primes Nettes Emises	135	132	137	111	119	142	70	90
G.6.3. Total	G.6.3. Total								
G.6.3.1. Gross Premiums	G.6.3.1. Primes Brutes	879	868	930	891	935	1 057	994	1 086
G.6.3.2. Ceded Premiums	G.6.3.2. Primes Cédées	322	307	317	269	269	302	194	269
G.6.3.3. Net Written Premiums	G.6.3.3. Primes Nettes Emises	557	561	613	622	666	755	800	817
G.7. Accident, Health	**G.7. Accident, Santé**								
G.7.1. Direct Business	G.7.1. Assurances Directes								
G.7.1.1. Gross Premiums	G.7.1.1. Primes Brutes	1 150	1 145	1 225	1 235	1 215	1 259	1 356	1 438
G.7.1.2. Ceded Premiums	G.7.1.2. Primes Cédées	425	431	478	458	421	460	497	428
G.7.1.3. Net Written Premiums	G.7.1.3. Primes Nettes Emises	725	814	747	777	794	799	859	1 010
G.7.2. Reinsurance Accepted	G.7.2. Réassurance Acceptée								
G.7.2.1. Gross Premiums	G.7.2.1. Primes Brutes	339	350	389	345	312	325	323	270
G.7.2.2. Ceded Premiums	G.7.2.2. Primes Cédées	140	141	156	134	111	115	107	71
G.7.2.3. Net Written Premiums	G.7.2.3. Primes Nettes Emises	199	209	233	211	201	210	216	199
G.7.3. Total	G.7.3. Total								
G.7.3.1. Gross Premiums	G.7.3.1. Primes Brutes	1 489	1 495	1 614	1 580	1 527	1 584	1 679	1 708
G.7.3.2. Ceded Premiums	G.7.3.2. Primes Cédées	565	572	634	592	532	575	604	499
G.7.3.3. Net Written Premiums	G.7.3.3. Primes Nettes Emises	924	923	980	988	995	1 009	1 075	1 209

Monetary Unit: million Icelandic kronur Unité monétaire : million de couronnes islandaises

		1992	1993	1994	1995	1996	1997	1998	1999
G.8. Others	G.8. Autres								
G.8.2. Reinsurance Accepted	G.8.2. Réassurance Acceptée								
G.8.2.1. Gross Premiums	G.8.2.1. Primes Brutes	76	73	3	0	0	0	0	128
G.8.2.2. Ceded Premiums	G.8.2.2. Primes Cédées	1	1	0	0	0	0	0	1
G.8.2.3. Net Written Premiums	G.8.2.3. Primes Nettes Emises	75	72	3	0	0	0	0	127
G.8.3. Total	G.8.3. Total								
G.8.3.1. Gross Premiums	G.8.3.1. Primes Brutes	76	73	3	0	0	0	0	128
G.8.3.2. Ceded Premiums	G.8.3.2. Primes Cédées	1	1	0	0	0	0	0	1
G.8.3.3. Net Written Premiums	G.8.3.3. Primes Nettes Emises	75	72	3	0	0	0	0	127
G.9. Treaty Reinsurance	G.9. Réassurance Obligatoire								
G.9.2. Reinsurance Accepted	G.9.2. Réassurance Acceptée								
G.9.2.1. Gross Premiums	G.9.2.1. Primes Brutes	0	0	..	103	0	0	129	0
G.9.2.2. Ceded Premiums	G.9.2.2. Primes Cédées							1	0
G.9.2.3. Net Written Premiums	G.9.2.3. Primes Nettes Emises	0	0	..	103	0	0	128	0
G.9.3. Total	G.9.3. Total								
G.9.3.1. Gross Premiums	G.9.3.1. Primes Brutes	0	0	..	103	0	0	129	0
G.9.3.2. Ceded Premiums	G.9.3.2. Primes Cédées							1	0
G.9.3.3. Net Written Premiums	G.9.3.3. Primes Nettes Emises	0	0	..	103	0	0	128	0
G.10. Total	G.10. Total								
G.10.1. Direct Business	G.10.1. Assurances Directes								
G.10.1.1. Gross Premiums	G.10.1.1. Primes Brutes	12 828	12 622	..	13 064	13 346	13 210	13 919	15 607
G.10.1.2. Ceded Premiums	G.10.1.2. Primes Cédées	3 780	3 665	..	3 770	3 575	3 490	3 454	3 422
G.10.1.3. Net Written Premiums	G.10.1.3. Primes Nettes Emises	9 048	8 957	..	9 294	9 771	9 720	10 464	12 185
G.10.2. Reinsurance Accepted	G.10.2. Réassurance Acceptée								
G.10.2.1. Gross Premiums	G.10.2.1. Primes Brutes	2 561	2 443	..	1 791	1 611	1 554	1 413	1 064
G.10.2.2. Ceded Premiums	G.10.2.2. Primes Cédées	1 541	1 388	..	903	828	735	576	332
G.10.2.3. Net Written Premiums	G.10.2.3. Primes Nettes Emises	1 020	1 055	..	888	783	819	838	732
G.10.3. Total	G.10.3. Total								
G.10.3.1. Gross Premiums	G.10.3.1. Primes Brutes	15 389	15 065	..	14 752	14 957	14 764	15 332	16 672
G.10.3.2. Ceded Premiums	G.10.3.2. Primes Cédées	5 321	5 053	..	4 673	4 403	4 225	4 030	3 754
G.10.3.3. Net Written Premiums	G.10.3.3. Primes Nettes Emises	10 068	10 012	..	10 079	10 554	10 539	11 302	12 918
H. GROSS CLAIMS PAYMENTS	**H. PAIEMENTS BRUTS DES SINISTRES**								
H.1. Life	**H.1. Vie**								
H.1.1. Domestic Companies	H.1.1. Entreprises Nationales					172	208	67	214
H.1. Total	H.1. Total					172	208	67	214
H.2. Non-Life	**H.2. Non-Vie**								
H.2.1. Domestic Companies	H.2.1. Entreprises Nationales					10 267	10 296	10 115	12 324
H.2.2. (Foreign Controlled Companies)	H.2.2. (Entreprises Sous Contrôle Etranger)					244	0	0	0
H.2. Total	H.2. Total					10 267	10 296	10 115	12 324
I. GROSS OPERATING EXPENSES	**I. DEPENSES BRUTES D'EXPLOITATION**								
I.1. Life	**I.1. Vie**								
I.1.1. Domestic Companies	I.1.1. Entreprises Nationales					217	255	329	416
I.1.2. (Foreign Controlled Companies)	I.1.2. (Entreprises Sous Contrôle Etranger)					15	0	0	0
I.1. Total	I.1. Total des Primes Nettes Vie					217	255	329	416
I.2. Non-Life	**I.2. Non-Vie**								
I.2.1. Domestic Companies	I.2.1. Entreprises Nationales					3 030	3 122	3 383	3 863
I.2.2. (Foreign Controlled Companies)	I.2.2. (Entreprises Sous Contrôle Etranger)					173	0	0	0
I.2. Total	I.2. Total					3 030	3 122	3 383	3 863

Monetary Unit: million Icelandic kronur   Unité monétaire : million de couronnes islandaises

	1992	1993	1994	1995	1996	1997	1998	1999	
J. COMMISSIONS									**J. COMMISSIONS**
J.1. Life									**J.1. Vie**
J.1.1. Direct Business									J.1.3. Assurance Directe
J.1.1.1. Domestic Companies						:	37	30	34 J.1.1.1. Entreprises Nationales
J.1.1. Total of Life Net Premiums						:	37	30	34 J.1.1. Total
J.2. Non-Life									**J.2. Non-Vie**
J.2.1. Direct Business									J.2.3. Assurance Directe
J.2.1.1. Domestic Companies						:	597	635	617 J.2.1.1. Entreprises Nationales
J.2.1. Total						:	597	635	617 J.2.1. Total

Monetary Unit: million Irish pounds
Unité monétaire : million de livres irlandaises

	1992	1993	1994	1995	1996	1997	1998	1999	
A. NUMBER OF COMPANIES IN THE REPORTING COUNTRY									**A. NOMBRE D'ENTREPRISES DANS LE PAYS DECLARANT**
A.1. Life									**A.1. Vie**
A.1.1. Domestic Companies	17	19	20	22	26	30	31	39	A.1.1. Entreprises Nationales
A.1.3. Branches & Agencies of Foreign Cies	14	14	14	13	14	14	14	14	A.1.3. Succursales et Agences d'Ent. Etrangères
A.1. All Companies	31	33	34	35	40	44	45	53	A.1. Ensemble des Entreprises
A.2. Non-Life									**A.2. Non-Vie**
A.2.1. Domestic Companies	34	44	52	61	72	83	88	121	A.2.1. Entreprises Nationales
A.2.3. Branches & Agencies of Foreign Cies	31	30	30	29	27	23	24	35	A.2.3. Succursales et Agences d'Ent. Etrangères
A.2. All Companies	65	74	82	90	99	106	112	156	A.2. Ensemble des Entreprises
A.5. Total									**A.5. Total**
A.5.1. Domestic Companies	51	63	72	83	98	113	119	160	A.5.1. Entreprises Nationales
A.5.3. Branches & Agencies of Foreign Cies	45	44	44	42	41	37	38	49	A.5.3. Succursales et Agences d'Ent. Etrangères
A.5. All Insurance Companies	96	107	116	125	139	150	157	209	A.5. Ensemble des Entreprises d'Assurances
B. NUMBER OF EMPLOYEES									**B. NOMBRE D'EMPLOYES**
B.1. Insurance Companies	10 118	10 085	10 402	10 386	10 231	10 031	10 478	11 320	B.1. Entreprises d'Assurances
C. BUSINESS WRITTEN IN THE REPORTING COUNTRY									**C. OPERATIONS CONCLUES DANS LE PAYS DECLARANT**
C.1. Life									**C.1. Vie**
C.1.1. Gross Premiums									C.1.1. Primes Brutes
C.1.1.1. Direct Business									C.1.1.1. Assurances Directes
C.1.1.1.1. Domestic Companies	920	1 244	1 359	1 438	1 846	2 626	4 099	6 587	C.1.1.1.1. Entreprises Nationales
C.1.1.1.3. Branches & Agencies of Foreign Cies	378	397	423	413	539	633	849	809	C.1.1.1.3. Succursales et Agences d'Ent. Etrangères
C.1.1.1. Total	1 298	1 641	1 782	1 851	2 385	3 259	4 948	7 396	C.1.1.1. Total
C.1.1.2. Reinsurance Accepted									C.1.1.2. Réassurance Acceptée
C.1.1.2.1. Domestic Companies	230	170	3	4	18	21	24	38	C.1.1.2.1. Entreprises Nationales
C.1.1.2.3. Branches & Agencies of Foreign Cies	0	0	0	4	5	6	7	6	C.1.1.2.3. Succursales et Agences d'Ent. Etrangères
C.1.1.2. Total	230	170	3	8	23	27	31	44	C.1.1.2. Total
C.1.1.3. Total									C.1.1.3. Total
C.1.1.3.1. Domestic Companies	1 150	1 414	1 362	1 442	1 864	2 647	4 123	6 625	C.1.1.3.1. Entreprises Nationales
C.1.1.3.3. Branches & Agencies of Foreign Cies	378	398	423	417	544	639	856	815	C.1.1.3.3. Succursales et Agences d'Ent. Etrangères
C.1.1.3. Total Gross Premiums	1 528	1 811	1 785	1 859	2 408	3 286	4 979	7 440	C.1.1.3. Total des Primes Brutes
C.1.2. Ceded Premiums									C.1.2. Primes Cédées
C.1.2.1. Domestic Companies	257	231	40	62	82	77	116	261	C.1.2.1. Entreprises Nationales
C.1.2.3. Branches & Agencies of Foreign Cies	12	13	14	14	16	9	22	75	C.1.2.3. Succursales et Agences d'Ent. Etrangères
C.1.2. Total	269	243	54	76	98	86	138	336	C.1.2. Total
C.1.3. Net Written Premiums									C.1.3. Primes Nettes Emises
C.1.3.1. Domestic Companies	893	1 183	1 322	1 380	1 782	2 570	4 007	6 364	C.1.3.1. Entreprises Nationales
C.1.3.3. Branches & Agencies of Foreign Cies	367	385	409	403	528	630	834	740	C.1.3.3. Succursales et Agences d'Ent. Etrangères
C.1.3. Total	1 259	1 568	1 731	1 783	2 310	3 200	4 841	7 104	C.1.3. Total
C.2. Non-Life									**C.2. Non-Vie**
C.2.1. Gross premiums									C.2.1. Primes Brutes
C.2.1.1. Direct Business									C.2.1.1. Assurances Directes
C.2.1.1.1. Domestic Companies	779	932	1 102	1 235	1 339	1 467	1 774	2 109	C.2.1.1.1. Entreprises Nationales
C.2.1.1.3. Branches & Agencies of Foreign Cies	432	384	384	305	366	348	430	528	C.2.1.1.3. Succursales et Agences d'Ent. Etrangères
C.2.1.1. Total	1 211	1 315	1 486	1 540	1 705	1 815	2 204	2 637	C.2.1.1. Total
C.2.1.2. Reinsurance Accepted									C.2.1.2. Réassurance Acceptée
C.2.1.2.1. Domestic Companies	47	72	65	148	155	359	364	556	C.2.1.2.1. Entreprises Nationales
C.2.1.2.3. Branches & Agencies of Foreign Cies	1	3	2	0	0	1	0	0	C.2.1.2.3. Succursales et Agences d'Ent. Etrangères
C.2.1.2. Total	48	75	67	148	155	360	364	556	C.2.1.2. Total

Monetary Unit: million Irish pounds   Unité monétaire : million de livres irlandaises

	1992	1993	1994	1995	1996	1997	1998	1999
C.2.1.3. Total								
C.2.1.3.1. Domestic Companies / Entreprises Nationales	826	1 004	1 167	1 383	1 494	1 826	2 138	2 665
C.2.1.3.3. Branches & Agencies of Foreign Cies / Succursales et Agences d'Ent. Etrangères	433	387	386	305	366	349	430	528
C.2.1.3. Total Gross Premiums / Total des Primes Brutes	1 259	1 390	1 553	1 688	1 860	2 175	2 568	3 193
C.2.2. Ceded Premiums / Primes Cédées								
C.2.2.1. Domestic Companies / Entreprises Nationales	167	202	242	313	324	315	371	604
C.2.2.3. Branches & Agencies of Foreign Cies / Succursales et Agences d'Ent. Etrangères	64	56	71	40	55	46	47	68
C.2.2. Total	230	257	312	353	379	361	418	672
C.2.3. Net Written Premiums / Primes Nettes Emises								
C.2.3.1. Domestic Companies / Entreprises Nationales	659	802	925	1 070	1 170	1 511	1 767	2 061
C.2.3.3. Branches & Agencies of Foreign Cies / Succursales et Agences d'Ent. Etrangères	369	331	316	265	311	303	383	460
C.2.3. Total	1 028	1 133	1 241	1 335	1 481	1 814	2 150	2 521
C.3. Total								
C.3.1. Gross Premiums / Primes Brutes								
C.3.1.1. Direct Business / Assurances Directes								
C.3.1.1.1. Domestic Companies / Entreprises Nationales	1 699	2 176	2 461	2 673	3 185	4 093	5 873	8 696
C.3.1.1.3. Branches & Agencies of Foreign Cies / Succursales et Agences d'Ent. Etrangères	810	781	807	718	905	981	1 279	1 337
C.3.1.1. Total	2 508	2 957	3 268	3 391	4 090	5 074	7 152	10 033
C.3.1.2. Reinsurance Accepted / Réassurance Acceptée								
C.3.1.2.1. Domestic Companies / Entreprises Nationales	277	242	68	152	173	380	388	594
C.3.1.2.3. Branches & Agencies of Foreign Cies / Succursales et Agences d'Ent. Etrangères	1	3	2	4	5	7	7	6
C.3.1.2. Total	278	245	70	156	178	387	395	600
C.3.1.3. Total								
C.3.1.3.1. Domestic Companies / Entreprises Nationales	1 976	2 417	2 529	2 825	3 358	4 473	6 261	9 290
C.3.1.3.3. Branches & Agencies of Foreign Cies / Succursales et Agences d'Ent. Etrangères	811	784	809	722	910	988	1 286	1 343
C.3.1.3. Total Gross Premiums / Total des Primes Brutes	2 786	3 201	3 338	3 547	4 268	5 461	7 547	10 633
C.3.2. Ceded Premiums / Primes Cédées								
C.3.2.1. Domestic Companies / Entreprises Nationales	424	432	282	375	406	392	487	865
C.3.2.3. Branches & Agencies of Foreign Cies / Succursales et Agences d'Ent. Etrangères	75	68	84	54	71	55	69	143
C.3.2. Total	499	501	366	429	477	447	556	1 008
C.3.3. Net Written Premiums / Primes Nettes Emises								
C.3.3.1. Domestic Companies / Entreprises Nationales	1 552	1 985	2 247	2 450	2 952	4 081	5 774	8 425
C.3.3.3. Branches & Agencies of Foreign Cies / Succursales et Agences d'Ent. Etrangères	735	716	725	668	839	933	1 217	1 200
C.3.3. Total	2 287	2 701	2 972	3 118	3 791	5 014	6 991	9 625
D. NET WRITTEN PREMIUMS IN THE REPORTING COUNTRY IN TERMS OF DOMESTIC AND FOREIGN RISKS / D. PRIMES NETTES EMISES DANS LE PAYS DÉCLARANT EN RISQUES NATIONAUX ET ETRANGERS								
D.1. Life / D.1. Vie								
D.1.1. Domestic Risks / Risques Nationaux								
D.1.1.1. Domestic Companies / Entreprises Nationales	893	1 129	1 240	1 219	1 470	1 890	2 631	3 789
D.1.1.3. Branches & Agencies of Foreign Cies / Succursales et Agences d'Ent. Etrangères	367	385	409	403	528	630	834	740
D.1.1. Total / Total des Primes Nettes Vie	1 259	1 514	1 649	1 622	1 998	2 520	3 465	4 529
D.1.2. Foreign Risks / Risques Etrangers								
D.1.2.1. Domestic Companies / Entreprises Nationales	..	54	82	161	312	680	1 376	2 575
D.1.2. Total / Total des Primes Nettes Vie	..	54	82	161	312	680	1 376	2 575
D.1.3. Total								
D.1.3.1. Domestic Companies / Entreprises Nationales	893	1 183	1 322	1 380	1 782	2 570	4 007	6 364
D.1.3.3. Branches & Agencies of Foreign Cies / Succursales et Agences d'Ent. Etrangères	367	385	409	403	528	630	834	740
D.1.3. Total of Life Net Premiums / Total des Primes Nettes Vie	1 259	1 568	1 731	1 783	2 310	3 200	4 841	7 104
D.2. Non-Life / D.2. Non-Vie								
D.2.1. Domestic Risks / Risques Nationaux								
D.2.1.1. Domestic Companies / Entreprises Nationales	596	697	818	854	910	997	1 128	1 244
D.2.1.3. Branches & Agencies of Foreign Cies / Succursales et Agences d'Ent. Etrangères	368	327	302	264	310	302	382	459
D.2.1. Total / Total des Primes Nettes Vie	964	1 024	1 120	1 118	1 220	1 299	1 510	1 703

Monetary Unit: million Irish pounds
Unité monétaire : million de livres irlandaises

	1992	1993	1994	1995	1996	1997	1998	1999
D.2.2. Foreign Risks / Risques Etrangers								
D.2.2.1. Domestic Companies / Entreprises Nationales	63	105	107	216	260	514	639	817
D.2.2.3. Branches & Agencies of Foreign Cies / Succursales et Agences d'Ent. Etrangères	1	4	14	1	1	1	1	1
D.2.2. Total / Total des Primes Nettes Vie	65	108	121	217	261	515	640	818
D.2.3. Total								
D.2.3.1. Domestic Companies / Entreprises Nationales	659	802	925	1 070	1 170	1 511	1 767	2 061
D.2.3.3. Branches & Agencies of Foreign Cies / Succursales et Agences d'Ent. Etrangères	369	331	316	265	311	303	383	460
D.2.3. Total / Total des Primes Nettes Vie	1 028	1 133	1 241	1 335	1 481	1 814	2 150	2 521

E. BUSINESS WRITTEN ABROAD / E. OPERATIONS A L'ETRANGER

E.1. Life / E.1. Vie

	1992	1993	1994	1995	1996	1997	1998	1999
E.1.1. Gross Premiums / Primes Brutes								
E.1.1.1. Direct Business / Assurance Directe								
E.1.1.1.1. Branches & Agencies / Succursales & Agences	104	136	114	89	70	10	44	87
E.1.1.1. Total	104	136	114	89	70	10	44	87
E.1.1.2. Reinsurance Accepted / Réassurance Acceptée								
E.1.1.2.1. Branches & Agencies / Succursales & Agences	0	0	0	0	0	-1	-3	-3
E.1.1.2. Total	0	0	0	0	0	-1	-3	-3
E.1.1.3. Total								
E.1.1.3.1. Branches & Agencies / Succursales & Agences	104	136	114	89	70	9	41	84
E.1.1.3. Total Gross Premiums / Total des Primes Brutes	104	136	114	89	70	9	41	84
E.1.2. Ceded Premiums / Primes Cédées								
E.1.2.1. Branches & Agencies / Succursales & Agences	1	1	1	63	1	0	4	5
E.1.2. Total	1	1	1	63	1	0	:	5
E.1.3. Net Written Premiums / Primes Nettes Emises								
E.1.3.1. Branches & Agencies / Succursales & Agences	103	135	112	26	69	9	37	79
E.1.3. Total	103	135	112	26	69	9	37	79

E.2. Non-Life / E.2. Non-Vie

	1992	1993	1994	1995	1996	1997	1998	1999
E.2.1. Gross Premiums / Primes Brutes								
E.2.1.1. Direct Business / Assurance Directe								
E.2.1.1.1. Branches & Agencies / Succursales & Agences	50	68	65	63	114	129	135	77
E.2.1.1. Total	50	68	65	63	114	129	135	77
E.2.1.2. Reinsurance Accepted / Réassurance Acceptée								
E.2.1.2.1. Branches & Agencies / Succursales & Agences	6	1	1	0	0	0	0	0
E.2.1.2. Total	6	1	1	0	0	0	0	0
E.2.1.3. Total								
E.2.1.3.1. Branches & Agencies / Succursales & Agences	56	67	66	63	114	129	135	77
E.2.1.3. Total Gross Premiums / Total des Primes Brutes	56	67	66	63	114	129	135	77
E.2.2. Ceded Premiums / Primes Cédées								
E.2.2.1. Branches & Agencies / Succursales & Agences	11	13	12	11	42	58	69	5
E.2.2. Total	11	13	12	11	42	58	:	5
E.2.3. Net Written Premiums / Primes Nettes Emises								
E.2.3.1. Branches & Agencies / Succursales & Agences	45	54	54	52	72	71	66	72
E.2.3. Total	45	54	54	52	72	71	66	72

F. OUTSTANDING INVESTMENT BY DIRECT INSURANCE COMPANIES / F. ENCOURS DES PLACEMENTS DES ENTREPRISES D'ASSURANCES DIRECTES

F.1. Life / F.1. Vie

	1992	1993	1994	1995	1996	1997	1998	1999
F.1.1. Real Estate / Immobilier								
F.1.1.1. Domestic Companies / Entreprises Nationales	571	586	631	625	631	785	982	1 272
F.1.1.3. Branches & Agencies of Foreign Cies / Succursales et Agences d'Ent. Etrangères	159	159	20	20	21	17	26	17
F.1.1.4. Domestic Investment / Placement dans le Pays	715	730	629	:	:	:	:	:
F.1.1.5. Foreign Investment / Placement à l'Etranger	15	16	21	:	:	:	:	:
F.1.1. Total	730	745	651	:	653	:	:	:

IRELAND   IRLANDE

Monetary Unit: million Irish pounds   Unité monétaire : million de livres irlandaises

English	French	1992	1993	1994	1995	1996	1997	1998	1999
F.1.3. Shares	**F.1.3. Actions**								
F.1.3.1. Domestic Companies	F.1.3.1. Entreprises Nationales	444	707	658	3 657	4 200	6 533	7 293	9 092
F.1.3.3. Branches & Agencies of Foreign Cies	F.1.3.3. Succursales et Agences d'Ent. Etrangères	709	1 140	72	78	145	225	273	302
F.1.3.4. Domestic Investment	F.1.3.4. Placement dans le Pays	946	1 553	482	:	:	:	:	:
F.1.3.5. Foreign Investment	F.1.3.5. Placement à l'Etranger	207	293	248	:	:	:	:	:
F.1.3. Total	F.1.3. Total	1 153	1 847	730	:	4 346	:	:	:
F.1.4. Bonds with Fixed Revenue	**F.1.4. Obligations**								
F.1.4.1. Domestic Companies	F.1.4.1. Entreprises Nationales	2 160	2 854	2 650	3 085	3 542	5 224	6 415	6 002
F.1.4.3. Branches & Agencies of Foreign Cies	F.1.4.3. Succursales et Agences d'Ent. Etrangères	1 314	1 682	130	125	165	208	320	246
F.1.4.4. Domestic Investment	F.1.4.4. Placement dans le Pays	3 321	4 362	2 733	:	:	:	:	:
F.1.4.5. Foreign Investment	F.1.4.5. Placement à l'Etranger	153	174	48	:	:	:	:	:
F.1.4. Total	F.1.4. Total	3 473	4 536	2 781	:	3 708	:	:	:
F.1.5. Loans other than Mortgage Loans	**F.1.5. Prêts Autres qu'Hypothécaires**								
F.1.5.1. Domestic Companies	F.1.5.1. Entreprises Nationales	233	219	400	456	665	64	65	63
F.1.5.3. Branches & Agencies of Foreign Cies	F.1.5.3. Succursales et Agences d'Ent. Etrangères	31	24	5	1	5	8	6	83
F.1.5.4. Domestic Investment	F.1.5.4. Placement dans le Pays	263	243	405	:	:	:	:	:
F.1.5. Total	F.1.5. Total	264	243	405	:	670	:	:	:
F.1.6. Other Investments	**F.1.6. Autres Placements**								
F.1.6.1. Domestic Companies	F.1.6.1. Entreprises Nationales	2 641	3 628	3 430	2 404	1 502	3 590	4 597	3 531
F.1.6.3. Branches & Agencies of Foreign Cies	F.1.6.3. Succursales et Agences d'Ent. Etrangères	479	694	87	26	40	37	25	22
F.1.6.4. Domestic Investment	F.1.6.4. Placement dans le Pays	2 950	4 188	3 480	:	:	:	:	:
F.1.6.5. Foreign Investment	F.1.6.5. Placement à l'Etranger	170	134	37	:	:	:	:	:
F.1.6. Total	F.1.6. Total	3 120	4 323	3 518	:	1 542	:	:	:
F.1.7. Total	**F.1.7. Total**								
F.1.7.1. Domestic Companies	F.1.7.1. Entreprises Nationales	6 047	7 995	7 769	10 227	10 540	16 196	19 352	19 960
F.1.7.3. Branches & Agencies of Foreign Cies	F.1.7.3. Succursales et Agences d'Ent. Etrangères	2 692	3 699	314	250	376	495	650	670
F.1.7.4. Domestic Investment	F.1.7.4. Placement dans le Pays	8 195	11 077	7 730	:	:	:	:	:
F.1.7.5. Foreign Investment	F.1.7.5. Placement à l'Etranger	545	617	354	:	:	:	:	:
F.1.7. Total of Life Investments	F.1.7. Total des Placements Vie	8 740	11 694	8 083	:	10 916	:	:	:
F.2. Non-Life	**F.2. Non-Vie**								
F.2.1. Real Estate	**F.2.1. Immobilier**								
F.2.1.1. Domestic Companies	F.2.1.1. Entreprises Nationales	46	41	54	89	90	64	93	134
F.2.1.3. Branches & Agencies of Foreign Cies	F.2.1.3. Succursales et Agences d'Ent. Etrangères	10	10	0	0	0	0	:	:
F.2.1.4. Domestic Investment	F.2.1.4. Placement dans le Pays	46	41	54	:	:	62	91	131
F.2.1.5. Foreign Investment	F.2.1.5. Placement à l'Etranger	10	10	0	:	:	2	2	3
F.2.1. Total	F.2.1. Total	56	50	54	:	90	64	93	134
F.2.3. Shares	**F.2.3. Actions**								
F.2.3.1. Domestic Companies	F.2.3.1. Entreprises Nationales	180	323	336	433	460	764	982	1 101
F.2.3.3. Branches & Agencies of Foreign Cies	F.2.3.3. Succursales et Agences d'Ent. Etrangères	52	56	0	0	0	0	:	:
F.2.3.4. Domestic Investment	F.2.3.4. Placement dans le Pays	180	323	336	:	:	555	714	580
F.2.3.5. Foreign Investment	F.2.3.5. Placement à l'Etranger	52	56	0	:	:	209	268	521
F.2.3. Total	F.2.3. Total	231	380	337	:	460	764	982	1 101
F.2.4. Bonds with Fixed Revenue	**F.2.4. Obligations**								
F.2.4.1. Domestic Companies	F.2.4.1. Entreprises Nationales	845	1 178	1 308	1 689	1 993	0	:	:
F.2.4.3. Branches & Agencies of Foreign Cies	F.2.4.3. Succursales et Agences d'Ent. Etrangères	588	595	4	0	0	0	:	:
F.2.4.4. Domestic Investment	F.2.4.4. Placement dans le Pays	845	1 178	1 308	:	:	:	:	:
F.2.4.5. Foreign Investment	F.2.4.5. Placement à l'Etranger	588	595	4	:	:	:	:	:
F.2.4. Total	F.2.4. Total	1 433	1 773	1 312	:	1 993	:	:	:
F.2.6. Other Investments	**F.2.6. Autres Placements**								
F.2.6.1. Domestic Companies	F.2.6.1. Entreprises Nationales	457	478	503	982	1 000	3 565	4 074	4 538
F.2.6.3. Branches & Agencies of Foreign Cies	F.2.6.3. Succursales et Agences d'Ent. Etrangères	55	42	1	9	7	5	4	:
F.2.6.4. Domestic Investment	F.2.6.4. Placement dans le Pays	457	478	503	:	:	2 673	2 129	2 431
F.2.6.5. Foreign Investment	F.2.6.5. Placement à l'Etranger	55	42	1	:	:	897	1 949	2 107
F.2.6. Total	F.2.6. Total	512	521	504	:	1 007	3 570	4 078	4 538

133

Monetary Unit: million Irish pounds — Unité monétaire : million de livres irlandaises

	1992	1993	1994	1995	1996	1997	1998	1999
F.2.7. Total								
F.2.7.1. Domestic Companies / F.2.7.1. Entreprises Nationales	1 528	2 020	2 201	3 193	3 543	4 393	5 149	5 773
F.2.7.3. Branches & Agencies of Foreign Cies / F.2.7.3. Succursales et Agences d'Ent. Etrangères	705	703	5	9	7	5	..	4
F.2.7.4. Domestic Investment / F.2.7.4. Placement dans le Pays	1 528	2 020	2 201	..	..	3 290	2 934	3 142
F.2.7.5. Foreign Investment / F.2.7.5. Placement à l'Etranger	705	703	5	..	..	1 108	2 219	2 631
F.2.7. Total of Non-Life Investments / F.2.7. Total des Placements Non-Vie	2 233	2 724	2 206	..	3 550	4 398	5 153	5 773
G. BREAKDOWN OF NON-LIFE PREMIUMS / G. VENTILATIONS DES PRIMES NON-VIE								
G.1. Motor vehicle / Assurance Automobile								
G.1.1. Direct Business / G.1.1. Assurances Directes								
G.1.1.1. Gross Premiums / G.1.1.1. Primes Brutes	582	607	646	692	757	781	898	1 038
G.1.1.2. Ceded Premiums / G.1.1.2. Primes Cédées	49	48	44	73	79	59	49	58
G.1.1.3. Net Written Premiums / G.1.1.3. Primes Nettes Emises	533	559	602	619	678	722	849	980
G.2. Marine, Aviation / Marine, Aviation								
G.2.1. Direct Business / G.2.1. Assurances Directes								
G.2.1.1. Gross Premiums / G.2.1.1. Primes Brutes	7	19	29	29	31	38	52	58
G.2.1.2. Ceded Premiums / G.2.1.2. Primes Cédées	3	7	16	12	13	16	19	31
G.2.1.3. Net Written Premiums / G.2.1.3. Primes Nettes Emises	5	11	13	17	19	22	33	27
G.4. Fire, Property Damages / Incendie, Dommages aux Biens								
G.4.1. Direct Business / G.4.1. Assurances Directes								
G.4.1.1. Gross Premiums / G.4.1.1. Primes Brutes	277	303	359	372	420	460	506	569
G.4.1.2. Ceded Premiums / G.4.1.2. Primes Cédées	80	87	114	123	141	147	146	163
G.4.1.3. Net Written Premiums / G.4.1.3. Primes Nettes Emises	198	216	246	249	279	313	360	406
G.5. Pecuniary Losses / Pertes Pécuniaires								
G.5.1. Direct Business / G.5.1. Assurances Directes								
G.5.1.1. Gross Premiums / G.5.1.1. Primes Brutes	42	47	55	19	..	..	..	..
G.5.1.2. Ceded Premiums / G.5.1.2. Primes Cédées	19	23	30	7	..	..	..	..
G.5.1.3. Net Written Premiums / G.5.1.3. Primes Nettes Emises	24	24	25	12	..	..	..	..
G.6. General Liability / Responsabilité Générale								
G.6.1. Direct Business / G.6.1. Assurances Directes								
G.6.1.1. Gross Premiums / G.6.1.1. Primes Brutes	263	295	347	327	352	350	430	541
G.6.1.2. Ceded Premiums / G.6.1.2. Primes Cédées	67	73	91	88	99	89	139	225
G.6.1.3. Net Written Premiums / G.6.1.3. Primes Nettes Emises	197	222	256	239	253	261	291	316
G.7. Accident, Health / Accident, Santé								
G.7.1. Direct Business / G.7.1. Assurances Directes								
G.7.1.1. Gross Premiums / G.7.1.1. Primes Brutes	39	45	50	56	73	101	148	179
G.7.1.2. Ceded Premiums / G.7.1.2. Primes Cédées	6	8	9	7	4	7	8	26
G.7.1.3. Net Written Premiums / G.7.1.3. Primes Nettes Emises	33	37	41	49	69	94	140	153
G.8. Others / Autres								
G.8.1. Direct Business / G.8.1. Assurances Directes								
G.8.1.1. Gross Premiums / G.8.1.1. Primes Brutes	..	..	..	45	72	85	170	252
G.8.1.2. Ceded Premiums / G.8.1.2. Primes Cédées	..	..	..	29	32	26	27	43
G.8.1.3. Net Written Premiums / G.8.1.3. Primes Nettes Emises	..	..	..	16	40	59	143	209
G.9. Treaty Reinsurance / Réassurance Obligatoire								
G.9.2. Reinsurance Accepted / G.9.2. Réassurance Acceptée								
G.9.2.1. Gross Premiums / G.9.2.1. Primes Brutes	48	75	..	148	155	360	364	556
G.9.2.2. Ceded Premiums / G.9.2.2. Primes Cédées	8	10	..	14	11	17	30	126
G.9.2.3. Net Written Premiums / G.9.2.3. Primes Nettes Emises	40	65	..	134	144	343	334	430
G.10. Total								
G.10.1. Direct Business / G.10.1. Assurances Directes								
G.10.1.1. Gross Premiums / G.10.1.1. Primes Brutes	1 211	1 315	1 486	1 540	1 705	1 815	2 204	2 637
G.10.1.2. Ceded Premiums / G.10.1.2. Primes Cédées	223	247	303	339	368	344	388	546
G.10.1.3. Net Written Premiums / G.10.1.3. Primes Nettes Emises	988	1 068	1 183	1 201	1 337	1 471	1 816	2 091
G.10.2. Reinsurance Accepted / G.10.2. Réassurance Acceptée								
G.10.2.1. Gross Premiums / G.10.2.1. Primes Brutes	..	75	67	148	155	360	364	556
G.10.2.2. Ceded Premiums / G.10.2.2. Primes Cédées	..	10	10	14	11	17	30	126
G.10.2.3. Net Written Premiums / G.10.2.3. Primes Nettes Emises	..	65	58	134	144	343	334	430

Monetary Unit: million Irish pounds — Unité monétaire : million de livres irlandaises

English	1992	1993	1994	1995	1996	1997	1998	1999	Français
G.10.3. Total									G.10.3. Total
G.10.3.1. Gross Premiums	1 259	1 390	1 553	1 688	1 860	2 175	2 568	3 193	G.10.3.1. Primes Brutes
G.10.3.2. Ceded Premiums	230	257	312	353	379	361	418	672	G.10.3.2. Primes Cédées
G.10.3.3. Net Written Premiums	1 028	1 133	1 241	1 335	1 481	1 814	2 150	2 521	G.10.3.3. Primes Nettes Emises
H. GROSS CLAIMS PAYMENTS									**H. PAIEMENTS BRUTS DES SINISTRES**
H.1. Life									**H.1. Vie**
H.1.1. Domestic Companies		1 143	1 553	1 127	1 124	1 363	2 079	1 968	H.1.1. Entreprises Nationales
H.1.3. Branches & Agencies of Foreign Cies		297	27	301	286	300	348	41	H.1.3. Succursales et Agences d'Ent. Etrangères
H.1. Total		1 441	1 580	1 428	1 410	1 663	2 427	2 009	H.1. Total
H.2. Non-Life									**H.2. Non-Vie**
H.2.1. Domestic Companies		683	679	750	929	1 149	1 229	1 477	H.2.1. Entreprises Nationales
H.2.3. Branches & Agencies of Foreign Cies		178	180	177	235	226	239	270	H.2.3. Succursales et Agences d'Ent. Etrangères
H.2. Total		861	859	927	1 164	1 375	1 468	1 747	H.2. Total
I. GROSS OPERATING EXPENSES									**I. DEPENSES BRUITES D'EXPLOITATION**
I.1. Life									**I.1. Vie**
I.1.1. Domestic Companies		194	188	207	222	280	319	393	I.1.1. Entreprises Nationales
I.1.3. Branches & Agencies of Foreign Cies		73	8	74	83	78	100	113	I.1.3. Succursales et Agences d'Ent. Etrangères
I.1. Total		267	196	281	305	358	419	506	I.1. Total des Primes Nettes Vie
I.2. Non-Life									**I.2. Non-Vie**
I.2.1. Domestic Companies		138	147	146	155	139	136	208	I.2.1. Entreprises Nationales
I.2.3. Branches & Agencies of Foreign Cies		35	33	37	41	40	48	37	I.2.3. Succursales et Agences d'Ent. Etrangères
I.2. Total		173	180	183	196	179	184	245	I.2. Total
J. COMMISSIONS									**J. COMMISSIONS**
J.1. Life									**J.1. Vie**
J.1.1. Direct Business									J.1.1. Assurance directe
J.1.1.1. Domestic Companies		84	88	97	120	177	261	365	J.1.1.1. Entreprises Nationales
J.1.1.3. Branches & Agencies of Foreign Cies		24	0	23	29	24	36	31	J.1.1.3. Succursales et Agences d'Ent. Etrangères
J.1.1. Total		108	88	120	149	201	297	396	J.1.1. Total
J.1.3. Total									J.1.3. Total
J.1.3.1. Domestic Companies		84	88	97	120	177	261	365	J.1.3.1. Entreprises Nationales
J.1.3.3. Branches & Agencies of Foreign Cies		24	0	23	29	24	36	31	J.1.3.3. Succursales et Agences d'Ent. Etrangères
J.1.3. Total of Life Net Premiums		108	88	120	149	201	297	396	J.1.3. Total
J.2. Non-Life									**J.2. Non-Vie**
J.2.1. Direct Business									J.2.1. Assurance directe
J.2.1.1. Domestic Companies		65	71	78	94	219	145	183	J.2.1.1. Entreprises Nationales
J.2.1.3. Branches & Agencies of Foreign Cies		31	34	36	44	44	54	67	J.2.1.3. Succursales et Agences d'Ent. Etrangères
J.2.1. Total		96	105	114	138	263	199	250	J.2.1. Total des Primes Nettes Vie
J.2.2. Reinsurance Accepted									J.2.2. Réassurances acceptées
J.2.2.1. Domestic Companies		12	16	36	38	108	98	139	J.2.2.1. Entreprises Nationales
J.2.2. Total		12	16	36	38	108	98	139	J.2.2. Total
J.2.3. Total									J.2.3. Total
J.2.3.1. Domestic Companies		77	87	114	132	327	243	322	J.2.3.1. Entreprises Nationales
J.2.3.3. Branches & Agencies of Foreign Cies		31	34	36	44	44	54	67	J.2.3.3. Succursales et Agences d'Ent. Etrangères
J.2.3. Total		108	121	150	176	371	297	389	J.2.3. Total

Monetary Unit: million lire　　　　　　　　　　　　Unité monétaire : million de lires

	1992	1993	1994	1995	1996	1997	1998	1999	
A. NUMBER OF COMPANIES IN THE REPORTING COUNTRY									**A. NOMBRE D'ENTREPRISES DANS LE PAYS DECLARANT**
A.1. Life									**A.1. Vie**
A.1.1. Domestic Companies	65	67	70	71	74	77	76	76	A.1.1. Entreprises Nationales
A.1.3. Branches & Agencies of Foreign Cies	6	7	6	6	9	10	11	12	A.1.3. Succursales et Agences d'Ent. Etrangères
A.1. All Companies	71	74	76	77	83	87	87	88	A.1. Ensemble des Entreprises
A.2. Non-Life									**A.2. Non-Vie**
A.2.1. Domestic Companies	119	124	122	122	122	111	102	100	A.2.1. Entreprises Nationales
A.2.3. Branches & Agencies of Foreign Cies	43	42	33	32	34	32	32	33	A.2.3. Succursales et Agences d'Ent. Etrangères
A.2. All Companies	162	166	155	154	156	143	134	133	A.2. Ensemble des Entreprises
A.3. Composite									**A.3. Mixte**
A.3.1. Domestic Companies	26	25	24	22	22	21	21	20	A.3.1. Entreprises Nationales
A.3. All Companies	26	25	24	22	22	21	21	20	A.3. Ensemble des Entreprises
A.4. Reinsurance									**A.4. Reassurance**
A.4.1. Domestic Companies	8	8	8	6	6	6	5	4	A.4.1. Entreprises Nationales
A.4.3. Branches & Agencies of Foreign Cies	1	1	2	2	4	4	5	5	A.4.3. Succursales et Agences d'Ent. Etrangères
A.4. All Companies	9	9	10	8	10	10	10	9	A.4. Ensemble des Entreprises
A.5. Total									**A.5. Total**
A.5.1. Domestic Companies	218	224	224	221	224	215	204	200	A.5.1. Entreprises Nationales
A.5.3. Branches & Agencies of Foreign Cies	50	50	41	40	47	46	9 147 624	50	A.5.3. Succursales et Agences d'Ent. Etrangères
A.5. All Insurance Companies	268	274	265	261	271	261	252	250	A.5. Ensemble des Entreprises d'Assurances
B. NUMBER OF EMPLOYEES									**B. NOMBRE D'EMPLOYES**
B.1. Insurance Companies	48 253	48 112	46 832	46 516	45 250	44 110	42 715	43 983	B.1. Entreprises d'Assurances
B.2. Intermediaries	90 000	90 000	90 200	90 200	90 200	90 200	90 500	90 500	B.2. Intermediaires
B. Total	138 253	138 112	137 032	136 716	135 450		133 215	134 483	B. Total
C. BUSINESS WRITTEN IN THE REPORTING COUNTRY									**C. OPERATIONS CONCLUES DANS LE PAYS DECLARANT**
C.1. Life									**C.1. Vie**
C.1.1. Gross Premiums									C.1.1. Primes Brutes
C.1.1.1. Direct Business									C.1.1.1. Assurances Directes
C.1.1.1.1. Domestic Companies	12 291 500	14 864 400	18 251 100	22 501 200	25 208 600	35 899 700	50 499 184	68 134 308	C.1.1.1.1. Entreprises Nationales
C.1.1.1.2. (Foreign Controlled Companies)	..					7 164 500			C.1.1.1.2. (Entreprises Sous Contrôle Etranger)
C.1.1.1.3. Branches & Agencies of Foreign Cies	216 800	278 600	374 300	554 000	609 100	782 500	1 032 444	1 375 126	C.1.1.1.3. Succursales et Agences d'Ent. Etrangères
C.1.1.1. Total	12 508 300	15 143 000	18 625 400	23 055 200	25 817 700	36 682 200	51 531 628	69 509 434	C.1.1.1. Total
C.1.1.2. Reinsurance Accepted									C.1.1.2. Réassurance Acceptée
C.1.1.2.1. Domestic Companies	2 813 100	2 671 700	2 328 900	2 514 800	2 836 000	3 195 400	3 194 428	3 381 073	C.1.1.2.1. Entreprises Nationales
C.1.1.2.3. Branches & Agencies of Foreign Cies	200	1 600	2 000	4 500	106 700	182 200	241 645	285 549	C.1.1.2.3. Succursales et Agences d'Ent. Etrangères
C.1.1.2. Total	2 813 300	2 673 300	2 330 900	2 519 300	2 942 700	3 377 600	3 436 073	3 666 622	C.1.1.2. Total
C.1.1.3. Total									C.1.1.3. Total
C.1.1.3.1. Domestic Companies	15 104 600	17 536 100	20 580 000	25 016 000	28 044 600	39 095 100	53 693 612	71 515 381	C.1.1.3.1. Entreprises Nationales
C.1.1.3.3. Branches & Agencies of Foreign Cies	217 000	280 200	376 300	558 500	715 800	964 700	1 274 089	1 660 675	C.1.1.3.3. Succursales et Agences d'Ent. Etrangères
C.1.1.3. Total Gross Premiums	15 321 600	17 816 300	20 956 300	25 574 500	28 760 400	40 059 800	54 967 701	73 176 056	C.1.1.3. Total des Primes Brutes
C.1.2. Ceded Premiums									C.1.2. Primes Cédées
C.1.2.1. Domestic Companies	2 840 200	2 970 300	2 157 700	2 379 100	2 591 500	3 081 900	3 111 513	3 326 901	C.1.2.1. Entreprises Nationales
C.1.2.3. Branches & Agencies of Foreign Cies	100	44 300	4 600	3 300	10 100	25 900	24 616	77 524	C.1.2.3. Succursales et Agences d'Ent. Etrangères
C.1.2. Total	2 840 300	3 014 600	2 162 300	2 382 400	2 601 600	3 107 800	3 136 129	3 404 425	C.1.2. Total
C.1.3. Net Written Premiums									C.1.3. Primes Nettes Emises
C.1.3.1. Domestic Companies	12 264 400	14 565 800	18 422 300	22 636 900	25 453 100	36 013 200	50 582 099	68 188 480	C.1.3.1. Entreprises Nationales
C.1.3.3. Branches & Agencies of Foreign Cies	216 900	235 900	371 700	555 200	705 700	938 800	1 249 473	1 583 151	C.1.3.3. Succursales et Agences d'Ent. Etrangères
C.1.3. Total	12 481 300	14 801 700	18 794 000	23 192 100	26 158 800	36 952 000	51 831 572	69 771 631	C.1.3. Total
C.2. Non-Life									**C.2. Non-Vie**
C.2.1. Gross premiums									C.2.1. Primes Brutes
C.2.1.1. Direct Business									C.2.1.1. Assurances Directes
C.2.1.1.1. Domestic Companies	31 430 700	33 637 000	35 634 900	37 249 900	39 296 000	41 697 100	45 491 122	48 993 205	C.2.1.1.1. Entreprises Nationales

Monetary Unit: million lire — Unité monétaire : million de lires

Code / Label	1992	1993	1994	1995	1996	1997	1998	1999
C.2.1.1.2. (Foreign Controlled Companies) / (Entreprises Sous Contrôle Etranger)	..	..	..	..	..	13 182 000	..	..
C.2.1.1.3. Branches & Agencies of Foreign Cies / Succursales et Agences d'Ent. Etrangères	1 414 500	1 473 200	1 158 800	1 511 700	1 559 700	1 921 000	2 283 609	2 661 983
C.2.1.1. Total	32 845 200	35 110 200	36 793 700	38 761 600	40 855 700	43 618 100	47 774 731	51 655 188
C.2.1.2. Reinsurance Accepted / Réassurance Acceptée								
C.2.1.2.1. Domestic Companies / Entreprises Nationales	5 320 100	5 361 100	5 038 500	5 047 800	4 624 100	4 593 600	4 557 401	4 079 424
C.2.1.2.3. Branches & Agencies of Foreign Cies / Succursales et Agences d'Ent. Etrangères	14 900	13 800	13 100	101 500	203 300	274 200	258 818	471 125
C.2.1.2. Total	5 335 000	5 374 900	5 051 600	5 149 300	4 827 400	4 867 800	4 816 219	4 550 549
C.2.1.3. Total								
C.2.1.3.1. Domestic Companies / Entreprises Nationales	36 750 800	38 998 100	40 673 400	42 297 700	43 920 100	46 290 700	50 048 523	53 072 629
C.2.1.3.3. Branches & Agencies of Foreign Cies / Succursales et Agences d'Ent. Etrangères	1 429 400	1 487 000	1 171 900	1 613 200	1 763 000	2 195 200	2 542 427	3 133 108
C.2.1.3. Total Gross Premiums / Total des Primes Brutes	38 180 200	40 485 100	41 845 300	43 910 900	45 683 100	48 485 900	52 590 950	56 205 737
C.2.2. Ceded Premiums / Primes Cédées								
C.2.2.1. Domestic Companies / Entreprises Nationales	8 016 700	7 619 300	7 103 900	7 013 100	6 796 200	6 944 700	7 164 065	7 202 096
C.2.2.3. Branches & Agencies of Foreign Cies / Succursales et Agences d'Ent. Etrangères	237 100	234 600	187 000	293 200	323 600	325 000	90 867	99 333
C.2.2. Total	8 253 800	7 853 900	7 290 900	7 306 300	7 119 800	7 269 700	7 254 932	7 301 429
C.2.3. Net Written Premiums / Primes Nettes Emises								
C.2.3.1. Domestic Companies / Entreprises Nationales	28 734 100	31 378 800	33 569 500	35 284 600	37 123 900	39 346 000	42 884 458	45 870 533
C.2.3.3. Branches & Agencies of Foreign Cies / Succursales et Agences d'Ent. Etrangères	1 192 300	1 252 400	984 900	1 320 000	1 439 400	1 870 200	2 451 560	3 033 775
C.2.3. Total	29 926 400	32 631 200	34 554 400	36 604 600	38 563 300	41 216 200	45 336 018	48 904 308
C.3. Total								
C.3.1. Gross Premiums / Primes Brutes								
C.3.1.1. Direct Business / Assurances Directes								
C.3.1.1.1. Domestic Companies / Entreprises Nationales	43 722 200	48 501 400	53 886 000	59 751 100	64 504 600	77 596 800	95 990 306	117 127 513
C.3.1.1.2. (Foreign Controlled Companies) / (Entreprises Sous Contrôle Etranger)	..	..	..	..	..	20 346 500	0	..
C.3.1.1.3. Branches & Agencies of Foreign Cies / Succursales et Agences d'Ent. Etrangères	1 631 300	1 751 800	1 533 100	2 065 700	2 168 800	2 703 500	3 316 053	4 037 109
C.3.1.1. Total	45 353 500	50 253 200	55 419 100	61 816 800	66 673 400	80 300 300	99 306 359	121 164 622
C.3.1.2. Reinsurance Accepted / Réassurance Acceptée								
C.3.1.2.1. Domestic Companies / Entreprises Nationales	8 133 200	8 032 800	7 367 400	7 562 600	7 460 100	7 789 000	7 751 829	7 460 497
C.3.1.2.3. Branches & Agencies of Foreign Cies / Succursales et Agences d'Ent. Etrangères	15 100	15 400	15 100	106 000	310 000	456 400	500 463	756 674
C.3.1.2. Total	8 148 300	8 048 200	7 382 500	7 668 600	7 770 100	8 245 400	8 252 292	8 217 171
C.3.1.3. Total								
C.3.1.3.1. Domestic Companies / Entreprises Nationales	51 855 400	56 534 200	61 253 400	67 313 700	71 964 700	85 385 800	103 742 135	124 588 010
C.3.1.3.3. Branches & Agencies of Foreign Cies / Succursales et Agences d'Ent. Etrangères	1 646 400	1 767 200	1 548 200	2 171 700	2 478 800	3 159 900	3 816 516	4 793 783
C.3.1.3. Total Gross Premiums / Total des Primes Brutes	53 501 800	58 301 400	62 801 600	69 485 400	74 443 500	88 545 700	107 558 651	129 381 793
C.3.2. Ceded Premiums / Primes Cédées								
C.3.2.1. Domestic Companies / Entreprises Nationales	10 856 900	10 589 600	9 261 600	9 392 200	9 387 700	10 026 600	10 275 578	10 528 997
C.3.2.3. Branches & Agencies of Foreign Cies / Succursales et Agences d'Ent. Etrangères	237 200	278 900	191 600	296 500	333 700	350 900	115 483	176 857
C.3.2. Total	11 094 100	10 868 500	9 453 200	9 688 700	9 721 400	10 377 500	10 391 061	10 705 854
C.3.3. Net Written Premiums / Primes Nettes Emises								
C.3.3.1. Domestic Companies / Entreprises Nationales	40 998 500	45 944 600	51 991 800	57 921 500	62 577 000	75 359 200	93 466 557	114 059 013
C.3.3.3. Branches & Agencies of Foreign Cies / Succursales et Agences d'Ent. Etrangères	1 409 200	1 488 300	1 356 600	1 875 200	2 145 100	2 809 000	3 701 033	4 616 926
C.3.3. Total	42 407 700	47 432 900	53 348 400	59 796 700	64 722 100	78 168 200	97 167 590	118 675 939

Monetary Unit: million lire — Unité monétaire : million de lires

D. NET WRITTEN PREMIUMS IN THE REPORTING COUNTRY IN TERMS OF DOMESTIC AND FOREIGN RISKS / D. PRIMES NETTES EMISES DANS LE PAYS DECLARANT EN RISQUES NATIONAUX ET ETRANGERS

	1992	1993	1994	1995	1996	1997	1998	1999
D.1. Life / D.1. Vie								
D.1.1. Domestic Risks / D.1.1. Risques Nationaux								
D.1.1.1. Domestic Companies / D.1.1.1. Entreprises Nationales	11 752 100	13 945 900	17 649 000	21 782 000	24 456 800	34 965 500	49 678 797	67 221 329
D.1.1.3. Branches & Agencies of Foreign Cies / D.1.1.3. Succursales et Agences d'Ent. Etrangères	216 900	235 900	371 700	555 200	705 700	938 800	1 249 473	1 583 151
D.1.1. Total / D.1.1. Total des Primes Nettes Vie	11 969 000	14 181 800	18 020 700	22 337 200	25 162 500	35 904 300	50 928 270	68 804 480
D.1.2. Foreign Risks / D.1.2. Risques Etrangers								
D.1.2.1. Domestic Companies / D.1.2.1. Entreprises Nationales	512 300	619 900	773 300	854 900	996 300	1 047 700	903 302	967 151
D.1.2. Total / D.1.2. Total des Primes Nettes Vie	512 300	619 900	773 300	854 900	996 300	1 047 700	903 302	967 151
D.1.3. Total								
D.1.3.1. Domestic Companies / D.1.3.1. Entreprises Nationales	12 284 400	14 565 800	18 422 300	22 636 900	25 453 100	36 013 200	50 582 099	68 188 480
D.1.3.3. Branches & Agencies of Foreign Cies / D.1.3.3. Succursales et Agences d'Ent. Etrangères	216 900	235 900	371 700	555 200	705 700	938 800	1 249 473	1 583 151
D.1.3. Total of Life Net Premiums / D.1.3. Total des Primes Nettes Vie	12 481 300	14 801 700	18 794 000	23 192 100	26 158 800	36 952 000	51 831 572	69 771 631
D.2. Non-Life / D.2. Non-Vie								
D.2.1. Domestic Risks / D.2.1. Risques Nationaux								
D.2.1.1. Domestic Companies / D.2.1.1. Entreprises Nationales	27 650 200	29 801 300	31 739 300	33 082 700	35 226 800	37 774 900	41 647 004	44 885 111
D.2.1.3. Branches & Agencies of Foreign Cies / D.2.1.3. Succursales et Agences d'Ent. Etrangères	1 192 300	1 252 400	984 900	1 320 000	1 439 400	1 870 200	2 451 560	3 033 775
D.2.1. Total / D.2.1. Total des Primes Nettes Vie	28 842 500	31 053 700	32 724 200	34 402 700	36 666 200	39 645 100	44 098 564	47 918 886
D.2.2. Foreign Risks / D.2.2. Risques Etrangers								
D.2.2.1. Domestic Companies / D.2.2.1. Entreprises Nationales	1 173 900	1 577 500	1 830 200	2 201 900	1 897 100	1 571 100	1 237 454	985 422
D.2.2. Total / D.2.2. Total des Primes Nettes Vie	1 173 900	1 577 500	1 830 200	2 201 900	1 897 100	1 571 100	1 237 454	985 422
D.2.3. Total								
D.2.3.1. Domestic Companies / D.2.3.1. Entreprises Nationales	28 734 100	31 378 800	33 569 500	35 284 600	37 123 900	39 346 000	42 884 458	45 870 533
D.2.3.3. Branches & Agencies of Foreign Cies / D.2.3.3. Succursales et Agences d'Ent. Etrangères	1 192 300	1 252 400	984 900	1 320 000	1 439 400	1 870 200	2 451 560	3 033 775
D.2.3. Total / D.2.3. Total des Primes Nettes Vie	29 926 400	32 631 200	34 554 400	36 604 600	38 563 300	41 216 200	45 336 018	48 904 308
E. BUSINESS WRITTEN ABROAD / E. OPERATIONS A L'ETRANGER								
E.1. Life / E.1. Vie								
E.1.1. Gross Premiums / E.1.1. Primes Brutes								
E.1.1.1. Direct Business / E.1.1.1. Assurance Directe								
E.1.1.1.1. Branches & Agencies / E.1.1.1.1. Succursales & Agences	423 700	330 000	156 400	191 500	269 100	329 300	218 579	127 223
E.1.1.1.2. Subsidiaries / E.1.1.1.2. Filliales	5 672 400	6 140 300	8 154 600	12 638 800	13 402 600	15 243 100	26 903 492	33 231 528
E.1.1.1. Total / E.1.1.1. Total	6 096 100	6 470 300	8 311 000	12 830 300	13 671 700	15 572 400	27 122 071	33 358 751
E.1.1.2. Reinsurance Accepted / E.1.1.2. Réassurance Acceptée								
E.1.1.2.1. Branches & Agencies / E.1.1.2.1. Succursales & Agences	422 600	590 800	652 400	759 000	897 300	1 050 700	1 075 906	2 032
E.1.1.2.2. Subsidiaries / E.1.1.2.2. Filliales	184 000	184 100	321 300	421 600	796 500	906 800	1 169 109	2 672 876
E.1.1.2. Total / E.1.1.2. Total	606 600	774 900	973 700	1 180 600	1 693 800	1 957 500	2 245 015	2 674 908
E.1.1.3. Total								
E.1.1.3.1. Branches & Agencies / E.1.1.3.1. Succursales & Agences	846 300	920 000	808 800	950 500	1 166 400	1 380 000	1 294 485	129 255
E.1.1.3.2. Subsidiaries / E.1.1.3.2. Filliales	5 856 400	6 324 400	8 475 900	13 060 400	14 199 100	16 149 900	28 072 601	35 904 404
E.1.1.3. Total Gross Premiums / E.1.1.3. Total des Primes Brutes	6 702 700	7 245 200	9 284 700	14 010 900	15 365 500	17 529 900	29 367 086	36 033 659
E.1.2. Ceded Premiums / E.1.2. Primes Cédées								
E.1.2.1. Branches & Agencies / E.1.2.1. Succursales & Agences	26 700	17 200	24 800	35 700	61 200	75 700	69 700	31 337
E.1.2.2. Subsidiaries / E.1.2.2. Filliales	1 031 600	1 336 600	1 906 500	1 836 500	2 287 400	2 543 800	2 848 700	4 376 633
E.1.2. Total / E.1.2. Total	1 058 300	1 353 800	1 931 300	1 872 200	2 348 600	2 619 500	2 918 400	4 407 970
E.1.3. Net Written Premiums / E.1.3. Primes Nettes Emises								
E.1.3.1. Branches & Agencies / E.1.3.1. Succursales & Agences	819 600	903 600	784 000	914 800	1 105 200	1 304 300	1 224 785	97 918
E.1.3.2. Subsidiaries / E.1.3.2. Filliales	4 824 800	4 987 800	6 569 400	11 223 900	11 911 700	13 606 100	25 223 901	31 527 771
E.1.3. Total / E.1.3. Total	5 644 400	5 891 400	7 353 400	12 138 700	13 016 900	14 910 400	26 448 686	31 625 689

ITALIE

Monetary Unit: million lire

Unité monétaire : million de lires

E.2. Non-Life / E.2. Non-Vie

	1992	1993	1994	1995	1996	1997	1998	1999
E.2.1. Gross Premiums / Primes Brutes								
E.2.1.1. Direct Business / Assurance Directe								
E.2.1.1.1. Branches & Agencies / Succursales & Agences	1 422 600	1 637 800	1 531 900	1 161 900	1 119 100	1 212 400	1 029 703	775 766
E.2.1.1.2. Subsidiaries / Filliales	10 357 000	12 223 900	13 051 000	17 087 400	15 524 100	16 053 900	23 500 083	29 756 079
E.2.1.1. Total	11 779 800	13 861 700	14 582 900	18 249 300	16 643 200	17 266 300	24 529 786	30 531 845
E.2.1.2. Reinsurance Accepted / Réassurance Acceptée								
E.2.1.2.1. Branches & Agencies / Succursales & Agences	773 100	760 000	860 800	1 021 000	795 200	801 600	806 712	837 856
E.2.1.2.2. Subsidiaries / Filliales	2 073 400	2 500 900	2 878 400	722 800	2 679 800	2 895 400	3 766 773	4 642 196
E.2.1.2. Total	2 846 500	3 260 900	3 739 200	1 743 800	3 475 000	3 697 000	4 573 485	5 480 052
E.2.1.3. Total								
E.2.1.3.1. Branches & Agencies / Succursales & Agences	2 195 700	2 397 800	2 392 700	2 182 900	1 914 300	2 014 000	1 836 415	1 613 622
E.2.1.3.2. Subsidiaries / Filliales	12 430 400	14 724 800	15 929 400	17 810 200	18 203 900	18 949 300	27 266 856	34 398 275
E.2.1.3. Total Gross Premiums / Total des Primes Brutes	14 626 100	17 122 600	18 322 100	19 993 100	20 118 200	20 963 300	29 103 271	36 011 897
E.2.2. Ceded Premiums / Primes Cédées								
E.2.2.1. Branches & Agencies / Succursales & Agences	345 300	509 300	479 600	374 900	365 200	418 800	340 100	305 446
E.2.2.2. Subsidiaries / Filliales	3 595 000	4 390 400	6 152 900	5 719 400	4 623 600	4 962 000	6 558 300	7 046 596
E.2.2. Total	3 940 300	4 899 700	6 632 500	6 094 300	4 988 800	5 380 800	6 898 400	7 352 042
E.2.3. Net Written Premiums / Primes Nettes Emises								
E.2.3.1. Branches & Agencies / Succursales & Agences	1 850 400	1 888 500	1 913 100	1 808 000	1 549 100	1 595 200	1 496 315	1 308 176
E.2.3.2. Subsidiaries / Filliales	8 835 400	10 334 400	9 776 500	12 090 800	13 580 300	13 987 300	20 708 556	27 351 679
E.2.3. Total	10 685 800	12 222 900	11 689 600	13 898 800	15 129 400	15 582 500	22 204 871	28 659 855

F. OUTSTANDING INVESTMENT BY DIRECT INSURANCE COMPANIES / F. ENCOURS DES PLACEMENTS DES ENTREPRISES D'ASSURANCES DIRECTES

F.1. Life / F.1. Vie

	1992	1993	1994	1995	1996	1997	1998	1999
F.1.1. Real Estate / Immobilier								
F.1.1.1. Domestic Companies / Entreprises Nationales	9 404 200	12 810 300	12 368 700	12 209 600	10 311 700	10 175 400	4 728 426	4 302 204
F.1.1.2. (Foreign Controlled Companies) / (Entreprises Sous Contrôle Etranger)	..	..	..	..	..	794 200	..	..
F.1.1.3. Branches & Agencies of Foreign Cies / Succursales et Agences d'Ent. Etrangères	2 900	8 900	7 200	7 200	7 300	1 200	1 039	1 039
F.1.1. Total	9 407 100	12 819 200	12 375 900	12 216 800	10 319 000	10 176 600	..	..
F.1.2. Mortgage Loans / Prêts Hypothécaires								
F.1.2.1. Domestic Companies / Entreprises Nationales	2 808 600	1 941 500	1 728 000	2 024 800	2 330 200	..	..	..
F.1.2.3. Branches & Agencies of Foreign Cies / Succursales et Agences d'Ent. Etrangères	6 300	11 100	14 500	17 400	20 100	..	0	..
F.1.2. Total	2 814 900	1 952 600	1 742 500	2 042 200	2 350 300	..	0	..
F.1.3. Shares / Actions								
F.1.3.1. Domestic Companies / Entreprises Nationales	6 436 300	10 484 500	12 643 700	14 787 200	16 964 100	24 004 200	29 350 070	41 749 087
F.1.3.2. (Foreign Controlled Companies) / (Entreprises Sous Contrôle Etranger)	..	..	..	..	..	3 700 600	..	..
F.1.3.3. Branches & Agencies of Foreign Cies / Succursales et Agences d'Ent. Etrangères	39 800	65 500	95 100	123 700	159 000	242 500	294 759	335 582
F.1.3.4. Domestic Investment / Placement dans le Pays	3 338 800	5 898 300	7 591 000	8 780 400	10 513 800	15 588 300	..	..
F.1.3.5. Foreign Investment / Placement à l' Etranger	3 137 300	4 651 700	5 147 900	6 130 500	6 609 300	8 658 400	..	..
F.1.3. Total	6 476 100	10 550 000	12 738 800	14 910 900	17 123 100	24 246 700	..	..
F.1.4. Bonds with Fixed Revenue / Obligations								
F.1.4.1. Domestic Companies / Entreprises Nationales	51 271 600	63 869 700	77 410 700	95 057 800	118 083 200	145 001 300	178 542 808	206 311 127
F.1.4.2. (Foreign Controlled Companies) / (Entreprises Sous Contrôle Etranger)	..	..	..	..	..	26 677 600	..	..
F.1.4.3. Branches & Agencies of Foreign Cies / Succursales et Agences d'Ent. Etrangères	651 200	888 100	1 110 400	1 557 800	2 114 300	1 690 200	1 635 845	2 299 863
F.1.4.4. Domestic Investment / Placement dans le Pays	48 743 500	60 560 800	73 593 800	89 939 400	106 737 000	124 911 800	..	..
F.1.4.5. Foreign Investment / Placement à l' Etranger	3 179 300	4 197 000	4 927 300	6 676 200	13 460 500	21 779 700	..	..
F.1.4. Total	51 922 800	64 757 800	78 521 100	96 615 600	120 197 500	146 691 500	..	..
F.1.5. Loans other than Mortgage Loans / Prêts Autres qu'Hypothécaires								
F.1.5.1. Domestic Companies / Entreprises Nationales	..	..	..	..	..	2 152 300	2 554 988	2 856 854
F.1.5.2. (Foreign Controlled Companies) / (Entreprises Sous Contrôle Etranger)	..	..	..	..	..	177 100	..	..
F.1.5.3. Branches & Agencies of Foreign Cies / Succursales et Agences d'Ent. Etrangères	..	..	..	..	..	16 400	16 474	16 281
F.1.5. Total	..	..	..	..	..	2 168 700	..	..

ITALY

Monetary Unit: million lire | Unité monétaire : million de lires

English Label	1992	1993	1994	1995	1996	1997	1998	1999	French Label
F.1.6. Other Investments									F.1.6. Autres Placements
F.1.6.1. Domestic Companies	2 031 200	1 833 300	2 371 300	2 673 200	1 956 300	2 807 800	21 439 101	45 504 739	F.1.6.1. Entreprises Nationales
F.1.6.2. (Foreign Controlled Companies)						641 200			F.1.6.2. (Entreprises Sous Contrôle Etranger)
F.1.6.3. Branches & Agencies of Foreign Cies	18 800	35 500	50 300	60 900	55 500	39 400	105 519	178 258	F.1.6.3. Succursales et Agences d'Ent. Etrangères
F.1.6. Total	2 050 000	1 868 800	2 421 600	2 734 100	2 011 800	2 847 200	..	..	F.1.6. Total
F.1.7. Total									F.1.7. Total
F.1.7.1. Domestic Companies	71 951 900	90 939 300	106 522 400	126 752 600	149 645 500	184 141 000	236 615 393	300 724 011	F.1.7.1. Entreprises Nationales
F.1.7.2. (Foreign Controlled Companies)						31 990 700			F.1.7.2. (Entreprises Sous Contrôle Etranger)
F.1.7.3. Branches & Agencies of Foreign Cies	719 000	1 009 100	1 277 500	1 767 000	2 356 200	1 989 700	2 053 636	2 831 023	F.1.7.3. Succursales et Agences d'Ent. Etrangères
F.1.7. Total of Life Investments	72 670 900	91 948 400	107 799 900	128 519 600	152 001 700	186 130 700	..	..	F.1.7. Total des Placements Vie
F.2. Non-Life									**F.2. Non-Vie**
F.2.1. Real Estate									F.2.1. Immobilier
F.2.1.1. Domestic Companies	10 549 200	10 544 800	11 390 800	11 968 500	12 821 900	12 856 700	11 604 178	11 703 925	F.2.1.1. Entreprises Nationales
F.2.1.2. (Foreign Controlled Companies)						2 677 000			F.2.1.2. (Entreprises Sous Contrôle Etranger)
F.2.1.3. Branches & Agencies of Foreign Cies	272 800	259 300	221 000	241 200	241 200	212 000	160 986	146 219	F.2.1.3. Succursales et Agences d'Ent. Etrangères
F.2.1. Total	10 822 000	10 804 100	11 611 800	12 209 700	13 063 100	13 068 700	..	..	F.2.1. Total
F.2.2. Mortgage Loans									F.2.2. Prêts Hypothécaires
F.2.2.1. Domestic Companies	1 810 000	2 095 300	1 756 400	1 615 800	1 654 800	..	5 019	4 948	F.2.2.1. Entreprises Nationales
F.2.2.3. Branches & Agencies of Foreign Cies	90 800	116 200	46 400	59 000	62 700	..	0	0	F.2.2.3. Succursales et Agences d'Ent. Etrangères
F.2.2. Total	1 900 800	2 211 500	1 802 800	1 674 800	1 717 500	..	..	..	F.2.2. Total
F.2.3. Shares									F.2.3. Actions
F.2.3.1. Domestic Companies	12 198 900	11 456 500	13 902 600	15 710 200	17 982 000	18 044 600	22 840 784	27 221 374	F.2.3.1. Entreprises Nationales
F.2.3.2. (Foreign Controlled Companies)						5 407 800			F.2.3.2. (Entreprises Sous Contrôle Etranger)
F.2.3.3. Branches & Agencies of Foreign Cies	127 500	147 300	251 200	290 200	307 300	456 800	451 868	537 363	F.2.3.3. Succursales et Agences d'Ent. Etrangères
F.2.3.4. Domestic Investment	8 984 600	8 768 300	10 157 900	9 883 100	10 928 300	11 451 900	..	..	F.2.3.4. Placement dans le Pays
F.2.3.5. Foreign Investment	3 341 800	2 835 500	3 995 900	6 117 300	7 361 000	7 049 500	..	..	F.2.3.5. Placement à l' Etranger
F.2.3. Total	12 326 400	11 603 800	14 153 800	16 000 400	18 289 300	18 501 400	..	..	F.2.3. Total
F.2.4. Bonds with Fixed Revenue									F.2.4. Obligations
F.2.4.1. Domestic Companies	28 122 100	34 243 600	36 887 400	40 850 800	43 140 200	43 798 900	47 529 211	47 554 402	F.2.4.1. Entreprises Nationales
F.2.4.2. (Foreign Controlled Companies)						14 894 100			F.2.4.2. (Entreprises Sous Contrôle Etranger)
F.2.4.3. Branches & Agencies of Foreign Cies	1 050 900	1 103 100	878 500	1 009 100	1 160 400	1 359 700	1 156 331	1 279 529	F.2.4.3. Succursales et Agences d'Ent. Etrangères
F.2.4.4. Domestic Investment	25 137 800	29 092 900	31 772 800	36 158 500	37 700 200	38 672 400	..	..	F.2.4.4. Placement dans le Pays
F.2.4.5. Foreign Investment	4 035 200	6 253 800	5 993 100	5 701 400	6 600 400	6 486 200	..	..	F.2.4.5. Placement a l' Etranger
F.2.4. Total	29 173 000	35 346 700	37 765 900	41 859 900	44 300 600	45 158 600	..	..	F.2.4. Total
F.2.5. Loans other than Mortgage Loans									F.2.5. Prêts Autres qu'Hypothécaires
F.2.5.1. Domestic Companies	..	..	..	..	..	1 703 700	1 069 652	834 635	F.2.5.1. Entreprises Nationales
F.2.5.2. (Foreign Controlled Companies)						298 300			F.2.5.2. (Entreprises Sous Contrôle Etranger)
F.2.5.3. Branches & Agencies of Foreign Cies	..	..	..	..	..	43 900	38 343	23 458	F.2.5.3. Succursales et Agences d'Ent. Etrangères
F.2.5. Total	..	..	..	..	..	1 747 600	..	..	F.2.5. Total
F.2.6. Other Investments									F.2.6. Autres Placements
F.2.6.1. Domestic Companies	2 219 500	2 174 900	2 963 200	2 911 000	2 935 200	2 690 700	2 892 273	3 793 172	F.2.6.1. Entreprises Nationales
F.2.6.2. (Foreign Controlled Companies)						584 200			F.2.6.2. (Entreprises Sous Contrôle Etranger)
F.2.6.3. Branches & Agencies of Foreign Cies	104 200	118 800	102 700	136 200	109 500	90 900	12 780	42 813	F.2.6.3. Succursales et Agences d'Ent. Etrangères
F.2.6. Total	2 323 700	2 293 700	3 065 900	3 047 200	3 044 700	2 781 600	..	..	F.2.6. Total
F.2.7. Total									F.2.7. Total
F.2.7.1. Domestic Companies	54 899 700	60 515 100	66 900 400	73 056 300	78 534 100	79 094 600	85 941 117	91 112 456	F.2.7.1. Entreprises Nationales
F.2.7.2. (Foreign Controlled Companies)						23 861 400			F.2.7.2. (Entreprises Sous Contrôle Etranger)
F.2.7.3. Branches & Agencies of Foreign Cies	1 646 200	1 744 700	1 499 800	1 735 700	1 881 100	2 163 300	1 820 308	2 029 382	F.2.7.3. Succursales et Agences d'Ent. Etrangères
F.2.7. Total of Non-Life Investments	56 545 900	62 259 800	68 400 200	74 792 000	80 415 200	81 257 900	..	..	F.2.7. Total des Placements Non-Vie

Monetary Unit: million lire

Unité monétaire : million de lires

G. BREAKDOWN OF NON-LIFE PREMIUMS / G. VENTILATIONS DES PRIMES NON-VIE

	1992	1993	1994	1995	1996	1997	1998	1999
G.1. Motor vehicle / G.1. Assurance Automobile								
G.1.1. Direct Business / G.1.1. Assurances Directes								
G.1.1.1. Gross Premiums / Primes Brutes	18 805 800	20 072 000	20 924 400	22 118 000	23 197 500	25 206 200	27 658 272	30 671 222
G.1.1.2. Ceded Premiums / Primes Cédées	990 800	762 300	638 300	737 300	711 200	816 100	1 332 756	1 440 553
G.1.1.3. Net Written Premiums / Primes Nettes Emises	1 781 500	19 309 700	20 286 100	21 380 700	22 486 300	24 390 100	26 325 519	29 230 669
G.1.2. Reinsurance Accepted / G.1.2. Réassurance Acceptée								
G.1.2.1. Gross Premiums / Primes Brutes	464 200	315 700	215 900	268 900	296 000	293 300	480 493	563 848
G.1.2.2. Ceded Premiums / Primes Cédées	69 900	57 500	49 100	50 300	55 900	56 400	82 770	150 493
G.1.2.3. Net Written Premiums / Primes Nettes Emises	394 300	258 200	166 800	218 600	240 100	236 900	397 723	413 355
G.1.3. Total								
G.1.3.1. Gross Premiums / Primes Brutes	19 270 000	20 387 700	21 140 300	22 386 900	23 493 500	25 499 500	28 138 765	31 235 070
G.1.3.2. Ceded Premiums / Primes Cédées	1 060 700	819 800	687 400	787 600	767 100	872 500	1 415 526	1 591 046
G.1.3.3. Net Written Premiums / Primes Nettes Emises	18 209 300	19 567 900	20 452 900	21 599 300	22 726 400	24 627 000	26 723 242	29 644 024
G.2. Marine, Aviation / G.2. Marine, Aviation								
G.2.1. Direct Business / G.2.1. Assurances Directes								
G.2.1.1. Gross Premiums / Primes Brutes	150 300	202 800	200 800	228 500	243 200	1 486 200	679 139	653 467
G.2.1.2. Ceded Premiums / Primes Cédées	134 900	184 300	180 100	211 000	227 400	904 300	485 298	474 168
G.2.1.3. Net Written Premiums / Primes Nettes Emises	15 400	18 500	20 700	17 500	15 800	581 900	193 841	179 299
G.2.2. Reinsurance Accepted / G.2.2. Réassurance Acceptée								
G.2.2.1. Gross Premiums / Primes Brutes	176 500	197 900	189 400	194 200	198 700	430 700	229 029	62 441
G.2.2.2. Ceded Premiums / Primes Cédées	116 800	135 700	129 400	136 000	140 200	268 100	124 125	15 506
G.2.2.3. Net Written Premiums / Primes Nettes Emises	59 700	62 200	60 000	58 200	58 500	162 600	104 904	46 935
G.2.3. Total								
G.2.3.1. Gross Premiums / Primes Brutes	326 800	400 700	390 200	422 700	441 900	1 916 900	908 168	715 908
G.2.3.2. Ceded Premiums / Primes Cédées	251 700	320 000	309 500	347 000	367 600	1 172 400	609 423	489 674
G.2.3.3. Net Written Premiums / Primes Nettes Emises	75 100	80 700	80 700	75 700	74 300	744 500	298 745	226 234
G.3. Freight / G.3. Fret								
G.3.1. Direct Business / G.3.1. Assurances Directes								
G.3.1.1. Gross Premiums / Primes Brutes	1 267 700	1 447 100	1 505 800	1 283 200	1 281 300	…	623 858	559 270
G.3.1.2. Ceded Premiums / Primes Cédées	813 200	900 800	934 800	737 100	737 000	…	264 563	246 320
G.3.1.3. Net Written Premiums / Primes Nettes Emises	454 500	546 300	571 000	546 100	544 300	…	359 292	312 950
G.3.2. Reinsurance Accepted / G.3.2. Réassurance Acceptée								
G.3.2.1. Gross Premiums / Primes Brutes	320 700	314 800	302 400	289 000	263 100	…	53 563	183 275
G.3.2.2. Ceded Premiums / Primes Cédées	205 300	212 300	214 400	185 600	166 900	…	27 351	118 472
G.3.2.3. Net Written Premiums / Primes Nettes Emises	115 400	102 500	88 000	103 400	96 200	…	26 212	64 803
G.3.3. Total								
G.3.3.1. Gross Premiums / Primes Brutes	1 588 400	1 761 900	1 808 200	1 572 200	1 544 400	…	677 421	742 545
G.3.3.2. Ceded Premiums / Primes Cédées	1 018 500	1 113 100	1 149 200	922 700	903 900	…	291 914	364 792
G.3.3.3. Net Written Premiums / Primes Nettes Emises	569 900	648 800	659 000	649 500	640 500	…	385 504	377 753
G.4. Fire, Property Damages / G.4. Incendie, Dommages aux Biens								
G.4.1. Direct Business / G.4.1. Assurances Directes								
G.4.1.1. Gross Premiums / Primes Brutes	4 539 100	4 662 400	4 865 400	5 159 100	5 482 000	5 984 900	6 289 820	6 408 866
G.4.1.2. Ceded Premiums / Primes Cédées	2 122 100	1 969 100	1 861 700	2 039 600	1 878 300	2 049 000	1 794 011	1 699 332
G.4.1.3. Net Written Premiums / Primes Nettes Emises	2 417 000	2 693 300	3 003 700	3 119 500	3 603 700	3 935 900	4 495 808	4 709 534
G.4.2. Reinsurance Accepted / G.4.2. Réassurance Acceptée								
G.4.2.1. Gross Premiums / Primes Brutes	1 559 500	1 314 800	1 185 700	1 186 200	1 032 600	1 165 000	1 366 504	1 084 363
G.4.2.2. Ceded Premiums / Primes Cédées	813 800	678 900	574 400	643 900	496 500	561 800	696 978	535 645
G.4.2.3. Net Written Premiums / Primes Nettes Emises	745 700	637 900	611 300	542 300	536 100	603 200	669 526	548 718
G.4.3. Total								
G.4.3.1. Gross Premiums / Primes Brutes	6 098 600	5 977 200	6 051 100	6 345 300	6 514 600	7 149 900	7 656 324	7 493 229
G.4.3.2. Ceded Premiums / Primes Cédées	2 935 900	2 646 000	2 436 100	2 683 500	2 374 800	2 610 800	2 490 989	2 234 977
G.4.3.3. Net Written Premiums / Primes Nettes Emises	3 162 700	3 331 200	3 615 000	3 661 800	4 139 800	4 539 100	5 165 334	5 258 252

ITALIE

Monetary Unit: million lire

Unité monétaire : million de lires

	1992	1993	1994	1995	1996	1997	1998	1999
G.5. Pecuniary Losses / Pertes Pécunières								
G.5.1. Direct Business / Assurances Directes								
G.5.1.1. Gross Premiums / Primes Brutes	830 800	819 600	939 400	1 019 800	1 137 800	1 300 500	1 676 168	1 605 711
G.5.1.2. Ceded Premiums / Primes Cédées	398 800	380 800	445 200	535 300	611 400	685 500	797 959	739 072
G.5.1.3. Net Written Premiums / Primes Nettes Emises	432 000	438 800	494 200	484 500	526 400	615 000	878 206	866 639
G.5.2. Reinsurance Accepted / Réassurance Acceptée								
G.5.2.1. Gross Premiums / Primes Brutes	196 700	192 800	188 600	216 400	240 600	268 500	322 824	309 621
G.5.2.2. Ceded Premiums / Primes Cédées	99 400	92 000	86 300	94 300	102 100	121 900	157 072	129 540
G.5.2.3. Net Written Premiums / Primes Nettes Emises	97 300	100 800	102 300	122 100	138 500	146 600	165 752	180 081
G.5.3. Total								
G.5.3.1. Gross Premiums / Primes Brutes	1 027 500	1 012 400	1 128 000	1 236 200	1 378 400	1 569 000	1 998 992	1 915 332
G.5.3.2. Ceded Premiums / Primes Cédées	498 200	472 800	531 500	629 600	713 500	807 400	955 031	868 612
G.5.3.3. Net Written Premiums / Primes Nettes Emises	529 300	539 600	596 500	606 600	664 900	761 600	1 043 958	1 046 720
G.6. General Liability / Responsabilité Générale								
G.6.1. Direct Business / Assurances Directes								
G.6.1.1. Gross Premiums / Primes Brutes	2 121 200	2 329 300	2 405 200	2 590 900	2 845 600	3 060 800	3 523 429	3 718 334
G.6.1.2. Ceded Premiums / Primes Cédées	340 900	303 400	281 200	295 900	328 600	313 800	346 099	365 571
G.6.1.3. Net Written Premiums / Primes Nettes Emises	1 780 300	2 025 900	2 123 800	2 295 000	2 517 000	2 746 500	3 177 332	3 352 763
G.6.2. Reinsurance Accepted / Réassurance Acceptée								
G.6.2.1. Gross Premiums / Primes Brutes	189 800	149 100	126 100	130 100	130 600	143 800	179 405	198 355
G.6.2.2. Ceded Premiums / Primes Cédées	58 600	56 700	43 700	44 400	41 700	45 900	71 913	62 237
G.6.2.3. Net Written Premiums / Primes Nettes Emises	131 200	92 400	82 400	85 700	88 900	97 900	107 492	136 118
G.6.3. Total								
G.6.3.1. Gross Premiums / Primes Brutes	2 311 000	2 478 400	2 531 100	2 721 000	2 976 200	3 204 100	3 702 834	3 916 689
G.6.3.2. Ceded Premiums / Primes Cédées	399 500	360 100	324 900	340 300	370 300	359 700	418 012	427 828
G.6.3.3. Net Written Premiums / Primes Nettes Emises	1 911 500	2 118 300	2 206 200	2 380 700	2 605 900	2 844 400	3 284 824	3 488 881
G.7. Accident, Health / Accident, Santé								
G.7.1. Direct Business / Assurances Directes								
G.7.1.1. Gross Premiums / Primes Brutes	4 620 200	4 996 700	5 252 700	5 542 500	5 762 100	6 108 600	6 457 818	6 635 446
G.7.1.2. Ceded Premiums / Primes Cédées	934 900	807 400	714 700	733 000	696 200	731 200	684 084	690 768
G.7.1.3. Net Written Premiums / Primes Nettes Emises	3 685 300	4 189 300	4 538 000	4 809 500	5 065 900	5 377 400	5 773 738	5 944 678
G.7.2. Reinsurance Accepted / Réassurance Acceptée								
G.7.2.1. Gross Premiums / Primes Brutes	588 000	514 300	436 800	417 700	420 700	506 400	626 063	527 753
G.7.2.2. Ceded Premiums / Primes Cédées	276 100	271 500	218 300	191 700	168 000	231 000	245 224	200 161
G.7.2.3. Net Written Premiums / Primes Nettes Emises	311 900	242 500	218 500	226 000	252 700	275 400	380 839	327 592
G.7.3. Total								
G.7.3.1. Gross Premiums / Primes Brutes	5 208 200	5 510 700	5 689 500	5 960 200	6 182 800	6 615 000	7 083 881	7 163 199
G.7.3.2. Ceded Premiums / Primes Cédées	1 211 000	1 078 900	933 000	924 700	864 200	962 200	929 308	890 929
G.7.3.3. Net Written Premiums / Primes Nettes Emises	3 997 200	4 431 800	4 756 500	5 035 500	5 318 600	5 652 800	6 154 577	6 272 270
G.8. Others / Autres								
G.8.1. Direct Business / Assurances Directes								
G.8.1.1. Gross Premiums / Primes Brutes	510 100	580 300	700 200	819 600	906 200	471 400	531 964	567 808
G.8.1.2. Ceded Premiums / Primes Cédées	243 700	246 500	292 900	355 000	370 800	142 200	137 812	153 852
G.8.1.3. Net Written Premiums / Primes Nettes Emises	266 400	333 800	407 300	464 600	535 400	329 200	394 152	413 956
G.8.2. Reinsurance Accepted / Réassurance Acceptée								
G.8.2.1. Gross Premiums / Primes Brutes	164 000	184 400	230 700	248 100	283 000	148 500	142 207	151 477
G.8.2.2. Ceded Premiums / Primes Cédées	79 500	88 700	74 700	69 600	86 300	10 200	6 934	3 261
G.8.2.3. Net Written Premiums / Primes Nettes Emises	84 500	95 700	155 400	178 500	196 700	138 300	135 273	148 216
G.8.3. Total								
G.8.3.1. Gross Premiums / Primes Brutes	674 100	764 700	930 300	1 067 700	1 189 200	619 900	674 171	719 285
G.8.3.2. Ceded Premiums / Primes Cédées	323 200	335 200	367 600	424 600	457 100	152 400	144 746	157 113
G.8.3.3. Net Written Premiums / Primes Nettes Emises	350 900	429 500	562 700	643 100	732 100	467 500	529 425	562 172
G.9. Treaty Reinsurance / Réassurance Obligatoire								
G.9.2. Reinsurance Accepted / Réassurance Acceptée								
G.9.2.1. Gross Premiums / Primes Brutes	1 675 600	2 191 400	2 176 600	2 198 700	1 962 100	1 911 600	1 416 131	1 448 223
G.9.2.2. Ceded Premiums / Primes Cédées	555 100	708 000	551 700	246 300	301 300	332 300	..	333 200
G.9.2.3. Net Written Premiums / Primes Nettes Emises	1 120 500	1 483 400	1 624 900	1 952 400	1 660 800	1 579 300	..	1 115 023
G.9.3. Total								
G.9.3.1. Gross Premiums / Primes Brutes	1 675 600	2 191 400	2 176 600	2 198 700	1 962 100	1 911 600	1 416 131	1 448 223
G.9.3.2. Ceded Premiums / Primes Cédées	555 100	708 000	551 700	246 300	301 300	332 300	0	333 200
G.9.3.3. Net Written Premiums / Primes Nettes Emises	1 120 500	1 483 400	1 624 900	1 952 400	1 660 800	1 579 300	0	1 115 023

Monetary Unit: million lire — Unité monétaire : million de lires

	1992	1993	1994	1995	1996	1997	1998	1999
G.10. Total								
G.10.1. Direct Business — G.10.1. Assurances Directes								
G.10.1.1. Gross Premiums — Primes Brutes	32 845 200	35 110 200	36 793 700	38 761 600	40 855 700	43 618 100	47 440 468	50 820 124
G.10.1.2. Ceded Premiums — Primes Cédées	5 979 300	5 554 600	5 348 900	5 644 200	5 560 900	5 642 100	5 842 582	5 809 636
G.10.1.3. Net Written Premiums — Primes Nettes Emises	26 865 900	29 555 600	31 444 800	33 117 400	35 294 800	37 976 000	41 597 886	45 010 488
G.10.2. Reinsurance Accepted — Réassurance Acceptée								
G.10.2.1. Gross Premiums — Primes Brutes	5 335 000	5 374 900	5 051 600	5 149 300	4 827 400	4 867 800	4 816 219	4 529 356
G.10.2.2. Ceded Premiums — Primes Cédées	2 274 500	2 299 300	1 942 000	1 662 100	1 558 900	1 627 600	1 412 367	1 548 515
G.10.2.3. Net Written Premiums — Primes Nettes Emises	3 060 500	3 075 600	3 109 600	3 487 200	3 268 500	3 240 200	3 403 852	2 980 841
G.10.3. Total								
G.10.3.1. Gross Premiums — Primes Brutes	38 180 200	40 485 100	41 845 300	43 910 900	45 683 100	48 485 900	52 256 687	55 349 480
G.10.3.2. Ceded Premiums — Primes Cédées	8 253 800	7 853 900	7 290 900	7 306 300	7 119 800	7 269 700	7 254 949	7 358 151
G.10.3.3. Net Written Premiums — Primes Nettes Emises	29 926 400	32 631 200	34 554 400	36 604 600	38 563 300	41 216 200	45 001 738	47 991 329
H. GROSS CLAIMS PAYMENTS — H. PAIEMENTS BRUTS DES SINISTRES								
H.1. Life — H.1. Vie								
H.1.1. Domestic Companies — Entreprises Nationales		4 428 000	5 583 000	6 832 000	8 967 000	11 204 000	13 873 788	16 711 546
H.1.2. (Foreign Controlled Companies) — (Entreprises Sous Contrôle Etranger)						2 044 000		
H.1.3. Branches & Agencies of Foreign Cies — Succursales et Agences d'Ent. Etrangères		53 000	76 000	114 000	145 000	164 000	127 004	185 985
H.1. Total		4 481 000	5 659 000	6 946 000	9 112 000	11 368 000	14 000 792	16 897 531
H.2. Non-Life — H.2. Non-Vie								
H.2.1. Domestic Companies — Entreprises Nationales		22 305 000	22 547 000	25 275 000	27 856 000	30 180 000	33 611 277	36 000 584
H.2.2. (Foreign Controlled Companies) — (Entreprises Sous Contrôle Etranger)						9 568 000		
H.2.3. Branches & Agencies of Foreign Cies — Succursales et Agences d'Ent. Etrangères		953 000	703 000	777 000	922 000	1 090 000	891 761	938 664
H.2. Total		23 258 000	23 250 000	26 052 000	28 778 000	31 270 000	34 503 038	36 939 248
I. GROSS OPERATING EXPENSES — I. DEPENSES BRUITES D'EXPLOITATION								
I.1. Life — I.1. Vie								
I.1.1. Domestic Companies — Entreprises Nationales		863 000	927 000	973 000	1 061 000	1 181 000	1 193 362	1 299 835
I.1.2. (Foreign Controlled Companies) — (Entreprises Sous Contrôle Etranger)						331 000		
I.1.3. Branches & Agencies of Foreign Cies — Succursales et Agences d'Ent. Etrangères		26 000	30 000	33 000	37 000	31 000	9 211	11 221
I.1. Total		889 000	957 000	1 006 000	1 098 000	1 212 000	1 202 573	1 311 056
I.2. Non-Life — I.2. Non-Vie								
I.2.1. Domestic Companies — Entreprises Nationales		2 415 000	2 519 000	2 627 000	2 785 000	2 772 000	2 487 440	2 555 896
I.2.2. (Foreign Controlled Companies) — (Entreprises Sous Contrôle Etranger)						1 013 000		
I.2.3. Branches & Agencies of Foreign Cies — Succursales et Agences d'Ent. Etrangères		141 000	107 000	133 000	140 000	159 000	99 755	91 398
I.2. Total		2 556 000	2 626 000	2 760 000	2 925 000	2 931 000	2 587 195	2 647 294
J. COMMISSIONS								
J.1. Life — J.1. Vie								
J.1.1. Direct Business — J.1.1. Assurance directe								
J.1.1.1. Domestic Companies — Entreprises Nationales		2 083 000	2 333 000	2 581 000	2 817 000	3 307 000	3 972 765	4 540 050
J.1.1.2. (Foreign Controlled Companies) — (Entreprises Sous Contrôle Etranger)						824 000		
J.1.1.3. Branches & Agencies of Foreign Cies — Succursales et Agences d'Ent. Etrangères		36 000	45 000	58 000	64 000	58 000	49 536	60 131
J.1.1. Total		2 119 000	2 378 000	2 639 000	2 881 000	3 365 000	4 022 301	4 600 181
J.1.2. Reinsurance Accepted — J.1.2. Réassurances acceptées								
J.1.2.1. Domestic Companies — Entreprises Nationales		507 000	441 000	502 000	535 000	553 000	:	:
J.1.2.2. (Foreign Controlled Companies) — (Entreprises Sous Contrôle Etranger)						170 000		
J.1.2.3. Branches & Agencies of Foreign Cies — Succursales et Agences d'Ent. Etrangères		0	0	2 000	45 000	87 000	:	:
J.1.2. Total		507 000	441 000	504 000	580 000	640 000	:	:

Monetary Unit: million lire   Unité monétaire : million de lires

	1992	1993	1994	1995	1996	1997	1998	1999	
J.1.3. Total									J.1.3. Total
J.1.3.1. Domestic Companies		2 590 000	2 774 000	3 083 000	3 352 000	3 860 000	..	..	J.1.3.1. Entreprises Nationales
J.1.3.2. (Foreign Controlled Companies)		..	..	..	..	994 000	..	..	J.1.3.2. (Entreprises Sous Contrôle Etranger)
J.1.3.3. Branches & Agencies of Foreign Cies		36 000	45 000	60 000	109 000	145 000	..	..	J.1.3.3. Succursales et Agences d'Ent. Etrangères
J.1.3. Total of Life Net Premiums		2 626 000	2 819 000	3 143 000	3 461 000	4 005 000	..	..	J.1.3. Total
J.2. Non-Life									**J.2. Non-Vie**
J.2.1. Direct Business									J.2.1. Assurance directe
J.2.1.1. Domestic Companies		6 062 000	6 219 000	6 982 000	7 519 000	7 810 000	8 754 387	9 147 624	J.2.1.1. Entreprises Nationales
J.2.1.2. (Foreign Controlled Companies)		..	..	..	..	2 474 000	..	..	J.2.1.2. (Entreprises Sous Contrôle Etranger)
J.2.1.3. Branches & Agencies of Foreign Cies		311 000	252 000	301 000	309 000	359 000	259 554	276 275	J.2.1.3. Succursales et Agences d'Ent. Etrangères
J.2.1. Total		6 373 000	6 471 000	7 283 000	7 828 000	8 169 000	9 013 941	9 423 899	J.2.1. Total des Primes Nettes Vie
J.2.2. Reinsurance Accepted									J.2.2. Réassurances acceptées
J.2.2.1. Domestic Companies		804 000	717 000	732 000	707 000	728 000	..	..	J.2.2.1. Entreprises Nationales
J.2.2.2. (Foreign Controlled Companies)		..	..	..	..	367 000	..	..	J.2.2.2. (Entreprises Sous Contrôle Etranger)
J.2.2.3. Branches & Agencies of Foreign Cies		2 000	2 000	44 000	56 000	75 000	..	..	J.2.2.3. Succursales et Agences d'Ent. Etrangères
J.2.2. Total		806 000	719 000	776 000	763 000	803 000	..	..	J.2.2. Total
J.2.3. Total									J.2.3. Total
J.2.3.1. Domestic Companies		6 866 000	2 774 000	7 714 000	8 226 000	8 538 000	..	..	J.2.3.1. Entreprises Nationales
J.2.3.2. (Foreign Controlled Companies)		..	..	..	..	2 841 000	..	..	J.2.3.2. (Entreprises Sous Contrôle Etranger)
J.2.3.3. Branches & Agencies of Foreign Cies		313 000	45 000	345 000	365 000	434 000	..	..	J.2.3.3. Succursales et Agences d'Ent. Etrangères
J.2.3. Total		7 179 000	2 819 000	8 059 000	8 591 000	8 972 000	..	..	J.2.3. Total

144

Monetary Unit: million Japanese yen

Unité monétaire : million de yen japonais

	1992	1993	1994	1995	1996	1997	1998	1999	(French)
A. NUMBER OF COMPANIES IN THE REPORTING COUNTRY									**A. NOMBRE D'ENTREPRISES DANS LE PAYS DECLARANT**
A.1. Life									**A.1. Vie**
A.1.1. Domestic Companies	27	27	27	29	41	41	42	43	A.1.1. Entreprises Nationales
A.1.2. (Foreign Controlled Companies)	3	3	3	5	6	5	6	11	A.1.2. (Entreprises Sous Contrôle Etranger)
A.1.3. Branches & Agencies of Foreign Cies	13	13	12	12	13	13	3	3	A.1.3. Succursales et Agences d'Ent. Etrangères
A.1. All Companies	40	40	39	41	54	54	45	46	A.1. Ensemble des Entreprises
A.2. Non-Life									**A.2. Non-Vie**
A.2.1. Domestic Companies	23	23	24	24	31	31	33	33	A.2.1. Entreprises Nationales
A.2.2. (Foreign Controlled Companies)	3	3	4	4	5	5	6	5	A.2.2. (Entreprises Sous Contrôle Etranger)
A.2.3. Branches & Agencies of Foreign Cies	33	27	27	28	27	28	26	25	A.2.3. Succursales et Agences d'Ent. Etrangères
A.2. All Companies	56	50	51	52	58	59	59	58	A.2. Ensemble des Entreprises
A.4. Reinsurance									**A.4. Réassurance**
A.4.1. Domestic Companies	2	2	2	2	2	2	2	2	A.4.1. Entreprises Nationales
A.4.3. Branches & Agencies of Foreign Cies	1	3	3	3	3	3	3	3	A.4.3. Succursales et Agences d'Ent. Etrangères
A.4. All Companies	3	5	5	5	5	5	5	5	A.4. Ensemble des Entreprises
A.5. Total									**A.5. Total**
A.5.1. Domestic Companies	52	52	53	55	74	74	77	78	A.5.1. Entreprises Nationales
A.5.2. (Foreign Controlled Companies)	6	6	7	9	11	10	12	16	A.5.2. (Entreprises Sous Contrôle Etranger)
A.5.3. Branches & Agencies of Foreign Cies	47	43	42	43	43	44	32	31	A.5.3. Succursales et Agences d'Ent. Etrangères
A.5. All Insurance Companies	99	95	95	98	117	118	109	109	A.5. Ensemble des Entreprises d'Assurances
B. NUMBER OF EMPLOYEES									**B. NOMBRE D'EMPLOYES**
B.1. Insurance Companies	648 000	649 653	629 432	622 200	597 305	544 756	527 513	515 937	B.1. Entreprises d'Assurances
B.2. Intermediaries	1 127 000	1 162 380	..	..	1 548 232	1 870 521	1 823 045	1 890 574	B.2. Intermediaires
B. Total	1 775 000	1 812 033	..	..	2 145 537	2 415 277	2 350 558	2 406 511	B. Total
C. BUSINESS WRITTEN IN THE REPORTING COUNTRY									**C. OPERATIONS CONCLUES DANS LE PAYS DECLARANT**
C.1. Life									**C.1. Vie**
C.1.1. Gross Premiums									C.1.1. Primes Brutes
C.1.1.1. Direct Business									C.1.1.1. Assurances Directes
C.1.1.1.1. Domestic Companies	28 924 314	29 715 907	29 723 454	30 010 633	28 528 700	29 473 151	27 790 373	26 037 757	C.1.1.1.1. Entreprises Nationales
C.1.1.1.2. (Foreign Controlled Companies)	159 506	169 839	208 121	335 228	337 788	301 470	441 849	1 295 642	C.1.1.1.2. (Entreprises Sous Contrôle Etranger)
C.1.1.1.3. Branches & Agencies of Foreign Cies	571 820	639 134	726 581	709 374	780 866	842 418	929 114	1 034 994	C.1.1.1.3. Succursales et Agences d'Ent. Etrangères
C.1.1.1. Total	29 496 134	30 355 041	30 450 036	30 720 007	29 309 566	30 315 569	28 719 485	27 072 751	C.1.1.1. Total
C.1.1.2. Reinsurance Accepted									C.1.1.2. Réassurance Acceptée
C.1.1.2.1. Domestic Companies	33 982	37 645	39 364	42 060	43 905	45 241	117 354	124 004	C.1.1.2.1. Entreprises Nationales
C.1.1.2.2. (Foreign Controlled Companies)	6	6	9	4	5	0	60 734	90 799	C.1.1.2.2. (Entreprises Sous Contrôle Etranger)
C.1.1.2.3. Branches & Agencies of Foreign Cies	2	2	3	5	7	0	2	0	C.1.1.2.3. Succursales et Agences d'Ent. Etrangères
C.1.1.2. Total	33 984	37 647	39 367	42 065	43 912	45 242	117 356	124 004	C.1.1.2. Total
C.1.1.3. Total									C.1.1.3. Total
C.1.1.3.1. Domestic Companies	28 958 296	29 753 552	29 762 818	30 052 693	28 572 605	29 518 393	27 907 727	26 161 761	C.1.1.3.1. Entreprises Nationales
C.1.1.3.2. (Foreign Controlled Companies)	159 512	169 845	208 130	335 232	337 793	301 470	502 583	1 386 441	C.1.1.3.2. (Entreprises Sous Contrôle Etranger)
C.1.1.3.3. Branches & Agencies of Foreign Cies	561 703	639 136	726 584	709 379	780 873	842 418	929 114	1 034 994	C.1.1.3.3. Succursales et Agences d'Ent. Etrangères
C.1.1.3. Total Gross Premiums	29 530 118	30 392 688	30 489 403	30 762 072	29 353 478	30 360 812	28 836 841	27 196 755	C.1.1.3. Total des Primes Brutes
C.1.2. Ceded Premiums									C.1.2. Primes Cédées
C.1.2.1. Domestic Companies	31 555	34 239	37 233	42 993	45 853	143 176	238 283	187 295	C.1.2.1. Entreprises Nationales
C.1.2.2. (Foreign Controlled Companies)	3 856	5 055	6 528	11 267	13 484	14 108	30 067	57 884	C.1.2.2. (Entreprises Sous Contrôle Etranger)
C.1.2.3. Branches & Agencies of Foreign Cies	10 119	12 819	11 038	8 506	8 496	8 753	9 202	16 995	C.1.2.3. Succursales et Agences d'Ent. Etrangères
C.1.2. Total	41 674	47 058	48 271	51 499	54 349	151 929	247 485	204 290	C.1.2. Total
C.1.3. Net Written Premiums									C.1.3. Primes Nettes Emises
C.1.3.1. Domestic Companies	28 926 741	29 719 313	29 725 585	30 009 700	28 526 752	29 375 217	27 669 444	25 974 466	C.1.3.1. Entreprises Nationales
C.1.3.2. (Foreign Controlled Companies)	155 656	164 790	201 602	323 965	324 309	287 362	472 516	1 328 557	C.1.3.2. (Entreprises Sous Contrôle Etranger)
C.1.3.3. Branches & Agencies of Foreign Cies	561 703	626 317	715 546	700 873	772 377	833 665	919 912	1 017 999	C.1.3.3. Succursales et Agences d'Ent. Etrangères
C.1.3. Total	29 488 444	30 345 630	30 441 132	30 710 573	29 299 129	30 208 883	28 589 356	26 992 465	C.1.3. Total

Monetary Unit: million Japanese yen — Unité monétaire : million de yen japonais

Label (EN)	1992	1993	1994	1995	1996	1997	1998	1999	Label (FR)
C.2. Non-Life									**C.2. Non-Vie**
C.2.1. Gross premiums									C.2.1. Primes Brutes
C.2.1.1. Direct Business									C.2.1.1. Assurances Directes
C.2.1.1.1. Domestic Companies	9 252 957	9 846 737	9 873 603	10 155 157	10 621 978	10 313 718	9 623 918	9 361 235	C.2.1.1.1. Entreprises Nationales
C.2.1.1.2. (Foreign Controlled Companies)	26 522	28 841	31 922	33 492	78 727	89 793	67 952	69 484	C.2.1.1.2. (Entreprises Sous Contrôle Etranger)
C.2.1.1.3. Branches & Agencies of Foreign Cies	279 286	292 685	306 023	320 052	281 771	290 372	295 591	313 149	C.2.1.1.3. Succursales et Agences d'Ent. Etrangères
C.2.1.1. Total	9 532 243	10 139 422	10 179 626	10 475 209	10 903 749	10 604 090	9 919 509	9 674 384	C.2.1.1. Total
C.2.1.2. Reinsurance Accepted									C.2.1.2. Réassurance Acceptée
C.2.1.2.1. Domestic Companies	962 123	893 771	875 667	918 124	694 410	648 403	578 168	538 789	C.2.1.2.1. Entreprises Nationales
C.2.1.2.2. (Foreign Controlled Companies)	4 418	4 355	4 331	4 580	7 065	6 355	5 572	4 752	C.2.1.2.2. (Entreprises Sous Contrôle Etranger)
C.2.1.2.3. Branches & Agencies of Foreign Cies	23 374	23 760	22 072	21 988	19 486	18 583	17 370	16 234	C.2.1.2.3. Succursales et Agences d'Ent. Etrangères
C.2.1.2. Total	985 497	917 531	897 739	940 112	713 896	666 986	595 538	555 023	C.2.1.2. Total
C.2.1.3. Total									C.2.1.3. Total
C.2.1.3.1. Domestic Companies	10 215 080	10 740 508	10 749 270	11 073 281	11 316 388	10 962 121	10 202 086	9 900 024	C.2.1.3.1. Entreprises Nationales
C.2.1.3.2. (Foreign Controlled Companies)	30 940	33 196	36 253	38 072	85 792	96 148	73 524	74 236	C.2.1.3.2. (Entreprises Sous Contrôle Etranger)
C.2.1.3.3. Branches & Agencies of Foreign Cies	302 660	316 445	328 095	342 040	301 257	308 955	312 961	329 383	C.2.1.3.3. Succursales et Agences d'Ent. Etrangères
C.2.1.3. Total Gross Premiums	10 517 740	11 056 953	11 077 365	11 415 321	11 617 645	11 271 076	10 515 047	10 229 407	C.2.1.3. Total des Primes Brutes
C.2.2. Ceded Premiums									C.2.2. Primes Cédées
C.2.2.1. Domestic Companies	1 490 300	1 402 215	1 404 968	1 459 484	1 400 400	1 309 117	1 222 612	1 202 917	C.2.2.1. Entreprises Nationales
C.2.2.2. (Foreign Controlled Companies)	5 091	4 946	4 393	3 312	10 218	32 660	36 770	34 553	C.2.2.2. (Entreprises Sous Contrôle Etranger)
C.2.2.3. Branches & Agencies of Foreign Cies	178 265	180 457	183 680	192 601	191 106	195 541	198 923	..	C.2.2.3. Succursales et Agences d'Ent. Etrangères
C.2.2. Total	1 668 565	1 582 672	1 588 648	1 652 085	1 591 506	1 504 658	1 421 535	..	C.2.2. Total
C.2.3. Net Written Premiums									C.2.3. Primes Nettes Emises
C.2.3.1. Domestic Companies	6 161 607	6 491 229	6 717 616	6 911 568	7 069 580	7 059 164	8 979 474	8 697 107	C.2.3.1. Entreprises Nationales
C.2.3.2. (Foreign Controlled Companies)	22 571	24 797	28 438	31 173	70 309	57 868	36 754	39 683	C.2.3.2. (Entreprises Sous Contrôle Etranger)
C.2.3.3. Branches & Agencies of Foreign Cies	113 175	121 713	129 279	134 230	94 966	98 365	114 038	..	C.2.3.3. Succursales et Agences d'Ent. Etrangères
C.2.3. Total	6 274 782	6 612 942	6 846 895	7 045 798	7 164 546	7 157 529	9 093 512	..	C.2.3. Total
C.3. Total									**C.3. Total**
C.3.1. Gross Premiums									C.3.1. Primes Brutes
C.3.1.1. Direct Business									C.3.1.1. Assurances Directes
C.3.1.1.1. Domestic Companies	38 177 271	39 562 644	39 597 057	40 165 790	39 150 678	39 786 869	37 414 291	35 398 992	C.3.1.1.1. Entreprises Nationales
C.3.1.1.2. (Foreign Controlled Companies)	186 028	198 680	240 043	368 720	416 515	391 263	509 801	1 365 126	C.3.1.1.2. (Entreprises Sous Contrôle Etranger)
C.3.1.1.3. Branches & Agencies of Foreign Cies	851 106	931 819	1 032 604	1 029 426	1 062 637	1 132 790	1 224 703	1 348 143	C.3.1.1.3. Succursales et Agences d'Ent. Etrangères
C.3.1.1. Total	39 028 377	40 494 463	40 629 662	41 195 216	40 213 315	40 919 659	38 638 994	36 747 135	C.3.1.1. Total
C.3.1.2. Reinsurance Accepted									C.3.1.2. Réassurance Acceptée
C.3.1.2.1. Domestic Companies	996 105	931 416	915 031	960 184	738 315	693 644	695 522	662 793	C.3.1.2.1. Entreprises Nationales
C.3.1.2.2. (Foreign Controlled Companies)	4 424	4 361	4 340	4 584	7 070	6 355	66 306	95 551	C.3.1.2.2. (Entreprises Sous Contrôle Etranger)
C.3.1.2.3. Branches & Agencies of Foreign Cies	23 376	23 762	22 075	21 993	19 493	18 583	17 372	16 234	C.3.1.2.3. Succursales et Agences d'Ent. Etrangères
C.3.1.2. Total	1 019 481	955 178	937 106	982 177	757 808	712 228	712 894	679 027	C.3.1.2. Total
C.3.1.3. Total									C.3.1.3. Total
C.3.1.3.1. Domestic Companies	39 173 376	40 494 060	40 512 088	41 125 974	39 888 993	40 480 514	38 109 813	36 061 785	C.3.1.3.1. Entreprises Nationales
C.3.1.3.2. (Foreign Controlled Companies)	190 452	203 041	244 383	373 304	423 585	397 618	576 107	1 460 677	C.3.1.3.2. (Entreprises Sous Contrôle Etranger)
C.3.1.3.3. Branches & Agencies of Foreign Cies	874 482	955 581	1 054 679	1 051 419	1 082 130	1 151 373	1 242 075	1 364 377	C.3.1.3.3. Succursales et Agences d'Ent. Etrangères
C.3.1.3. Total Gross Premiums	40 047 858	41 449 641	41 566 768	42 177 393	40 971 123	41 631 888	39 351 888	37 426 162	C.3.1.3. Total des Primes Brutes
C.3.2. Ceded Premiums									C.3.2. Primes Cédées
C.3.2.1. Domestic Companies	1 521 855	1 436 454	1 442 201	1 502 477	1 446 253	1 452 293	1 460 895	1 390 212	C.3.2.1. Entreprises Nationales
C.3.2.2. (Foreign Controlled Companies)	8 947	10 001	10 921	14 579	23 702	46 768	66 837	92 437	C.3.2.2. (Entreprises Sous Contrôle Etranger)
C.3.2.3. Branches & Agencies of Foreign Cies	188 384	193 276	194 718	201 107	199 602	204 294	208 125	..	C.3.2.3. Succursales et Agences d'Ent. Etrangères
C.3.2. Total	1 710 239	1 629 730	1 636 919	1 703 584	1 645 855	1 656 587	1 669 020	..	C.3.2. Total
C.3.3. Net Written Premiums									C.3.3. Primes Nettes Emises
C.3.3.1. Domestic Companies	35 088 348	36 210 542	36 443 201	36 921 268	35 596 332	36 434 381	36 648 918	34 671 573	C.3.3.1. Entreprises Nationales
C.3.3.2. (Foreign Controlled Companies)	178 227	189 587	230 040	355 138	394 618	345 230	509 270	1 368 240	C.3.3.2. (Entreprises Sous Contrôle Etranger)
C.3.3.3. Branches & Agencies of Foreign Cies	674 878	748 030	844 825	835 103	867 343	932 030	1 033 950	..	C.3.3.3. Succursales et Agences d'Ent. Etrangères
C.3.3. Total	35 763 226	36 958 572	37 288 027	37 756 371	36 463 675	37 366 412	37 682 868	..	C.3.3. Total

Monetary Unit: million Japanese yen　　　　　　　　　　　　　　　　Unité monétaire : million de yen japonais

D. NET WRITTEN PREMIUMS IN THE REPORTING COUNTRY IN TERMS OF DOMESTIC AND FOREIGN RISKS
D. PRIMES NETTES EMISES DANS LE PAYS DECLARANT EN RISQUES NATIONAUX ET ETRANGERS

D.1. Life / D.1. Vie

	1992	1993	1994	1995	1996	1997	1998	1999
D.1.1. Domestic Risks / Risques Nationaux								
D.1.1.1. Domestic Companies / Entreprises Nationales	28 926 741	29 719 313	29 725 585	30 009 700	28 526 752	29 395 217	27 669 444	25 974 466
D.1.1.2. (Foreign Controlled Companies) / (Entreprises Sous Contrôle Etranger)	155 656	164 790	201 602	323 965	324 309	287 362	472 516	1 328 557
D.1.1.3. Branches & Agencies of Foreign Cies / Succursales et Agences d'Ent. Etrangères	561 703	626 317	715 546	700 873	772 377	833 665	919 912	1 017 999
D.1.1. Total / Total des Primes Nettes Vie	29 488 444	30 345 630	30 441 132	30 710 573	29 299 129	30 208 883	28 589 356	26 992 465
D.1.3. Total / Total								
D.1.3.1. Domestic Companies / Entreprises Nationales	28 926 741	29 719 313	29 725 585	30 009 700	28 526 752	29 395 217	27 669 444	25 974 466
D.1.3.2. (Foreign Controlled Companies) / (Entreprises Sous Contrôle Etranger)	155 656	164 790	201 602	323 965	324 309	287 362	472 516	1 328 557
D.1.3.3. Branches & Agencies of Foreign Cies / Succursales et Agences d'Ent. Etrangères	561 703	626 317	715 546	700 873	772 377	833 665	919 912	1 017 999
D.1.3. Total of Life Net Premiums / Total des Primes Nettes Vie	29 488 444	30 345 630	30 441 132	30 710 573	29 299 129	30 208 883	28 589 356	26 992 465

E. BUSINESS WRITTEN ABROAD / E. OPERATIONS A L'ETRANGER

E.1. Life / E.1. Vie

	1992	1993	1994	1995	1996	1997	1998	1999
E.1.1. Gross Premiums / Primes Brutes								
E.1.1.1. Direct Business / Assurance Directe								
E.1.1.1.2. Subsidiaries / Filliales	:	:	:	10 015	:	:	0	0
E.1.1.2. Reinsurance Accepted / Réassurance Acceptée								
E.1.1.2.2. Subsidiaries / Filliales	:	:	:	117	:	:	0	0
E.1.1.3. Total / Total								
E.1.1.3.2. Subsidiaries / Filliales	:	:	:	10 132	:	:	0	0
E.1.2. Ceded Premiums / Primes Cédées								
E.1.2.2. Subsidiaries / Filliales	:	:	:	2 586	:	:	0	0
E.1.3. Net Written Premiums / Primes Nettes Emises								
E.1.3.2. Subsidiaries / Filliales	:	:	:	7 546	:	:	0	0

E.2. Non-Life / E.2. Non-Vie

	1992	1993	1994	1995	1996	1997	1998	1999
E.2.1. Gross Premiums / Primes Brutes								
E.2.1.1. Direct Business / Assurance Directe								
E.2.1.1.1. Branches & Agencies / Succursales & Agences	69 920	60 505	54 561	56 575	65 202	77 873	:	:
E.2.1.2. Reinsurance Accepted / Réassurance Acceptée								
E.2.1.2.1. Branches & Agencies / Succursales & Agences	3 275	5 216	5 683	10 436	32 787	28 031	:	:
E.2.1.3. Total / Total								
E.2.1.3.1. Branches & Agencies / Succursales & Agences	73 195	65 720	60 244	67 011	97 991	105 904	100 318	84 403
E.2.1.3.2. Subsidiaries / Filliales	167 745	138 941	123 500	140 491	166 038	186 927	182 145	134 509
E.2.1.3. Total Gross Premiums / Total des Primes Brutes	240 940	204 661	183 744	207 502	264 029	292 831	282 463	218 912
E.2.2. Ceded Premiums / Primes Cédées								
E.2.2.1. Branches & Agencies / Succursales & Agences	5 761	5 363	12 562	19 273	49 268	38 342	46 301	39 232
E.2.2.2. Subsidiaries / Filliales	98 155	77 443	63 460	71 156	83 339	104 704	65 227	31 292
E.2.2. Total / Total	103 916	82 806	76 022	90 429	132 607	143 046	111 528	70 524
E.2.3. Net Written Premiums / Primes Nettes Emises								
E.2.3.1. Branches & Agencies / Succursales & Agences	67 434	60 358	47 682	47 738	48 724	67 562	54 017	45 171
E.2.3.2. Subsidiaries / Filliales	69 590	61 498	60 040	69 335	82 697	82 222	116 918	103 217
E.2.3. Total / Total	137 024	121 856	107 722	117 073	131 421	149 784	170 935	148 388

F. OUTSTANDING INVESTMENT BY DIRECT INSURANCE COMPANIES / F. ENCOURS DES PLACEMENTS DES ENTREPRISES D'ASSURANCES DIRECTES

F.1. Life / F.1. Vie

	1992	1993	1994	1995	1996	1997	1998	1999
F.1.1. Real Estate / Immobilier								
F.1.1.1. Domestic Companies / Entreprises Nationales	8 364 646	8 958 853	9 442 685	9 734 839	9 698 235	9 832 165	9 692 786	8 959 010
F.1.1.2. (Foreign Controlled Companies) / (Entreprises Sous Contrôle Etranger)	9 045	8 688	8 690	8 899	9 193	1 100	1 571	225 124
F.1.1.3. Branches & Agencies of Foreign Cies / Succursales et Agences d'Ent. Etrangères	25 259	25 538	32 383	30 284	28 789	27 358	25 998	24 928
F.1.1. Total / Total	8 398 950	8 993 079	9 475 068	9 765 123	9 727 024	9 859 523	9 718 784	8 983 938

Monetary Unit: million Japanese yen　　　　　　　　　　　　　Unité monétaire : million de yen japonais

	1992	1993	1994	1995	1996	1997	1998	1999
F.1.2. Mortgage Loans / Prêts Hypothécaires								
F.1.2.1. Domestic Companies / Entreprises Nationales	4 680 784	7 342 258	7 249 375	7 251 368	:	:	:	:
F.1.2.2. (Foreign Controlled Companies) / (Entreprises Sous Contrôle Etranger)	3 398	33 217	40 897	44 733	:	:	:	:
F.1.2.3. Branches & Agencies of Foreign Cies / Succursales et Agences d'Ent. Etrangères	4 115	1 272	1 556	1 625	:	:	:	:
F.1.2. Total	4 688 297	7 376 747	7 250 931	7 252 993	:	:	:	:
F.1.3. Shares / Actions								
F.1.3.1. Domestic Companies / Entreprises Nationales	35 354 398	36 803 814	46 695 106	46 948 933	35 518 308	33 731 496	32 905 427	28 141 874
F.1.3.2. (Foreign Controlled Companies) / (Entreprises Sous Contrôle Etranger)	34 568	42 428	180 515	241 753	52 510	28 857	31 740	394 426
F.1.3.3. Branches & Agencies of Foreign Cies / Succursales et Agences d'Ent. Etrangères	177 732	182 793	635 030	738 907	128 052	108 128	105 894	116 142
F.1.3.4. Domestic Investment / Placement dans le Pays	31 506 834	33 070 784	41 434 636	42 250 550	31 896 190	29 913 175	28 542 623	
F.1.3.5. Foreign Investment / Placement à l' Etranger	4 059 864	3 958 251	5 895 500	5 437 290	3 750 171	3 927 449	4 468 698	
F.1.3. Total	35 566 698	37 029 035	47 330 136	47 687 840	35 646 361	33 840 624	33 011 321	28 258 016
F.1.4. Bonds with Fixed Revenue / Obligations								
F.1.4.1. Domestic Companies / Entreprises Nationales	28 116 446	31 822 130	30 696 666	40 454 441	53 703 298	54 930 528	59 997 459	50 211 552
F.1.4.2. (Foreign Controlled Companies) / (Entreprises Sous Contrôle Etranger)	292 558	340 555	265 294	460 993	789 174	642 328	861 846	2 385 340
F.1.4.3. Branches & Agencies of Foreign Cies / Succursales et Agences d'Ent. Etrangères	1 306 793	1 519 899	1 374 582	1 498 751	2 343 168	2 639 225	2 941 686	1 736 337
F.1.4.4. Domestic Investment / Placement dans le Pays	19 332 480	25 832 185	7 164 759	33 535 970	44 116 584	44 585 995	47 356 891	
F.1.4.5. Foreign Investment / Placement à l' Etranger	10 383 317	7 842 899	24 906 489	8 417 222	11 929 886	12 983 755	15 582 254	
F.1.4. Total	29 715 797	33 682 084	32 071 248	41 953 192	56 046 470	57 569 751	62 939 145	51 947 889
F.1.5. Loans other than Mortgage Loans / Prêts Autres qu'Hypothécaires								
F.1.5.1. Domestic Companies / Entreprises Nationales	56 275 657	56 561 705	59 602 542	59 919 564	65 092 898	63 299 798	58 882 683	53 884 780
F.1.5.2. (Foreign Controlled Companies) / (Entreprises Sous Contrôle Etranger)	118 615	111 502	140 751	156 705	206 355	21 558	23 193	2 110 601
F.1.5.3. Branches & Agencies of Foreign Cies / Succursales et Agences d'Ent. Etrangères	65 367	117 121	131 009	162 354	202 507	216 963	243 194	307 163
F.1.5.4. Domestic Investment / Placement dans le Pays	50 551 854	50 759 241	52 729 967	52 886 372			54 159 498	49 796 196
F.1.5.5. Foreign Investment / Placement à l' Etranger	5 907 785	6 031 087	7 003 575	7 195 546			4 966 379	4 395 747
F.1.5. Total	56 459 639	56 790 328	59 733 551	60 081 918	65 295 405	63 516 761	59 125 877	54 191 943
F.1.6. Other Investments / Autres Placements								
F.1.6.1. Domestic Companies / Entreprises Nationales	20 900 645	24 973 418	21 969 815	20 666 939	21 819 596	25 203 711	26 793 808	43 275 594
F.1.6.2. (Foreign Controlled Companies) / (Entreprises Sous Contrôle Etranger)	84 935	33 102	78 618	136 352	139 379	104 886	373 663	3 949 709
F.1.6.3. Branches & Agencies of Foreign Cies / Succursales et Agences d'Ent. Etrangères	196 133	189 337	134 730	84 486	124 109	120 619	179 469	1 759 942
F.1.6. Total	21 181 713	25 250 857	22 104 545	20 751 425	21 943 700	25 324 329	26 973 277	45 035 536
F.1.7. Total								
F.1.7.1. Domestic Companies / Entreprises Nationales	153 692 576	166 462 178	175 656 189	184 976 084	185 832 335	186 997 695	188 272 163	184 472 810
F.1.7.2. (Foreign Controlled Companies) / (Entreprises Sous Contrôle Etranger)	543 119	624 492	714 765	1 049 435	1 196 611	798 729	1 292 013	9 065 200
F.1.7.3. Branches & Agencies of Foreign Cies / Succursales et Agences d'Ent. Etrangères	1 775 399	2 035 460	2 309 290	2 516 407	2 826 625	3 113 293	3 496 241	3 944 512
F.1.7.4. Domestic Investment / Placement dans le Pays	133 211 321	151 289 893						
F.1.7.5. Foreign Investment / Placement à l' Etranger	22 799 773	17 832 237						
F.1.7. Total of Life Investments / Total des Placements Vie	156 011 094	169 122 130	177 965 479	187 492 491	188 658 960	190 110 988	191 768 404	188 417 322
F.2. Non-Life / F.2. Non-Vie								
F.2.1. Real Estate / Immobilier								
F.2.1.1. Domestic Companies / Entreprises Nationales	1 562 915	1 625 669	1 815 981	1 811 907	1 837 566	1 814 999	1 805 464	1 773 841
F.2.1.2. (Foreign Controlled Companies) / (Entreprises Sous Contrôle Etranger)	146	141	159	146	839	822	993	1 006
F.2.1.3. Branches & Agencies of Foreign Cies / Succursales et Agences d'Ent. Etrangères			644	641	397	436	526	
F.2.1.4. Domestic Investment / Placement dans le Pays								
F.2.1. Total	1 563 061	1 625 810	1 816 625	1 812 548	1 837 963	1 815 435	1 805 990	1 773 841
F.2.2. Mortgage Loans / Prêts Hypothécaires								
F.2.2.1. Domestic Companies / Entreprises Nationales	558 069	577 286	594 299	594 384	:	:	:	:
F.2.2.4. Domestic Investment / Placement dans le Pays	558 069	577 246	594 299	594 384	:	:	:	:
F.2.2. Total								
F.2.3. Shares / Actions								
F.2.3.1. Domestic Companies / Entreprises Nationales	4 735 973	4 929 577	5 241 857	5 338 027	5 889 262	5 793 385	5 908 999	5 972 356
F.2.3.2. (Foreign Controlled Companies) / (Entreprises Sous Contrôle Etranger)	285	191	310	1 147	5 772	6 167	3 388	5 109
F.2.3.3. Branches & Agencies of Foreign Cies / Succursales et Agences d'Ent. Etrangères			23 451	28 492	25 903	19 157	18 389	
F.2.3.4. Domestic Investment / Placement dans le Pays	4 736 258	4 929 768				5 391 456	5 575 874	5 596 066
F.2.3.5. Foreign Investment / Placement à l' Etranger						421 086	351 514	376 290
F.2.3. Total	4 736 258	4 929 768	5 265 308	5 366 519	5 915 165	5 812 542	5 927 388	5 972 356

Monetary Unit: million Japanese yen — Unité monétaire : million de yen japonais

	1992	1993	1994	1995	1996	1997	1998	1999
F.2.4. Bonds with Fixed Revenue — F.2.4. Obligations								
F.2.4.1. Domestic Companies — Entreprises Nationales	7 085 551	7 377 112	8 230 846	8 957 926	8 226 935	8 816 265	8 774 546	9 003 985
F.2.4.2. (Foreign Controlled Companies) — (Entreprises Sous Contrôle Etranger)	26 764	31 559	36 247	38 953	81 695	70 038	47 478	38 016
F.2.4.3. Branches & Agencies of Foreign Cies — Succursales et Agences d'Ent. Etrangères	..	..	110 865	322 671	186 940	145 933	151 160	..
F.2.4.4. Domestic Investment — Placement dans le Pays	..	..	..	..	..	5 519 590	5 793 838	6 237 863
F.2.4.5. Foreign Investment — Placement à l'Etranger	..	..	..	..	..	3 442 608	3 131 868	2 766 122
F.2.4. Total	7 112 315	7 408 621	8 341 711	9 280 597	8 413 875	8 962 198	8 925 706	9 003 985
F.2.5. Loans other than Mortgage Loans — F.2.5. Prêts Autres qu'Hypothécaires								
F.2.5.1. Domestic Companies — Entreprises Nationales	6 641 347	6 143 748	5 967 958	5 944 453	6 547 114	6 651 665	6 260 155	5 478 088
F.2.5.2. (Foreign Controlled Companies) — (Entreprises Sous Contrôle Etranger)	2 996	1 883	1 323	1 264	1 491	1 474	295	193
F.2.5.3. Branches & Agencies of Foreign Cies — Succursales et Agences d'Ent. Etrangères	..	..	10 251	9 234	8 532	4 854	2 098	..
F.2.5.4. Domestic Investment — Placement dans le Pays	..	..	..	..	..	..	..	..
F.2.5. Total	6 644 343	6 145 631	5 978 209	5 953 687	6 555 646	6 656 519	6 262 253	5 478 088
F.2.6. Other Investments — F.2.6. Autres Placements								
F.2.6.1. Domestic Companies — Entreprises Nationales	3 962 072	4 043 040	3 806 328	4 016 581	4 930 403	7 291 713	7 287 593	8 251 577
F.2.6.2. (Foreign Controlled Companies) — (Entreprises Sous Contrôle Etranger)	8 627	6 942	7 701	7 103	15 174	44 047	30 999	40 380
F.2.6.3. Branches & Agencies of Foreign Cies — Succursales et Agences d'Ent. Etrangères	..	..	52 060	35 499	36 360	39 593	32 982	..
F.2.6.4. Domestic Investment — Placement dans le Pays	..	..	..	..	..	..	..	..
F.2.6. Total	3 970 699	4 054 982	3 858 388	4 052 080	4 966 763	7 331 306	7 320 575	8 251 577
F.2.7. Total — F.2.7. Total								
F.2.7.1. Domestic Companies — Entreprises Nationales	24 545 927	24 701 392	25 657 269	26 663 278	27 431 280	30 368 027	30 036 757	30 479 847
F.2.7.2. (Foreign Controlled Companies) — (Entreprises Sous Contrôle Etranger)	38 818	40 716	45 740	48 613	104 971	122 548	83 153	84 704
F.2.7.3. Branches & Agencies of Foreign Cies — Succursales et Agences d'Ent. Etrangères	..	..	197 271	396 537	258 132	209 973	205 155	197 366
F.2.7.4. Domestic Investment — Placement dans le Pays	..	..	..	..	..	..	..	..
F.2.7. Total of Non-Life Investments — F.2.7. Total des Placements Non-Vie	24 584 745	24 742 108	25 854 540	27 059 815	27 689 412	30 578 000	30 241 912	30 677 213
G. BREAKDOWN OF NON-LIFE PREMIUMS — G. VENTILATIONS DES PRIMES NON-VIE								
G.1. Motor vehicle — G.1. Assurance Automobile								
G.1.1. Direct Business — Assurances Directes								
G.1.1.1. Gross Premiums — Primes Brutes	4 160 318	4 379 638	4 537 409	4 658 804	4 792 901	4 742 745	4 619 120	4 685 811
G.1.2. Reinsurance Accepted — Réassurance Acceptée								
G.1.2.1. Gross Premiums — Primes Brutes	437 627	396 614	382 980	397 242	347 311	326 806	302 978	307 648
G.1.3. Total								
G.1.3.1. Gross Premiums — Primes Brutes	4 597 945	4 776 252	4 920 389	5 056 046	5 140 212	5 069 551	4 922 098	4 888 029
G.1.3.2. Ceded Premiums — Primes Cédées	937 462	841 095	843 301	870 157	888 349	810 622	795 525	751 721
G.1.3.3. Net Written Premiums — Primes Nettes Emises	3 660 483	3 935 157	4 077 088	4 185 889	4 251 863	4 258 929	4 126 573	4 136 308
G.2. Marine, Aviation — G.2. Marine, Aviation								
G.2.1. Direct Business — Assurances Directes								
G.2.1.1. Gross Premiums — Primes Brutes	260 037	251 394	254 829	255 125	278 771	268 497	233 478	207 355
G.2.2. Reinsurance Accepted — Réassurance Acceptée								
G.2.2.1. Gross Premiums — Primes Brutes	148 985	143 894	146 914	162 370	120 650	108 093	83 681	65 740
G.2.3. Total								
G.2.3.1. Gross Premiums — Primes Brutes	409 022	395 288	401 743	417 495	399 421	376 590	317 159	268 142
G.2.3.2. Ceded Premiums — Primes Cédées	176 800	176 739	177 740	194 926	161 870	144 448	109 271	91 860
G.2.3.3. Net Written Premiums — Primes Nettes Emises	232 222	218 549	224 003	222 569	237 551	232 142	207 888	176 282
G.3. Freight — G.3. Fret								
G.3.1. Direct Business — Assurances Directes								
G.3.1.1. Gross Premiums — Primes Brutes	68 256	66 448	66 897	68 497	70 212	70 667	66 976	66 087
G.3.2. Reinsurance Accepted — Réassurance Acceptée								
G.3.2.1. Gross Premiums — Primes Brutes	17 508	16 632	15 765	16 105	8 681	7 452	6 311	4 732
G.3.3. Total								
G.3.3.1. Gross Premiums — Primes Brutes	85 764	83 080	82 662	84 602	78 893	78 119	73 287	68 605
G.3.3.2. Ceded Premiums — Primes Cédées	24 519	23 574	22 307	22 255	16 632	15 614	13 127	9 735
G.3.3.3. Net Written Premiums — Primes Nettes Emises	61 245	59 506	60 355	62 347	62 261	62 505	60 160	58 870
G.4. Fire, Property Damages — G.4. Incendie, Dommages aux Biens								
G.4.1. Direct Business — Assurances Directes								
G.4.1.1. Gross Premiums — Primes Brutes	1 808 733	1 955 794	1 994 506	2 004 317	2 065 268	2 067 196	1 932 150	1 903 028
G.4.2. Reinsurance Accepted — Réassurance Acceptée								
G.4.2.1. Gross Premiums — Primes Brutes	258 221	245 244	240 491	258 823	158 319	160 523	147 183	119 446
G.4.3. Total								
G.4.3.1. Gross Premiums — Primes Brutes	2 066 954	2 201 038	2 234 997	2 263 140	2 223 587	2 227 719	2 079 333	1 982 209
G.4.3.2. Ceded Premiums — Primes Cédées	304 403	316 923	324 012	343 963	305 431	324 796	297 300	256 000
G.4.3.3. Net Written Premiums — Primes Nettes Emises	1 080 928	1 109 737	1 177 744	1 216 085	1 220 011	1 234 662	1 782 033	1 726 209

JAPAN

Monetary Unit: million Japanese yen

JAPON

Unité monétaire : million de yen japonais

	1992	1993	1994	1995	1996	1997	1998	1999	
G.5. Pecuniary Losses									G.5. Pertes Pécunières
G.5.1. Direct Business									G.5.1. Assurances Directes
G.5.1.1. Gross Premiums	114 641	80 878	76 920	75 940	99 962	76 249	87 601	89 598	G.5.1.1. Primes Brutes
G.5.2. Reinsurance Accepted									G.5.2. Réassurance Acceptée
G.5.2.1. Gross Premiums	833	745	752	619	3 984	4 479	4 843	4 512	G.5.2.1. Primes Brutes
G.5.3. Total									G.5.3. Total
G.5.3.1. Gross Premiums	115 474	81 623	77 672	76 559	103 946	80 728	92 444	84 584	G.5.3.1. Primes Brutes
G.5.3.2. Ceded Premiums	1 566	1 896	1 917	2 229	6 520	7 206	7 455	8 522	G.5.3.2. Primes Cédées
G.5.3.3. Net Written Premiums	81 630	58 802	56 269	53 206	77 050	59 272	84 989	76 062	G.5.3.3. Primes Nettes Emises
G.6. General Liability									G.6. Responsabilité Générale
G.6.1. Direct Business									G.6.1. Assurances Directes
G.6.1.1. Gross Premiums	234 247	242 830	256 320	285 090	312 436	327 888	323 813	325 568	G.6.1.1. Primes Brutes
G.6.2. Reinsurance Accepted									G.6.2. Réassurance Acceptée
G.6.2.1. Gross Premiums	25 560	24 029	24 041	23 761	14 950	14 713	15 024	9 152	G.6.2.1. Primes Brutes
G.6.3. Total									G.6.3. Total
G.6.3.1. Gross Premiums	259 807	266 859	280 361	308 851	327 386	342 601	338 837	314 215	G.6.3.1. Primes Brutes
G.6.3.2. Ceded Premiums	36 351	36 535	38 357	40 061	38 937	38 760	37 954	20 499	G.6.3.2. Primes Cédées
G.6.3.3. Net Written Premiums	223 456	230 324	242 004	268 790	288 449	303 841	300 883	293 716	G.6.3.3. Primes Nettes Emises
G.7. Accident, Health									G.7. Accident, Santé
G.7.1. Direct Business									G.7.1. Assurances Directes
G.7.1.1. Gross Premiums	2 664 135	2 921 896	2 754 119	2 871 398	3 153 041	2 919 457	2 530 295	2 276 325	G.7.1.1. Primes Brutes
G.7.2. Reinsurance Accepted									G.7.2. Réassurance Acceptée
G.7.2.1. Gross Premiums	16 862	16 628	17 971	15 929	16 280	13 550	12 344	8 937	G.7.2.1. Primes Brutes
G.7.3. Total									G.7.3. Total
G.7.3.1. Gross Premiums	2 680 997	2 938 524	2 772 090	2 887 327	3 169 321	2 933 007	2 542 639	2 155 177	G.7.3.1. Primes Brutes
G.7.3.2. Ceded Premiums	97 804	96 150	97 059	98 091	104 853	110 401	112 771	27 788	G.7.3.2. Primes Cédées
G.7.3.3. Net Written Premiums	736 267	797 494	806 741	832 461	921 394	896 228	2 429 868	2 127 389	G.7.3.3. Primes Nettes Emises
G.8. Others									G.8. Autres
G.8.1. Direct Business									G.8.1. Assurances Directes
G.8.1.1. Gross Premiums	221 876	240 544	238 626	256 038	131 155	131 387	126 076	120 612	G.8.1.1. Primes Brutes
G.8.2. Reinsurance Accepted									G.8.2. Réassurance Acceptée
G.8.2.1. Gross Premiums	79 901	73 745	68 825	65 263	43 717	31 367	23 174	18 622	G.8.2.1. Primes Brutes
G.8.3. Total									G.8.3. Total
G.8.3.1. Gross Premiums	301 777	314 289	307 451	321 301	174 872	162 754	149 250	139 063	G.8.3.1. Primes Brutes
G.8.3.2. Ceded Premiums	89 660	89 760	83 955	80 403	68 911	52 808	48 132	36 792	G.8.3.2. Primes Cédées
G.8.3.3. Net Written Premiums	198 551	203 373	202 691	204 451	105 961	109 946	101 118	102 271	G.8.3.3. Primes Nettes Emises
G.10. Total									G.10. Total
G.10.1. Direct Business									G.10.1. Assurances Directes
G.10.1.1. Gross Premiums	9 532 243	10 139 422	10 179 626	10 475 209	10 903 749	10 604 090	9 919 509	9 674 384	G.10.1.1. Primes Brutes
G.10.2. Reinsurance Accepted									G.10.2. Réassurance Acceptée
G.10.2.1. Gross Premiums	985497	917531	897739	940112	713896	666986	595538	538 789	G.10.2.1. Primes Brutes
G.10.3. Total									G.10.3. Total
G.10.3.1. Gross Premiums	10517740	11056953	11077365	11415321	11617645	11271076	10515047	9 900 024	G.10.3.1. Primes Brutes
G.10.3.2. Ceded Premiums	1668565	1582672	1588648	1652085	1591506	1504658	1421535	1 202 917	G.10.3.2. Primes Cédées
G.10.3.3. Net Written Premiums	6274782	6612942	6846895	7045798	7164546	9157529	9093512	8 697 107	G.10.3.3. Primes Nettes Emises

Monetary Unit: million won
Unité monétaire : million de won

A. NUMBER OF COMPANIES IN THE REPORTING COUNTRY — A. NOMBRE D'ENTREPRISES DANS LE PAYS DECLARANT

	1992	1993	1994	1995	1996	1997	1998	1999
A.1. Life — A.1. Vie								
A.1.1. Domestic Companies — A.1.1. Entreprises Nationales	..	..	31	31	31	31	27	27
A.1.2. (Foreign Controlled Companies) — A.1.2. (Entreprises Sous Contrôle Etranger)	..	..	3	3	3	3	4	8
A.1.3. Branches & Agencies of Foreign Cies — A.1.3. Succursales et Agences d'Ent. Etrangères	..	..	2	2	2	2	2	2
A.1. All Companies — A.1. Ensemble des Entreprises	..	..	33	33	33	33	29	29
A.2. Non-Life — A.2. Non-Vie								
A.2.1. Domestic Companies — A.2.1. Entreprises Nationales	..	..	13	13	13	13	12	12
A.2.3. Branches & Agencies of Foreign Cies — A.2.3. Succursales et Agences d'Ent. Etrangères	..	..	3	3	3	3	3	4
A.2. All Companies — A.2. Ensemble des Entreprises	..	..	16	16	16	16	15	16
A.4. Reinsurance — A.4. Réassurance								
A.4.1. Domestic Companies — A.4.1. Entreprises Nationales	..	..	1	1	1	1	1	1
A.4. All Companies — A.4. Ensemble des Entreprises	..	..	1	1	1	1	1	1
A.5. Total								
A.5.1. Domestic Companies — A.5.1. Entreprises Nationales	..	..	45	45	45	45	40	40
A.5.2. (Foreign Controlled Companies) — A.5.2. (Entreprises Sous Contrôle Etranger)	..	..	3	3	3	3	4	8
A.5.3. Branches & Agencies of Foreign Cies — A.5.3. Succursales et Agences d'Ent. Etrangères	..	..	5	5	5	5	5	6
A.5. All Insurance Companies — A.5. Ensemble des Entreprises d'Assurances	..	..	50	50	50	50	45	46

B. NUMBER OF EMPLOYEES — B. NOMBRE D'EMPLOYES

	1992	1993	1994	1995	1996	1997	1998	1999
B.1. Insurance Companies — B.1. Entreprises d'Assurances	..	..	74 632	79 948	87 218	84 451	64 894	61 745
B.2. Intermediaries — B.2. Intermediaires	..	..	43 782	46 186	46 385	74 801	79 937	389 611
B. Total	..	..	118 414	126 134	133 603	159 252	144 831	451 356

C. BUSINESS WRITTEN IN THE REPORTING COUNTRY — C. OPERATIONS CONCLUES DANS LE PAYS DECLARANT

C.1. Life — C.1. Vie

	1992	1993	1994	1995	1996	1997	1998	1999
C.1.1. Gross Premiums — C.1.1. Primes Brutes								
C.1.1.1. Direct Business — C.1.1.1. Assurances Directes								
C.1.1.1.1. Domestic Companies — C.1.1.1.1. Entreprises Nationales	..	..	26 855 269	33 689 944	37 206 444	41 916 538	51 430 419	46 923 369
C.1.1.1.2. (Foreign Controlled Companies) — C.1.1.1.2. (Entreprises Sous Contrôle Etranger)	..	..	67 883	79 878	97 090	118 226	418 890	2 734 979
C.1.1.1.3. Branches & Agencies of Foreign Cies — C.1.1.1.3. Succursales et Agences d'Ent. Etrangères	..	..	35 304	36 098	37 596	42 816	42 251	63 242
C.1.1.1. Total — C.1.1.1. Total	..	..	26 890 573	33 726 042	37 244 040	41 959 354	51 472 670	46 986 611
C.1.1.2. Reinsurance Accepted — C.1.1.2. Réassurance Acceptée								
C.1.1.2.1. Domestic Companies — C.1.1.2.1. Entreprises Nationales	..	..	876	1 890	43 164	1 370	2 162	4 382
C.1.1.2.2. (Foreign Controlled Companies) — C.1.1.2.2. (Entreprises Sous Contrôle Etranger)	..	..						29
C.1.1.2. Total — C.1.1.2. Total	..	..	876	1 890	43 164	1 370	2 162	4 382
C.1.1.3. Total								
C.1.1.3.1. Domestic Companies — C.1.1.3.1. Entreprises Nationales	..	..	26 856 145	33 691 834	37 249 608	41 917 908	51 432 581	46 927 751
C.1.1.3.2. (Foreign Controlled Companies) — C.1.1.3.2. (Entreprises Sous Contrôle Etranger)	..	..	67 883	79 878	97 090	118 226	418 890	2 735 008
C.1.1.3.3. Branches & Agencies of Foreign Cies — C.1.1.3.3. Succursales et Agences d'Ent. Etrangères	..	..	35 304	36 098	37 596	42 816	42 251	63 242
C.1.1.3. Total Gross Premiums — C.1.1.3. Total des Primes Brutes	..	..	26 891 449	33 727 932	37 287 204	41 960 724	51 474 832	46 990 993
C.1.2. Ceded Premiums — C.1.2. Primes Cédées								
C.1.2.1. Domestic Companies — C.1.2.1. Entreprises Nationales	..	..	73 703	90 941	112 644	207 905	147 143	207 957
C.1.2.2. (Foreign Controlled Companies) — C.1.2.2. (Entreprises Sous Contrôle Etranger)	..	..	973	2 616	4 857	3 241	9 583	37 932
C.1.2.3. Branches & Agencies of Foreign Cies — C.1.2.3. Succursales et Agences d'Ent. Etrangères	..	..	1 145	519	1 907	1 226	2 433	2 491
C.1.2. Total — C.1.2. Total	..	..	74 848	91 460	114 551	209 132	149 576	210 448
C.1.3. Net Written Premiums — C.1.3. Primes Nettes Emises								
C.1.3.1. Domestic Companies — C.1.3.1. Entreprises Nationales	..	..	26 782 442	33 600 893	37 136 964	41 710 003	51 285 437	46 719 794
C.1.3.2. (Foreign Controlled Companies) — C.1.3.2. (Entreprises Sous Contrôle Etranger)	..	..	66 910	77 262	93 850	113 964	409 307	2 697 076
C.1.3.3. Branches & Agencies of Foreign Cies — C.1.3.3. Succursales et Agences d'Ent. Etrangères	..	..	34 159	35 579	35 689	41 590	39 819	60 751
C.1.3. Total — C.1.3. Total	..	..	26 816 601	33 636 472	37 172 653	41 751 592	51 325 256	46 780 545

Monetary Unit: million won   Unité monétaire : million de won

C.2. Non-Life / C.2. Non-Vie

	1992	1993	1994	1995	1996	1997	1998	1999
C.2.1. Gross premiums / C.2.1. Primes Brutes								
C.2.1.1. Direct Business / C.2.1.1. Assurances Directes								
C.2.1.1.1. Domestic Companies / Entreprises Nationales	...	...	7 881 422	10 240 861	12 814 382	15 374 350	15 179 698	14 434 255
C.2.1.1.3. Branches & Agencies of Foreign Cies / Succursales et Agences d'Ent. Etrangères	...	...	14 988	53 328	44 383	47 596	42 822	48 580
C.2.1.1. Total	...	...	7 896 410	10 294 189	12 858 765	15 421 946	15 222 520	14 482 835
C.2.1.2. Reinsurance Accepted / C.2.1.2. Réassurance Acceptée								
C.2.1.2.1. Domestic Companies / Entreprises Nationales	...	...	955 857	1 081 115	1 174 816	1 255 636	1 324 430	1 483 380
C.2.1.2.3. Branches & Agencies of Foreign Cies / Succursales et Agences d'Ent. Etrangères	...	...	5 911	14 310	13 463	13 018	13 320	10 987
C.2.1.2. Total	...	...	961 768	1 095 425	1 188 279	1 268 654	1 337 750	1 494 367
C.2.1.3. Total								
C.2.1.3.1. Domestic Companies / Entreprises Nationales	...	...	8 837 279	11 321 976	13 989 199	16 629 986	16 504 128	15 917 635
C.2.1.3.3. Branches & Agencies of Foreign Cies / Succursales et Agences d'Ent. Etrangères	...	...	20 899	67 638	57 846	60 614	56 142	59 567
C.2.1.3. Total Gross Premiums / Total des Primes Brutes	...	...	8 858 178	11 389 614	14 047 045	16 690 600	16 560 270	15 977 202
C.2.2. Ceded Premiums / C.2.2. Primes Cédées								
C.2.2.1. Domestic Companies / Entreprises Nationales	...	...	1 256 508	1 462 248	1 574 205	1 657 733	1 872 671	2 006 792
C.2.2.3. Branches & Agencies of Foreign Cies / Succursales et Agences d'Ent. Etrangères	...	...	3 366	12 521	12 793	12 474	13 440	13 822
C.2.2. Total	...	...	1 259 874	1 474 769	1 586 998	1 670 207	1 886 111	2 020 614
C.2.3. Net Written Premiums / C.2.3. Primes Nettes Emises								
C.2.3.1. Domestic Companies / Entreprises Nationales	...	...	7 580 771	9 859 728	12 414 993	14 972 253	14 631 457	13 910 843
C.2.3.3. Branches & Agencies of Foreign Cies / Succursales et Agences d'Ent. Etrangères	...	...	17 533	55 117	45 054	48 140	42 702	45 745
C.2.3. Total	...	...	7 598 304	9 914 845	12 460 047	15 020 393	14 674 159	13 956 588

C.3. Total / C.3. Total

	1992	1993	1994	1995	1996	1997	1998	1999
C.3.1. Gross Premiums / C.3.1. Primes Brutes								
C.3.1.1. Direct Business / C.3.1.1. Assurances Directes								
C.3.1.1.1. Domestic Companies / Entreprises Nationales	...	...	34 736 691	43 930 805	50 020 826	57 290 888	66 610 117	61 357 624
C.3.1.1.2. (Foreign Controlled Companies) / (Entreprises Sous Contrôle Etranger)	...	...	67 883	79 878	97 090	118 226	418 890	2 734 979
C.3.1.1.3. Branches & Agencies of Foreign Cies / Succursales et Agences d'Ent. Etrangères	...	...	50 292	89 426	81 979	90 412	85 073	111 822
C.3.1.1. Total	...	...	34 786 983	44 020 231	50 102 805	57 381 300	66 695 190	61 469 446
C.3.1.2. Reinsurance Accepted / C.3.1.2. Réassurance Acceptée								
C.3.1.2.1. Domestic Companies / Entreprises Nationales	...	...	956 733	1 083 005	1 217 980	1 257 006	1 326 592	1 487 762
C.3.1.2.3. Branches & Agencies of Foreign Cies / Succursales et Agences d'Ent. Etrangères	...	...	5 911	14 310	13 463	13 018	13 320	21 974
C.3.1.2. Total	...	...	962 644	1 097 315	1 231 443	1 270 024	1 339 912	1 498 749
C.3.1.3. Total								
C.3.1.3.1. Domestic Companies / Entreprises Nationales	...	...	35 693 424	45 013 810	51 238 807	58 547 894	67 936 709	62 845 386
C.3.1.3.2. (Foreign Controlled Companies) / (Entreprises Sous Contrôle Etranger)	...	...	67 883	79 878	97 090	118 226	418 890	2 735 008
C.3.1.3.3. Branches & Agencies of Foreign Cies / Succursales et Agences d'Ent. Etrangères	...	...	56 203	103 736	95 442	103 430	98 393	122 809
C.3.1.3. Total Gross Premiums / Total des Primes Brutes	...	...	35 749 627	45 117 546	51 334 249	58 651 324	68 035 102	62 968 195
C.3.2. Ceded Premiums / C.3.2. Primes Cédées								
C.3.2.1. Domestic Companies / Entreprises Nationales	...	...	1 330 211	1 553 189	1 686 849	1 865 638	2 019 814	2 214 749
C.3.2.2. (Foreign Controlled Companies) / (Entreprises Sous Contrôle Etranger)	...	...	973	2 616	3 241	4 857	9 583	37 932
C.3.2.3. Branches & Agencies of Foreign Cies / Succursales et Agences d'Ent. Etrangères	...	...	4 511	13 040	14 700	13 700	15 873	16 313
C.3.2. Total	...	...	1 334 722	1 566 229	1 701 549	1 879 339	2 035 687	2 231 062
C.3.3. Net Written Premiums / C.3.3. Primes Nettes Emises								
C.3.3.1. Domestic Companies / Entreprises Nationales	...	...	34 363 213	43 460 621	49 551 957	56 682 256	65 916 894	60 630 637
C.3.3.2. (Foreign Controlled Companies) / (Entreprises Sous Contrôle Etranger)	...	...	66 910	77 262	93 850	113 369	409 307	2 697 076
C.3.3.3. Branches & Agencies of Foreign Cies / Succursales et Agences d'Ent. Etrangères	...	...	51 692	90 696	80 743	89 730	82 521	106 496
C.3.3. Total	...	...	34 414 905	43 551 317	49 632 700	56 771 985	65 999 415	60 737 133

Monetary Unit: million won   Unité monétaire : million de won

D. NET WRITTEN PREMIUMS IN THE REPORTING COUNTRY IN TERMS OF DOMESTIC AND FOREIGN RISKS
D. PRIMES NETTES EMISES DANS LE PAYS DECLARANT EN RISQUES NATIONAUX ET ETRANGERS

	1992	1993	1994	1995	1996	1997	1998	1999
D.1. Life / D.1. Vie								
D.1.1. Domestic Risks / D.1.1. Risques Nationaux								
D.1.1.1. Domestic Companies / D.1.1.1. Entreprises Nationales	..	..	26 781 566	33 599 003	37 093 800	41 708 633	51 283 275	46 715 433
D.1.1.2. (Foreign Controlled Companies) / D.1.1.2. (Entreprises Sous Contrôle Etranger)	..	..	66 910	77 262	93 850	113 369	409 307	2 697 047
D.1.1.3. Branches & Agencies of Foreign Cies / D.1.1.3. Succursales et Agences d'Ent. Etrangères	..	..	34 159	35 579	35 689	41 590	39 819	60 751
D.1.1. Total / D.1.1. Total des Primes Nettes Vie	..	..	26 815 725	33 634 582	37 129 489	41 750 222	51 323 094	46 776 184
D.1.2. Foreign Risks / D.1.2. Risques Etrangers								
D.1.2.1. Domestic Companies / D.1.2.1. Entreprises Nationales	..	..	876	1 890	43 164	1 370	2 162	4 361
D.1.2.2. (Foreign Controlled Companies) / D.1.2.2. (Entreprises Sous Contrôle Etranger)								29
D.1.2. Total / D.1.2. Total des Primes Nettes Vie	..	..	876	1 890	43 164	1 370	2 162	4 361
D.1.3. Total								
D.1.3.1. Domestic Companies / D.1.3.1. Entreprises Nationales	..	..	26 782 442	33 600 893	37 136 964	41 710 003	51 285 437	46 719 794
D.1.3.2. (Foreign Controlled Companies) / D.1.3.2. (Entreprises Sous Contrôle Etranger)	..	..	66 910	77 262	93 850	113 369	409 307	2 697 076
D.1.3.3. Branches & Agencies of Foreign Cies / D.1.3.3. Succursales et Agences d'Ent. Etrangères	..	..	34 159	35 579	35 689	41 590	39 819	60 751
D.1.3. Total of Life Net Premiums / D.1.3. Total des Primes Nettes Vie	..	..	26 816 601	33 636 472	37 172 653	41 751 592	51 325 256	46 780 545
D.2. Non-Life / D.2. Non-Vie								
D.2.1. Domestic Risks / D.2.1. Risques Nationaux								
D.2.1.1. Domestic Companies / D.2.1.1. Entreprises Nationales	..	..	7 508 382	9 829 164	12 377 730	14 921 240	14 554 864	13 813 502
D.2.1.3. Branches & Agencies of Foreign Cies / D.2.1.3. Succursales et Agences d'Ent. Etrangères	..	..	17 421	53 089	44 736	43 700	40 603	45 341
D.2.1. Total / D.2.1. Total des Primes Nettes Vie	..	..	7 525 803	9 882 253	12 422 466	14 964 940	14 595 467	13 858 843
D.2.2. Foreign Risks / D.2.2. Risques Etrangers								
D.2.2.1. Domestic Companies / D.2.2.1. Entreprises Nationales	..	..	72 389	30 564	37 263	51 013	76 593	97 341
D.2.2.3. Branches & Agencies of Foreign Cies / D.2.2.3. Succursales et Agences d'Ent. Etrangères	..	..	112	2 028	318	4 440	2 099	404
D.2.2. Total / D.2.2. Total des Primes Nettes Vie	..	..	72 501	32 592	37 581	55 453	78 692	97 745
D.2.3. Total								
D.2.3.1. Domestic Companies / D.2.3.1. Entreprises Nationales	..	..	7 580 771	9 859 728	12 414 993	14 972 253	14 631 457	13 910 843
D.2.3.3. Branches & Agencies of Foreign Cies / D.2.3.3. Succursales et Agences d'Ent. Etrangères	..	..	17 533	55 117	45 054	48 140	42 702	45 745
D.2.3. Total / D.2.3. Total des Primes Nettes Vie	..	..	7 598 304	9 914 845	12 460 047	15 020 393	14 674 159	13 956 588

E. BUSINESS WRITTEN ABROAD
E. OPERATIONS A L'ETRANGER

	1992	1993	1994	1995	1996	1997	1998	1999
E.2. Non-Life / E.2. Non-Vie								
E.2.1. Gross Premiums / E.2.1. Primes Brutes								
E.2.1.1. Direct Business / E.2.1.1. Assurance Directe								
E.2.1.1.1. Branches & Agencies / E.2.1.1.1. Succursales & Agences	..	..	38 497	29 588	41 699	56 555	70 001	39 424
E.2.1.1.2. Subsidiaries / E.2.1.1.2. Filliales	..	..	996	896	1 182	13 718	16 457	27 189
E.2.1.1. Total / E.2.1.1. Total	..	..	39 493	30 484	42 881	70 273	86 458	66 613
E.2.1.2. Reinsurance Accepted / E.2.1.2. Réassurance Acceptée								
E.2.1.2.1. Branches & Agencies / E.2.1.2.1. Succursales & Agences	..	..	6 223	5 588	7 357	8 235	11 874	36 471
E.2.1.2.2. Subsidiaries / E.2.1.2.2. Filliales	..	..	0	5	4	1	670	1
E.2.1.2. Total / E.2.1.2. Total	..	..	6 223	5 593	7 361	8 236	12 544	36 472
E.2.1.3. Total								
E.2.1.3.1. Branches & Agencies / E.2.1.3.1. Succursales & Agences	..	..	44 720	35 176	49 056	64 790	81 875	75 895
E.2.1.3.2. Subsidiaries / E.2.1.3.2. Filliales	..	..	996	901	1 186	13 719	17 127	27 190
E.2.1.3. Total Gross Premiums / E.2.1.3. Total des Primes Brutes	..	..	45 716	36 077	50 242	78 509	99 002	103 085
E.2.2. Ceded Premiums / E.2.2. Primes Cédées								
E.2.2.1. Branches & Agencies / E.2.2.1. Succursales & Agences	..	..	19 487	17 352	22 650	30 188	34 837	33 376
E.2.2.2. Subsidiaries / E.2.2.2. Filliales	..	..	501	358	334	10 186	10 699	14 953
E.2.2. Total / E.2.2. Total	..	..	19 988	17 710	22 984	40 374	45 536	48 329
E.2.3. Net Written Premiums / E.2.3. Primes Nettes Emises								
E.2.3.1. Branches & Agencies / E.2.3.1. Succursales & Agences	..	..	25 233	17 824	26 406	34 602	47 038	42 519
E.2.3.2. Subsidiaries / E.2.3.2. Filliales	..	..	495	543	852	3 533	6 428	12 237
E.2.3. Total / E.2.3. Total	..	..	25 728	18 367	27 258	38 135	53 466	54 756

Monetary Unit: million won

F. OUTSTANDING INVESTMENT BY DIRECT INSURANCE COMPANIES

F.1. Life

	1992	1993	1994	1995	1996	1997	1998	1999
F.1.1. Real Estate								
F.1.1.1. Domestic Companies			4 229 015	4 763 520	5 788 271	6 984 429	8 369 953	9 252 581
F.1.1.2. (Foreign Controlled Companies)							3 394	489 548
F.1.1.4. Domestic Investment			4 229 015	..	5 788 271	6 984 429	8 369 953	9 252 581
F.1.1. Total			4 229 015	..	5 788 271	6 984 429	8 369 953	9 252 581
F.1.2. Mortgage Loans								
F.1.2.1. Domestic Companies			180 555	199 709	195 860	207 600	108 965	8 117 720
F.1.2.4. Domestic Investment			180 555	..	195 860	207 600	108 965	8 117 848
F.1.2. Total			180 555	..	195 860	207 600	108 965	8 117 848
F.1.3. Shares								
F.1.3.1. Domestic Companies			7 157 134	8 492 186	9 720 103	10 278 321	8 479 346	6 818 960
F.1.3.2. (Foreign Controlled Companies)			951	1 270	2 674	3 755	17 509	783 154
F.1.3.3. Branches & Agencies of Foreign Cies				299	829	1 025	239	926
F.1.3.4. Domestic Investment			7 100 399	..	9 578 354	10 069 080	8 160 278	6 557 464
F.1.3.5. Foreign Investment			56 735	..	142 578	210 266	319 307	262 422
F.1.3. Total			7 157 134	..	9 720 932	10 279 346	8 479 585	6 819 886
F.1.4. Bonds with Fixed Revenue								
F.1.4.1. Domestic Companies			7 880 393	7 766 041	10 000 073	12 696 700	26 192 289	16 943 805
F.1.4.2. (Foreign Controlled Companies)			56 273	50 263	75 729	105 689	383 095	1 867 840
F.1.4.3. Branches & Agencies of Foreign Cies			31 903	36 536	44 525	50 928	44 713	42 335
F.1.4.4. Domestic Investment			7 885 890	..	9 976 779	12 592 556	24 976 404	15 431 790
F.1.4.5. Foreign Investment			26 406	..	67 819	155 072	1 260 598	1 554 350
F.1.4. Total			7 912 296	..	10 044 598	12 747 628	26 237 002	16 986 140
F.1.5. Loans other than Mortgage Loans								
F.1.5.1. Domestic Companies			27 364 435	30 431 824	36 388 349	43 277 907	34 955 629	27 592 671
F.1.5.2. (Foreign Controlled Companies)			7 692	9 927	11 715	14 134	96 756	1 086 943
F.1.5.3. Branches & Agencies of Foreign Cies			5 522	5 695	6 637	7 477	7 121	8 455
F.1.5.4. Domestic Investment			27 369 957	..				27 601 126
F.1.5. Total			27 369 957	..	36 394 986	43 285 384	34 962 750	27 601 126
F.1.6. Other Investments								
F.1.6.1. Domestic Companies			9 037 516	10 757 511	13 422 664	18 851 574	14 112 385	26 411 759
F.1.6.2. (Foreign Controlled Companies)			54 784	45 559	47 986	88 284	197 598	1 345 204
F.1.6.3. Branches & Agencies of Foreign Cies			23 668	15 651	9 733	31 047	27 597	34 146
F.1.6.4. Domestic Investment			9 061 184	..				25 804 123
F.1.6. Total			9 061 184	..	13 432 397	18 882 621	14 139 982	26 445 905
F.1.7. Total								
F.1.7.1. Domestic Companies			55 849 048	62 410 791	75 515 320	92 296 531	92 218 567	95 137 496
F.1.7.2. (Foreign Controlled Companies)			119 700	107 019	138 104	211 861	698 352	5 742 344
F.1.7.3. Branches & Agencies of Foreign Cies			61 093	58 181	61 724	90 477	79 670	85 990
F.1.7.4. Domestic Investment			55 827 000	..				92 764 932
F.1.7.5. Foreign Investment			83 141	..				2 458 554
F.1.7. Total of Life Investments			55 910 141	..	75 577 044	92 387 008	92 298 237	95 223 486
F.2. Non-Life								
F.2.1. Real Estate								
F.2.1.1. Domestic Companies			887 925	1 049 975	1 228 719	1 509 759	2 052 755	2 444 568
F.2.1.4. Domestic Investment			887 925	..	1 228 719	1 509 759	2 051 272	2 443 110
F.2.1.5. Foreign Investment							1 483	1 458
F.2.1. Total			887 925	..	1 228 719	1 509 759	2 052 755	2 444 568
F.2.3. Shares								
F.2.3.1. Domestic Companies			1 687 103	1 985 240	2 060 126	2 372 230	1 724 055	2 521 232
F.2.3.3. Branches & Agencies of Foreign Cies			3 010	2 815	2 616	619	2 389	5 687
F.2.3.4. Domestic Investment			1 681 900	..	2 053 513	2 369 818	1 725 897	2 496 332
F.2.3.5. Foreign Investment			8 213	..	9 229	3 031	547	30 587
F.2.3. Total			1 690 113	..	2 062 742	2 372 849	1 726 444	2 526 919

F. ENCOURS DES PLACEMENTS DES ENTREPRISES D'ASSURANCES DIRECTES

F.1. Vie

F.1.1. Immobilier
- F.1.1.1. Entreprises Nationales
- F.1.1.2. (Entreprises Sous Contrôle Etranger)
- F.1.1.4. Placement dans le Pays
- F.1.1. Total

F.1.2. Prêts Hypothécaires
- F.1.2.1. Entreprises Nationales
- F.1.2.4. Placement dans le Pays
- F.1.2. Total

F.1.3. Actions
- F.1.3.1. Entreprises Nationales
- F.1.3.2. (Entreprises Sous Contrôle Etranger)
- F.1.3.3. Succursales et Agences d'Ent. Etrangères
- F.1.3.4. Placement dans le Pays
- F.1.3.5. Placement à l' Etranger
- F.1.3. Total

F.1.4. Obligations
- F.1.4.1. Entreprises Nationales
- F.1.4.2. (Entreprises Sous Contrôle Etranger)
- F.1.4.3. Succursales et Agences d'Ent. Etrangères
- F.1.4.4. Placement dans le Pays
- F.1.4.5. Placement à l' Etranger
- F.1.4. Total

F.1.5. Prêts Autres qu'Hypothécaires
- F.1.5.1. Entreprises Nationales
- F.1.5.2. (Entreprises Sous Contrôle Etranger)
- F.1.5.3. Succursales et Agences d'Ent. Etrangères
- F.1.5.4. Placement dans le Pays
- F.1.5. Total

F.1.6. Autres Placements
- F.1.6.1. Entreprises Nationales
- F.1.6.2. (Entreprises Sous Contrôle Etranger)
- F.1.6.3. Succursales et Agences d'Ent. Etrangères
- F.1.6.4. Placement dans le Pays
- F.1.6. Total

F.1.7. Total
- F.1.7.1. Entreprises Nationales
- F.1.7.2. (Entreprises Sous Contrôle Etranger)
- F.1.7.3. Succursales et Agences d'Ent. Etrangères
- F.1.7.4. Placement dans le Pays
- F.1.7.5. Placement à l' Etranger
- F.1.7. Total des Placements Vie

F.2. Non-Vie

F.2.1. Immobilier
- F.2.1.1. Entreprises Nationales
- F.2.1.4. Placement dans le Pays
- F.2.1.5. Placement à l' Etranger
- F.2.1. Total

F.2.3. Actions
- F.2.3.1. Entreprises Nationales
- F.2.3.3. Succursales et Agences d'Ent. Etrangères
- F.2.3.4. Placement dans le Pays
- F.2.3.5. Placement à l' Etranger
- F.2.3. Total

Monetary Unit: million won — Unité monétaire : million de won

F. (continued) / G. BREAKDOWN OF NON-LIFE PREMIUMS — G. VENTILATIONS DES PRIMES NON-VIE

Label (EN)	Label (FR)	1992	1993	1994	1995	1996	1997	1998	1999
F.2.4. Bonds with Fixed Revenue	F.2.4. Obligations								
F.2.4.1. Domestic Companies	F.2.4.1. Entreprises Nationales			1 268 593	1 676 319	2 257 999	2 926 245	6 889 349	5 128 166
F.2.4.3. Branches & Agencies of Foreign Cies	F.2.4.3. Succursales et Agences d'Ent. Etrangères			14 959	17 260	16 352	16 668	18 732	25 826
F.2.4.4. Domestic Investment	F.2.4.4. Placement dans le Pays			1 254 584	..	2 263 803	2 865 304	6 307 139	4 648 946
F.2.4.5. Foreign Investment	F.2.4.5. Placement à l'Etranger			28 968	..	10 548	77 609	600 942	505 046
F.2.4. Total	F.2.4. Total			1 283 552	..	2 274 351	2 942 913	6 908 081	5 153 992
F.2.5. Loans other than Mortgage Loans	F.2.5. Prêts Autres qu'Hypothécaires								
F.2.5.1. Domestic Companies	F.2.5.1. Entreprises Nationales			1 881 036	2 589 958	3 390 687	4 533 109	3 481 600	2 281 197
F.2.5.3. Branches & Agencies of Foreign Cies	F.2.5.3. Succursales et Agences d'Ent. Etrangères			2 703	2 959	3 585	3 849	3 516	3 388
F.2.5.4. Domestic Investment	F.2.5.4. Placement dans le Pays			1 883 739	..	3 394 272	4 536 958	3 485 116	2 284 585
F.2.5. Total	F.2.5. Total			1 883 739	..	3 394 272	4 536 958	3 485 116	2 284 585
F.2.6. Other Investments	F.2.6. Autres Placements								
F.2.6.1. Domestic Companies	F.2.6.1. Entreprises Nationales			3 287 273	2 521 097	2 950 892	6 897 707	6 679 885	7 474 601
F.2.6.3. Branches & Agencies of Foreign Cies	F.2.6.3. Succursales et Agences d'Ent. Etrangères			30 305	17 996	22 586	46 282	40 584	14 288
F.2.6.4. Domestic Investment	F.2.6.4. Placement dans le Pays			3 317 578	..	..	..	..	7 280 010
F.2.6.5. Foreign Investment	F.2.6.5. Placement à l'Etranger			..	..	..	..	..	208 879
F.2.6. Total	F.2.6. Total			3 317 578	..	2 973 478	6 943 989	6 720 469	7 488 889
F.2.7. Total	F.2.7. Total								
F.2.7.1. Domestic Companies	F.2.7.1. Entreprises Nationales			9 011 930	9 822 589	11 888 423	18 239 050	20 827 644	21 091 852
F.2.7.3. Branches & Agencies of Foreign Cies	F.2.7.3. Succursales et Agences d'Ent. Etrangères			50 977	41 030	45 139	67 418	65 221	49 984
F.2.7.4. Domestic Investment	F.2.7.4. Placement dans le Pays			9 025 726	..	..	..	..	20 395 866
F.2.7.5. Foreign Investment	F.2.7.5. Placement à l'Etranger			37 181	..	..	..	..	745 970
F.2.7. Total of Non-Life Investments	F.2.7. Total des Placements Non-Vie			9 062 907	..	11 933 562	18 306 468	20 892 865	21 141 836
G. BREAKDOWN OF NON-LIFE PREMIUMS	**G. VENTILATIONS DES PRIMES NON-VIE**								
G.1. Motor vehicle	G.1. Assurance Automobile								
G.1.1. Direct Business	G.1.1. Assurances Directes								
G.1.1.1. Gross Premiums	G.1.1.1. Primes Brutes			3 861 280	4 724 527	5 958 147	6 283 431	5 430 449	5 300 580
G.1.2. Reinsurance Accepted	G.1.2. Réassurance Accepté								
G.1.2.1. Gross Premiums	G.1.2.1. Primes Brutes			50 157	56 484	66 168	88 664	205 264	189 527
G.1.3. Total	G.1.3. Total								
G.1.3.1. Gross Premiums	G.1.3.1. Primes Brutes			3 911 436	4 781 011	6 024 315	6 372 095	5 635 713	5 490 107
G.1.3.2. Ceded Premiums	G.1.3.2. Primes Cédées			58 583	64 382	75 723	97 963	238 662	222 848
G.1.3.3. Net Written Premiums	G.1.3.3. Primes Nettes Emises			3 852 853	4 716 629	5 948 591	6 274 132	5 397 051	5 267 259
G.2. Marine, Aviation	G.2. Marine, Aviation								
G.2.1. Direct Business	G.2.1. Assurances Directes								
G.2.1.1. Gross Premiums	G.2.1.1. Primes Brutes			186 285	233 001	210 750	191 549	230 877	282 256
G.2.2. Reinsurance Accepted	G.2.2. Réassurance Accepté								
G.2.2.1. Gross Premiums	G.2.2.1. Primes Brutes			96 903	105 450	88 731	63 630	73 689	71 904
G.2.3. Total	G.2.3. Total								
G.2.3.1. Gross Premiums	G.2.3.1. Primes Brutes			283 188	338 451	299 481	255 179	304 566	354 160
G.2.3.2. Ceded Premiums	G.2.3.2. Primes Cédées			223 761	264 859	225 871	192 518	234 075	179 633
G.2.3.3. Net Written Premiums	G.2.3.3. Primes Nettes Emises			59 426	73 592	73 610	62 661	70 491	174 527
G.3. Freight	G.3. Fret								
G.3.1. Direct Business	G.3.1. Assurances Directes								
G.3.1.1. Gross Premiums	G.3.1.1. Primes Brutes			225 646	234 608	212 648	183 290	165 949	160 640
G.3.2. Reinsurance Accepted	G.3.2. Réassurance Accepté								
G.3.2.1. Gross Premiums	G.3.2.1. Primes Brutes			44 351	45 492	41 504	33 385	32 218	30 537
G.3.3. Total	G.3.3. Total								
G.3.3.1. Gross Premiums	G.3.3.1. Primes Brutes			269 997	280 100	254 153	216 675	198 167	191 177
G.3.3.2. Ceded Premiums	G.3.3.2. Primes Cédées			56 061	59 395	53 694	45 381	43 408	42 988
G.3.3.3. Net Written Premiums	G.3.3.3. Primes Nettes Emises			213 936	220 705	200 458	171 295	154 759	148 189
G.4. Fire, Property Damages	G.4. Incendie, Dommages aux Biens								
G.4.1. Direct Business	G.4.1. Assurances Directes								
G.4.1.1. Gross Premiums	G.4.1.1. Primes Brutes			620 938	424 546	399 130	519 873	460 386	429 998
G.4.2. Reinsurance Accepted	G.4.2. Réassurance Accepté								
G.4.2.1. Gross Premiums	G.4.2.1. Primes Brutes			347 254	258 201	240 925	467 067	424 726	478 507
G.4.3. Total	G.4.3. Total								
G.4.3.1. Gross Premiums	G.4.3.1. Primes Brutes			968 191	682 747	640 055	986 940	885 112	908 505
G.4.3.2. Ceded Premiums	G.4.3.2. Primes Cédées			539 647	357 401	326 032	478 725	440 364	412 156

Monetary Unit: million won

Unité monétaire : million de won

	1992	1993	1994	1995	1996	1997	1998	1999	
G.4.3.3. Net Written Premiums			428 544	325 346	314 023	508 215	444 748	496 349	G.4.3.3. Primes Nettes Emises
G.5. Pecuniary Losses									G.5. Pertes Pécunières
G.5.1. Direct Business									G.5.1. Assurances Directes
G.5.1.1. Gross Premiums			709 268	680 005	667 306	841 639	1 187 571	616 457	G.5.1.1. Primes Brutes
G.5.2. Reinsurance Accepted									G.5.2. Réassurance Acceptée
G.5.2.1. Gross Premiums			220 051	204 973	192 520	141 662	78 097	117 837	G.5.2.1. Primes Brutes
G.5.3. Total									G.5.3. Total
G.5.3.1. Gross Premiums			929 318	884 978	859 826	983 301	1 265 668	734 294	G.5.3.1. Primes Brutes
G.5.3.2. Ceded Premiums			234 345	218 586	208 468	165 821	112 615	151 376	G.5.3.2. Primes Cédées
G.5.3.3. Net Written Premiums			694 973	666 392	651 359	817 480	1 153 053	582 918	G.5.3.3. Primes Nettes Emises
G.6. General Liability									G.6. Responsabilité Générale
G.6.1. Direct Business									G.6.1. Assurances Directes
G.6.1.1. Gross Premiums			58 616	178 276	187 963	199 815	215 820	251 437	G.6.1.1. Primes Brutes
G.6.2. Reinsurance Accepted									G.6.2. Réassurance Acceptée
G.6.2.1. Gross Premiums			33 773	73 294	82 926	89 769	116 982	140 667	G.6.2.1. Primes Brutes
G.6.3. Total									G.6.3. Total
G.6.3.1. Gross Premiums			92 389	251 570	270 889	289 584	332 802	392 104	G.6.3.1. Primes Brutes
G.6.3.2. Ceded Premiums			48 934	92 931	100 576	112 008	159 234	193 781	G.6.3.2. Primes Cédées
G.6.3.3. Net Written Premiums			43 455	158 639	170 312	177 576	173 568	198 323	G.6.3.3. Primes Nettes Emises
G.7. Accident, Health									G.7. Accident, Santé
G.7.1. Direct Business									G.7.1. Assurances Directes
G.7.1.1. Gross Premiums			1 348 959	2 082 951	2 869 366	3 823 836	4 976 877	4 546 675	G.7.1.1. Primes Brutes
G.7.2. Reinsurance Accepted									G.7.2. Réassurance Acceptée
G.7.2.1. Gross Premiums			42 900	47 818	63 859	230 928	249 238	262 214	G.7.2.1. Primes Brutes
G.7.3. Total									G.7.3. Total
G.7.3.1. Gross Premiums			1 391 859	2 130 769	2 933 225	4 054 764	5 226 115	4 808 889	G.7.3.1. Primes Brutes
G.7.3.2. Ceded Premiums			46 296	51 888	71 393	439 706	518 299	538 881	G.7.3.2. Primes Cédées
G.7.3.3. Net Written Premiums			1 345 563	2 078 881	2 861 832	3 615 058	4 707 816	4 270 008	G.7.3.3. Primes Nettes Emises
G.8. Others									G.8. Autres
G.8.1. Direct Business									G.8.1. Assurances Directes
G.8.1.1. Gross Premiums			885 420	1 736 275	2 353 455	3 378 513	2 554 591	2 894 792	G.8.1.1. Primes Brutes
G.8.2. Reinsurance Accepted									G.8.2. Réassurance Acceptée
G.8.2.1. Gross Premiums			92 481	303 713	411 646	153 549	157 536	203 174	G.8.2.1. Primes Brutes
G.8.3. Total									G.8.3. Total
G.8.3.1. Gross Premiums			977 901	2 039 988	2 765 102	3 532 062	2 712 127	3 097 966	G.8.3.1. Primes Brutes
G.8.3.2. Ceded Premiums			52 144	365 327	525 240	138 085	139 454	278 952	G.8.3.2. Primes Cédées
G.8.3.3. Net Written Premiums			925 757	1 674 661	2 239 862	3 393 976	2 572 673	2 819 014	G.8.3.3. Primes Nettes Emises
G.9. Treaty Reinsurance									G.9. Réassurance Obligatoire
G.9.2. Reinsurance Accepted									G.9.2. Réassurance Acceptée
G.9.2.1. Gross Premiums			33 899	..	0	0	..	..	G.9.2.1. Primes Brutes
G.9.3. Total									G.9.3. Total
G.9.3.1. Gross Premiums			33 899	..	0	0	..	..	G.9.3.1. Primes Brutes
G.9.3.2. Ceded Premiums			103	..	0	0	..	..	G.9.3.2. Primes Cédées
G.9.3.3. Net Written Premiums			33 796	..	0	0	..	..	G.9.3.3. Primes Nettes Emises
G.10. Total									G.10. Total
G.10.1. Direct Business									G.10.1. Assurances Directes
G.10.1.1. Gross Premiums			7 896 410	10 294 189	12 858 765	15 421 946	15 222 520	14 482 835	G.10.1.1. Primes Brutes
G.10.2. Reinsurance Accepted									G.10.2. Réassurance Acceptée
G.10.2.1. Gross Premiums			961 768	1 095 425	1 188 279	1 268 654	1 337 750	1 494 367	G.10.2.1. Primes Brutes
G.10.3. Total									G.10.3. Total
G.10.3.1. Gross Premiums			8 858 178	11 389 614	14 047 046	16 690 600	16 560 270	15 977 202	G.10.3.1. Primes Brutes
G.10.3.2. Ceded Premiums			1 259 874	1 474 769	1 586 997	1 670 207	1 886 111	2 020 614	G.10.3.2. Primes Cédées
G.10.3.3. Net Written Premiums			7 598 304	9 914 845	12 460 047	15 020 393	14 674 159	13 956 588	G.10.3.3. Primes Nettes Emises
H. GROSS CLAIMS PAYMENTS									**H. PAIEMENTS BRUTS DES SINISTRES**
H.1. Life									**H.1. Vie**
H.1.1. Domestic Companies					23 772 421	30 102 052	52 252 419	40 230 160	H.1.1. Entreprises Nationales
H.1.2. (Foreign Controlled Companies)					41 623	52 216	404 401	2 494 362	H.1.2. (Entreprises Sous Contrôle Etranger)
H.1.3. Branches & Agencies of Foreign Cies					20 450	22 799	41 495	20 485	H.1.3. Succursales et Agences d'Ent. Etrangères

KOREA

Monetary Unit: million won · Unité monétaire : million de won

	1992	1993	1994	1995	1996	1997	1998	1999	
H.1. Total					23 792 871	30 124 851	52 293 913	40 250 645	H.1. Total
H.2. Non-Life									**H.2. Non-Vie**
H.2.1. Domestic Companies					6 226 401	7 122 791	7 651 091	9 165 453	H.2.1. Entreprises Nationales
H.2.3. Branches & Agencies of Foreign Cies					14 680	21 868	17 135	16 816	H.2.3. Succursales et Agences d'Ent. Etrangères
H.2. Total					6 241 081	7 144 659	7 668 226	9 182 269	H.2. Total
I. GROSS OPERATING EXPENSES									**I. DEPENSES BRUTES D'EXPLOITATION**
I.1. Life									**I.1. Vie**
I.1.1. Domestic Companies					6 822 858	7 589 381	6 777 946	4 544 780	I.1.1. Entreprises Nationales
I.1.2. (Foreign Controlled Companies)					35 583	58 374	132 540	509 215	I.1.2. (Entreprises Sous Contrôle Etranger)
I.1.3. Branches & Agencies of Foreign Cies					18 213	23 880	26 261	27 439	I.1.3. Succursales et Agences d'Ent. Etrangères
I.1. Total					6 841 071	7 613 261	6 804 207	4 572 219	I.1. Total des Primes Nettes Vie
I.2. Non-Life									**I.2. Non-Vie**
I.2.1. Domestic Companies					2 637 812	3 121 658	2 986 498	2 813 982	I.2.1. Entreprises Nationales
I.2.3. Branches & Agencies of Foreign Cies					13 380	15 950	16 379	15 931	I.2.3. Succursales et Agences d'Ent. Etrangères
I.2. Total					2 651 192	3 137 608	3 002 877	2 829 913	I.2. Total
J. COMMISSIONS									**J. COMMISSIONS**
J.1. Life									**J.1. Vie**
J.1.1. Direct Business									J.1.1. Assurance directe
J.1.1.1. Domestic Companies					3 811 943	4 635 956	3 391 358	3 541 124	J.1.1.1. Entreprises Nationales
J.1.1.2. (Foreign Controlled Companies)					19 322	34 402	62 085	334 384	J.1.1.2. (Entreprises Sous Contrôle Etranger)
J.1.1.3. Branches & Agencies of Foreign Cies					5 824	12 462	10 550	12 708	J.1.1.3. Succursales et Agences d'Ent. Etrangères
J.1.1. Total					3 817 767	4 648 418	3 401 908	3 553 832	J.1.1. Total
J.1.2. Reinsurance Accepted									J.1.2. Réassurances acceptées
J.1.2.1. Domestic Companies					144	12 376	124	1 218	J.1.2.1. Entreprises Nationales
J.1.2.3. Branches & Agencies of Foreign Cies					0	1	0	1	J.1.2.3. Succursales et Agences d'Ent. Etrangères
J.1.2. Total					144	12 377	124	1 219	J.1.2. Total
J.1.3. Total									J.1.3. Total
J.1.3.1. Domestic Companies					3 812 088	4 648 332	3 391 482	3 542 342	J.1.3.1. Entreprises Nationales
J.1.3.2. (Foreign Controlled Companies)					19 322	34 402	62 085	334 407	J.1.3.2. (Entreprises Sous Contrôle Etranger)
J.1.3.3. Branches & Agencies of Foreign Cies					5 824	12 463	10 550	334 407	J.1.3.3. Succursales et Agences d'Ent. Etrangères
J.1.3. Total of Life Net Premiums					3 817 911	4 660 795	3 402 032	3 555 051	J.1.3. Total
J.2. Non-Life									**J.2. Non-Vie**
J.2.1. Direct Business									J.2.1. Assurance directe
J.2.1.1. Domestic Companies					1 323 980	1 323 980	1 623 554	667 067	J.2.1.1. Entreprises Nationales
J.2.1.3. Branches & Agencies of Foreign Cies					10 022	10 022	9 077	814	J.2.1.3. Succursales et Agences d'Ent. Etrangères
J.2.1. Total					1 334 002	1 334 002	1 632 631	667 881	J.2.1. Total des Primes Nettes Vie
J.2.2. Reinsurance Accepted									J.2.2. Réassurances acceptées
J.2.2.1. Domestic Companies					271 113	271 113	283 252	334 748	J.2.2.1. Entreprises Nationales
J.2.2.3. Branches & Agencies of Foreign Cies					4 885	4 885	4 206	3 267	J.2.2.3. Succursales et Agences d'Ent. Etrangères
J.2.2. Total					275 998	275 998	287 458	338 015	J.2.2. Total
J.2.3. Total									J.2.3. Total
J.2.3.1. Domestic Companies					1 595 093	1 595 093	1 906 806	1 001 815	J.2.3.1. Entreprises Nationales
J.2.3.3. Branches & Agencies of Foreign Cies					14 907	14 907	13 283	4 081	J.2.3.3. Succursales et Agences d'Ent. Etrangères
J.2.3. Total					1 610 000	1 610 000	1 920 089	1 005 896	J.2.3. Total

Monetary Unit: million Luxembourg francs

Unité monétaire : million de Francs luxembourgeois

	1992	1993	1994	1995	1996	1997	1998	1999		Code FR
A. NUMBER OF COMPANIES IN THE REPORTING COUNTRY										**A. NOMBRE D'ENTREPRISES DANS LE PAYS DECLARANT**
A.1. Life										**A.1. Vie**
A.1.1. Domestic Companies	27	30	34	39	50	51	54	57	57	A.1.1. Entreprises Nationales
A.1.2. (Foreign Controlled Companies)	..	..	..	..	38	37	41	43	43	A.1.2. (Entreprises Sous Contrôle Etranger)
A.1.3. Branches & Agencies of Foreign Cies	7	6	5	6	4	4	4	3	3	A.1.3. Succursales et Agences d'Ent. Etrangères
A.1. Total	34	36	39	45	54	55	58	60	60	A.1. Ensemble des Entreprises
A.2. Non-Life										**A.2. Non-Vie**
A.2.1. Domestic Companies	16	20	20	21	21	21	21	21	21	A.2.1. Entreprises Nationales
A.2.2. (Foreign Controlled Companies)	..	..	..	2	15	13	10	11	11	A.2.2. (Entreprises Sous Contrôle Etranger)
A.2.3. Branches & Agencies of Foreign Cies	16	15	14	12	12	11	10	9	9	A.2.3. Succursales et Agences d'Ent. Etrangères
A.2. Total	32	35	34	33	33	32	31	30	30	A.2. Ensemble des Entreprises
A.3. Composite										**A.3. Mixte**
A.3.1. Domestic Companies	1	1	1	1	0	0	0	0	0	A.3.1. Entreprises Nationales
A.3.3. Branches & Agencies of Foreign Cies	1	1	2	2	3	4	4	4	4	A.3.3. Succursales et Agences d'Ent. Etrangères
A.3. All Companies	2	2	3	3	3	4	4	4	4	A.3. Ensemble des Entreprises
A.4. Reinsurance										**A.4. Réassurance**
A.4.1. Domestic Companies	173	184	213	234	244	255	255	257	257	A.4.1. Entreprises Nationales
A.4.2. (Foreign Controlled Companies)	..	..	..	206	0	217	230	231	231	A.4.2. (Entreprises Sous Contrôle Etranger)
A.4. All Companies	173	184	213	234	244	255	255	257	257	A.4. Ensemble des Entreprises
A.5. Total										**A.5. Total**
A.5.1. Domestic Companies	217	235	268	295	315	327	330	335	335	A.5.1. Entreprises Nationales
A.5.2. (Foreign Controlled Companies)	..	..	..	210	53	267	281	285	285	A.5.2. (Entreprises Sous Contrôle Etranger)
A.5.3. Branches & Agencies of Foreign Cies	24	22	21	20	19	19	18	16	16	A.5.3. Succursales et Agences d'Ent. Etrangères
A.5. All Insurance Companies	241	257	289	315	334	346	348	351	351	A.5. Ensemble des Entreprises d'Assurances
B. NUMBER OF EMPLOYEES										**B. NOMBRE D'EMPLOYES**
B.1. Insurance Companies	1 190	1 208	1 277	1 304	1 592	1 720	1 760	1 923	1 923	B.1. Entreprises d'Assurances
B.2. Intermediaries	6 000	6 200	6 620	6 800	6 985	7 157	7 175	7 441	7 441	B.2. Intermediaires
B. Total	7 190	7 408	7 897	8 104	8 577	8 877	8 935	9 364	9 364	B. Total
C. BUSINESS WRITTEN IN THE REPORTING COUNTRY										**C. OPERATIONS CONCLUES DANS LE PAYS DECLARANT**
C.1. Life										**C.1. Vie**
C.1.1. Gross Premiums										**C.1.1. Primes Brutes**
C.1.1.1. Direct Business										C.1.1.1. Assurances Directes
C.1.1.1.1. Domestic Companies	3 971	5 259	36 791	105 136	93 123	150 874	164 738	177 332	177 332	C.1.1.1.1. Entreprises Nationales
C.1.1.1.2. (Foreign Controlled Companies)	..	0	..	..	85 383	124 594	138 617	121 478	121 478	C.1.1.1.2. (Entreprises Sous Contrôle Etranger)
C.1.1.1.3. Branches & Agencies of Foreign Cies	1 831	564	1 559	2 430	2 182	4 292	7 683	15 067	15 067	C.1.1.1.3. Succursales et Agences d'Ent. Etrangères
C.1.1.1. Total	5 803	5 823	38 350	107 566	95 305	155 166	172 420	192 399	192 399	C.1.1.1. Total
C.1.1.2. Reinsurance Accepted										C.1.1.2. Réassurance Acceptée
C.1.1.2.1. Domestic Companies	..	..	132	67	195	213	20	4	4	C.1.1.2.1. Entreprises Nationales
C.1.1.2.2. (Foreign Controlled Companies)	..	0	..	..	6	5	5	0	0	C.1.1.2.2. (Entreprises Sous Contrôle Etranger)
C.1.1.2.3. Branches & Agencies of Foreign Cies	..	..	0	0	0	99	25	2	2	C.1.1.2.3. Succursales et Agences d'Ent. Etrangères
C.1.1.2. Total	..	..	132	67	195	312	46	6	6	C.1.1.2. Total
C.1.1.3. Total										C.1.1.3. Total
C.1.1.3.1. Domestic Companies	..	..	36 923	105 203	93 318	151 087	164 758	177 336	177 336	C.1.1.3.1. Entreprises Nationales
C.1.1.3.2. (Foreign Controlled Companies)	..	0	..	..	85 389	124 599	138 622	121 478	121 478	C.1.1.3.2. (Entreprises Sous Contrôle Etranger)
C.1.1.3.3. Branches & Agencies of Foreign Cies			1 559	2 430	2 182	4 391	7 708	15 069	15 069	C.1.1.3.3. Succursales et Agences d'Ent. Etrangères
C.1.1.3. Total Gross Premiums			38 482	107 633	95 500	155 478	172 466	192 405	192 405	C.1.1.3. Total des Primes Brutes
C.1.2. Ceded Premiums										**C.1.2. Primes Cédées**
C.1.2.1. Domestic Companies	..	..	1 713	1 923	11 441	9 054	4 308	2 927	2 927	C.1.2.1. Entreprises Nationales
C.1.2.2. (Foreign Controlled Companies)	..	0	..	..	10 879	6 602	4 088	2 103	2 103	C.1.2.2. (Entreprises Sous Contrôle Etranger)
C.1.2.3. Branches & Agencies of Foreign Cies	..	..	18	18	18	17	78	4	4	C.1.2.3. Succursales et Agences d'Ent. Etrangères
C.1.2. Total	..	..	1 731	1 941	11 459	9 071	4 385	2 931	2 931	C.1.2. Total

Monetary Unit: million Luxembourg francs

Unité monétaire : million de Francs luxembourgeois

	1992	1993	1994	1995	1996	1997	1998	1999
C.1.3. Net Written Premiums / C.1.3. Primes Nettes Emises								
C.1.3.1. Domestic Companies / C.1.3.1. Entreprises Nationales	..	..	35 210	103 280	81 877	142 033	160 450	174 409
C.1.3.2. (Foreign Controlled Companies) / C.1.3.2. (Entreprises Sous Contrôle Etranger)	..	0	..	..	74 510	117 997	134 534	119 375
C.1.3.3. Branches & Agencies of Foreign Cies / C.1.3.3. Succursales et Agences d'Ent. Etrangères	..	..	1 541	2 412	2 164	4 374	7 630	15 065
C.1.3. Total / C.1.3. Total	..	..	36 751	105 692	84 041	146 407	168 081	189 474
C.2. Non-Life / C.2. Non-Vie								
C.2.1. Gross premiums / C.2.1. Primes Brutes								
C.2.1.1. Direct Business / C.2.1.1. Assurances Directes								
C.2.1.1.1. Domestic Companies / C.2.1.1.1. Entreprises Nationales	9 543	9 899	11 653	12 553	14 252	14 050	23 914	25 786
C.2.1.1.2. (Foreign Controlled Companies) / C.2.1.1.2. (Entreprises Sous Contrôle Etranger)	..	0	..	..	3 430	2 782	3 609	3 993
C.2.1.1.3. Branches & Agencies of Foreign Cies / C.2.1.1.3. Succursales et Agences d'Ent. Etrangères	2 713	2 502	2 703	2 380	2 678	2 464	3 267	2 781
C.2.1.1. Total / C.2.1.1. Total	12 256	12 402	14 356	14 933	16 930	16 514	27 181	28 567
C.2.1.2. Reinsurance Accepted / C.2.1.2. Réassurance Acceptée								
C.2.1.2.1. Domestic Companies / C.2.1.2.1. Entreprises Nationales	..	..	95	28	36	34	72	46
C.2.1.2.2. (Foreign Controlled Companies) / C.2.1.2.2. (Entreprises Sous Contrôle Etranger)	..	0	..	..	5	..	8	5
C.2.1.2.3. Branches & Agencies of Foreign Cies / C.2.1.2.3. Succursales et Agences d'Ent. Etrangères	..	..	0	0	0	9	109	92
C.2.1.2. Total / C.2.1.2. Total	..	..	95	28	36	43	180	138
C.2.1.3. Total								
C.2.1.3.1. Domestic Companies / C.2.1.3.1. Entreprises Nationales	..	..	11 748	12 582	14 288	14 084	23 985	25 832
C.2.1.3.2. (Foreign Controlled Companies) / C.2.1.3.2. (Entreprises Sous Contrôle Etranger)	..	0	..	..	3 435	2 782	3 617	3 998
C.2.1.3.3. Branches & Agencies of Foreign Cies / C.2.1.3.3. Succursales et Agences d'Ent. Etrangères	..	..	2 703	2 380	2 678	2 473	3 375	2 873
C.2.1.3. Total Gross Premiums / C.2.1.3. Total des Primes Brutes	..	..	14 451	14 962	16 966	16 557	27 361	28 705
C.2.2. Ceded Premiums / C.2.2. Primes Cédées								
C.2.2.1. Domestic Companies / C.2.2.1. Entreprises Nationales	..	..	4 379	4 070	3 499	3 513	5 866	6 012
C.2.2.2. (Foreign Controlled Companies) / C.2.2.2. (Entreprises Sous Contrôle Etranger)	..	0	..	..	1 064	804	673	880
C.2.2.3. Branches & Agencies of Foreign Cies / C.2.2.3. Succursales et Agences d'Ent. Etrangères	..	..	1 017	600	758	898	1 074	1 064
C.2.2. Total / C.2.2. Total	..	..	5 396	4 670	4 257	4 411	6 940	7 076
C.2.3. Net Written Premiums / C.2.3. Primes Nettes Emises								
C.2.3.1. Domestic Companies / C.2.3.1. Entreprises Nationales	..	..	7 369	8 512	10 789	10 571	18 119	19 820
C.2.3.2. (Foreign Controlled Companies) / C.2.3.2. (Entreprises Sous Contrôle Etranger)	..	0	..	..	2 371	1 978	2 944	3 118
C.2.3.3. Branches & Agencies of Foreign Cies / C.2.3.3. Succursales et Agences d'Ent. Etrangères	..	..	1 686	1 780	1 920	1 575	2 301	1 809
C.2.3. Total / C.2.3. Total	..	..	9 055	10 292	12 709	12 146	20 420	21 629
C.3. Total								
C.3.1. Gross Premiums / C.3.1. Primes Brutes								
C.3.1.1. Direct Business / C.3.1.1. Assurances Directes								
C.3.1.1.1. Domestic Companies / C.3.1.1.1. Entreprises Nationales	13 514	15 158	48 444	117 689	107 375	164 924	188 652	203 118
C.3.1.1.2. (Foreign Controlled Companies) / C.3.1.1.2. (Entreprises Sous Contrôle Etranger)	..	0	..	..	88 813	127 376	142 226	125 471
C.3.1.1.3. Branches & Agencies of Foreign Cies / C.3.1.1.3. Succursales et Agences d'Ent. Etrangères	4 544	3 066	4 262	4 810	4 860	6 756	10 949	17 848
C.3.1.1. Total / C.3.1.1. Total	18 059	18 225	52 706	122 499	112 235	171 680	199 601	220 966
C.3.1.2. Reinsurance Accepted / C.3.1.2. Réassurance Acceptée								
C.3.1.2.1. Domestic Companies / C.3.1.2.1. Entreprises Nationales	..	..	227	95	231	247	92	50
C.3.1.2.2. (Foreign Controlled Companies) / C.3.1.2.2. (Entreprises Sous Contrôle Etranger)	..	0	..	..	11	..	12	5
C.3.1.2.3. Branches & Agencies of Foreign Cies / C.3.1.2.3. Succursales et Agences d'Ent. Etrangères	..	..	0	0	0	108	134	94
C.3.1.2. Total / C.3.1.2. Total	..	..	227	95	231	355	226	144
C.3.1.3. Total								
C.3.1.3.1. Domestic Companies / C.3.1.3.1. Entreprises Nationales	..	..	48 671	117 785	107 606	165 171	188 743	203 168
C.3.1.3.2. (Foreign Controlled Companies) / C.3.1.3.2. (Entreprises Sous Contrôle Etranger)	..	0	..	..	88 824	127 381	142 238	125 476
C.3.1.3.3. Branches & Agencies of Foreign Cies / C.3.1.3.3. Succursales et Agences d'Ent. Etrangères	..	..	4 262	4 810	4 860	6 864	11 083	17 942
C.3.1.3. Total Gross Premiums / C.3.1.3. Total des Primes Brutes	..	..	52 933	122 595	112 466	172 035	199 827	221 110
C.3.2. Ceded Premiums / C.3.2. Primes Cédées								
C.3.2.1. Domestic Companies / C.3.2.1. Entreprises Nationales	..	..	6 092	5 993	14 940	12 567	10 174	8 939
C.3.2.2. (Foreign Controlled Companies) / C.3.2.2. (Entreprises Sous Contrôle Etranger)	..	0	..	..	11 943	7 406	4 761	2 984
C.3.2.3. Branches & Agencies of Foreign Cies / C.3.2.3. Succursales et Agences d'Ent. Etrangères	..	..	1 035	618	776	915	1 152	1 068
C.3.2. Total / C.3.2. Total	..	..	7 127	6 611	15 716	13 482	11 326	10 007

Monetary Unit: million Luxembourg francs

	1992	1993	1994	1995	1996	1997	1998	1999
C.3.3. Net Written Premiums / Primes Nettes Emises								
C.3.3.1. Domestic Companies / Entreprises Nationales	::	::	42 579	111 792	92 666	152 604	178 570	194 229
C.3.3.2. (Foreign Controlled Companies) / (Entreprises Sous Contrôle Etranger)	::	0	::		76 881	119 975	137 477	122 493
C.3.3.3. Branches & Agencies of Foreign Cies / Succursales et Agences d'Ent. Etrangères	::	::	3 227	4 192	4 084	5 949	9 932	16 874
C.3.3. Total	::	::	45 806	115 984	96 750	158 553	188 501	211 103
E. BUSINESS WRITTEN ABROAD / E. OPERATIONS A L'ETRANGER								
E.1. Life / E.1. Vie								
E.1.1. Gross Premiums / E.1.1. Primes Brutes								
E.1.1.1. Direct Business / E.1.1.1. Assurance Directe								
E.1.1.1.1. Branches & Agencies / E.1.1.1.1. Succursales & Agences							4 029	11 788
E.1.1.1. Total / E.1.1.1. Total							4 029	11 788
E.1.1.3. Total / E.1.1.3. Total								
E.1.1.3.1. Branches & Agencies / E.1.1.3.1. Succursales & Agences							4 029	11 788
E.1.1.3. Total Gross Premiums / E.1.1.3. Total des Primes Brutes							4 029	11 788
E.1.2. Ceded Premiums / E.1.2. Primes Cédées								
E.1.2.1. Branches & Agencies / E.1.2.1. Succursales & Agences							105	- 2
E.1.2. Total / E.1.2. Total							105	- 2
E.1.3. Net Written Premiums / E.1.3. Primes Nettes Emises								
E.1.3.1. Branches & Agencies / E.1.3.1. Succursales & Agences							3 924	11 790
E.1.3. Total / E.1.3. Total							3 924	11 790
E.2. Non-Life / E.2. Non-Vie								
E.2.1. Gross Premiums / E.2.1. Primes Brutes								
E.2.1.1. Direct Business / E.2.1.1. Assurance Directe								
E.2.1.1.1. Branches & Agencies / E.2.1.1.1. Succursales & Agences							316	271
E.2.1.1. Total / E.2.1.1. Total							316	271
E.2.1.3. Total / E.2.1.3. Total								
E.2.1.3.1. Branches & Agencies / E.2.1.3.1. Succursales & Agences							316	271
E.2.1.3. Total Gross Premiums / E.2.1.3. Total des Primes Brutes							316	271
E.2.2. Ceded Premiums / E.2.2. Primes Cédées								
E.2.2.1. Branches & Agencies / E.2.2.1. Succursales & Agences							77	16
E.2.2. Total / E.2.2. Total							77	16
E.2.3. Net Written Premiums / E.2.3. Primes Nettes Emises								
E.2.3.1. Branches & Agencies / E.2.3.1. Succursales & Agences							239	255
E.2.3. Total / E.2.3. Total							239	255
F. OUTSTANDING INVESTMENT BY DIRECT INSURANCE COMPANIES / F. ENCOURS DES PLACEMENTS DES ENTREPRISES D'ASSURANCES DIRECTES								
F.1. Life / F.1. Vie								
F.1.1. Real Estate / F.1.1. Immobilier								
F.1.1.1. Domestic Companies / F.1.1.1. Entreprises Nationales	::	::	941	1 109	781	1 316	882	870
F.1.1.2. (Foreign Controlled Companies) / F.1.1.2. (Entreprises Sous Contrôle Etranger)	::	::	::	::	328	845	::	::
F.1.1.3. Branches & Agencies of Foreign Cies / F.1.1.3. Succursales et Agences d'Ent. Etrangères	::	::	::	::	::	::	::	::
F.1.1.4. Domestic Investment / F.1.1.4. Placement dans le Pays	905	1 020	::	1 109	::	::	::	::
F.1.1. Total / F.1.1. Total				1 109	781		882	870
F.1.2. Mortgage Loans / F.1.2. Prêts Hypothécaires								
F.1.2.1. Domestic Companies / F.1.2.1. Entreprises Nationales	::	::	::	8	15	14	0	0
F.1.2.2. (Foreign Controlled Companies) / F.1.2.2. (Entreprises Sous Contrôle Etranger)	::	::	::	8	15	14	::	::
F.1.2.4. Domestic Investment / F.1.2.4. Placement dans le Pays	::	::	::	::	::	::	::	::
F.1.2. Total / F.1.2. Total				8	15		0	0

Monetary Unit: million Luxembourg francs

Unité monétaire : million de Francs luxembourgeois

Label (EN)	1992	1993	1994	1995	1996	1997	1998	1999	Label (FR)
F.1.3. Shares									F.1.3. Actions
F.1.3.1. Domestic Companies	:	:	2 411	26 101	4 670	7 346	150 765	289 053	F.1.3.1. Entreprises Nationales
F.1.3.2. (Foreign Controlled Companies)	:	:	:	:	2 099	3 996	:	:	F.1.3.2. (Entreprises Sous Contrôle Etranger)
F.1.3.3. Branches & Agencies of Foreign Cies	:	:	:	:	:	:	:	:	F.1.3.3. Succursales et Agences d'Ent. Etrangères
F.1.3.4. Domestic Investment	:	:	:	1 930	:	:	:	:	F.1.3.4. Placement dans le Pays
F.1.3.5. Foreign Investment	4 160	:	:	24 171	:	:	:	:	F.1.3.5. Placement à l' Etranger
F.1.3. Total	4 160	3 010	:	26 101	4 670	:	150 765	289 053	F.1.3. Total
F.1.4. Bonds with Fixed Revenue									F.1.4. Obligations
F.1.4.1. Domestic Companies	:	:	12 762	141 374	181 035	243 575	378 884	413 462	F.1.4.1. Entreprises Nationales
F.1.4.2. (Foreign Controlled Companies)	:	:	:	:	164 175	212 309	:	:	F.1.4.2. (Entreprises Sous Contrôle Etranger)
F.1.4.3. Branches & Agencies of Foreign Cies	:	:	:	:	:	:	:	:	F.1.4.3. Succursales et Agences d'Ent. Etrangères
F.1.4.4. Domestic Investment	:	:	:	:	:	:	:	:	F.1.4.4. Placement dans le Pays
F.1.4.5. Foreign Investment	:	:	:	:	:	:	:	:	F.1.4.5. Placement à l' Etranger
F.1.4. Total	19 982	21 766	:	141 374	181 035	:	378 884	413 462	F.1.4. Total
F.1.5. Loans other than Mortgage Loans									F.1.5. Prêts Autres qu'Hypothécaires
F.1.5.1. Domestic Companies	:	:	:	0	695	685	774	883	F.1.5.1. Entreprises Nationales
F.1.5.2. (Foreign Controlled Companies)	:	:	:	:	533	550	:	:	F.1.5.2. (Entreprises Sous Contrôle Etranger)
F.1.5. Total	:	:	:	0	695	:	774	883	F.1.5. Total
F.1.6. Other Investments									F.1.6. Autres Placements
F.1.6.1. Domestic Companies	:	:	4 041	24 882	15 444	19 272	58 996	64 789	F.1.6.1. Entreprises Nationales
F.1.6.2. (Foreign Controlled Companies)	:	:	:	:	12 694	1 972	:	:	F.1.6.2. (Entreprises Sous Contrôle Etranger)
F.1.6.3. Branches & Agencies of Foreign Cies	:	:	:	:	:	:	:	:	F.1.6.3. Succursales et Agences d'Ent. Etrangères
F.1.6. Total	3 806	3 949	:	24 882	15 444	:	58 996	64 789	F.1.6. Total
F.1.7. Total									F.1.7. Total
F.1.7.1. Domestic Companies	:	:	20 155	193 474	202 640	272 208	590 301	769 057	F.1.7.1. Entreprises Nationales
F.1.7.2. (Foreign Controlled Companies)	:	:	:	:	179 844	219 686	:	:	F.1.7.2. (Entreprises Sous Contrôle Etranger)
F.1.7.3. Branches & Agencies of Foreign Cies	:	:	:	:	:	:	:	:	F.1.7.3. Succursales et Agences d'Ent. Etrangères
F.1.7. Total of Life Investments	28 855	29 745	:	193 474	202 640	:	590 301	769 057	F.1.7. Total des Placements Vie
F.2. Non-Life									**F.2. Non-Vie**
F.2.1. Real Estate									F.2.1. Immobilier
F.2.1.1. Domestic Companies	:	:	1 411	946	831	1 982	1 816	1 967	F.2.1.1. Entreprises Nationales
F.2.1.2. (Foreign Controlled Companies)	:	:	:	:	266	1 125	:	:	F.2.1.2. (Entreprises Sous Contrôle Etranger)
F.2.1.3. Branches & Agencies of Foreign Cies	:	:	:	:	:	:	:	:	F.2.1.3. Succursales et Agences d'Ent. Etrangères
F.2.1.4. Domestic Investment	:	:	:	946	:	:	:	:	F.2.1.4. Placement dans le Pays
F.2.1. Total	1 134	1 178	:	946	831	:	1 816	1 967	F.2.1. Total
F.2.2. Mortgage Loans									F.2.2. Prêts Hypothécaires
F.2.2.1. Domestic Companies	:	:	:	30	41	31	87	20	F.2.2.1. Entreprises Nationales
F.2.2.2. (Foreign Controlled Companies)	:	:	:	:	11	:	:	:	F.2.2.2. (Entreprises Sous Contrôle Etranger)
F.2.2.4. Domestic Investment	:	:	:	30	:	:	:	:	F.2.2.4. Placement dans le Pays
F.2.2. Total	:	:	:	30	41	:	87	20	F.2.2. Total
F.2.3. Shares									F.2.3. Actions
F.2.3.1. Domestic Companies	:	:	3 802	5 352	7 944	9 852	14 870	17 360	F.2.3.1. Entreprises Nationales
F.2.3.2. (Foreign Controlled Companies)	:	:	:	:	5 531	4 210	:	:	F.2.3.2. (Entreprises Sous Contrôle Etranger)
F.2.3.3. Branches & Agencies of Foreign Cies	:	:	:	:	:	:	:	:	F.2.3.3. Succursales et Agences d'Ent. Etrangères
F.2.3.4. Domestic Investment	:	:	:	2 558	:	:	:	:	F.2.3.4. Placement dans le Pays
F.2.3.5. Foreign Investment	1 613	:	:	2 794	:	:	:	:	F.2.3.5. Placement à l' Etranger
F.2.3. Total	1 613	:	:	5 352	7 944	:	14 870	17 360	F.2.3. Total
F.2.4. Bonds with Fixed Revenue									F.2.4. Obligations
F.2.4.1. Domestic Companies	:	:	26 732	21 069	30 467	34 375	40 779	39 114	F.2.4.1. Entreprises Nationales
F.2.4.2. (Foreign Controlled Companies)	:	:	:	:	18 639	15 609	:	:	F.2.4.2. (Entreprises Sous Contrôle Etranger)
F.2.4.3. Branches & Agencies of Foreign Cies	:	:	:	:	:	:	:	:	F.2.4.3. Succursales et Agences d'Ent. Etrangères
F.2.4.4. Domestic Investment	:	:	:	:	:	:	:	:	F.2.4.4. Placement dans le Pays
F.2.4.5. Foreign Investment	:	:	:	:	:	:	:	:	F.2.4.5. Placement à l' Etranger
F.2.4. Total	12 261	14 444	:	21 069	30 467	:	40 779	39 114	F.2.4. Total
F.2.5. Loans other than Mortgage Loans									F.2.5. Prêts Autres qu'Hypothécaires
F.2.5.1. Domestic Companies	:	:	:	0	160	171	0	0	F.2.5.1. Entreprises Nationales
F.2.5.2. (Foreign Controlled Companies)	:	:	:	:	13	:	0	0	F.2.5.2. (Entreprises Sous Contrôle Etranger)
F.2.5. Total	:	:	:	0	160	:	0	0	F.2.5. Total

Monetary Unit: million Luxembourg francs

Unité monétaire : million de Francs luxembourgeois

	1992	1993	1994	1995	1996	1997	1998	1999	
F.2.6. Other Investments									F.2.6. Autres Placements
F.2.6.1. Domestic Companies	..	..	5 119	7 545	8 034	8 254	13 657	11 637	F.2.6.1. Entreprises Nationales
F.2.6.2. (Foreign Controlled Companies)	..	..	..	..	4 569	1 700	..	..	F.2.6.2. (Entreprises Sous Contrôle Etranger)
F.2.6.3. Branches & Agencies of Foreign Cies	..	..	..	..	..	..	..	..	F.2.6.3. Succursales et Agences d'Ent. Etrangères
F.2.6.4. Domestic Investment	..	..	..	..	..	..	..	..	F.2.6.4. Placement dans le Pays
F.2.6. Total	2 350	3 345	..	7 546	8 034	..	..	11 637	F.2.6. Total
F.2.7. Total									F.2.7. Total
F.2.7.1. Domestic Companies	..	..	37 064	34 942	47 477	54 665	71 209	70 097	F.2.7.1. Entreprises Nationales
F.2.7.2. (Foreign Controlled Companies)	..	..	..	..	29 029	22 644	..	..	F.2.7.2. (Entreprises Sous Contrôle Etranger)
F.2.7.3. Branches & Agencies of Foreign Cies	..	..	..	..	..	..	..	..	F.2.7.3. Succursales et Agences d'Ent. Etrangères
F.2.7. Total of Non-Life Investments	17 360	21 662	..	34 943	47 477	..	71 209	70 097	F.2.7. Total des Placements Non-Vie
G. BREAKDOWN OF NON-LIFE PREMIUMS									**G. VENTILATIONS DES PRIMES NON-VIE**
G.1. Motor vehicle									G.1. Assurance Automobile
G.1.1. Direct Business									G.1.1. Assurances Directes
G.1.1.1. Gross Premiums	5 732	5 821	6 524	6 832	7 847	7 206	8 111	8 495	G.1.1.1. Primes Brutes
G.1.1.2. Ceded Premiums	..	..	..	1 264	746	845	1 085	1 390	G.1.1.2. Primes Cédées
G.1.1.3. Net Written Premiums	..	..	..	5 568	7 101	6 361	7 026	7 105	G.1.1.3. Primes Nettes Emises
G.2. Marine, Aviation									G.2. Marine, Aviation
G.2.1. Direct Business									G.2.1. Assurances Directes
G.2.1.1. Gross Premiums	43	83	81	10	9	69	7 990	7 776	G.2.1.1. Primes Brutes
G.2.1.2. Ceded Premiums	..	..	..	5	3	4	1 833	1 290	G.2.1.2. Primes Cédées
G.2.1.3. Net Written Premiums	..	..	..	4	6	65	6 157	6 486	G.2.1.3. Primes Nettes Emises
G.3. Freight									G.3. Fret
G.3.1. Direct Business									G.3.1. Assurances Directes
G.3.1.1. Gross Premiums	429	252	275	356	319	420	507	478	G.3.1.1. Primes Brutes
G.3.1.2. Ceded Premiums	..	..	..	263	227	326	376	345	G.3.1.2. Primes Cédées
G.3.1.3. Net Written Premiums	..	..	..	93	92	94	131	133	G.3.1.3. Primes Nettes Emises
G.4. Fire, Property Damages									G.4. Incendie, Dommages aux Biens
G.4.1. Direct Business									G.4.1. Assurances Directes
G.4.1.1. Gross Premiums	3 050	3 352	3 533	3 712	3 888	3 991	4 479	4 731	G.4.1.1. Primes Brutes
G.4.1.2. Ceded Premiums	..	..	..	1 590	1 109	1 217	1 334	1 420	G.4.1.2. Primes Cédées
G.4.1.3. Net Written Premiums	..	..	..	2 121	2 779	2 774	3 145	3 310	G.4.1.3. Primes Nettes Emises
G.5. Pecuniary Losses									G.5. Pertes Pécunières
G.5.1. Direct Business									G.5.1. Assurances Directes
G.5.1.1. Gross Premiums	944	716	807	1 292	1 805	1 755	1 691	2 403	G.5.1.1. Primes Brutes
G.5.1.2. Ceded Premiums	..	..	..	558	1 228	1 020	1 079	1 311	G.5.1.2. Primes Cédées
G.5.1.3. Net Written Premiums	..	..	..	733	577	735	612	1 092	G.5.1.3. Primes Nettes Emises
G.6. General Liability									G.6. Responsabilité Générale
G.6.1. Direct Business									G.6.1. Assurances Directes
G.6.1.1. Gross Premiums	1 030	1 270	1 630	1 580	1 666	1 843	2 013	2 163	G.6.1.1. Primes Brutes
G.6.1.2. Ceded Premiums	..	..	..	787	686	845	908	990	G.6.1.2. Primes Cédées
G.6.1.3. Net Written Premiums	..	..	..	793	980	998	1 105	1 174	G.6.1.3. Primes Nettes Emises
G.7. Accident, Health									G.7. Accident, Santé
G.7.1. Direct Business									G.7.1. Assurances Directes
G.7.1.1. Gross Premiums	682	665	783	845	901	887	1 018	1 092	G.7.1.1. Primes Brutes
G.7.1.2. Ceded Premiums	..	..	..	140	84	102	113	134	G.7.1.2. Primes Cédées
G.7.1.3. Net Written Premiums	..	..	..	705	817	785	905	958	G.7.1.3. Primes Nettes Emises
G.8. Others									G.8. Autres
G.8.1. Direct Business									G.8.1. Assurances Directes
G.8.1.1. Gross Premiums	346	239	280	307	495	343	1 371	1 430	G.8.1.1. Primes Brutes
G.8.1.2. Ceded Premiums	..	..	..	59	171	46	147	140	G.8.1.2. Primes Cédées
G.8.1.3. Net Written Premiums	..	..	..	248	324	297	1 225	1 290	G.8.1.3. Primes Nettes Emises
G.10. Total									G.10. Total
G.10.1. Direct Business									G.10.1. Assurances Directes
G.10.1.1. Gross Premiums	12 256	12 398	13 913	14 935	16 930	16 514	27 181	28 567	G.10.1.1. Primes Brutes
G.10.1.2. Ceded Premiums	..	..	..	4 666	4 254	4 405	6 876	7 020	G.10.1.2. Primes Cédées
G.10.1.3. Net Written Premiums	..	..	..	10 265	12 676	12 109	20 305	21 547	G.10.1.3. Primes Nettes Emises

LUXEMBOURG

Monetary Unit: million Luxembourg francs — Unité monétaire : million de Francs luxembourgeois

	1992	1993	1994	1995	1996	1997	1998	1999
G.10.2. Reinsurance Accepted / Réassurance Acceptée								
G.10.2.1. Gross Premiums / Primes Brutes	:	:	:	28	36	43	180	138
G.10.2.2. Ceded Premiums / Primes Cédées	:	:	:	1	3	6	65	55
G.10.2.3. Net Written Premiums / Primes Nettes Emises	:	:	:	27	33	37	116	82
G.10.3. Total								
G.10.3.1. Gross Premiums / Primes Brutes	:	:	:	14 963	16 966	16 557	27 361	28 705
G.10.3.2. Ceded Premiums / Primes Cédées	:	:	:	4 667	4 257	4 411	6 940	7 076
G.10.3.3. Net Written Premiums / Primes Nettes Emises	:	:	:	10 292	12 709	12 146	20 420	21 629

H. GROSS CLAIMS PAYMENTS / H. PAIEMENTS BRUTS DES SINISTRES

H.1. Life / H.1. Vie

	1992	1993	1994	1995	1996	1997	1998	1999
H.1.1. Domestic Companies / Entreprises Nationales		4 069	5 601	8 167	17 741	27 582	70 769	71 365
H.1.2. (Foreign Controlled Companies) / (Entreprises Sous Contrôle Etranger)		1 830	3 957	6 053	14 811	24 475	66 438	57 250
H.1.3. Branches & Agencies of Foreign Cies / Succursales et Agences d'Ent. Etrangères		522	593	743	1 105	1 950	1 010	22 857
H.1. Total		4 591	6 194	8 910	18 846	29 532	71 780	94 222

H.2. Non-Life / H.2. Non-Vie

	1992	1993	1994	1995	1996	1997	1998	1999
H.2.1. Domestic Companies / Entreprises Nationales		5 922	5 492	6 940	7 889	6 592	15 427	19 076
H.2.2. (Foreign Controlled Companies) / (Entreprises Sous Contrôle Etranger)		1 305	965	1 968	2 349	1 215	1 470	1 522
H.2.3. Branches & Agencies of Foreign Cies / Succursales et Agences d'Ent. Etrangères		1 280	1 353	1 153	1 198	1 147	1 307	1 322
H.2. Total		7 202	6 845	8 093	9 087	7 739	16 734	20 398

I. GROSS OPERATING EXPENSES / I. DEPENSES BRUTES D'EXPLOITATION

I.1. Life / I.1. Vie

	1992	1993	1994	1995	1996	1997	1998	1999
I.1.1. Domestic Companies / Entreprises Nationales		2 057	2 852	3 573	1 253	5 748	7 645	10 478
I.1.2. (Foreign Controlled Companies) / (Entreprises Sous Contrôle Etranger)		1 429	2 114	2 840	893	4 629	6 232	7 803
I.1.3. Branches & Agencies of Foreign Cies / Succursales et Agences d'Ent. Etrangères		168	186	218	103	592	1 050	1 609
I.1. Total / Total des Primes Nettes Vie		2 225	3 038	3 791	1 356	6 340	8 695	12 087

I.2. Non-Life / I.2. Non-Vie

	1992	1993	1994	1995	1996	1997	1998	1999
I.2.1. Domestic Companies / Entreprises Nationales		3 147	3 344	2 694	738	3 127	4 757	5 285
I.2.2. (Foreign Controlled Companies) / (Entreprises Sous Contrôle Etranger)		837	702	585	237	709	1 048	1 022
I.2.3. Branches & Agencies of Foreign Cies / Succursales et Agences d'Ent. Etrangères		735	737	612	211	784	895	712
I.2. Total		3 882	4 081	3 306	949	3 911	5 652	5 997

J. COMMISSIONS

J.1. Life / J.1. Vie

	1992	1993	1994	1995	1996	1997	1998	1999
J.1.1. Direct Business / Assurance directe								
J.1.1.1. Domestic Companies / Entreprises Nationales		818	1 202	2 546	2 826	3 964	5 346	7 711
J.1.1.2. (Foreign Controlled Companies) / (Entreprises Sous Contrôle Etranger)		620	968	2 130	2 366	3 321	4 427	5 943
J.1.1.3. Branches & Agencies of Foreign Cies / Succursales et Agences d'Ent. Etrangères		53	57	131	256	479	924	1 508
J.1.1. Total		871	1 259	2 677	3 082	4 443	6 270	9 219
J.1.2. Reinsurance Accepted / Réassurances acceptées								
J.1.2.1. Domestic Companies / Entreprises Nationales		0	14	0	2	2	0	1
J.1.2.2. (Foreign Controlled Companies) / (Entreprises Sous Contrôle Etranger)		0	0	0	0	1	0	0
J.1.2.3. Branches & Agencies of Foreign Cies / Succursales et Agences d'Ent. Etrangères		0	14	0	2	3	0	1
J.1.2. Total								
J.1.3. Total								
J.1.3.1. Domestic Companies / Entreprises Nationales		818	1 216	2 546	2 828	3 966	5 346	7 711
J.1.3.2. (Foreign Controlled Companies) / (Entreprises Sous Contrôle Etranger)		620	968	2 130	2 366	3 321	4 427	5 943
J.1.3.3. Branches & Agencies of Foreign Cies / Succursales et Agences d'Ent. Etrangères		53	57	131	256	480	924	1 508
J.1.3. Total of Life Net Premiums / Total		871	1 273	2 677	3 084	4 446	6 270	9 220

Monetary Unit: million Luxembourg francs

Unité monétaire : million de Francs luxembourgeois

J.2. Non-Life　　　　　　　　　　　　　　　　　　　　　　**J.2. Non-Vie**

	1992	1993	1994	1995	1996	1997	1998	1999	
J.2.1. Direct Business									J.2.1. Assurance directe
J.2.1.1. Domestic Companies		1 306	1 299	2 050	2 492	2 676	3 413	3 897	J.2.1.1. Entreprises Nationales
J.2.1.2. (Foreign Controlled Companies)		361	275	385	674	787	846	783	J.2.1.2. (Entreprises Sous Contrôle Etranger)
J.2.1.3. Branches & Agencies of Foreign Cies		316	284	419	470	544	606	521	J.2.1.3. Succursales et Agences d'Ent. Etrangères
J.2.1. Total		1 622	1 583	2 469	2 962	3 220	4 019	4 419	J.2.1. Total des Primes Nettes Vie
J.2.2. Reinsurance Accepted									J.2.2. Réassurances acceptées
J.2.2.1. Domestic Companies		0	24	7	7	9	22	14	J.2.2.1. Entreprises Nationales
J.2.2.2. (Foreign Controlled Companies)							2	2	J.2.2.2. (Entreprises Sous Contrôle Etranger)
J.2.2.3. Branches & Agencies of Foreign Cies		0	0	0	0	2	22	18	J.2.2.3. Succursales et Agences d'Ent. Etrangères
J.2.2. Total		0	24	7	7	11	44	32	J.2.2. Total
J.2.3. Total									J.2.3. Total
J.2.3.1. Domestic Companies		1 306	1 323	2 057	2 499	2 685	3 435	3 911	J.2.3.1. Entreprises Nationales
J.2.3.2. (Foreign Controlled Companies)		361	275	385	674	787	847	786	J.2.3.2. (Entreprises Sous Contrôle Etranger)
J.2.3.3. Branches & Agencies of Foreign Cies		316	284	419	470	546	628	539	J.2.3.3. Succursales et Agences d'Ent. Etrangères
J.2.3. Total		1 622	1 607	2 476	2 969	3 231	4 063	4 451	J.2.3. Total

Monetary Unit: million pesos   Unité monétaire : million de pesos

A. NUMBER OF COMPANIES IN THE REPORTING COUNTRY
A. NOMBRE D'ENTREPRISES DANS LE PAYS DECLARANT

	1992	1993	1994	1995	1996	1997	1998	1999
A.1. Life / A.1. Vie								
A.1.1. Domestic Companies / Entreprises Nationales	1	4	3	5	3	3	9	11
A.1.2. (Foreign Controlled Companies) / (Entreprises Sous Contrôle Etranger)	0	0	0	3	2	1	2	4
A.1. All Companies / Ensemble des Entreprises	1	4	3	5	3	3	9	11
A.2. Non-Life / A.2. Non-Vie								
A.2.1. Domestic Companies / Entreprises Nationales	9	7	13	16	13	14	15	13
A.2.2. (Foreign Controlled Companies) / (Entreprises Sous Contrôle Etranger)	0	0	1	5	4	6	5	5
A.2. All Companies / Ensemble des Entreprises	9	7	13	16	13	14	15	13
A.3. Composite / A.3. Mixte								
A.3.1. Domestic Companies / Entreprises Nationales	31	33	29	33	43	44	41	41
A.3.2. (Foreign Controlled Companies) / (Entreprises Sous Contrôle Etranger)	0	0	0	5	12	15	17	18
A.3. All Companies / Ensemble des Entreprises	31	33	29	33	43	44	41	41
A.4. Reinsurance / A.4. Réassurance								
A.4.1. Domestic Companies / Entreprises Nationales	2	2	2	2	2	3	3	3
A.4.2. (Foreign Controlled Companies) / (Entreprises Sous Contrôle Etranger)							1	1
A.4. All Companies / A.4.4. Ensemble des Entreprises	2	2	2	2	2	3	3	3
A.5. Total								
A.5.1. Domestic Companies / Entreprises Nationales	43	45	47	56	61	64	68	68
A.5.2. (Foreign Controlled Companies) / (Entreprises Sous Contrôle Etranger)	0	0	1	13	18	22	25	28
A.5. All Insurance Companies / Ensemble des Entreprises d'Assurances	43	45	47	56	61	64	68	68

B. NUMBER OF EMPLOYEES / B. NOMBRE D'EMPLOYES

	1992	1993	1994	1995	1996	1997	1998	1999
B.1. Insurance Companies / Entreprises d'Assurances	20 687	20 067	20 348	19 398	19 661	20 539	22 325	21 920
B.2. Intermediaries / Intermediaires	..	28 418	27 827	30 587	25 163	29 466	27 970	27 190
B. Total	..	48 485	48 175	49 985	44 824	50 005	50 295	49 110

C. BUSINESS WRITTEN IN THE REPORTING COUNTRY
C. OPERATIONS CONCLUES DANS LE PAYS DECLARANT

C.1. Life / C.1. Vie

	1992	1993	1994	1995	1996	1997	1998	1999
C.1.1. Gross Premiums / C.1.1. Primes Brutes								
C.1.1.1. Direct Business / C.1.1.1. Assurances Directes								
C.1.1.1.1. Domestic Companies / Entreprises Nationales	5 193	6 053	7 159	8 053	10 672	14 496	26 112	38 023
C.1.1.1.2. (Foreign Controlled Companies) / (Entreprises Sous Contrôle Etranger)	0	0	0	92	137	1 447	2 561	2 292
C.1.1.1. Total	5 193	6 053	7 159	8 053	10 672	14 496	26 112	38 023
C.1.1.2. Reinsurance Accepted / C.1.1.2. Réassurance Acceptée								
C.1.1.2.1. Domestic Companies / Entreprises Nationales	52	69	82	93	116	193	247	286
C.1.1.2.2. (Foreign Controlled Companies) / (Entreprises Sous Contrôle Etranger)	0	0	0	1	83	1	1	236
C.1.1.2. Total	52	69	82	93	116	193	247	286
C.1.1.3. Total								
C.1.1.3.1. Domestic Companies / Entreprises Nationales	5 246	6 122	7 241	8 146	10 787	14 689	26 359	38 308
C.1.1.3.2. (Foreign Controlled Companies) / (Entreprises Sous Contrôle Etranger)	0	0	0	92	220	1 447	2 562	2 528
C.1.1.3. Total Gross Premiums / Total des Primes Brutes	5 246	6 122	7 241	8 146	10 787	14 689	26 359	38 308
C.1.2. Ceded Premiums / C.1.2. Primes Cedées								
C.1.2.1. Domestic Companies / Entreprises Nationales	292	337	463	548	801	1 088	1 667	1 928
C.1.2.2. (Foreign Controlled Companies) / (Entreprises Sous Contrôle Etranger)	0	0	0	14	18	74	81	372
C.1.2. Total	292	337	463	548	801	1 088	1 667	1 928
C.1.3. Net Written Premiums / C.1.3. Primes Nettes Emises								
C.1.3.1. Domestic Companies / Entreprises Nationales	4 953	5 785	6 778	7 598	9 987	13 601	24 691	36 380
C.1.3.2. (Foreign Controlled Companies) / (Entreprises Sous Contrôle Etranger)	0	0	0	78	202	1 373	2 481	2 156
C.1.3. Total	4 953	5 785	6 778	7 598	9 987	13 601	24 691	36 380

Monetary Unit: million pesos

Unité monétaire : million de pesos

C.2. Non-Life / C.2. Non-Vie

	1992	1993	1994	1995	1996	1997	1998	1999
C.2.1. Gross premiums / C.2.1. Primes Brutes								
C.2.1.1. Direct Business / C.2.1.1. Assurances Directes								
C.2.1.1.1. Domestic Companies / C.2.1.1.1. Entreprises Nationales	10 018	11 934	13 367	15 755	20 197	25 318	31 644	40 492
C.2.1.1.2. (Foreign Controlled Companies) / C.2.1.1.2. (Entreprises Sous Contrôle Etranger)	0	0	7	635	1 444	2 771	3 272	4 976
C.2.1.1. Total / C.2.1.1. Total	10 018	11 934	13 367	15 755	20 197	25 318	31 644	40 492
C.2.1.2. Reinsurance Accepted / C.2.1.2. Réassurance Acceptée								
C.2.1.2.1. Domestic Companies / C.2.1.2.1. Entreprises Nationales	603	719	762	1 030	1 065	1 160	1 242	1 579
C.2.1.2.2. (Foreign Controlled Companies) / C.2.1.2.2. (Entreprises Sous Contrôle Etranger)	0	0	0	15	42	136	124	835
C.2.1.2. Total / C.2.1.2. Total	603	719	762	1 030	1 065	1 160	1 242	1 579
C.2.1.3. Total / C.2.1.3. Total								
C.2.1.3.1. Domestic Companies / C.2.1.3.1. Entreprises Nationales	10 621	12 652	14 129	16 784	21 263	26 478	32 886	42 071
C.2.1.3.2. (Foreign Controlled Companies) / C.2.1.3.2. (Entreprises Sous Contrôle Etranger)	0	0	7	650	1 486	2 908	3 395	5 811
C.2.1.3. Total Gross Premiums / C.2.1.3. Total des Primes Brutes	10 621	12 652	14 129	16 784	21 263	26 478	32 886	42 071
C.2.2. Ceded Premiums / C.2.2. Primes Cédées								
C.2.2.1. Domestic Companies / C.2.2.1. Entreprises Nationales	2 765	3 455	3 689	4 959	6 410	7 366	8 327	10 267
C.2.2.2. (Foreign Controlled Companies) / C.2.2.2. (Entreprises Sous Contrôle Etranger)	0	0	4	336	670	1 112	1 345	2 254
C.2.2. Total / C.2.2. Total	2 765	3 455	3 689	4 959	6 410	7 366	8 327	10 267
C.2.3. Net Written Premiums / C.2.3. Primes Nettes Emises								
C.2.3.1. Domestic Companies / C.2.3.1. Entreprises Nationales	7 857	9 198	10 440	11 826	14 853	19 112	24 559	31 804
C.2.3.2. (Foreign Controlled Companies) / C.2.3.2. (Entreprises Sous Contrôle Etranger)	0	0	3	314	816	1 796	2 051	3 557
C.2.3. Total / C.2.3. Total	7 857	9 198	10 440	11 826	14 853	19 112	24 559	31 804

C.3. Total

	1992	1993	1994	1995	1996	1997	1998	1999
C.3.1. Gross Premiums / C.3.1. Primes Brutes								
C.3.1.1. Direct Business / C.3.1.1. Assurances Directes								
C.3.1.1.1. Domestic Companies / C.3.1.1.1. Entreprises Nationales	15 211	17 987	20 527	23 807	30 869	39 814	57 756	78 515
C.3.1.1.2. (Foreign Controlled Companies) / C.3.1.1.2. (Entreprises Sous Contrôle Etranger)	0	0	7	727	1 580	4 218	5 832	7 269
C.3.1.1. Total / C.3.1.1. Total	15 211	17 987	20 527	23 807	30 869	39 814	57 756	78 515
C.3.1.2. Reinsurance Accepted / C.3.1.2. Réassurance Acceptée								
C.3.1.2.1. Domestic Companies / C.3.1.2.1. Entreprises Nationales	656	788	844	1 123	1 181	1 353	1 489	1 865
C.3.1.2.2. (Foreign Controlled Companies) / C.3.1.2.2. (Entreprises Sous Contrôle Etranger)	0	0	0	16	125	137	125	1 071
C.3.1.2. Total / C.3.1.2. Total	656	788	844	1 123	1 181	1 353	1 489	1 865
C.3.1.3. Total / C.3.1.3. Total								
C.3.1.3.1. Domestic Companies / C.3.1.3.1. Entreprises Nationales	15 867	18 774	21 371	24 930	32 050	41 167	59 245	80 380
C.3.1.3.2. (Foreign Controlled Companies) / C.3.1.3.2. (Entreprises Sous Contrôle Etranger)	0	0	7	742	1 705	4 355	5 957	8 339
C.3.1.3. Total Gross Premiums / C.3.1.3. Total des Primes Brutes	15 867	18 774	21 371	24 930	32 050	41 167	59 245	80 380
C.3.2. Ceded Premiums / C.3.2. Primes Cédées								
C.3.2.1. Domestic Companies / C.3.2.1. Entreprises Nationales	3 057	3 792	4 152	5 506	7 210	8 454	9 995	12 195
C.3.2.2. (Foreign Controlled Companies) / C.3.2.2. (Entreprises Sous Contrôle Etranger)	0	0	4	350	688	1 186	1 426	2 626
C.3.2. Total / C.3.2. Total	3 057	3 792	4 152	5 506	7 210	8 454	9 995	12 195
C.3.3. Net Written Premiums / C.3.3. Primes Nettes Emises								
C.3.3.1. Domestic Companies / C.3.3.1. Entreprises Nationales	12 810	14 982	17 219	19 424	24 840	32 712	49 250	68 185
C.3.3.2. (Foreign Controlled Companies) / C.3.3.2. (Entreprises Sous Contrôle Etranger)	0	0	3	392	1 017	3 169	3 170	5 713
C.3.3. Total / C.3.3. Total	12 810	14 982	17 219	19 424	24 840	32 712	49 250	68 185

D. NET WRITTEN PREMIUMS IN THE REPORTING COUNTRY IN TERMS OF DOMESTIC AND FOREIGN RISKS
D. PRIMES NETTES EMISES DANS LE PAYS DECLARANT EN RISQUES NATIONAUX ET ETRANGERS

	1992	1993	1994	1995	1996	1997	1998	1999
D.1. Life — D.1. Vie								
D.1.1. Domestic Risks — D.1.1. Risques Nationaux								
D.1.1.1. Domestic Companies — D.1.1.1. Entreprises Nationales	4 953	..	..	..	..	..	..	..
D.1.1. Total — D.1.1. Total des Primes Nettes Vie	4 953	..	..	..	..	..	..	..
D.1.3. Total								
D.1.3.1. Domestic Companies — D.1.3.1. Entreprises Nationales	4 953	5 785	6 778	7 598	9 987	13 601	24 691	36 380
D.1.3.2. (Foreign Controlled Companies) — D.1.3.2. (Entreprises Sous Contrôle Etranger)		0	0	78	202	1 373	2 481	2 156
D.1.3. Total of Life Net Premiums — D.1.3. Total des Primes Nettes Vie	4 953	5 785	6 778	7 598	9 987	13 601	24 691	36 380
D.2. Non-Life — D.2. Non-Vie								
D.2.1. Domestic Risks — D.2.1. Risques Nationaux								
D.2.1.1. Domestic Companies — D.2.1.1. Entreprises Nationales	7 857	..	..	..	..	..	..	..
D.2.1. Total — D.2.1. Total des Primes Nettes Vie	7 857	..	..	..	..	..	..	..
D.2.3. Total								
D.2.3.1. Domestic Companies — D.2.3.1. Entreprises Nationales	7 857	9 198	10 440	11 826	14 853	19 112	24 559	31 804
D.2.3.2. (Foreign Controlled Companies) — D.2.3.2. (Entreprises Sous Contrôle Etranger)		0	..	314	816	1 796	2 051	3 557
D.2.3. Total — D.2.3. Total des Primes Nettes Vie	7 857	9 198	10 440	11 826	14 853	19 112	24 559	31 804

G. BREAKDOWN OF NON-LIFE PREMIUMS
G. VENTILATIONS DES PRIMES NON-VIE

	1992	1993	1994	1995	1996	1997	1998	1999
G.1. Motor vehicle — G.1. Assurance Automobile								
G.1.1. Direct Business — G.1.1. Assurances Directes								
G.1.1.1. Gross Premiums — G.1.1.1. Primes Brutes	5 018	5 695	6 070	6 300	7 825	10 612	14 707	18 797
G.1.1.2. Ceded Premiums — G.1.1.2. Primes Cédées	34	66	38	70	75	134	197	266
G.1.1.3. Net Written Premiums — G.1.1.3. Primes Nettes Emises	4 983	5 629	6 032	6 231	7 750	10 478	14 509	18 530
G.1.2. Reinsurance Accepted — G.1.2. Réassurance Acceptée								
G.1.2.1. Gross Premiums — G.1.2.1. Primes Brutes	0	43	27	41	40	44	56	140
G.1.2.2. Ceded Premiums — G.1.2.2. Primes Cédées	0	2	2	0	3	7	7	20
G.1.2.3. Net Written Premiums — G.1.2.3. Primes Nettes Emises	0	41	25	41	37	36	49	120
G.1.3. Total								
G.1.3.1. Gross Premiums — G.1.3.1. Primes Brutes	5 018	5 738	6 096	6 342	7 866	10 655	14 763	18 936
G.1.3.2. Ceded Premiums — G.1.3.2. Primes Cédées	35	68	40	70	78	141	204	286
G.1.3.3. Net Written Premiums — G.1.3.3. Primes Nettes Emises	44 983	5 670	6 057	6 272	7 787	10 514	14 559	18 650
G.2. Marine, Aviation — G.2. Marine, Aviation								
G.2.1. Direct Business — G.2.1. Assurances Directes								
G.2.1.1. Gross Premiums — G.2.1.1. Primes Brutes	1 031	950	1 173	1 479	2 324	2 696	2 835	3 312
G.2.1.2. Ceded Premiums — G.2.1.2. Primes Cédées	667	710	733	918	1 462	1 601	1 713	2 051
G.2.1.3. Net Written Premiums — G.2.1.3. Primes Nettes Emises	364	240	440	560	862	1 096	1 122	1 261
G.2.2. Reinsurance Accepted — G.2.2. Réassurance Acceptée								
G.2.2.1. Gross Premiums — G.2.2.1. Primes Brutes	0	183	212	354	355	401	392	250
G.2.2.2. Ceded Premiums — G.2.2.2. Primes Cédées	0	109	115	185	207	239	225	121
G.2.2.3. Net Written Premiums — G.2.2.3. Primes Nettes Emises	0	73	97	168	148	162	166	130
G.2.3. Total								
G.2.3.1. Gross Premiums — G.2.3.1. Primes Brutes	1 031	1 132	1 385	1 832	2 679	3 097	3 227	3 562
G.2.3.2. Ceded Premiums — G.2.3.2. Primes Cédées	667	819	848	1 104	1 669	1 840	1 938	2 172
G.2.3.3. Net Written Premiums — G.2.3.3. Primes Nettes Emises	364	313	537	729	1 010	1 258	1 288	1 390

Monetary Unit: million pesos   Unité monétaire : million de pesos

	1992	1993	1994	1995	1996	1997	1998	1999	
G.4. Fire, Property Damages									**G.4. Incendie, Dommages aux Biens**
G.4.1. Direct Business									G.4.1. Assurances Directes
G.4.1.1. Gross Premiums	1 808	2 029	2 292	2 898	3 408	3 866	2 451	3 000	G.4.1.1. Primes Brutes
G.4.1.2. Ceded Premiums	1 227	1 540	1 389	1 778	2 120	2 535	1 772	2 144	G.4.1.2. Primes Cédées
G.4.1.3. Net Written Premiums	581	489	902	1 121	1 288	1 331	679	856	G.4.1.3. Primes Nettes Emises
G.4.2. Reinsurance Accepted									G.4.2. Réassurance Acceptée
G.4.2.1. Gross Premiums	0	306	347	459	455	425	316	499	G.4.2.1. Primes Brutes
G.4.2.2. Ceded Premiums	0	114	60	107	160	156	83	123	G.4.2.2. Primes Cédées
G.4.2.3. Net Written Premiums	0	192	287	351	294	269	233	376	G.4.2.3. Primes Nettes Emises
G.4.3. Total									G.4.3. Total
G.4.3.1. Gross Premiums	1 808	2 335	2 638	3 357	3 863	4 291	2 767	3 499	G.4.3.1. Primes Brutes
G.4.3.2. Ceded Premiums	1 227	1 654	1 449	1 885	2 281	2 691	1 855	2 267	G.4.3.2. Primes Cédées
G.4.3.3. Net Written Premiums	581	681	1 189	1 472	1 582	1 600	912	1 232	G.4.3.3. Primes Nettes Emises
G.5. Pecuniary Losses									**G.5. Pertes Pécunières**
G.5.1. Direct Business									G.5.1. Assurances Directes
G.5.1.1. Gross Premiums	37	23	26	48	61	74	87	111	G.5.1.1. Primes Brutes
G.5.1.2. Ceded Premiums	19	19	22	40	51	63	74	95	G.5.1.2. Primes Cédées
G.5.1.3. Net Written Premiums	17	4	4	8	9	11	13	16	G.5.1.3. Primes Nettes Emises
G.5.2. Reinsurance Accepted									G.5.2. Réassurance Acceptée
G.5.2.1. Gross Premiums	0	21	17	14	14	21	24	26	G.5.2.1. Primes Brutes
G.5.2.2. Ceded Premiums	0	0	0	0	0	1	2	1	G.5.2.2. Primes Cédées
G.5.2.3. Net Written Premiums	0	21	17	14	14	21	23	25	G.5.2.3. Primes Nettes Emises
G.5.3. Total									G.5.3. Total
G.5.3.1. Gross Premiums	37	44	43	62	74	95	111	137	G.5.3.1. Primes Brutes
G.5.3.2. Ceded Premiums	19	19	22	40	51	63	76	96	G.5.3.2. Primes Cédées
G.5.3.3. Net Written Premiums	17	25	21	21	23	32	36	41	G.5.3.3. Primes Nettes Emises
G.6. General Liability									**G.6. Responsabilité Générale**
G.6.1. Direct Business									G.6.1. Assurances Directes
G.6.1.1. Gross Premiums	217	292	377	644	788	997	1 368	1 662	G.6.1.1. Primes Brutes
G.6.1.2. Ceded Premiums	125	176	226	393	543	742	1 044	1 300	G.6.1.2. Primes Cédées
G.6.1.3. Net Written Premiums	92	117	151	251	244	256	324	362	G.6.1.3. Primes Nettes Emises
G.6.2. Reinsurance Accepted									G.6.2. Réassurance Acceptée
G.6.2.1. Gross Premiums	0	12	11	18	24	34	64	76	G.6.2.1. Primes Brutes
G.6.2.2. Ceded Premiums	0	2	1	1	7	15	22	25	G.6.2.2. Primes Cédées
G.6.2.3. Net Written Premiums	0	10	10	18	17	20	42	51	G.6.2.3. Primes Nettes Emises
G.6.3. Total									G.6.3. Total
G.6.3.1. Gross Premiums	217	305	388	662	811	1 032	1 432	1 737	G.6.3.1. Primes Brutes
G.6.3.2. Ceded Premiums	125	178	227	393	550	756	1 066	1 325	G.6.3.2. Primes Cédées
G.6.3.3. Net Written Premiums	92	126	161	269	261	275	366	413	G.6.3.3. Primes Nettes Emises
G.7. Accident, Health									**G.7. Accident, Santé**
G.7.1. Direct Business									G.7.1. Assurances Directes
G.7.1.1. Gross Premiums	1 231	1 435	1 734	2 101	3 019	4 046	5 158	7 389	G.7.1.1. Primes Brutes
G.7.1.2. Ceded Premiums	71	79	80	65	85	137	225	327	G.7.1.2. Primes Cédées
G.7.1.3. Net Written Premiums	1 161	1 355	1 654	2 036	2 934	3 908	4 932	7 061	G.7.1.3. Primes Nettes Emises
G.7.2. Reinsurance Accepted									G.7.2. Réassurance Acceptée
G.7.2.1. Gross Premiums	0	47	40	30	10	17	35	59	G.7.2.1. Primes Brutes
G.7.2.2. Ceded Premiums	0	0	0	0	0	1	3	4	G.7.2.2. Primes Cédées
G.7.2.3. Net Written Premiums	0	46	40	30	10	16	33	54	G.7.2.3. Primes Nettes Emises
G.7.3. Total									G.7.3. Total
G.7.3.1. Gross Premiums	1 231	1 481	1 773	2 131	3 029	4 062	5 193	7 447	G.7.3.1. Primes Brutes
G.7.3.2. Ceded Premiums	71	80	80	66	85	139	228	332	G.7.3.2. Primes Cédées
G.7.3.3. Net Written Premiums	1 161	1 402	1 693	2 066	2 944	3 924	4 965	7 116	G.7.3.3. Primes Nettes Emises

Monetary Unit: million pesos   Unité monétaire : million de pesos

		1992	1993	1994	1995	1996	1997	1998	1999
G.8. Others	G.8. Autres								
G.8.1. Direct Business	G.8.1. Assurances Directes								
G.8.1.1. Gross Premiums	G.8.1.1. Primes Brutes	1 280	1 510	1 696	2 284	2 773	3 027	5 038	6 223
G.8.1.2. Ceded Premiums	G.8.1.2. Primes Cédées	621	865	1 001	1 386	1 664	1 691	2 879	3 688
G.8.1.3. Net Written Premiums	G.8.1.3. Primes Nettes Emises	658	645	696	898	1 109	1 336	2 159	2 535
G.8.2. Reinsurance Accepted	G.8.2. Réassurance Acceptée								
G.8.2.1. Gross Premiums	G.8.2.1. Primes Brutes	0	107	109	114	168	218	355	529
G.8.2.2. Ceded Premiums	G.8.2.2. Primes Cédées	0	26	23	15	31	45	81	101
G.8.2.3. Net Written Premiums	G.8.2.3. Primes Nettes Emises	0	81	87	99	137	173	273	428
G.8.3. Total	G.8.3. Total								
G.8.3.1. Gross Premiums	G.8.3.1. Primes Brutes	1 280	1 617	1 806	2 399	2 941	3 245	5 393	6 752
G.8.3.2. Ceded Premiums	G.8.3.2. Primes Cédées	621	891	1 024	1 401	1 696	1 736	2 960	3 789
G.8.3.3. Net Written Premiums	G.8.3.3. Primes Nettes Emises	658	726	782	998	1 246	1 509	2 433	2 963
G.10. Total	G.10. Total								
G.10.1. Direct Business	G.10.1. Assurances Directes								
G.10.1.1. Gross Premiums	G.10.1.1. Primes Brutes	10 621	11 934	13 367	15 755	20 197	25 318	31 644	40 492
G.10.1.2. Ceded Premiums	G.10.1.2. Primes Cédées	2 765	3 455	3 489	4 650	6 001	6 903	7 905	9 872
G.10.1.3. Net Written Premiums	G.10.1.3. Primes Nettes Emises	7 857	8 479	9 878	11 105	14 196	18 415	23 740	30 620
G.10.2. Reinsurance Accepted	G.10.2. Réassurance Acceptée								
G.10.2.1. Gross Premiums	G.10.2.1. Primes Brutes	0	719	762	1 030	1 065	1 160	1 242	1 579
G.10.2.2. Ceded Premiums	G.10.2.2. Primes Cédées	0	254	200	309	409	464	423	395
G.10.2.3. Net Written Premiums	G.10.2.3. Primes Nettes Emises	0	465	562	721	657	696	819	1 184
G.10.3. Total	G.10.3. Total								
G.10.3.1. Gross Premiums	G.10.3.1. Primes Brutes	10 621	12 652	14 129	16 784	21 263	26 478	32 886	42 071
G.10.3.2. Ceded Premiums	G.10.3.2. Primes Cédées	2 765	3 709	3 689	4 959	6 410	7 366	8 327	10 267
G.10.3.3. Net Written Premiums	G.10.3.3. Primes Nettes Emises	7 857	8 943	10 440	11 826	14 853	19 112	24 559	31 804
H. GROSS CLAIMS PAYMENTS	**H. PAIEMENTS BRUTS DES SINISTRES**								
H.1. Life	**H.1. Vie**								
H.1.1. Domestic Companies	H.1.1. Entreprises Nationales		4 483	5 403	5 949	7 327	9 363	12 603	19 403
H.1.2. (Foreign Controlled Companies)	H.1.2. (Entreprises Sous Contrôle Etranger)		0			125	593	794	1 557
H.1. Total	H.1. Total		4 483	5 403	5 949	7 327	9 363	12 603	19 403
H.2. Non-Life	**H.2. Non-Vie**								
H.2.1. Domestic Companies	H.2.1. Entreprises Nationales		6 736	7 755	11 615	14 564	16 209	20 648	28 095
H.2.2. (Foreign Controlled Companies)	H.2.2. (Entreprises Sous Contrôle Etranger)		0			526	1 286	1 633	2 164
H.2. Total	H.2. Total		6 736	7 755	11 615	14 564	16 209	20 648	28 095
I. GROSS OPERATING EXPENSES	**I. DEPENSES BRUTES D'EXPLOITATION**								
I.1. Life	**I.1. Vie**								
I.1.1. Domestic Companies	I.1.1. Entreprises Nationales		863	1 063	1 169	1 516	2 058	2 334	4 405
I.1.2. (Foreign Controlled Companies)	I.1.2. (Entreprises Sous Contrôle Etranger)		0				248	281	675
I.1. Total	I.1. Total des Primes Nettes Vie		863	1 063	1 169	1 516	2 058	2 334	4 405
I.2. Non-Life	**I.2. Non-Vie**								
I.2.1. Domestic Companies	I.2.1. Entreprises Nationales		1 785	2 074	2 414	2 988	3 161	4 213	4 691
I.2.2. (Foreign Controlled Companies)	I.2.2. (Entreprises Sous Contrôle Etranger)		0				487	647	762
I.2. Total	I.2. Total		1 785	2 074	2 414	2 988	3 161	4 213	4 691

Monetary Unit: million pesos   Unité monétaire : million de pesos

J. COMMISSIONS — J. COMMISSIONS

J.1. Life — J.1. Vie

	1992	1993	1994	1995	1996	1997	1998	1999		
J.1.1. Direct Business									J.1.1. Assurance directe	
J.1.1.1. Domestic Companies		870	927	1 082	1 448	1 931	2 832	3 725	J.1.1.1. Entreprises Nationales	
J.1.1.2. (Foreign Controlled Companies)		0	..	..	37	142	208	351	J.1.1.2. (Entreprises Sous Contrôle Etranger)	
J.1.1. Total		870	927	1 082	1 448	1 931	2 832	3 725	J.1.1. Total	
J.1.2. Reinsurance Accepted									J.1.2. Réassurances acceptées	
J.1.2.1. Domestic Companies		18	29	37	53	84	124	153	J.1.2.1. Entreprises Nationales	
J.1.2.2. (Foreign Controlled Companies)		0	..	..	0	0	2	130	J.1.2.2. (Entreprises Sous Contrôle Etranger)	
J.1.2. Total		18	29	37	53	84	124	153	J.1.2. Total	
J.1.3. Total									J.1.3. Total	
J.1.3.1. Domestic Companies		888	956	1 118	1 501	2 014	2 956	3 878	J.1.3.1. Entreprises Nationales	
J.1.3.2. (Foreign Controlled Companies)		0	..	..	37	142	209	481	J.1.3.2. (Entreprises Sous Contrôle Etranger)	
J.1.3. Total of Life Net Premiums		888	956	1 118	1 501	2 014	2 956	3 878	J.1.3. Total	

J.2. Non-Life — J.2. Non-Vie

	1992	1993	1994	1995	1996	1997	1998	1999		
J.2.1. Direct Business									J.2.1. Assurance directe	
J.2.1.1. Domestic Companies		1 614	1 879	2 243	2 998	4 364	5 693	7 162	J.2.1.1. Entreprises Nationales	
J.2.1.2. (Foreign Controlled Companies)		0	..	..	139	427	555	547	J.2.1.2. (Entreprises Sous Contrôle Etranger)	
J.2.1. Total		1 614	1 879	2 243	2 998	4 364	5 693	7 162	J.2.1. Total des Primes Nettes Vie	
J.2.2. Reinsurance Accepted									J.2.2. Réassurances acceptées	
J.2.2.1. Domestic Companies		203	209	280	237	301	336	453	J.2.2.1. Entreprises Nationales	
J.2.2.2. (Foreign Controlled Companies)		0	..	..	0	1	1	165	J.2.2.2. (Entreprises Sous Contrôle Etranger)	
J.2.2. Total		203	209	280	237	301	336	453	J.2.2. Total	
J.2.3. Total									J.2.3. Total	
J.2.3.1. Domestic Companies		1 816	2 089	2 523	3 234	4 665	6 029	7 615	J.2.3.1. Entreprises Nationales	
J.2.3.2. (Foreign Controlled Companies)		0	..	..	139	428	556	712	J.2.3.2. (Entreprises Sous Contrôle Etranger)	
J.2.3. Total		1 816	2 089	2 523	3 234	4 665	6 029	7 615	J.2.3. Total	

170

Monetary Unit: million guilders — Unité monétaire : million de florins

A. NUMBER OF COMPANIES IN THE REPORTING COUNTRY — A. NOMBRE D'ENTREPRISES DANS LE PAYS DECLARANT

	1992	1993	1994	1995	1996	1997	1998	1999
A.1. Life — A.1. Vie								
A.1.1. Domestic Companies — A.1.1. Entreprises Nationales	87	89	90	92	96	104	105	106
A.1.2. (Foreign Controlled Companies) — A.1.2. (Entreprises Sous Contrôle Etranger)	17	16	17	20	17	36	36	36
A.1.3. Branches & Agencies of Foreign Cies — A.1.3. Succursales et Agences d'Ent. Etrangères	10	10	5	4	3	7	3	3
A.1. All Companies — A.1. Ensemble des Entreprises	97	99	95	96	99	111	108	109
A.2. Non-Life — A.2. Non-Vie								
A.2.1. Domestic Companies — A.2.1. Entreprises Nationales	533	532	523	277	286	293	277	274
A.2.2. (Foreign Controlled Companies) — A.2.2. (Entreprises Sous Contrôle Etranger)	36	36	32	34	32	50	50	50
A.2.3. Branches & Agencies of Foreign Cies — A.2.3. Succursales et Agences d'Ent. Etrangères	140	136	131	23	22	18	17	17
A.2. All Companies — A.2. Ensemble des Entreprises	673	668	654	300	308	311	294	291
A.4. Reinsurance — A.4. Réassurance								
A.4.1. Domestic Companies — A.4.1. Entreprises Nationales	15	15	8	:	:	0	:	:
A.4.2. (Foreign Controlled Companies) — A.4.2. (Entreprises Sous Contrôle Etranger)	2	2	0	:	:	0	:	:
A.4.3. Branches & Agencies of Foreign Cies — A.4.3. Succursales et Agences d'Ent. Etrangères	2	2	0	:	:	0	:	:
A.4. All Companies — A.4. Ensemble des Entreprises	17	17	8	:	:	0	:	:
A.5. Total — A.5. Total								
A.5.1. Domestic Companies — A.5.1. Entreprises Nationales	634	636	621	369	382	397	382	:
A.5.2. (Foreign Controlled Companies) — A.5.2. (Entreprises Sous Contrôle Etranger)	54	54	49	54	49	62	62	:
A.5.3. Branches & Agencies of Foreign Cies — A.5.3. Succursales et Agences d'Ent. Etrangères	152	148	136	27	25	25	20	:
A.5. All Insurance Companies — A.5. Ensemble des Entreprises d'Assurances	786	784	757	396	407	422	402	:
B. NUMBER OF EMPLOYEES — B. NOMBRE D'EMPLOYES								
B.1. Insurance Companies — B.1. Entreprises d'Assurances	58 500	:	:	47 900	51 700	53 300	54 700	47 900
B.2. Intermediaries — B.2. Intermediaires	10 500	:	:	19 000	20 700	23 200	27 300	31 300
B. Total — B. Total	69 000	70 500	77 400	66 900	72 400	76 500	82 000	79 200

C. BUSINESS WRITTEN IN THE REPORTING COUNTRY — C. OPERATIONS CONCLUES DANS LE PAYS DECLARANT

	1992	1993	1994	1995	1996	1997	1998	1999
C.1. Life — C.1. Vie								
C.1.1. Gross Premiums — C.1.1. Primes Brutes								
C.1.1.1. Direct Business — C.1.1.1. Assurances Directes								
C.1.1.1.1. Domestic Companies — C.1.1.1.1. Entreprises Nationales	:	:	:	28 370	31 325	35 159	40 838	43 469
C.1.1.1.2. (Foreign Controlled Companies) — C.1.1.1.2. (Entreprises Sous Contrôle Etranger)	:	:	:	4 894	4 877	10 921	12 752	12 386
C.1.1.1.3. Branches & Agencies of Foreign Cies — C.1.1.1.3. Succursales et Agences d'Ent. Etrangères	:	:	:	1 759	1 858	1 928	1 859	2 228
C.1.1.1. Total — C.1.1.1. Total	:	:	:	30 129	33 183	37 087	42 697	45 697
C.1.1.2. Reinsurance Accepted — C.1.1.2. Réassurance Acceptée								
C.1.1.2.1. Domestic Companies — C.1.1.2.1. Entreprises Nationales	:	:	:	1 086	606	446	823	1 006
C.1.1.2.2. (Foreign Controlled Companies) — C.1.1.2.2. (Entreprises Sous Contrôle Etranger)	:	:	:	284	283	0	322	369
C.1.1.2. Total — C.1.1.2. Total	:	:	:	1 086	606	446	823	1 006
C.1.1.3. Total — C.1.1.3. Total								
C.1.1.3.1. Domestic Companies — C.1.1.3.1. Entreprises Nationales	23 838	23 880	26 112	29 456	31 931	35 605	41 661	44 475
C.1.1.3.2. (Foreign Controlled Companies) — C.1.1.3.2. (Entreprises Sous Contrôle Etranger)	4 425	4 174	4 617	5 178	5 160	10 921	13 074	12 755
C.1.1.3.3. Branches & Agencies of Foreign Cies — C.1.1.3.3. Succursales et Agences d'Ent. Etrangères	1 472	1 664	1 572	1 759	1 858	1 928	1 859	2 228
C.1.1.3. Total Gross Premiums — C.1.1.3. Total des Primes Brutes	25 310	25 544	27 684	31 215	33 789	37 533	43 520	46 703
C.1.2. Ceded Premiums — C.1.2. Primes Cédées								
C.1.2.1. Domestic Companies — C.1.2.1. Entreprises Nationales	1 192	2 374	2 553	2 193	1 859	2 063	2 481	1 754
C.1.2.2. (Foreign Controlled Companies) — C.1.2.2. (Entreprises Sous Contrôle Etranger)	303	234	209	274	196	436	885	451
C.1.2.3. Branches & Agencies of Foreign Cies — C.1.2.3. Succursales et Agences d'Ent. Etrangères	21	18	31	24	21	49	14	12
C.1.2. Total — C.1.2. Total	1 213	2 392	2 584	2 216	1 880	2 113	2 495	1 766
C.1.3. Net Written Premiums — C.1.3. Primes Nettes Emises								
C.1.3.1. Domestic Companies — C.1.3.1. Entreprises Nationales	22 646	21 506	23 559	27 263	30 072	33 542	39 180	42 721
C.1.3.2. (Foreign Controlled Companies) — C.1.3.2. (Entreprises Sous Contrôle Etranger)	4 122	3 940	4 408	4 904	4 964	10 485	12 189	12 304
C.1.3.3. Branches & Agencies of Foreign Cies — C.1.3.3. Succursales et Agences d'Ent. Etrangères	1 451	1 646	1 541	1 735	1 837	1 879	1 845	2 216
C.1.3. Total — C.1.3. Total	24 097	23 152	25 100	28 998	31 909	35 420	41 025	44 937

Monetary Unit: million guilders — Unité monétaire : million de florins

C.2. Non-Life / C.2. Non-Vie

Label (EN) / (FR)	1992	1993	1994	1995	1996	1997	1998	1999
C.2.1. Gross premiums / Primes Brutes								
C.2.1.1. Direct Business / Assurances Directes								
C.2.1.1.1. Domestic Companies / Entreprises Nationales	19 629	21 813	24 570	25 715	27 145	28 430	30 240	32 648
C.2.1.1.2. (Foreign Controlled Companies) / (Entreprises Sous Contrôle Etranger)	4 747	4 589	4 705	4 998	5 006	9 842	10 534	11 070
C.2.1.1.3. Branches & Agencies of Foreign Cies / Succursales et Agences d'Ent. Etrangères	1 279	1 299	1 280	808	644	752	765	724
C.2.1.1. Total	20 908	23 112	25 850	26 522	27 789	29 182	31 005	33 372
C.2.1.2. Reinsurance Accepted / Réassurance Acceptée								
C.2.1.2.1. Domestic Companies / Entreprises Nationales	804	744	809	827	916	889	825	894
C.2.1.2.2. (Foreign Controlled Companies) / (Entreprises Sous Contrôle Etranger)	219	212	217	267	296	420	379	476
C.2.1.2.3. Branches & Agencies of Foreign Cies / Succursales et Agences d'Ent. Etrangères	87	89	87	32	91	1	1	1
C.2.1.2. Total	891	833	896	859	1 007	890	826	895
C.2.1.3. Total								
C.2.1.3.1. Domestic Companies / Entreprises Nationales	20 433	22 557	25 379	26 541	28 061	29 319	31 065	33 542
C.2.1.3.2. (Foreign Controlled Companies) / (Entreprises Sous Contrôle Etranger)	4 966	4 801	4 922	5 265	5 302	10 262	10 913	11 546
C.2.1.3.3. Branches & Agencies of Foreign Cies / Succursales et Agences d'Ent. Etrangères	1 366	1 388	1 367	839	735	753	766	725
C.2.1.3. Total Gross Premiums / Total des Primes Brutes	21 799	23 945	26 746	27 381	28 796	30 072	31 831	34 267
C.2.2. Ceded Premiums / Primes Cédées								
C.2.2.1. Domestic Companies / Entreprises Nationales	2 897	3 082	3 386	3 320	3 375	3 320	3 798	3 945
C.2.2.2. (Foreign Controlled Companies) / (Entreprises Sous Contrôle Etranger)	1 145	974	892	889	833	1 534	2 126	2 238
C.2.2.3. Branches & Agencies of Foreign Cies / Succursales et Agences d'Ent. Etrangères	289	332	360	158	126	120	102	115
C.2.2. Total	3 186	3 414	3 746	3 478	3 501	3 440	3 900	4 060
C.2.3. Net Written Premiums / Primes Nettes Emises								
C.2.3.1. Domestic Companies / Entreprises Nationales	17 536	19 475	21 993	23 221	24 686	25 999	27 267	29 597
C.2.3.2. (Foreign Controlled Companies) / (Entreprises Sous Contrôle Etranger)	3 821	3 827	4 030	4 376	4 469	8 728	8 787	9 308
C.2.3.3. Branches & Agencies of Foreign Cies / Succursales et Agences d'Ent. Etrangères	1 077	1 056	1 007	681	609	633	664	610
C.2.3. Total	18 613	20 531	23 000	23 902	25 295	26 632	27 931	30 207

C.3. Total

Label (EN) / (FR)	1992	1993	1994	1995	1996	1997	1998	1999
C.3.1. Gross Premiums / Primes Brutes								
C.3.1.1. Direct Business / Assurances Directes								
C.3.1.1.1. Domestic Companies / Entreprises Nationales	:	:	:	54 085	58 470	63 589	71 078	76 117
C.3.1.1.2. (Foreign Controlled Companies) / (Entreprises Sous Contrôle Etranger)	:	:	:	9 892	9 883	20 763	23 286	23 456
C.3.1.1.3. Branches & Agencies of Foreign Cies / Succursales et Agences d'Ent. Etrangères	:	:	:	2 567	2 502	2 680	2 624	2 952
C.3.1.1. Total	:	:	:	56 651	60 972	66 269	73 702	79 069
C.3.1.2. Reinsurance Accepted / Réassurance Acceptée								
C.3.1.2.1. Domestic Companies / Entreprises Nationales	:	:	:	1 913	1 522	1 335	1 648	1 900
C.3.1.2.2. (Foreign Controlled Companies) / (Entreprises Sous Contrôle Etranger)	:	:	:	551	579	420	701	845
C.3.1.2.3. Branches & Agencies of Foreign Cies / Succursales et Agences d'Ent. Etrangères	:	:	:	32	91	1	1	1
C.3.1.2. Total	:	:	:	1 945	1 613	1 336	1 649	1 901
C.3.1.3. Total								
C.3.1.3.1. Domestic Companies / Entreprises Nationales	44 271	46 437	51 491	55 997	59 992	64 924	72 726	78 017
C.3.1.3.2. (Foreign Controlled Companies) / (Entreprises Sous Contrôle Etranger)	9 391	8 975	9 539	10 443	10 462	21 183	23 987	24 301
C.3.1.3.3. Branches & Agencies of Foreign Cies / Succursales et Agences d'Ent. Etrangères	2 838	3 052	2 939	2 598	2 593	2 681	2 625	2 953
C.3.1.3. Total Gross Premiums / Total des Primes Brutes	47 109	49 489	54 430	58 596	62 585	67 605	75 351	80 970
C.3.2. Ceded Premiums / Primes Cédées								
C.3.2.1. Domestic Companies / Entreprises Nationales	4 089	5 456	5 939	5 513	5 234	5 383	6 279	5 699
C.3.2.2. (Foreign Controlled Companies) / (Entreprises Sous Contrôle Etranger)	1 448	1 208	1 101	1 163	1 029	1 970	3 011	2 689
C.3.2.3. Branches & Agencies of Foreign Cies / Succursales et Agences d'Ent. Etrangères	310	350	391	182	147	169	116	127
C.3.2. Total	4 399	5 806	6 330	5 694	5 381	5 553	6 395	5 826
C.3.3. Net Written Premiums / Primes Nettes Emises								
C.3.3.1. Domestic Companies / Entreprises Nationales	40 182	40 981	45 552	50 484	54 758	59 541	66 447	72 318
C.3.3.2. (Foreign Controlled Companies) / (Entreprises Sous Contrôle Etranger)	7 943	7 767	8 438	9 280	9 433	19 213	20 976	21 612
C.3.3.3. Branches & Agencies of Foreign Cies / Succursales et Agences d'Ent. Etrangères	2 528	2 702	2 548	2 416	2 446	2 512	2 509	2 826
C.3.3. Total	42 710	43 683	48 100	52 900	57 204	62 052	68 956	75 144

Monetary Unit: million guilders — Unité monétaire : million de florins

E. BUSINESS WRITTEN ABROAD — E. OPERATIONS A L'ETRANGER

English label	French label	1992	1993	1994	1995	1996	1997	1998	1999
E.1. Life	**E.1. Vie**								
E.1.1. Gross Premiums	E.1.1. Primes Brutes								
E.1.1.1. Direct Business	E.1.1.1. Assurance Directe								
E.1.1.1.2. Subsidiaries	E.1.1.1.2. Filliales	:	128	:	:	:	:	:	:
E.1.1.3. Total	E.1.1.3. Total								
E.1.1.3.1. Branches & Agencies	E.1.1.3.1. Succursales & Agences	1 000	1 337	:	:	:	:	:	:
E.1.1.3.2. Subsidiaries	E.1.1.3.2. Filliales	8 069	13 022	:	:	:	:	:	:
E.1.1.3. Total Gross Premiums	E.1.1.3. Total des Primes Brutes	9 069	14 359	:	:	:	:	:	:
E.1.2. Ceded Premiums	E.1.2. Primes Cédées								
E.1.2.1. Branches & Agencies	E.1.2.1. Succursales & Agences	22	35	:	:	:	:	:	:
E.1.2.2. Subsidiaries	E.1.2.2. Filliales	529	649	:	:	:	:	:	:
E.1.2. Total	E.1.2. Total	551	684	:	:	:	:	:	:
E.1.3. Net Written Premiums	E.1.3. Primes Nettes Emises								
E.1.3.1. Branches & Agencies	E.1.3.1. Succursales & Agences	978	1 302	:	:	:	:	:	:
E.1.3.2. Subsidiaries	E.1.3.2. Filliales	7 540	12 373	:	:	:	:	:	:
E.1.3. Total	E.1.3. Total	8 518	13 675	:	:	:	:	:	:
E.2. Non-Life	**E.2. Non-Vie**								
E.2.1. Gross Premiums	E.2.1. Primes Brutes								
E.2.1.3. Total	E.2.1.3. Total								
E.2.1.3.1. Branches & Agencies	E.2.1.3.1. Succursales & Agences	133	155	:	:	:	:	:	:
E.2.1.3.2. Subsidiaries	E.2.1.3.2. Filliales	16 044	14 644	:	:	:	:	:	:
E.2.1.3. Total Gross Premiums	E.2.1.3. Total des Primes Brutes	16 177	14 799	:	:	:	:	:	:
E.2.2. Ceded Premiums	E.2.2. Primes Cédées								
E.2.2.1. Branches & Agencies	E.2.2.1. Succursales & Agences	24	27	:	:	:	:	:	:
E.2.2.2. Subsidiaries	E.2.2.2. Filliales	2 510	1 867	:	:	:	:	:	:
E.2.2. Total	E.2.2. Total	2 534	1 894	:	:	:	:	:	:
E.2.3. Net Written Premiums	E.2.3. Primes Nettes Emises								
E.2.3.1. Branches & Agencies	E.2.3.1. Succursales & Agences	109	128	:	:	:	:	:	:
E.2.3.2. Subsidiaries	E.2.3.2. Filliales	13 534	12 777	:	:	:	:	:	:
E.2.3. Total	E.2.3. Total	13 643	12 905	:	:	:	:	:	:

F. OUTSTANDING INVESTMENT BY DIRECT INSURANCE COMPANIES — F. ENCOURS DES PLACEMENTS DES ENTREPRISES D'ASSURANCES DIRECTES

English label	French label	1992	1993	1994	1995	1996	1997	1998	1999
F.1. Life	**F.1. Vie**								
F.1.1. Real Estate	F.1.1. Immobilier								
F.1.1.1. Domestic Companies	F.1.1.1. Entreprises Nationales	15 396	15 430	14 459	16 981	16 147	19 325	20 554	23 160
F.1.1.2. (Foreign Controlled Companies)	F.1.1.2. (Entreprises Sous Contrôle Etranger)	2 420	2 454	2 495	2 641	2 524	5 849	5 858	7 027
F.1.1.3. Branches & Agencies of Foreign Cies	F.1.1.3. Succursales et Agences d'Ent. Etrangères	523	648	507	478	526	212	612	772
F.1.1.4. Domestic Investment	F.1.1.4. Placement dans le Pays	15 018	15 199	14 155	:	16 270	19 334	20 954	23 826
F.1.1.5. Foreign Investment	F.1.1.5. Placement à l' Etranger	901	879	811	:	403	203	212	106
F.1.1. Total	F.1.1. Total	15 919	16 078	14 966	:	16 673	19 537	21 166	23 932
F.1.2. Mortgage Loans	F.1.2. Prêts Hypothécaires								
F.1.2.1. Domestic Companies	F.1.2.1. Entreprises Nationales	35 997	34 599	38 187	41 569	43 903	43 331	48 206	51 747
F.1.2.2. (Foreign Controlled Companies)	F.1.2.2. (Entreprises Sous Contrôle Etranger)	3 779	4 245	4 711	5 919	4 096	11 629	10 257	10 883
F.1.2.3. Branches & Agencies of Foreign Cies	F.1.2.3. Succursales et Agences d'Ent. Etrangères	354	968	1 069	1 780	1 199	1 687	2 104	2 682
F.1.2.4. Domestic Investment	F.1.2.4. Placement dans le Pays	36 351	35 567	39 256	:	45 102	45 018	50 310	54 429
F.1.2. Total	F.1.2. Total	36 351	35 567	39 256	:	45 102	45 018	50 310	54 429
F.1.3. Shares	F.1.3. Actions								
F.1.3.1. Domestic Companies	F.1.3.1. Entreprises Nationales	21 668	33 640	35 404	56 913	60 826	86 093	110 518	150 018
F.1.3.2. (Foreign Controlled Companies)	F.1.3.2. (Entreprises Sous Contrôle Etranger)	2 163	2 994	3 883	4 627	5 062	15 771	22 098	17 195
F.1.3.3. Branches & Agencies of Foreign Cies	F.1.3.3. Succursales et Agences d'Ent. Etrangères	340	618	860	1 227	2 065	4 248	4 161	5 102
F.1.3.4. Domestic Investment	F.1.3.4. Placement dans le Pays	18 941	29 238	31 507	:	56 968	82 964	102 824	142 088
F.1.3.5. Foreign Investment	F.1.3.5. Placement à l' Etranger	3 067	5 020	4 757	:	5 923	7 377	11 855	13 032
F.1.3. Total	F.1.3. Total	22 008	34 258	36 264	:	62 891	90 341	114 679	155 120

Monetary Unit: million guilders   Unité monétaire : million de florins

	1992	1993	1994	1995	1996	1997	1998	1999
F.1.4. Obligations / Bonds with Fixed Revenue								
F.1.4.1. Entreprises Nationales / Domestic Companies	34 864	47 059	62 431	64 657	81 951	107 791	119 132	123 311
F.1.4.2. (Entreprises Sous Contrôle Etranger) / (Foreign Controlled Companies)	7 968	9 931	10 571	13 822	17 595	33 956	39 450	43 935
F.1.4.3. Succursales et Agences d'Ent. Etrangères / Branches & Agencies of Foreign Cies	3 602	4 745	5 108	7 629	9 562	10 511	10 304	10 727
F.1.4.4. Placement dans le Pays / Domestic Investment	30 540	37 877	58 938	..	69 217	91 369	100 753	102 257
F.1.4.5. Placement à l'Etranger / Foreign Investment	7 926	13 927	8 601	..	22 296	26 933	28 683	31 781
F.1.4. Total	38 466	51 804	67 539	..	91 513	118 302	129 436	134 038
F.1.5. Prêts Autres qu'Hypothécaires / Loans other than Mortgage Loans								
F.1.5.1. Entreprises Nationales / Domestic Companies	80 919	87 358	90 111	85 203	82 829	78 629	73 624	61 948
F.1.5.2. (Entreprises Sous Contrôle Etranger) / (Foreign Controlled Companies)	10 942	11 664	12 565	12 689	10 830	21 484	20 292	20 645
F.1.5.3. Succursales et Agences d'Ent. Etrangères / Branches & Agencies of Foreign Cies	3 180	3 773	3 784	1 809	1 969	1 464	2 068	1 027
F.1.5.4. Placement dans le Pays / Domestic Investment	81 431	88 050	91 105	..	80 981	77 941	73 485	59 335
F.1.5.5. Placement à l'Etranger / Foreign Investment	2 668	3 081	2 790	..	3 817	2 151	2 207	3 640
F.1.5. Total	84 099	91 131	93 895	..	84 798	80 093	75 692	62 975
F.1.6. Autres Placements / Other Investments								
F.1.6.1. Entreprises Nationales / Domestic Companies	11 851	16 435	15 421	22 375	28 239	30 524	36 291	42 064
F.1.6.2. (Entreprises Sous Contrôle Etranger) / (Foreign Controlled Companies)	2 293	3 132	2 712	5 347	2 644	8 547	9 500	14 860
F.1.6.3. Succursales et Agences d'Ent. Etrangères / Branches & Agencies of Foreign Cies	17	19	19	312	331	256	684	1 430
F.1.6. Total	11 868	16 454	15 440	..	28 570	30 780	36 975	43 494
F.1.7. Total								
F.1.7.1. Entreprises Nationales / Domestic Companies	200 695	234 521	256 013	287 698	313 895	365 693	408 325	452 248
F.1.7.2. (Entreprises Sous Contrôle Etranger) / (Foreign Controlled Companies)	29 565	34 420	36 937	45 045	42 751	97 236	15 216	114 545
F.1.7.3. Succursales et Agences d'Ent. Etrangères / Branches & Agencies of Foreign Cies	8 016	10 771	11 347	13 235	15 652	18 378	19 933	21 740
F.1.7. Total des Placements Vie / Total of Life Investments	208 711	245 292	267 360	..	329 547	384 071	428 258	473 988
F.2. Non-Vie / Non-Life								
F.2.1. Immobilier / Real Estate								
F.2.1.1. Entreprises Nationales / Domestic Companies	1 024	1 115	692	979	923	973	912	946
F.2.1.2. (Entreprises Sous Contrôle Etranger) / (Foreign Controlled Companies)	433	349	301	308	295	290	213	245
F.2.1.3. Succursales et Agences d'Ent. Etrangères / Branches & Agencies of Foreign Cies	95	113	45	50	54	37	43	37
F.2.1.4. Placement dans le Pays / Domestic Investment	1 103	1 205	737	..	967	966	939	954
F.2.1.5. Placement à l'Etranger / Foreign Investment	16	23	0	..	10	44	16	29
F.2.1. Total	1 119	1 228	737	..	977	1 010	955	983
F.2.2. Prêts Hypothécaires / Mortgage Loans								
F.2.2.1. Entreprises Nationales / Domestic Companies	1 054	891	908	860	739	704	746	626
F.2.2.2. (Entreprises Sous Contrôle Etranger) / (Foreign Controlled Companies)	57	40	38	58	43	205	202	148
F.2.2.3. Succursales et Agences d'Ent. Etrangères / Branches & Agencies of Foreign Cies	31	29	29	27	24	26	24	24
F.2.2.4. Placement dans le Pays / Domestic Investment	1 085	920	937	..	763	730	770	650
F.2.2. Total	1 085	920	937	..	763	730	770	650
F.2.3. Actions / Shares								
F.2.3.1. Entreprises Nationales / Domestic Companies	3 276	4 578	5 049	5 794	8 489	11 908	13 888	16 539
F.2.3.2. (Entreprises Sous Contrôle Etranger) / (Foreign Controlled Companies)	725	999	905	1 033	1 335	3 170	3 674	4 510
F.2.3.3. Succursales et Agences d'Ent. Etrangères / Branches & Agencies of Foreign Cies	249	344	292	188	221	319	399	343
F.2.3.4. Placement dans le Pays / Domestic Investment	3 122	4 320	4 826	..	7 965	9 873	11 437	13 400
F.2.3.5. Placement à l'Etranger / Foreign Investment	403	602	515	..	745	2 354	2 850	3 482
F.2.3. Total	3 525	4 922	5 341	..	8 710	12 227	14 287	16 882
F.2.4. Obligations / Bonds with Fixed Revenue								
F.2.4.1. Entreprises Nationales / Domestic Companies	9 619	11 273	11 826	13 975	19 309	23 050	26 510	26 889
F.2.4.2. (Entreprises Sous Contrôle Etranger) / (Foreign Controlled Companies)	2 773	2 698	2 850	3 262	3 946	7 563	8 537	8 462
F.2.4.3. Succursales et Agences d'Ent. Etrangères / Branches & Agencies of Foreign Cies	1 453	1 390	1 858	888	853	822	906	890
F.2.4.4. Placement dans le Pays / Domestic Investment	9 774	10 610	11 200	..	15 717	17 882	19 726	22 770
F.2.4.5. Placement à l'Etranger / Foreign Investment	1 298	2 053	..	..	4 445	5 990	7 690	5 009
F.2.4. Total	11 072	12 663	13 058	..	20 162	23 872	27 416	27 779
F.2.5. Prêts Autres qu'Hypothécaires / Loans other than Mortgage Loans								
F.2.5.1. Entreprises Nationales / Domestic Companies	9 423	9 705	10 398	9 569	8 172	7 076	6 534	5 562
F.2.5.2. (Entreprises Sous Contrôle Etranger) / (Foreign Controlled Companies)	1 327	1 148	1 180	1 198	1 087	1 750	1 752	1 612
F.2.5.3. Succursales et Agences d'Ent. Etrangères / Branches & Agencies of Foreign Cies	147	186	183	129	118	117	120	95
F.2.5.4. Placement dans le Pays / Domestic Investment	9 360	9 605	10 281	..	7 944	6 905	6 429	5 565
F.2.5.5. Placement à l'Etranger / Foreign Investment	210	286	300	..	346	288	225	92
F.2.5. Total	9 570	9 891	10 581	..	8 290	7 193	6 654	5 657

NETHERLANDS
PAYS-BAS
Monetary Unit: million guilders
Unité monétaire : million de florins

	1992	1993	1994	1995	1996	1997	1998	1999
F.2.6. Other Investments — F.2.6. Autres Placements								
F.2.6.1. Domestic Companies — F.2.6.1. Entreprises Nationales	88	208	164	6 281	5 942	6 504	7 029	7 132
F.2.6.2. (Foreign Controlled Companies) — F.2.6.2. (Entreprises Sous Contrôle Etranger)	10	160	20	643	499	780	838	1 063
F.2.6.3. Branches & Agencies of Foreign Cies — F.2.6.3. Succursales et Agences d'Ent. Etrangères	0	..	0	129	71	38	25	35
F.2.6.4. Domestic Investment — F.2.6.4. Placement dans le Pays	..	89	..	..	..	6 441	7 016	7 023
F.2.6.5. Foreign Investment — F.2.6.5. Placement à l' Etranger	..	119	..	..	..	101	38	144
F.2.6. Total — F.2.6. Total	88	208	164	..	6 013	6 542	7 054	7 167
F.2.7. Total								
F.2.7.1. Domestic Companies — F.2.7.1. Entreprises Nationales	24 484	27 770	29 037	37 458	43 574	50 215	55 619	57 694
F.2.7.2. (Foreign Controlled Companies) — F.2.7.2. (Entreprises Sous Contrôle Etranger)	5 325	5 394	5 294	6 502	7 204	13 713	15 216	16 040
F.2.7.3. Branches & Agencies of Foreign Cies — F.2.7.3. Succursales et Agences d'Ent. Etrangères	1 975	2 062	1 781	1 411	1 341	1 359	1 517	1 424
F.2.7.4. Domestic Investment — F.2.7.4. Placement dans le Pays	..	..	..	..	..	42 797	46 317	50 362
F.2.7.5. Foreign Investment — F.2.7.5. Placement à l' Etranger	..	..	..	..	..	8 777	10 819	8 756
F.2.7. Total of Non-Life Investments — F.2.7. Total des Placements Non-Vie	26 459	29 832	30 818	..	44 915	51 574	57 136	59 118
G. BREAKDOWN OF NON-LIFE PREMIUMS — G. VENTILATIONS DES PRIMES NON-VIE								
G.1. Motor vehicle — G.1. Assurance Automobile								
G.1.1. Direct Business — G.1.1. Assurances Directes								
G.1.1.1. Gross Premiums — G.1.1.1. Primes Brutes	5 215	5 073	6 415	6 414	6 825	7 023	7 160	7 588
G.1.1.2. Ceded Premiums — G.1.1.2. Primes Cédées	328	257	312	273	260	242	217	243
G.1.1.3. Net Written Premiums — G.1.1.3. Primes Nettes Emises	4 887	4 816	6 103	6 140	6 565	6 781	6 943	7 345
G.1.2. Reinsurance Accepted — G.1.2. Réassurance Acceptée								
G.1.2.1. Gross Premiums — G.1.2.1. Primes Brutes	88	70	83	73	70	44	40	45
G.1.2.2. Ceded Premiums — G.1.2.2. Primes Cédées	30	3	6	3	2	3	9	12
G.1.2.3. Net Written Premiums — G.1.2.3. Primes Nettes Emises	58	67	77	71	68	41	31	33
G.1.3. Total								
G.1.3.1. Gross Premiums — G.1.3.1. Primes Brutes	5 303	5 143	6 498	6 487	6 895	7 067	7 200	7 633
G.1.3.2. Ceded Premiums — G.1.3.2. Primes Cédées	358	260	318	276	262	245	226	255
G.1.3.3. Net Written Premiums — G.1.3.3. Primes Nettes Emises	4 945	4 883	6 180	6 211	6 633	6 822	6 974	7 378
G.2. Marine, Aviation — G.2. Marine, Aviation								
G.2.1. Direct Business — G.2.1. Assurances Directes								
G.2.1.1. Gross Premiums — G.2.1.1. Primes Brutes	1 010	818	1 205	1 024	1 039	1 055	1 045	1 015
G.2.1.2. Ceded Premiums — G.2.1.2. Primes Cédées	271	246	326	320	302	308	279	286
G.2.1.3. Net Written Premiums — G.2.1.3. Primes Nettes Emises	739	572	879	704	737	747	766	729
G.2.2. Reinsurance Accepted — G.2.2. Réassurance Acceptée								
G.2.2.1. Gross Premiums — G.2.2.1. Primes Brutes	70	70	78	92	109	109	111	79
G.2.2.2. Ceded Premiums — G.2.2.2. Primes Cédées	24	19	19	25	38	35	40	40
G.2.2.3. Net Written Premiums — G.2.2.3. Primes Nettes Emises	46	51	59	67	71	74	71	39
G.2.3. Total								
G.2.3.1. Gross Premiums — G.2.3.1. Primes Brutes	1 080	888	1 283	1 116	1 148	1 164	1 156	1 094
G.2.3.2. Ceded Premiums — G.2.3.2. Primes Cédées	295	265	345	345	340	343	319	326
G.2.3.3. Net Written Premiums — G.2.3.3. Primes Nettes Emises	785	623	938	771	808	821	837	768
G.4. Fire, Property Damages — G.4. Incendie, Dommages aux Biens								
G.4.1. Direct Business — G.4.1. Assurances Directes								
G.4.1.1. Gross Premiums — G.4.1.1. Primes Brutes	4 190	4 289	5 004	4 969	5 057	5 252	5 392	5 429
G.4.1.2. Ceded Premiums — G.4.1.2. Primes Cédées	1 253	1 316	1 426	1 431	1 389	1 337	1 376	1 355
G.4.1.3. Net Written Premiums — G.4.1.3. Primes Nettes Emises	2 937	2 973	3 578	3 538	3 668	3 915	4 016	4 074
G.4.2. Reinsurance Accepted — G.4.2. Réassurance Acceptée								
G.4.2.1. Gross Premiums — G.4.2.1. Primes Brutes	218	190	301	237	284	203	182	226
G.4.2.2. Ceded Premiums — G.4.2.2. Primes Cédées	68	61	144	106	144	84	85	125
G.4.2.3. Net Written Premiums — G.4.2.3. Primes Nettes Emises	150	129	157	131	140	119	97	101
G.4.3. Total								
G.4.3.1. Gross Premiums — G.4.3.1. Primes Brutes	4 408	4 479	5 305	5 205	5 341	5 455	5 574	5 655
G.4.3.2. Ceded Premiums — G.4.3.2. Primes Cédées	1 321	1 377	1 570	1 536	1 533	1 421	1 461	1 480
G.4.3.3. Net Written Premiums — G.4.3.3. Primes Nettes Emises	3 087	3 102	3 735	3 669	3 808	4 034	4 113	4 175

NETHERLANDS   PAYS-BAS

Monetary Unit: million guilders — Unité monétaire : million de florins

	1992	1993	1994	1995	1996	1997	1998	1999
G.7. Accident, Health — G.7. Accident, Santé								
G.7.1. Direct Business — G.7.1. Assurances Directes								
G.7.1.1. Gross Premiums — G.7.1.1. Primes Brutes	7 997	9 413	10 154	11 289	12 043	12 795	13 756	15 548
G.7.1.2. Ceded Premiums — G.7.1.2. Primes Cédées	494	555	628	547	671	700	749	801
G.7.1.3. Net Written Premiums — G.7.1.3. Primes Nettes Emises	7 483	8 858	9 526	10 742	11 373	12 095	13 007	14 747
G.7.2. Reinsurance Accepted — G.7.2. Réassurance Acceptée								
G.7.2.1. Gross Premiums — G.7.2.1. Primes Brutes	309	231	216	225	294	315	286	310
G.7.2.2. Ceded Premiums — G.7.2.2. Primes Cédées	7	7	2	6	4	33	34	35
G.7.2.3. Net Written Premiums — G.7.2.3. Primes Nettes Emises	302	224	214	220	290	282	252	275
G.7.3. Total								
G.7.3.1. Gross Premiums — G.7.3.1. Primes Brutes	3 286	9 644	10 370	11 514	12 337	13 110	14 042	15 858
G.7.3.2. Ceded Premiums — G.7.3.2. Primes Cédées	501	562	630	553	675	733	783	836
G.7.3.3. Net Written Premiums — G.7.3.3. Primes Nettes Emises	7 765	9 082	9 740	10 962	11 662	12 377	13 259	15 022
G.8. Others — G.8. Autres								
G.8.1. Direct Business — G.8.1. Assurances Directes								
G.8.1.1. Gross Premiums — G.8.1.1. Primes Brutes	2 515	2 220	3 072	2 826	2 827	3 057	3 652	3 792
G.8.1.2. Ceded Premiums — G.8.1.2. Primes Cédées	672	578	837	736	647	672	1 051	1 081
G.8.1.3. Net Written Premiums — G.8.1.3. Primes Nettes Emises	1 843	1 642	2 235	2 090	2 180	2 385	2 601	2 711
G.8.2. Reinsurance Accepted — G.8.2. Réassurance Acceptée								
G.8.2.1. Gross Premiums — G.8.2.1. Primes Brutes	207	183	218	232	250	219	207	235
G.8.2.2. Ceded Premiums — G.8.2.2. Primes Cédées	39	40	46	32	46	26	60	82
G.8.2.3. Net Written Premiums — G.8.2.3. Primes Nettes Emises	168	143	172	200	204	193	147	153
G.8.3. Total								
G.8.3.1. Gross Premiums — G.8.3.1. Primes Brutes	2 722	2 403	3 290	3 058	3 077	3 276	3 859	4 027
G.8.3.2. Ceded Premiums — G.8.3.2. Primes Cédées	711	618	883	768	693	698	1 111	1 163
G.8.3.3. Net Written Premiums — G.8.3.3. Primes Nettes Emises	2 011	1 785	2 407	2 290	2 384	2 578	2 748	2 864
G.10. Total								
G.10.1. Direct Business — G.10.1. Assurances Directes								
G.10.1.1. Gross Premiums — G.10.1.1. Primes Brutes	20 908	21 813	25 850	26 522	27 791	29 182	31 005	33 372
G.10.1.2. Ceded Premiums — G.10.1.2. Primes Cédées	3 018	2 952	3 529	3 308	3 269	3 259	3 672	3 766
G.10.1.3. Net Written Premiums — G.10.1.3. Primes Nettes Emises	17 889	18 861	22 321	23 215	24 523	25 923	27 333	29 606
G.10.2. Reinsurance Accepted — G.10.2. Réassurance Acceptée								
G.10.2.1. Gross Premiums — G.10.2.1. Primes Brutes	891	744	896	859	1 007	890	826	895
G.10.2.2. Ceded Premiums — G.10.2.2. Primes Cédées	168	130	217	171	234	181	228	294
G.10.2.3. Net Written Premiums — G.10.2.3. Primes Nettes Emises	725	614	679	688	773	709	598	601
G.10.3. Total								
G.10.3.1. Gross Premiums — G.10.3.1. Primes Brutes	21 799	28 557	26 746	27 381	28 798	30 072	31 831	34 267
G.10.3.2. Ceded Premiums — G.10.3.2. Primes Cédées	3 186	3 082	3 746	3 478	3 503	3 440	3 900	4 060
G.10.3.3. Net Written Premiums — G.10.3.3. Primes Nettes Emises	18 613	19 475	23 000	23 902	25 295	26 632	27 931	30 207
H. GROSS CLAIMS PAYMENTS — H. PAIEMENTS BRUTS DES SINISTRES								
H.1. Life — H.1. Vie								
H.1.1. Domestic Companies — H.1.1. Entreprises Nationales	..	..	..	12 412	16 962	17 923	18 741	22 870
H.1.2. (Foreign Controlled Companies) — H.1.2. (Entreprises Sous Contrôle Etranger)	..	..	..	..	2 595	6 442	6 454	8 221
H.1.3. Branches & Agencies of Foreign Cies — H.1.3. Succursales et Agences d'Ent. Etrangères	..	..	..	632	759	950	986	1 276
H.1. Total	..	..	..	13 044	17 721	18 873	19 727	24 146
H.2. Non-Life — H.2. Non-Vie								
H.2.1. Domestic Companies — H.2.1. Entreprises Nationales	..	..	..	17 485	18 195	20 028	21 523	23 397
H.2.2. (Foreign Controlled Companies) — H.2.2. (Entreprises Sous Contrôle Etranger)	..	..	..	..	3 329	6 985	7 404	7 866
H.2.3. Branches & Agencies of Foreign Cies — H.2.3. Succursales et Agences d'Ent. Etrangères	..	..	..	487	416	543	524	518
H.2. Total	..	..	..	17 972	18 611	20 571	22 047	23 915

Monetary Unit: million guilders

Unité monétaire : million de florins

I. GROSS OPERATING EXPENSES / **I. DEPENSES BRUITES D'EXPLOITATION**

	1992	1993	1994	1995	1996	1997	1998	1999	
I.1. Life / **I.1. Vie**									
I.1.1. Domestic Companies / I.1.1. Entreprises Nationales		:	:	3 709	4 032	4 649	5 418	5 877	
I.1.2. (Foreign Controlled Companies) / I.1.2. (Entreprises Sous Contrôle Etranger)		:	:	:	777	1 655	1 885	2 093	
I.1.3. Branches & Agencies of Foreign Cies / I.1.3. Succursales et Agences d'Ent. Etrangères		:	:	262	283	350	414	422	
I.1. Total / I.1. Total des Primes Nettes Vie		:	:	3 971	4 315	4 999	5 832	6 299	
I.2. Non-Life / **I.2. Non-Vie**									
I.2.1. Domestic Companies / I.2.1. Entreprises Nationales		:	:	5 549	6 229	6 603	6 842	7 319	
I.2.2. (Foreign Controlled Companies) / I.2.2. (Entreprises Sous Contrôle Etranger)		:	:	:	2 890	2 473	2 598	2 653	
I.2.3. Branches & Agencies of Foreign Cies / I.2.3. Succursales et Agences d'Ent. Etrangères		:	:	207	285	262	264	265	
I.2. Total / I.2. Total		:	:	5 756	6 514	6 865	7 106	7 584	
J. COMMISSIONS / **J. COMMISSIONS**									
J.1. Life / **J.1. Vie**									
J.1.1. Direct Business / J.1.1. Assurance directe									
J.1.1.1. Domestic Companies / J.1.1.1. Entreprises Nationales		:	:	:	:	1 973	2 507	2 089	
J.1.1.2. (Foreign Controlled Companies) / J.1.1.2. (Entreprises Sous Contrôle Etranger)		:	:	:	:	703	870	720	
J.1.1.3. Branches & Agencies of Foreign Cies / J.1.1.3. Succursales et Agences d'Ent. Etrangères		:	:	:	:	15	40	32	
J.1.1. Total / J.1.1. Total		:	:	:	:	1 988	2 547	2 121	
J.2. Non-Life / **J.2. Non-Vie**									
J.2.1. Direct Business / J.2.1. Assurance directe									
J.2.1.1. Domestic Companies / J.2.1.1. Entreprises Nationales		:	:	:	:	2 090	2 508	1 911	
J.2.1.2. (Foreign Controlled Companies) / J.2.1.2. (Entreprises Sous Contrôle Etranger)		:	:	:	:	783	852	693	
J.2.1.3. Branches & Agencies of Foreign Cies / J.2.1.3. Succursales et Agences d'Ent. Etrangères		:	:	:	:	15	147	139	
J.2.1. Total / J.2.1. Total des Primes Nettes Vie		:	:	:	:	2 100	2 655	2 050	

Monetary Unit: million New Zealand dollars   Unité monétaire : million de dollars de Nouvelle-Zélande

English	1992	1993	1994	1995	1996	1997	1998	1999	Français
A. NUMBER OF COMPANIES IN THE REPORTING COUNTRY									**A. NOMBRE D'ENTREPRISES DANS LE PAYS DECLARANT**
A.1. Life									**A.1. Vie**
A.1.1. Domestic Companies	29	..	46	43	40	38	38	22	A.1.1. Entreprises Nationales
A.1.2. (Foreign Controlled Companies)	0	..	21	25	22	21	23	9	A.1.2. (Entreprises Sous Contrôle Etranger)
A.1.3. Branches & Agencies of Foreign Cies	10	..	..	..	0	0	..	12	A.1.3. Succursales et Agences d'Ent. Etrangères
A.1. All Companies	39	..	46	43	40	38	38	34	A.1. Ensemble des Entreprises
A.2. Non-Life									**A.2. Non-Vie**
A.2.1. Domestic Companies	104	..	186	182	182	156	163	69	A.2.1. Entreprises Nationales
A.2.2. (Foreign Controlled Companies)	0	..	37	32	36	39	41	15	A.2.2. (Entreprises Sous Contrôle Etranger)
A.2.3. Branches & Agencies of Foreign Cies	24	..	..	..	0	0	..	20	A.2.3. Succursales et Agences d'Ent. Etrangères
A.2. All Companies	128	..	186	182	182	156	163	89	A.2. Ensemble des Entreprises
A.5. Total									**A.5. Total**
A.5.1. Domestic Companies	133	..	232	225	222	194	201	91	A.5.1. Entreprises Nationales
A.5.2. (Foreign Controlled Companies)	0	..	58	57	58	60	..	24	A.5.2. (Entreprises Sous Contrôle Etranger)
A.5.3. Branches & Agencies of Foreign Cies	34	..	..	..	0	0	..	32	A.5.3. Succursales et Agences d'Ent. Etrangères
A.5. All Insurance Companies	167	..	232	225	222	194	201	123	A.5. Ensemble des Entreprises d'Assurances
B. NUMBER OF EMPLOYEES									**B. NOMBRE D'EMPLOYES**
B.1. Insurance Companies	9 045	8 823	8 926	9 280	9 362	9 801	8 520	..	B.1. Entreprises d'Assurances
B. Total	..	..	..	..	..	..	..	..	B. Total
C. BUSINESS WRITTEN IN THE REPORTING COUNTRY									**C. OPERATIONS CONCLUES DANS LE PAYS DECLARANT**
C.1. Life									**C.1. Vie**
C.1.1. Gross Premiums									C.1.1. Primes Brutes
C.1.1.1. Direct Business									C.1.1.1. Assurances Directes
C.1.1.1.1. Domestic Companies	1 168	1 182	1 240	1 004	..	..	..	..	C.1.1.1.1. Entreprises Nationales
C.1.1.1. Total	1 168	1 182	1 240	1 004	..	..	..	..	C.1.1.1. Total
C.1.1.3. Total	1 168	1 182	1 240	1 004	..	..	..	..	C.1.1.3. Total
C.1.1.3.1. Domestic Companies	..	..	..	..	..	..	..	..	C.1.1.3.1. Entreprises Nationales
C.1.1.3.3. Branches & Agencies of Foreign Cies	..	..	..	..	..	..	..	..	C.1.1.3.3. Succursales et Agences d'Ent. Etrangères
C.1.1.3. Total Gross Premiums	1 168	1 182	1 240	1 004	1 263	1 410	1 304	1 327	C.1.1.3. Total des Primes Brutes
C.1.3. Net Written Premiums									C.1.3. Primes Nettes Emises
C.1.3.1. Domestic Companies	1 168	1 182	1 240	1 004	..	..	..	..	C.1.3.1. Entreprises Nationales
C.1.3. Total	1 168	1 182	1 240	1 004	..	..	..	..	C.1.3. Total
C.2. Non-Life									**C.2. Non-Vie**
C.2.1. Gross premiums									C.2.1. Primes Brutes
C.2.1.1. Direct Business									C.2.1.1. Assurances Directes
C.2.1.1.1. Domestic Companies	..	..	..	..	..	..	..	..	C.2.1.1.1. Entreprises Nationales
C.2.1.1. Total	..	..	..	..	2 374	2 503	2 480	..	C.2.1.1. Total
C.2.1.2. Reinsurance Accepted									C.2.1.2. Réassurance Accepté
C.2.1.2.1. Domestic Companies	..	..	..	..	..	..	..	..	C.2.1.2.1. Entreprises Nationales
C.2.1.2.3. Branches & Agencies of Foreign Cies	..	..	..	..	..	..	..	..	C.2.1.2.3. Succursales et Agences d'Ent. Etrangères
C.2.1.2. Total	..	..	..	..	37	36	27	..	C.2.1.2. Total
C.2.1.3. Total									C.2.1.3. Total
C.2.1.3.1. Domestic Companies	1 813	1 574	1 608	1 822	..	..	..	..	C.2.1.3.1. Entreprises Nationales
C.2.1.3. Total Gross Premiums	1 813	1 574	1 608	1 822	2 411	2 539	2 507	1 827	C.2.1.3. Total des Primes Brutes

Monetary Unit: million New Zealand dollars — Unité monétaire : million de dollars de Nouvelle-Zélande

Label (EN)	Label (FR)	1992	1993	1994	1995	1996	1997	1998	1999
C.2.2. Ceded Premiums	C.2.2. Primes Cédées								
C.2.2.1. Domestic Companies	C.2.2.1. Entreprises Nationales	64	..						
C.2.2.3. Branches & Agencies of Foreign Cies	C.2.2.3. Succursales et Agences d'Ent. Etrangères	120	237	286	347	318	306	274	..
C.2.2. Total	C.2.2. Total	184	237	286	347	318	306	274	..
C.2.3. Net Written Premiums	C.2.3. Primes Nettes Emises								
C.2.3.1. Domestic Companies	C.2.3.1. Entreprises Nationales	1 750	1 336	1 322	1 475				
C.2.3.3. Branches & Agencies of Foreign Cies	C.2.3.3. Succursales et Agences d'Ent. Etrangères								
C.2.3. Total	C.2.3. Total	1 750	1 336	1 322	1 475	2 093	2 233	2 234	..
C.3. Total	**C.3. Total**								
C.3.1. Gross Premiums	C.3.1. Primes Brutes								
C.3.1.1. Direct Business	C.3.1.1. Assurances Directes								
C.3.1.1.1. Domestic Companies	C.3.1.1.1. Entreprises Nationales	..	..	..	..	..	..	..	..
C.3.1.1.3. Branches & Agencies of Foreign Cies	C.3.1.1.3. Succursales et Agences d'Ent. Etrangères	..	..	..	..	..	..	..	..
C.3.1.1. Total	C.3.1.1. Total	2 982	2 756	2 848	2 826	..	..	..	..
C.3.1.3. Total	C.3.1.3. Total								
C.3.1.3.1. Domestic Companies	C.3.1.3.1. Entreprises Nationales	..	..	..	..	..	..	..	..
C.3.1.3.3. Branches & Agencies of Foreign Cies	C.3.1.3.3. Succursales et Agences d'Ent. Etrangères	..	..	..	..	..	..	..	..
C.3.1.3. Total Gross Premiums	C.3.1.3. Total des Primes Brutes	2 982	2 756	2 848	2 826	3 674	3 949	3 811	3 155
C.3.3. Net Written Premiums	C.3.3. Primes Nettes Emises								
C.3.3.1. Domestic Companies	C.3.3.1. Entreprises Nationales	2 918	2 518	2 562	2 479	..	..	..	..
C.3.3.3. Branches & Agencies of Foreign Cies	C.3.3.3. Succursales et Agences d'Ent. Etrangères	..	..	..	..	..	..	..	..
C.3.3. Total	C.3.3. Total	2 918	2 518	2 562	2 479	..	..	..	..
G. BREAKDOWN OF NON-LIFE PREMIUMS	**G. VENTILATIONS DES PRIMES NON-VIE**								
G.1. Motor vehicle	G.1. Assurance Automobile								
G.1.1. Direct Business	G.1.1. Assurances Directes								
G.1.1.1. Gross Premiums	G.1.1.1. Primes Brutes	517	535	524	549	..	628	579	..
G.1.3. Total	G.1.3. Total								
G.1.3.1. Gross Premiums	G.1.3.1. Primes Brutes	..	..	..	..	516	..	..	..
G.2. Marine, Aviation	G.2. Marine, Aviation								
G.2.1. Direct Business	G.2.1. Assurances Directes								
G.2.1.1. Gross Premiums	G.2.1.1. Primes Brutes	24	32	45	34	..	32	20	..
G.2.3. Total	G.2.3. Total								
G.2.3.1. Gross Premiums	G.2.3.1. Primes Brutes	..	..	..	..	22	..	..	..
G.3. Freight	G.3. Fret								
G.3.1. Direct Business	G.3.1. Assurances Directes								
G.3.1.1. Gross Premiums	G.3.1.1. Primes Brutes	39	33	28	27	..	30	14	..
G.3.3. Total	G.3.3. Total								
G.3.3.1. Gross Premiums	G.3.3.1. Primes Brutes	..	..	..	..	21	..	..	..
G.4. Fire, Property Damages	G.4. Incendie, Dommages aux Biens								
G.4.1. Direct Business	G.4.1. Assurances Directes								
G.4.1.1. Gross Premiums	G.4.1.1. Primes Brutes	571	628	644	729	..	767	623	..
G.4.3. Total	G.4.3. Total								
G.4.3.1. Gross Premiums	G.4.3.1. Primes Brutes	..	..	..	..	625	..	..	..
G.7. Accident, Health	G.7. Accident, Santé								
G.7.1. Direct Business	G.7.1. Assurances Directes								
G.7.1.1. Gross Premiums	G.7.1.1. Primes Brutes	..	..	..	..	..	752	712	..
G.7.3. Total	G.7.3. Total								
G.7.3.1. Gross Premiums	G.7.3.1. Primes Brutes	..	..	..	..	445	..	..	..

Monetary Unit: million New Zealand dollars

Unité monétaire : million de dollars de Nouvelle-Zélande

		1992	1993	1994	1995	1996	1997	1998	1999
G.8. Others	G.8. Autres								
G.8.1. Direct Business	G.8.1. Assurances Directes								
G.8.1.1. Gross Premiums	G.8.1.1. Primes Brutes	122	132	172	142	:	136	138	
G.8.3. Total	G.8.3. Total								
G.8.3.1. Gross Premiums	G.8.3.1. Primes Brutes	:	:	:	:	129	:	:	
G.10. Total	G.10. Total								
G.10.1. Direct Business	G.10.1. Assurances Directes								
G.10.1.1. Gross Premiums	G.10.1.1. Primes Brutes	:	1 509	1 413	1 481	:	:	:	
G.10.1.2. Ceded Premiums	G.10.1.2. Primes Cédées	64	:	:	:	:	:	:	
G.10.1.3. Net Written Premiums	G.10.1.3. Primes Nettes Emises	:	:	:	:	:	:	:	
G.10.2. Reinsurance Accepted	G.10.2. Reassurance Acceptée								
G.10.2.1. Gross Premiums	G.10.2.1. Primes Brutes	:	237	:	:	:	36	27	
G.10.2.3. Net Written Premiums	G.10.2.3. Primes Nettes Emises	:	:	:	:	:	:	:	
G.10.3. Total	G.10.3. Total								
G.10.3.1. Gross Premiums	G.10.3.1. Primes Brutes	1 813	1 574	1 608	:	1 757	:	:	
G.10.3.2. Ceded Premiums	G.10.3.2. Primes Cédées	64	237	286	:	:	306	274	
G.10.3.3. Net Written Premiums	G.10.3.3. Primes Nettes Emises	1 750	1 336	1 322	:	:	:	:	
H. GROSS CLAIMS PAYMENTS	**H. PAIEMENTS BRUTS DES SINISTRES**								
H.1. Life	**H.1. Vie**								
H.1. Total	H.1. Total		998	1 076	1 211	1 178	1 477	1 342	
H.2. Non-Life	**H.2. Non-Vie**								
H.2. Total	H.2. Total		866	1 150	1 348	1 435	1 606	1 508	
I. GROSS OPERATING EXPENSES	**I. DEPENSES BRUTES D'EXPLOITATION**								
I.1. Life	**I.1. Vie**								
I.1. Total	I.1. Total des Primes Nettes Vie		1 213	1 292	1 131	1 113	1 115	880	
I.2. Non-Life	**I.2. Non-Vie**								
I.2. Total	I.2. Total		642	542	542	629	601	642	
J. COMMISSIONS	**J. COMMISSIONS**								
J.1. Life	**J.1. Vie**								
J.1.3. Total — Total of Life Net Premiums	J.1.3. Total		:	:	:	49	221	217	
J.2. Non-Life	**J.2. Non-Vie**								
J.2.3. Total	J.2.3. Total	128	128	98	118	105	184	192	

180

Monetary Unit: million Norwegian kroner — Unité monétaire : million de couronnes norvégiennes

	1992	1993	1994	1995	1996	1997	1998	1999
A. NUMBER OF COMPANIES IN THE REPORTING COUNTRY / A. NOMBRE D'ENTREPRISES DANS LE PAYS DECLARANT								
A.1. Life / A.1. Vie								
A.1.1. Domestic Companies / A.1.1. Entreprises Nationales	10	10	10	9	9	16	16	15
A.1.2. (Foreign Controlled Companies) / A.1.2. (Entreprises Sous Contrôle Etranger)	2	1	1	1	1	1	1	1
A.1.3. Branches & Agencies of Foreign Cies / A.1.3. Succursales et Agences d'Ent. Etrangères	0	0	0	0	0	1	6	7
A.1. All Companies / A.1. Ensemble des Entreprises	10	10	10	9	10	17	22	22
A.2. Non-Life / A.2. Non-Vie								
A.2.1. Domestic Companies / A.2.1. Entreprises Nationales	111	113	104	107	106	110	105	89
A.2.2. (Foreign Controlled Companies) / A.2.2. (Entreprises Sous Contrôle Etranger)	2	2	2	1	5	7	7	6
A.2.3. Branches & Agencies of Foreign Cies / A.2.3. Succursales et Agences d'Ent. Etrangères	22	14	18	18	12	13	17	21
A.2. All Companies / A.2. Ensemble des Entreprises	133	127	122	125	118	123	122	110
A.4. Reinsurance / A.4. Réassurance								
A.4.1. Domestic Companies / A.4.1. Entreprises Nationales	2	2	2	2	2	2	2	2
A.4.2. (Foreign Controlled Companies) / A.4.2. (Entreprises Sous Contrôle Etranger)	0	0	0	0	1	1	1	1
A.4. All Companies / A.4. Ensemble des Entreprises	2	2	2	2	2	2	2	2
A.5. Total								
A.5.1. Domestic Companies / A.5.1. Entreprises Nationales	123	125	116	118	117	128	123	106
A.5.2. (Foreign Controlled Companies) / A.5.2. (Entreprises Sous Contrôle Etranger)	4	3	3	3	7	9	9	8
A.5.3. Branches & Agencies of Foreign Cies / A.5.3. Succursales et Agences d'Ent. Etrangères	22	14	18	18	13	14	23	28
A.5. All Insurance Companies / A.5. Ensemble des Entreprises d'Assurances	145	139	134	136	130	142	146	134
B. NUMBER OF EMPLOYEES / B. NOMBRE D'EMPLOYES								
B.1. Insurance Companies / B.1. Entreprises d'Assurances	12 000	11 640	8 083	7 817	9 319	9 132	10 677	10 268
B.2. Intermediaries / B.2. Intermediaires	..	..	..	..	..	..	..	
B. Total	..	..	..	..	..	..	..	
C. BUSINESS WRITTEN IN THE REPORTING COUNTRY / C. OPERATIONS CONCLUES DANS LE PAYS DECLARANT								
C.1. Life / C.1. Vie								
C.1.1. Gross Premiums / C.1.1. Primes Brutes								
C.1.1.1. Direct Business / C.1.1.1. Assurances Directes								
C.1.1.1.1. Domestic Companies / C.1.1.1.1. Entreprises Nationales	..	15 862	19 255	18 893	19 787	25 211	26 526	26 075
C.1.1.1.2. (Foreign Controlled Companies) / C.1.1.1.2. (Entreprises Sous Contrôle Etranger)	..	281	434	468	551	707	912	928
C.1.1.1.3. Branches & Agencies of Foreign Cies / C.1.1.1.3. Succursales et Agences d'Ent. Etrangères	0	0	..	0	3	3	52	119
C.1.1.1. Total	..	15 862	19 255	18 893	19 790	25 214	26 578	26 194
C.1.1.2. Reinsurance Accepted / C.1.1.2. Réassurance Acceptée								
C.1.1.2.1. Domestic Companies / C.1.1.2.1. Entreprises Nationales	..	0	0	0	0	0	0	0
C.1.1.2. Total	..	0	0	0	0	0	0	0
C.1.1.3. Total								
C.1.1.3.1. Domestic Companies / C.1.1.3.1. Entreprises Nationales	15 546	15 862	19 255	18 893	19 787	25 211	26 526	26 075
C.1.1.3.2. (Foreign Controlled Companies) / C.1.1.3.2. (Entreprises Sous Contrôle Etranger)	346	281	434	468	551	707	912	928
C.1.1.3.3. Branches & Agencies of Foreign Cies / C.1.1.3.3. Succursales et Agences d'Ent. Etrangères	0	0	..	0	3	3	52	119
C.1.1.3. Total Gross Premiums / C.1.1.3. Total des Primes Brutes	15 892	15 862	19 255	18 893	19 790	25 214	26 578	26 194
C.1.2. Ceded Premiums / C.1.2. Primes Cédées								
C.1.2.1. Domestic Companies / C.1.2.1. Entreprises Nationales	8	0	0	0	245	272	862	929
C.1.2.2. (Foreign Controlled Companies) / C.1.2.2. (Entreprises Sous Contrôle Etranger)	7	0	0	0	1	2	2	6
C.1.2.3. Branches & Agencies of Foreign Cies / C.1.2.3. Succursales et Agences d'Ent. Etrangères							2	4
C.1.2. Total	15	0	0	0	245	272	864	933
C.1.3. Net Written Premiums / C.1.3. Primes Nettes Emises								
C.1.3.1. Domestic Companies / C.1.3.1. Entreprises Nationales	15 538	15 862	19 255	18 893	19 542	24 939	25 664	25 146
C.1.3.2. (Foreign Controlled Companies) / C.1.3.2. (Entreprises Sous Contrôle Etranger)	339	281	434	468	550	705	910	922
C.1.3.3. Branches & Agencies of Foreign Cies / C.1.3.3. Succursales et Agences d'Ent. Etrangères	0	0	..	0	3	3	50	115
C.1.3. Total	15 877	15 862	19 255	18 893	19 545	24 942	25 714	25 261

Monetary Unit: million Norwegian kroner

Unité monétaire : million de couronnes norvégiennes

C.2. Non-Life / C.2. Non-Vie

	1992	1993	1994	1995	1996	1997	1998	1999
C.2.1. Gross premiums / **C.2.1. Primes Brutes**								
C.2.1.1. Direct Business / C.2.1.1. Assurances Directes								
C.2.1.1.1. Domestic Companies / C.2.1.1.1. Entreprises Nationales	22 752	24 057	24 741	23 837	24 576	25 079	26 838	29 238
C.2.1.1.2. (Foreign Controlled Companies) / C.2.1.1.2. (Entreprises Sous Contrôle Etranger)	3 418	3 807	3 825	3 766	4 418	4 684	5 535	5 471
C.2.1.1.3. Branches & Agencies of Foreign Cies / C.2.1.1.3. Succursales et Agences d'Ent. Etrangères	345	386	:	:	444	742	775	857
C.2.1.1. Total / C.2.1.1. Total	23 097	24 443	:	:	25 020	25 821	27 613	30 095
C.2.1.2. Reinsurance Accepted / C.2.1.2. Réassurance Acceptée								
C.2.1.2.1. Domestic Companies / C.2.1.2.1. Entreprises Nationales	2 389	2 233	1 081	678	253	277	337	349
C.2.1.2.2. (Foreign Controlled Companies) / C.2.1.2.2. (Entreprises Sous Contrôle Etranger)	239	236	165	207	2	61	85	87
C.2.1.2.3. Branches & Agencies of Foreign Cies / C.2.1.2.3. Succursales et Agences d'Ent. Etrangères	5	0	:	:	0	0	0	0
C.2.1.2. Total / C.2.1.2. Total	2 394	2 233	:	:	253	277	337	349
C.2.1.3. Total / C.2.1.3. Total								
C.2.1.3.1. Domestic Companies / C.2.1.3.1. Entreprises Nationales	25 141	26 290	25 822	24 514	24 829	25 356	27 175	29 587
C.2.1.3.2. (Foreign Controlled Companies) / C.2.1.3.2. (Entreprises Sous Contrôle Etranger)	3 657	4 043	3 990	3 973	4 420	4 745	5 620	5 558
C.2.1.3.3. Branches & Agencies of Foreign Cies / C.2.1.3.3. Succursales et Agences d'Ent. Etrangères	349	386	:	:	444	742	775	857
C.2.1.3. Total Gross Premiums / C.2.1.3. Total des Primes Brutes	25 490	26 676	:	:	25 273	26 098	27 950	30 444
C.2.2. Ceded Premiums / **C.2.2. Primes Cédées**								
C.2.2.1. Domestic Companies / C.2.2.1. Entreprises Nationales	5 767	6 529	6 169	5 141	3 954	4 226	4 657	5 114
C.2.2.2. (Foreign Controlled Companies) / C.2.2.2. (Entreprises Sous Contrôle Etranger)	813	1 052	833	708	678	722	1 316	1 531
C.2.2.3. Branches & Agencies of Foreign Cies / C.2.2.3. Succursales et Agences d'Ent. Etrangères	34	83	:	:	44	100	139	183
C.2.2. Total / C.2.2. Total	5 801	6 612	:	:	3 998	4 326	4 796	5 297
C.2.3. Net Written Premiums / **C.2.3. Primes Nettes Emises**								
C.2.3.1. Domestic Companies / C.2.3.1. Entreprises Nationales	19 374	19 761	19 653	19 373	20 875	21 130	22 518	24 473
C.2.3.2. (Foreign Controlled Companies) / C.2.3.2. (Entreprises Sous Contrôle Etranger)	2 844	2 991	3 157	3 265	3 742	4 023	4 304	4 027
C.2.3.3. Branches & Agencies of Foreign Cies / C.2.3.3. Succursales et Agences d'Ent. Etrangères	315	303	:	:	400	642	636	674
C.2.3. Total / C.2.3. Total	19 689	20 064	:	:	21 275	21 772	23 154	25 147

C.3. Total / C.3. Total

	1992	1993	1994	1995	1996	1997	1998	1999
C.3.1. Gross Premiums / **C.3.1. Primes Brutes**								
C.3.1.1. Direct Business / C.3.1.1. Assurances Directes								
C.3.1.1.1. Domestic Companies / C.3.1.1.1. Entreprises Nationales	:	39 919	43 996	42 730	44 363	50 290	53 364	55 313
C.3.1.1.2. (Foreign Controlled Companies) / C.3.1.1.2. (Entreprises Sous Contrôle Etranger)	:	4 088	4 259	4 234	4 969	5 391	6 447	6 399
C.3.1.1.3. Branches & Agencies of Foreign Cies / C.3.1.1.3. Succursales et Agences d'Ent. Etrangères	345	386	:	:	447	745	827	976
C.3.1.1. Total / C.3.1.1. Total	:	40 305	:	:	44 810	51 035	54 191	56 289
C.3.1.2. Reinsurance Accepted / C.3.1.2. Réassurance Acceptée								
C.3.1.2.1. Domestic Companies / C.3.1.2.1. Entreprises Nationales	:	2 233	1 081	678	253	277	337	349
C.3.1.2.2. (Foreign Controlled Companies) / C.3.1.2.2. (Entreprises Sous Contrôle Etranger)	:	236	165	207	2	61	85	87
C.3.1.2.3. Branches & Agencies of Foreign Cies / C.3.1.2.3. Succursales et Agences d'Ent. Etrangères	5	0	:	:	0	0	0	0
C.3.1.2. Total / C.3.1.2. Total	:	2 233	:	:	253	277	337	349
C.3.1.3. Total / C.3.1.3. Total								
C.3.1.3.1. Domestic Companies / C.3.1.3.1. Entreprises Nationales	40 687	42 152	45 077	43 407	44 616	50 567	53 701	55 662
C.3.1.3.2. (Foreign Controlled Companies) / C.3.1.3.2. (Entreprises Sous Contrôle Etranger)	4 003	4 324	4 424	4 441	4 971	5 452	6 531	6 486
C.3.1.3.3. Branches & Agencies of Foreign Cies / C.3.1.3.3. Succursales et Agences d'Ent. Etrangères	349	386	:	:	447	745	827	976
C.3.1.3. Total Gross Premiums / C.3.1.3. Total des Primes Brutes	41 382	42 538	:	:	45 063	51 312	54 528	56 638
C.3.2. Ceded Premiums / **C.3.2. Primes Cédées**								
C.3.2.1. Domestic Companies / C.3.2.1. Entreprises Nationales	5 775	6 529	6 169	5 141	4 199	4 498	5 519	6 043
C.3.2.2. (Foreign Controlled Companies) / C.3.2.2. (Entreprises Sous Contrôle Etranger)	820	1 052	833	708	679	724	1 317	1 537
C.3.2.3. Branches & Agencies of Foreign Cies / C.3.2.3. Succursales et Agences d'Ent. Etrangères	34	83	:	:	:	100	141	187
C.3.2. Total / C.3.2. Total	5 816	6 612	:	:	4 243	4 598	5 660	6 230
C.3.3. Net Written Premiums / **C.3.3. Primes Nettes Emises**								
C.3.3.1. Domestic Companies / C.3.3.1. Entreprises Nationales	34 912	35 623	38 908	38 266	40 417	46 069	48 182	49 619
C.3.3.2. (Foreign Controlled Companies) / C.3.3.2. (Entreprises Sous Contrôle Etranger)	3 183	3 272	3 591	3 733	4 292	4 728	5 214	4 949
C.3.3.3. Branches & Agencies of Foreign Cies / C.3.3.3. Succursales et Agences d'Ent. Etrangères	315	303	:	:	403	645	686	789
C.3.3. Total / C.3.3. Total	35 566	35 926	:	:	40 820	46 714	48 868	50 408

Monetary Unit: million Norwegian kroner — Unité monétaire : million de couronnes norvégiennes

D. NET WRITTEN PREMIUMS IN THE REPORTING COUNTRY IN TERMS OF DOMESTIC AND FOREIGN RISKS / D. PRIMES NETTES EMISES DANS LE PAYS DECLARANT EN RISQUES NATIONAUX ET ETRANGERS

	1992	1993	1994	1995	1996	1997	1998	1999
D.1. Life / D.1. Vie								
D.1.1. Domestic Risks / D.1.1. Risques Nationaux								
D.1.1.3. Branches & Agencies of Foreign Cies / Succursales et Agences d'Ent. Etrangères	0	..	..	..	..	3	..	..
D.1.3. Total								
D.1.3.1. Domestic Companies / Entreprises Nationales	15 538	15 862	19 255	18 893	19 542	24 939	25 664	25 146
D.1.3.2. (Foreign Controlled Companies / Entreprises Sous Contrôle Etranger)	339	281	434	468	550	705	910	922
D.1.3.3. Branches & Agencies of Foreign Cies / Succursales et Agences d'Ent. Etrangères	0	0	0	3	3	3	50	115
D.1.3. Total of Life Net Premiums / Total des Primes Nettes Vie	15 877	15 862	19 255	18 893	19 545	24 942	25 714	25 261
E. BUSINESS WRITTEN ABROAD / E. OPERATIONS A L'ETRANGER								
E.2. Non-Life / E.2. Non-Vie								
E.2.1. Gross Premiums / E.2.1. Primes Brutes								
E.2.1.1. Direct Business / E.2.1.1. Assurance Directe								
E.2.1.1.1. Branches & Agencies / Succursales & Agences	..	..	..	..	441	496	500	561
E.2.1.1.2. Subsidiaries / Filliales	..	..	..	..	368	402	358	412
E.2.1.1. Total	..	..	..	..	809	898	..	..
E.2.1.3. Total								
E.2.1.3.1. Branches & Agencies / Succursales & Agences	..	..	..	..	441	496	..	..
E.2.1.3.2. Subsidiaries / Filliales	..	..	..	..	368	402	..	..
E.2.1.3. Total Gross Premiums / Total des Primes Brutes	..	..	..	..	809	898	..	..
F. OUTSTANDING INVESTMENT BY DIRECT INSURANCE COMPANIES / F. ENCOURS DES PLACEMENTS DES ENTREPRISES D'ASSURANCES DIRECTES								
F.1. Life / F.1. Vie								
F.1.1. Real Estate / F.1.1. Immobilier								
F.1.1.1. Domestic Companies / Entreprises Nationales	9 726	10 330	12 461	14 459	18 191	19 347	21 820	33 140
F.1.1.2. (Foreign Controlled Companies / Entreprises Sous Contrôle Etranger)	2	9	132	264	265	385	374	591
F.1.1.4. Domestic Investment / Placement dans le Pays	9 726	..	..	..	..	..	..	..
F.1.1.5. Foreign Investment / Placement à l'Etranger	2	..	..	..	..	..	..	..
F.1.1. Total	9 728	10 330	12 461	14 459	18 919	19 347	..	..
F.1.2. Mortgage Loans / Prêts Hypothécaires								
F.1.2.1. Domestic Companies / Entreprises Nationales	37 683	67 773	51 960	39 091	37 285	31 593	15 792	13 413
F.1.2.2. (Foreign Controlled Companies / Entreprises Sous Contrôle Etranger)	0	343	529	484	..	..	0	0
F.1.2.4. Domestic Investment / Placement dans le Pays	37 683	..	..	..	..	31 336	..	..
F.1.2.5. Foreign Investment / Placement à l'Etranger	0	..	..	..	..	257	..	..
F.1.2. Total	37 683	67 773	51 960	39 091	37 285	31 593	..	..
F.1.3. Shares / F.1.3. Actions								
F.1.3.1. Domestic Companies / Entreprises Nationales	14 357	22 021	20 460	26 080	35 174	56 596	73 580	113 172
F.1.3.2. (Foreign Controlled Companies / Entreprises Sous Contrôle Etranger)	51	182	348	458	803	1 084	1 820	3 060
F.1.3.4. Domestic Investment / Placement dans le Pays	14 357	..	..	..	22 602	32 739	..	..
F.1.3.5. Foreign Investment / Placement à l'Etranger	51	..	..	..	12 572	23 857	..	..
F.1.3. Total	14 408	22 021	20 460	26 080	35 174	56 596	..	..
F.1.4. Bonds with Fixed Revenue / Obligations								
F.1.4.1. Domestic Companies / Entreprises Nationales	71 014	95 616	102 724	125 200	121 368	140 055	160 779	171 830
F.1.4.2. (Foreign Controlled Companies / Entreprises Sous Contrôle Etranger)	1 580	1 511	1 594	2 287	3 803	4 578	5 738	5 946
F.1.4.4. Domestic Investment / Placement dans le Pays	71 014	..	..	..	88 910	96 508	..	..
F.1.4.5. Foreign Investment / Placement à l'Etranger	1 580	..	..	..	32 458	43 547	..	..
F.1.4. Total	72 594	95 616	102 724	125 200	121 368	140 055	..	..

Monetary Unit: million Norwegian kroner — Unité monétaire : million de couronnes norvégiennes

Item	1992	1993	1994	1995	1996	1997	1998	1 999
F.1.5. Loans other than Mortgage Loans / Prêts Autres qu'Hypothécaires								
F.1.5.1. Domestic Companies / Entreprises Nationales	36 219	0	11 030	13 624	13 002	14 257	12 689	12 019
F.1.5.2. (Foreign Controlled Companies) / (Entreprises Sous Contrôle Etranger)	335	0	0	:	:	:	0	0
F.1.5.4. Domestic Investment / Placement dans le Pays	36 219	:	:	:	:	:	:	:
F.1.5.5. Foreign Investment / Placement à l'Etranger	335	:	:	:	:	:	:	:
F.1.5. Total	36 554	0	11 030	13 624	13 002	14 257	:	12 019
F.1.6. Other Investments / Autres Placements								
F.1.6.1. Domestic Companies / Entreprises Nationales	17 193	13 548	20 496	18 324	26 381	21 326	4 229	5 002
F.1.6.2. (Foreign Controlled Companies) / (Entreprises Sous Contrôle Etranger)	368	127	366	312	:	831	4	54
F.1.6.4. Domestic Investment / Placement dans le Pays	17 193	:	:	:	:	:	:	:
F.1.6.5. Foreign Investment / Placement à l'Etranger	368	:	:	:	:	:	:	:
F.1.6. Total	17 561	13 548	20 496	18 324	26 381	21 326	4 229	:
F.1.7. Total								
F.1.7.1. Domestic Companies / Entreprises Nationales	186 192	209 288	219 131	236 778	251 401	283 174	288 888	348 576
F.1.7.2. (Foreign Controlled Companies) / (Entreprises Sous Contrôle Etranger)	2 336	2 172	2 969	3 805	4 871	6 878	7 936	9 651
F.1.7.4. Domestic Investment / Placement dans le Pays	186 192	:	:	:	:	:	:	:
F.1.7.5. Foreign Investment / Placement à l'Etranger	2 336	:	:	:	:	:	:	:
F.1.7. Total of Life Investments / Total des Placements Vie	188 528	209 288	219 131	236 778	251 401	283 174	:	:
F.2. Non-Life / Non-Vie								
F.2.1. Real Estate / Immobilier								
F.2.1.1. Domestic Companies / Entreprises Nationales	2 939	2 767	2 756	3 227	3 069	3 719	2 946	3 109
F.2.1.2. (Foreign Controlled Companies) / (Entreprises Sous Contrôle Etranger)	279	274	484	474	461	470	614	586
F.2.1. Total	3 218	2 767	:	:	3 069	3 719	:	:
F.2.2. Mortgage Loans / Prêts Hypothécaires								
F.2.2.1. Domestic Companies / Entreprises Nationales	2 824	3 352	3 628	3 585	4 269	3 925	3 092	1 221
F.2.2.2. (Foreign Controlled Companies) / (Entreprises Sous Contrôle Etranger)	0	518	655	533	1 180	1 448	1 762	14
F.2.2.4. Domestic Investment / Placement dans le Pays	2 824	2 974	:	:	:	:	:	:
F.2.2.5. Foreign Investment / Placement à l'Etranger	0	378	:	:	:	:	:	:
F.2.2. Total	2 824	3 352	:	:	4 269	3 925	:	:
F.2.3. Shares / Actions								
F.2.3.1. Domestic Companies / Entreprises Nationales	5 620	8 804	11 211	12 821	13 224	19 037	20 191	26 321
F.2.3.2. (Foreign Controlled Companies) / (Entreprises Sous Contrôle Etranger)	554	1 600	2 075	2 319	2 640	3 211	3 706	3 638
F.2.3.4. Domestic Investment / Placement dans le Pays	4 507	5 979	:	:	:	12 604	:	:
F.2.3.5. Foreign Investment / Placement à l'Etranger	1 667	2 825	:	:	:	6 433	:	:
F.2.3. Total	6 174	8 804	:	:	13 224	19 037	:	:
F.2.4. Bonds with Fixed Revenue / Obligations								
F.2.4.1. Domestic Companies / Entreprises Nationales	12 347	20 529	17 112	30 260	31 269	33 570	33 714	27 687
F.2.4.2. (Foreign Controlled Companies) / (Entreprises Sous Contrôle Etranger)	2 546	3 334	3 100	3 849	4 321	4 220	3 257	4 094
F.2.4.4. Domestic Investment / Placement dans le Pays	11 502	14 616	:	:	:	:	:	:
F.2.4.5. Foreign Investment / Placement à l'Etranger	3 391	5 913	:	:	:	:	:	:
F.2.4. Total	14 893	20 529	:	:	31 269	33 570	:	:
F.2.5. Loans other than Mortgage Loans / Prêts Autres qu'Hypothécaires								
F.2.5.1. Domestic Companies / Entreprises Nationales	4 363	1 379	2 440	441	334	330	203	101
F.2.5.2. (Foreign Controlled Companies) / (Entreprises Sous Contrôle Etranger)	624	82	29	0	1	70	52	1
F.2.5.4. Domestic Investment / Placement dans le Pays	4 987	1 379	:	:	:	:	:	:
F.2.5. Total	4 987	1 379	:	:	334	330	:	:
F.2.6. Other Investments / Autres Placements								
F.2.6.1. Domestic Companies / Entreprises Nationales	13 162	20 393	19 575	18 319	16 438	17 378	3 383	17 090
F.2.6.2. (Foreign Controlled Companies) / (Entreprises Sous Contrôle Etranger)	1 909	1 482	1 374	1 444	1 811	136	109	856
F.2.6. Total	15 071	20 393	:	:	16 438	17 378	:	:

	1992	1993	1994	1995	1996	1997	1998	1999
F.2.7. Total	41 255	57 224	56 722	68 653	68 603	77 959	63 529	75 529
F.2.7.1. Domestic Companies	5 912	7 290	7 717	8 619	10 414	9 555	9 500	9 189
F.2.7.2. (Foreign Controlled Companies)	:	:	:	:	:	:	:	:
F.2.7. Total of Non-Life Investments	47 167	57 224	:	:	68 603	77 959	:	:
G. BREAKDOWN OF NON-LIFE PREMIUMS								
G.1. Motor vehicle								
G.1.1. Direct Business								
G.1.1.1. Gross Premiums	5 929	6 401	5 725	7 207	7 506	7 760	8 615	9 190
G.1.1.2. Ceded Premiums	173	223	76	145	149	128	462	551
G.1.1.3. Net Written Premiums	5 756	6 178	5 649	7 062	7 357	7 632	8 154	8 639
G.1.3. Total								
G.1.3.1. Gross Premiums	:	6 401	:	:	7 506	7 760	8 615	9 190
G.1.3.2. Ceded Premiums	:	223	:	:	149	128	462	551
G.1.3.3. Net Written Premiums	:	6 178	:	:	7 357	7 632	8 154	8 639
G.2. Marine, Aviation								
G.2.1. Direct Business								
G.2.1.1. Gross Premiums	4 578	7 503	7 451	6 110	6 679	6 451	6 377	6 486
G.2.1.2. Ceded Premiums	2 109	3 669	3 894	3 149	2 374	2 495	2 202	2 288
G.2.1.3. Net Written Premiums	2 469	3 834	3 557	2 961	4 305	3 956	4 175	4 198
G.2.3. Total								
G.2.3.1. Gross Premiums	:	7 503	:	:	6 679	6 451	6 377	6 486
G.2.3.2. Ceded Premiums	:	3 669	:	:	2 374	2 495	2 202	2 288
G.2.3.3. Net Written Premiums	:	3 834	:	:	4 305	3 956	4 175	4 198
G.3. Freight								
G.3.1. Direct Business								
G.3.1.1. Gross Premiums	278	285	312	335	:	1	0	0
G.3.1.2. Ceded Premiums	42	233	64	44	:	0	0	0
G.3.1.3. Net Written Premiums	236	52	248	291	:	1	0	0
G.3.3. Total								
G.3.3.1. Gross Premiums	:	285	:	:	:	1	0	0
G.3.3.2. Ceded Premiums	:	233	:	:	:	0	0	0
G.3.3.3. Net Written Premiums	:	52	:	:	:	1	0	0
G.4. Fire, Property Damages								
G.4.1. Direct Business								
G.4.1.1. Gross Premiums	6 245	5 963	5 832	5 766	6 093	6 199	6 833	7 433
G.4.1.2. Ceded Premiums	1 102	1 177	965	826	680	701	746	835
G.4.1.3. Net Written Premiums	5 143	4 786	4 867	4 940	5 413	5 498	6 088	6 598
G.4.3. Total								
G.4.3.1. Gross Premiums	:	5 963	:	:	6 093	6 199	6 833	7 433
G.4.3.2. Ceded Premiums	:	1 177	:	:	680	701	746	835
G.4.3.3. Net Written Premiums	:	4 786	:	:	5 413	5 498	6 088	6 598
G.5. Pecuniary Losses								
G.5.1. Direct Business								
G.5.1.1. Gross Premiums	139	115	94	91	70	80	85	132
G.5.1.2. Ceded Premiums	86	71	59	60	46	56	61	92
G.5.1.3. Net Written Premiums	53	44	35	31	24	24	25	40
G.5.3. Total								
G.5.3.1. Gross Premiums	:	115	:	:	70	80	85	132
G.5.3.2. Ceded Premiums	:	71	:	:	46	54	61	92
G.5.3.3. Net Written Premiums	:	44	:	:	24	24	25	40
G.6. General Liability								
G.6.1. Direct Business								
G.6.1.1. Gross Premiums	691	672	613	647	694	737	756	861
G.6.1.2. Ceded Premiums	111	148	115	113	139	166	332	358
G.6.1.3. Net Written Premiums	580	524	498	534	555	571	425	503
G.6.3. Total								
G.6.3.1. Gross Premiums	:	672	:	:	694	737	756	861
G.6.3.2. Ceded Premiums	:	148	:	:	139	166	332	358
G.6.3.3. Net Written Premiums	:	524	:	:	555	571	425	503

French row labels (right column):

F.2.7. Total
F.2.7.1. Entreprises Nationales
F.2.7.2. (Entreprises Sous Contrôle Etranger)
F.2.7. Total des Placements Non-Vie

G. VENTILATIONS DES PRIMES NON-VIE

G.1. Assurance Automobile
G.1.1. Assurances Directes
G.1.1.1. Primes Brutes
G.1.1.2. Primes Cédées
G.1.1.3. Primes Nettes Emises
G.1.3. Total
G.1.3.1. Primes Brutes
G.1.3.2. Primes Cédées
G.1.3.3. Primes Nettes Emises

G.2. Marine, Aviation
G.2.1. Assurances Directes
G.2.1.1. Primes Brutes
G.2.1.2. Primes Cédées
G.2.1.3. Primes Nettes Emises
G.2.3. Total
G.2.3.1. Primes Brutes
G.2.3.2. Primes Cédées
G.2.3.3. Primes Nettes Emises

G.3. Fret
G.3.1. Assurances Directes
G.3.1.1. Primes Brutes
G.3.1.2. Primes Cédées
G.3.1.3. Primes Nettes Emises
G.3.3. Total
G.3.3.1. Primes Brutes
G.3.3.2. Primes Cédées
G.3.3.3. Primes Nettes Emises

G.4. Incendie, Dommages aux Biens
G.4.1. Assurances Directes
G.4.1.1. Primes Brutes
G.4.1.2. Primes Cédées
G.4.1.3. Primes Nettes Emises
G.4.3. Total
G.4.3.1. Primes Brutes
G.4.3.2. Primes Cédées
G.4.3.3. Primes Nettes Emises

G.5. Pertes Pécunières
G.5.1. Assurances Directes
G.5.1.1. Primes Brutes
G.5.1.2. Primes Cédées
G.5.1.3. Primes Nettes Emises
G.5.3. Total
G.5.3.1. Primes Brutes
G.5.3.2. Primes Cédées
G.5.3.3. Primes Nettes Emises

G.6. Responsabilité Générale
G.6.1. Assurances Directes
G.6.1.1. Primes Brutes
G.6.1.2. Primes Cédées
G.6.1.3. Primes Nettes Emises
G.6.3. Total
G.6.3.1. Primes Brutes
G.6.3.2. Primes Cédées
G.6.3.3. Primes Nettes Emises

Monetary Unit: million Norwegian kroner — Unité monétaire : million de couronnes norvégiennes

		1992	1993	1994	1995	1996	1997	1998	1999
G.7. Accident, Health	G.7. Accident, Santé								
G.7.1. Direct Business	G.7.1. Assurances Directes								
G.7.1.1. Gross Premiums	G.7.1.1. Primes Brutes	1 919	1 877	1 827	1 734	1 837	2 138	2 047	2 315
G.7.1.2. Ceded Premiums	G.7.1.2. Primes Cédées	246	313	227	165	139	176	393	586
G.7.1.3. Net Written Premiums	G.7.1.3. Primes Nettes Emises	1 673	1 564	1 600	1 569	1 698	1 962	1 655	1 729
G.7.3. Total	G.7.3. Total								
G.7.3.1. Gross Premiums	G.7.3.1. Primes Brutes	..	1 877	..	..	1 837	2 138	2 047	2 315
G.7.3.2. Ceded Premiums	G.7.3.2. Primes Cédées	..	313	..	..	139	176	393	586
G.7.3.3. Net Written Premiums	G.7.3.3. Primes Nettes Emises	..	1 564	..	..	1 698	1 962	1 655	1 729
G.8. Others	G.8. Autres								
G.8.1. Direct Business	G.8.1. Assurances Directes								
G.8.1.1. Gross Premiums	G.8.1.1. Primes Brutes	3 318	1 627	2 887	1 947	2 141	2 455	2 899	3 677
G.8.1.2. Ceded Premiums	G.8.1.2. Primes Cédées	1 686	387	461	404	399	532	521	510
G.8.1.3. Net Written Premiums	G.8.1.3. Primes Nettes Emises	1 632	1 240	2 426	1 543	1 742	1 923	2 378	3 167
G.8.3. Total	G.8.3. Total								
G.8.3.1. Gross Premiums	G.8.3.1. Primes Brutes	..	1 627	..	..	2 141	2 455	2 899	3 677
G.8.3.2. Ceded Premiums	G.8.3.2. Primes Cédées	..	387	..	..	399	532	521	510
G.8.3.3. Net Written Premiums	G.8.3.3. Primes Nettes Emises	..	1 240	..	..	1 742	1 923	2 378	3 167
G.9. Treaty Reinsurance	G.9. Réassurance Obligatoire								
G.9.1. Direct Business	G.9.1. Assurances Directes								
G.9.1.1. Gross Premiums	G.9.1.1. Primes Brutes	2 394	..	..	..	..	..	..	..
G.9.1.2. Ceded Premiums	G.9.1.2. Primes Cédées	246	..	..	..	..	..	..	..
G.9.1.3. Net Written Premiums	G.9.1.3. Primes Nettes Emises	2 148	..	..	..	..	..	..	..
G.9.2. Reinsurance Accepted	G.9.2. Réassurance Acceptée								
G.9.2.1. Gross Premiums	G.9.2.1. Primes Brutes	..	2 233	1 081	678	253	277	337	349
G.9.2.2. Ceded Premiums	G.9.2.2. Primes Cédées	..	391	308	236	72	72	81	77
G.9.2.3. Net Written Premiums	G.9.2.3. Primes Nettes Emises	..	1 842	773	442	181	205	256	272
G.9.3. Total	G.9.3. Total								
G.9.3.1. Gross Premiums	G.9.3.1. Primes Brutes	..	2 233	..	..	253	277	337	349
G.9.3.2. Ceded Premiums	G.9.3.2. Primes Cédées	..	391	..	..	72	72	81	77
G.9.3.3. Net Written Premiums	G.9.3.3. Primes Nettes Emises	..	1 842	..	..	181	205	256	272
G.10. Total	G.10. Total								
G.10.1. Direct Business	G.10.1. Assurances Directes								
G.10.1.1. Gross Premiums	G.10.1.1. Primes Brutes	25 491	24 443	24 741	23 837	25 020	25 821	27 613	30 094
G.10.1.2. Ceded Premiums	G.10.1.2. Primes Cédées	5 801	6 221	5 861	4 906	3 926	4 254	4 715	5 220
G.10.1.3. Net Written Premiums	G.10.1.3. Primes Nettes Emises	19 690	18 222	18 880	18 931	21 094	21 567	22 898	24 874
G.10.2. Reinsurance Accepted	G.10.2. Réassurance Acceptée								
G.10.2.1. Gross Premiums	G.10.2.1. Primes Brutes	..	2 233	1 081	678	253	277	337	349
G.10.2.2. Ceded Premiums	G.10.2.2. Primes Cédées	..	391	308	236	72	72	81	77
G.10.2.3. Net Written Premiums	G.10.2.3. Primes Nettes Emises	..	1 842	773	442	181	205	256	272
G.10.3. Total	G.10.3. Total								
G.10.3.1. Gross Premiums	G.10.3.1. Primes Brutes	..	26 676	25 822	..	25 273	26 098	27 950	30 443
G.10.3.2. Ceded Premiums	G.10.3.2. Primes Cédées	..	6 612	6 169	..	3 998	4 326	4 796	5 297
G.10.3.3. Net Written Premiums	G.10.3.3. Primes Nettes Emises	..	20 064	19 653	..	21 275	21 772	23 154	25 146

Monetary Unit: million Norwegian kroner — Unité monétaire : million de couronnes norvégiennes

	1992	1993	1994	1995	1996	1997	1998	1999
H. GROSS CLAIMS PAYMENTS / **H. PAIEMENTS BRUTS DES SINISTRES**								
H.1. Life / **H.1. Vie**								
H.1.1. Domestic Companies / H.1.1. Entreprises Nationales					12 995	13 947	18 235	16 848
H.1.2. (Foreign Controlled Companies) / H.1.2. (Entreprises Sous Contrôle Etranger)					152	136	241	264
H.1. Total					12 995	13 947	..	..
H.2. Non-Life / **H.2. Non-Vie**								
H.2.1. Domestic Companies / H.2.1. Entreprises Nationales					18 214	20 311	21 959	26 234
H.2.2. (Foreign Controlled Companies) / H.2.2. (Entreprises Sous Contrôle Etranger)					3 120	3 556	4 593	5 220
H.2.3. Branches & Agencies of Foreign Cies / H.2.3. Succursales et Agences d'Ent. Etrangères					304	664	495	770
H.2. Total					18 518	20 975	22 454	27 004
I. GROSS OPERATING EXPENSES / **I. DEPENSES BRUTES D'EXPLOITATION**								
I.1. Life / **I.1. Vie**								
I.1.1. Domestic Companies / I.1.1. Entreprises Nationales					2 618	2 631	2 728	2 626
I.1.2. (Foreign Controlled Companies) / I.1.2. (Entreprises Sous Contrôle Etranger)					53	69	74	78
I.2. Non-Life / **I.2. Non-Vie**								
I.2.1. Domestic Companies / I.2.1. Entreprises Nationales					6 021	5 912	6 494	7 365
I.2.2. (Foreign Controlled Companies) / I.2.2. (Entreprises Sous Contrôle Etranger)					994	1 151	1 411	1 357
J. COMMISSIONS / **J. COMMISSIONS**								
J.2. Non-Life / **J.2. Non-Vie**								
J.2.1. Direct Business / J.2.1. Assurance directe								
J.2.1.1. Domestic Companies / J.2.1.1. Entreprises Nationales					563	474	623	586
J.2.1.2. (Foreign Controlled Companies) / J.2.1.2. (Entreprises Sous Contrôle Etranger)					99	119	259	236
J.2.1.3. Branches & Agencies of Foreign Cies / J.2.1.3. Succursales et Agences d'Ent. Etrangères					17	20	31	126
J.2.1. Total / J.2.1. Total des Primes Nettes Vie					580	494	654	712
J.2.3. Total								
J.2.3.1. Domestic Companies / J.2.3.1. Entreprises Nationales					563	474	623	586
J.2.3.2. (Foreign Controlled Companies) / J.2.3.2. (Entreprises Sous Contrôle Etranger)					99	119	259	236
J.2.3.3. Branches & Agencies of Foreign Cies / J.2.3.3. Succursales et Agences d'Ent. Etrangères					17	20	31	126
J.2.3. Total					580	494	654	712

Monetary Unit: million zlotys | Unité monétaire : million de zlotys

Item	Libellé	1992	1993	1994	1995	1996	1997	1998	1999
A. NUMBER OF COMPANIES IN THE REPORTING COUNTRY	**A. NOMBRE D'ENTREPRISES DANS LE PAYS DECLARANT**								
A.1. Life	**A.1. Vie**								
A.1.1. Domestic Companies	A.1.1. Entreprises Nationales	..	6	9	13	15	21	24	30
A.1.2. (Foreign Controlled Companies)	A.1.2. (Entreprises Sous Contrôle Etranger)	..	5	5	6	6	11	13	20
A.1. All Companies	A.1. Ensemble des Entreprises	..	6	9	13	15	21	24	30
A.2. Non-Life	**A.2. Non-Vie**								
A.2.1. Domestic Companies	A.2.1. Entreprises Nationales	..	22	21	27	29	29	30	32
A.2.2. (Foreign Controlled Companies)	A.2.2. (Entreprises Sous Contrôle Etranger)	..	4	4	5	9	10	12	17
A.2. All Companies	A.2. Ensemble des Entreprises	..	22	21	27	29	29	30	32
A.4. Reinsurance	**A.4. Réassurance**								
A.4.1. Domestic Companies	A.4.1. Entreprises Nationales	..		..	..	1	1	1	1
A.4. All Companies	A.4. Ensemble des Entreprises	..	0	0	0	1	1	1	1
A.5. Total	**A.5. Total**								
A.5.1. Domestic Companies	A.5.1. Entreprises Nationales	..	28	30	40	45	51	55	63
A.5.2. (Foreign Controlled Companies)	A.5.2. (Entreprises Sous Contrôle Etranger)	..	9	9	11	15	21	25	37
A.5. All Insurance Companies	A.5. Ensemble des Entreprises d'Assurances	..	28	30	40	45	51	55	63
B. NUMBER OF EMPLOYEES	**B. NOMBRE D'EMPLOYES**								
B.1. Insurance Companies	B.1. Entreprises d'Assurances	..	..	..	26 211	25 762	25 902	29 245	30 401
B.2. Intermediaries	B.2. Intermediaires	..	..	..	..	..	46 082	67 514	90 248
B. Total	B. Total	..	..	..	..	..	71 984	96 759	120 649
C. BUSINESS WRITTEN IN THE REPORTING COUNTRY	**C. OPERATIONS CONCLUES DANS LE PAYS DECLARANT**								
C.1. Life	**C.1. Vie**								
C.1.1. Gross Premiums	C.1.1. Primes Brutes								
C.1.1.1. Direct Business	C.1.1.1. Assurances Directes								
C.1.1.1.1. Domestic Companies	C.1.1.1.1. Entreprises Nationales	..	887	1 284	1 538	2 342	3 407	4 530	5 885
C.1.1.1.2. (Foreign Controlled Companies)	C.1.1.1.2. (Entreprises Sous Contrôle Etranger)	..	10	68	216	559	1 127	1 736	2 684
C.1.1.1. Total	C.1.1.1. Total	..	887	1 284	1 538	2 342	3 407	4 530	5 885
C.1.1.3. Total	C.1.1.3. Total								
C.1.1.3.1. Domestic Companies	C.1.1.3.1. Entreprises Nationales	..	887	1 284	1 538	2 342	3 407	4 530	5 885
C.1.1.3.2. (Foreign Controlled Companies)	C.1.1.3.2. (Entreprises Sous Contrôle Etranger)	..	10	68	216	559	1 127	1 736	2 684
C.1.1.3. Total Gross Premiums	C.1.1.3. Total des Primes Brutes	..	887	1 284	1 538	2 342	3 407	4 530	5 885
C.1.2. Ceded Premiums	C.1.2. Primes Cédées								
C.1.2.1. Domestic Companies	C.1.2.1. Entreprises Nationales	..	..	1	2	7	39	104	148
C.1.2.2. (Foreign Controlled Companies)	C.1.2.2. (Entreprises Sous Contrôle Etranger)	..	..	1	2	7	39	103	148
C.1.2. Total	C.1.2. Total	..	0	1	2	7	39	104	148
C.1.3. Net Written Premiums	C.1.3. Primes Nettes Emises								
C.1.3.1. Domestic Companies	C.1.3.1. Entreprises Nationales	..	887	1 283	1 536	2 335	3 368	4 427	5 737
C.1.3.2. (Foreign Controlled Companies)	C.1.3.2. (Entreprises Sous Contrôle Etranger)	..	10	67	214	553	1 088	1 633	2 536
C.1.3. Total	C.1.3. Total	..	887	1 283	1 536	2 335	3 368	4 427	5 737

Monetary Unit: million zlotys / Unité monétaire : million de zlotys

C.2. Non-Life / C.2. Non-Vie

	1992	1993	1994	1995	1996	1997	1998	1999
C.2.1. Gross premiums / C.2.1. Primes Brutes								
C.2.1.1. Direct Business / C.2.1.1. Assurances Directes								
C.2.1.1.1. Domestic Companies / C.2.1.1.1. Entreprises Nationales		:	:	4 020	5 811	8 756	10 902	12 259
C.2.1.1.2. (Foreign Controlled Companies) / C.2.1.1.2. (Entreprises Sous Contrôle Etranger)		:	:	:	174	699	1 328	2 044
C.2.1.1. Total / C.2.1.1. Total		:	:	4 020	5 811	8 756	10 902	12 259
C.2.1.2. Reinsurance Accepted / C.2.1.2. Réassurance Acceptée								
C.2.1.2.1. Domestic Companies / C.2.1.2.1. Entreprises Nationales		:	:	25	36	147	157	344
C.2.1.2.2. (Foreign Controlled Companies) / C.2.1.2.2. (Entreprises Sous Contrôle Etranger)		:	:	:	2	4	6	4
C.2.1.2. Total / C.2.1.2. Total		:	:	25	36	147	157	344
C.2.1.3. Total / C.2.1.3. Total								
C.2.1.3.1. Domestic Companies / C.2.1.3.1. Entreprises Nationales		2 209	2 862	4 046	5 847	8 903	11 059	12 603
C.2.1.3.2. (Foreign Controlled Companies) / C.2.1.3.2. (Entreprises Sous Contrôle Etranger)		27	30	70	176	702	1 334	2 048
C.2.1.3. Total Gross Premiums / C.2.1.3. Total des Primes Brutes		2 209	2 862	4 046	5 847	8 903	11 059	12 603
C.2.2. Ceded Premiums / C.2.2. Primes Cédées								
C.2.2.1. Domestic Companies / C.2.2.1. Entreprises Nationales		834	1 132	1 381	2 022	3 022	2 783	3 581
C.2.2.2. (Foreign Controlled Companies) / C.2.2.2. (Entreprises Sous Contrôle Etranger)		15	18	33	67	211	413	748
C.2.2. Total / C.2.2. Total		834	1 132	1 381	2 022	3 022	2 783	3 581
C.2.3. Net Written Premiums / C.2.3. Primes Nettes Emises								
C.2.3.1. Domestic Companies / C.2.3.1. Entreprises Nationales		1 375	1 730	2 664	3 825	5 881	8 276	9 021
C.2.3.2. (Foreign Controlled Companies) / C.2.3.2. (Entreprises Sous Contrôle Etranger)		12	13	37	108	491	921	1 300
C.2.3. Total / C.2.3. Total		1 375	1 730	2 664	3 825	5 881	8 276	9 021

C.3. Total / C.3. Total

	1992	1993	1994	1995	1996	1997	1998	1999
C.3.1. Gross Premiums / C.3.1. Primes Brutes								
C.3.1.1. Direct Business / C.3.1.1. Assurances Directes								
C.3.1.1.1. Domestic Companies / C.3.1.1.1. Entreprises Nationales		:	:	:	8 154	12 163	15 432	18 144
C.3.1.1.2. (Foreign Controlled Companies) / C.3.1.1.2. (Entreprises Sous Contrôle Etranger)		:	:	:	733	1 825	3 063	4 728
C.3.1.1. Total / C.3.1.1. Total		:	:	:	8 154	12 163	15 432	18 144
C.3.1.2. Reinsurance Accepted / C.3.1.2. Réassurance Acceptée								
C.3.1.2.1. Domestic Companies / C.3.1.2.1. Entreprises Nationales		:	:	:	36	147	157	344
C.3.1.2.2. (Foreign Controlled Companies) / C.3.1.2.2. (Entreprises Sous Contrôle Etranger)		:	:	:	2	4	6	4
C.3.1.2. Total / C.3.1.2. Total		:	:	:	36	147	157	344
C.3.1.3. Total / C.3.1.3. Total								
C.3.1.3.1. Domestic Companies / C.3.1.3.1. Entreprises Nationales		3 096	4 146	5 583	8 189	12 310	15 589	18 488
C.3.1.3.2. (Foreign Controlled Companies) / C.3.1.3.2. (Entreprises Sous Contrôle Etranger)		37	98	286	735	1 829	3 070	4 731
C.3.1.3. Total Gross Premiums / C.3.1.3. Total des Primes Brutes		3 096	4 146	5 583	8 189	12 310	15 589	18 488
C.3.2. Ceded Premiums / C.3.2. Primes Cédées								
C.3.2.1. Domestic Companies / C.3.2.1. Entreprises Nationales			1 133	1 383	2 029	3 061	2 887	3 730
C.3.2.2. (Foreign Controlled Companies) / C.3.2.2. (Entreprises Sous Contrôle Etranger)			19	35	74	250	516	895
C.3.2. Total / C.3.2. Total		834	1 133	1 383	2 029	3 061	2 887	3 730
C.3.3. Net Written Premiums / C.3.3. Primes Nettes Emises								
C.3.3.1. Domestic Companies / C.3.3.1. Entreprises Nationales		2 262	3 013	4 200	6 160	9 249	12 702	14 758
C.3.3.2. (Foreign Controlled Companies) / C.3.3.2. (Entreprises Sous Contrôle Etranger)		22	80	251	661	1 579	2 554	3 836
C.3.3. Total / C.3.3. Total		2 262	3 013	4 200	6 160	9 249	12 702	14 758

F. OUTSTANDING INVESTMENT BY DIRECT INSURANCE COMPANIES / F. ENCOURS DES PLACEMENTS DES ENTREPRISES D'ASSURANCES DIRECTES

F.1. Life / F.1. Vie

	1992	1993	1994	1995	1996	1997	1998	1999
F.1.1. Real Estate / F.1.1. Immobilier								
F.1.1.1. Domestic Companies / F.1.1.1. Entreprises Nationales		6	23	78	103	147	291	251
F.1.1.2. (Foreign Controlled Companies) / F.1.1.2. (Entreprises Sous Contrôle Etranger)		:	:	0	0	15	103	51
F.1.1.4. Domestic Investment / F.1.1.4. Placement dans le Pays		6	23	78	103	147	291	251
F.1.1. Total / F.1.1. Total		6	23	78	103	147	291	251

Monetary Unit: million zlotys

Unité monétaire : million de zlotys

	1992	1993	1994	1995	1996	1997	1998	1999
F.1.2. Mortgage Loans / F.1.2. Prêts Hypothécaires								
F.1.2.1. Domestic Companies / F.1.2.1. Entreprises Nationales	..	..	..	..	1	1	14	146
F.1.2.2. (Foreign Controlled Companies) / F.1.2.2. (Entreprises Sous Contrôle Etranger)					1	1	0	2
F.1.2.4. Domestic Investment / F.1.2.4. Placement dans le Pays					1	1	14	146
F.1.2. Total / F.1.2. Total					1	1	14	146
F.1.3. Shares / F.1.3. Actions								
F.1.3.1. Domestic Companies / F.1.3.1. Entreprises Nationales		11	21	480	904	2 311	3 562	1 560
F.1.3.2. (Foreign Controlled Companies) / F.1.3.2. (Entreprises Sous Contrôle Etranger)			..	3	10	29	211	409
F.1.3.4. Domestic Investment / F.1.3.4. Placement dans le Pays		11	21	480	904	2 311	3 426	1 560
F.1.3.5. Foreign Investment / F.1.3.5. Placement à l'Etranger							136	0
F.1.3. Total / F.1.3. Total		11	21	480	904	2 311	3 562	1 560
F.1.4. Bonds with Fixed Revenue / F.1.4. Obligations								
F.1.4.1. Domestic Companies / F.1.4.1. Entreprises Nationales		249	900	1 355	2 245	2 975	4 834	9 490
F.1.4.2. (Foreign Controlled Companies) / F.1.4.2. (Entreprises Sous Contrôle Etranger)		2	29	119	431	1 062	1 891	3 187
F.1.4.4. Domestic Investment / F.1.4.4. Placement dans le Pays		249	900	1 355	2 245	2 971	4 827	9 486
F.1.4.5. Foreign Investment / F.1.4.5. Placement à l'Etranger				0	0	5	7	5
F.1.4. Total / F.1.4. Total		249	900	1 355	2 245	2 975	4 834	9 490
F.1.5. Loans other than Mortgage Loans / F.1.5. Prêts Autres qu'Hypothécaires								
F.1.5.1. Domestic Companies / F.1.5.1. Entreprises Nationales					..	1	6	153
F.1.5.2. (Foreign Controlled Companies) / F.1.5.2. (Entreprises Sous Contrôle Etranger)					..	1	4	9
F.1.5.4. Domestic Investment / F.1.5.4. Placement dans le Pays					..	1	6	153
F.1.5. Total / F.1.5. Total					..	1	6	153
F.1.6. Other Investments / F.1.6. Autres Placements								
F.1.6.1. Domestic Companies / F.1.6.1. Entreprises Nationales		324	231	189	372	573	904	2 056
F.1.6.2. (Foreign Controlled Companies) / F.1.6.2. (Entreprises Sous Contrôle Etranger)		14	23	29	71	169	443	978
F.1.6.4. Domestic Investment / F.1.6.4. Placement dans le Pays		324	231	189	372	573	904	2 055
F.1.6.5. Foreign Investment / F.1.6.5. Placement à l'Etranger								1
F.1.6. Total / F.1.6. Total		324	231	189	372	573	904	2 056
F.1.7. Total								
F.1.7.1. Domestic Companies / F.1.7.1. Entreprises Nationales		591	1 175	2 102	3 625	6 008	9 610	13 656
F.1.7.2. (Foreign Controlled Companies) / F.1.7.2. (Entreprises Sous Contrôle Etranger)		16	53	152	513	1 277	2 652	4 637
F.1.7.4. Domestic Investment / F.1.7.4. Placement dans le Pays		591	1 175	2 102	3 625	6 003	9 467	13 651
F.1.7.5. Foreign Investment / F.1.7.5. Placement à l'Etranger						5	143	5
F.1.7. Total of Life Investments / F.1.7. Total des Placements Vie				2 102	3 625	6 008	9 610	13 656
F.2. Non-Life / F.2. Non-Vie								
F.2.1. Real Estate / F.2.1. Immobilier								
F.2.1.1. Domestic Companies / F.2.1.1. Entreprises Nationales		50	78	140	180	221	293	393
F.2.1.2. (Foreign Controlled Companies) / F.2.1.2. (Entreprises Sous Contrôle Etranger)			..	..	1	12	17	22
F.2.1.4. Domestic Investment / F.2.1.4. Placement dans le Pays		50	78	140	180	221	293	393
F.2.1. Total / F.2.1. Total		50	78	140	180	221	293	393
F.2.2. Mortgage Loans / F.2.2. Prêts Hypothécaires								
F.2.2.1. Domestic Companies / F.2.2.1. Entreprises Nationales		2	3	30	51	51	54	57
F.2.2.2. (Foreign Controlled Companies) / F.2.2.2. (Entreprises Sous Contrôle Etranger)			..	..	..	7	17	15
F.2.2.4. Domestic Investment / F.2.2.4. Placement dans le Pays		2	3	30	51	51	54	57
F.2.2. Total / F.2.2. Total		2	3	30	51	51	54	57
F.2.3. Shares / F.2.3. Actions								
F.2.3.1. Domestic Companies / F.2.3.1. Entreprises Nationales		95	249	320	374	839	859	1 476
F.2.3.2. (Foreign Controlled Companies) / F.2.3.2. (Entreprises Sous Contrôle Etranger)		0	0	1	10	32	67	174
F.2.3.4. Domestic Investment / F.2.3.4. Placement dans le Pays		95	249	320	374	835	855	1 473
F.2.3.5. Foreign Investment / F.2.3.5. Placement à l'Etranger						4	4	4
F.2.3. Total / F.2.3. Total		95	249	320	374	839	859	1 476
F.2.4. Bonds with Fixed Revenue / F.2.4. Obligations								
F.2.4.1. Domestic Companies / F.2.4.1. Entreprises Nationales		129	376	773	1 645	2 562	4 690	7 276
F.2.4.2. (Foreign Controlled Companies) / F.2.4.2. (Entreprises Sous Contrôle Etranger)		0	1	19	56	273	563	742
F.2.4.4. Domestic Investment / F.2.4.4. Placement dans le Pays		129	376	773	1 645	2 562	4 690	7 276
F.2.4. Total / F.2.4. Total			376	773	1 645	2 562	4 690	7 276

Monetary Unit: million zlotys Unité monétaire : million de zlotys

	1992	1993	1994	1995	1996	1997	1998	1999	
F.2.5. Loans other than Mortgage Loans									F.2.5. Prêts Autres qu'Hypothécaires
F.2.5.1. Domestic Companies	..	..	..	..	1	2	2	156	F.2.5.1. Entreprises Nationales
F.2.5.2. (Foreign Controlled Companies)	..	..	..	..	1	1	2	2	F.2.5.2. (Entreprises Sous Contrôle Etranger)
F.2.5.4. Domestic Investment	..	..	..	..	1	2	2	156	F.2.5.4. Placement dans le Pays
F.2.5. Total	..	..	..	..	1	2	2	156	F.2.5. Total
F.2.6. Other Investments									F.2.6. Autres Placements
F.2.6.1. Domestic Companies	..	529	624	502	561	902	1 404	1 157	F.2.6.1. Entreprises Nationales
F.2.6.2. (Foreign Controlled Companies)	..	10	17	40	41	44	154	208	F.2.6.2. (Entreprises Sous Contrôle Etranger)
F.2.6.4. Domestic Investment	..	529	624	502	561	895	1 381	1 134	F.2.6.4. Placement dans le Pays
F.2.6.5. Foreign Investment	..			0	0	7	23	23	F.2.6.5. Placement à l' Etranger
F.2.6. Total	..	529	624	502	561	902	1 404	1 157	F.2.6. Total
F.2.7. Total									F.2.7. Total
F.2.7.1. Domestic Companies	..	804	1 331	1 765	2 813	4 577	7 303	10 516	F.2.7.1. Entreprises Nationales
F.2.7.2. (Foreign Controlled Companies)	..	11	18	61	109	370	820	1 163	F.2.7.2. (Entreprises Sous Contrôle Etranger)
F.2.7.4. Domestic Investment	..	804	1 331	1 765	2 813	4 566	7 275	10 488	F.2.7.4. Placement dans le Pays
F.2.7.5. Foreign Investment	..			..		11	27	27	F.2.7.5. Placement à l' Etranger
F.2.7. Total of Non-Life Investments	..	804	1 331	1 765	2 813	4 577	7 303	10 516	F.2.7. Total des Placements Non-Vie
G. BREAKDOWN OF NON-LIFE PREMIUMS									**G. VENTILATIONS DES PRIMES NON-VIE**
G.1. Motor vehicle									G.1. Assurance Automobile
G.1.1. Direct Business									G.1.1. Assurances Directes
G.1.1.1. Gross Premiums	..	..	..	2 225	3 464	5 714	7 108	7 900	G.1.1.1. Primes Brutes
G.1.1.2. Ceded Premiums	..	..	..	855	1 390	2 281	1 920	2 552	G.1.1.2. Primes Cédées
G.1.1.3. Net Written Premiums	..	..	..	1 369	2 074	3 433	5 189	5 348	G.1.1.3. Primes Nettes Emises
G.1.2. Reinsurance Accepted									G.1.2. Réassurance Acceptée
G.1.2.1. Gross Premiums								147	G.1.2.1. Primes Brutes
G.1.2.2. Ceded Premiums								90	G.1.2.2. Primes Cédées
G.1.2.3. Net Written Premiums								58	G.1.2.3. Primes Nettes Emises
G.1.3. Total									G.1.3. Total
G.1.3.1. Gross Premiums	..	..	..	2 225	3 464	:::	:::	8 047	G.1.3.1. Primes Brutes
G.1.3.2. Ceded Premiums	..	..	..	855	1 390	:::	:::	2 641	G.1.3.2. Primes Cédées
G.1.3.3. Net Written Premiums	..	..	..	1 369	2 074	:::	:::	5 406	G.1.3.3. Primes Nettes Emises
G.2. Marine, Aviation									G.2. Marine, Aviation
G.2.1. Direct Business									G.2.1. Assurances Directes
G.2.1.1. Gross Premiums	..	..	..	130	123	124	120	110	G.2.1.1. Primes Brutes
G.2.1.2. Ceded Premiums	..	..	..	79	49	50	42	38	G.2.1.2. Primes Cédées
G.2.1.3. Net Written Premiums	..	..	..	51	74	74	78	73	G.2.1.3. Primes Nettes Emises
G.2.2. Reinsurance Accepted									G.2.2. Réassurance Acceptée
G.2.2.1. Gross Premiums								66	G.2.2.1. Primes Brutes
G.2.2.2. Ceded Premiums								7	G.2.2.2. Primes Cédées
G.2.2.3. Net Written Premiums								59	G.2.2.3. Primes Nettes Emises
G.2.3. Total									G.2.3. Total
G.2.3.1. Gross Premiums	..	..	..	130	123	:::	:::	176	G.2.3.1. Primes Brutes
G.2.3.2. Ceded Premiums	..	..	..	79	49	:::	:::	44	G.1.2. Réassurance Acceptée
G.2.3.3. Net Written Premiums	..	..	..	51	74	:::	:::	132	G.1.3.1. Primes Brutes
G.3. Freight									G.3. Fret
G.3.1. Direct Business									G.3.1. Assurances Directes
G.3.1.1. Gross Premiums	..	..	..	55	75	91	108	98	G.3.1.1. Primes Brutes
G.3.1.2. Ceded Premiums	..	..	..	12	13	22	23	20	G.3.1.2. Primes Cédées
G.3.1.3. Net Written Premiums	..	..	..	43	62	69	85	78	G.3.1.3. Primes Nettes Emises
G.3.2. Reinsurance Accepted									G.3.2. Réassurance Acceptée
G.3.2.1. Gross Premiums								8	G.3.2.1. Primes Brutes
G.3.2.2. Ceded Premiums								2	G.3.2.2. Primes Cédées
G.3.2.3. Net Written Premiums								6	G.3.2.3. Primes Nettes Emises
G.3.3. Total									G.3.3.Total
G.3.3.1. Gross Premiums	..	..	..	55	75	:::	:::	106	G.3.3.1. Primes Brutes
G.3.3.2. Ceded Premiums	..	..	..	12	13	:::	:::	22	G.3.3.2. Primes Cédées
G.3.3.3. Net Written Premiums	..	..	..	43	62	:::	:::	84	G.3.3.3. Primes Nettes Emises

Monetary Unit: million zlotys   Unité monétaire : million de zlotys

	1992	1993	1994	1995	1996	1997	1998	1999
G.4. Fire, Property Damages / G.4. Incendie, Dommages aux Biens								
G.4.1. Direct Business / G.4.1. Assurances Directes								
G.4.1.1. Gross Premiums / G.4.1.1. Primes Brutes	..	..	..	846	1 099	1 402	1 714	1 856
G.4.1.2. Ceded Premiums / G.4.1.2. Primes Cédées	..	..	..	345	440	481	602	534
G.4.1.3. Net Written Premiums / G.4.1.3. Primes Nettes Emises	..	..	..	501	658	922	1 112	1 322
G.4.2. Reinsurance Accepted / G.4.2. Réassurance Acceptée								
G.4.2.1. Gross Premiums / G.4.2.1. Primes Brutes								2
G.4.2.2. Ceded Premiums / G.4.2.2. Primes Cédées								2
G.4.2.3. Net Written Premiums / G.4.2.3. Primes Nettes Emises								0
G.4.3. Total								
G.4.3.1. Gross Premiums / G.4.3.1. Primes Brutes	..	..	..	846	1 099	..	..	1 858
G.4.3.2. Ceded Premiums / G.4.3.2. Primes Cédées	..	..	..	345	440	..	..	536
G.4.3.3. Net Written Premiums / G.4.3.3. Primes Nettes Emises	..	..	..	501	658	..	..	1 322
G.5. Pecuniary Losses / G.5. Pertes Pécuniaires								
G.5.1. Direct Business / G.5.1. Assurances Directes								
G.5.1.1. Gross Premiums / G.5.1.1. Primes Brutes	..	..	..	76	123	151	212	270
G.5.1.2. Ceded Premiums / G.5.1.2. Primes Cédées	..	..	..	6	11	30	58	111
G.5.1.3. Net Written Premiums / G.5.1.3. Primes Nettes Emises	..	..	..	70	112	121	154	159
G.5.3. Total								
G.5.3.1. Gross Premiums / G.5.3.1. Primes Brutes	..	..	..	76	123	..	..	270
G.5.3.2. Ceded Premiums / G.5.3.2. Primes Cédées	..	..	..	6	11	..	..	111
G.5.3.3. Net Written Premiums / G.5.3.3. Primes Nettes Emises	..	..	..	70	112	..	..	159
G.6. General Liability / G.6. Responsabilité Générale								
G.6.1. Direct Business / G.6.1. Assurances Directes								
G.6.1.1. Gross Premiums / G.6.1.1. Primes Brutes	..	..	..	99	121	170	238	305
G.6.1.2. Ceded Premiums / G.6.1.2. Primes Cédées	..	..	..	11	15	26	45	70
G.6.1.3. Net Written Premiums / G.6.1.3. Primes Nettes Emises	..	..	..	88	106	144	193	235
G.6.3. Total								
G.6.3.1. Gross Premiums / G.6.3.1. Primes Brutes	..	..	..	99	121	..	..	305
G.6.3.2. Ceded Premiums / G.6.3.2. Primes Cédées	..	..	..	11	15	..	..	70
G.6.3.3. Net Written Premiums / G.6.3.3. Primes Nettes Emises	..	..	..	88	106	..	..	235
G.7. Accident, Health / G.7. Accident, Santé								
G.7.1. Direct Business / G.7.1. Assurances Directes								
G.7.1.1. Gross Premiums / G.7.1.1. Primes Brutes	..	..	..	550	756	1 058	1 345	1 647
G.7.1.2. Ceded Premiums / G.7.1.2. Primes Cédées	..	..	..	32	51	68	22	40
G.7.1.3. Net Written Premiums / G.7.1.3. Primes Nettes Emises	..	..	..	518	704	990	1 323	1 607
G.7.2. Reinsurance Accepted / G.7.2. Réassurance Acceptée								
G.7.2.1. Gross Premiums / G.7.2.1. Primes Brutes								120
G.7.2.2. Ceded Premiums / G.7.2.2. Primes Cédées								69
G.7.2.3. Net Written Premiums / G.7.2.3. Primes Nettes Emises								51
G.7.3. Total								
G.7.3.1. Gross Premiums / G.7.3.1. Primes Brutes	..	..	..	550	756	..	..	1 767
G.7.3.2. Ceded Premiums / G.7.3.2. Primes Cédées	..	..	..	32	51	..	..	109
G.7.3.3. Net Written Premiums / G.7.3.3. Primes Nettes Emises	..	..	..	518	704	..	..	1 657
G.8. Others / G.8. Autres								
G.8.1. Direct Business / G.8.1. Assurances Directes								
G.8.1.1. Gross Premiums / G.8.1.1. Primes Brutes	..	..	..	40	52	44	58	73
G.8.1.2. Ceded Premiums / G.8.1.2. Primes Cédées	..	..	..	40	50	43	41	47
G.8.1.3. Net Written Premiums / G.8.1.3. Primes Nettes Emises	..	..	..	0	2	1	16	26
G.8.3. Total								
G.8.3.1. Gross Premiums / G.8.3.1. Primes Brutes	..	..	..	40	52	..	..	73
G.8.3.2. Ceded Premiums / G.8.3.2. Primes Cédées	..	..	..	40	50	..	..	47
G.8.3.3. Net Written Premiums / G.8.3.3. Primes Nettes Emises	..	..	..	0	2	..	..	26
G.9. Treaty Reinsurance / G.9. Réassurance Obligatoire								
G.9.2. Reinsurance Accepted / G.9.2. Réassurance Acceptée								
G.9.2.1. Gross Premiums / G.9.2.1. Primes Brutes	..	..	..	25	36	147	157	...
G.9.2.2. Ceded Premiums / G.9.2.2. Primes Cédées	..	..	..	1	3	19	30	...
G.9.2.3. Net Written Premiums / G.9.2.3. Primes Nettes Emises	..	..	..	25	33	128	127	...
G.9.3. Total								
G.9.3.1. Gross Premiums / G.9.3.1. Primes Brutes	..	..	..	25	36	147	157	...
G.9.3.2. Ceded Premiums / G.9.3.2. Primes Cédées	..	..	..	1	3	19	30	...
G.9.3.3. Net Written Premiums / G.9.3.3. Primes Nettes Emises	..	..	..	25	33	128	127	...

	1992	1993	1994	1995	1996	1997	1998	1999
G.10. Total — G.10. Total								
G.10.1. Direct Business — G.10.1. Assurances Directes								
G.10.1.1. Gross Premiums — G.10.1.1. Primes Brutes	..	..	..	4 020	5 811	8 756	10 902	12 259
G.10.1.2. Ceded Premiums — G.10.1.2. Primes Cédées	..	..	..	1 380	2 019	3 002	2 753	3 412
G.10.1.3. Net Written Premiums — G.10.1.3. Primes Nettes Emises	..	..	..	2 640	3 792	5 754	8 149	8 847
G.10.2. Reinsurance Accepted — G.10.2. Réassurance Acceptée								
G.10.2.1. Gross Premiums — G.10.2.1. Primes Brutes	..	..	..	25	36	147	157	344
G.10.2.2. Ceded Premiums — G.10.2.2. Primes Cédées	..	..	..	1	3	19	30	170
G.10.2.3. Net Written Premiums — G.10.2.3. Primes Nettes Emises	..	..	..	25	33	128	127	174
G.10.3. Total — G.10.3. Total								
G.10.3.1. Gross Premiums — G.10.3.1. Primes Brutes	..	..	..	4 046	5 847	8 903	11 059	12 603
G.10.3.2. Ceded Premiums — G.10.3.2. Primes Cédées	..	..	..	1 381	2 022	3 022	2 783	3 581
G.10.3.3. Net Written Premiums — G.10.3.3. Primes Nettes Emises	..	..	..	2 664	3 825	5 881	8 276	9 021
H. GROSS CLAIMS PAYMENTS — **H. PAIEMENTS BRUTS DES SINISTRES**								
H.1. Life — **H.1. Vie**								
H.1.1. Domestic Companies — H.1.1. Entreprises Nationales		1	695	750	963	1 176	1 428	1 654
H.1.2. (Foreign Controlled Companies) — H.1.2. (Entreprises Sous Contrôle Etranger)		..	4	8	13	33	73	137
H.1. Total — H.1. Total		1	695	750	963	1 176	1 428	1 654
H.2. Non-Life — **H.2. Non-Vie**								
H.2.1. Domestic Companies — H.2.1. Entreprises Nationales		2	1 670	2 364	3 271	5 256	6 127	7 498
H.2.2. (Foreign Controlled Companies) — H.2.2. (Entreprises Sous Contrôle Etranger)		..	7	18	34	358	472	1 106
H.2. Total — H.2. Total		2	1 670	2 364	3 271	5 256	6 127	7 498
I. GROSS OPERATING EXPENSES — **I. DEPENSES BRUTES D'EXPLOITATION**								
I.1. Life — **I.1. Vie**								
I.1.1. Domestic Companies — I.1.1. Entreprises Nationales		133	216	349	606	905	1 290	1 752
I.1.2. (Foreign Controlled Companies) — I.1.2. (Entreprises Sous Contrôle Etranger)		..	44	136	274	492	742	1 118
I.1. Total — I.1. Total des Primes Nettes Vie		133	216	349	606	905	1 290	1 752
I.2. Non-Life — **I.2. Non-Vie**								
I.2.1. Domestic Companies — I.2.1. Entreprises Nationales		497	707	1 081	1 468	2 048	2 753	3 465
I.2.2. (Foreign Controlled Companies) — I.2.2. (Entreprises Sous Contrôle Etranger)		..	9	27	71	258	487	792
I.2. Total — I.2. Total		497	707	1 081	1 468	2 048	2 753	3 465
J. COMMISSIONS — **J. COMMISSIONS**								
J.1. Life — **J.1. Vie**								
J.1.1. Direct Business — J.1.1. Assurance directe								
J.1.1.1. Domestic Companies — J.1.1.1. Entreprises Nationales		..	..	..	368	556	709	837
J.1.1.2. (Foreign Controlled Companies) — J.1.1.2. (Entreprises Sous Contrôle Etranger)		..	..	..	204	344	456	580
J.1.1. Total — J.1.1. Total		..	..	..	368	556	709	837
J.1.3. Total — J.1.3. Total								
J.1.3.1. Domestic Companies — J.1.3.1. Entreprises Nationales		..	..	..	368	556	709	837
J.1.3.2. (Foreign Controlled Companies) — J.1.3.2. (Entreprises Sous Contrôle Etranger)		..	..	..	204	344	456	580
J.1.3. Total of Life Net Premiums — J.1.3. Total		..	..	..	368	556	709	837
J.2. Non-Life — **J.2. Non-Vie**								
J.2.1. Direct Business — J.2.1. Assurance directe								
J.2.1.1. Domestic Companies — J.2.1.1. Entreprises Nationales		..	..	..	406	648	823	
J.2.1.2. (Foreign Controlled Companies) — J.2.1.2. (Entreprises Sous Contrôle Etranger)		..	..	..	18	86	176	
J.2.1. Total — J.2.1. Total des Primes Nettes Vie		..	..	..	406	648	823	

Monetary Unit: million zlotys

Unité monétaire : million de zlotys

	1992	1993	1994	1995	1996	1997	1998	1999
J.2.2. Reinsurance Accepted								
J.2.2.1. Domestic Companies		:	:	:	10	18	21	:
J.2.2.2. (Foreign Controlled Companies)							1	:
J.2.2. Total		:	:	:	10	18	21	:
J.2.3. Total								
J.2.3.1. Domestic Companies		:	:	:	416	666	844	1 089
J.2.3.2. (Foreign Controlled Companies)		:	:	:	18	86	177	269
J.2.3. Total		:	:	:	416	666	844	1 089

J.2.2. Réassurances acceptées
J.2.2.1. Entreprises Nationales
J.2.2.2. (Entreprises Sous Contrôle Etranger)
J.2.2. Total
J.2.3. Total
J.2.3.1. Entreprises Nationales
J.2.3.2. (Entreprises Sous Contrôle Etranger)
J.2.3. Total

PORTUGAL

Monetary Unit: million escudos — Unité monétaire : million de escudos

Item (EN)	1992	1993	1994	1995	1996	1997	1998	1999	Item (FR)
A. NUMBER OF COMPANIES IN THE REPORTING COUNTRY									**A. NOMBRE D'ENTREPRISES DANS LE PAYS DECLARANT**
A.1. Life									**A.1. Vie**
A.1.1. Domestic Companies	11	12	15	15	16	16	16	16	A.1.1. Entreprises Nationales
A.1.2. (Foreign Controlled Companies)	3	5	5	5	6	6	6	6	A.1.2. (Entreprises Sous Contrôle Etranger)
A.1.3. Branches & Agencies of Foreign Cies	13	14	14	15	14	15	15	14	A.1.3. Succursales et Agences d'Ent. Etrangères
A.1. All Companies	24	26	29	30	30	31	31	30	A.1. Ensemble des Entreprises
A.2. Non-Life									**A.2. Non-Vie**
A.2.1. Domestic Companies	22	22	21	24	27	26	27	28	A.2.1. Entreprises Nationales
A.2.2. (Foreign Controlled Companies)	3	5	6	6	6	7	7	8	A.2.2. (Entreprises Sous Contrôle Etranger)
A.2.3. Branches & Agencies of Foreign Cies	32	32	34	32	29	33	31	28	A.2.3. Succursales et Agences d'Ent. Etrangères
A.2. All Companies	54	54	55	56	56	59	58	56	A.2. Ensemble des Entreprises
A.3. Composite									**A.3. Mixte**
A.3.1. Domestic Companies	8	9	9	8	8	7	7	6	A.3.1. Entreprises Nationales
A.3.2. (Foreign Controlled Companies)	4	4	4	4	4	3	3	2	A.3.2. (Entreprises Sous Contrôle Etranger)
A.3.3. Branches & Agencies of Foreign Cies	1	1	1	0	0	1	1	1	A.3.3. Succursales et Agences d'Ent. Etrangères
A.3. All Companies	9	10	10	8	8	8	8	7	A.3. Ensemble des Entreprises
A.4. Reinsurance									**A.4. Réassurance**
A.4.1. Domestic Companies	1	1	1	1	1	1	1	1	A.4.1. Entreprises Nationales
A.4. All Companies	1	1	1	1	1	1	1	1	A.4. Ensemble des Entreprises
A.5. Total									**A.5. Total**
A.5.1. Domestic Companies	42	44	46	48	52	50	51	51	A.5.1. Entreprises Nationales
A.5.2. (Foreign Controlled Companies)	10	14	15	15	16	16	16	16	A.5.2. (Entreprises Sous Contrôle Etranger)
A.5.3. Branches & Agencies of Foreign Cies	46	47	49	47	43	49	47	43	A.5.3. Succursales et Agences d'Ent. Etrangères
A.5. All Insurance Companies	88	91	95	95	95	99	98	94	A.5. Ensemble des Entreprises d'Assurances
B. NUMBER OF EMPLOYEES									**B. NOMBRE D'EMPLOYES**
B.1. Insurance Companies	14 941	14 592	14 008	14 037	13 677	14 578	14 271	12 989	B.1. Entreprises d'Assurances
B.2. Intermediaries	42 907	43 176	44 202	44 987	41 766	41 842	41 962	41 855	B.2. Intermediaires
B. Total	57 848	57 768	58 210	59 024	55 443	56 420	56 233	54 844	B. Total
C. BUSINESS WRITTEN IN THE REPORTING COUNTRY									**C. OPERATIONS CONCLUES DANS LE PAYS DECLARANT**
C.1. Life									**C.1. Vie**
C.1.1. Gross Premiums									C.1.1. Primes Brutes
C.1.1.1. Direct Business									C.1.1.1. Assurances Directes
C.1.1.1.1. Domestic Companies	101 726	144 356	195 427	306 567	393 192	395 632	528 157	717 511	C.1.1.1.1. Entreprises Nationales
C.1.1.1.2. (Foreign Controlled Companies)	11 321	26 311	48 723	..	40 864	43 946	70 318	76 003	C.1.1.1.2. (Entreprises Sous Contrôle Etranger)
C.1.1.1.3. Branches & Agencies of Foreign Cies	23 472	21 306	12 232	6 955	7 752	9 447	12 087	12 167	C.1.1.1.3. Succursales et Agences d'Ent. Etrangères
C.1.1.1. Total	125 198	165 662	207 659	313 522	400 944	405 079	520 244	729 678	C.1.1.1. Total
C.1.1.2. Reinsurance Accepted									C.1.1.2. Réassurance Acceptée
C.1.1.2.1. Domestic Companies	143	24	28	74	617	792	1 249	3 377	C.1.1.2.1. Entreprises Nationales
C.1.1.2.2. (Foreign Controlled Companies)	124	0	0	..	0	..	0	0	C.1.1.2.2. (Entreprises Sous Contrôle Etranger)
C.1.1.2.3. Branches & Agencies of Foreign Cies	0	105	0	0	0	0	0	0	C.1.1.2.3. Succursales et Agences d'Ent. Etrangères
C.1.1.2. Total	143	129	28	74	617	792	1 249	3 377	C.1.1.2. Total
C.1.1.3. Total									C.1.1.3. Total
C.1.1.3.1. Domestic Companies	101 869	144 380	195 455	306 641	393 809	396 424	529 406	720 888	C.1.1.3.1. Entreprises Nationales
C.1.1.3.2. (Foreign Controlled Companies)	11 445	26 311	48 723	31 138	40 864	43 946	70 318	76 003	C.1.1.3.2. (Entreprises Sous Contrôle Etranger)
C.1.1.3.3. Branches & Agencies of Foreign Cies	23 472	21 411	12 232	6 955	7 752	9 447	12 087	12 167	C.1.1.3.3. Succursales et Agences d'Ent. Etrangères
C.1.1.3. Total Gross Premiums	125 341	165 791	207 687	313 596	401 561	405 871	541 493	733 055	C.1.1.3. Total des Primes Brutes
C.1.2. Ceded Premiums									C.1.2. Primes Cédées
C.1.2.1. Domestic Companies	2 689	3 456	4 047	6 817	7 289	6 690	8 524	12 128	C.1.2.1. Entreprises Nationales
C.1.2.2. (Foreign Controlled Companies)	73	676	963	715	1 888	1 904	3 081	2 732	C.1.2.2. (Entreprises Sous Contrôle Etranger)
C.1.2.3. Branches & Agencies of Foreign Cies	586	417	291	276	293	352	432	477	C.1.2.3. Succursales et Agences d'Ent. Etrangères
C.1.2. Total	3 275	3 873	4 338	7 093	7 582	7 042	8 956	12 605	C.1.2. Total

PORTUGAL

Monetary Unit: million escudos — Unité monétaire : million de escudos

Code		1992	1993	1994	1995	1996	1997	1998	1999
C.1.3.	**Net Written Premiums / Primes Nettes Emises**								
C.1.3.1.	Domestic Companies / Entreprises Nationales	99 180	140 924	191 408	299 824	386 520	389 734	520 882	708 760
C.1.3.2.	(Foreign Controlled Companies) / (Entreprises Sous Contrôle Etranger)	11 372	25 635	47 760	30 423	38 976	42 042	67 237	73 271
C.1.3.3.	Branches & Agencies of Foreign Cies / Succursales et Agences d'Ent. Etrangères	22 886	20 994	11 941	6 679	7 459	9 095	11 655	11 690
C.1.3.	Total	122 066	161 918	203 349	306 503	393 979	398 829	532 537	720 450
C.2.	**Non-Life / Non-Vie**								
C.2.1.	**Gross premiums / Primes Brutes**								
C.2.1.1.	Direct Business / Assurances Directes								
C.2.1.1.1.	Domestic Companies / Entreprises Nationales	284 908	334 744	374 679	403 429	445 040	469 684	504 492	543 951
C.2.1.1.2.	(Foreign Controlled Companies) / (Entreprises Sous Contrôle Etranger)	57 116	18 318	20 911	...	64 007	68 099	136 940	149 655
C.2.1.1.3.	Branches & Agencies of Foreign Cies / Succursales et Agences d'Ent. Etrangères	21 374	26 402	13 978	2 791	3 107	3 436	4 020	292
C.2.1.1.	Total	306 282	361 146	388 657	406 220	448 147	473 120	508 512	544 243
C.2.1.2.	Reinsurance Accepted / Réassurance Acceptée								
C.2.1.2.1.	Domestic Companies / Entreprises Nationales	3 833	5 072	6 130	8 138	11 422	14 210	31 191	25 963
C.2.1.2.2.	(Foreign Controlled Companies) / (Entreprises Sous Contrôle Etranger)	80	505	650	...	1 405	1 583	1 588	2 351
C.2.1.2.3.	Branches & Agencies of Foreign Cies / Succursales et Agences d'Ent. Etrangères	1 603	1 728	511	128	144	152	166	0
C.2.1.2.	Total	5 436	6 800	6 641	8 266	11 566	14 362	31 357	25 963
C.2.1.3.	Total								
C.2.1.3.1.	Domestic Companies / Entreprises Nationales	288 741	339 816	380 809	411 567	456 462	483 894	535 683	569 914
C.2.1.3.2.	(Foreign Controlled Companies) / (Entreprises Sous Contrôle Etranger)	57 196	18 823	21 561	60 708	65 412	69 682	138 528	152 006
C.2.1.3.3.	Branches & Agencies of Foreign Cies / Succursales et Agences d'Ent. Etrangères	22 977	28 130	14 489	2 919	3 251	3 588	4 186	292
C.2.1.3.	Total Gross Premiums / Total des Primes Brutes	311 718	367 946	395 298	414 486	459 713	487 482	539 869	570 206
C.2.2.	**Ceded Premiums / Primes Cédées**								
C.2.2.1.	Domestic Companies / Entreprises Nationales	38 752	44 690	47 745	53 221	67 159	74 206	92 633	95 722
C.2.2.2.	(Foreign Controlled Companies) / (Entreprises Sous Contrôle Etranger)	7 389	2 630	2 788	6 952	8 221	8 486	9 685	15 025
C.2.2.3.	Branches & Agencies of Foreign Cies / Succursales et Agences d'Ent. Etrangères	4 309	5 333	2 140	761	1 054	1 128	1 265	16
C.2.2.	Total	43 061	50 023	49 885	53 982	68 213	75 334	93 898	95 738
C.2.3.	**Net Written Premiums / Primes Nettes Emises**								
C.2.3.1.	Domestic Companies / Entreprises Nationales	249 989	295 126	333 064	358 346	389 303	409 688	443 050	474 192
C.2.3.2.	(Foreign Controlled Companies) / (Entreprises Sous Contrôle Etranger)	49 807	16 193	18 773	53 756	57 191	61 196	128 843	136 981
C.2.3.3.	Branches & Agencies of Foreign Cies / Succursales et Agences d'Ent. Etrangères	18 668	22 797	12 349	2 158	2 197	2 460	2 921	276
C.2.3.	Total	268 657	317 923	345 413	360 504	391 500	412 148	445 971	474 468
C.3.	**Total**								
C.3.1.	**Gross Premiums / Primes Brutes**								
C.3.1.1.	Direct Business / Assurances Directes								
C.3.1.1.1.	Domestic Companies / Entreprises Nationales	386 634	479 100	570 106	709 996	838 232	865 316	1 032 649	1 261 462
C.3.1.1.2.	(Foreign Controlled Companies) / (Entreprises Sous Contrôle Etranger)	68 437	44 629	69 634	...	104 871	112 045	207 258	225 658
C.3.1.1.3.	Branches & Agencies of Foreign Cies / Succursales et Agences d'Ent. Etrangères	44 846	47 708	26 210	9 746	10 859	12 883	16 107	12 459
C.3.1.1.	Total	431 480	526 808	596 316	719 742	849 091	878 199	1 048 756	1 273 921
C.3.1.2.	Reinsurance Accepted / Réassurance Acceptée								
C.3.1.2.1.	Domestic Companies / Entreprises Nationales	3 976	5 096	6 158	8 212	12 039	15 002	32 440	29 340
C.3.1.2.2.	(Foreign Controlled Companies) / (Entreprises Sous Contrôle Etranger)	204	505	650	...	1 405	1 583	1 583	2 351
C.3.1.2.3.	Branches & Agencies of Foreign Cies / Succursales et Agences d'Ent. Etrangères	1 603	1 833	511	128	144	152	152	0
C.3.1.2.	Total	5 579	6 929	6 669	8 340	12 183	15 154	32 606	29 340
C.3.1.3.	Total								
C.3.1.3.1.	Domestic Companies / Entreprises Nationales	390 610	484 196	576 264	718 208	850 271	880 318	1 065 089	1 290 802
C.3.1.3.2.	(Foreign Controlled Companies) / (Entreprises Sous Contrôle Etranger)	68 641	45 134	70 284	91 846	106 276	113 628	208 846	228 009
C.3.1.3.3.	Branches & Agencies of Foreign Cies / Succursales et Agences d'Ent. Etrangères	46 449	49 541	26 721	9 874	11 003	13 035	16 273	12 459
C.3.1.3.	Total Gross Premiums / Total des Primes Brutes	437 059	533 737	602 985	728 082	861 274	893 353	1 081 362	1 303 261
C.3.2.	**Ceded Premiums / Primes Cédées**								
C.3.2.1.	Domestic Companies / Entreprises Nationales	41 441	48 146	51 792	60 038	74 448	80 896	101 157	107 850
C.3.2.2.	(Foreign Controlled Companies) / (Entreprises Sous Contrôle Etranger)	7 462	3 306	3 751	7 667	10 109	10 390	12 766	17 757
C.3.2.3.	Branches & Agencies of Foreign Cies / Succursales et Agences d'Ent. Etrangères	4 895	5 750	2 431	1 037	1 347	1 480	1 697	493
C.3.2.	Total	46 336	53 896	54 223	61 075	75 795	82 376	102 854	108 343

Monetary Unit: million escudos

Unité monétaire : million de escudos

	1992	1993	1994	1995	1996	1997	1998	1999	
C.3.3. Net Written Premiums									C.3.3. Primes Nettes Emises
C.3.3.1. Domestic Companies	349 169	436 050	524 472	658 170	775 823	799 422	963 932	1 182 952	C.3.3.1. Entreprises Nationales
C.3.3.2. (Foreign Controlled Companies)	61 179	41 828	66 533	84 179	96 167	103 238	196 080	210 252	C.3.3.2. (Entreprises Sous Contrôle Etranger)
C.3.3.3. Branches & Agencies of Foreign Cies	41 554	43 791	24 290	8 837	9 656	11 555	14 576	11 966	C.3.3.3. Succursales et Agences d'Ent. Etrangères
C.3.3. Total	390 723	479 841	548 762	667 007	785 479	810 977	978 508	1 194 918	C.3.3. Total
E. BUSINESS WRITTEN ABROAD									**E. OPERATIONS A L'ETRANGER**
E.1. Life	..	..							E.1. Vie
E.1.1. Gross Premiums									E.1.1. Primes Brutes
E.1.1.3. Total									E.1.1.3. Total
E.1.1.3.1. Branches & Agencies	0	0	0	7	1 897	992	6 076	8 017	E.1.1.3.1. Succursales & Agences
E.1.1.3. Total Gross Premiums	0	0	..	..	..	992	6 076	8 017	E.1.1.3. Total des Primes Brutes
E.2. Non-Life									E.2. Non-Vie
E.2.1. Gross Premiums									E.2.1. Primes Brutes
E.2.1.1. Direct Business									E.2.1.1. Assurance Directe
E.2.1.1.1. Branches & Agencies	1 467	1 916	2 229	..	..	..	..	..	E.2.1.1.1. Succursales & Agences
E.2.1.1. Total	1 467	1 916	..	..	..	..	..	..	E.2.1.1. Total
E.2.1.2. Reinsurance Accepted									E.2.1.2. Réassurance Acceptée
E.2.1.2.1. Branches & Agencies	15	13	169	..	..	..	..	..	E.2.1.2.1. Succursales & Agences
E.2.1.2. Total	15	13	..	..	..	..	..	..	E.2.1.2. Total
E.2.1.3. Total									E.2.1.3. Total
E.2.1.3.1. Branches & Agencies	1 482	1 929	2 398	3 759	6 117	6 302	6 021	5 679	E.2.1.3.1. Succursales & Agences
E.2.1.3. Total Gross Premiums	1 482	1 929	..	..	..	6 302	6 021	5 679	E.2.1.3. Total des Primes Brutes
E.2.2. Ceded Premiums									E.2.2. Primes Cédées
E.2.2.1. Branches & Agencies	261	306	449	..	..	..	..	..	E.2.2.1. Succursales & Agences
E.2.2. Total	261	306	..	..	..	..	..	..	E.2.2. Total
E.2.3. Net Written Premiums									E.2.3. Primes Nettes Emises
E.2.3.1. Branches & Agencies	1 221	1 623	1 949	..	..	..	..	..	E.2.3.1. Succursales & Agences
E.2.3. Total	1 221	1 623	..	..	..	..	..	..	E.2.3. Total
F. OUTSTANDING INVESTMENT BY DIRECT INSURANCE COMPANIES									**F. ENCOURS DES PLACEMENTS DES ENTREPRISES D'ASSURANCES DIRECTES**
F.1. Life									F.1. Vie
F.1.1. Real Estate									F.1.1. Immobilier
F.1.1.1. Domestic Companies	4 078	17 408	16 879	23 183	25 817	28 428	29 420	29 830	F.1.1.1. Entreprises Nationales
F.1.1.2. (Foreign Controlled Companies)	581	1 096	2 173	11 293	13 048	17 695	17 619	17 491	F.1.1.2. (Entreprises Sous Contrôle Etranger)
F.1.1.3. Branches & Agencies of Foreign Cies	2 530	2 220	1 513	536	553	0	0	0	F.1.1.3. Succursales et Agences d'Ent. Etrangères
F.1.1.4. Domestic Investment	6 608	19 628	18 392	23 719	26 370	28 428	29 420	29 830	F.1.1.4. Placement dans le Pays
F.1.1. Total	6 608	19 628	18 392	23 719	26 370	28 428	29 420	29 830	F.1.1. Total
F.1.2. Mortgage Loans									F.1.2. Prêts Hypothécaires
F.1.2.1. Domestic Companies	167	1 031	1 065	776	775	757	672	529	F.1.2.1. Entreprises Nationales
F.1.2.2. (Foreign Controlled Companies)	71	988	1 015	250	296	323	339	373	F.1.2.2. (Entreprises Sous Contrôle Etranger)
F.1.2.3. Branches & Agencies of Foreign Cies	339	238	145	178	158	0	0	0	F.1.2.3. Succursales et Agences d'Ent. Etrangères
F.1.2.4. Domestic Investment	506	1 269	1 210	954	933	757	672	529	F.1.2.4. Placement dans le Pays
F.1.2. Total	506	1 269	1 210	954	933	757	672	529	F.1.2. Total

Monetary Unit: million escudos

Unité monétaire : million de escudos

	1992	1993	1994	1995	1996	1997	1998	1999	
F.1.3. Shares									**F.1.3. Actions**
F.1.3.1. Domestic Companies	74 539	322 291	481 772	30 884	94 938	163 457	217 526	282 320	F.1.3.1. Entreprises Nationales
F.1.3.2. (Foreign Controlled Companies)	27 505	61 573	120 166	6 222	7 870	16 749	21 528	30 617	F.1.3.2. (Entreprises Sous Contrôle Etranger)
F.1.3.3. Branches & Agencies of Foreign Cies	42 342	44 010	21 210	554	835	1 633	2 520	3 030	F.1.3.3. Succursales et Agences d'Ent. Etrangères
F.1.3.4. Domestic Investment	116 881	366 301	:	:	:	:	:	:	F.1.3.4. Placement dans le Pays
F.1.3. Total	116 881	366 301	502 982	31 438	95 773	165 090	220 046	285 350	F.1.3. Total
F.1.4. Bonds with Fixed Revenue									**F.1.4. Obligations**
F.1.4.1. Domestic Companies	:	:	:	393 419	554 356	671 107	847 146	1 026 351	F.1.4.1. Entreprises Nationales
F.1.4.2. (Foreign Controlled Companies)	:	:	:	106 801	149 329	172 751	196 231	213 164	F.1.4.2. (Entreprises Sous Contrôle Etranger)
F.1.4.3. Branches & Agencies of Foreign Cies	:	:	:	19 925	26 148	6 502	8 957	10 587	F.1.4.3. Succursales et Agences d'Ent. Etrangères
F.1.4. Total	:	:	:	413 344	580 504	677 609	856 103	1 036 938	F.1.4. Total
F.1.5. Loans other than Mortgage Loans									**F.1.5. Prêts Autres qu'Hypothécaires**
F.1.5.1. Domestic Companies	76	342	749	532	1 314	1 375	1 605	1 604	F.1.5.1. Entreprises Nationales
F.1.5.2. (Foreign Controlled Companies)	0	261	574	312	329	307	548	632	F.1.5.2. (Entreprises Sous Contrôle Etranger)
F.1.5.3. Branches & Agencies of Foreign Cies	1 395	60	105	32	49	0	0	0	F.1.5.3. Succursales et Agences d'Ent. Etrangères
F.1.5.4. Domestic Investment	1 471	402	:	:	:	:	:	:	F.1.5.4. Placement dans le Pays
F.1.5. Total	1 471	402	854	564	1 363	1 375	1 605	1 604	F.1.5. Total
F.1.6. Other Investments									**F.1.6. Autres Placements**
F.1.6.1. Domestic Companies	3 968	25 231	49 818	78 726	132 925	186 476	232 266	321 629	F.1.6.1. Entreprises Nationales
F.1.6.2. (Foreign Controlled Companies)	:	1 898	11 150	6 374	9 527	3 087	7 000	9 550	F.1.6.2. (Entreprises Sous Contrôle Etranger)
F.1.6.3. Branches & Agencies of Foreign Cies	2 147	4 237	817	1 308	697	35	79	93	F.1.6.3. Succursales et Agences d'Ent. Etrangères
F.1.6.4. Domestic Investment	6 115	29 469	:	:	:	:	:	:	F.1.6.4. Placement dans le Pays
F.1.6. Total	6 115	29 469	50 635	80 034	133 622	186 511	232 345	321 722	F.1.6. Total
F.1.7. Total									**F.1.7. Total**
F.1.7.1. Domestic Companies	82 828	366 303	550 283	527 520	810 125	1 051 600	1 328 635	1 662 263	F.1.7.1. Entreprises Nationales
F.1.7.2. (Foreign Controlled Companies)	28 157	65 816	135 078	131 252	180 399	210 912	243 265	271 827	F.1.7.2. (Entreprises Sous Contrôle Etranger)
F.1.7.3. Branches & Agencies of Foreign Cies	48 753	50 765	23 790	22 533	28 440	8 170	11 556	13 710	F.1.7.3. Succursales et Agences d'Ent. Etrangères
F.1.7.4. Domestic Investment	131 581	417 069	:	:	:	:	:	:	F.1.7.4. Placement dans le Pays
F.1.7. Total of Life Investments	131 581	417 069	574 073	550 053	838 565	1 059 770	1 340 191	1 675 973	F.1.7. Total des Placements Vie
F.2. Non-Life									**F.2. Non-Vie**
F.2.1. Real Estate									**F.2.1. Immobilier**
F.2.1.1. Domestic Companies	157 310	152 781	165 823	203 904	217 708	223 387	229 229	236 265	F.2.1.1. Entreprises Nationales
F.2.1.2. (Foreign Controlled Companies)	17 659	5 216	7 161	34 312	38 905	34 319	57 905	57 582	F.2.1.2. (Entreprises Sous Contrôle Etranger)
F.2.1.3. Branches & Agencies of Foreign Cies	5 259	5 533	1 666	1 312	1 284	1 369	1 400	553	F.2.1.3. Succursales et Agences d'Ent. Etrangères
F.2.1.4. Domestic Investment	162 569	158 314	:	:	:	:	:	:	F.2.1.4. Placement dans le Pays
F.2.1. Total	162 569	158 314	167 489	205 216	218 992	224 756	230 629	236 818	F.2.1. Total
F.2.2. Mortgage Loans									**F.2.2. Prêts Hypothécaires**
F.2.2.1. Domestic Companies	1 129	2 024	3 963	3 444	3 334	4 907	6 442	6 316	F.2.2.1. Entreprises Nationales
F.2.2.2. (Foreign Controlled Companies)	461	0	0	94	108	427	1 659	1 675	F.2.2.2. (Entreprises Sous Contrôle Etranger)
F.2.2.3. Branches & Agencies of Foreign Cies	56	0	0	0	0	183	201	212	F.2.2.3. Succursales et Agences d'Ent. Etrangères
F.2.2.4. Domestic Investment	1 185	2 024	:	:	:	:	:	:	F.2.2.4. Placement dans le Pays
F.2.2. Total	1 185	2 024	3 963	3 444	3 334	5 090	6 643	6 528	F.2.2. Total
F.2.3. Shares									**F.2.3. Actions**
F.2.3.1. Domestic Companies	314 423	237 648	275 737	61 240	74 692	182 503	149 942	230 221	F.2.3.1. Entreprises Nationales
F.2.3.2. (Foreign Controlled Companies)	51 043	10 208	16 126	6 167	7 809	12 348	36 961	59 973	F.2.3.2. (Entreprises Sous Contrôle Etranger)
F.2.3.3. Branches & Agencies of Foreign Cies	12 228	15 774	4 335	776	116	130	165	0	F.2.3.3. Succursales et Agences d'Ent. Etrangères
F.2.3.4. Domestic Investment	326 651	253 422	:	:	:	:	:	:	F.2.3.4. Placement dans le Pays
F.2.3. Total	326 651	253 422	280 072	62 016	74 808	182 633	150 107	230 221	F.2.3. Total
F.2.4. Bonds with Fixed Revenue									**F.2.4. Obligations**
F.2.4.1. Domestic Companies	:	:	:	458 185	583 167	696 156	879 026	1 038 585	F.2.4.1. Entreprises Nationales
F.2.4.2. (Foreign Controlled Companies)	:	:	:	52 122	60 963	63 852	206 968	222 246	F.2.4.2. (Entreprises Sous Contrôle Etranger)
F.2.4.3. Branches & Agencies of Foreign Cies	:	:	:	1 614	2 246	28 562	34 927	37 764	F.2.4.3. Succursales et Agences d'Ent. Etrangères
F.2.4. Total	:	:	:	459 799	585 413	724 718	913 953	1 076 349	F.2.4. Total
F.2.5. Loans other than Mortgage Loans									**F.2.5. Prêts Autres qu'Hypothécaires**
F.2.5.1. Domestic Companies	288	0	0	9 864	865	943	894	1 226	F.2.5.1. Entreprises Nationales
F.2.5.2. (Foreign Controlled Companies)	:	0	0	:	:	:	185	182	F.2.5.2. (Entreprises Sous Contrôle Etranger)
F.2.5.3. Branches & Agencies of Foreign Cies	0	0	0	0	0	88	166	194	F.2.5.3. Succursales et Agences d'Ent. Etrangères
F.2.5.4. Domestic Investment	288	0	:	:	:	:	:	:	F.2.5.4. Placement dans le Pays
F.2.5. Total	288	0	0	9 864	865	1 031	1 060	1 420	F.2.5. Total

Monetary Unit: million escudos — Unité monétaire : million de escudos

	1992	1993	1994	1995	1996	1997	1998	1999
F.2.6. Other Investments / Autres Placements								
F.2.6.1. Domestic Companies / Entreprises Nationales	14 404	12 169	25 325	386 175	419 026	437 096	509 551	637 969
F.2.6.2. (Foreign Controlled Companies) / (Entreprises Sous Contrôle Etranger)	1 685	375	280	7 361	5 343	4 898	16 647	16 476
F.2.6.3. Branches & Agencies of Foreign Cies / Succursales et Agences d'Ent. Etrangères	853	1 033	405	0	0	478	232	844
F.2.6.4. Domestic Investment / Placement dans le Pays	15 257	13 201						
F.2.6. Total	15 257	13 201	25 730	386 175	419 026	437 574	509 783	638 813
F.2.7. Total								
F.2.7.1. Domestic Companies / Entreprises Nationales	487 554	404 622	470 848	1 122 812	1 298 792	1 544 992	1 775 084	2 150 582
F.2.7.2. (Foreign Controlled Companies) / (Entreprises Sous Contrôle Etranger)	70 848	15 799	23 567	100 056	113 128	155 844	320 325	358 134
F.2.7.3. Branches & Agencies of Foreign Cies / Succursales et Agences d'Ent. Etrangères	18 396	22 340	6 406	3 702	3 646	30 810	37 091	39 567
F.2.7.4. Domestic Investment / Placement dans le Pays	505 950	426 961	426 961					
F.2.7. Total of Non-Life Investments / Total des Placements Non-Vie	505 950	426 961	477 254	1 126 514	1 302 438	1 575 802	1 812 175	2 190 149

G. BREAKDOWN OF NON-LIFE PREMIUMS / G. VENTILATIONS DES PRIMES NON-VIE

	1992	1993	1994	1995	1996	1997	1998	1999
G.1. Motor vehicle / G.1. Assurance Automobile								
G.1.1. Direct Business / G.1.1. Assurances Directes								
G.1.1.1. Gross Premiums / Primes Brutes	150 098	190 287	210 418	220 494	240 542	249 062	261 502	276 449
G.1.1.2. Ceded Premiums / Primes Cédées							20 428	14 394
G.1.1.3. Net Written Premiums / Primes Nettes Emises							241 074	262 055
G.1.2. Reinsurance Accepted / G.1.2. Réassurance Acceptée								
G.1.2.1. Gross Premiums / Primes Brutes	179	266	300	277	256	358	12 486	4 932
G.1.2.2. Ceded Premiums / Primes Cédées							424	102
G.1.2.3. Net Written Premiums / Primes Nettes Emises							12 062	4 830
G.1.3. Total								
G.1.3.1. Gross Premiums / Primes Brutes	150 277	190 553	210 718	220 771	240 798	249 420	273 988	281 381
G.1.3.2. Ceded Premiums / Primes Cédées	3 844	5 671	5 577	6 443	7 360	8 494	20 852	14 496
G.1.3.3. Net Written Premiums / Primes Nettes Emises	146 433	184 882	205 141	214 328	233 438	240 926	253 136	266 885
G.2. Marine, Aviation								
G.2.1. Direct Business / G.2.1. Assurances Directes								
G.2.1.1. Gross Premiums / Primes Brutes	4 143	4 885	4 976	6 331	7 199	6 824	5 360	5 157
G.2.1.2. Ceded Premiums / Primes Cédées							3 838	3 795
G.2.1.3. Net Written Premiums / Primes Nettes Emises							1 522	1 362
G.2.2. Reinsurance Accepted / G.2.2. Réassurance Acceptée								
G.2.2.1. Gross Premiums / Primes Brutes	575	729	838	1 685	1 472	2 137	1 497	1 295
G.2.2.2. Ceded Premiums / Primes Cédées							862	868
G.2.2.3. Net Written Premiums / Primes Nettes Emises							635	427
G.2.3. Total								
G.2.3.1. Gross Premiums / Primes Brutes	4 718	5 614	5 814	8 016	8 671	8 961	6 857	6 452
G.2.3.2. Ceded Premiums / Primes Cédées	3 554	3 991	4 232	5 507	5 981	6 320	4 700	4 663
G.2.3.3. Net Written Premiums / Primes Nettes Emises	1 164	1 623	1 582	2 509	2 690	2 641	2 157	1 789
G.3. Freight / G.3. Fret								
G.3.1. Direct Business / G.3.1. Assurances Directes								
G.3.1.1. Gross Premiums / Primes Brutes	6 360	6 042	5 271	3 130	3 781	4 269	5 660	5 579
G.3.1.2. Ceded Premiums / Primes Cédées							3 005	3 177
G.3.1.3. Net Written Premiums / Primes Nettes Emises							2 655	2 402
G.3.2. Reinsurance Accepted / G.3.2. Réassurance Acceptée								
G.3.2.1. Gross Premiums / Primes Brutes	394	415	255	3	10	4	75	391
G.3.2.2. Ceded Premiums / Primes Cédées							130	124
G.3.2.3. Net Written Premiums / Primes Nettes Emises							- 55	267
G.3.3. Total								
G.3.3.1. Gross Premiums / Primes Brutes	6 754	6 457	5 526	3 133	3 791	4 273	5 735	5 970
G.3.3.2. Ceded Premiums / Primes Cédées	3 124	2 606	2 641	1 495	1 996	2 337	3 135	3 301
G.3.3.3. Net Written Premiums / Primes Nettes Emises	3 630	3 851	2 885	1 638	1 795	1 936	2 600	2 669
G.4. Fire, Property Damages / G.4. Incendie, Dommages aux Biens								
G.4.1. Direct Business / G.4.1. Assurances Directes								
G.4.1.1. Gross Premiums / Primes Brutes	42 559	47 675	49 175	52 092	62 367	68 258	77 810	84 126
G.4.1.2. Ceded Premiums / Primes Cédées							32 917	35 639
G.4.1.3. Net Written Premiums / Primes Nettes Emises							44 893	48 487

PORTUGAL

Monetary Unit: million escudos

Unité monétaire : million de escudos

	1992	1993	1994	1995	1996	1997	1998	1999	
G.4.2. Reinsurance Accepted									G.4.2. Réassurance Acceptée
G.4.2.1. Gross Premiums	1 544	1 462	1 914	2 866	4 384	4 410	4 258	4 181	G.4.2.1. Primes Brutes
G.4.2.2. Ceded Premiums							2 229	2 251	G.4.2.2. Primes Cédées
G.4.2.3. Net Written Premiums							2 029	1 930	G.4.2.3. Primes Nettes Emises
G.4.3. Total									G.4.3. Total
G.4.3.1. Gross Premiums	44 103	49 137	51 089	54 958	66 751	72 668	82 068	88 307	G.4.3.1. Primes Brutes
G.4.3.2. Ceded Premiums	19 073	23 000	24 974	26 312	32 711	34 563	35 146	37 890	G.4.3.2. Primes Cédées
G.4.3.3. Net Written Premiums	25 030	26 137	26 115	28 646	34 040	38 105	46 922	50 417	G.4.3.3. Primes Nettes Emises
G.5. Pecuniary Losses									G.5. Pertes Pécunières
G.5.1. Direct Business									G.5.1. Assurances Directes
G.5.1.1. Gross Premiums	8 027	8 033	7 384	6 836	7 653	8 236	8 678	7 573	G.5.1.1. Primes Brutes
G.5.1.2. Ceded Premiums							6 282	5 500	G.5.1.2. Primes Cédées
G.5.1.3. Net Written Premiums							2 396	2 073	G.5.1.3. Primes Nettes Emises
G.5.2. Reinsurance Accepted									G.5.2. Réassurance Acceptée
G.5.2.1. Gross Premiums	940	1 106	1 330	1 470	1 121	1 186	1 271	1 248	G.5.2.1. Primes Brutes
G.5.2.2. Ceded Premiums							62	45	G.5.2.2. Primes Cédées
G.5.2.3. Net Written Premiums							1 209	1 203	G.5.2.3. Primes Nettes Emises
G.5.3. Total									G.5.3. Total
G.5.3.1. Gross Premiums	8 967	9 139	8 714	8 306	8 774	9 422	9 949	8 821	G.5.3.1. Primes Brutes
G.5.3.2. Ceded Premiums	5 164	5 013	4 622	4 535	5 570	6 310	6 344	5 545	G.5.3.2. Primes Cédées
G.5.3.3. Net Written Premiums	3 803	4 126	4 092	3 771	3 204	3 112	3 605	3 276	G.5.3.3. Primes Nettes Emises
G.6. General Liability									G.6. Responsabilité Générale
G.6.1. Direct Business									G.6.1. Assurances Directes
G.6.1.1. Gross Premiums	4 772	5 490	5 553	5 939	6 835	7 350	8 297	9 496	G.6.1.1. Primes Brutes
G.6.1.2. Ceded Premiums							2 464	3 148	G.6.1.2. Primes Cédées
G.6.1.3. Net Written Premiums							5 833	6 348	G.6.1.3. Primes Nettes Emises
G.6.2. Reinsurance Accepted									G.6.2. Réassurance Acceptée
G.6.2.1. Gross Premiums	115	290	214	334	316	307	341	431	G.6.2.1. Primes Brutes
G.6.2.2. Ceded Premiums							200	314	G.6.2.2. Primes Cédées
G.6.2.3. Net Written Premiums							141	117	G.6.2.3. Primes Nettes Emises
G.6.3. Total									G.6.3. Total
G.6.3.1. Gross Premiums	4 887	5 780	5 767	6 273	7 151	7 657	8 638	9 927	G.6.3.1. Primes Brutes
G.6.3.2. Ceded Premiums	1 864	2 279	2 053	1 921	2 419	2 418	2 664	3 462	G.6.3.2. Primes Cédées
G.6.3.3. Net Written Premiums	3 023	3 501	3 714	4 352	4 732	5 239	5 974	6 465	G.6.3.3. Primes Nettes Emises
G.7. Accident, Health									G.7. Accident, Santé
G.7.1. Direct Business									G.7.1. Assurances Directes
G.7.1.1. Gross Premiums	89 493	97 712	104 808	110 082	118 056	127 194	137 368	151 260	G.7.1.1. Primes Brutes
G.7.1.2. Ceded Premiums							18 855	22 954	G.7.1.2. Primes Cédées
G.7.1.3. Net Written Premiums							118 513	128 306	G.7.1.3. Primes Nettes Emises
G.7.2. Reinsurance Accepted									G.7.2. Réassurance Acceptée
G.7.2.1. Gross Premiums	308	357	444	399	2 048	3 701	7 486	9 337	G.7.2.1. Primes Brutes
G.7.2.2. Ceded Premiums							288	949	G.7.2.2. Primes Cédées
G.7.2.3. Net Written Premiums							7 198	8 388	G.7.2.3. Primes Nettes Emises
G.7.3. Total									G.7.3. Total
G.7.3.1. Gross Premiums	89 801	98 069	105 252	110 481	120 104	130 895	144 854	160 597	G.7.3.1. Primes Brutes
G.7.3.2. Ceded Premiums	6 060	6 866	5 140	6 943	11 189	13 750	19 143	23 903	G.7.3.2. Primes Cédées
G.7.3.3. Net Written Premiums	83 741	91 203	100 112	103 538	108 915	117 145	125 711	136 694	G.7.3.3. Primes Nettes Emises
G.8. Others									G.8. Autres
G.8.1. Direct Business									G.8.1. Assurances Directes
G.8.1.1. Gross Premiums	830	1 022	1 072	1 316	1 714	1 927	3 837	4 603	G.8.1.1. Primes Brutes
G.8.1.2. Ceded Premiums							1 705	2 201	G.8.1.2. Primes Cédées
G.8.1.3. Net Written Premiums							2 132	2 402	G.8.1.3. Primes Nettes Emises
G.8.2. Reinsurance Accepted									G.8.2. Réassurance Acceptée
G.8.2.1. Gross Premiums	1 381	2 175	1 346	1 232	1 959	2 259	3 943	4 148	G.8.2.1. Primes Brutes
G.8.2.2. Ceded Premiums							209	277	G.8.2.2. Primes Cédées
G.8.2.3. Net Written Premiums							3 734	3 871	G.8.2.3. Primes Nettes Emises
G.8.3. Total									G.8.3. Total
G.8.3.1. Gross Premiums	2 211	3 197	2 418	2 548	3 673	4 186	7 780	8 751	G.8.3.1. Primes Brutes
G.8.3.2. Ceded Premiums	378	597	646	826	987	1 142	1 914	2 478	G.8.3.2. Primes Cédées
G.8.3.3. Net Written Premiums	1 833	2 600	1 772	1 722	2 686	3 044	5 866	6 273	G.8.3.3. Primes Nettes Emises

Monetary Unit: million escudos — Unité monétaire : million de escudos

	1992	1993	1994	1995	1996	1997	1998	1999
G.10. Total								
G.10.1. Direct Business / G.10.1. Assurances Directes								
G.10.1.1. Gross Premiums / Primes Brutes	306 282	361 146	388 657	406 220	448 147	473 120	508 512	544 243
G.10.1.2. Ceded Premiums / Primes Cédées							89 494	90 808
G.10.1.3. Net Written Premiums / Primes Nettes Emises							419 018	453 435
G.10.2. Reinsurance Accepted / Réassurance Acceptée								
G.10.2.1. Gross Premiums / Primes Brutes	5 436	6 800	6 641	8 266	11 566	14 362	31 357	25 963
G.10.2.2. Ceded Premiums / Primes Cédées							4 404	4 930
G.10.2.3. Net Written Premiums / Primes Nettes Emises							26 953	21 033
G.10.3. Total								
G.10.3.1. Gross Premiums / Primes Brutes	311 718	367 946	395 298	414 486	459 713	487 482	539 869	570 206
G.10.3.2. Ceded Premiums / Primes Cédées	43 061	50 023	49 885	53 982	68 213	75 334	93 898	95 738
G.10.3.3. Net Written Premiums / Primes Nettes Emises	268 657	317 923	345 413	360 504	391 500	412 148	445 971	474 468
H. GROSS CLAIMS PAYMENTS / H. PAIEMENTS BRUTS DES SINISTRES								
H.1. Life / H.1. Vie								
H.1.1. Domestic Companies / Entreprises Nationales		42 968	57 113	78 819	104 988	120 204	146 442	193 630
H.1.2. (Foreign Controlled Companies) / (Entreprises Sous Contrôle Etranger)		9 747	19 156	13 405	19 493	20 368	31 496	36 477
H.1.3. Branches & Agencies of Foreign Cies / Succursales et Agences d'Ent. Etrangères		7 950	4 593	3 105	3 005	3 254	3 973	4 705
H.1. Total		50 918	61 706	81 924	107 993	123 458	150 415	198 335
H.2. Non-Life / H.2. Non-Vie								
H.2.1. Domestic Companies / Entreprises Nationales		229 218	255 172	283 511	313 591	361 425	390 081	396 973
H.2.2. (Foreign Controlled Companies) / (Entreprises Sous Contrôle Etranger)		40 049	41 154	41 668	45 975	48 728	110 422	105 922
H.2.3. Branches & Agencies of Foreign Cies / Succursales et Agences d'Ent. Etrangères		17 610	10 078	1 994	2 088	2 510	3 520	123
H.2. Total		246 828	265 250	285 505	315 679	363 935	393 601	397 096
I. GROSS OPERATING EXPENSES / I. DEPENSES BRUITES D'EXPLOITATION								
I.1. Life / I.1. Vie								
I.1.1. Domestic Companies / Entreprises Nationales		14 022	15 324	19 350	22 594	26 229	31 862	30 671
I.1.2. (Foreign Controlled Companies) / (Entreprises Sous Contrôle Etranger)		4 207	4 569	5 200	6 336	5 824	11 696	10 889
I.1.3. Branches & Agencies of Foreign Cies / Succursales et Agences d'Ent. Etrangères		3 778	2 556	1 208	1 303	1 265	1 472	1 477
I.1. Total / Total des Primes Nettes Vie		17 800	17 880	20 558	23 897	27 494	33 334	32 148
I.2. Non-Life / I.2. Non-Vie								
I.2.1. Domestic Companies / Entreprises Nationales		87 142	87 760	109 727	119 313	126 565	153 702	141 186
I.2.2. (Foreign Controlled Companies) / (Entreprises Sous Contrôle Etranger)		4 160	4 799	19 206	20 189	19 029	39 640	39 467
I.2.3. Branches & Agencies of Foreign Cies / Succursales et Agences d'Ent. Etrangères		8 585	3 264	1 035	1 060	1 040	1 559	78
I.2. Total		95 727	91 024	110 762	120 373	127 605	155 261	141 264
J. COMMISSIONS								
J.1. Life / J.1. Vie								
J.1.1. Direct Business / Assurance directe								
J.1.1.1. Domestic Companies / Entreprises Nationales		4 765	5 595	..	5 284	7 786	7 257	7 455
J.1.1.2. (Foreign Controlled Companies) / (Entreprises Sous Contrôle Etranger)		1 541	1 577	..	3 899	3 222	4 398	3 199
J.1.1.3. Branches & Agencies of Foreign Cies / Succursales et Agences d'Ent. Etrangères		1 201	661	..	439	468	511	566
J.1.1. Total		5 966	6 256	..	5 723	8 254	7 768	8 021
J.1.2. Reinsurance Accepted / Réassurances acceptées								
J.1.2.1. Domestic Companies / Entreprises Nationales		6	9	..	..	..	..	..
J.1.2. Total		6	9	..	..	..	..	..

PORTUGAL

Monetary Unit: million escudos

Unité monétaire : million de escudos

	1992	1993	1994	1995	1996	1997	1998	1999
J.1.3. Total								
J.1.3.1. Domestic Companies / Entreprises Nationales		4 771	5 604	:	:	:	:	:
J.1.3.2. (Foreign Controlled Companies) / (Entreprises Sous Contrôle Etranger)		1 541	1 577	:	:	:	:	:
J.1.3.3. Branches & Agencies of Foreign Cies / Succursales et Agences d'Ent. Etrangères		1 201	661	:	:	:	:	:
J.1.3. Total of Life Net Premiums / Total		5 972	6 265	:	:	:	:	:
J.2. Non-Life / J.2. Non-Vie								
J.2.1. Direct Business / Assurance directe								
J.2.1.1. Domestic Companies / Entreprises Nationales		29 813	33 836	:	32 063	37 050	37 301	39 657
J.2.1.2. (Foreign Controlled Companies) / (Entreprises Sous Contrôle Etranger)		1 809	2 276	:	8 624	10 515	10 428	11 236
J.2.1.3. Branches & Agencies of Foreign Cies / Succursales et Agences d'Ent. Etrangères		2 906	1 279	:	276	344	392	77
J.2.1. Total / Total des Primes Nettes Vie		32 719	35 115	:	32 339	37 394	37 693	39 734
J.2.2. Reinsurance Accepted / Réassurances acceptées								
J.2.2.1. Domestic Companies / Entreprises Nationales		1 039	1 191	:	:	:	:	:
J.2.2.2. (Foreign Controlled Companies) / (Entreprises Sous Contrôle Etranger)		17	8	:	:	:	:	:
J.2.2.3. Branches & Agencies of Foreign Cies / Succursales et Agences d'Ent. Etrangères		126	49	:	:	:	:	:
J.2.2. Total		1 165	1 240	:	:	:	:	:
J.2.3. Total								
J.2.3.1. Domestic Companies / Entreprises Nationales		30 852	35 027	:	:	:	:	:
J.2.3.2. (Foreign Controlled Companies) / (Entreprises Sous Contrôle Etranger)		1 826	2 284	:	:	:	:	:
J.2.3.3. Branches & Agencies of Foreign Cies / Succursales et Agences d'Ent. Etrangères		3 032	1 328	:	:	:	:	:
J.2.3. Total		33 884	36 355	:	:	:	:	:

Monetary Unit: million Slovak koruna

Unité monétaire : million de couronnes slovaques

	1992	1993	1994	1995	1996	1997	1998	1999
A. NUMBER OF COMPANIES IN THE REPORTING COUNTRY / A. NOMBRE D'ENTREPRISES DANS LE PAYS DECLARANT								
A.1. Life / A.1. Vie								
A.1.1. Domestic Companies / A.1.1. Entreprises Nationales						2	3	3
A.1.2. (Foreign Controlled Companies) / A.1.2. (Entreprises Sous Contrôle Etranger)						1	2	2
A.1. All Companies / A.1. Ensemble des Entreprises						2	3	3
A.2. Non-Life / A.2. Non-Vie								
A.2.1. Domestic Companies / A.2.1. Entreprises Nationales						5	6	7
A.2.2. (Foreign Controlled Companies) / A.2.2. (Entreprises Sous Contrôle Etranger)						3	4	5
A.2. All Companies / A.2. Ensemble des Entreprises						5	6	7
A.3. Composite / A.3. Mixte								
A.3.1. Domestic Companies / A.3.1. Entreprises Nationales						16	17	17
A.3.2. (Foreign Controlled Companies) / A.3.2. (Entreprises Sous Contrôle Etranger)						7	8	8
A.3. All Companies / A.3. Ensemble des Entreprises						16	17	17
A.5. Total / A.5. Total								
A.5.1. Domestic Companies / A.5.1. Entreprises Nationales						23	26	28
A.5.2. (Foreign Controlled Companies) / A.5.2. (Entreprises Sous Contrôle Etranger)						11	14	18
A.5. All Insurance Companies / A.5. Ensemble des Entreprises d'Assurances						23	26	28
B. NUMBER OF EMPLOYEES / B. NOMBRE D'EMPLOYES								
B.1. Insurance Companies / B.1. Entreprises d'Assurances						6 412	8 538	7 788
B.2. Intermediaries / B.2. Intermediaries						19 789	24 217	366 210
B. Total / B. Total						26 201	32 755	373 998
C. BUSINESS WRITTEN IN THE REPORTING COUNTRY / C. OPERATIONS CONCLUES DANS LE PAYS DECLARANT								
C.1. Life / C.1. Vie								
C.1.1. Gross Premiums / C.1.1. Primes Brutes								
C.1.1.1. Direct Business / C.1.1.1. Assurances Directes								
C.1.1.1.1. Domestic Companies / C.1.1.1.1. Entreprises Nationales						4 603	6 297	7 860
C.1.1.1.2. (Foreign Controlled Companies) / C.1.1.1.2. (Entreprises Sous Contrôle Etranger)						1 157	2 108	3 637
C.1.1.1. Total / C.1.1.1. Total						4 603	6 297	7 860
C.1.1.3. Total / C.1.1.3. Total								
C.1.1.3.1. Domestic Companies / C.1.1.3.1. Entreprises Nationales						4 603	6 297	7 860
C.1.1.3.2. (Foreign Controlled Companies) / C.1.1.3.2. (Entreprises Sous Contrôle Etranger)						1 157	2 108	3 637
C.1.1.3. Total Gross Premiums / C.1.1.3. Total des Primes Brutes						4 603	6 297	7 860
C.1.2. Ceded Premiums / C.1.2. Primes Cédées								
C.1.2.1. Domestic Companies / C.1.2.1. Entreprises Nationales						40	36	60
C.1.2.2. (Foreign Controlled Companies) / C.1.2.2. (Entreprises Sous Contrôle Etranger)						39	29	48
C.1.2. Total / C.1.2. Total						40	36	60
C.1.3. Net Written Premiums / C.1.3. Primes Nettes Emises								
C.1.3.1. Domestic Companies / C.1.3.1. Entreprises Nationales						4 564	6 261	7 799
C.1.3.2. (Foreign Controlled Companies) / C.1.3.2. (Entreprises Sous Contrôle Etranger)						1 119	2 080	3 589
C.1.3. Total / C.1.3. Total						4 564	6 261	7 799
C.2. Non-Life / C.2. Non-Vie								
C.2.1. Gross premiums / C.2.1. Primes Brutes								
C.2.1.1. Direct Business / C.2.1.1. Assurances Directes								
C.2.1.1.1. Domestic Companies / C.2.1.1.1. Entreprises Nationales						12 389	15 063	15 807
C.2.1.1.2. (Foreign Controlled Companies) / C.2.1.1.2. (Entreprises Sous Contrôle Etranger)						3 866	4 050	6 156
C.2.1.1. Total / C.2.1.1. Total						12 389	15 063	15 807
C.2.1.2. Reinsurance Accepted / C.2.1.2. Réassurance Acceptée								
C.2.1.2.1. Domestic Companies / C.2.1.2.1. Entreprises Nationales						95	64	62
C.2.1.2.2. (Foreign Controlled Companies) / C.2.1.2.2. (Entreprises Sous Contrôle Etranger)						49	1	7
C.2.1.2. Total / C.2.1.2. Total						95	64	62

Monetary Unit : million Slovak koruna

Unité monétaire : million de couronnes slovaques

	1992	1993	1994	1995	1996	1997	1998	1999
C.2.1.3. Total						12 484	15 127	15 869
C.2.1.3.1. Domestic Companies C.2.1.3.1. Entreprises Nationales						12 484	15 127	15 869
C.2.1.3.2. (Foreign Controlled Companies) C.2.1.3.2. (Entreprises Sous Contrôle Etranger)						3 915	4 051	6 163
C.2.1.3. Total Gross Premiums C.2.1.3. Total des Primes Brutes						12 484	15 127	15 869
C.2.2. Ceded Premiums C.2.2. Primes Cédées								
C.2.2.1. Domestic Companies C.2.2.1. Entreprises Nationales						3 107	4 029	3 602
C.2.2.2. (Foreign Controlled Companies) C.2.2.2. (Entreprises Sous Contrôle Etranger)						1 707	1 642	2 445
C.2.2. Total C.2.2. Total						3 107	4 029	3 602
C.2.3. Net Written Premiums C.2.3. Primes Nettes Emises						9 377	11 098	12 267
C.2.3.1. Domestic Companies C.2.3.1. Entreprises Nationales						9 377	11 098	12 267
C.2.3.2. (Foreign Controlled Companies) C.2.3.2. (Entreprises Sous Contrôle Etranger)						2 208	2 410	3 718
C.2.3. Total C.2.3. Total						9 377	11 098	12 267
C.3. Total								
C.3.1. Gross Premiums C.3.1. Primes Brutes								
C.3.1.1. Direct Business C.3.1.1. Assurances Directes								
C.3.1.1.1. Domestic Companies C.3.1.1.1. Entreprises Nationales						16 992	21 360	23 666
C.3.1.1.2. (Foreign Controlled Companies) C.3.1.1.2. (Entreprises Sous Contrôle Etranger)						5 023	6 158	9 793
C.3.1.1. Total C.3.1.1. Total						16 992	21 360	23 666
C.3.1.2. Reinsurance Accepted C.3.1.2. Réassurance Acceptée								
C.3.1.2.1. Domestic Companies C.3.1.2.1. Entreprises Nationales						95	64	62
C.3.1.2.2. (Foreign Controlled Companies) C.3.1.2.2. (Entreprises Sous Contrôle Etranger)						49	1	7
C.3.1.2. Total C.3.1.2. Total						95	64	62
C.3.1.3. Total						17 087	21 424	23 728
C.3.1.3.1. Domestic Companies C.3.1.3.1. Entreprises Nationales						17 087	21 424	23 728
C.3.1.3.2. (Foreign Controlled Companies) C.3.1.3.2. (Entreprises Sous Contrôle Etranger)						5 073	6 160	9 799
C.3.1.3. Total Gross Premiums C.3.1.3. Total des Primes Brutes						17 087	21 424	23 728
C.3.2. Ceded Premiums C.3.2. Primes Cédées								
C.3.2.1. Domestic Companies C.3.2.1. Entreprises Nationales						3 147	4 065	3 662
C.3.2.2. (Foreign Controlled Companies) C.3.2.2. (Entreprises Sous Contrôle Etranger)						1 746	1 670	2 492
C.3.2. Total C.3.2. Total						3 147	4 065	3 662
C.3.3. Net Written Premiums C.3.3. Primes Nettes Emises						13 941	17 358	20 066
C.3.3.1. Domestic Companies C.3.3.1. Entreprises Nationales						13 941	17 358	20 066
C.3.3.2. (Foreign Controlled Companies) C.3.3.2. (Entreprises Sous Contrôle Etranger)						3 326	4 489	7 307
C.3.3. Total C.3.3. Total						13 941	17 358	20 066
D. NET WRITTEN PREMIUMS IN THE REPORTING COUNTRY IN TERMS OF DOMESTIC AND FOREIGN RISKS **D. PRIMES NETTES EMISES DANS LE PAYS DECLARANT EN RISQUES NATIONAUX ET ETRANGERS**								
D.1. Life **D.1. Vie**								
D.1.1. Domestic Risks D.1.1. Risques Nationaux						4 564	6 261	7 799
D.1.1.1. Domestic Companies D.1.1.1. Entreprises Nationales						4 564	6 261	7 799
D.1.1.2. (Foreign Controlled Companies) D.1.1.2. (Entreprises Sous Contrôle Etranger)						1 119	2 080	:
D.1.1. Total D.1.1. Total des Primes Nettes Vie						4 564	6 261	:
D.1.3. Total						4 564	6 261	7 799
D.1.3.1. Domestic Companies D.1.3.1. Entreprises Nationales						4 564	6 261	7 799
D.1.3.2. (Foreign Controlled Companies) D.1.3.2. (Entreprises Sous Contrôle Etranger)						1 119	2 080	3 589
D.1.3. Total of Life Net Premiums D.1.3. Total des Primes Nettes Vie						4 564	6 261	7 799
D.2. Non-Life **D.2. Non-Vie**								
D.2.1. Domestic Risks D.2.1. Risques Nationaux						9 377	11 098	11 993
D.2.1.1. Domestic Companies D.2.1.1. Entreprises Nationales						9 377	11 098	11 993
D.2.1.2. (Foreign Controlled Companies) D.2.1.2. (Entreprises Sous Contrôle Etranger)						2 208	2 410	3 533
D.2.1. Total D.2.1. Total des Primes Nettes Vie						9 377	11 098	11 993
D.2.2. Foreign Risks D.2.2. Risques Etrangers								
D.2.2.1. Domestic Companies D.2.2.1. Entreprises Nationales								274
D.2.2.2. (Foreign Controlled Companies) D.2.2.2. (Entreprises Sous Contrôle Etranger)								185
D.2.2. Total D.2.2. Total des Primes Nettes Vie								274
D.2.3. Total						9 377	11 098	12 267
D.2.3.1. Domestic Companies D.2.3.1. Entreprises Nationales						9 377	11 098	12 267
D.2.3.2. (Foreign Controlled Companies) D.2.3.2. (Entreprises Sous Contrôle Etranger)						2 208	2 410	3 718
D.2.3. Total D.2.3. Total des Primes Nettes Vie						9 377	11 098	12 267

Monetary Unit: million Slovak koruna

Unité monétaire : million de couronnes slovaques

F. OUTSTANDING INVESTMENT BY DIRECT INSURANCE COMPANIES
F. ENCOURS DES PLACEMENTS DES ENTREPRISES D'ASSURANCES DIRECTES

F.1. Life — F.1. Vie

Code	Label (EN)	Label (FR)	1992	1993	1994	1995	1996	1997	1998	1999
F.1.1.	Real Estate	Immobilier								
F.1.1.1.	Domestic Companies	Entreprises Nationales							3 578	3 089
F.1.1.2.	(Foreign Controlled Companies)	(Entreprises Sous Contrôle Etranger)							200	263
F.1.1.4.	Domestic Investment	Placement dans le Pays							3 578	3 089
F.1.1.	Total	Total							3 578	3 089
F.1.3.	Shares	Actions								
F.1.3.1.	Domestic Companies	Entreprises Nationales							3 712	6 627
F.1.3.2.	(Foreign Controlled Companies)	(Entreprises Sous Contrôle Etranger)							57	11
F.1.3.4.	Domestic Investment	Placement dans le Pays							3 655	6 539
F.1.3.5.	Foreign Investment	Placement à l' Etranger							57	88
F.1.3.	Total	Total							3 712	6 627
F.1.4.	Bonds with Fixed Revenue	Obligations								
F.1.4.1.	Domestic Companies	Entreprises Nationales							4 355	5 102
F.1.4.2.	(Foreign Controlled Companies)	(Entreprises Sous Contrôle Etranger)							1 233	2 898
F.1.4.4.	Domestic Investment	Placement dans le Pays							4 355	5 079
F.1.4.5.	Foreign Investment	Placement à l' Etranger								23
F.1.4.	Total	Total							4 355	5 102
F.1.5.	Loans other than Mortgage Loans	Prêts Autres qu'Hypothécaires								
F.1.5.1.	Domestic Companies	Entreprises Nationales							2 282	1 050
F.1.5.4.	Domestic Investment	Placement dans le Pays							2 282	1 050
F.1.5.	Total	Total							2 282	1 050
F.1.6.	Other Investments	Autres Placements								
F.1.6.1.	Domestic Companies	Entreprises Nationales							11 912	9 843
F.1.6.2.	(Foreign Controlled Companies)	(Entreprises Sous Contrôle Etranger)							1 054	2 932
F.1.6.4.	Domestic Investment	Placement dans le Pays							11 812	9 843
F.1.6.5.	Foreign Investment	Placement à l' Etranger							100	0
F.1.6.	Total	Total							11 912	9 843
F.1.7.	Total	Total								
F.1.7.1.	Domestic Companies	Entreprises Nationales						24 114	25 839	25 710
F.1.7.2.	(Foreign Controlled Companies)	(Entreprises Sous Contrôle Etranger)						1 562	2 544	6 104
F.1.7.4.	Domestic Investment	Placement dans le Pays							25 682	25 600
F.1.7.5.	Foreign Investment	Placement à l' Etranger							157	110
F.1.7.	Total of Life Investments	Total des Placements Vie							25 839	25 710

F.2. Non-Life — F.2. Non-Vie

Code	Label (EN)	Label (FR)	1992	1993	1994	1995	1996	1997	1998	1999
F.2.1.	Real Estate	Immobilier								
F.2.1.1.	Domestic Companies	Entreprises Nationales							133	437
F.2.1.2.	(Foreign Controlled Companies)	(Entreprises Sous Contrôle Etranger)							133	406
F.2.1.4.	Domestic Investment	Placement dans le Pays							133	437
F.2.1.	Total	Total							133	437
F.2.3.	Shares	Actions								
F.2.3.1.	Domestic Companies	Entreprises Nationales							219	257
F.2.3.2.	(Foreign Controlled Companies)	(Entreprises Sous Contrôle Etranger)							135	95
F.2.3.4.	Domestic Investment	Placement dans le Pays							105	257
F.2.3.5.	Foreign Investment	Placement à l' Etranger							114	0
F.2.3.	Total	Total							219	257
F.2.4.	Bonds with Fixed Revenue	Obligations								
F.2.4.1.	Domestic Companies	Entreprises Nationales							1 399	2 113
F.2.4.2.	(Foreign Controlled Companies)	(Entreprises Sous Contrôle Etranger)							152	494
F.2.4.4.	Domestic Investment	Placement dans le Pays							1 399	2 106
F.2.4.5.	Foreign Investment	Placement à l' Etranger								7
F.2.4.	Total	Total							1 399	2 113

Monetary Unit: million Slovak koruna   Unité monétaire : million de couronnes slovaques

	1992	1993	1994	1995	1996	1997	1998	1999	
F.2.5. Loans other than Mortgage Loans									F.2.5. Prêts Autres qu'Hypothécaires
F.2.5.1. Domestic Companies							1 538	1 193	F.2.5.1. Entreprises Nationales
F.2.5.4. Domestic Investment							1 538	1 193	F.2.5.4. Placement dans le Pays
F.2.5. Total							1 538	1 193	F.2.5. Total
F.2.6. Other Investments									F.2.6. Autres Placements
F.2.6.1. Domestic Companies							4 760	6 614	F.2.6.1. Entreprises Nationales
F.2.6.2. (Foreign Controlled Companies)							2 141	2 360	F.2.6.2. (Entreprises Sous Contrôle Etranger)
F.2.6.4. Domestic Investment							4 760	6 614	F.2.6.4. Placement dans le Pays
F.2.6. Total							4 760	6 614	F.2.6. Total
F.2.7. Total									F.2.7. Total
F.2.7.1. Domestic Companies						6 384	8 048	10 614	F.2.7.1. Entreprises Nationales
F.2.7.2. (Foreign Controlled Companies)						2 572	2 561	3 356	F.2.7.2. (Entreprises Sous Contrôle Etranger)
F.2.7.4. Domestic Investment							7 934	10 607	F.2.7.4. Placement dans le Pays
F.2.7.5. Foreign Investment							114	7	F.2.7.5. Placement à l' Etranger
F.2.7. Total of Non-Life Investments							8 048	10 614	F.2.7. Total des Placements Non-Vie
G. BREAKDOWN OF NON-LIFE PREMIUMS									**G. VENTILATIONS DES PRIMES NON-VIE**
G.1. Motor vehicle									G.1. Assurance Automobile
G.1.1. Direct Business									G.1.1. Assurances Directes
G.1.1.1. Gross Premiums							7 557	8 183	G.1.1.1. Primes Brutes
G.1.1.2. Ceded Premiums							1 812	986	G.1.1.2. Primes Cédées
G.1.1.3. Net Written Premiums							5 746	7 197	G.1.1.3. Primes Nettes Emises
G.1.2. Reinsurance Accepted									G.1.2. Réassurance Acceptée
G.1.2.1. Gross Premiums								3	G.1.2.1. Primes Brutes
G.1.2.3. Net Written Premiums								3	G.1.2.3. Primes Nettes Emises
G.1.3. Total									G.1.3. Total
G.1.3.1. Gross Premiums						5 427	7 557	8 186	G.1.3.1. Primes Brutes
G.1.3.2. Ceded Premiums							1 812	986	G.1.3.2. Primes Cédées
G.1.3.3. Net Written Premiums							5 746	7 200	G.1.3.3. Primes Nettes Emises
G.2. Marine, Aviation									G.2. Marine, Aviation
G.2.1. Direct Business									G.2.1. Assurances Directes
G.2.1.1. Gross Premiums							84	84	G.2.1.1. Primes Brutes
G.2.1.2. Ceded Premiums							37	60	G.2.1.2. Primes Cédées
G.2.1.3. Net Written Premiums							46	23	G.2.1.3. Primes Nettes Emises
G.2.3. Total									G.2.3. Total
G.2.3.1. Gross Premiums						26	84	84	G.2.3.1. Primes Brutes
G.2.3.2. Ceded Premiums							37	60	G.2.3.2. Primes Cédées
G.2.3.3. Net Written Premiums							46	24	G.2.3.3. Primes Nettes Emises
G.3. Freight									G.3. Fret
G.3.1. Direct Business									G.3.1. Assurances Directes
G.3.1.1. Gross Premiums							157	137	G.3.1.1. Primes Brutes
G.3.1.2. Ceded Premiums							50	80	G.3.1.2. Primes Cédées
G.3.1.3. Net Written Premiums							108	57	G.3.1.3. Primes Nettes Emises
G.3.2. Reinsurance Accepted									G.3.2. Réassurance Acceptée
G.3.2.1. Gross Premiums								1	G.3.2.1. Primes Brutes
G.3.2.3. Net Written Premiums								1	G.3.2.3. Primes Nettes Emises
G.3.3. Total									G.3.3. Total
G.3.3.1. Gross Premiums						151	157	139	G.3.3.1. Primes Brutes
G.3.3.2. Ceded Premiums							50	80	G.3.3.2. Primes Cédées
G.3.3.3. Net Written Premiums							108	59	G.3.3.3. Primes Nettes Emises
G.4. Fire, Property Damages									G.4. Incendie, Dommages aux Biens
G.4.1. Direct Business									G.4.1. Assurances Directes
G.4.1.1. Gross Premiums							3 682	3 612	G.4.1.1. Primes Brutes
G.4.1.2. Ceded Premiums							1 702	1 223	G.4.1.2. Primes Cédées
G.4.1.3. Net Written Premiums							1 980	2 389	G.4.1.3. Primes Nettes Emises
G.4.2. Reinsurance Accepted									G.4.2. Réassurance Acceptée
G.4.2.1. Gross Premiums							62	8	G.4.2.1. Primes Brutes
G.4.2.2. Ceded Premiums								4	G.4.2.2. Primes Cédées
G.4.2.3. Net Written Premiums							62	4	G.4.2.3. Primes Nettes Emises
G.4.3. Total									G.4.3. Total
G.4.3.1. Gross Premiums						2 132	3 744	3 620	G.4.3.1. Primes Brutes
G.4.3.2. Ceded Premiums							1 702	1 227	G.4.3.2. Primes Cédées
G.4.3.3. Net Written Premiums							2 042	2 394	G.4.3.3. Primes Nettes Emises
G.5. Pecuniary Losses									G.5. Pertes Pécuniaires
G.5.1. Direct Business									G.5.1. Assurances Directes

Monetary Unit: million Slovak koruna

Unité monétaire : million de couronnes slovaques

	1992	1993	1994	1995	1996	1997	1998	1999	
G.5.1.1. Gross Premiums							11	35	G.5.1.1. Primes Brutes
G.5.1.2. Ceded Premiums							7	15	G.5.1.2. Primes Cédées
G.5.1.3. Net Written Premiums							5	20	G.5.1.3. Primes Nettes Emises
G.5.3. Total						77			G.5.3. Total
G.5.3.1. Gross Premiums							11	35	G.5.3.1. Primes Brutes
G.5.3.2. Ceded Premiums							7	15	G.5.3.2. Primes Cédées
G.5.3.3. Net Written Premiums							5	20	G.5.3.3. Primes Nettes Emises
G.6. General Liability									G.6. Responsabilité Générale
G.6.1. Direct Business									G.6.1. Assurances Directes
G.6.1.1. Gross Premiums							1 677	1 104	G.6.1.1. Primes Brutes
G.6.1.2. Ceded Premiums							93	192	G.6.1.2. Primes Cédées
G.6.1.3. Net Written Premiums							1 583	911	G.6.1.3. Primes Nettes Emises
G.6.2. Reinsurance Accepted									G.6.2. Réassurance Acceptée
G.6.2.1. Gross Premiums								2	G.6.2.1. Primes Brutes
G.6.2.3. Net Written Premiums								2	G.6.2.3. Primes Nettes Emises
G.6.3. Total						1 520			G.6.3. Total
G.6.3.1. Gross Premiums							1 677	1 105	G.6.3.1. Primes Brutes
G.6.3.2. Ceded Premiums							93	192	G.6.3.2. Primes Cédées
G.6.3.3. Net Written Premiums							1 583	913	G.6.3.3. Primes Nettes Emises
G.7. Accident, Health									G.7. Accident, Santé
G.7.1. Direct Business									G.7.1. Assurances Directes
G.7.1.1. Gross Premiums							1 609	1 292	G.7.1.1. Primes Brutes
G.7.1.2. Ceded Premiums							164	212	G.7.1.2. Primes Cédées
G.7.1.3. Net Written Premiums							1 446	1 080	G.7.1.3. Primes Nettes Emises
G.7.3. Total						949			G.7.3. Total
G.7.3.1. Gross Premiums							1 609	1 292	G.7.3.1. Primes Brutes
G.7.3.2. Ceded Premiums							164	212	G.7.3.2. Primes Cédées
G.7.3.3. Net Written Premiums							1 446	1 080	G.7.3.3. Primes Nettes Emises
G.8. Others									G.8. Autres
G.8.1. Direct Business									G.8.1. Assurances Directes
G.8.1.1. Gross Premiums							286	1 360	G.8.1.1. Primes Brutes
G.8.1.2. Ceded Premiums							165	830	G.8.1.2. Primes Cédées
G.8.1.3. Net Written Premiums							120	530	G.8.1.3. Primes Nettes Emises
G.8.2. Reinsurance Accepted									G.8.2. Réassurance Acceptée
G.8.2.1. Gross Premiums							1	47	G.8.2.1. Primes Brutes
G.8.2.3. Net Written Premiums							1	47	G.8.2.3. Primes Nettes Emises
G.8.3. Total						2 203			G.8.3. Total
G.8.3.1. Gross Premiums							287	1 407	G.8.3.1. Primes Brutes
G.8.3.2. Ceded Premiums							165	830	G.8.3.2. Primes Cédées
G.8.3.3. Net Written Premiums							122	577	G.8.3.3. Primes Nettes Emises
G.10. Total									G.10. Total
G.10.1. Direct Business									G.10.1. Assurances Directes
G.10.1.1. Gross Premiums							15 063	15 807	G.10.1.1. Primes Brutes
G.10.1.2. Ceded Premiums							4 029	3 598	G.10.1.2. Primes Cédées
G.10.1.3. Net Written Premiums							11 034	12 209	G.10.1.3. Primes Nettes Emises
G.10.2. Reinsurance Accepted									G.10.2. Réassurance Acceptée
G.10.2.1. Gross Premiums							64	62	G.10.2.1. Primes Brutes
G.10.2.2. Ceded Premiums								4	G.10.2.2. Primes Cédées
G.10.2.3. Net Written Premiums							64	58	G.10.2.3. Primes Nettes Emises
G.10.3. Total						12 484			G.10.3. Total
G.10.3.1. Gross Premiums							15 127	15 869	G.10.3.1. Primes Brutes
G.10.3.2. Ceded Premiums							4 029	3 602	G.10.3.2. Primes Cédées
G.10.3.3. Net Written Premiums							11 098	12 267	G.10.3.3. Primes Nettes Emises

Monetary Unit: million Slovak koruna

Unité monétaire : million de couronnes slovaques

	1992	1993	1994	1995	1996	1997	1998	1999	
H. GROSS CLAIMS PAYMENTS									**H. PAIEMENTS BRUTS DES SINISTRES**
H.1. Life									**H.1. Vie**
H.1.1. Domestic Companies		1 950	2 059	2 116	::	2 618	3 180	3 642	H.1.1. Entreprises Nationales
H.1.2. (Foreign Controlled Companies)		::	537	::	::	32	74	431	H.1.2. (Entreprises Sous Contrôle Etranger)
H.1. Total		1 950	2 059	2 116	::	2 618	3 180	3 642	H.1. Total
H.2. Non-Life									**H.2. Non-Vie**
H.2.1. Domestic Companies		4 816	4 522	4 388	::	7 032	8 170	9 561	H.2.1. Entreprises Nationales
H.2.2. (Foreign Controlled Companies)		::	0	::	::	1 542	2 063	3 085	H.2.2. (Entreprises Sous Contrôle Etranger)
H.2. Total		4 816	4 522	4 388	::	7 032	8 170	9 561	H.2. Total
I. GROSS OPERATING EXPENSES									**I. DEPENSES BRUITES D'EXPLOITATION**
I.1. Life									**I.1. Vie**
I.1.1. Domestic Companies		8	638	771	2 014	2 713	2 669	3 101	I.1.1. Entreprises Nationales
I.1.2. (Foreign Controlled Companies)		0	20	39	141	833	1 200	1 637	I.1.2. (Entreprises Sous Contrôle Etranger)
I.1. Total		8	638	771	2 014	2 713	2 669	3 101	I.1. Total des Primes Nettes Vie
I.2. Non-Life									**I.2. Non-Vie**
I.2.1. Domestic Companies		128	1 413	1 747	2 283	3 330	4 207	4 514	I.2.1. Entreprises Nationales
I.2.2. (Foreign Controlled Companies)		5	23	97	637	1 356	1 647	2 211	I.2.2. (Entreprises Sous Contrôle Etranger)
I.2. Total		128	1 413	1 747	2 283	3 330	4 207	4 514	I.2. Total
J. COMMISSIONS									**J. COMMISSIONS**
J.1. Life									**J.1. Vie**
J.1.3. Total									J.1.3. Total
J.1.3.1. Domestic Companies		4 771	5 604	::	::	::	::	459	J.1.3.1. Entreprises Nationales
J.1.3.2. (Foreign Controlled Companies)		1 541	1 577	::	::	::	::	315	J.1.3.2. (Entreprises Sous Contrôle Etranger)
J.1.3. Total of Life Net Premiums		5 972	6 265	::	::	::	::	459	J.1.3. Total
J.2. Non-Life									**J.2. Non-Vie**
J.2.3. Total									J.2.3. Total
J.2.3.1. Domestic Companies		30 852	35 027	::	::	::	::	652	J.2.3.1. Entreprises Nationales
J.2.3.2. (Foreign Controlled Companies)		1 826	2 284	::	::	::	::	498	J.2.3.2. (Entreprises Sous Contrôle Etranger)
J.2.3. Total		33 884	36 355	::	::	::	::	652	J.2.3. Total

Monetary Unit: million pesetas

Unité monétaire : million de pesetas

A. NUMBER OF COMPANIES IN THE REPORTING COUNTRY
A. NOMBRE D'ENTREPRISES DANS LE PAYS DECLARANT

	1992	1993	1994	1995	1996	1997	1998	1999		(French label)
A.1. Life									**A.1. Vie**	
A.1.1. Domestic Companies	63	56	57	56	56	54	49	51	A.1.1. Entreprises Nationales	
A.1.2. (Foreign Controlled Companies)	18	19	18	18	17	13	14	12	A.1.2. (Entreprises Sous Contrôle Etranger)	
A.1.3. Branches & Agencies of Foreign Cies	5	5	5	3	3	3	1	1	A.1.3. Succursales et Agences d'Ent. Etrangères	
A.1. All Companies	68	61	62	59	58	57	50	52	A.1. Ensemble des Entreprises	
A.2. Non-Life									**A.2. Non-Vie**	
A.2.1. Domestic Companies	291	278	261	244	238	228	211	203	A.2.1. Entreprises Nationales	
A.2.2. (Foreign Controlled Companies)	33	30	28	30	27	25	25	24	A.2.2. (Entreprises Sous Contrôle Etranger)	
A.2.3. Branches & Agencies of Foreign Cies	24	21	17	10	8	8	1	1	A.2.3. Succursales et Agences d'Ent. Etrangères	
A.2. All Companies	315	299	278	254	246	236	212	204	A.2. Ensemble des Entreprises	
A.3. Composite									**A.3. Mixte**	
A.3.1. Domestic Companies	82	81	73	71	66	65	67	60	A.3.1. Entreprises Nationales	
A.3.2. (Foreign Controlled Companies)	29	32	26	24	24	19	20	15	A.3.2. (Entreprises Sous Contrôle Etranger)	
A.3.3. Branches & Agencies of Foreign Cies	2	2	2	2	2	2	1	1	A.3.3. Succursales et Agences d'Ent. Etrangères	
A.3. All Companies	84	83	75	73	68	67	68	61	A.3. Ensemble des Entreprises	
A.4. Reinsurance									**A.4. Reassurance**	
A.4.1. Domestic Companies	6	6	5	5	5	4	4	4	A.4.1. Entreprises Nationales	
A.4.3. Branches & Agencies of Foreign Cies	1	1	1	1	0	..	0	0	A.4.3. Succursales et Agences d'Ent. Etrangères	
A.4. All Companies	7	7	6	6	5	4	4	4	A.4. Ensemble des Entreprises	
A.5. Total									**A.5. Total**	
A.5.1. Domestic Companies	442	421	396	376	365	351	331	318	A.5.1. Entreprises Nationales	
A.5.2. (Foreign Controlled Companies)	80	81	72	72	68	57	59	51	A.5.2. (Entreprises Sous Contrôle Etranger)	
A.5.3. Branches & Agencies of Foreign Cies	32	29	25	16	12	13	3	3	A.5.3. Succursales et Agences d'Ent. Etrangères	
A.5. All Insurance Companies	474	450	421	392	377	364	334	321	A.5. Ensemble des Entreprises d'Assurances	

B. NUMBER OF EMPLOYEES
B. NOMBRE D'EMPLOYES

	1992	1993	1994	1995	1996	1997	1998	1999	(French label)
B.1. Insurance Companies	46 803	44 570	45 851	47 773	48 269	40 852	43 007	42 380	B.1. Entreprises d'Assurances
B.2. Intermediaries	..	21 132	19 173	17 603	16 296	..	..	..	B.2. Intermediaires
B. Total	..	65 702	65 024	65 376	64 565	..	..	..	B. Total

C. BUSINESS WRITTEN IN THE REPORTING COUNTRY
C. OPERATIONS CONCLUES DANS LE PAYS DECLARANT

C.1. Life / C.1. Vie

	1992	1993	1994	1995	1996	1997	1998	1999	(French label)
C.1.1. Gross Premiums									**C.1.1. Primes Brutes**
C.1.1.1. Direct Business									C.1.1.1. Assurances Directes
C.1.1.1.1. Domestic Companies	760 297	830 007	1 338 439	1 322 217	1 569 674	1 838 247	2 024 043	2 771 960	C.1.1.1.1. Entreprises Nationales
C.1.1.1.2. (Foreign Controlled Companies)	..	188 973	177 865	317 388	289 012	322 055	569 073	427 614	C.1.1.1.2. (Entreprises Sous Contrôle Etranger)
C.1.1.1.3. Branches & Agencies of Foreign Cies	51 481	48 295	103 141	50 384	65 973	69 690	19 592	21 250	C.1.1.1.3. Succursales et Agences d'Ent. Etrangères
C.1.1.1. Total	811 778	878 302	1 441 580	1 372 601	1 635 647	1 907 937	2 043 635	2 793 210	C.1.1.1. Total
C.1.1.2. Reinsurance Accepted									C.1.1.2. Réassurance Acceptée
C.1.1.2.1. Domestic Companies	5 022	5 570	6 605	8 711	8 554	13 087	5 563	58 573	C.1.1.2.1. Entreprises Nationales
C.1.1.2.2. (Foreign Controlled Companies)	..	2 161	538	716	499	277	215	283	C.1.1.2.2. (Entreprises Sous Contrôle Etranger)
C.1.1.2.3. Branches & Agencies of Foreign Cies	- 57	452	- 228	259	- 1 320	0	0	0	C.1.1.2.3. Succursales et Agences d'Ent. Etrangères
C.1.1.2. Total	4 965	6 022	6 377	8 970	7 234	13 087	5 563	58 573	C.1.1.2. Total
C.1.1.3.									C.1.1.3. Total
C.1.1.3.1. Domestic Companies	765 319	835 577	1 345 044	1 330 928	1 578 228	1 851 334	2 029 606	2 830 533	C.1.1.3.1. Entreprises Nationales
C.1.1.3.2. (Foreign Controlled Companies)	..	191 134	178 403	318 104	289 511	322 332	569 288	427 897	C.1.1.3.2. (Entreprises Sous Contrôle Etranger)
C.1.1.3.3. Branches & Agencies of Foreign Cies	51 424	48 747	102 913	50 643	64 653	69 690	19 592	21 250	C.1.1.3.3. Succursales et Agences d'Ent. Etrangères
C.1.1.3. Total Gross Premiums	816 743	884 324	1 447 957	1 381 571	1 642 881	1 921 024	2 049 198	2 851 783	C.1.1.3. Total des Primes Brutes
C.1.2. Ceded Premiums									**C.1.2. Primes Cédées**
C.1.2.1. Domestic Companies	22 244	24 382	25 196	31 584	34 849	33 118	34 183	35 163	C.1.2.1. Entreprises Nationales
C.1.2.2. (Foreign Controlled Companies)	..	14 153	8 595	11 389	11 787	8 770	12 818	7 040	C.1.2.2. (Entreprises Sous Contrôle Etranger)
C.1.2.3. Branches & Agencies of Foreign Cies	2 955	4 256	5 780	4 854	3 236	588	648	1 001	C.1.2.3. Succursales et Agences d'Ent. Etrangères
C.1.2. Total	25 199	28 638	30 976	36 438	38 085	33 706	34 831	36 164	C.1.2. Total

209

Monetary Unit: million pesetas · Unité monétaire : million de pesetas

	1992	1993	1994	1995	1996	1997	1998	1999
C.1.3. Net Written Premiums / C.1.3. Primes Nettes Emises								
C.1.3.1. Domestic Companies / C.1.3.1. Entreprises Nationales	743 075	811 195	1 319 848	1 299 344	1 543 379	1 818 216	1 995 423	2 795 370
C.1.3.2. (Foreign Controlled Companies) / C.1.3.2. (Entreprises Sous Contrôle Etranger)	..	176 981	169 808	306 715	277 724	313 562	556 470	420 857
C.1.3.3. Branches & Agencies of Foreign Cies / C.1.3.3. Succursales et Agences d'Ent. Etrangères	448 469	44 491	97 133	45 789	61 417	69 102	18 944	20 249
C.1.3. Total	791 544	855 686	1 416 981	1 345 133	1 604 796	1 887 318	2 014 367	2 815 619
C.2. Non-Life / C.2. Non-Vie								
C.2.1. Gross premiums / C.2.1. Primes Brutes								
C.2.1.1. Direct Business / C.2.1.1. Assurances Directes								
C.2.1.1.1. Domestic Companies / C.2.1.1.1. Entreprises Nationales	1 481 544	1 630 146	1 739 438	1 907 641	2 010 594	2 049 219	2 245 263	2 498 966
C.2.1.1.2. (Foreign Controlled Companies) / C.2.1.1.2. (Entreprises Sous Contrôle Etranger)	..	621 668	492 555	598 320	558 664	525 459	617 502	651 930
C.2.1.1.3. Branches & Agencies of Foreign Cies / C.2.1.1.3. Succursales et Agences d'Ent. Etrangères	124 681	111 977	125 554	73 067	69 866	73 725	1 303	1 720
C.2.1.1. Total	1 606 225	1 742 128	1 864 992	1 980 708	2 080 460	2 122 944	2 246 566	2 500 686
C.2.1.2. Reinsurance Accepted / C.2.1.2. Réassurance Acceptée								
C.2.1.2.1. Domestic Companies / C.2.1.2.1. Entreprises Nationales	96 617	120 944	122 829	119 005	124 647	130 252	140 470	163 159
C.2.1.2.2. (Foreign Controlled Companies) / C.2.1.2.2. (Entreprises Sous Contrôle Etranger)	..	32 112	14 930	19 259	17 578	13 953	17 402	17 111
C.2.1.2.3. Branches & Agencies of Foreign Cies / C.2.1.2.3. Succursales et Agences d'Ent. Etrangères	6 740	6 126	7 436	6 333	592	2 474	0	0
C.2.1.2. Total	103 357	127 070	130 265	125 338	125 239	132 726	140 470	163 159
C.2.1.3.1. Domestic Companies / C.2.1.3.1. Entreprises Nationales	1 578 161	1 751 090	1 862 267	2 026 646	2 135 241	2 179 471	2 385 733	2 662 125
C.2.1.3.2. (Foreign Controlled Companies) / C.2.1.3.2. (Entreprises Sous Contrôle Etranger)	..	653 780	507 485	617 579	576 242	539 412	634 904	669 041
C.2.1.3.3. Branches & Agencies of Foreign Cies / C.2.1.3.3. Succursales et Agences d'Ent. Etrangères	131 421	118 103	132 990	79 400	70 458	76 199	1 303	1 720
C.2.1.3. Total Gross Premiums / C.2.1.3. Total des Primes Brutes	1 709 582	1 869 200	1 995 257	2 106 046	2 205 699	2 255 670	2 387 036	2 663 845
C.2.2. Ceded Premiums / C.2.2. Primes Cédées								
C.2.2.1. Domestic Companies / C.2.2.1. Entreprises Nationales	281 278	304 794	307 521	292 105	308 994	305 114	320 516	355 048
C.2.2.2. (Foreign Controlled Companies) / C.2.2.2. (Entreprises Sous Contrôle Etranger)	..	118 866	90 618	91 228	90 773	82 897	92 398	93 792
C.2.2.3. Branches & Agencies of Foreign Cies / C.2.2.3. Succursales et Agences d'Ent. Etrangères	22 036	27 275	21 704	16 485	9 622	7 654	284	422
C.2.2. Total	303 314	332 070	329 225	308 590	318 616	312 768	320 800	355 470
C.2.3. Net Written Premiums / C.2.3. Primes Nettes Emises								
C.2.3.1. Domestic Companies / C.2.3.1. Entreprises Nationales	1 296 883	1 446 296	1 554 746	1 734 541	1 826 247	1 874 357	2 065 217	2 307 077
C.2.3.2. (Foreign Controlled Companies) / C.2.3.2. (Entreprises Sous Contrôle Etranger)	..	534 914	416 867	526 351	458 469	456 515	542 506	575 248
C.2.3.3. Branches & Agencies of Foreign Cies / C.2.3.3. Succursales et Agences d'Ent. Etrangères	109 385	90 828	111 286	62 915	60 836	68 545	1 019	1 298
C.2.3. Total	1 406 268	1 537 124	1 666 032	1 797 456	1 887 083	1 942 902	2 066 236	2 308 375
C.3. Total								
C.3.1. Gross Premiums / C.3.1. Primes Brutes								
C.3.1.1. Direct Business / C.3.1.1. Assurances Directes								
C.3.1.1.1. Domestic Companies / C.3.1.1.1. Entreprises Nationales	2 241 841	2 460 153	3 077 877	3 229 858	3 580 268	3 887 466	4 269 306	5 270 926
C.3.1.1.2. (Foreign Controlled Companies) / C.3.1.1.2. (Entreprises Sous Contrôle Etranger)	..	810 641	670 420	915 708	847 676	847 544	1 186 575	1 079 544
C.3.1.1.3. Branches & Agencies of Foreign Cies / C.3.1.1.3. Succursales et Agences d'Ent. Etrangères	176 162	160 272	228 695	123 451	135 839	143 415	20 895	22 970
C.3.1.1. Total	2 418 003	2 620 430	3 306 572	3 353 309	3 716 107	4 030 881	4 290 201	5 293 896
C.3.1.2. Reinsurance Accepted / C.3.1.2. Réassurance Acceptée								
C.3.1.2.1. Domestic Companies / C.3.1.2.1. Entreprises Nationales	101 639	126 514	129 434	127 716	133 201	143 339	146 033	221 732
C.3.1.2.2. (Foreign Controlled Companies) / C.3.1.2.2. (Entreprises Sous Contrôle Etranger)	..	34 273	15 468	19 975	18 077	14 230	17 617	17 394
C.3.1.2.3. Branches & Agencies of Foreign Cies / C.3.1.2.3. Succursales et Agences d'Ent. Etrangères	6 683	6 578	7 208	6 592	- 728	2 474	0	0
C.3.1.2. Total	108 322	133 092	136 642	134 308	132 473	145 813	146 033	221 732
C.3.1.3.1. Domestic Companies / C.3.1.3.1. Entreprises Nationales	2 343 480	2 586 667	3 207 311	3 357 574	3 713 469	4 030 805	4 415 339	5 492 658
C.3.1.3.2. (Foreign Controlled Companies) / C.3.1.3.2. (Entreprises Sous Contrôle Etranger)	..	844 914	685 888	935 683	865 753	861 744	1 204 192	1 096 938
C.3.1.3.3. Branches & Agencies of Foreign Cies / C.3.1.3.3. Succursales et Agences d'Ent. Etrangères	182 845	166 850	235 903	130 043	135 111	145 889	20 895	22 970
C.3.1.3. Total Gross Premiums / C.3.1.3. Total des Primes Brutes	2 526 325	2 753 524	3 443 214	3 487 617	3 848 580	4 176 694	4 436 234	5 515 628
C.3.2. Ceded Premiums / C.3.2. Primes Cédées								
C.3.2.1. Domestic Companies / C.3.2.1. Entreprises Nationales	303 522	329 176	332 717	323 689	343 843	338 232	354 699	390 211
C.3.2.2. (Foreign Controlled Companies) / C.3.2.2. (Entreprises Sous Contrôle Etranger)	..	133 019	99 213	102 617	102 560	91 667	105 216	100 832
C.3.2.3. Branches & Agencies of Foreign Cies / C.3.2.3. Succursales et Agences d'Ent. Etrangères	24 991	31 531	27 484	21 339	12 858	8 242	932	1 423
C.3.2. Total	328 513	360 708	360 201	345 028	356 701	346 474	355 631	391 634

Monetary Unit: million pesetas   Unité monétaire : million de pesetas

	1992	1993	1994	1995	1996	1997	1998	1999
C.3.3. Net Written Premiums / Primes Nettes Emises								
C.3.3.1. Domestic Companies / Entreprises Nationales	2 039 958	2 257 491	2 874 594	3 033 885	3 369 626	3 692 573	4 060 640	5 102 447
C.3.3.2. (Foreign Controlled Companies) / (Entreprises Sous Contrôle Etranger)	..	711 895	586 675	833 066	736 193	770 077	1 098 976	996 105
C.3.3.3. Branches & Agencies of Foreign Cies / Succursales et Agences d'Ent. Etrangères	557 854	135 319	208 419	108 704	122 253	137 647	19 963	21 547
C.3.3. Total	2 197 812	2 392 810	3 083 013	3 142 589	3 491 879	3 830 220	4 080 603	5 123 994

E. BUSINESS WRITTEN ABROAD / E. OPERATIONS A L'ETRANGER

E.1. Life / E.1. Vie

	1992	1993	1994	1995	1996	1997	1998	1999
E.1.1. Gross Premiums / Primes Brutes								
E.1.1.1. Direct Business / Assurance Directe								
E.1.1.1.1. Branches & Agencies / Succursales & Agences	1 992	3 153	4 585	14 306	29 071	41 488	39 053	16 844
E.1.1.1. Total	1 992	3 153	4 585	14 306	29 071	:	39 053	16 844
E.1.1.2. Reinsurance Accepted / Réassurance Acceptée								
E.1.1.2.1. Branches & Agencies / Succursales & Agences	..	..	..	0	0	:	0	84
E.1.1.2. Total	..	..	..	0	0	:	0	84
E.1.1.3. Total								
E.1.1.3.1. Branches & Agencies / Succursales & Agences	1 992	3 153	4 585	14 306	29 071	41 488	39 053	16 928
E.1.1.3. Total Gross Premiums / Total des Primes Brutes	1 992	3 153	4 585	14 306	29 071	:	39 053	16 928
E.1.2. Ceded Premiums / Primes Cédées								
E.1.2.1. Branches & Agencies / Succursales & Agences	60	71	86	1 534	109	105	99	63
E.1.2. Total	60	71	86	1 534	109	:	99	63
E.1.3. Net Written Premiums / Primes Nettes Emises								
E.1.3.1. Branches & Agencies / Succursales & Agences	1 932	3 082	4 499	12 772	28 962	41 383	38 954	16 865
E.1.3. Total	1 932	3 082	4 499	12 772	28 962	:	38 954	16 865

E.2. Non-Life / E.2. Non-Vie

	1992	1993	1994	1995	1996	1997	1998	1999
E.2.1. Gross Premiums / Primes Brutes								
E.2.1.1. Direct Business / Assurance Directe								
E.2.1.1.1. Branches & Agencies / Succursales & Agences	3 309	5 648	11 587	13 731	12 925	14 640	12 168	9 665
E.2.1.1. Total	3 309	5 648	11 587	13 731	12 925	:	12 168	9 665
E.2.1.2. Reinsurance Accepted / Réassurance Acceptée								
E.2.1.2.1. Branches & Agencies / Succursales & Agences	168	342	473	2 603	5 331	6 819	5 674	16 132
E.2.1.2. Total	168	342	473	2 603	5 331	:	5 674	16 132
E.2.1.3. Total								
E.2.1.3.1. Branches & Agencies / Succursales & Agences	3 447	5 990	12 060	16 334	18 256	21 459	17 842	25 797
E.2.1.3. Total Gross Premiums / Total des Primes Brutes	3 477	5 990	12 060	16 334	18 256	:	17 842	25 797
E.2.2. Ceded Premiums / Primes Cédées								
E.2.2.1. Branches & Agencies / Succursales & Agences	892	1 025	1 411	2 966	2 577	2 727	2 267	2 691
E.2.2. Total	892	1 025	1 411	2 966	2 577	:	2 267	2 691
E.2.3. Net Written Premiums / Primes Nettes Emises								
E.2.3.1. Branches & Agencies / Succursales & Agences	2 585	4 965	10 649	13 368	15 679	18 732	15 575	23 106
E.2.3. Total	2 585	4 965	10 649	13 368	15 679	:	15 575	23 106

G. BREAKDOWN OF NON-LIFE PREMIUMS / G. VENTILATIONS DES PRIMES NON-VIE

G.1. Motor vehicle / G.1. Assurance Automobile

	1992	1993	1994	1995	1996	1997	1998	1999
G.1.1. Direct Business / Assurances Directes								
G.1.1.1. Gross Premiums / Primes Brutes	747 024	800 071	831 523	859 081	864 618	846 551	896 853	1 125 592
G.1.1.2. Ceded Premiums / Primes Cédées	58 814	69 226	60 224	45 208	47 363	42 362	46 726	65 213
G.1.1.3. Net Written Premiums / Primes Nettes Emises	688 210	730 845	771 299	813 873	817 255	804 189	850 127	1 060 379
G.1.2. Reinsurance Accepted / Réassurance Acceptée								
G.1.2.1. Gross Premiums / Primes Brutes	21 468	29 184	29 303	24 803	25 510	22 444	13 122	18 985
G.1.2.2. Ceded Premiums / Primes Cédées	3 253	3 788	3 946	3 642	3 129	3 242	374	2 563
G.1.2.3. Net Written Premiums / Primes Nettes Emises	18 215	25 396	25 357	21 161	22 381	19 201	12 748	16 422
G.1.3. Total								
G.1.3.1. Gross Premiums / Primes Brutes	768 492	829 255	860 826	883 884	890 128	868 995	909 975	1 144 577
G.1.3.2. Ceded Premiums / Primes Cédées	62 047	73 014	64 170	48 850	50 492	45 604	47 100	67 776
G.1.3.3. Net Written Premiums / Primes Nettes Emises	706 425	756 241	796 656	835 034	839 636	823 390	862 875	1 076 801

Monetary Unit: million pesetas

Unité monétaire : million de pesetas

	1992	1993	1994	1995	1996	1997	1998	1999
G.2. Marine, Aviation								
G.2.1. Direct Business								
G.2.1.1. Gross Premiums	22 585	24 242	24 476	23 362	23 908	23 864	20 002	22 343
G.2.1.2. Ceded Premiums	17 210	19 357	19 023	16 489	16 915	15 854	13 499	14 427
G.2.1.3. Net Written Premiums	5 375	4 885	5 453	6 873	6 993	8 010	6 503	7 916
G.2.2. Reinsurance Accepted								
G.2.2.1. Gross Premiums	5 521	9 371	9 373	10 178	8 819	7 285	8 801	10 115
G.2.2.2. Ceded Premiums	2 565	4 111	4 521	3 935	4 130	3 309	3 527	4 552
G.2.2.3. Net Written Premiums	2 956	5 227	4 852	6 243	4 689	3 977	5 274	5 563
G.2.3. Total								
G.2.3.1. Gross Premiums	28 106	33 613	33 849	33 540	32 727	31 149	28 803	32 458
G.2.3.2. Ceded Premiums	19 775	23 501	23 544	20 424	21 045	19 163	17 026	18 979
G.2.3.3. Net Written Premiums	8 331	10 112	10 305	13 116	11 682	11 986	11 777	13 479
G.3. Freight								
G.3.1. Direct Business								
G.3.1.1. Gross Premiums	35 142	24 102	27 204	29 068	29 586	26 308	27 523	28 878
G.3.1.2. Ceded Premiums	12 510	12 038	13 412	13 719	13 409	11 555	12 077	12 756
G.3.1.3. Net Written Premiums	12 632	12 064	13 792	15 349	16 177	14 753	15 446	16 122
G.3.2. Reinsurance Accepted								
G.3.2.1. Gross Premiums	1 508	2 731	3 132	2 458	2 977	3 059	3 525	3 490
G.3.2.2. Ceded Premiums	477	713	696	607	586	787	1 108	907
G.3.2.3. Net Written Premiums	1 031	2 018	2 436	1 851	2 391	2 272	2 417	2 583
G.3.3. Total								
G.3.3.1. Gross Premiums	26 650	26 833	30 336	31 526	32 563	29 367	31 048	32 368
G.3.3.2. Ceded Premiums	12 987	12 751	14 108	14 326	13 995	12 342	13 185	13 663
G.3.3.3. Net Written Premiums	13 663	14 082	16 228	17 200	18 568	17 025	17 863	18 705
G.4. Fire, Property Damages								
G.4.1. Direct Business								
G.4.1.1. Gross Premiums	87 527	87 180	85 598	86 195	94 238	89 859	92 699	92 572
G.4.1.2. Ceded Premiums	45 696	44 316	41 471	38 325	40 943	36 707	38 025	31 273
G.4.1.3. Net Written Premiums	41 831	42 864	44 127	47 870	53 295	53 151	54 674	61 299
G.4.2. Reinsurance Accepted								
G.4.2.1. Gross Premiums	31 151	35 343	34 020	30 782	35 269	37 305	41 396	48 239
G.4.2.2. Ceded Premiums	11 353	12 384	13 153	11 470	11 747	12 685	9 488	16 062
G.4.2.3. Net Written Premiums	19 798	22 959	20 867	19 312	23 522	24 620	31 908	32 177
G.4.3. Total								
G.4.3.1. Gross Premiums	118 678	122 523	119 618	116 977	129 507	127 167	134 095	140 811
G.4.3.2. Ceded Premiums	57 049	56 700	54 624	49 795	52 690	49 393	47 513	47 335
G.4.3.3. Net Written Premiums	61 629	65 823	64 994	67 182	76 817	77 771	86 582	93 476
G.5. Pecuniary Losses								
G.5.1. Direct Business								
G.5.1.1. Gross Premiums	43 805	45 861	47 412	46 940	50 934	7 749	10 145	66 520
G.5.1.2. Ceded Premiums	31 345	31 148	32 974	34 036	34 822	3 718	4 713	40 044
G.5.1.3. Net Written Premiums	12 460	14 713	14 438	12 904	16 112	4 032	5 432	26 476
G.5.2. Reinsurance Accepted								
G.5.2.1. Gross Premiums	6 035	5 847	4 883	5 264	6 245	41	165	8 711
G.5.2.2. Ceded Premiums	2 041	2 400	2 077	2 791	3 644	22	60	4 364
G.5.2.3. Net Written Premiums	3 994	3 447	2 806	2 473	2 601	18	105	4 347
G.5.3. Total								
G.5.3.1. Gross Premiums	49 840	51 708	52 295	52 204	57 179	7 790	10 310	75 231
G.5.3.2. Ceded Premiums	33 386	33 548	35 051	36 827	38 466	3 740	4 773	44 408
G.5.3.3. Net Written Premiums	16 454	18 160	17 244	15 377	18 713	4 050	5 537	30 823
G.6. General Liability								
G.6.1. Direct Business								
G.6.1.1. Gross Premiums	51 111	60 469	72 746	81 214	87 413	68 275	97 409	110 196
G.6.1.2. Ceded Premiums	22 324	24 595	25 831	25 355	26 767	21 450	29 271	40 030
G.6.1.3. Net Written Premiums	28 787	35 874	46 915	55 859	60 646	46 825	68 138	70 166
G.6.2. Reinsurance Accepted								
G.6.2.1. Gross Premiums	6 166	7 134	5 063	6 091	5 024	1 913	5 977	6 688
G.6.2.2. Ceded Premiums	2 904	3 725	2 840	2 302	1 322	549	5 800	1 338
G.6.2.3. Net Written Premiums	3 262	3 409	2 223	3 789	3 702	1 364	177	5 350

French labels (Assurances Directes / Réassurance Acceptée / Total):
G.2. Marine, Aviation — G.2.1. Assurances Directes; G.2.1.1. Primes Brutes; G.2.1.2. Primes Cédées; G.2.1.3. Primes Nettes Emises; G.2.2. Réassurance Acceptée; G.2.2.1. Primes Brutes; G.2.2.2. Primes Cédées; G.2.2.3. Primes Nettes Emises; G.2.3. Total; G.2.3.1. Primes Brutes; G.2.3.2. Primes Cédées; G.2.3.3. Primes Nettes Emises.
G.3. Fret — G.3.1. Assurances Directes; G.3.1.1. Primes Brutes; G.3.1.2. Primes Cédées; G.3.1.3. Primes Nettes Emises; G.3.2. Réassurance Acceptée; G.3.2.1. Primes Brutes; G.3.2.2. Primes Cédées; G.3.2.3. Primes Nettes Emises; G.3.3. Total; G.3.3.1. Primes Brutes; G.3.3.2. Primes Cédées; G.3.3.3. Primes Nettes Emises.
G.4. Incendie, Dommages aux Biens — G.4.1. Assurances Directes; G.4.1.1. Primes Brutes; G.4.1.2. Primes Cédées; G.4.1.3. Primes Nettes Emises; G.4.2. Réassurance Acceptée; G.4.2.1. Primes Brutes; G.4.2.2. Primes Cédées; G.4.2.3. Primes Nettes Emises; G.4.3. Total; G.4.3.1. Primes Brutes; G.4.3.2. Primes Cédées; G.4.3.3. Primes Nettes Emises.
G.5. Pertes Pécunières — G.5.1. Assurances Directes; G.5.1.1. Primes Brutes; G.5.1.2. Primes Cédées; G.5.1.3. Primes Nettes Emises; G.5.2. Réassurance Acceptée; G.5.2.1. Primes Brutes; G.5.2.2. Primes Cédées; G.5.2.3. Primes Nettes Emises; G.5.3. Total; G.5.3.1. Primes Brutes; G.5.3.2. Primes Cédées; G.5.3.3. Primes Nettes Emises.
G.6. Responsabilité Générale — G.6.1. Assurances Directes; G.6.1.1. Primes Brutes; G.6.1.2. Primes Cédées; G.6.1.3. Primes Nettes Emises; G.6.2. Réassurance Acceptée; G.6.2.1. Primes Brutes; G.6.2.2. Primes Cédées; G.6.2.3. Primes Nettes Emises.

Monetary Unit: million pesetas — Unité monétaire : million de pesetas

	1992	1993	1994	1995	1996	1997	1998	1999
G.6.3. Total								
G.6.3.1. Gross Premiums / Primes Brutes	57 277	67 603	77 809	87 305	92 437	70 188	103 386	116 884
G.6.3.2. Ceded Premiums / Primes Cédées	25 228	28 320	28 671	27 657	28 089	21 999	35 071	41 368
G.6.3.3. Net Written Premiums / Primes Nettes Emises	32 049	39 283	49 138	59 648	64 348	48 189	68 315	75 516
G.7. Accident, Health / Accident, Santé								
G.7.1. Direct Business / Assurances Directes								
G.7.1.1. Gross Premiums / Primes Brutes	316 539	349 898	385 479	422 441	454 246	480 861	508 797	514 663
G.7.1.2. Ceded Premiums / Primes Cédées	13 741	14 202	15 892	15 340	18 124	18 349	19 843	18 399
G.7.1.3. Net Written Premiums / Primes Nettes Emises	302 798	335 696	369 587	407 101	436 122	462 512	488 954	496 264
G.7.2. Reinsurance Accepted / Réassurance Acceptée								
G.7.2.1. Gross Premiums / Primes Brutes	6 023	6 846	8 083	7 834	5 243	7 769	9 054	10 637
G.7.2.2. Ceded Premiums / Primes Cédées	909	1 132	1 140	1 079	710	933	280	1 072
G.7.2.3. Net Written Premiums / Primes Nettes Emises	5 114	5 714	6 943	6 755	4 533	6 837	8 774	9 565
G.7.3. Total								
G.7.3.1. Gross Premiums / Primes Brutes	322 562	356 744	393 562	430 275	459 489	488 630	517 851	525 300
G.7.3.2. Ceded Premiums / Primes Cédées	14 650	15 334	17 032	16 419	18 834	19 281	20 123	19 471
G.7.3.3. Net Written Premiums / Primes Nettes Emises	307 912	341 410	376 530	413 856	440 655	469 349	497 728	505 829
G.8. Others / Autres								
G.8.1. Direct Business / Assurances Directes								
G.8.1.1. Gross Premiums / Primes Brutes	312 492	350 300	390 554	432 407	475 517	579 478	593 138	539 921
G.8.1.2. Ceded Premiums / Primes Cédées	73 048	80 578	84 840	84 753	88 198	129 959	133 291	100 526
G.8.1.3. Net Written Premiums / Primes Nettes Emises	239 444	269 722	305 714	347 654	387 319	449 519	459 847	439 395
G.8.2. Reinsurance Accepted / Réassurance Acceptée								
G.8.2.1. Gross Premiums / Primes Brutes	25 485	30 614	36 408	37 928	36 152	52 910	58 430	56 294
G.8.2.2. Ceded Premiums / Primes Cédées	5 124	5 737	7 185	9 539	6 807	11 285	2 718	1 943
G.8.2.3. Net Written Premiums / Primes Nettes Emises	20 361	24 877	29 223	28 389	29 345	41 624	55 712	54 351
G.8.3. Total								
G.8.3.1. Gross Premiums / Primes Brutes	337 977	380 914	426 962	470 335	511 669	632 388	651 568	596 216
G.8.3.2. Ceded Premiums / Primes Cédées	78 172	86 315	92 025	94 292	95 005	141 245	136 009	102 470
G.8.3.3. Net Written Premiums / Primes Nettes Emises	259 805	294 599	334 937	376 043	416 664	491 144	515 559	493 746
G.10. Total								
G.10.1. Direct Business / Assurances Directes								
G.10.1.1. Gross Premiums / Primes Brutes	1 606 225	1 742 128	1 864 992	1 980 708	2 080 460	:	2 246 566	2 500 685
G.10.1.2. Ceded Premiums / Primes Cédées	274 688	295 450	293 667	273 225	286 541	:	297 445	322 668
G.10.1.3. Net Written Premiums / Primes Nettes Emises	1 331 537	1 446 673	1 571 325	1 707 483	1 793 919	:	1 949 121	2 178 017
G.10.2. Reinsurance Accepted / Réassurance Acceptée								
G.10.2.1. Gross Premiums / Primes Brutes	103 357	127 070	130 265	125 338	125 239	:	140 470	163 159
G.10.2.2. Ceded Premiums / Primes Cédées	28 626	34 023	35 559	35 365	32 075	:	23 355	32 801
G.10.2.3. Net Written Premiums / Primes Nettes Emises	74 731	93 047	94 707	89 973	93 164	:	117 115	130 358
G.10.3. Total								
G.10.3.1. Gross Premiums / Primes Brutes	1 709 582	1 869 193	1 995 257	2 106 046	2 205 699		2 387 036	2 663 845
G.10.3.2. Ceded Premiums / Primes Cédées	303 314	329 483	329 225	308 590	318 616		320 800	355 470
G.10.3.3. Net Written Premiums / Primes Nettes Emises	1 406 268	1 539 710	1 666 032	1 797 456	1 887 083		2 066 236	2 308 375

H. GROSS CLAIMS PAYMENTS / H. PAIEMENTS BRUTS DES SINISTRES

H.1. Life / H.1. Vie

	1992	1993	1994	1995	1996	1997	1998	1999
H.1.1. Domestic Companies / Entreprises Nationales		533 722	591 826	765 976	836 372	993 337	1 271 429	1 442 260
H.1.2. (Foreign Controlled Companies) / (Entreprises Sous Contrôle Etranger)					147 238	152 532	345 627	398 669
H.1.3. Branches & Agencies of Foreign Cies / Succursales et Agences d'Ent. Etrangères		25 473	28 841	19 000	23 826	29 045	15 242	13 063
H.1. Total		559 195	620 667	784 976	860 198	1 022 382	1 286 671	1 455 323

H.2. Non-Life / H.2. Non-Vie

	1992	1993	1994	1995	1996	1997	1998	1999
H.2.1. Domestic Companies / Entreprises Nationales	1 266 582	1 303 217	1 413 739	1 464 696	1 523 414	1 636 636	1 795 411	
H.2.2. (Foreign Controlled Companies) / (Entreprises Sous Contrôle Etranger)				395 774	379 651	450 059	457 073	
H.2.3. Branches & Agencies of Foreign Cies / Succursales et Agences d'Ent. Etrangères	77 719	85 745	50 648	46 044	52 673	513	578	
H.2. Total	1 344 301	1 388 962	1 464 387	1 510 740	1 576 087	1 637 149	1 795 989	

SPAIN

Monetary Unit: million pesetas — Unité monétaire : million de pesetas

I. GROSS OPERATING EXPENSES — I. DEPENSES BRUTES D'EXPLOITATION

I.1. Life — I.1. Vie

	1992	1993	1994	1995	1996	1997	1998	1999	
I.1.1. Domestic Companies		99 261	107 238	124 955	133 252	149 736	130 020	141 540	I.1.1. Entreprises Nationales
I.1.2. (Foreign Controlled Companies)					47 308	43 115	45 443	42 615	I.1.2. (Entreprises Sous Contrôle Etranger)
I.1.3. Branches & Agencies of Foreign Cies		16 288	18 686	16 043	17 769	17 998	4 147	4 072	I.1.3. Succursales et Agences d'Ent. Etrangères
I.1. Total		115 549	125 924	140 998	151 021	167 734	134 167	145 612	I.1. Total des Primes Nettes Vie

I.2. Non-Life — I.2. Non-Vie

	1992	1993	1994	1995	1996	1997	1998	1999	
I.2.1. Domestic Companies		549 047	577 991	625 402	662 150	686 410	661 581	641 796	I.2.1. Entreprises Nationales
I.2.2. (Foreign Controlled Companies)					235 814	192 878	193 575	181 646	I.2.2. (Entreprises Sous Contrôle Etranger)
I.2.3. Branches & Agencies of Foreign Cies		42 400	47 484	27 300	23 992	25 546	516	376	I.2.3. Succursales et Agences d'Ent. Etrangères
I.2. Total		591 447	625 475	652 702	686 142	711 956	662 097	642 172	I.2. Total

J. COMMISSIONS — J. COMMISSIONS

J.1. Life — J.1. Vie

	1992	1993	1994	1995	1996	1997	1998	1999	
J.1.1. Direct Business									J.1.1. Assurance directe
J.1.1.1. Domestic Companies		29 719	33 855	42 762	49 685	57 708	..	105 502	J.1.1.1. Entreprises Nationales
J.1.1.2. (Foreign Controlled Companies)					16 791	15 671	..	29 998	J.1.1.2. (Entreprises Sous Contrôle Etranger)
J.1.1.3. Branches & Agencies of Foreign Cies		6 876	8 388	7 038	7 718	7 745	..	2 868	J.1.1.3. Succursales et Agences d'Ent. Etrangères
J.1.1. Total		36 595	42 243	49 800	57 403	65 453	..	108 370	J.1.1. Total
J.1.2. Reinsurance Accepted									J.1.2. Réassurances acceptées
J.1.2.1. Domestic Companies		795	835	1 253	1 259	1 153	..		J.1.2.1. Entreprises Nationales
J.1.2.2. (Foreign Controlled Companies)		99	- 40	69	166	97	..		J.1.2.2. (Entreprises Sous Contrôle Etranger)
J.1.2.3. Branches & Agencies of Foreign Cies							..		J.1.2.3. Succursales et Agences d'Ent. Etrangères
J.1.2. Total		894	795	1 322	1 327	1 153	..		J.1.2. Total
J.1.3. Total									J.1.3. Total
J.1.3.1. Domestic Companies		30 514	34 690	44 015	50 944	58 861	97 787	105 502	J.1.3.1. Entreprises Nationales
J.1.3.2. (Foreign Controlled Companies)					16 957	15 768	33 821	29 998	J.1.3.2. (Entreprises Sous Contrôle Etranger)
J.1.3.3. Branches & Agencies of Foreign Cies		6 975	8 348	7 107	7 786	7 745	2 731	2 868	J.1.3.3. Succursales et Agences d'Ent. Etrangères
J.1.3. Total of Life Net Premiums		97 489	43 038	51 122	58 730	66 606	100 518	108 370	J.1.3. Total

J.2. Non-Life — J.2. Non-Vie

	1992	1993	1994	1995	1996	1997	1998	1999	
J.2.1. Direct Business									J.2.1. Assurance directe
J.2.1.1. Domestic Companies		226 503	240 098	263 795	281 276	285 559	..	428 510	J.2.1.1. Entreprises Nationales
J.2.1.2. (Foreign Controlled Companies)					90 799	81 974	..	121 970	J.2.1.2. (Entreprises Sous Contrôle Etranger)
J.2.1.3. Branches & Agencies of Foreign Cies		18 959	21 391	12 002	11 457	12 279	..	221	J.2.1.3. Succursales et Agences d'Ent. Etrangères
J.2.1. Total		245 462	261 489	275 797	292 733	297 838	..	428 731	J.2.1. Total
J.2.2. Reinsurance Accepted									J.2.2. Réassurances acceptées
J.2.2.1. Domestic Companies		26 051	26 222	23 899	23 695	26 628	..		J.2.2.1. Entreprises Nationales
J.2.2.2. (Foreign Controlled Companies)		764	1 269	1 404	1 056	1 380	..		J.2.2.2. (Entreprises Sous Contrôle Etranger)
J.2.2.3. Branches & Agencies of Foreign Cies					137	486			J.2.2.3. Succursales et Agences d'Ent. Etrangères
J.2.2. Total		26 815	27 491	25 303	23 832	27 114	..		J.2.2. Total
J.2.3. Total									J.2.3. Total
J.2.3.1. Domestic Companies		252 554	266 320	287 694	304 971	312 187	457 758	428 510	J.2.3.1. Entreprises Nationales
J.2.3.2. (Foreign Controlled Companies)					91 855	83 354	133 342	121 970	J.2.3.2. (Entreprises Sous Contrôle Etranger)
J.2.3.3. Branches & Agencies of Foreign Cies		19 723	22 660	13 406	11 594	12 765	241	221	J.2.3.3. Succursales et Agences d'Ent. Etrangères
J.2.3. Total		272 277	288 980	301 100	316 565	324 952	457 999	428 731	J.2.3. Total

214

Monetary Unit: million Swedish kroner

SUEDE

Unité monétaire : million de couronnes suédoises

A. NUMBER OF COMPANIES IN THE REPORTING COUNTRY
A. NOMBRE D'ENTREPRISES DANS LE PAYS DECLARANT

		1992	1993	1994	1995	1996	1997	1998	1999
A.1. Life	**A.1. Vie**								
A.1.1. Domestic Companies	A.1.1. Entreprises Nationales	29	31	29	28	29	30	37	39
A.1. All Companies	A.1. Ensemble des Entreprises	29	31	29	28	29	30	37	..
A.2. Non-Life	**A.2. Non-Vie**								
A.2.1. Domestic Companies	A.2.1. Entreprises Nationales	93	100	107	110	98	100	113	114
A.2.2. (Foreign Controlled Companies)	A.2.2. (Entreprises Sous Contrôle Etranger)	2	2	2	3	3	4	4	5
A.2.3. Branches & Agencies of Foreign Cies	A.2.3. Succursales et Agences d'Ent. Etrangères	12	13	2	2	1	0	0	..
A.2. All Companies	A.2. Ensemble des Entreprises	105	113	109	111	99	100	113	..
A.4. Reinsurance	**A.4. Réassurance**								
A.4.1. Domestic Companies	A.4.1. Entreprises Nationales	6	5	6	6	8	8	8	7
A.4. All Companies	A.4. Ensemble des Entreprises	..	..	..	..	..	8	8	..
A.5. Total	**A.5. Total**								
A.5.1. Domestic Companies	A.5.1. Entreprises Nationales	128	136	142	144	135	138	158	160
A.5.2. (Foreign Controlled Companies)	A.5.2. (Entreprises Sous Contrôle Etranger)	2	2	2	3	3	4	4	5
A.5.3. Branches & Agencies of Foreign Cies	A.5.3. Succursales et Agences d'Ent. Etrangères	..	..	..	..	..	..	..	..
A.5. All Insurance Companies	A.5. Ensemble des Entreprises d'Assurances	..	..	..	..	..	138	158	..

B. NUMBER OF EMPLOYEES
B. NOMBRE D'EMPLOYES

		1992	1993	1994	1995	1996	1997	1998	1999
B.1. Insurance Companies	B.1. Entreprises d'Assurances	40 100	40 000	19 000	18 750	18 500	16 520	16 500	16 500
B.2. Intermediaries	B.2. Intermediaires	500	600	900	1 094	1 102	1 180	880	930
B. Total	B. Total	40 600	40 600	19 900	19 844	19 602	17 700	17 380	17 430

C. BUSINESS WRITTEN IN THE REPORTING COUNTRY
C. OPERATIONS CONCLUES DANS LE PAYS DECLARANT

C.1. Life / C.1. Vie

		1992	1993	1994	1995	1996	1997	1998	1999
C.1.1. Gross Premiums	**C.1.1. Primes Brutes**								
C.1.1.1. Direct Business	C.1.1.1. Assurances Directes								
C.1.1.1. Domestic Companies	C.1.1.1. Entreprises Nationales	42 030	42 414	52 794	53 947	60 038	64 709	75 143	95 134
C.1.1.1. Total	C.1.1.1. Total	42 030	42 414	52 794	53 947	60 038	64 709	75 143	95 134
C.1.1.2. Reinsurance Accepted	C.1.1.2. Réassurance Acceptée								
C.1.1.2.1. Domestic Companies	C.1.1.2.1. Entreprises Nationales	2 882	2 415	1 579	2 398	79	200	181	371
C.1.1.2. Total	C.1.1.2. Total	2 882	2 416	1 579	2 398	79	200	181	371
C.1.1.3. Total	C.1.1.3. Total								
C.1.1.3.1. Domestic Companies	C.1.1.3.1. Entreprises Nationales	44 912	44 829	54 373	56 345	60 117	64 909	75 324	95 505
C.1.1.3. Total Gross Premiums	C.1.1.3. Total des Primes Brutes	44 912	44 829	54 373	56 345	60 117	64 909	75 324	95 505
C.1.2. Ceded Premiums	**C.1.2. Primes Cédées**								
C.1.2.1. Domestic Companies	C.1.2.1. Entreprises Nationales	426	1 381	725	1 242	613	726	777	411
C.1.2. Total	C.1.2. Total	426	1 381	725	1 242	613	726	777	411
C.1.3. Net Written Premiums	**C.1.3. Primes Nettes Emises**								
C.1.3.1. Domestic Companies	C.1.3.1. Entreprises Nationales	44 486	43 448	53 648	55 103	59 504	64 183	74 547	95 094
C.1.3. Total	C.1.3. Total	44 486	43 448	53 648	55 103	59 504	64 183	74 547	95 094

Monetary Unit: million Swedish kroner

Unité monétaire : million de couronnes suédoises

C.2. Non-Life — C.2. Non-Vie

	1992	1993	1994	1995	1996	1997	1998	1999
C.2.1. Gross premiums — C.2.1. Primes Brutes								
C.2.1.1. Direct Business — C.2.1.1. Assurances Directes								
C.2.1.1.1. Domestic Companies — C.2.1.1.1. Entreprises Nationales	36 422	45 606	35 611	36 103	34 994	36 368	36 070	44 864
C.2.1.1.2. (Foreign Controlled Companies) — C.2.1.1.2. (Entreprises Sous Contrôle Etranger)	659	766	656	1 048	1 124	1 152	1 327	5 553
C.2.1.1.3. Branches & Agencies of Foreign Cies — C.2.1.1.3. Succursales et Agences d'Ent. Etrangères	750	791	198	205	205	..	..	1 556
C.2.1.1. Total — C.2.1.1. Total	37 172	46 397	35 809	36 308	35 199	36 368	36 070	46 420
C.2.1.2. Reinsurance Accepted — C.2.1.2. Réassurance Acceptée								
C.2.1.2.1. Domestic Companies — C.2.1.2.1. Entreprises Nationales	14 189	5 553	10 816	10 176	9 971	10 479	8 692	10 793
C.2.1.2.2. (Foreign Controlled Companies) — C.2.1.2.2. (Entreprises Sous Contrôle Etranger)	41	46	43	51	57	109	168	94
C.2.1.2. Total — C.2.1.2. Total	..	..	..	..	..	10 479	8 692	..
C.2.1.3. Total — C.2.1.3. Total								
C.2.1.3.1. Domestic Companies — C.2.1.3.1. Entreprises Nationales	50 611	51 159	46 427	46 279	44 965	46 847	44 762	55 657
C.2.1.3.2. (Foreign Controlled Companies) — C.2.1.3.2. (Entreprises Sous Contrôle Etranger)	700	812	699	1 099	1 181	1 261	1 495	5 647
C.2.1.3. Total Gross Premiums — C.2.1.3. Total des Primes Brutes	..	..	..	..	..	46 847	44 762	..
C.2.2. Ceded Premiums — C.2.2. Primes Cédées								
C.2.2.1. Domestic Companies — C.2.2.1. Entreprises Nationales	9 027	8 724	9 624	9 900	9 884	9 601	9 351	9 337
C.2.2.2. (Foreign Controlled Companies) — C.2.2.2. (Entreprises Sous Contrôle Etranger)	376	458	300	273	241	284	376	297
C.2.2. Total — C.2.2. Total	..	..	..	..	..	9 601	9 351	..
C.2.3. Net Written Premiums — C.2.3. Primes Nettes Emises								
C.2.3.1. Domestic Companies — C.2.3.1. Entreprises Nationales	41 584	42 435	36 803	36 379	35 081	37 246	35 411	46 320
C.2.3.2. (Foreign Controlled Companies) — C.2.3.2. (Entreprises Sous Contrôle Etranger)	324	354	399	826	940	977	1 119	5 350
C.2.3. Total — C.2.3. Total	..	..	..	..	..	37 246	35 411	..

C.3. Total — C.3. Total

	1992	1993	1994	1995	1996	1997	1998	1999
C.3.1. Gross Premiums — C.3.1. Primes Brutes								
C.3.1.1. Direct Business — C.3.1.1. Assurances Directes								
C.3.1.1.1. Domestic Companies — C.3.1.1.1. Entreprises Nationales	78 452	88 020	88 405	90 050	95 032	101 077	111 213	139 998
C.3.1.1.2. (Foreign Controlled Companies) — C.3.1.1.2. (Entreprises Sous Contrôle Etranger)	659	766	656	1 048	1 124	1 152	1 327	5 553
C.3.1.1.3. Branches & Agencies of Foreign Cies — C.3.1.1.3. Succursales et Agences d'Ent. Etrangères	750	791	198	205	205	..	..	..
C.3.1.1. Total — C.3.1.1. Total	79 202	88 811	88 603	90 255	95 237	101 077	111 213	141 554
C.3.1.2. Reinsurance Accepted — C.3.1.2. Réassurance Acceptée								
C.3.1.2.1. Domestic Companies — C.3.1.2.1. Entreprises Nationales	17 071	7 968	12 395	12 574	10 050	10 679	8 873	11 164
C.3.1.2.2. (Foreign Controlled Companies) — C.3.1.2.2. (Entreprises Sous Contrôle Etranger)	..	46	43	51	57	109	168	94
C.3.1.2. Total — C.3.1.2. Total	..	..	..	..	..	10 679	8 873	..
C.3.1.3. Total — C.3.1.3. Total								
C.3.1.3.1. Domestic Companies — C.3.1.3.1. Entreprises Nationales	95 523	95 988	100 800	102 624	105 082	111 756	120 086	151 162
C.3.1.3.2. (Foreign Controlled Companies) — C.3.1.3.2. (Entreprises Sous Contrôle Etranger)	700	812	699	1 099	1 181	1 261	1 495	5 647
C.3.1.3. Total Gross Premiums — C.3.1.3. Total des Primes Brutes	..	..	..	..	..	111 756	120 086	..
C.3.2. Ceded Premiums — C.3.2. Primes Cédées								
C.3.2.1. Domestic Companies — C.3.2.1. Entreprises Nationales	9 453	10 105	10 349	11 142	10 497	10 327	10 128	9 748
C.3.2.2. (Foreign Controlled Companies) — C.3.2.2. (Entreprises Sous Contrôle Etranger)	376	458	300	273	241	284	376	297
C.3.2. Total — C.3.2. Total	..	..	..	..	..	10 327	10 128	..
C.3.3. Net Written Premiums — C.3.3. Primes Nettes Emises								
C.3.3.1. Domestic Companies — C.3.3.1. Entreprises Nationales	86 070	85 883	90 451	91 482	94 585	101 429	109 958	141 414
C.3.3.2. (Foreign Controlled Companies) — C.3.3.2. (Entreprises Sous Contrôle Etranger)	324	354	399	826	940	977	1 119	5 350
C.3.3. Total — C.3.3. Total	..	..	..	..	..	101 429	109 958	..

D. NET WRITTEN PREMIUMS IN THE REPORTING COUNTRY IN TERMS OF DOMESTIC AND FOREIGN RISKS — D. PRIMES NETTES EMISES DANS LE PAYS DECLARANT EN RISQUES NATIONAUX ET ETRANGERS

D.1. Life — D.1. Vie

	1992	1993	1994	1995	1996	1997	1998	1999
D.1.1. Domestic Risks — D.1.1. Risques Nationaux								
D.1.1.1. Domestic Companies — D.1.1.1. Entreprises Nationales	..	..	..	..	59 504	64 183	74 432	95 071
D.1.1. Total — D.1.1. Total des Primes Nettes Vie	..	..	..	..	59 504	64 183	74 432	95 071

216

Monetary Unit: million Swedish kroner　　　　Unité monétaire : million de couronnes suédoises

	1992	1993	1994	1995	1996	1997	1998	1999
D.1.2. Foreign Risks / Risques Etrangers								
D.1.2.1. Domestic Companies / Entreprises Nationales	:	:	:	:	:	:	115	23
D.1.2. Total / Total des Primes Nettes Vie	:	:	:	:	:	:	115	23
D.1.3. Total								
D.1.3.1. Domestic Companies / Entreprises Nationales	44 486	43 448	53 648	55 103	59 504	64 183	74 547	95 094
D.1.3. Total / Total des Primes Nettes Vie	44 486	43 448	53 648	55 103	59 504	64 183	74 547	95 094

D.2. Non Life / D.2. Non Vie

	1992	1993	1994	1995	1996	1997	1998	1999
D.2.1. Domestic Risks / Risques Nationaux								
D.2.1.1. Domestic Companies / Entreprises Nationales	:	:				:	32 072	:
D.2.1.2. Foreign Controlled Companies / Entreprises Sous Controle Etranger	:	:				:	1 039	:
D.2.1. Total / Total des Primes Nettes Vie	:	:				:	32 072	:
D.2.2. Foreign Risks / Risques Etrangers								
D.2.2.1. Domestic Companies / Entreprises Nationales	:	:				:	3 339	:
D.2.2.2. Foreign Controlled Companies / Entreprises Sous Controle Etranger	:	:				:	80	:
D.2.2 Total / Total des Primes Nettes Vie	:	:				:	3 339	:
D.2.3. Total								
D.2.3.1. Domestic Companies / Entreprises Nationales	:	:				:	35 411	46 320
D.2.3.2. Foreign Controlled Companies / Entreprises Sous Controle Etranger	:	:				:	1 119	5 350
D.2.3. Total / Total des Primes Nettes Vie	:	:				:	35 411	

E. BUSINESS WRITTEN ABROAD / E. OPERATIONS A L'ETRANGER

E.1. Life / E.1. Vie

	1992	1993	1994	1995	1996	1997	1998	1999
E.1.1. Gross Premiums / Primes Brutes								
E.1.1.1. Direct Business / Assurance Directe								
E.1.1.1.1. Branches & Agencies / Succursales & Agences	:	:				:	96	23
E.1.1.1. Total	:	:				:	96	:
E.1.1.3. Total								
E.1.1.3.1. Branches & Agencies / Succursales & Agences	:	:				:	96	:
E.1.1.3. Total Gross Premiums / Total des Primes Brutes	:	:				:	96	:
E.1.3. Net Written Premiums / Primes Nettes Emises								
E.1.3.1. Branches & Agencies / Succursales & Agences	:	:				:	96	:
E.1.3. Total	:	:				:	96	:

E.2. Non-Life / E.2. Non-Vie

	1992	1993	1994	1995	1996	1997	1998	1999
E.2.1. Gross Premiums / Primes Brutes								
E.2.1.1. Direct Business / Assurance Directe								
E.2.1.1.1. Branches & Agencies / Succursales & Agences	690	833	1 096	928		:	604	9 483
E.2.1.1. Total	:	:				:	604	:
E.2.1.3. Total								
E.2.1.3.1. Branches & Agencies / Succursales & Agences	:	:				:	604	:
E.2.1.3. Total Gross Premiums / Total des Primes Brutes	:	:				:	604	:
E.2.2. Ceded Premiums / Primes Cédées								
E.2.2.1. Branches & Agencies / Succursales & Agences	230	231	331	386		:	:	:
E.2.3. Net Written Premiums / Primes Nettes Emises								
E.2.3.1. Branches & Agencies / Succursales & Agences	:	:				:	604	:
E.2.3. Total	:	:				:	604	:

F. OUTSTANDING INVESTMENT BY DIRECT INSURANCE COMPANIES / F. ENCOURS DES PLACEMENTS DES ENTREPRISES D'ASSURANCES DIRECTES

F.1. Life / F.1. Vie

	1992	1993	1994	1995	1996	1997	1998	1999
F.1.1. Real Estate / Immobilier								
F.1.1.1. Domestic Companies / Entreprises Nationales	34 864	34 887	36 486	37 629	51 130	51 566	59 575	73 766
F.1.1. Total	34 864	34 887	36 486	37 629	51 130	51 566	59 575	73 766

Monetary Unit: million Swedish kroner

Unité monétaire : million de couronnes suédoises

English label	1992	1993	1994	1995	1996	1997	1998	1999	French label
F.1.2. Mortgage Loans									**F.1.2. Prêts Hypothécaires**
F.1.2.1. Domestic Companies	..	..	..	..	10 064	8 217	4 106	2 511	F.1.2.1. Entreprises Nationales
F.1.2. Total	..	..	..	..	10 064	8 217	4 106	2 511	F.1.2. Total
F.1.3. Shares									**F.1.3. Actions**
F.1.3.1. Domestic Companies	83 697	103 284	116 284	148 993	308 918	393 967	452 869	598 598	F.1.3.1. Entreprises Nationales
F.1.3. Total	83 697	103 289	116 284	148 993	308 918	393 967	452 869	598 598	F.1.3. Total
F.1.4. Bonds with Fixed Revenue									**F.1.4. Obligations**
F.1.4.1. Domestic Companies	248 621	292 285	268 988	300 504	398 321	445 279	501 101	547 560	F.1.4.1. Entreprises Nationales
F.1.4.2. (Foreign Controlled Companies)	0	0	0	0	0	19	0	0	F.1.4.2. (Entreprises Sous Contrôle Etranger)
F.1.4. Total	248 621	292 285	268 988	300 504	398 321	445 279	501 101	547 560	F.1.4. Total
F.1.5. Loans other than Mortgage Loans									**F.1.5. Prêts Autres qu'Hypothécaires**
F.1.5.1. Domestic Companies	41 919	38 151	35 177	32 577	8 498	17 530	11 001	13 254	F.1.5.1. Entreprises Nationales
F.1.5. Total	41 919	38 151	35 177	32 577	8 498	17 530	11 001	13 254	F.1.5. Total
F.1.6. Other Investments									**F.1.6. Autres Placements**
F.1.6.1. Domestic Companies	39 883	41 793	46 121	40 503	39 453	52 623	22 677	180 316	F.1.6.1. Entreprises Nationales
F.1.6. Total	39 883	41 793	46 121	40 503	39 453	52 623	22 677	180 316	F.1.6. Total
F.1.7. Total									**F.1.7. Total**
F.1.7.1. Domestic Companies	448 984	510 400	503 056	560 206	816 384	969 182	1 051 329	1 416 005	F.1.7.1. Entreprises Nationales
F.1.7.2. (Foreign Controlled Companies)	0	0	0	0	0	19	0	0	F.1.7.2. (Entreprises Sous Contrôle Etranger)
F.1.7. Total of Life Investments	448 984	510 400	503 056	560 206	816 384	969 182	1 051 329	1 416 005	F.1.7. Total des Placements Vie
F.2. Non-Life									**F.2. Non-Vie**
F.2.1. Real Estate									**F.2.1. Immobilier**
F.2.1.1. Domestic Companies	8 126	8 205	8 235	7 345	10 593	8 518	8 926	8 580	F.2.1.1. Entreprises Nationales
F.2.1.2. (Foreign Controlled Companies)								59	F.2.1.2. (Entreprises Sous Contrôle Etranger)
F.2.1. Total	8 126	8 205	8 235	7 345	10 593	8 518	8 926	8 580	F.2.1. Total
F.2.2. Mortgage Loans									**F.2.2. Prêts Hypothécaires**
F.2.2.1. Domestic Companies	..	..	..	..	2 900	2 912	229	104	F.2.2.1. Entreprises Nationales
F.2.2.2. (Foreign Controlled Companies)	..	..	..	..	4	118	114	11	F.2.2.2. (Entreprises Sous Contrôle Etranger)
F.2.2. Total	..	..	..	..	2 900	2 912	229	104	F.2.2. Total
F.2.3. Shares									**F.2.3. Actions**
F.2.3.1. Domestic Companies	31 210	40 863	55 757	57 487	96 207	113 504	90 086	125 244	F.2.3.1. Entreprises Nationales
F.2.3.2. (Foreign Controlled Companies)	48	107	165	140	324	473	531	1 457	F.2.3.2. (Entreprises Sous Contrôle Etranger)
F.2.3. Total	31 258	40 970	55 757	57 487	96 207	113 504	90 086	125 244	F.2.3. Total
F.2.4. Bonds with Fixed Revenue									**F.2.4. Obligations**
F.2.4.1. Domestic Companies	26 474	37 867	79 767	91 057	128 604	136 830	128 084	151 372	F.2.4.1. Entreprises Nationales
F.2.4.2. (Foreign Controlled Companies)	339	846	855	1 073	1 667	1 891	1 835	10 518	F.2.4.2. (Entreprises Sous Contrôle Etranger)
F.2.4. Total	26 813	38 713	79 767	91 057	128 604	136 830	128 084	151 372	F.2.4. Total
F.2.5. Loans other than Mortgage Loans									**F.2.5. Prêts Autres qu'Hypothécaires**
F.2.5.1. Domestic Companies	7 680	6 884	7 051	5 042	1 342	5 467	551	840	F.2.5.1. Entreprises Nationales
F.2.5.2. (Foreign Controlled Companies)	156	163	162	142	240	8	9	31	F.2.5.2. (Entreprises Sous Contrôle Etranger)
F.2.5. Total	7 836	7 047	7 051	5 042	1 342	5 467	551	840	F.2.5. Total
F.2.6. Other Investments									**F.2.6. Autres Placements**
F.2.6.1. Domestic Companies	8 654	9 328	13 823	14 376	5 314	6 003	80 790	45 530	F.2.6.1. Entreprises Nationales
F.2.6.2. (Foreign Controlled Companies)	575	166	126	339	0	0	131	52	F.2.6.2. (Entreprises Sous Contrôle Etranger)
F.2.6.3. Branches & Agencies of Foreign Cies	746	791	198	205	205	..	..	..	F.2.6.3. Succursales et Agences d'Ent. Etrangères
F.2.6. Total	9 229	9 494	14 021	14 581	5 519	6 003	80 790	45 530	F.2.6. Total
F.2.7. Total									**F.2.7. Total**
F.2.7.1. Domestic Companies	82 144	103 147	164 633	175 307	244 960	273 234	308 666	331 670	F.2.7.1. Entreprises Nationales
F.2.7.2. (Foreign Controlled Companies)	1 118	1 282	1 308	1 694	2 235	2 490	2 620	12 128	F.2.7.2. (Entreprises Sous Contrôle Etranger)
F.2.7.3. Branches & Agencies of Foreign Cies	746	791	198	205	205	..	..	..	F.2.7.3. Succursales et Agences d'Ent. Etrangères
F.2.7. Total of Non-Life Investments	83 262	104 429	164 831	175 512	245 165	273 234	308 666	331 670	F.2.7. Total des Placements Non-Vie
G. BREAKDOWN OF NON-LIFE PREMIUMS									**G. VENTILATIONS DES PRIMES NON-VIE**
G.1. Motor vehicle									**G.1. Assurance Automobile**
G.1.1. Direct Business									G.1.1. Assurances Directes
G.1.1.1. Gross Premiums	10 910	11 019	10 056	10 252	10 386	10 263	11 668	12 048	G.1.1.1. Primes Brutes
G.1.1.2. Ceded Premiums	870	886	839	669	734	676	1 017	1 296	G.1.1.2. Primes Cédées
G.1.1.3. Net Written Premiums	9 320	9 223	9 217	9 583	9 652	9 587	10 651	10 752	G.1.1.3. Primes Nettes Emises

Monetary Unit: million Swedish kroner — Unité monétaire : million de couronnes suédoises

	1992	1993	1994	1995	1996	1997	1998	1999
G.2. Marine, Aviation — G.2. Marine, Aviation								
G.2.1. Direct Business — G.2.1. Assurances Directes								
G.2.1.1. Gross Premiums — G.2.1.1. Primes Brutes	912	1 178	1 314	1 193	1 003	935	1 509	609
G.2.1.2. Ceded Premiums — G.2.1.2. Primes Cédées	523	613	725	607	499	442	607	289
G.2.1.3. Net Written Premiums — G.2.1.3. Primes Nettes Emises	389	665	589	586	504	493	902	320
G.3. Freight — G.3. Fret								
G.3.1. Direct Business — G.3.1. Assurances Directes								
G.3.1.1. Gross Premiums — G.3.1.1. Primes Brutes	752	687	763	834	810	747	..	580
G.3.1.2. Ceded Premiums — G.3.1.2. Primes Cédées	258	209	308	303	317	260	..	164
G.3.1.3. Net Written Premiums — G.3.1.3. Primes Nettes Emises	493	478	455	531	493	487	..	416
G.4. Fire, Property Damages — G.4. Incendie, Dommages aux Biens								
G.4.1. Direct Business — G.4.1. Assurances Directes								
G.4.1.1. Gross Premiums — G.4.1.1. Primes Brutes	15 715	16 539	15 903	15 843	15 462	14 978	11 965	13 376
G.4.1.2. Ceded Premiums — G.4.1.2. Primes Cédées	3 519	3 645	4 127	4 388	3 972	3 399	3 992	2 853
G.4.1.3. Net Written Premiums — G.4.1.3. Primes Nettes Emises	12 196	11 894	11 776	11 455	11 490	11 579	7 973	10 523
G.5. Pecuniary Losses — G.5. Pertes Pécunières								
G.5.1. Direct Business — G.5.1. Assurances Directes								
G.5.1.1. Gross Premiums — G.5.1.1. Primes Brutes	384	660	528	489	570	603	624	583
G.5.1.2. Ceded Premiums — G.5.1.2. Primes Cédées	- 169	61	79	177	159	75	99	122
G.5.1.3. Net Written Premiums — G.5.1.3. Primes Nettes Emises	553	599	449	312	411	528	525	461
G.6. General Liability — G.6. Responsabilité Générale								
G.6.1. Direct Business — G.6.1. Assurances Directes								
G.6.1.1. Gross Premiums — G.6.1.1. Primes Brutes							1 974	..
G.6.1.2. Ceded Premiums — G.6.1.2. Primes Cédées							714	..
G.6.1.3. Net Written Premiums — G.6.1.3. Primes Nettes Emises							1 260	..
G.7. Accident, Health — G.7. Accident, Santé								
G.7.1. Direct Business — G.7.1. Assurances Directes								
G.7.1.1. Gross Premiums — G.7.1.1. Primes Brutes	8 576	17 514	6 274	6 613	6 421	7 089	7 127	6 425
G.7.1.2. Ceded Premiums — G.7.1.2. Primes Cédées	101	168	141	167	1 402	137	95	52
G.7.1.3. Net Written Premiums — G.7.1.3. Primes Nettes Emises	8 475	17 346	6 133	6 446	5 019	6 952	7 032	6 373
G.8. Others — G.8. Autres								
G.8.1. Direct Business — G.8.1. Assurances Directes								
G.8.1.1. Gross Premiums — G.8.1.1. Primes Brutes	643	710	970	1 084	547	1 753	1 203	772
G.8.1.2. Ceded Premiums — G.8.1.2. Primes Cédées	11	10	5	6	6	6	8	11
G.8.1.3. Net Written Premiums — G.8.1.3. Primes Nettes Emises	632	700	965	1 079	541	1 747	1 195	761
G.9. Treaty Reinsurance — G.9. Réassurance Obligatoire								
G.9.2. Reinsurance Accepted — G.9.2. Réassurance Acceptée								
G.9.2.1. Gross Premiums — G.9.2.1. Primes Brutes	14 174	5 553	10 816	10 176	9 971	10 479	8 692	9 862
G.9.2.2. Ceded Premiums — G.9.2.2. Primes Cédées	3 917	3 132	3 400	3 584	2 795	4 606	2 819	2 872
G.9.2.3. Net Written Premiums — G.9.2.3. Primes Nettes Emises	10 257	2 421	7 416	6 592	7 176	5 873	5 873	6 990
G.9.3. Total — G.9.3. Total								
G.9.3.1. Gross Premiums — G.9.3.1. Primes Brutes	14 174	5 553	10 816	10 176	9 971	..	..	..
G.9.3.2. Ceded Premiums — G.9.3.2. Primes Cédées	3 917	3 132	3 400	3 584	2 795	..	..	..
G.9.3.3. Net Written Premiums — G.9.3.3. Primes Nettes Emises	10 257	2 421	7 416	6 592	7 176	..	..	..
G.10. Total — G.10. Total								
G.10.1. Direct Business — G.10.1. Assurances Directes								
G.10.1.1. Gross Premiums — G.10.1.1. Primes Brutes	37 172	46 397	35 809	36 308	35 199	36 368	36 070	34 394
G.10.1.2. Ceded Premiums — G.10.1.2. Primes Cédées	5 113	5 592	6 224	6 316	7 089	4 995	6 532	4 788
G.10.1.3. Net Written Premiums — G.10.1.3. Primes Nettes Emises	32 059	40 805	29 584	29 992	28 110	31 373	29 538	29 606
G.10.2. Reinsurance Accepted — G.10.2. Réassurance Acceptée								
G.10.2.1. Gross Premiums — G.10.2.1. Primes Brutes	..	..	..	..	9 971	10 479	8 692	9 862
G.10.2.2. Ceded Premiums — G.10.2.2. Primes Cédées	..	..	..	..	2 795	4 606	2 819	2 872
G.10.2.3. Net Written Premiums — G.10.2.3. Primes Nettes Emises	..	..	..	..	7 176	5 873	5 873	6 990
G.10.3. Total — G.10.3. Total								
G.10.3.1. Gross Premiums — G.10.3.1. Primes Brutes	..	..	..	..	45 170	46 847	44 762	44 256
G.10.3.2. Ceded Premiums — G.10.3.2. Primes Cédées	..	..	..	..	9 884	9 601	9 351	7 660
G.10.3.3. Net Written Premiums — G.10.3.3. Primes Nettes Emises	..	..	..	..	35 286	37 246	35 411	36 596

Monetary Unit: million Swedish kroner · Unité monétaire : million de couronnes suédoises

H. GROSS CLAIMS PAYMENTS — H. PAIEMENTS BRUTS DES SINISTRES

	1992	1993	1994	1995	1996	1997	1998	1999
H.1. Life — H.1. Vie								
H.1.1. Domestic Companies — H.1.1. Entreprises Nationales					22 961	24 035	30 700	33 493
H.1. Total					22 961	24 035	30 700	33 493
H.2. Non-Life — H.2. Non-Vie								
H.2.1. Domestic Companies — H.2.1. Entreprises Nationales					38 089	37 502	36 568	49 002
H.2.2. (Foreign Controlled Companies) — H.2.2. (Entreprises Sous Contrôle Etranger)					704	835	897	4 810
H.2.3. Branches & Agencies of Foreign Cies — H.2.3. Succursales et Agences d'Ent. Etrangères					67	0	..	..
H.2. Total					38 156	37 502	36 568	..

I. GROSS OPERATING EXPENSES — I. DEPENSES BRUTES D'EXPLOITATION

	1992	1993	1994	1995	1996	1997	1998	1999
I.1. Life — I.1. Vie								
I.1.1. Domestic Companies — I.1.1. Entreprises Nationales					5 305	5 656	6 616	7 324
I.1. Total — I.1. Total des Primes Nettes Vie					5 305	5 656	6 616	7 324
I.2. Non-Life — I.2. Non-Vie								
I.2.1. Domestic Companies — I.2.1. Entreprises Nationales					8 430	8 406	8 100	10 578
I.2.2. (Foreign Controlled Companies) — I.2.2. (Entreprises Sous Contrôle Etranger)					292	312	379	1 401
I.2.3. Branches & Agencies of Foreign Cies — I.2.3. Succursales et Agences d'Ent. Etrangères					55	0	..	..
I.2. Total					8 485	8 406	8 100	..

J. COMMISSIONS — J. COMMISSIONS

	1992	1993	1994	1995	1996	1997	1998	1999
J.1. Life — J.1. Vie								
J.1.1. Direct Business — J.1.1. Assurance directe								
J.1.1.1. Domestic Companies — J.1.1.1. Entreprises Nationales					1 906	2 249	2 707	3 390
J.1.1. Total					1 906	2 249	2 707	3 390
J.1.2. Reinsurance Accepted — J.1.2. Réassurances acceptées								
J.1.2.1. Domestic Companies — J.1.2.1. Entreprises Nationales					5	4	2	9
J.1.2. Total					5	4	2	9
J.1.3. Total								
J.1.3.1. Domestic Companies — J.1.3.1. Entreprises Nationales					1 911	2 253	2 709	3 399
J.1.3. Total of Life Net Premiums					1 911	2 253	2 709	3 399
J.2. Non-Life — J.2. Non-Vie								
J.2.1. Direct Business — J.2.1. Assurance directe								
J.2.1.1. Domestic Companies — J.2.1.1. Entreprises Nationales					1 324	1 545	1 612	..
J.2.1.2. (Foreign Controlled Companies) — J.2.1.2. (Entreprises Sous Contrôle Etranger)					92	94	144	..
J.2.1. Total — J.2.1. Total des Primes Nettes Vie					1 324	1 545	1 612	..
J.2.2. Reinsurance Accepted — J.2.2. Réassurances acceptées								
J.2.2.1. Domestic Companies — J.2.2.1. Entreprises Nationales					2 362	2 125	1 556	..
J.2.2.2. (Foreign Controlled Companies) — J.2.2.2. (Entreprises Sous Contrôle Etranger)					11	4	0	..
J.2.2. Total					2 362	2 125	1 556	..
J.2.3. Total								
J.2.3.1. Domestic Companies — J.2.3.1. Entreprises Nationales					3 686	3 670	3 168	..
J.2.3.2. (Foreign Controlled Companies) — J.2.3.2. (Entreprises Sous Contrôle Etranger)					103	98	144	..
J.2.3. Total					3 686	3 670	3 168	2 299

Monetary Unit: million Swiss francs — Unité monétaire : million de francs suisses

	1992	1993	1994	1995	1996	1997	1998	1999
A. NUMBER OF COMPANIES IN THE REPORTING COUNTRY / A. NOMBRE D'ENTREPRISES DANS LE PAYS DECLARANT								
A.1. Life / A.1. Vie								
A.1.1. Domestic Companies / Entreprises Nationales	30	30	30	31	31	31	30	28
A.1.2. Foreign Controlled Companies / Entreprises Sous Contrôle Etranger	6	7	8	8	..	..	..	..
A.1.3. Branches & Agencies of Foreign Cies / Succursales et Agences d'Ent. Etrangères	0	0	..	0	0	1	1	2
A.1. All Companies / Ensemble des Entreprises	30	30	30	31	31	32	31	30
A.2. Non-Life / A.2. Non-Vie								
A.2.1. Domestic Companies / Entreprises Nationales	67	70	71	71	71	73	74	73
A.2.2. Foreign Controlled Companies / Entreprises Sous Contrôle Etranger	9	12	17	15	..	..	..	..
A.2.3. Branches & Agencies of Foreign Cies / Succursales et Agences d'Ent. Etrangères	26	25	27	25	25	27	31	35
A.2. All Companies / Ensemble des Entreprises	93	95	98	96	96	100	105	108
A.4. Reinsurance / A.4. Réassurance								
A.4.1. Domestic Companies / Entreprises Nationales	19	21	23	26	26	27	28	35
A.4.2. Foreign Controlled Companies / Entreprises Sous Contrôle Etranger	12	13	15	13	..	..	..	..
A.4. All Companies / Ensemble des Entreprises	19	21	23	26	26	27	28	35
A.5. Total								
A.5.1. Domestic Companies / Entreprises Nationales	116	121	124	128	128	131	132	136
A.5.2. Foreign Controlled Companies / Entreprises Sous Contrôle Etranger	27	32	40	36	..	..	..	..
A.5.3. Branches & Agencies of Foreign Cies / Succursales et Agences d'Ent. Etrangères	26	25	27	25	25	28	32	37
A.5. All Insurance Companies / Ensemble des Entreprises d'Assurances	142	146	151	153	153	159	164	173
B. NUMBER OF EMPLOYEES / B. NOMBRE D'EMPLOYES								
B.1. Insurance Companies / Entreprises d'Assurances	37 313	37 241	36 510	36 619	..	..	41 891	40 725
B.2. Intermediaries / Intermediaires	11 756	11 078	11 144	10 654	..	..	..	..
B. Total	49 069	48 319	47 654	47 273	43 511	43 512	..	..
C. BUSINESS WRITTEN IN THE REPORTING COUNTRY / C. OPERATIONS CONCLUES DANS LE PAYS DECLARANT								
C.1. Life / C.1. Vie								
C.1.1. Gross Premiums / Primes Brutes								
C.1.1.1. Direct Business / Assurances Directes								
C.1.1.1.1. Domestic Companies / Entreprises Nationales	17 002	18 938	21 088	24 102	27 158	30 869	34 958	31 334
C.1.1.1.2. Foreign Controlled Companies / Entreprises Sous Contrôle Etranger	348	479	978	946	..	..	1	7
C.1.1.1.3. Branches & Agencies of Foreign Cies / Succursales et Agences d'Ent. Etrangères								
C.1.1.1. Total	17 002	18 938	21 088	24 102	27 158	30 869	34 959	31 341
C.1.1.2. Reinsurance Accepted / Réassurance Acceptée								
C.1.1.2.1. Domestic Companies / Entreprises Nationales	1 734	1 890	1 661	1 881	1 058	555	588	347
C.1.1.2.2. Foreign Controlled Companies / Entreprises Sous Contrôle Etranger	92	100	69	965	..	..	..	..
C.1.1.2. Total	1 734	1 890	1 661	1 881	1 058	555	588	347
C.1.1.3. Total								
C.1.1.3.1. Domestic Companies / Entreprises Nationales	18 736	20 828	22 749	25 983	28 216	31 424	35 546	31 681
C.1.1.3.2. Foreign Controlled Companies / Entreprises Sous Contrôle Etranger	440	579	1 047	1 911	..	1	1	7
C.1.1.3.3. Branches & Agencies of Foreign Cies / Succursales et Agences d'Ent. Etrangères								
C.1.1.3. Total Gross Premiums / Total des Primes Brutes	18 736	20 828	22 749	25 983	28 216	31 424	35 547	31 688
C.1.2. Ceded Premiums / Primes Cédées								
C.1.2.1. Domestic Companies / Entreprises Nationales	616	679	748	740	525	425	749	569
C.1.2.2. Foreign Controlled Companies / Entreprises Sous Contrôle Etranger	90	74	72	82	..	..	..	..
C.1.2. Total	616	679	748	740	525	425	749	569
C.1.3. Net Written Premiums / Primes Nettes Emises								
C.1.3.1. Domestic Companies / Entreprises Nationales	18 120	20 149	22 001	25 243	27 691	30 999	34 797	31 112
C.1.3.2. Foreign Controlled Companies / Entreprises Sous Contrôle Etranger							1	7
C.1.3.3. Branches & Agencies of Foreign Cies / Succursales et Agences d'Ent. Etrangères								
C.1.3. Total	18 120	20 149	22 001	25 243	27 691	30 999	34 798	31 119

Monetary Unit: million Swiss francs — Unité monétaire : million de francs suisses

C.2. Non-Life — C.2. Non-Vie

	1992	1993	1994	1995	1996	1997	1998	1999
C.2.1. Gross premiums — Primes Brutes								
C.2.1.1. Direct Business — Assurances Directes								
C.2.1.1.1. Domestic Companies — Entreprises Nationales	12 100	12 542	12 932	13 200	13 301	13 039	12 842	18 201
C.2.1.1.2. (Foreign Controlled Companies — Entreprises Sous Contrôle Etranger)	554	581	637	1 072	..	..	..	..
C.2.1.1.3. Branches & Agencies of Foreign Cies — Succursales et Agences d'Ent. Etrangères	264	273	268	236	319	333	327	391
C.2.1.1. Total	12 364	12 815	13 200	13 436	13 620	13 372	13 170	18 592
C.2.1.2. Reinsurance Accepted — Réassurance Acceptée								
C.2.1.2.1. Domestic Companies — Entreprises Nationales	14 776	16 141	15 936	14 266	6 327	5 528	4 172	3 337
C.2.1.2.2. (Foreign Controlled Companies — Entreprises Sous Contrôle Etranger)	1 860	2 652	2 231	825	..	..	..	..
C.2.1.2.3. Branches & Agencies of Foreign Cies — Succursales et Agences d'Ent. Etrangères	33	37	43	33	..	10	12	..
C.2.1.2. Total	14 809	16 178	15 979	14 299	6 327	5 538	4 184	3 337
C.2.1.3. Total								
C.2.1.3.1. Domestic Companies — Entreprises Nationales	26 876	28 683	28 868	27 466	19 628	18 567	17 014	21 538
C.2.1.3.2. (Foreign Controlled Companies — Entreprises Sous Contrôle Etranger)	2 364	3 233	2 868	1 897	..	..	..	..
C.2.1.3.3. Branches & Agencies of Foreign Cies — Succursales et Agences d'Ent. Etrangères	297	310	311	269	319	343	339	391
C.2.1.3. Total Gross Premiums — Total des Primes Brutes	27 173	28 993	29 179	27 735	19 947	18 910	17 354	21 929
C.2.2. Ceded Premiums — Primes Cédées								
C.2.2.1. Domestic Companies — Entreprises Nationales	5 376	5 983	5 324	5 297	5 666	4 094	5 445	3 130
C.2.2.2. (Foreign Controlled Companies — Entreprises Sous Contrôle Etranger)	794	1 329	841	1 583	..	..	..	..
C.2.2. Total	5 376	5 983	..	..	5 666	4 094	5 445	3 130
C.2.3. Net Written Premiums — Primes Nettes Emises								
C.2.3.1. Domestic Companies — Entreprises Nationales	21 500	22 700	23 544	22 169	13 962	14 473	11 569	18 408
C.2.3.2. (Foreign Controlled Companies — Entreprises Sous Contrôle Etranger)	1 570	1 904	2 027	314	..	..	..	..
C.2.3.3. Branches & Agencies of Foreign Cies — Succursales et Agences d'Ent. Etrangères	297	310	..	..	319	343	339	391
C.2.3. Total	21 797	23 010	..	..	14 281	14 816	11 909	18 799

C.3. Total — C.3. Total

	1992	1993	1994	1995	1996	1997	1998	1999
C.3.1. Gross Premiums — Primes Brutes								
C.3.1.1. Direct Business — Assurances Directes								
C.3.1.1.1. Domestic Companies — Entreprises Nationales	29 102	31 480	34 020	37 302	40 459	43 908	47 800	49 535
C.3.1.1.2. (Foreign Controlled Companies — Entreprises Sous Contrôle Etranger)	902	1 060	1 615	2 018	..	..	..	..
C.3.1.1.3. Branches & Agencies of Foreign Cies — Succursales et Agences d'Ent. Etrangères	264	273	268	236	319	333	328	398
C.3.1.1. Total	29 366	31 753	34 288	37 538	40 778	44 241	48 129	49 933
C.3.1.2. Reinsurance Accepted — Réassurance Acceptée								
C.3.1.2.1. Domestic Companies — Entreprises Nationales	16 510	18 031	17 597	16 147	7 385	6 083	4 760	3 684
C.3.1.2.2. (Foreign Controlled Companies — Entreprises Sous Contrôle Etranger)	1 952	2 752	2 300	1 790	..	..	..	..
C.3.1.2.3. Branches & Agencies of Foreign Cies — Succursales et Agences d'Ent. Etrangères	33	37	43	33	..	10	12	..
C.3.1.2. Total	16 543	18 068	17 640	16 180	7 385	6 093	4 772	3 684
C.3.1.3. Total								
C.3.1.3.1. Domestic Companies — Entreprises Nationales	45 612	49 511	51 617	53 449	47 844	49 991	52 560	53 219
C.3.1.3.2. (Foreign Controlled Companies — Entreprises Sous Contrôle Etranger)	2 804	3 812	3 915	3 808	..	..	..	..
C.3.1.3.3. Branches & Agencies of Foreign Cies — Succursales et Agences d'Ent. Etrangères	297	310	311	269	319	343	340	398
C.3.1.3. Total Gross Premiums — Total des Primes Brutes	45 909	49 821	51 928	53 718	48 163	50 334	52 901	53 617
C.3.2. Ceded Premiums — Primes Cédées								
C.3.2.1. Domestic Companies — Entreprises Nationales	5 992	6 662	6 072	6 037	6 191	4 519	6 194	3 699
C.3.2.2. (Foreign Controlled Companies — Entreprises Sous Contrôle Etranger)	884	1 403	913	1 665	..	..	..	..
C.3.2. Total	5 992	6 662	..	..	6 191	4 519	6 194	3 699
C.3.3. Net Written Premiums — Primes Nettes Emises								
C.3.3.1. Domestic Companies — Entreprises Nationales	39 620	42 849	45 545	47 412	41 653	45 472	46 366	49 520
C.3.3.2. (Foreign Controlled Companies — Entreprises Sous Contrôle Etranger)	1 570	1 904	2 027	314	..	..	..	..
C.3.3.3. Branches & Agencies of Foreign Cies — Succursales et Agences d'Ent. Etrangères	297	310	..	..	319	343	340	398
C.3.3. Total	39 917	43 159	..	..	41 972	45 815	46 707	49 918

Monetary Unit: million Swiss francs　　　　　　　　　Unité monétaire : million de francs suisses

E. BUSINESS WRITTEN ABROAD — E. OPERATIONS A L'ETRANGER

E.1. Life — E.1. Vie

	1992	1993	1994	1995	1996	1997	1998	1999
E.1.1. Gross Premiums — E.1.1. Primes Brutes								
E.1.1.1. Direct Business — E.1.1.1. Assurance Directe								
E.1.1.1.1. Branches & Agencies — E.1.1.1.1. Succursales & Agences	6 100	6 450	7 100	5 800	:	:	:	:
E.1.1.1.2. Subsidiaries — E.1.1.1.2. Filliales	4 800	5 300	6 500	6 800	:	:	:	:
E.1.1.1. Total — E.1.1.1. Total	10 900	11 750	13 600	12 600	:	:	:	:
E.1.1.2. Reinsurance Accepted — E.1.1.2. Réassurance Acceptée								
E.1.1.2.1. Branches & Agencies — E.1.1.2.1. Succursales & Agences	1 500	1 700	1 750	1 200	:	:	:	:
E.1.1.2.2. Subsidiaries — E.1.1.2.2. Filliales	350	400	450	1 200	:	:	:	:
E.1.1.2. Total — E.1.1.2. Total	1 850	2 100	2 200	2 400	:	:	:	:
E.1.1.3. Total								
E.1.1.3.1. Branches & Agencies — E.1.1.3.1. Succursales & Agences	7 600	8 150	8 850	7 000	6 183	5 963	6 608	7 233
E.1.1.3.2. Subsidiaries — E.1.1.3.2. Filliales	5 150	5 700	6 950	8 000	:	:	:	:
E.1.1.3. Total Gross Premiums — E.1.1.3. Total des Primes Brutes	12 750	13 850	15 800	15 000	:	:	:	:
E.1.2. Ceded Premiums — E.1.2. Primes Cédées								
E.1.2.1. Branches & Agencies — E.1.2.1. Succursales & Agences	380	400	1 800	300	:	:	:	:
E.1.2.2. Subsidiaries — E.1.2.2. Filliales	250	280	350	1 200	:	:	:	:
E.1.2. Total — E.1.2. Total	630	680	2 150	1 500	:	:	:	:
E.1.3. Net Written Premiums — E.1.3. Primes Nettes Emises								
E.1.3.1. Branches & Agencies — E.1.3.1. Succursales & Agences	7 220	7 750	7 050	6 700	:	:	:	:
E.1.3.2. Subsidiaries — E.1.3.2. Filliales	4 900	5 420	6 600	6 800	:	:	:	:
E.1.3. Total — E.1.3. Total	12 120	13 170	13 650	13 500	:	:	:	:

E.2. Non-Life — E.2. Non-Vie

	1992	1993	1994	1995	1996	1997	1998	1999
E.2.1. Gross Premiums — E.2.1. Primes Brutes								
E.2.1.1. Direct Business — E.2.1.1. Assurance Directe								
E.2.1.1.1. Branches & Agencies — E.2.1.1.1. Succursales & Agences	8 700	9 300	9 200	8 300	:	:	:	:
E.2.1.1.2. Subsidiaries — E.2.1.1.2. Filliales	20 500	22 000	25 100	18 300	:	:	:	:
E.2.1.1. Total — E.2.1.1. Total	29 200	31 300	34 300	26 600	:	:	:	:
E.2.1.2. Reinsurance Accepted — E.2.1.2. Réassurance Acceptée								
E.2.1.2.1. Branches & Agencies — E.2.1.2.1. Succursales & Agences	13 700	15 000	16 500	8 900	:	:	:	:
E.2.1.2.2. Subsidiaries — E.2.1.2.2. Filliales	3 050	3 300	3 700	11 100	:	:	:	:
E.2.1.2. Total — E.2.1.2. Total	16 750	18 300	20 200	20 000	:	:	:	:
E.2.1.3. Total								
E.2.1.3.1. Branches & Agencies — E.2.1.3.1. Succursales & Agences	22 400	24 300	25 700	17 200	8 695	8 618	10 414	8 358
E.2.1.3.2. Subsidiaries — E.2.1.3.2. Filliales	23 550	25 300	28 800	29 400	:	:	:	:
E.2.1.3. Total Gross Premiums — E.2.1.3. Total des Primes Brutes	45 950	49 600	54 500	46 600	:	:	:	:
E.2.2. Ceded Premiums — E.2.2. Primes Cédées								
E.2.2.1. Branches & Agencies — E.2.2.1. Succursales & Agences	2 900	3 200	3 300	2 200	:	:	:	:
E.2.2.2. Subsidiaries — E.2.2.2. Filliales	3 050	3 300	3 700	3 800	:	:	:	:
E.2.2. Total — E.2.2. Total	5 950	6 500	7 000	6 000	:	:	:	:
E.2.3. Net Written Premiums — E.2.3. Primes Nettes Emises								
E.2.3.1. Branches & Agencies — E.2.3.1. Succursales & Agences	19 500	21 100	22 400	15 000	:	:	:	:
E.2.3.2. Subsidiaries — E.2.3.2. Filliales	20 500	22 000	25 100	25 600	:	:	:	:
E.2.3. Total — E.2.3. Total	40 000	43 100	47 500	40 600	:	:	:	:

Monetary Unit: million Swiss francs

Unité monétaire : million de francs suisses

F. OUTSTANDING INVESTMENT BY DIRECT INSURANCE COMPANIES
F. ENCOURS DES PLACEMENTS DES ENTREPRISES D'ASSURANCES DIRECTES

F.1. Life / F.1. Vie

	1992	1993	1994	1995	1996	1997	1998	1999
F.1.1. Real Estate — F.1.1. Immobilier								
F.1.1.1. Domestic Companies — F.1.1.1. Entreprises Nationales	19 754	20 818	21 789	22 502	23 493	24 311	24 997	25 578
F.1.1.2. (Foreign Controlled Companies) — F.1.1.2. (Entreprises Sous Contrôle Etranger)	273	398	1 027	899	:	:	:	:
F.1.2. Mortgage Loans — F.1.2. Prêts Hypothécaires								
F.1.2.1. Domestic Companies — F.1.2.1. Entreprises Nationales	27 477	27 183	27 134	26 683	26 407	26 568	26 907	26 665
F.1.2.2. (Foreign Controlled Companies) — F.1.2.2. (Entreprises Sous Contrôle Etranger)	358	481	798	609	:	:	:	:
F.1.3. Shares — F.1.3. Actions								
F.1.3.1. Domestic Companies — F.1.3.1. Entreprises Nationales	11 154	16 284	20 330	24 965	32 885	33 973	41 207	51 190
F.1.3.2. (Foreign Controlled Companies) — F.1.3.2. (Entreprises Sous Contrôle Etranger)	52	369	498	616	:	:	:	:
F.1.4. Bonds with Fixed Revenue — F.1.4. Obligations								
F.1.4.1. Domestic Companies — F.1.4.1. Entreprises Nationales	52 990	58 585	64 843	72 125	83 187	94 680	102 273	111 892
F.1.4.2. (Foreign Controlled Companies) — F.1.4.2. (Entreprises Sous Contrôle Etranger)	813	1 259	1 889	1 707	:	:	:	:
F.1.5. Loans other than Mortgage Loans — F.1.5. Prêts Autres qu'Hypothécaires								
F.1.5.1. Domestic Companies — F.1.5.1. Entreprises Nationales	20 878	22 477	23 647	25 917	34 344	27 547	34 431	21 750
F.1.5.2. (Foreign Controlled Companies) — F.1.5.2. (Entreprises Sous Contrôle Etranger)	92	213	342	562	:	:	:	:
F.1.6. Other Investments — F.1.6. Autres Placements								
F.1.6.1. Domestic Companies — F.1.6.1. Entreprises Nationales	4 709	4 723	5 612	14 302	2 434	1 629	2 693	10 923
F.1.6.2. (Foreign Controlled Companies) — F.1.6.2. (Entreprises Sous Contrôle Etranger)	314	391	487	442	:	:	:	:
F.1.7. Total — F.1.7. Total								
F.1.7.1. Domestic Companies — F.1.7.1. Entreprises Nationales	136 962	150 070	163 355	186 494	202 750	208 708	232 508	247 998
F.1.7.2. (Foreign Controlled Companies) — F.1.7.2. (Entreprises Sous Contrôle Etranger)	1 905	3 727	5 041	4 835	:	:	:	:

F.2. Non-Life / F.2. Non-Vie

	1992	1993	1994	1995	1996	1997	1998	1999
F.2.1. Real Estate — F.2.1. Immobilier								
F.2.1.1. Domestic Companies — F.2.1.1. Entreprises Nationales	7 620	7 904	8 420	8 158	7 880	7 703	7 381	6 999
F.2.1.2. (Foreign Controlled Companies) — F.2.1.2. (Entreprises Sous Contrôle Etranger)	179	180	182	191	:	:	:	:
F.2.2. Mortgage Loans — F.2.2. Prêts Hypothécaires								
F.2.2.1. Domestic Companies — F.2.2.1. Entreprises Nationales	3 829	3 715	3 602	3 590	3 492	3 537	3 516	3 548
F.2.2.2. (Foreign Controlled Companies) — F.2.2.2. (Entreprises Sous Contrôle Etranger)	28	25	23	20	:	:	:	:
F.2.3. Shares — F.2.3. Actions								
F.2.3.1. Domestic Companies — F.2.3.1. Entreprises Nationales	12 385	13 906	15 381	17 071	23 777	9 908	9 984	11 081
F.2.3.2. (Foreign Controlled Companies) — F.2.3.2. (Entreprises Sous Contrôle Etranger)	141	296	423	412	:	:	:	:
F.2.4. Bonds with Fixed Revenue — F.2.4. Obligations								
F.2.4.1. Domestic Companies — F.2.4.1. Entreprises Nationales	20 415	21 037	21 561	21 935	23 021	25 472	21 796	24 358
F.2.4.2. (Foreign Controlled Companies) — F.2.4.2. (Entreprises Sous Contrôle Etranger)	514	564	641	750	:	:	:	:
F.2.5. Loans other than Mortgage Loans — F.2.5. Prêts Autres qu'Hypothécaires								
F.2.5.1. Domestic Companies — F.2.5.1. Entreprises Nationales	5 171	5 565	6 225	5 736	8 479	5 820	4 712	2 358
F.2.5.2. (Foreign Controlled Companies) — F.2.5.2. (Entreprises Sous Contrôle Etranger)	59	59	985	1 119	:	:	:	:
F.2.6. Other Investments — F.2.6. Autres Placements								
F.2.6.1. Domestic Companies — F.2.6.1. Entreprises Nationales	0	0	:	10 238	1 629	6 723	8 211	1 605
F.2.6.2. (Foreign Controlled Companies) — F.2.6.2. (Entreprises Sous Contrôle Etranger)	0	0	:	592	:	:	:	:
F.2.7. Total — F.2.7. Total								
F.2.7.1. Domestic Companies — F.2.7.1. Entreprises Nationales	49 420	52 127	55 189	66 728	68 278	59 163	55 600	49 949
F.2.7.2. (Foreign Controlled Companies) — F.2.7.2. (Entreprises Sous Contrôle Etranger)	921	1 007	2 254	3 084	:	:	:	:

G. BREAKDOWN OF NON-LIFE PREMIUMS
G. VENTILATIONS DES PRIMES NON-VIE

	1992	1993	1994	1995	1996	1997	1998	1999
G.1. Motor vehicle — G.1. Assurance Automobile								
G.1.1. Direct Business — G.1.1. Assurances Directes								
G.1.1.1. Gross Premiums — G.1.1.1. Primes Brutes	3 871	4 025	4 127	4 206	3 990	3 878	3 917	3 962
G.2. Marine, Aviation — G.2. Marine, Aviation								
G.2.1. Direct Business — G.2.1. Assurances Directes								
G.2.1.1. Gross Premiums — G.2.1.1. Primes Brutes	41	50	43	59	390	372	356	353

Monetary Unit: million Swiss francs — Unité monétaire : million de francs suisses

	1992	1993	1994	1995	1996	1997	1998	1999
G.3. Freight — G.3. Fret								
G.3.1. Direct Business — G.3.1. Assurances Directes								
G.3.1.1. Gross Premiums — G.3.1.1. Primes Brutes	298	306	308	602	:	:	:	:
G.4. Fire, Property Damages — G.4. Incendie, Dommages aux Biens								
G.4.1. Direct Business — G.4.1. Assurances Directes								
G.4.1.1. Gross Premiums — G.4.1.1. Primes Brutes	2 600	2 693	2 745	2 804	3 135	3 069	3 076	3 053
G.5. Pecuniary Losses — G.5. Pertes Pécunières								
G.5.1. Direct Business — G.5.1. Assurances Directes								
G.5.1.1. Gross Premiums — G.5.1.1. Primes Brutes	75	63	66	101	222	260	93	111
G.6. General Liability — G.6. Responsabilité Générale								
G.6.1. Direct Business — G.6.1. Assurances Directes								
G.6.1.1. Gross Premiums — G.6.1.1. Primes Brutes	1 224	1 295	1 319	1 387	1 384	1 383	1 402	1 392
G.7. Accident, Health — G.7. Accident, Santé								
G.7.1. Direct Business — G.7.1. Assurances Directes								
G.7.1.1. Gross Premiums — G.7.1.1. Primes Brutes	3 630	3 749	3 904	3 867	4 230	4 125	3 930	9 265
G.8. Others — G.8. Autres								
G.8.1. Direct Business — G.8.1. Assurances Directes								
G.8.1.1. Gross Premiums — G.8.1.1. Primes Brutes	625	634	688	410	269	285	396	455
G.9. Treaty Reinsurance — G.9. Réassurance Obligatoire								
G.9.2. Reinsurance Accepted — G.9.2. Réassurance Acceptée								
G.9.2.1. Gross Premiums — G.9.2.1. Primes Brutes								3 338
G.9.3. Total — G.9.3. Total								
G.9.3.1. Gross Premiums — G.9.3.1. Primes Brutes								3 338
G.10. Total — G.10. Total								
G.10.1. Direct Business — G.10.1. Assurances Directes								
G.10.1.1. Gross Premiums — G.10.1.1. Primes Brutes	12 364	12 815	13 200	13 436	13 620	13 372	13 170	18 592
G.10.2. Reinsurance Accepted — G.10.2. Réassurance Acceptée								
G.10.2.1. Gross Premiums — G.10.2.1. Primes Brutes	14 809	16 178	15 979	14 299	6 327	5 538	4 184	3 338
G.10.2.2. Ceded Premiums — G.10.2.2. Primes Cédées	:	:	:	:	3 419	4 094	:	:
G.10.2.3. Net Written Premiums — G.10.2.3. Primes Nettes Emises	:	:	:	:	2 908	1 444	:	:
G.10.3. Total — G.10.3. Total								
G.10.3.1. Gross Premiums — G.10.3.1. Primes Brutes	27 173	28 993	29 179	27 735	19 947	18 910	17 354	21 929
G.10.3.2. Ceded Premiums — G.10.3.2. Primes Cédées	:	:	:	:	5 666	4 094	5 445	:
G.10.3.3. Net Written Premiums — G.10.3.3. Primes Nettes Emises	:	:	:	:	14 281	14 816	11 909	:
H. GROSS CLAIMS PAYMENTS — H. PAIEMENTS BRUTS DES SINISTRES								
H.1. Life — H.1. Vie								
H.1.1. Domestic Companies — H.1.1. Entreprises Nationales					19 718	20 707	22 400	20 997
H.1.3. Branches & Agencies of Foreign Cies — H.1.3. Succursales et Agences d'Ent. Etrangères								1
H.1. Total — H.1. Total					19 718	20 707	:	20 998
H.2. Non-Life — H.2. Non-Vie								
H.2.1. Domestic Companies — H.2.1. Entreprises Nationales					16 126	17 218	18 160	11 860
H.2.3. Branches & Agencies of Foreign Cies — H.2.3. Succursales et Agences d'Ent. Etrangères					169	:	:	333
H.2. Total — H.2. Total					16 295	17 218	:	12 193
I. GROSS OPERATING EXPENSES — I. DEPENSES BRUITES D'EXPLOITATION								
I.1. Life — I.1. Vie								
I.1.1. Domestic Companies — I.1.1. Entreprises Nationales					1 899		:	:
I.1. Total — I.1. Total des Primes Nettes Vie					1 899		:	:

Monetary Unit: million Turkish liras — Unité monétaire : million de livres turques

A. NUMBER OF COMPANIES IN THE REPORTING COUNTRY — A. NOMBRE D'ENTREPRISES DANS LE PAYS DECLARANT

	1992	1993	1994	1995	1996	1997	1998	1999
A.1. Life — A.1. Vie								
A.1.1. Domestic Companies — A.1.1. Entreprises Nationales	9	12	12	17	17	14	23	22
A.1.2. (Foreign Controlled Companies) — A.1.2. (Entreprises Sous Contrôle Etranger)	3	4	3			4	4	4
A.1. All Companies — A.1. Ensemble des Entreprises	9	12	12	17	17	14	23	22
A.2. Non-Life — A.2. Non-Vie								
A.2.1. Domestic Companies — A.2.1. Entreprises Nationales	21	20	24	19	22	19	24	23
A.2.2. (Foreign Controlled Companies) — A.2.2. (Entreprises Sous Contrôle Etranger)	10	6	7	6	6	5	5	2
A.2.3. Branches & Agencies of Foreign Cies — A.2.3. Succursales et Agences d'Ent. Etrangères	1	2	1	2	2	0	0	0
A.2. All Companies — A.2. Ensemble des Entreprises	22	22	25	21	24	19	24	23
A.3. Composite — A.3. Mixte								
A.3.1. Domestic Companies — A.3.1. Entreprises Nationales	19	19	15	17	17	16	17	17
A.3.2. (Foreign Controlled Companies) — A.3.2. (Entreprises Sous Contrôle Etranger)	3	3	1	1	1	1	1	1
A.3. All Companies — A.3. Ensemble des Entreprises	19	19	15	17	17	16	17	17
A.4. Reinsurance — A.4. Réassurance								
A.4.1. Domestic Companies — A.4.1. Entreprises Nationales	4	4	4	4	4	4	4	4
A.4. All Companies — A.4. Ensemble des Entreprises	4	4	4	4	4	4	4	4
A.5. Total — A.5. Total								
A.5.1. Domestic Companies — A.5.1. Entreprises Nationales	53	55	55	57	60	53	68	66
A.5.2. (Foreign Controlled Companies) — A.5.2. (Entreprises Sous Contrôle Etranger)	16	13	11	11	11	10	10	5
A.5.3. Branches & Agencies of Foreign Cies — A.5.3. Succursales et Agences d'Ent. Etrangères	1	2	1	2	2	0	0	0
A.5. All Insurance Companies — A.5. Ensemble des Entreprises d'Assurances	54	57	56	59	62	53	68	66

B. NUMBER OF EMPLOYEES — B. NOMBRE D'EMPLOYES

	1992	1993	1994	1995	1996	1997	1998	1999
B.1. Insurance Companies — B.1. Entreprises d'Assurances	5 215	5 932	5 598	6 578	7 453	8 076	8 239	9 715
B.2. Intermediaries — B.2. Intermédiaires	..	9 948	10 995	10 723	12 191	13 862	14 010	13 567
B. Total — B. Total	..	..	16 593	..	19 644	21 938	22 249	23 282

C. BUSINESS WRITTEN IN THE REPORTING COUNTRY — C. OPERATIONS CONCLUES DANS LE PAYS DECLARANT

C.1. Life — C.1. Vie

	1992	1993	1994	1995	1996	1997	1998	1999
C.1.1. Gross Premiums — C.1.1. Primes Brutes								
C.1.1.1. Direct Business — C.1.1.1. Assurances Directes								
C.1.1.1.1. Domestic Companies — C.1.1.1.1. Entreprises Nationales	1 533 808	2 478 185	3 862 596	8 108 208	18 793 268	44 701 566	94 193 081	177 053 102
C.1.1.1.2. (Foreign Controlled Companies) — C.1.1.1.2. (Entreprises Sous Contrôle Etranger)	37 611	120 962	223 739	496 977	1 596 764	3 039 653	6 665 905	18 415 204
C.1.1.1. Total — C.1.1.1. Total	1 571 419	2 478 185	3 862 596	8 108 208	18 793 268	44 701 566	94 193 081	177 053 102
C.1.1.2. Reinsurance Accepted — C.1.1.2. Réassurance Acceptée								
C.1.1.2.1. Domestic Companies — C.1.1.2.1. Entreprises Nationales	288	446	1 332	46 751	102 227	248 807	6 083	1 488
C.1.1.2.2. (Foreign Controlled Companies) — C.1.1.2.2. (Entreprises Sous Contrôle Etranger)	0	0	244	41 533	95 741	0	0	- 199
C.1.1.2. Total — C.1.1.2. Total	288	446	1 332	46 751	102 227	248 807	6 083	1 488
C.1.1.3. Total — C.1.1.3. Total								
C.1.1.3.1. Domestic Companies — C.1.1.3.1. Entreprises Nationales	1 534 096	2 478 631	3 863 928	8 154 959	18 895 495	44 950 373	94 199 164	177 054 590
C.1.1.3.2. (Foreign Controlled Companies) — C.1.1.3.2. (Entreprises Sous Contrôle Etranger)	37 611	120 962	223 983	538 510	1 692 505	3 039 653	6 665 905	18 415 005
C.1.1.3. Total Gross Premiums — C.1.1.3. Total des Primes Brutes	1 571 707	2 478 631	3 863 928	8 154 959	18 895 495	44 950 373	94 199 164	177 054 590
C.1.2. Ceded Premiums — C.1.2. Primes Cédées								
C.1.2.1. Domestic Companies — C.1.2.1. Entreprises Nationales	54 956	35 058	62 153	205 715	468 374	1 005 923	4 308 523	1 471 222
C.1.2.2. (Foreign Controlled Companies) — C.1.2.2. (Entreprises Sous Contrôle Etranger)	4 663	2 175	1 429	24 031	88 408	33 741	924 012	116 327
C.1.2. Total — C.1.2. Total	59 619	35 058	62 153	205 715	468 374	1 005 923	4 308 523	1 471 222
C.1.3. Net Written Premiums — C.1.3. Primes Nettes Emises								
C.1.3.1. Domestic Companies — C.1.3.1. Entreprises Nationales	1 479 140	2 443 573	3 801 775	7 949 244	18 427 121	43 944 450	89 890 641	175 583 368
C.1.3.2. (Foreign Controlled Companies) — C.1.3.2. (Entreprises Sous Contrôle Etranger)	32 948	118 787	222 554	514 479	1 604 097	3 005 912	5 741 893	18 298 678
C.1.3. Total — C.1.3. Total	1 512 088	2 443 543	3 801 775	7 949 244	18 427 121	43 944 450	89 890 641	175 583 368

Monetary Unit: million Turkish liras

Unité monétaire : million de livres turques

Label	1992	1993	1994	1995	1996	1997	1998	1999
C.2. Non-Life / C.2. Non-Vie								
C.2.1. Gross premiums / C.2.1. Primes Brutes								
C.2.1.1. Direct Business / C.2.1.1. Assurances Directes								
C.2.1.1.1. Domestic Companies / Entreprises Nationales	5 776 740	14 377 303	27 904 903	54 842 768	109 012 293	237 841 036	459 270 161	892 616 232
C.2.1.1.2. (Foreign Controlled Companies) / (Entreprises Sous Contrôle Etranger)	815 436	1 626 184	2 761 653	5 352 774	11 170 228	20 715 654	35 949 714	31 394 065
C.2.1.1.3. Branches & Agencies of Foreign Cies / Succursales et Agences d'Ent. Etrangères	8 258	44 464	57 640	57 985	- 1 172	0	0	0
C.2.1.1. Total	6 600 434	14 421 767	27 962 543	54 900 753	109 011 121	237 841 036	459 270 161	892 616 232
C.2.1.2. Reinsurance Accepted / C.2.1.2. Réassurance Acceptée								
C.2.1.2.1. Domestic Companies / Entreprises Nationales	161 085	251 422	447 730	724 448	1 383 443	2 595 257	4 435 887	33 184 991
C.2.1.2.2. (Foreign Controlled Companies) / (Entreprises Sous Contrôle Etranger)	9 233	12 283	25 789	51 587	70 142	290 669	84 828	480 657
C.2.1.2.3. Branches & Agencies of Foreign Cies / Succursales et Agences d'Ent. Etrangères	16	0	0	0	0	0	0	0
C.2.1.2. Total	170 334	251 422	447 730	724 448	1 383 443	2 595 257	4 435 887	33 184 991
C.2.1.3. Total								
C.2.1.3.1. Domestic Companies / Entreprises Nationales	5 937 825	14 628 725	28 352 633	55 567 216	110 395 735	240 436 293	463 706 048	925 801 223
C.2.1.3.2. (Foreign Controlled Companies) / (Entreprises Sous Contrôle Etranger)	824 669	1 638 467	2 787 442	5 404 361	11 240 370	21 006 323	36 034 542	31 874 722
C.2.1.3.3. Branches & Agencies of Foreign Cies / Succursales et Agences d'Ent. Etrangères	8 274	44 464	57 640	57 985	- 1 172	0	0	0
C.2.1.3. Total Gross Premiums / Total des Primes Brutes	6 770 768	14 673 189	28 410 273	55 625 201	110 394 563	240 436 293	463 706 048	925 801 223
C.2.2. Ceded Premiums / C.2.2. Primes Cédées								
C.2.2.1. Domestic Companies / Entreprises Nationales	2 785 063	2 387 800	6 402 240	12 249 783	23 627 767	53 222 246	188 163 005	144 847 984
C.2.2.2. (Foreign Controlled Companies) / (Entreprises Sous Contrôle Etranger)	379 232	216 286	723 951	1 338 494	2 999 246	5 491 231	14 165 589	4 053 721
C.2.2.3. Branches & Agencies of Foreign Cies / Succursales et Agences d'Ent. Etrangères	6 802	15 594	32 319	25 909	- 542	0	0	0
C.2.2. Total	3 171 097	2 403 394	6 434 559	12 275 692	23 627 225	53 222 246	188 163 005	144 847 984
C.2.3. Net Written Premiums / C.2.3. Primes Nettes Emises								
C.2.3.1. Domestic Companies / Entreprises Nationales	3 152 762	12 240 925	21 950 393	43 317 433	86 767 969	187 214 047	275 543 043	780 953 239
C.2.3.2. (Foreign Controlled Companies) / (Entreprises Sous Contrôle Etranger)	445 437	1 422 181	2 063 491	4 065 867	8 241 124	15 515 092	21 868 953	27 821 001
C.2.3.3. Branches & Agencies of Foreign Cies / Succursales et Agences d'Ent. Etrangères	1 472	28 870	25 321	32 076	- 630	0	0	0
C.2.3. Total	3 599 671	12 269 795	21 975 714	43 349 509	86 767 339	187 214 047	275 543 043	780 953 239
C.3. Total								
C.3.1. Gross Premiums / C.3.1. Primes Brutes								
C.3.1.1. Direct Business / C.3.1.1. Assurances Directes								
C.3.1.1.1. Domestic Companies / Entreprises Nationales	7 310 548	16 855 488	31 767 499	62 950 976	127 805 561	282 542 602	553 463 242	1 069 669 334
C.3.1.1.2. (Foreign Controlled Companies) / (Entreprises Sous Contrôle Etranger)	853 047	1 747 146	2 985 392	5 849 751	12 766 992	23 755 307	42 615 619	49 809 269
C.3.1.1.3. Branches & Agencies of Foreign Cies / Succursales et Agences d'Ent. Etrangères	8 258	44 464	57 640	57 985	- 1 172	0	0	0
C.3.1.1. Total	8 171 853	16 899 952	31 825 139	63 008 961	127 804 389	282 542 602	553 463 242	1 069 669 334
C.3.1.2. Reinsurance Accepted / C.3.1.2. Réassurance Acceptée								
C.3.1.2.1. Domestic Companies / Entreprises Nationales	161 373	251 868	449 062	771 199	1 485 670	2 844 064	4 441 970	33 186 479
C.3.1.2.2. (Foreign Controlled Companies) / (Entreprises Sous Contrôle Etranger)	9 233	12 283	26 033	93 120	165 883	290 669	84 828	480 458
C.3.1.2.3. Branches & Agencies of Foreign Cies / Succursales et Agences d'Ent. Etrangères	16	0	0	0	0	0	0	0
C.3.1.2. Total	170 622	251 868	449 062	771 199	1 485 670	2 844 064	4 441 970	33 186 479
C.3.1.3. Total								
C.3.1.3.1. Domestic Companies / Entreprises Nationales	7 471 921	17 107 356	32 216 561	63 722 175	129 291 230	285 386 666	557 905 212	1 102 855 813
C.3.1.3.2. (Foreign Controlled Companies) / (Entreprises Sous Contrôle Etranger)	862 280	1 759 429	3 011 425	5 942 871	12 932 875	24 045 976	42 700 447	50 289 727
C.3.1.3.3. Branches & Agencies of Foreign Cies / Succursales et Agences d'Ent. Etrangères	8 274	44 464	57 640	57 985	- 1 172	0	0	0
C.3.1.3. Total Gross Premiums / Total des Primes Brutes	8 342 475	17 151 820	32 274 201	63 780 160	129 290 058	285 386 666	557 905 212	1 102 855 813
C.3.2. Ceded Premiums / C.3.2. Primes Cédées								
C.3.2.1. Domestic Companies / Entreprises Nationales	2 840 019	2 422 858	6 464 393	12 455 498	24 096 141	54 228 169	192 471 528	146 319 206
C.3.2.2. (Foreign Controlled Companies) / (Entreprises Sous Contrôle Etranger)	383 895	218 461	725 380	1 362 525	3 087 654	5 524 972	15 089 601	4 170 048
C.3.2.3. Branches & Agencies of Foreign Cies / Succursales et Agences d'Ent. Etrangères	6 802	15 594	32 319	25 909	- 542	0	0	0
C.3.2. Total	3 230 716	2 438 452	6 496 712	12 481 407	24 095 599	54 228 169	192 471 528	146 319 206
C.3.3. Net Written Premiums / C.3.3. Primes Nettes Emises								
C.3.3.1. Domestic Companies / Entreprises Nationales	4 631 902	14 684 498	25 752 168	51 266 677	105 195 090	231 158 497	365 433 684	956 536 607
C.3.3.2. (Foreign Controlled Companies) / (Entreprises Sous Contrôle Etranger)	478 385	1 540 968	2 286 045	4 580 346	9 845 221	18 521 004	27 610 846	46 119 679
C.3.3.3. Branches & Agencies of Foreign Cies / Succursales et Agences d'Ent. Etrangères	28 870	28 870	25 321	32 076	- 630	0	0	0
C.3.3. Total	5 111 759	14 713 338	25 777 489	51 298 753	105 194 460	231 158 497	365 433 684	956 536 607

Monetary Unit: million Turkish liras   Unité monétaire : million de livres turques

D. NET WRITTEN PREMIUMS IN THE REPORTING COUNTRY IN TERMS OF DOMESTIC AND FOREIGN RISKS
D. PRIMES NETTES EMISES DANS LE PAYS DECLARANT EN RISQUES NATIONAUX ET ETRANGERS

D.1. Life / D.1. Vie

Item (EN)	1992	1993	1994	1995	1996	1997	1998	1999	Poste (FR)
D.1.1. Domestic Risks									**D.1.1. Risques Nationaux**
D.1.1.1. Domestic Companies	1 479 140	2 443 573	3 801 775	7 949 244	18 427 121	43 944 450	89 781 207	175 467 702	D.1.1.1. Entreprises Nationales
D.1.1.2. (Foreign Controlled Companies)	32 948	118 787	222 554	514 479	1 604 097	3 005 912	5 741 893	18 298 678	D.1.1.2. (Entreprises Sous Contrôle Etranger)
D.1.1. Total	1 512 088	2 443 543	3 801 775	7 949 244	18 427 121	43 944 450	89 781 207	175 467 702	D.1.1. Total des Primes Nettes Vie
D.1.2. Foreign Risks									**D.1.2. Risques Etrangers**
D.1.2.1. Domestic Companies	..	..	..	..	..	..	109 434	115 666	D.1.2.1. Entreprises Nationales
D.1.2. Total	..	..	..	..	..	..	109 434	115 666	D.1.2. Total des Primes Nettes Vie
D.1.3. Total									**D.1.3. Total**
D.1.3.1. Domestic Companies	1 479 140	2 443 573	3 801 775	7 949 244	18 427 121	43 944 450	89 890 641	175 583 368	D.1.3.1. Entreprises Nationales
D.1.3.2. (Foreign Controlled Companies)	32 948	118 787	222 554	514 479	1 604 097	3 005 912	5 741 893	18 298 678	D.1.3.2. (Entreprises Sous Contrôle Etranger)
D.1.3. Total of Life Net Premiums	1 512 088	2 443 543	3 801 775	7 949 244	18 427 121	43 944 450	89 890 641	175 583 368	D.1.3. Total des Primes Nettes Vie

D.2. Non-Life / D.2. Non-Vie

Item (EN)	1992	1993	1994	1995	1996	1997	1998	1999	Poste (FR)
D.2.1. Domestic Risks									**D.2.1. Risques Nationaux**
D.2.1.1. Domestic Companies	3 220 660	12 240 925	21 950 393	43 317 433	86 767 969	187 214 047	274 432 558	780 007 452	D.2.1.1. Entreprises Nationales
D.2.1.2. (Foreign Controlled Companies)	448 737	1 422 181	2 063 491	4 065 867	8 241 124	15 515 092	21 868 953	27 821 001	D.2.1.2. (Entreprises Sous Contrôle Etranger)
D.2.1.3. Branches & Agencies of Foreign Cies	1 472	28 870	25 321	32 076	- 630	0	0	0	D.2.1.3. Succursales et Agences d'Ent. Etrangères
D.2.1. Total	3 670 869	12 269 795	21 975 714	43 349 509	86 767 339	187 214 047	274 432 558	780 007 452	D.2.1. Total des Primes Nettes Vie
D.2.2. Foreign Risks									**D.2.2. Risques Etrangers**
D.2.2.1. Domestic Companies	..	..	..	..	..	..	1 110 484	945 787	D.2.2.1. Entreprises Nationales
D.2.2 Total	..	..	..	..	..	..	1 110 484	945 787	D.2.2. Total des Primes Nettes Vie
D.2.3. Total									**D.2.3. Total**
D.2.3.1. Domestic Companies	3 220 660	12 240 925	21 950 393	43 317 433	86 767 969	187 214 047	275 543 043	780 953 239	D.2.3.1. Entreprises Nationales
D.2.3.2. (Foreign Controlled Companies)	..	1 422 181	2 063 491	4 065 867	8 241 124	15 515 092	21 868 953	27 821 001	D.2.3.2. (Entreprises Sous Contrôle Etranger)
D.2.3.3. Branches & Agencies of Foreign Cies	1 472	28 870	25 321	32 076	- 630	0	0	0	D.2.3.3. Succursales et Agences d'Ent. Etrangères
D.2.3. Total	3 670 869	12 269 795	21 975 714	43 349 509	86 767 339	187 214 047	275 543 043	780 953 239	D.2.3. Total des Primes Nettes Vie

E. BUSINESS WRITTEN ABROAD / E. OPERATIONS A L'ETRANGER

E.2. Non-Life / E.2. Non-Vie

Item (EN)	1992	1993	1994	1995	1996	1997	1998	1999	Poste (FR)
E.2.1. Gross Premiums									**E.2.1. Primes Brutes**
E.2.1.1. Branches & Agencies	29 200	31 300	55 640	26 600	..	..	518 702	956 541	E.2.1.1.1. Succursales & Agences
E.2.1.1. Total			34 300		..	..	518 702	956 541	E.2.1.1. Total
E.2.1.3. Total									E.2.1.3. Total
E.2.1.3.1. Branches & Agencies			55 640		..	..	518 702	956 541	E.2.1.3.1. Succursales & Agences
E.2.1.3. Total Gross Premiums	45 950	49 600	54 500	46 600	..	..	518 702	956 541	E.2.1.3. Total des Primes Brutes
E.2.2. Ceded Premiums									**E.2.2. Primes Cédées**
E.2.2.1. Branches & Agencies	..	..	..	..	..	..	121 191	146 081	E.2.2.1. Succursales & Agences
E.2.2. Total	..	..	..	..	..	..	121 191	146 081	E.2.2. Total
E.2.3. Net Written Premiums									**E.2.3. Primes Nettes Emises**
E.2.3.1. Branches & Agencies	..	..	55 640	..	..	..	397 511	810 460	E.2.3.1. Succursales & Agences
E.2.3. Total	..	..	..	..	..	..	397 511	810 460	E.2.3. Total

Monetary Unit: million Turkish liras · Unité monétaire : million de livres turques

F. OUTSTANDING INVESTMENT BY DIRECT INSURANCE COMPANIES
F. ENCOURS DES PLACEMENTS DES ENTREPRISES D'ASSURANCES DIRECTES

F.1. Life / F.1. Vie

	1992	1993	1994	1995	1996	1997	1998	1999
F.1.1. Real Estate								
F.1.1.1. Domestic Companies	224 504	333 331	561 670	1 317 825	2 474 726	5 010 910	8 455 943	13 296 224
F.1.1.2. (Foreign Controlled Companies)	7 439	0	0	57 874	99 089	178 557	331 857	507 280
F.1.1.4. Domestic Investment	224 504	333 331						
F.1.1.5. Foreign Investment	7 439	0						
F.1.1. Total	231 943	333 331	561 670	1 317 825	2 474 726	5 010 910	8 455 943	13 296 224
F.1.2. Mortgage Loans								
F.1.2.1. Domestic Companies	0	58 604	0	0	0	484 779	0	0
F.1.2.2. (Foreign Controlled Companies)	0	0	0	0	0	2 258	0	0
F.1.2.4. Domestic Investment		58 578						
F.1.2.5. Foreign Investment		26						
F.1.2. Total		58 604	0	0	0	484 779	0	0
F.1.3. Shares								
F.1.3.1. Domestic Companies	56 199	262 218	723 774	1 088 633	1 312 105	803 057	1 024 404	2 836 793
F.1.3.2. (Foreign Controlled Companies)	790	9 833	20 327	6 831	9 848	0	0	0
F.1.3.4. Domestic Investment	56 199	252 385						
F.1.3.5. Foreign Investment	790	24 728						
F.1.3. Total	56 989	277 113	723 774	1 088 633	1 312 105	803 057	1 024 404	2 836 793
F.1.4. Bonds with Fixed Revenue								
F.1.4.1. Domestic Companies	1 574 911	3 641 539	9 047 607	20 825 388	53 210 966	124 252 658	244 506 207	479 672 246
F.1.4.2. (Foreign Controlled Companies)	26 682	70 083	1 820	449 076	1 727 703	3 100 875	7 135 916	32 346 612
F.1.4.4. Domestic Investment	1 574 911	3 571 456						
F.1.4.5. Foreign Investment	26 682	70 083						
F.1.4. Total	1 601 593	3 641 539	9 047 607	20 825 388	53 210 966	124 252 658	244 506 207	479 672 246
F.1.5. Loans other than Mortgage Loans								
F.1.5.1. Domestic Companies	34 947	58 347	91 169	154 387	85 420	794	885 838	2 021 290
F.1.5.2. (Foreign Controlled Companies)	2	26	0	7	66		19 445	107 625
F.1.5.4. Domestic Investment	34 947	58 321						
F.1.5.5. Foreign Investment	2	26						
F.1.5. Total	34 949	58 347	91 169	154 387	85 420	794	885 838	2 021 290
F.1.6. Other Investments								
F.1.6.1. Domestic Companies	0	0	0	1 151 375	2 645 701	2 729 069	6 934 951	5 610 731
F.1.6.2. (Foreign Controlled Companies)	0	0	0	62 915	244 675			1 674 057
F.1.6. Total		0	0	1 151 375	2 645 701	2 729 069	6 934 951	5 610 731
F.1.7. Total								
F.1.7.1. Domestic Companies	1 890 561	4 354 039	10 424 220	24 537 608	59 728 918	133 281 267	261 807 343	503 437 284
F.1.7.2. (Foreign Controlled Companies)	34 913	79 968	22 147	576 703	2 081 381	3 281 690	7 487 218	34 635 574
F.1.7.4. Domestic Investment	1 890 561	4 274 071						
F.1.7.5. Foreign Investment	34 913	94 863						
F.1.7. Total of Life Investments	1 925 474	4 368 934	10 424 220	24 537 608	59 728 918	133 281 267	261 807 343	503 437 284

F.2. Non-Life / F.2. Non-Vie

	1992	1993	1994	1995	1996	1997	1998	1999
F.2.1. Real Estate								
F.2.1.1. Domestic Companies	534 165	1 051 882	3 635 879	4 783 632	9 562 351	20 734 970	37 060 847	60 721 792
F.2.1.2. (Foreign Controlled Companies)	75 135	147 142	335 407	450 267	988 377	1 646 499	2 799 993	1 890 118
F.2.1.3. Branches & Agencies of Foreign Cies	16	16	9	9	0	0	0	0
F.2.1.4. Domestic Investment	534 165	904 740						
F.2.1.5. Foreign Investment	75 151	147 158						
F.2.1. Total	609 316	1 051 898	3 635 879	4 783 641	9 562 351	20 734 970	37 060 847	60 721 792
F.2.2. Mortgage Loans								
F.2.2.1. Domestic Companies	2 236	1 401	2 573	1 148	1 285	6 689 768	0	0
F.2.2.2. (Foreign Controlled Companies)	1 246	147 142	150	0	- 210	470 854	0	0
F.2.2.4. Domestic Investment	2 236	1 401						
F.2.2.5. Foreign Investment	1 246	0						
F.2.2. Total	3 482	1 401	2 573	1 148	1 285	6 689 768	0	0

Monetary Unit: million Turkish liras   Unité monétaire : million de livres turques

	1992	1993	1994	1995	1996	1997	1998	1999
F.2.3. Shares — F.2.3. Actions								
F.2.3.1. Domestic Companies — F.2.3.1. Entreprises Nationales	498 518	1 095 404	2 932 468	2 629 248	9 311 723	12 937 083	24 248 038	21 852 347
F.2.3.2. (Foreign Controlled Companies) — F.2.3.2. (Entreprises Sous Contrôle Etranger)	30 761	24 485	4 721	12 133	25 460	5 144	126	5 157
F.2.3.3. Branches & Agencies of Foreign Cies — F.2.3.3. Succursales et Agences d'Ent. Etrangères	10 077	10 076	0	0	0	..	0	0
F.2.3.4. Domestic Investment — F.2.3.4. Placement dans le Pays	498 518	818 534	..	..	..	..	..	..
F.2.3.5. Foreign Investment — F.2.3.5. Placement à l' Etranger	40 838	9 833	..	..	..	..	..	..
F.2.3. Total — F.2.3. Total	539 356	828 367	2 932 468	2 629 248	9 311 723	12 937 083	24 248 038	21 852 347
F.2.4. Bonds with Fixed Revenue — F.2.4. Obligations								
F.2.4.1. Domestic Companies — F.2.4.1. Entreprises Nationales	863 379	3 126 035	15 894 949	14 127 804	39 076 358	71 692 979	122 273 754	229 377 741
F.2.4.2. (Foreign Controlled Companies) — F.2.4.2. (Entreprises Sous Contrôle Etranger)	195 443	402 035	622 635	1 437 508	2 175 287	3 516 038	5 762 548	11 000 094
F.2.4.3. Branches & Agencies of Foreign Cies — F.2.4.3. Succursales et Agences d'Ent. Etrangères	1 946	19 899	21 256	93 012	122 601	..	0	0
F.2.4.4. Domestic Investment — F.2.4.4. Placement dans le Pays	863 379	2 724 000	..	..	..	..	..	..
F.2.4.5. Foreign Investment — F.2.4.5. Placement à l' Etranger	197 389	421 934	..	..	..	..	..	..
F.2.4. Total — F.2.4. Total	1 060 768	3 145 934	15 916 205	14 220 816	39 198 959	71 692 979	122 273 754	229 377 741
F.2.5. Loans other than Mortgage Loans — F.2.5. Prêts Autres qu'Hypothécaires								
F.2.5.1. Domestic Companies — F.2.5.1. Entreprises Nationales	0	0	0	0	0	2 652	102 634	1 163
F.2.5. Total — F.2.5. Total	..	0	0	0	0	2 652	102 634	1 163
F.2.6. Other Investments — F.2.6. Autres Placements								
F.2.6.1. Domestic Companies — F.2.6.1. Entreprises Nationales	0	0	0	1 353 002	2 677 492	4 776 894	6 173 017	16 033 543
F.2.6.2. (Foreign Controlled Companies) — F.2.6.2. (Entreprises Sous Contrôle Etranger)	0	0	0	6 926	202 794	347 152	120 481	938 988
F.2.6.3. Branches & Agencies of Foreign Cies — F.2.6.3. Succursales et Agences d'Ent. Etrangères	0	0	0	237	2 335	..	0	..
F.2.6. Total — F.2.6. Total	..	0	0	1 353 239	2 679 827	4 776 894	6 173 017	16 033 543
F.2.7. Total — F.2.7.								
F.2.7.1. Domestic Companies — F.2.7.1. Entreprises Nationales	1 898 298	5 274 722	22 465 869	22 894 834	60 629 208	116 834 346	189 858 290	327 986 586
F.2.7.2. (Foreign Controlled Companies) — F.2.7.2. (Entreprises Sous Contrôle Etranger)	4 091 442	5 848 384	962 913	1 906 834	3 391 708	5 985 687	8 683 148	13 834 357
F.2.7.3. Branches & Agencies of Foreign Cies — F.2.7.3. Succursales et Agences d'Ent. Etrangères	12 039	29 975	21 256	93 258	124 936	..	0	0
F.2.7.4. Domestic Investment — F.2.7.4. Placement dans le Pays	1 898 298	4 448 675	..	..	..	..	..	..
F.2.7.5. Foreign Investment — F.2.7.5. Placement à l' Etranger	314 624	578 925	..	..	..	..	..	..
F.2.7. Total of Non-Life Investments — F.2.7. Total des Placements Non-Vie	2 212 922	5 027 600	22 487 125	22 988 092	60 754 144	116 834 346	189 858 290	327 986 586
G. BREAKDOWN OF NON-LIFE PREMIUMS — G. VENTILATIONS DES PRIMES NON-VIE								
G.1. Motor vehicle — G.1. Assurance Automobile								
G.1.1. Direct Business — G.1.1. Assurances Directes								
G.1.1.1. Gross Premiums — G.1.1.1. Primes Brutes	3 564 840	676 554	16 058 939	30 966 343	58 505 007	133 019 709	234 629 022	440 389 007
G.1.1.2. Ceded Premiums — G.1.1.2. Primes Cédées	..	109 391	..	6 652 476	11 808 885	26 468 671	57 889 148	..
G.1.1.3. Net Written Premiums — G.1.1.3. Primes Nettes Emises	..	567 163	..	24 313 867	46 696 122	106 551 038	176 739 874	..
G.1.2. Reinsurance Accepted — G.1.2. Réassurance Acceptée								
G.1.2.1. Gross Premiums — G.1.2.1. Primes Brutes	..	25 514	305 698	491 740	902 888	1 196 335	1 141 399	14 374 779
G.1.2.2. Ceded Premiums — G.1.2.2. Primes Cédées	..	47 533	..	20 083	96 129	378 074	281 613	..
G.1.2.3. Net Written Premiums — G.1.2.3. Primes Nettes Emises	..	20 761	..	471 657	806 759	818 281	859 786	..
G.1.3. Total								
G.1.3.1. Gross Premiums — G.1.3.1. Primes Brutes	..	702 068	16 364 637	31 458 083	59 407 895	134 216 064	235 770 421	454 763 785
G.1.3.2. Ceded Premiums — G.1.3.2. Primes Cédées	..	114 144	..	6 672 559	11 905 014	26 846 745	58 170 761	..
G.1.3.3. Net Written Premiums — G.1.3.3. Primes Nettes Emises	..	587 924	..	24 785 524	47 502 881	107 369 319	177 599 659	..
G.2. Marine, Aviation — G.2. Marine, Aviation								
G.2.1. Direct Business — G.2.1. Assurances Directes								
G.2.1.1. Gross Premiums — G.2.1.1. Primes Brutes	553 617	1 517 006	3 360 400	6 903 263	12 915 147	21 935 836	11 846 094	23 018 704
G.2.1.2. Ceded Premiums — G.2.1.2. Primes Cédées	..	346 079	..	1 493 555	2 591 451	4 865 270	10 562 128	..
G.2.1.3. Net Written Premiums — G.2.1.3. Primes Nettes Emises	..	1 170 927	..	5 409 708	10 323 696	17 070 566	1 283 966	..
G.2.2. Reinsurance Accepted — G.2.2. Réassurance Acceptée								
G.2.2.1. Gross Premiums — G.2.2.1. Primes Brutes	..	22 336	27 481	57 606	122 440	481 870	242 271	666 363
G.2.2.2. Ceded Premiums — G.2.2.2. Primes Cédées	..	12 606	..	602	5 956	19 165	216 012	..
G.2.2.3. Net Written Premiums — G.2.2.3. Primes Nettes Emises	..	9 730	..	57 004	116 484	462 705	26 259	..
G.2.3. Total								
G.2.3.1. Gross Premiums — G.2.3.1. Primes Brutes	..	1 539 342	3 587 881	6 960 869	13 037 587	22 417 706	12 088 365	23 685 066
G.2.3.2. Ceded Premiums — G.2.3.2. Primes Cédées	..	358 685	..	1 494 157	2 597 407	4 884 435	10 778 140	..
G.2.3.3. Net Written Premiums — G.2.3.3. Primes Nettes Emises	..	1 180 657	..	5 466 712	10 440 180	17 533 271	1 310 225	..

Monetary Unit: million Turkish liras   Unité monétaire : million de livres turques

Label (EN)	1992	1993	1994	1995	1996	1997	1998	1999	Label (FR)
G.3. Freight									G.3. Fret
G.3.1. Direct Business									G.3.1. Assurances Directes
G.3.1.1. Gross Premiums	253 823	..	0	..	..	..	25 649 333	36 392 236	G.3.1.1. Primes Brutes
G.3.1.2. Ceded Premiums							9 967 205	..	G.3.1.2. Primes Cédées
G.3.1.3. Net Written Premiums							15 682 128		G.3.1.3. Primes Nettes Emises
G.3.2. Reinsurance Accepted									G.3.2. Réassurance Acceptée
G.3.2.1. Gross Premiums							433 827	1 712 974	G.3.2.1. Primes Brutes
G.3.2.2. Ceded Premiums							168 583		G.3.2.2. Primes Cédées
G.3.2.3. Net Written Premiums							265 244	..	G.3.2.3. Primes Nettes Emises
G.3.3. Total									G.3.3. Total
G.3.3.1. Gross Premiums							26 083 160	38 105 210	G.3.3.1. Primes Brutes
G.3.3.2. Ceded Premiums							10 135 788		G.3.3.2. Primes Cédées
G.3.3.3. Net Written Premiums							15 947 372	..	G.3.3.3. Primes Nettes Emises
G.4. Fire, Property Damages									G.4. Incendie, Dommages aux Biens
G.4.1. Direct Business									G.4.1. Assurances Directes
G.4.1.1. Gross Premiums	1 216 068	2 713 231	5 847 291	10 876 987	21 429 179	42 464 160	114 311 894	245 699 689	G.4.1.1. Primes Brutes
G.4.1.2. Ceded Premiums	..	426 564	..	2 750 789	5 169 588	12 483 718	78 115 610	..	G.4.1.2. Primes Cédées
G.4.1.3. Net Written Premiums	..	2 286 667	..	8 126 198	16 259 591	29 980 442	36 196 284		G.4.1.3. Primes Nettes Emises
G.4.2. Reinsurance Accepted									G.4.2. Réassurance Acceptée
G.4.2.1. Gross Premiums	..	71 542	81 225	130 647	271 462	620 722	2 349 047	14 223 530	G.4.2.1. Primes Brutes
G.4.2.2. Ceded Premiums	..	15 571	..	9 926	17 545	138 572	1 605 233		G.4.2.2. Primes Cédées
G.4.2.3. Net Written Premiums	..	55 971	..	120 721	253 917	482 150	743 814		G.4.2.3. Primes Nettes Emises
G.4.3. Total									G.4.3. Total
G.4.3.1. Gross Premiums	..	2 784 773	5 928 516	11 007 634	21 700 641	43 084 882	116 660 941	259 923 220	G.4.3.1. Primes Brutes
G.4.3.2. Ceded Premiums	..	442 135	..	2 760 715	5 187 133	12 622 290	79 720 843	..	G.4.3.2. Primes Cédées
G.4.3.3. Net Written Premiums	..	2 342 638	..	8 246 919	16 513 508	30 462 592	36 940 098		G.4.3.3. Primes Nettes Emises
G.5. General Liability									G.6. Responsabilité Générale
G.5.1. Direct Business									
G.5.1.1. Gross Premiums								75 299	G.6.1.1. Primes Brutes
G.5.2. Reinsurance Accepted									G.6.2. Réassurance Acceptée
G.5.2.1. Gross Premiums								0	G.6.2.1. Primes Brutes
G.5.3. Total									
G.5.3.1. Gross Premiums								75 299	G.6.3.1. Primes Brutes
G.6. General Liability									G.6. Responsabilité Générale
G.6.1. Direct Business									G.6.1. Assurances Directes
G.6.1.1. Gross Premiums	96 774	..				..	6 480 716	11 774 729	G.6.1.1. Primes Brutes
G.6.1.2. Ceded Premiums							3 715 920		G.6.1.2. Primes Cédées
G.6.1.3. Net Written Premiums							2 764 796		G.6.1.3. Primes Nettes Emises
G.6.2. Reinsurance Accepted									G.6.2. Réassurance Acceptée
G.6.2.1. Gross Premiums							58 617	551 301	G.6.2.1. Primes Brutes
G.6.2.2. Ceded Premiums							33 610		G.6.2.2. Primes Cédées
G.6.2.3. Net Written Premiums							25 007		G.6.2.3. Primes Nettes Emises
G.6.3. Total									G.6.3. Total
G.6.3.1. Gross Premiums							6 539 333	12 326 030	G.6.3.1. Primes Brutes
G.6.3.2. Ceded Premiums							3 749 530		G.6.3.2. Primes Cédées
G.6.3.3. Net Written Premiums							2 789 803	..	G.6.3.3. Primes Nettes Emises
G.7. Accident, Health									G.7. Accident, Santé
G.7.1. Direct Business									G.7.1. Assurances Directes
G.7.1.1. Gross Premiums	394 476	9 514 976	941 660	3 021 806	8 358 317	24 197 625	66 039 612	134 744 140	G.7.1.1. Primes Brutes
G.7.1.2. Ceded Premiums	..	1 456 737	..	494 985	1 442 730	3 491 499	25 526 490	..	G.7.1.2. Primes Cédées
G.7.1.3. Net Written Premiums	..	8 058 239	..	2 526 821	6 915 587	20 706 126	40 513 122		G.7.1.3. Primes Nettes Emises
G.7.2. Reinsurance Accepted									G.7.2. Réassurance Acceptée
G.7.2.1. Gross Premiums	..	132 030	672	1 899	4 358	27 943	210 726	1 656 044	G.7.2.1. Primes Brutes
G.7.2.2. Ceded Premiums	..	31 693	..	0	1 060	3 093	81 453		G.7.2.2. Primes Cédées
G.7.2.3. Net Written Premiums	..	100 337	..	1 899	3 298	24 850	129 273		G.7.2.3. Primes Nettes Emises
G.7.3. Total									G.7.3. Total
G.7.3.1. Gross Premiums	..	9 647 006	942 332	3 023 705	8 362 675	24 225 568	66 250 338	136 400 185	G.7.3.1. Primes Brutes
G.7.3.2. Ceded Premiums	..	14 884 300	..	494 985	1 443 790	3 494 592	25 607 943	..	G.7.3.2. Primes Cédées
G.7.3.3. Net Written Premiums	..	8 158 576	..	2 528 720	6 918 885	20 730 976	40 642 395		G.7.3.3. Primes Nettes Emises

Monetary Unit: million Turkish liras / Unité monétaire : million de livres turques

	1992	1993	1994	1995	1996	1997	1998	1999
G.8. Others / G.8. Autres								
G.8.1. Direct Business / Assurances Directes								
G.8.1.1. Gross Premiums / Primes Brutes	557 164	:	1 554 253	3 132 354	7 803 470	16 223 707	313 490	522 428
G.8.1.2. Ceded Premiums / Primes Cédées		:	:	850 830	2 489 769	5 495 214	0	:
G.8.1.3. Net Written Premiums / Primes Nettes Emises		:	:	2 281 524	5 313 700	10 728 493	313 490	:
G.8.2. Reinsurance Accepted / Réassurance Acceptée								
G.8.2.1. Gross Premiums / Primes Brutes	:	:	32 654	42 555	82 295	268 367	0	0
G.8.2.2. Ceded Premiums / Primes Cédées	:	:	:	2 445	4 111	2 228	0	0
G.8.2.3. Net Written Premiums / Primes Nettes Emises	:	:	:	40 110	78 184	266 139	0	:
G.8.3. Total								
G.8.3.1. Gross Premiums / Primes Brutes	:	:	1 586 907	3 174 910	7 885 765	16 492 074	313 490	522 428
G.8.3.2. Ceded Premiums / Primes Cédées	:	:	:	853 276	2 493 880	5 497 442	0	:
G.8.3.3. Net Written Premiums / Primes Nettes Emises	:	:	:	2 321 634	5 391 885	10 994 632	313 490	:
G.10. Total								
G.10.1. Direct Business / Assurances Directes								
G.10.1.1. Gross Premiums / Primes Brutes	6 636 762	14 421 767	27 962 543	54 900 753	109 011 121	..	459 270 161	892 616 232
G.10.1.2. Ceded Premiums / Primes Cédées	2 997 312	2 338 771	:	12 242 635	23 502 424	..	185 776 501	:
G.10.1.3. Net Written Premiums / Primes Nettes Emises	363 450	12 082 995	:	42 658 118	85 508 697	..	273 493 659	:
G.10.2. Reinsurance Accepted / Réassurance Acceptée								
G.10.2.1. Gross Premiums / Primes Brutes	205 204	251 422	447 730	724 448	1 383 443	..	4 435 887	33 184 991
G.10.2.2. Ceded Premiums / Primes Cédées	173 785	64 623	:	33 056	124 801	..	2 386 504	:
G.10.2.3. Net Written Premiums / Primes Nettes Emises	31 419	186 799	:	691 391	1 258 642	..	2 049 383	:
G.10.3. Total								
G.10.3.1. Gross Premiums / Primes Brutes	6 841 965	14 673 189	28 410 273	55 625 201	110 394 563	..	463 706 048	925 801 223
G.10.3.2. Ceded Premiums / Primes Cédées	3 171 097	2 403 394	6 434 559	12 275 692	23 627 225	..	188 163 005	144 847 984
G.10.3.3. Net Written Premiums / Primes Nettes Emises	3 670 868	12 269 795	21 975 714	43 349 509	86 767 339	..	275 543 043	780 953 239
H. GROSS CLAIMS PAYMENTS / PAIEMENTS BRUTS DES SINISTRES								
H.1. Life / Vie								
H.1.1. Domestic Companies / Entreprises Nationales		288 168	288 168	1 201 227	3 786 216	8 153 946	29 157 975	101 914 934
H.1.2. (Foreign Controlled Companies) / (Entreprises Sous Contrôle Etranger)		4 319	4 319	56 909	143 017	321 625	791 216	2 818 431
H.1. Total		288 168	288 168	1 201 227	3 786 216	8 153 946	29 157 975	101 914 934
H.2. Non-Life / Non-Vie								
H.2.1. Domestic Companies / Entreprises Nationales		5 304 585	5 304 585	23 915 750	49 649 218	119 528 287	265 325 339	650 433 561
H.2.2. (Foreign Controlled Companies) / (Entreprises Sous Contrôle Etranger)		516 801	516 801	2 806 011	4 783 056	14 123 791	20 939 042	18 232 790
H.2.3. Branches & Agencies of Foreign Cies / Succursales et Agences d'Ent. Etrangères		22 113	22 113	80 780	8 564	0	0	
H.2. Total		5 326 698	5 326 698	23 996 530	49 657 782	119 528 287	265 325 339	650 433 561
I. GROSS OPERATING EXPENSES / DEPENSES BRUTES D'EXPLOITATION								
I.1. Life / Vie								
I.1.1. Domestic Companies / Entreprises Nationales		668 312	1 331 610	1 540 379	5 462 770	7 926 090	19 263 099	46 991 530
I.1.2. (Foreign Controlled Companies) / (Entreprises Sous Contrôle Etranger)		67 726	157 354	152 384	632 622	1 177 499	3 726 054	10 439 199
I.1. Total / Total des Primes Nettes Vie		668 312	1 331 610	1 540 379	5 462 770	7 926 090	19 263 099	46 991 530
I.2. Non-Life / Non-Vie								
I.2.1. Domestic Companies / Entreprises Nationales	2 944 862		5 311 156	5 516 003	20 517 098	25 140 851	58 835 172	:
I.2.2. (Foreign Controlled Companies) / (Entreprises Sous Contrôle Etranger)	402 854		648 470	708 022	2 370 638	2 660 007	4 989 534	:
I.2.3. Branches & Agencies of Foreign Cies / Succursales et Agences d'Ent. Etrangères	21 350		36 440	33 362	20 864	0	0	0
I.2. Total	2 966 212		5 347 596	5 549 365	20 537 962	25 140 851	58 835 172	:

Monetary Unit: million Turkish liras

Unité monétaire : million de livres turques

J. COMMISSIONS

J.1. Life / J.1. Vie

	1992	1993	1994	1995	1996	1997	1998	1999	
J.1.1. Direct Business									J.1.1. Assurance directe
J.1.1.1. Domestic Companies		30 249	57 181	137 188	2 009 854	722 482	10 268 070	17 985 800	J.1.1.1. Entreprises Nationales
J.1.1.2. (Foreign Controlled Companies)		18 519	19 582	47 182	294 649	185 185	1 512 865	4 170 887	J.1.1.2. (Entreprises Sous Contrôle Etranger)
J.1.1. Total		30 249	57 181	137 188	2 009 854	722 482	10 268 070	17 985 800	J.1.1. Total
J.1.2. Reinsurance Accepted									J.1.2. Réassurances acceptées
J.1.2.1. Domestic Companies		0	727	289	9 108	63 865	1 829	964	J.1.2.1. Entreprises Nationales
J.1.2.2. (Foreign Controlled Companies)		0	288	5 208	5 365	0	0	- 50	J.1.2.2. (Entreprises Sous Contrôle Etranger)
J.1.2. Total		0	727	289	9 108	63 865	1 829	964	J.1.2. Total
J.1.3. Total									J.1.3. Total
J.1.3.1. Domestic Companies		30 249	57 908	137 477	2 018 962	786 347	10 269 899	17 986 764	J.1.3.1. Entreprises Nationales
J.1.3.2. (Foreign Controlled Companies)		18 519	19 870	52 390	300 014	185 185	1 512 865	4 170 837	J.1.3.2. (Entreprises Sous Contrôle Etranger)
J.1.3. Total of Life Net Premiums		30 249	57 908	137 477	2 018 962	786 347	10 269 899	17 986 764	J.1.3. Total des Primes Nettes Vie

J.2. Non-Life / J.2. Non-Vie

	1992	1993	1994	1995	1996	1997	1998	1999	
J.2.1. Direct Business									J.2.1. Assurance directe
J.2.1.1. Domestic Companies		1 718 328	3 033 042	5 746 114	8 889 525	24 449 467	60 323 457	132 106 049	J.2.1.1. Entreprises Nationales
J.2.1.2. (Foreign Controlled Companies)		207 625	374 340	638 670	855 135	2 021 584	4 718 626	4 341 972	J.2.1.2. (Entreprises Sous Contrôle Etranger)
J.2.1.3. Branches & Agencies of Foreign Cies		9 075	0	9 806	- 3	0	0	0	J.2.1.3. Succursales et Agences d'Ent. Etrangères
J.2.1. Total		1 727 403	3 033 042	5 755 920	8 889 522	24 449 467	60 323 457	132 106 049	J.2.1. Total
J.2.2. Reinsurance Accepted									J.2.2. Réassurances acceptées
J.2.2.1. Domestic Companies		20 106	172 373	28 405	343 793	118 107	945 399	4 381 949	J.2.2.1. Entreprises Nationales
J.2.2.2. (Foreign Controlled Companies)		3 769	9 645	18 541	11 577	25 472	25 321	39 977	J.2.2.2. (Entreprises Sous Contrôle Etranger)
J.2.2.3. Branches & Agencies of Foreign Cies		0	1	0	0	0	0	0	J.2.2.3. Succursales et Agences d'Ent. Etrangères
J.2.2. Total		20 106	172 374	28 405	343 793	118 107	945 399	4 381 949	J.2.2. Total
J.2.3. Total									J.2.3. Total
J.2.3.1. Domestic Companies		1 738 434	3 205 415	5 774 519	9 233 319	24 567 574	61 268 856	136 487 998	J.2.3.1. Entreprises Nationales
J.2.3.2. (Foreign Controlled Companies)		211 394	383 985	657 211	866 712	2 047 056	4 743 947	4 381 949	J.2.3.2. (Entreprises Sous Contrôle Etranger)
J.2.3.3. Branches & Agencies of Foreign Cies		9 075	1	9 806	- 3	0	0	0	J.2.3.3. Succursales et Agences d'Ent. Etrangères
J.2.3. Total		1 747 509	3 205 416	5 784 325	9 233 316	24 567 574	61 268 856	136 487 998	J.2.3. Total

Monetary Unit: million pounds sterling — Unité monétaire : million de livres sterling

A. NUMBER OF COMPANIES IN THE REPORTING COUNTRY / A. NOMBRE D'ENTREPRISES DANS LE PAYS DECLARANT

	1992	1993	1994	1995	1996	1997	1998	1999
A.1. Life / A.1. Vie								
A.1.1. Domestic Companies / Entreprises Nationales	182	180	173	160	163	162	270	198
A.1.2. (Foreign Controlled Companies) / (Entreprises Sous Contrôle Etranger)	..	3	4	3	..	..	..	..
A.1.3. Branches & Agencies of Foreign Cies / Succursales et Agences d'Ent. Etrangères	14	11	14	14	14	15	10	..
A.1. All Companies / Ensemble des Entreprises	196	194	191	174	177	177	280	..
A.2. Non-Life / A.2. Non-Vie								
A.2.1. Domestic Companies / Entreprises Nationales	449	453	449	457	443	452	432	362
A.2.2. (Foreign Controlled Companies) / (Entreprises Sous Contrôle Etranger)	..	60	63	73	..	..	..	..
A.2.3. Branches & Agencies of Foreign Cies / Succursales et Agences d'Ent. Etrangères	117	63	62	64	135	147	58	58
A.2. All Companies / Ensemble des Entreprises	566	576	574	594	578	599	490	..
A.3. Composite / A.3. Mixte								
A.3.1. Domestic Companies / Entreprises Nationales	52	50	50	51	52	58	49	76
A.3.2. (Foreign Controlled Companies) / (Entreprises Sous Contrôle Etranger)	..	6	4	4	7	7	3	..
A.3.3. Branches & Agencies of Foreign Cies / Succursales et Agences d'Ent. Etrangères	10	..	3	3	..	..	..	..
A.3. All Companies / Ensemble des Entreprises	62	59	57	58	59	65	52	..
A.4. Reinsurance / A.4. Réassurance								
A.4.1. Domestic Companies / Entreprises Nationales							38	49
A.4.3. Branches & Agencies of Foreign Cies / Succursales et Agences d'Ent. Etrangères							10	..
A.4. All Companies / Ensemble des Entreprises							48	..
A.5. Total / A.5. Total								
A.5.1. Domestic Companies / Entreprises Nationales	683	683	672	668	658	672	789	685
A.5.2. (Foreign Controlled Companies) / (Entreprises Sous Contrôle Etranger)	..	66	71	80	..	..	..	93
A.5.3. Branches & Agencies of Foreign Cies / Succursales et Agences d'Ent. Etrangères	141	80	79	78	156	169	81	27
A.5. All Insurance Companies / Ensemble des Entreprises d'Assurances	824	829	822	826	814	841	870	712

B. NUMBER OF EMPLOYEES / B. NOMBRE D'EMPLOYES

	1992	1993	1994	1995	1996	1997	1998	1999
B.1. Insurance Companies / Entreprises d'Assurances	260 000	267 800	221 031	203 500	200 400	228 500	234 591	223 000
B.2. Intermediaries / Intermediaires	102 000	100 900	101 700	134 300	133 500	124 500	116 275	143 700
B. Total	362 000	368 700	322 731	337 800	333 900	353 000	350 866	366 700

C. BUSINESS WRITTEN IN THE REPORTING COUNTRY / C. OPERATIONS CONCLUES DANS LE PAYS DECLARANT

C.1. Life / C.1. Vie

	1992	1993	1994	1995	1996	1997	1998	1999
C.1.1. Gross Premiums / Primes Brutes								
C.1.1.1. Direct Business / Assurances Directes								
C.1.1.1.1. Domestic Companies / Entreprises Nationales	..	..	..	..	53 652	59 908	70 357	87 511
C.1.1.1.2. (Foreign Controlled Companies) / (Entreprises Sous Contrôle Etranger)	..	..	..	..	10 131	10 406	15 501	19 769
C.1.1.1.3. Branches & Agencies of Foreign Cies / Succursales et Agences d'Ent. Etrangères	..	..	..	..	1 615	1 485	3 468	3 528
C.1.1.1. Total	..	..	..	..	55 267	61 393	73 825	91 039
C.1.1.2. Reinsurance Accepted / Réassurance Acceptée								
C.1.1.2.1. Domestic Companies / Entreprises Nationales	..	..	..	..	335	370	500	395
C.1.1.2.2. (Foreign Controlled Companies) / (Entreprises Sous Contrôle Etranger)	..	..	..	..	140	370	500	395
C.1.1.2.3. Branches & Agencies of Foreign Cies / Succursales et Agences d'Ent. Etrangères	..	..	..	..	90	68	116	180
C.1.1.2. Total	..	..	..	..	425	438	616	575
C.1.1.3. Total								
C.1.1.3.1. Domestic Companies / Entreprises Nationales	..	48 706	47 653	46 706	53 987	60 278	70 857	87 906
C.1.1.3.2. (Foreign Controlled Companies) / (Entreprises Sous Contrôle Etranger)	..	..	..	..	10 271	10 776	16 001	20 164
C.1.1.3.3. Branches & Agencies of Foreign Cies / Succursales et Agences d'Ent. Etrangères	..	1 129	1 033	1 288	1 705	1 553	3 584	3 708
C.1.1.3. Total Gross Premiums / Total des Primes Brutes	..	49 835	48 686	47 994	55 692	61 831	74 441	91 614

Monetary Unit: million pounds sterling

Unité monétaire : million de livres sterling

	1992	1993	1994	1995	1996	1997	1998	1999
C.1.2. Ceded Premiums								
C.1.2.1. Domestic Companies	..	2 232	4 480	1 896	1 595	1 363	3 645	4 918
C.1.2.2. (Foreign Controlled Companies)	..				290	403	919	1 688
C.1.2.3. Branches & Agencies of Foreign Cies	..	85	21	23	98	57	- 1 605	1 691
C.1.2. Total	..	2 317	4 501	1 919	1 693	1 420	2 040	3 227
C.1.3. Net Written Premiums								
C.1.3.1. Domestic Companies	41 751	46 474	43 173	44 810	52 392	58 915	67 212	82 998
C.1.3.2. (Foreign Controlled Companies)					9 981	10 373	15 082	18 476
C.1.3.3. Branches & Agencies of Foreign Cies	1 959	1 044	1 012	1 265	1 607	1 496	5 189	5 399
C.1.3. Total	43 710	47 518	44 185	46 075	53 999	60 411	72 401	88 387
C.2. Non-Life								
C.2.1. Gross premiums								
C.2.1.1. Direct Business								
C.2.1.1.1. Domestic Companies	30 819	32 751	33 296	32 750	31 650	32 053	32 049	32 628
C.2.1.1.2. (Foreign Controlled Companies)						9 662	9 689	11 698
C.2.1.1.3. Branches & Agencies of Foreign Cies	1 760	2 356	2 351	2 266	2 218	2 426	2 390	2 245
C.2.1.1. Total	32 579	35 109	35 647	35 016	33 868	34 479	34 439	34 873
C.2.1.2. Reinsurance Accepted								
C.2.1.2.1. Domestic Companies	7 799	7 074	5 595	5 587	5 282	4 516	4 438	4 661
C.2.1.2.2. (Foreign Controlled Companies)						2 161	2 192	2 595
C.2.1.2.3. Branches & Agencies of Foreign Cies	377	298	288	290	390	498	2 072	1 864
C.2.1.2. Total	8 176	7 372	5 883	5 877	5 672	5 014	6 510	6 525
C.2.1.3.1. Domestic Companies	38 618	39 825	38 891	38 337	36 932	36 569	36 487	37 289
C.2.1.3.2. (Foreign Controlled Companies)						11 823	11 881	14 293
C.2.1.3.3. Branches & Agencies of Foreign Cies	2 137	2 656	2 639	2 556	2 608	2 924	4 462	4 109
C.2.1.3. Total Gross Premiums	40 755	42 481	41 530	40 893	39 540	39 493	40 949	41 398
C.2.2. Ceded Premiums								
C.2.2.1. Domestic Companies	8 413	7 943	8 026	8 099	7 378	7 054	6 696	6 867
C.2.2.2. (Foreign Controlled Companies)						3 606	3 377	4 239
C.2.2.3. Branches & Agencies of Foreign Cies	874	1 045	1 048	971	1 120	1 321	1 747	1 475
C.2.2. Total	9 287	8 988	9 074	9 070	8 498	8 375	8 443	8 342
C.2.3. Net Written Premiums								
C.2.3.1. Domestic Companies	30 205	31 882	30 865	30 238	29 554	29 515	29 791	30 422
C.2.3.2. (Foreign Controlled Companies)						8 217	8 504	10 054
C.2.3.3. Branches & Agencies of Foreign Cies	1 263	1 611	1 591	1 585	1 488	1 603	2 715	2 634
C.2.3. Total	31 468	33 493	32 456	31 823	31 042	31 118	32 506	33 056
C.3. Total								
C.3.1. Gross Premiums								
C.3.1.1. Direct Business								
C.3.1.1.1. Domestic Companies	..	88 531	86 544	85 043	85 302	91 961	102 406	120 139
C.3.1.1.2. (Foreign Controlled Companies)						20 068	25 190	31 467
C.3.1.1.3. Branches & Agencies of Foreign Cies	..	3 785	3 672	3 844	3 833	3 911	5 858	5 773
C.3.1.1. Total	..	92 316	90 216	88 887	89 135	95 872	108 284	125 912
C.3.1.2. Reinsurance Accepted								
C.3.1.2.1. Domestic Companies					5 617	4 886	4 938	5 056
C.3.1.2.2. (Foreign Controlled Companies)						2 531	2 692	2 990
C.3.1.2.3. Branches & Agencies of Foreign Cies					480	566	2 188	2 044
C.3.1.2. Total					6 097	5 452	7 126	7 100
C.3.1.3.1. Domestic Companies					90 919	96 847	107 344	125 195
C.3.1.3.2. (Foreign Controlled Companies)						22 599	27 882	34 457
C.3.1.3.3. Branches & Agencies of Foreign Cies					4 313	4 477	8 046	7 817
C.3.1.3. Total Gross Premiums					95 232	101 324	115 390	133 012

French row labels (right-hand side of table):

C.1.2. Primes Cédées
- C.1.2.1. Entreprises Nationales
- C.1.2.2. (Entreprises Sous Contrôle Etranger)
- C.1.2.3. Succursales et Agences d'Ent. Etrangères
- C.1.2. Total

C.1.3. Primes Nettes Emises
- C.1.3.1. Entreprises Nationales
- C.1.3.2. (Entreprises Sous Contrôle Etranger)
- C.1.3.3. Succursales et Agences d'Ent. Etrangères
- C.1.3. Total

C.2. Non-Vie
C.2.1. Primes Brutes
- C.2.1.1. Assurances Directes
  - C.2.1.1.1. Entreprises Nationales
  - C.2.1.1.2. (Entreprises Sous Contrôle Etranger)
  - C.2.1.1.3. Succursales et Agences d'Ent. Etrangères
  - C.2.1.1. Total
- C.2.1.2. Réassurance Acceptée
  - C.2.1.2.1. Entreprises Nationales
  - C.2.1.2.2. (Entreprises Sous Contrôle Etranger)
  - C.2.1.2.3. Succursales et Agences d'Ent. Etrangères
  - C.2.1.2. Total
- C.2.1.3.1. Entreprises Nationales
- C.2.1.3.2. (Entreprises Sous Contrôle Etranger)
- C.2.1.3.3. Succursales et Agences d'Ent. Etrangères
- C.2.1.3. Total des Primes Brutes

C.2.2. Primes Cédées
- C.2.2.1. Entreprises Nationales
- C.2.2.2. (Entreprises Sous Contrôle Etranger)
- C.2.2.3. Succursales et Agences d'Ent. Etrangères
- C.2.2. Total

C.2.3. Primes Nettes Emises
- C.2.3.1. Entreprises Nationales
- C.2.3.2. (Entreprises Sous Contrôle Etranger)
- C.2.3.3. Succursales et Agences d'Ent. Etrangères
- C.2.3. Total

C.3. Total
C.3.1. Primes Brutes
- C.3.1.1. Assurances Directes
  - C.3.1.1.1. Entreprises Nationales
  - C.3.1.1.2. (Entreprises Sous Contrôle Etranger)
  - C.3.1.1.3. Succursales et Agences d'Ent. Etrangères
  - C.3.1.1. Total
- C.3.1.2. Réassurance Acceptée
  - C.3.1.2.1. Entreprises Nationales
  - C.3.1.2.2. (Entreprises Sous Contrôle Etranger)
  - C.3.1.2.3. Succursales et Agences d'Ent. Etrangères
  - C.3.1.2. Total
- C.3.1.3. Total
  - C.3.1.3.1. Entreprises Nationales
  - C.3.1.3.2. (Entreprises Sous Contrôle Etranger)
  - C.3.1.3.3. Succursales et Agences d'Ent. Etrangères
  - C.3.1.3. Total des Primes Brutes

Label (English)	1992	1993	1994	1995	1996	1997	1998	1999	Label (French)
C.3.2. Ceded Premiums									C.3.2. Primes Cédées
C.3.2.1. Domestic Companies	..	10 175	12 506	9 995	8 973	8 417	10 341	11 785	C.3.2.1. Entreprises Nationales
C.3.2.2. (Foreign Controlled Companies)	..					4 009	4 296	5 927	C.3.2.2. (Entreprises Sous Contrôle Etranger)
C.3.2.3. Branches & Agencies of Foreign Cies	..	1 130	1 069	994	1 218	1 378	3 352	3 166	C.3.2.3. Succursales et Agences d'Ent. Etrangères
C.3.2. Total	..	11 305	13 575	10 989	10 191	9 795	10 483	11 569	C.3.2. Total
C.3.3. Net Written Premiums									C.3.3. Primes Nettes Emises
C.3.3.1. Domestic Companies	71 956	78 356	74 038	75 048	81 946	88 430	97 003	113 410	C.3.3.1. Entreprises Nationales
C.3.3.2. (Foreign Controlled Companies)		..				18 590	23 586	28 530	C.3.3.2. (Entreprises Sous Contrôle Etranger)
C.3.3.3. Branches & Agencies of Foreign Cies	3 222	2 655	2 603	2 850	3 095	3 099	7 904	8 033	C.3.3.3. Succursales et Agences d'Ent. Etrangères
C.3.3. Total	75 178	81 011	76 641	77 898	85 041	91 529	104 907	121 443	C.3.3. Total

D. NET WRITTEN PREMIUMS IN THE REPORTING COUNTRY IN TERMS OF DOMESTIC AND FOREIGN RISKS — **D. PRIMES NETTES EMISES DANS LE PAYS DECLARANT EN RISQUES NATIONAUX ET ETRANGERS**

D.2. Non-Life — **D.2. Non-Vie**

Label (English)	1992	1993	1994	1995	1996	1997	1998	1999	Label (French)
D.2.1. Domestic Risks									D.2.1. Risques Nationaux
D.2.1.1. Domestic Companies	20 524	22 015	22 406	21 785	21 443	22 042	22 786	23 181	D.2.1.1. Entreprises Nationales
D.2.1.2. (Foreign Controlled Companies)							6 504	7 661	D.2.1.2. (Entreprises Sous Contrôle Etranger)
D.2.1.3. Branches & Agencies of Foreign Cies	923	1 250	1 260	1 241	1 076	1 120	1 441	1 324	D.2.1.3. Succursales et Agences d'Ent. Etrangères
D.2.1. Total	21 447	23 265	23 666	23 026	22 519	23 162	24 227	24 505	D.2.1. Total des Primes Nettes Vie
D.2.2. Foreign Risks									D.2.2. Risques Etrangers
D.2.2.1. Domestic Companies	9 681	9 867	8 459	8 453	8 111	7 473	7 005	7 241	D.2.2.1. Entreprises Nationales
D.2.2.2. Foreign Controlled Companies							2 000	2 393	D.2.2.2. Entreprises Sous Controle Etranger
D.2.2.3. Branches & Agencies of Foreign Cies	340	361	331	344	412	483	1 274	1 310	D.2.2.3. Succursales et Agences d'Ent. Etrangères
D.2.2. Total	10 021	10 228	8 790	8 797	8 523	7 956	8 279	8 551	D.2.2. Total des Primes Nettes Vie
D.2.3. Total									D.2.3. Total
D.2.3.1. Domestic Companies	30 205	31 882	30 865	30 238	29 554	29 515	29 791	30 422	D.2.3.1. Entreprises Nationales
D.2.3.2. (Foreign Controlled Companies)							8 504	10 054	D.2.3.2. (Entreprises Sous Controle Etranger)
D.2.3.3. Branches & Agencies of Foreign Cies	1 263	1 611	1 591	1 585	1 488	1 603	2 715	2 634	D.2.3.3. Succursales et Agences d'Ent. Etrangères
D.2.3. Total	31 468	33 493	32 456	31 823	31 042	31 118	32 506	33 056	D.2.3. Total des Primes Nettes Vie

E. BUSINESS WRITTEN ABROAD — **E. OPERATIONS A L'ETRANGER**

E.1. Life — **E.1. Vie**

Label (English)	1992	1993	1994	1995	1996	1997	1998	1999	Label (French)
E.1.1. Gross Premiums									E.1.1. Primes Brutes
E.1.1.1. Direct Business / E.1.1.1. Total					12 744	14 326	15 082	18 585	E.1.1.1. Assurance Directe / E.1.1.1. Total
E.1.1.2. Reinsurance Accepted / E.1.1.2. Total					1 206	826	402	168	E.1.1.2. Réassurance Acceptée / E.1.1.2. Total
E.1.1.3. Total Gross Premiums	..	10 397	11 537	12 808	13 950	15 152	15 484	18 753	E.1.1.3. Total des Primes Brutes
E.1.2. Ceded Premiums / E.1.2. Total		994	715	1 494	241	714	554	698	E.1.2. Primes Cédées / E.1.2. Total
E.1.3. Net Written Premiums / E.1.3. Total	9 224	9 403	10 822	11 314	13 709	14 438	14 930	18 055	E.1.3. Primes Nettes Emises / E.1.3. Total

E.2. Non-Life — **E.2. Non-Vie**

Label (English)	1992	1993	1994	1995	1996	1997	1998	1999	Label (French)
E.2.1. Gross Premiums									E.2.1. Primes Brutes
E.2.1.1. Direct Business									E.2.1.1. Assurance Directe
E.2.1.1.1 Branches & Agencies							1 411	1 138	E.2.1.1.1. Succursales & Agences
E.2.1.1.2. Subsidiaries							12 402	10 845	E.2.1.1.2. Filliales
E.2.1.1. Total				15 039	14 406	13 333	13 813	11 983	E.2.1.1. Total
E.2.1.2. Reinsurance Accepted									E.2.1.2. Réassurance Acceptée
E.2.1.2.1. Branches & Agencies							71	70	E.2.1.2.1. Succursales & Agences
E.2.1.2.2. Subsidiaries							632	662	E.2.1.2.2. Filliales
E.2.1.2. Total				1 472	702	792	703	732	E.2.1.2. Total
E.2.1.3. Total									E.2.1.3. Total
E.2.1.3.1. Branches & Agencies							1 482	1 208	E.2.1.3.1. Succursales & Agences
E.2.1.3.2. Subsidiaries							13 034	11 507	E.2.1.3.2. Filliales
E.2.1.3. Total Gross Premiums	..	..	..	16 511	15 108	14 125	14 516	12 715	E.2.1.3. Total des Primes Brutes

English Label	1992	1993	1994	1995	1996	1997	1998	1999	French Label
E.2.2. Ceded Premiums									E.2.2. Primes Cédées
E.2.2.1. Branches & Agencies							194	99	E.2.2.1. Succursales & Agences
E.2.2.2. Subsidiaries							1 710	940	E.2.2.2. Filliales
E.2.2. Total	..	..	..	2 285	2 155	1 964	1 904	1 039	E.2.2. Total
E.2.3. Net Written Premiums									E.2.3. Primes Nettes Emises
E.2.3.1. Branches & Agencies	..	..	..	..	2 244	..	1 288	1 109	E.2.3.1. Succursales & Agences
E.2.3.2. Subsidiaries	..	..	..	..	10 709	..	11 324	10 567	E.2.3.2. Filliales
E.2.3. Total	10 421	11 918	11 705	14 226	12 953	12 161	12 612	11 676	E.2.3. Total

F. OUTSTANDING INVESTMENT BY DIRECT INSURANCE COMPANIES / F. ENCOURS DES PLACEMENTS DES ENTREPRISES D'ASSURANCES DIRECTES

F.1. Life / F.1. Vie

English Label	1992	1993	1994	1995	1996	1997	1998	1999	French Label
F.1.1. Real Estate									F.1.1. Immobilier
F.1.1.1. Domestic Companies	30 074	33 939	35 914	35 596	36 209	42 275	66 224	50 005	F.1.1.1. Entreprises Nationales
F.1.1.4. Domestic Investment	2 299	144	151	118	114	98	65 562	49 697	F.1.1.4. Placement dans le Pays
F.1.1.5. Foreign Investment							662	308	F.1.1.5. Placement à l' Etranger
F.1.1. Total	32 373	34 083	36 065	35 714	36 323	42 373	66 224	50 005	F.1.1. Total
F.1.2. Mortgage Loans									F.1.2. Prêts Hypothécaires
F.1.2.1. Domestic Companies	2 733	2 113	1 441	1 184	1 089	1 000	13 662	1 120	F.1.2.1. Entreprises Nationales
F.1.2.4. Domestic Investment	651	..	0	0	0	0	13 662	..	F.1.2.4. Placement dans le Pays
F.1.2.5. Foreign Investment								..	F.1.2.5. Placement à l' Etranger
F.1.2. Total	3 384	2 113	1 441	1 184	1 089	1 000	13 662	1 120	F.1.2. Total
F.1.3. Shares									F.1.3. Actions
F.1.3.1. Domestic Companies	149 962	204 035	189 019	237 345	266 320	333 354	427 351	536 717	F.1.3.1. Entreprises Nationales
F.1.3.4. Domestic Investment	7 502	46 359	45 127	57 141	59 371	68 763	358 975	466 235	F.1.3.4. Placement dans le Pays
F.1.3.5. Foreign Investment							68 376	70 482	F.1.3.5. Placement à l' Etranger
F.1.3. Total	157 464	250 394	234 146	294 486	325 691	402 117	427 351	536 717	F.1.3. Total
F.1.4. Bonds with Fixed Revenue									F.1.4. Obligations
F.1.4.1. Domestic Companies	68 518	97 441	86 630	107 976	119 282	149 349	301 495	222 030	F.1.4.1. Entreprises Nationales
F.1.4.4. Domestic Investment	11 050	11 602	9 939	11 602	10 561	13 136	265 316	189 426	F.1.4.4. Placement dans le Pays
F.1.4.5. Foreign Investment							36 179	32 604	F.1.4.5. Placement à l' Etranger
F.1.4. Total	79 568	109 043	96 569	119 578	129 843	162 485	301 495	222 030	F.1.4. Total
F.1.5. Loans other than Mortgage Loans									F.1.5. Prêts Autres qu'Hypothécaires
F.1.5.1. Domestic Companies	5 552	6 463	5 340	6 053	5 318	7 035	6 698	8 694	F.1.5.1. Entreprises Nationales
F.1.5.4. Domestic Investment	561	55	52	68	246	236	6 430	8 177	F.1.5.4. Placement dans le Pays
F.1.5.5. Foreign Investment							268	517	F.1.5.5. Placement à l' Etranger
F.1.5. Total	6 123	6 518	5 392	6 121	5 564	7 271	6 698	8 694	F.1.5. Total
F.1.6. Other Investments									F.1.6. Autres Placements
F.1.6.1. Domestic Companies	7 699	11 456	10 723	10 630	14 803	15 964	4 835	27 894	F.1.6.1. Entreprises Nationales
F.1.6.4. Domestic Investment	965	528	1 042	355	152	244	4 787	26 392	F.1.6.4. Placement dans le Pays
F.1.6.5. Foreign Investment							48	1 502	F.1.6.5. Placement à l' Etranger
F.1.6. Total	8 664	11 984	11 765	10 985	14 955	16 208	4 835	27 894	F.1.6. Total
F.1.7. Total									F.1.7. Total
F.1.7.1. Domestic Companies	264 548	355 447	329 067	398 784	443 021	548 977	820 265	846 460	F.1.7.1. Entreprises Nationales
F.1.7.4. Domestic Investment	23 028	58 688	56 311	69 284	70 444	82 477	714 732	741 047	F.1.7.4. Placement dans le Pays
F.1.7.5. Foreign Investment							105 533	105 413	F.1.7.5. Placement à l' Etranger
F.1.7. Total of Life Investments	287 576	414 135	385 378	468 068	513 465	631 454	820 265	846 460	F.1.7. Total des Placements Vie

F.2. Non-Life / F.2. Non-Vie

English Label	1992	1993	1994	1995	1996	1997	1998	1999	French Label
F.2.1. Real Estate									F.2.1. Immobilier
F.2.1.1. Domestic Companies	124	2 375	2 121	2 100	2 077	2 842	1 678	1 224	F.2.1.1. Entreprises Nationales
F.2.1.4. Domestic Investment	185	80	89	128	120	149	1 527	1 085	F.2.1.4. Placement dans le Pays
F.2.1.5. Foreign Investment							151	139	F.2.1.5. Placement à l' Etranger
F.2.1. Total	309	2 455	2 210	2 228	2 197	2 991	1 678	1 224	F.2.1. Total
F.2.2. Mortgage Loans									F.2.2. Prêts Hypothécaires
F.2.2.1. Domestic Companies	..	815	808	691	620	653	4 007	587	F.2.2.1. Entreprises Nationales
F.2.2.4. Domestic Investment	..	815	808	691	620	653	4 007	..	F.2.2.4. Placement dans le Pays
F.2.2. Total		815	808	691	620	653	4 007	587	F.2.2. Total

	1992	1993	1994	1995	1996	1997	1998	1999	
F.2.3. Shares									**F.2.3. Actions**
F.2.3.1. Domestic Companies	29 900	10 587	10 439	13 182	13 691	15 464	17 916	20 015	F.2.3.1. Entreprises Nationales
F.2.3.4. Domestic Investment	1 890	2 154	2 158	2 714	2 636	3 508	12 183	15 424	F.2.3.4. Placement dans le Pays
F.2.3.5. Foreign Investment							5 733	4 591	F.2.3.5. Placement à l' Etranger
F.2.3. Total	31 790	12 741	12 597	15 896	16 327	18 972	17 916	20 015	F.2.3. Total
F.2.4. Bonds with Fixed Revenue									**F.2.4. Obligations**
F.2.4.1. Domestic Companies	10 994	15 197	15 947	18 293	20 564	18 885	46 683	37 602	F.2.4.1. Entreprises Nationales
F.2.4.4. Domestic Investment	6 517	7 333	6 484	8 219	11 982	11 301	28 477	17 918	F.2.4.4. Placement dans le Pays
F.2.4.5. Foreign Investment							18 206	19 684	F.2.4.5. Placement à l' Etranger
F.2.4. Total	17 511	22 530	22 431	26 512	32 546	30 186	46 683	37 602	F.2.4. Total
F.2.5. Loans other than Mortgage Loans									**F.2.5. Prêts Autres qu'Hypothécaires**
F.2.5.1. Domestic Companies	55	415	510	549	963	634	590	1 383	F.2.5.1. Entreprises Nationales
F.2.5.4. Domestic Investment	4	3	3	97	7	98	519	823	F.2.5.4. Placement dans le Pays
F.2.5.5. Foreign Investment							71	560	F.2.5.5. Placement à l' Etranger
F.2.5. Total	59	418	513	646	970	732	590	1 383	F.2.5. Total
F.2.6. Other Investments									**F.2.6. Autres Placements**
F.2.6.1. Domestic Companies	325	672	800	870	1 133	2 598	2 347	3 658	F.2.6.1. Entreprises Nationales
F.2.6.4. Domestic Investment	23	28	32	164	88	45	2 324	1 317	F.2.6.4. Placement dans le Pays
F.2.6.5. Foreign Investment							23	2 341	F.2.6.5. Placement à l' Etranger
F.2.6. Total	348	700	832	1 034	1 221	2 643	2 347	3 658	F.2.6. Total
F.2.7. Total	41 398	30 061	30 625	35 685	39 048	41 076	73 221	64 469	**F.2.7. Total**
F.2.7.4. Domestic Investment	8 619	9 598	8 766	11 322	14 833	15 101	49 037	37 154	F.2.7.4. Placement dans le Pays
F.2.7.5. Foreign Investment	50 017	39 659	39 391	47 007	53 881	56 177	24 184	27 315	F.2.7.5. Placement à l' Etranger
F.2.7. Total of Non-Life Investments							73 221	64 469	F.2.7. Total des Placements Non-Vie
G. BREAKDOWN OF NON-LIFE PREMIUMS									**G. VENTILATIONS DES PRIMES NON-VIE**
G.1. Motor vehicle									**G.1. Assurance Automobile**
G.1.1. Direct Business									G.1.1. Assurances Directes
G.1.1.1. Gross Premiums	7 713	8 518	8 432	8 155	7 912	8 091	9 632	10 769	G.1.1.1. Primes Brutes
G.1.1.2. Ceded Premiums	506	528	660	914	674	751	883	:	G.1.1.2. Primes Cédées
G.1.1.3. Net Written Premiums	7 207	7 990	7 772	7 241	7 238	7 340	8 749	:	G.1.1.3. Primes Nettes Emises
G.1.3. Total									G.1.3. Total
G.1.3.1. Gross Premiums	7 713	8 518	8 432	8 155	7 912	8 091	9 632	10 769	G.1.3.1. Primes Brutes
G.1.3.2. Ceded Premiums	506	528	660	914	674	751	883	:	G.1.3.2. Primes Cédées
G.1.3.3. Net Written Premiums	7 207	7 990	7 772	7 241	7 238	7 340	8 749	:	G.1.3.3. Primes Nettes Emises
G.2. Marine, Aviation									**G.2. Marine, Aviation**
G.2.1. Direct Business									G.2.1. Assurances Directes
G.2.1.1. Gross Premiums	5 695	5 713	5 489	4 931	4 199	3 933	3 892	3 121	G.2.1.1. Primes Brutes
G.2.1.2. Ceded Premiums	3 230	2 642	2 314	1 844	1 276	1 066	1 549	:	G.2.1.2. Primes Cédées
G.2.1.3. Net Written Premiums	2 465	3 071	3 175	3 087	2 923	2 867	2 343	:	G.2.1.3. Primes Nettes Emises
G.2.2. Reinsurance Accepted									G.2.2. Réassurance Acceptée
G.2.2.1. Gross Premiums	2 769	2 114	1 455	1 443	1 183	1 093	1 108	932	G.2.2.1. Primes Brutes
G.2.2.2. Ceded Premiums	0	0	0		380	285	175	:	G.2.2.2. Primes Cédées
G.2.2.3. Net Written Premiums	2 769	2 114	1 455	1 443	803	808	933	:	G.2.2.3. Primes Nettes Emises
G.2.3. Total									G.2.3. Total
G.2.3.1. Gross Premiums	8 464	7 827	6 944	6 374	5 382	5 026	5 000	4 053	G.2.3.1. Primes Brutes
G.2.3.2. Ceded Premiums	3 230	2 642	2 314	1 844	1 656	1 351	1 724	:	G.2.3.2. Primes Cédées
G.2.3.3. Net Written Premiums	5 234	5 185	4 630	4 530	3 726	3 675	3 276	:	G.2.3.3. Primes Nettes Emises
G.4. Fire, Property Damages									**G.4. Incendie, Dommages aux Biens**
G.4.1. Direct Business									G.4.1. Assurances Directes
G.4.1.1. Gross Premiums	9 709	10 647	10 833	10 453	10 048	10 614	9 352	8 706	G.4.1.1. Primes Brutes
G.4.1.2. Ceded Premiums	2 175	2 638	2 546	2 338	2 278	2 581	1 771	:	G.4.1.2. Primes Cédées
G.4.1.3. Net Written Premiums	7 534	8 009	8 287	8 115	7 770	8 033	7 581	:	G.4.1.3. Primes Nettes Emises
G.4.3. Total									G.4.3. Total
G.4.3.1. Gross Premiums	9 709	10 647	10 833	10 453	10 048	10 614	9 352	8 706	G.4.3.1. Primes Brutes
G.4.3.2. Ceded Premiums	2 175	2 638	2 546	2 338	2 278	2 581	1 771	:	G.4.3.2. Primes Cédées
G.4.3.3. Net Written Premiums	7 534	8 009	8 287	8 115	7 770	8 033	7 581	:	G.4.3.3. Primes Nettes Emises

Monetary Unit: million pounds sterling — Unité monétaire : million de livres sterling

		1992	1993	1994	1995	1996	1997	1998	1999
G.5. Pecuniary Losses	**G.5. Pertes Pécunières**								
G.5.1. Direct Business	G.5.1. Assurances Directes								
G.5.1.1. Gross Premiums	G.5.1.1. Primes Brutes	2 471	2 699	3 323	3 419	3 687	3 629	3 612	3 950
G.5.1.2. Ceded Premiums	G.5.1.2. Primes Cédées	747	871	996	1 100	1 258	1 126	1 004	:
G.5.1.3. Net Written Premiums	G.5.1.3. Primes Nettes Emises	1 724	1 828	2 327	2 319	2 429	2 503	2 608	:
G.5.3. Total	G.5.3. Total								
G.5.3.1. Gross Premiums	G.5.3.1. Primes Brutes	2 471	2 699	3 323	3 419	3 687	3 629	3 612	3 950
G.5.3.2. Ceded Premiums	G.5.3.2. Primes Cédées	747	871	996	1 100	1 258	1 126	1 004	:
G.5.3.3. Net Written Premiums	G.5.3.3. Primes Nettes Emises	1 724	1 828	2 327	2 319	2 429	2 503	2 608	:
G.6. General Liability	**G.6. Responsabilité Générale**								
G.6.1. Direct Business	G.6.1. Assurances Directes								
G.6.1.1. Gross Premiums	G.6.1.1. Primes Brutes	3 693	4 048	3 976	4 034	3 981	3 923	3 527	3 674
G.6.1.2. Ceded Premiums	G.6.1.2. Primes Cédées	901	952	980	971	1 088	1 070	992	:
G.6.1.3. Net Written Premiums	G.6.1.3. Primes Nettes Emises	2 792	3 096	2 996	3 063	2 893	2 853	2 535	:
G.6.3. Total	G.6.3. Total								
G.6.3.1. Gross Premiums	G.6.3.1. Primes Brutes	3 693	4 048	3 976	4 034	3 981	3 923	3 527	3 674
G.6.3.2. Ceded Premiums	G.6.3.2. Primes Cédées	901	952	980	971	1 088	1 070	992	:
G.6.3.3. Net Written Premiums	G.6.3.3. Primes Nettes Emises	2 792	3 096	2 996	3 063	2 893	2 853	2 535	:
G.7. Accident, Health	**G.7. Accident, Santé**								
G.7.1. Direct Business	G.7.1. Assurances Directes								
G.7.1.1. Gross Premiums	G.7.1.1. Primes Brutes	3 299	3 484	3 594	4 024	4 041	4 289	4 424	4 653
G.7.1.2. Ceded Premiums	G.7.1.2. Primes Cédées	246	274	539	848	756	734	788	:
G.7.1.3. Net Written Premiums	G.7.1.3. Primes Nettes Emises	3 053	3 210	3 055	3 176	3 285	3 555	3 636	:
G.7.3. Total	G.7.3. Total								
G.7.3.1. Gross Premiums	G.7.3.1. Primes Brutes	3 299	3 484	3 594	4 024	4 041	4 289	4 424	4 653
G.7.3.2. Ceded Premiums	G.7.3.2. Primes Cédées	246	274	539	848	756	734	788	:
G.7.3.3. Net Written Premiums	G.7.3.3. Primes Nettes Emises	3 053	3 210	3 055	3 176	3 285	3 555	3 636	:
G.9. Treaty Reinsurance	**G.9. Réassurance Obligatoire**								
G.9.2. Reinsurance Accepted	G.9.2. Réassurance Acceptée								
G.9.2.1. Gross Premiums	G.9.2.1. Primes Brutes	5 407	5 258	4 428	4 434	4 489	3 921	5 402	5 593
G.9.2.2. Ceded Premiums	G.9.2.2. Primes Cédées	1 483	1 083	1 039	1 055	788	762	1 281	:
G.9.2.3. Net Written Premiums	G.9.2.3. Primes Nettes Emises	3 924	4 175	3 389	3 379	3 701	3 159	4 121	:
G.9.3. Total	G.9.3. Total								
G.9.3.1. Gross Premiums	G.9.3.1. Primes Brutes	5 407	5 258	4 428	4 434	4 489	3 921	5 402	5 593
G.9.3.2. Ceded Premiums	G.9.3.2. Primes Cédées	1 483	1 083	1 039	1 055	788	762	1 281	:
G.9.3.3. Net Written Premiums	G.9.3.3. Primes Nettes Emises	3 924	4 175	3 389	3 379	3 701	3 159	4 121	:
G.10. Total	**G.10. Total**								
G.10.1. Direct Business	G.10.1. Assurances Directes								
G.10.1.1. Gross Premiums	G.10.1.1. Primes Brutes	32 580	35 109	35 647	35 016	33 868	34 479	34 439	34 873
G.10.1.2. Ceded Premiums	G.10.1.2. Primes Cédées	7 805	7 905	8 035	8 015	7 330	7 328	6 987	:
G.10.1.3. Net Written Premiums	G.10.1.3. Primes Nettes Emises	24 775	27 204	27 612	27 001	26 538	27 151	27 452	:
G.10.2. Reinsurance Accepted	G.10.2. Réassurance Acceptée								
G.10.2.1. Gross Premiums	G.10.2.1. Primes Brutes	8 176	7 372	5 883	5 877	5 672	5 014	6 510	6 525
G.10.2.2. Ceded Premiums	G.10.2.2. Primes Cédées	1 483	1 083	1 039	1 055	1 168	1 047	1 456	:
G.10.2.3. Net Written Premiums	G.10.2.3. Primes Nettes Emises	6 693	6 289	4 844	4 822	4 504	3 967	5 054	:
G.10.3. Total	G.10.3. Total								
G.10.3.1. Gross Premiums	G.10.3.1. Primes Brutes	40 756	42 481	41 530	40 893	39 540	39 493	40 949	41 398
G.10.3.2. Ceded Premiums	G.10.3.2. Primes Cédées	9 288	8 988	9 074	9 070	8 498	8 375	8 443	8 342
G.10.3.3. Net Written Premiums	G.10.3.3. Primes Nettes Emises	31 468	33 493	32 456	31 823	31 042	31 118	32 506	33 056

UNITED KINGDOM   **ROYAUME UNI**

Monetary Unit: million pounds sterling   Unité monétaire : million de livres sterling

H. GROSS CLAIMS PAYMENTS — H. PAIEMENTS BRUTS DES SINISTRES

H.1. Life — H.1. Vie

	1992	1993	1994	1995	1996	1997	1998	1999	
H.1.1. Domestic Companies					41 136	45 504	51 749	56 665	H.1.1. Entreprises Nationales
H.1.2. (Foreign Controlled Companies)					8 375	6 794	11 161	13 579	H.1.2. (Entreprises Sous Contrôle Etranger)
H.1.3. Branches & Agencies of Foreign Cies					452	1 170	2 798	4 011	H.1.3. Succursales et Agences d'Ent. Etrangères
H.1. Total					41 588	46 674	54 547	60 676	H.1. Total

H.2. Non-Life — H.2. Non-Vie

	1992	1993	1994	1995	1996	1997	1998	1999	
H.2.1. Domestic Companies							31 347	24 117	H.2.1. Entreprises Nationales

I. GROSS OPERATING EXPENSES — I. DEPENSES BRUITES D'EXPLOITATION

I.1. Life — I.1. Vie

	1992	1993	1994	1995	1996	1997	1998	1999	
I.1.1. Domestic Companies					5 926	6 120	7 134	7 653	I.1.1. Entreprises Nationales
I.1.2. (Foreign Controlled Companies)					1 259	977	1 440	1 960	I.1.2. (Entreprises Sous Contrôle Etranger)
I.1.3. Branches & Agencies of Foreign Cies					17	4	153	172	I.1.3. Succursales et Agences d'Ent. Etrangères
I.1. Total					5 943	6 124	7 287	7 825	I.1. Total des Primes Nettes Vie

I.2. Non-Life — I.2. Non-Vie

	1992	1993	1994	1995	1996	1997	1998	1999	
I.2.1. Domestic Companies							10 719	9 863	I.2.1. Entreprises Nationales

J. COMMISSIONS — J. COMMISSIONS

J.1. Life — J.1. Vie

	1992	1993	1994	1995	1996	1997	1998	1999	
J.1.1. Direct Business									J.1.1. Assurance directe
J.1.1.1. Domestic Companies					2 740	3 077	3 139	3 581	J.1.1.1. Entreprises Nationales
J.1.1.2. (Foreign Controlled Companies)					636	729	800	1 002	J.1.1.2. (Entreprises Sous Contrôle Etranger)
J.1.1.3. Branches & Agencies of Foreign Cies					9	23	39	60	J.1.1.3. Succursales et Agences d'Ent. Etrangères
J.1.1. Total					2 749	3 100	3 178	3 641	J.1.1. Total
J.1.2. Reinsurance Accepted									J.1.2. Réassurances acceptées
J.1.2.1. Domestic Companies					56	63	69	123	J.1.2.1. Entreprises Nationales
J.1.2.2. (Foreign Controlled Companies)					29	63	69	123	J.1.2.2. (Entreprises Sous Contrôle Etranger)
J.1.2.3. Branches & Agencies of Foreign Cies					6	5	5	6	J.1.2.3. Succursales et Agences d'Ent. Etrangères
J.1.2. Total					62	68	74	129	J.1.2. Total
J.1.3. Total									J.1.3. Total
J.1.3.1. Domestic Companies					2 796	3 140	3 208	3 704	J.1.3.1. Entreprises Nationales
J.1.3.2. (Foreign Controlled Companies)					665	792	869	1 125	J.1.3.2. (Entreprises Sous Contrôle Etranger)
J.1.3.3. Branches & Agencies of Foreign Cies					15	28	44	66	J.1.3.3. Succursales et Agences d'Ent. Etrangères
J.1.3. Total of Life Net Premiums					2 811	3 168	3 252	3 770	J.1.3. Total

UNITED STATES / ETATS-UNIS

Monetary Unit: million US dollars — Unité monétaire : million de dollars des EU

A. NUMBER OF COMPANIES IN THE REPORTING COUNTRY / A. NOMBRE D'ENTREPRISES DANS LE PAYS DECLARANT

	1992	1993	1994	1995	1996	1997	1998	1999
A.1. Life / A.1. Vie								
A.1.1. Domestic Companies / A.1.1. Entreprises Nationales	1 667	1 608	1 556	1 515	1 488	1 442	1 390	1 320
A.1.2. (Foreign Controlled Companies) / A.1.2. (Entreprises Sous Contrôle Etranger)	109	113	105	93	87	76	95	109
A.1.3. Branches & Agencies of Foreign Cies / A.1.3. Succursales et Agences d'Ent. Etrangères	11	11	10	9	8	6	6	0
A.1. All Companies / A.1. Ensemble des Entreprises	1 678	1 619	1 566	1 524	1 496	1 448	1 396	1 320
A.2. Non-Life / A.2. Non-Vie								
A.2.1. Domestic Companies / A.2.1. Entreprises Nationales	2 675	2 686	2 724	2 745	3 255	3 342	3 132	3 291
A.2.2. (Foreign Controlled Companies) / A.2.2. (Entreprises Sous Contrôle Etranger)	270	270	244	243	260	249	274	334
A.2.3. Branches & Agencies of Foreign Cies / A.2.3. Succursales et Agences d'Ent. Etrangères	19	19	21	20	21	21	19	18
A.2. All Companies / A.2. Ensemble des Entreprises	2 694	2 705	2 745	2 765	3 276	3 363	3 151	3 309
A.4. Reassurance / A.4. Réassurance								
A.4.1. Domestic Companies / A.4.1. Entreprises Nationales	450	470	419	400	381	297	267	276
A.4.2. (Foreign Controlled Companies) / A.4.2. (Entreprises Sous Contrôle Etranger)	51	55	48	44	44	39	48	55
A.4.3. Branches & Agencies of Foreign Cies / A.4.3. Succursales et Agences d'Ent. Etrangères	15	15	11	11	9	6	4	2
A.4. All Companies / A.4. Ensemble des Entreprises	465	485	430	411	390	303	271	278
A.5. Total / A.5. Total								
A.5.1. Domestic Companies / A.5.1. Entreprises Nationales	4 792	4 764	4 699	4 660	5 124	5 081	4 789	4 887
A.5.2. (Foreign Controlled Companies) / A.5.2. (Entreprises Sous Contrôle Etranger)	430	438	397	380	391	364	417	498
A.5.3. Branches & Agencies of Foreign Cies / A.5.3. Succursales et Agences d'Ent. Etrangères	45	45	42	40	38	33	29	20
A.5. All Insurance Companies / A.5. Ensemble des Entreprises d'Assurances	4 837	4 809	4 741	4 700	5 162	5 114	4 818	4 907

B. NUMBER OF EMPLOYEES / B. NOMBRE D'EMPLOYES

	1992	1993	1994	1995	1996	1997	1998	1999
B.1. Insurance Companies / B.1. Entreprises d'Assurances	1 480 000	1 518 400	1 550 700	1 541 200	..	..	..	..
B.2. Intermediaries / B.2. Intermediaires	652 200	662 100	686 400	696 800	..	..	..	..
B. Total / B. Total	2 132 200	2 180 500	2 237 100	2 238 000	..	..	..	..

C. BUSINESS WRITTEN IN THE REPORTING COUNTRY / C. OPERATIONS CONCLUES DANS LE PAYS DECLARANT

	1992	1993	1994	1995	1996	1997	1998	1999
C.1. Life / C.1. Vie								
C.1.1. Gross Premiums / C.1.1. Primes Brutes								
C.1.1.1. Direct Business / C.1.1.1. Assurances Directes								
C.1.1.1.1. Domestic Companies / C.1.1.1.1. Entreprises Nationales	218 372	241 566	262 276	270 315	291 646	319 434	357 552	461 802
C.1.1.1.2. (Foreign Controlled Companies) / C.1.1.1.2. (Entreprises Sous Contrôle Etranger)	22 008	28 940	32 294	31 269	36 625	37 665	60 002	86 270
C.1.1.1.3. Branches & Agencies of Foreign Cies / C.1.1.1.3. Succursales et Agences d'Ent. Etrangères	4 701	4 571	2 533	2 534	2 455	1 573	1 691	0
C.1.1.1. Total / C.1.1.1. Total	223 073	246 137	264 809	272 849	294 101	321 007	359 243	461 802
C.1.1.2. Reinsurance Accepted / C.1.1.2. Réassurance Acceptée								
C.1.1.2.1. Domestic Companies / C.1.1.2.1. Entreprises Nationales	16 659	19 709	12 293	20 521	20 607	16 928	41 094	37 826
C.1.1.2.2. (Foreign Controlled Companies) / C.1.1.2.2. (Entreprises Sous Contrôle Etranger)	1 353	5 752	1 780	2 445	5 335	4 236	7 004	12 586
C.1.1.2.3. Branches & Agencies of Foreign Cies / C.1.1.2.3. Succursales et Agences d'Ent. Etrangères	1 172	1 180	642	983	830	408	351	0
C.1.1.2. Total / C.1.1.2. Total	17 831	20 889	12 935	21 504	21 437	17 336	41 445	37 826
C.1.1.3. Total / C.1.1.3. Total								
C.1.1.3.1. Domestic Companies / C.1.1.3.1. Entreprises Nationales	235 031	261 275	274 569	290 836	312 253	336 362	398 646	499 628
C.1.1.3.2. (Foreign Controlled Companies) / C.1.1.3.2. (Entreprises Sous Contrôle Etranger)	23 361	34 692	34 074	33 714	41 960	41 901	67 006	98 856
C.1.1.3.3. Branches & Agencies of Foreign Cies / C.1.1.3.3. Succursales et Agences d'Ent. Etrangères	5 873	5 751	3 175	3 517	3 285	1 981	2 042	0
C.1.1.3. Total Gross Premiums / C.1.1.3. Total des Primes Brutes	240 904	267 026	277 744	294 353	315 538	338 343	400 688	499 628
C.1.2. Ceded Premiums / C.1.2. Primes Cédées								
C.1.2.1. Domestic Companies / C.1.2.1. Entreprises Nationales	16 654	19 985	14 266	25 485	23 319	14 914	33 451	43 326
C.1.2.2. (Foreign Controlled Companies) / C.1.2.2. (Entreprises Sous Contrôle Etranger)	3 544	5 353	3 762	2 572	2 159	1 768	5 604	12 072
C.1.2.3. Branches & Agencies of Foreign Cies / C.1.2.3. Succursales et Agences d'Ent. Etrangères	500	558	225	226	188	103	943	0
C.1.2. Total / C.1.2. Total	17 154	20 543	14 491	25 711	23 507	15 017	34 394	43 326
C.1.3. Net Written Premiums / C.1.3. Primes Nettes Emises								
C.1.3.1. Domestic Companies / C.1.3.1. Entreprises Nationales	218 377	241 290	260 303	265 351	288 934	321 448	365 195	456 302
C.1.3.2. (Foreign Controlled Companies) / C.1.3.2. (Entreprises Sous Contrôle Etranger)	19 817	29 339	30 312	31 142	39 801	40 133	61 402	86 784
C.1.3.3. Branches & Agencies of Foreign Cies / C.1.3.3. Succursales et Agences d'Ent. Etrangères	5 373	5 193	2 950	3 291	3 097	1 878	1 099	0
C.1.3. Total / C.1.3. Total	223 750	246 483	263 253	268 642	292 031	323 326	366 293	456 302

Monetary Unit: million US dollars   Unité monétaire : million de dollars des EU

C.2. Non-Life / C.2. Non-Vie

	1992	1993	1994	1995	1996	1997	1998	1999
C.2.1. Gross premiums / C.2.1. Primes Brutes								
C.2.1.1. Direct Business / C.2.1.1. Assurances Directes								
C.2.1.1.1. Domestic Companies / C.2.1.1.1. Entreprises Nationales	375 017	395 702	409 146	419 913	430 809	506 719	541 845	504 301
C.2.1.1.2. (Foreign Controlled Companies) / C.2.1.1.2. (Entreprises Sous Contrôle Etranger)	31 667	34 268	33 189	33 440	36 324	34 355	36 788	41 401
C.2.1.1.3. Branches & Agencies of Foreign Cies / C.2.1.1.3. Succursales et Agences d'Ent. Etrangères	1 658	1 934	1 971	2 726	2 538	2 376	2 175	3 049
C.2.1.1. Total	376 675	397 636	411 117	422 639	433 347	509 095	544 019	507 350
C.2.1.2. Reinsurance Accepted / C.2.1.2. Réassurance Acceptée								
C.2.1.2.1. Domestic Companies / C.2.1.2.1. Entreprises Nationales	34 536	37 900	40 949	44 407	44 219	43 028	49 138	47 852
C.2.1.2.2. (Foreign Controlled Companies) / C.2.1.2.2. (Entreprises Sous Contrôle Etranger)	6 192	6 873	7 485	8 525	10 560	10 439	11 431	12 960
C.2.1.2.3. Branches & Agencies of Foreign Cies / C.2.1.2.3. Succursales et Agences d'Ent. Etrangères	1 956	2 446	1 863	2 240	2 011	1 228	1 116	215
C.2.1.2. Total	36 492	40 346	42 812	46 647	46 230	44 256	50 254	48 067
C.2.1.3. Total								
C.2.1.3.1. Domestic Companies / C.2.1.3.1. Entreprises Nationales	409 553	433 602	450 095	464 320	475 028	549 747	590 983	552 153
C.2.1.3.2. (Foreign Controlled Companies) / C.2.1.3.2. (Entreprises Sous Contrôle Etranger)	37 859	41 141	40 674	41 965	46 904	44 794	48 219	54 361
C.2.1.3.3. Branches & Agencies of Foreign Cies / C.2.1.3.3. Succursales et Agences d'Ent. Etrangères	3 614	4 380	3 834	4 966	4 549	3 604	3 291	3 264
C.2.1.3. Total Gross Premiums / C.2.1.3. Total des Primes Brutes	413 167	437 982	453 929	469 286	479 577	553 351	594 274	555 417
C.2.2. Ceded Premiums / C.2.2. Primes Cédées								
C.2.2.1. Domestic Companies / C.2.2.1. Entreprises Nationales	46 873	49 228	53 782	56 537	55 594	54 226	62 783	61 994
C.2.2.2. (Foreign Controlled Companies) / C.2.2.2. (Entreprises Sous Contrôle Etranger)	6 213	6 763	7 270	7 963	7 560	7 560	9 254	12 451
C.2.2.3. Branches & Agencies of Foreign Cies / C.2.2.3. Succursales et Agences d'Ent. Etrangères	1 220	1 430	1 492	2 130	1 615	1 174	1 088	1 386
C.2.2. Total	48 093	50 658	55 274	58 667	57 209	55 400	63 871	63 380
C.2.3. Net Written Premiums / C.2.3. Primes Nettes Emises								
C.2.3.1. Domestic Companies / C.2.3.1. Entreprises Nationales	362 680	384 374	396 313	407 783	419 434	495 521	528 200	490 159
C.2.3.2. (Foreign Controlled Companies) / C.2.3.2. (Entreprises Sous Contrôle Etranger)	31 646	34 378	33 404	34 002	39 389	37 234	38 965	41 910
C.2.3.3. Branches & Agencies of Foreign Cies / C.2.3.3. Succursales et Agences d'Ent. Etrangères	2 394	2 950	2 342	2 836	2 934	2 430	2 203	1 878
C.2.3. Total	365 074	387 324	398 655	410 619	422 368	497 951	530 403	492 037

C.3. Total

	1992	1993	1994	1995	1996	1997	1998	1999
C.3.1. Gross Premiums / C.3.1. Primes Brutes								
C.3.1.1. Direct Business / C.3.1.1. Assurances Directes								
C.3.1.1.1. Domestic Companies / C.3.1.1.1. Entreprises Nationales	593 389	637 268	671 422	690 228	722 455	826 153	899 396	966 103
C.3.1.1.2. (Foreign Controlled Companies) / C.3.1.1.2. (Entreprises Sous Contrôle Etranger)	53 675	63 208	65 483	64 709	72 949	72 020	96 790	127 671
C.3.1.1.3. Branches & Agencies of Foreign Cies / C.3.1.1.3. Succursales et Agences d'Ent. Etrangères	6 359	6 505	4 504	5 260	4 993	3 949	3 866	3 049
C.3.1.1. Total	599 748	643 773	675 926	695 488	727 448	830 102	903 262	969 152
C.3.1.2. Reinsurance Accepted / C.3.1.2. Réassurance Acceptée								
C.3.1.2.1. Domestic Companies / C.3.1.2.1. Entreprises Nationales	51 195	57 609	53 242	64 928	64 826	59 956	90 232	85 678
C.3.1.2.2. (Foreign Controlled Companies) / C.3.1.2.2. (Entreprises Sous Contrôle Etranger)	7 545	12 625	9 265	10 970	15 915	14 675	18 435	25 546
C.3.1.2.3. Branches & Agencies of Foreign Cies / C.3.1.2.3. Succursales et Agences d'Ent. Etrangères	3 128	3 626	2 505	3 223	2 841	1 636	1 467	215
C.3.1.2. Total	54 323	61 235	55 747	68 151	67 667	61 592	91 699	85 893
C.3.1.3. Total								
C.3.1.3.1. Domestic Companies / C.3.1.3.1. Entreprises Nationales	644 584	694 877	724 664	755 156	787 281	886 109	989 629	1 051 781
C.3.1.3.2. (Foreign Controlled Companies) / C.3.1.3.2. (Entreprises Sous Contrôle Etranger)	61 220	75 833	74 748	75 679	88 864	86 695	115 225	153 217
C.3.1.3.3. Branches & Agencies of Foreign Cies / C.3.1.3.3. Succursales et Agences d'Ent. Etrangères	9 487	10 131	7 009	8 483	7 834	5 585	5 333	3 264
C.3.1.3. Total Gross Premiums / C.3.1.3. Total des Primes Brutes	654 071	705 008	731 673	763 639	795 115	891 694	994 961	1 055 045
C.3.2. Ceded Premiums / C.3.2. Primes Cédées								
C.3.2.1. Domestic Companies / C.3.2.1. Entreprises Nationales	63 527	69 213	68 048	82 022	78 913	69 140	96 234	105 320
C.3.2.2. (Foreign Controlled Companies) / C.3.2.2. (Entreprises Sous Contrôle Etranger)	9 757	12 116	11 032	10 535	9 674	9 328	14 858	24 523
C.3.2.3. Branches & Agencies of Foreign Cies / C.3.2.3. Succursales et Agences d'Ent. Etrangères	1 720	1 988	1 717	2 356	1 803	1 277	2 031	1 386
C.3.2. Total	65 247	71 201	69 765	84 378	80 716	70 417	98 265	106 706
C.3.3. Net Written Premiums / C.3.3. Primes Nettes Emises								
C.3.3.1. Domestic Companies / C.3.3.1. Entreprises Nationales	581 057	625 664	656 616	673 134	708 368	816 969	893 395	946 461
C.3.3.2. (Foreign Controlled Companies) / C.3.3.2. (Entreprises Sous Contrôle Etranger)	51 463	63 717	63 716	65 144	79 190	77 367	100 367	128 694
C.3.3.3. Branches & Agencies of Foreign Cies / C.3.3.3. Succursales et Agences d'Ent. Etrangères	7 767	8 143	5 292	6 127	6 031	4 308	3 301	1 878
C.3.3. Total	588 824	633 807	661 908	679 261	714 399	821 277	896 696	948 339

242

Monetary Unit: million US dollars   Unité monétaire : million de dollars des EU

F. OUTSTANDING INVESTMENT BY DIRECT INSURANCE COMPANIES
F. ENCOURS DES PLACEMENTS DES ENTREPRISES D'ASSURANCES DIRECTES

F.1. Life — F.1. Vie

	1992	1993	1994	1995	1996	1997	1998	1999
F.1.1. Real Estate — Immobilier								
F.1.1.1. Domestic Companies — Entreprises Nationales	40 232	43 856	43 087	41 632	38 452	33 850	27 957	29 012
F.1.1.2. (Foreign Controlled Companies)	3 100	4 321	4 386	3 739	3 815	1 403	2 801	3 159
F.1.1.3. Branches & Agencies of Foreign Cies	1 515	1 122	890	360	375	416	409	0
F.1.1. Total	..	44 978	43 977	41 992	38 827	34 266	28 366	29 012
F.1.2. Mortgage Loans — Prêts Hypothécaires								
F.1.2.1. Domestic Companies — Entreprises Nationales	244 172	226 859	218 797	216 614	212 680	210 102	216 212	265 626
F.1.2.2. (Foreign Controlled Companies)	19 526	22 136	20 282	19 418	19 602	17 953	27 029	32 259
F.1.2.3. Branches & Agencies of Foreign Cies	10 574	8 023	4 120	3 708	3 283	2 865	2 788	0
F.1.2. Total	..	234 882	222 917	220 322	215 964	212 967	219 000	265 626
F.1.3. Shares — Actions								
F.1.3.1. Domestic Companies — Entreprises Nationales	73 664	80 885	81 920	91 250	101 954	118 922	127 497	162 549
F.1.3.2. (Foreign Controlled Companies)	6 944	8 858	8 232	8 942	10 724	10 088	14 124	22 508
F.1.3.3. Branches & Agencies of Foreign Cies	2 083	3 193	2 500	2 926	1 010	1 434	843	0
F.1.3.4. Domestic Investment — Placement dans le Pays	..	..	..	90 309	98 138	114 004	..	..
F.1.3.5. Foreign Investment — Placement à l'Etranger	..	..	..	3 867	4 826	6 352	..	..
F.1.3. Total	..	84 078	84 420	94 176	102 964	120 356	128 341	162 549
F.1.4. Bonds with Fixed Revenue — Obligations								
F.1.4.1. Domestic Companies — Entreprises Nationales	892 553	1 010 262	1 086 740	1 171 598	1 238 683	1 300 704	1 349 667	1 592 762
F.1.4.2. (Foreign Controlled Companies)	76 702	99 813	107 060	116 806	133 523	122 291	164 352	202 192
F.1.4.3. Branches & Agencies of Foreign Cies	13 875	9 596	7 588	8 684	5 755	5 647	5 840	0
F.1.4.4. Domestic Investment — Placement dans le Pays	..	..	..	1 080 481	1 109 981	1 138 809	..	..
F.1.4.5. Foreign Investment — Placement à l'Etranger	..	..	..	99 801	134 457	167 542	..	..
F.1.4. Total	..	1 019 858	1 094 328	1 180 282	1 244 438	1 306 351	1 355 507	1 592 762
F.1.5. Loans other than Mortgage Loans — Prêts Autres qu'Hypothécaires								
F.1.5.1. Domestic Companies — Entreprises Nationales	70 059	76 376	87 824	96 685	101 085	103 954	104 241	111 746
F.1.5.2. (Foreign Controlled Companies)	7 112	8 521	8 997	9 605	11 776	9 114	13 194	14 045
F.1.5.3. Branches & Agencies of Foreign Cies	1 853	2 174	1 623	1 741	614	628	520	0
F.1.5. Total	..	78 550	89 447	98 426	101 699	104 582	104 760	111 746
F.1.6. Other Investments — Autres Placements								
F.1.6.1. Domestic Companies — Entreprises Nationales	73 054	69 860	75 092	70 713	67 963	90 383	98 843	121 524
F.1.6.2. (Foreign Controlled Companies)	7 611	8 523	7 643	6 810	7 492	7 969	13 261	15 128
F.1.6.3. Branches & Agencies of Foreign Cies	1 711	1 727	1 129	1 214	621	484	583	0
F.1.6. Total	..	71 587	76 221	71 927	68 584	90 867	99 426	121 524
F.1.7. Total								
F.1.7.1. Domestic Companies — Entreprises Nationales	1 393 734	1 508 098	1 593 460	1 688 491	1 760 818	1 857 915	1 924 418	2 283 219
F.1.7.2. (Foreign Controlled Companies)	120 994	152 172	156 599	165 319	186 932	168 818	234 761	289 291
F.1.7.3. Branches & Agencies of Foreign Cies	31 611	25 835	17 850	18 633	11 658	11 474	10 983	0
F.1.7. Total of Life Investments — Total des Placements Vie	..	1 533 933	1 611 310	1 707 125	1 772 476	1 869 389	1 935 400	2 283 219

F.2. Non-Life — F.2. Non-Vie

	1992	1993	1994	1995	1996	1997	1998	1999
F.2.1. Real Estate — Immobilier								
F.2.1.1. Domestic Companies — Entreprises Nationales	9 576	10 213	10 723	10 411	10 918	10 710	11 965	11 336
F.2.1.2. (Foreign Controlled Companies)	473	482	481	495	579	498	485	456
F.2.1.3. Branches & Agencies of Foreign Cies	96	93	91	89	87	85	4	2
F.2.1. Total	..	10 306	10 814	10 500	11 005	10 795	11 969	11 338

Monetary Unit: million US dollars — Unité monétaire : million de dollars des EU

	1992	1993	1994	1995	1996	1997	1998	1999
F.2.2. Mortgage Loans — Prêts Hypothécaires								
F.2.2.1. Domestic Companies — Entreprises Nationales	5 848	4 704	3 921	2 962	2 615	2 368	2 224	2 551
F.2.2.2. (Foreign Controlled Companies) — (Entreprises Sous Contrôle Etranger)	64	70	68	138	182	246	155	201
F.2.2. Total	..	4 704	3 921	2 962	2 615	2 368	2 224	2 551
F.2.3. Shares — Actions								
F.2.3.1. Domestic Companies — Entreprises Nationales	105 093	112 483	116 069	137 576	164 476	198 482	289 130	324 211
F.2.3.2. (Foreign Controlled Companies) — (Entreprises Sous Contrôle Etranger)	10 739	12 825	12 008	14 467	16 733	22 477	25 981	27 285
F.2.3.3. Branches & Agencies of Foreign Cies — Succursales et Agences d'Ent. Etrangères	1 003	1 151	1 020	943	901	1 069	1 440	4 518
F.2.3.4. Domestic Investment — Placement dans le Pays	..	..	..	133 994	159 749	192 217	..	..
F.2.3.5. Foreign Investment — Placement à l'Etranger	..	..	..	4 525	5 628	7 334	..	..
F.2.3. Total	..	113 634	117 089	138 519	165 377	199 551	290 571	328 729
F.2.4. Bonds with Fixed Revenue — Obligations								
F.2.4.1. Domestic Companies — Entreprises Nationales	411 961	449 001	471 081	495 560	516 841	553 867	561 126	620 866
F.2.4.2. (Foreign Controlled Companies) — (Entreprises Sous Contrôle Etranger)	66 136	48 756	44 620	46 118	54 911	56 202	60 486	66 190
F.2.4.3. Branches & Agencies of Foreign Cies — Succursales et Agences d'Ent. Etrangères	5 098	5 606	5 724	5 960	5 980	4 867	5 088	8 847
F.2.4.4. Domestic Investment — Placement dans le Pays	..	..	..	481 776	501 534	534 921	..	..
F.2.4.5. Foreign Investment — Placement à l'Etranger	..	..	..	19 744	21 287	23 813	..	..
F.2.4. Total	..	454 607	476 805	501 520	522 821	558 734	566 214	629 713
F.2.5. Loans other than Mortgage Loans — Prêts Autres qu'Hypothécaires								
F.2.5.1. Domestic Companies — Entreprises Nationales	218	109	434	984	182	154	..	0
F.2.5.2. (Foreign Controlled Companies) — (Entreprises Sous Contrôle Etranger)	4	8	13	7	7	9	..	0
F.2.5. Total	..	109	434	984	182	154	..	0
F.2.6. Other Investments — Autres Placements								
F.2.6.1. Domestic Companies — Entreprises Nationales	51 979	50 188	47 315	56 775	57 079	67 798	80 353	78 162
F.2.6.2. (Foreign Controlled Companies) — (Entreprises Sous Contrôle Etranger)	4 293	4 505	5 115	5 641	6 825	6 437	7 412	6 911
F.2.6.3. Branches & Agencies of Foreign Cies — Succursales et Agences d'Ent. Etrangères	610	453	486	441	967	1 001	951	725
F.2.6. Total	..	50 641	47 801	57 216	58 046	68 799	81 304	78 887
F.2.7. Total								
F.2.7.1. Domestic Companies — Entreprises Nationales	584 675	626 698	649 543	704 268	752 111	833 379	944 798	1 037 126
F.2.7.2. (Foreign Controlled Companies) — (Entreprises Sous Contrôle Etranger)	59 709	66 646	62 306	66 867	79 238	85 839	94 519	101 043
F.2.7.3. Branches & Agencies of Foreign Cies — Succursales et Agences d'Ent. Etrangères	6 806	7 303	7 321	7 433	7 935	7 022	7 484	14 092
F.2.7. Total of Non-Life Investments — Total des Placements Non-Vie	..	634 001	656 864	711 701	760 046	840 401	952 282	1 051 218

G. BREAKDOWN OF NON-LIFE PREMIUMS — G. VENTILATIONS DES PRIMES NON-VIE

	1992	1993	1994	1995	1996	1997	1998	1999
G.1. Motor vehicle — Assurance Automobile								
G.1.1. Direct Business — Assurances Directes								
G.1.1.1. Gross Premiums — Primes Brutes	112 155	..	123 112	129 563	130 039	135 916	138 391	140 451
G.1.1.2. Ceded Premiums — Primes Cédées	7 670	8 055	9 738	10 595	..	..	..	..
G.1.1.3. Net Written Premiums — Primes Nettes Emises	104 485	109 957	113 374	118 968	130 039	..	..	..
G.1.2. Reinsurance Accepted — Réassurance Acceptée								
G.1.2.1. Gross Premiums — Primes Brutes	1 019	931	1 150	1 200	6 495	6 575	6 230	7 623
G.1.2.2. Ceded Premiums — Primes Cédées	117	94	133	131	..	..	..	..
G.1.2.3. Net Written Premiums — Primes Nettes Emises	902	837	1 017	1 069	6 495	..	..	..
G.1.3. Total								
G.1.3.1. Gross Premiums — Primes Brutes	113 174	118 943	124 262	130 763	136 534	142 491	144 621	148 074
G.1.3.2. Ceded Premiums — Primes Cédées	7 787	8 149	9 871	10 726	10 217	9 887	8 597	10 167
G.1.3.3. Net Written Premiums — Primes Nettes Emises	105 387	110 794	114 391	120 037	126 317	132 604	136 024	137 907
G.2. Marine, Aviation								
G.2.1. Direct Business — Assurances Directes								
G.2.1.1. Gross Premiums — Primes Brutes	3 402	4 115	4 644	4 858	3 660	3 611	3 538	3 426
G.2.1.2. Ceded Premiums — Primes Cédées	1 623	1 873	1 958	2 025	..	..	..	..
G.2.1.3. Net Written Premiums — Primes Nettes Emises	1 779	2 242	2 686	2 833	3 660	..	..	..
G.2.2. Reinsurance Accepted — Réassurance Acceptée								
G.2.2.1. Gross Premiums — Primes Brutes	116	104	149	150	1 479	1 325	1 241	1 269
G.2.2.2. Ceded Premiums — Primes Cédées	15	14	13	14	..	..	..	..
G.2.2.3. Net Written Premiums — Primes Nettes Emises	101	90	136	136	1 479	..	..	..
G.2.3. Total								
G.2.3.1. Gross Premiums — Primes Brutes	3 518	4 219	4 793	5 008	5 139	4 936	4 779	4 695
G.2.3.2. Ceded Premiums — Primes Cédées	1 638	1 887	1 971	2 039	2 092	2 000	1 942	1 993
G.2.3.3. Net Written Premiums — Primes Nettes Emises	1 880	2 332	2 822	2 969	3 047	2 936	2 837	2 702

UNITED STATES

Monetary Unit: million US dollars

	1992	1993	1994	1995	1996	1997	1998	1999
G.3. Freight								
G.3.1. Direct Business								
G.3.1.1. Gross Premiums	6 317	6 834	7 496	7 988	7 297	7 317	7 365	8 063
G.3.1.2. Ceded Premiums	2 016	2 219	2 475	2 724	:	:	:	:
G.3.1.3. Net Written Premiums	4 301	4 615	5 021	5 264	7 297	:	:	:
G.3.2. Reinsurance Accepted								
G.3.2.1. Gross Premiums	174	146	118	124	877	788	697	972
G.3.2.2. Ceded Premiums	26	16	11	15	:	:	:	:
G.3.2.3. Net Written Premiums	148	130	107	109	877	:	:	:
G.3.3. Total								
G.3.3.1. Gross Premiums	6 491	6 980	7 614	8 112	8 174	8 105	8 063	9 035
G.3.3.2. Ceded Premiums	2 042	2 235	2 486	2 739	2 384	2 273	2 227	2 699
G.3.3.3. Net Written Premiums	4 449	4 745	5 128	5 373	5 790	5 832	5 836	6 336
G.4. Fire, Property Damages								
G.4.1. Direct Business								
G.4.1.1. Gross Premiums	33 742	36 523	40 374	42 966	41 292	43 031	44 914	47 083
G.4.1.2. Ceded Premiums	5 613	6 664	7 854	8 757	:	:	:	:
G.4.1.3. Net Written Premiums	28 129	29 859	32 520	34 209	41 292	:	:	:
G.4.2. Reinsurance Accepted								
G.4.2.1. Gross Premiums	1 046	1 271	1 359	1 282	4 819	4 362	4 779	5 211
G.4.2.2. Ceded Premiums	327	297	386	464	:	:	:	:
G.4.2.3. Net Written Premiums	719	974	973	818	4 819	:	:	:
G.4.3. Total								
G.4.3.1. Gross Premiums	34 788	37 794	41 733	44 248	46 111	47 393	49 694	52 294
G.4.3.2. Ceded Premiums	5 940	6 961	8 240	9 221	8 764	9 244	9 668	10 291
G.4.3.3. Net Written Premiums	28 848	30 833	33 493	35 027	37 347	38 149	40 026	42 003
G.5. Pecuniary Losses								
G.5.1. Direct Business								
G.5.1.1. Gross Premiums	6 391	7 264	7 448	7 969	8 104	8 707	9 349	10 801
G.5.1.2. Ceded Premiums	1 154	1 289	1 253	1 303	:	:	:	:
G.5.1.3. Net Written Premiums	5 237	5 975	6 195	6 666	8 104	:	:	:
G.5.2. Reinsurance Accepted								
G.5.2.1. Gross Premiums	274	280	299	336	1 057	1 054	983	1 067
G.5.2.2. Ceded Premiums	44	29	26	76	:	:	:	:
G.5.2.3. Net Written Premiums	230	251	273	260	1 057	:	:	:
G.5.3. Total								
G.5.3.1. Gross Premiums	6 665	7 544	7 747	8 305	9 161	9 761	10 332	11 868
G.5.3.2. Ceded Premiums	1 198	1 318	1 279	1 379	1 378	1 522	1 550	2 380
G.5.3.3. Net Written Premiums	5 467	6 226	6 468	6 926	7 783	8 239	8 782	9 488
G.6. General Liability								
G.6.1. Direct Business								
G.6.1.1. Gross Premiums	19 899	21 384	22 257	23 307	22 010	21 893	22 188	22 268
G.6.1.2. Ceded Premiums	3 190	3 496	3 760	3 665	:	:	:	:
G.6.1.3. Net Written Premiums	16 709	17 888	18 497	19 642	22 010	:	:	:
G.6.2. Reinsurance Accepted								
G.6.2.1. Gross Premiums	517	464	489	451	1 510	1 367	1 408	1 586
G.6.2.2. Ceded Premiums	103	60	68	77	:	:	:	:
G.6.2.3. Net Written Premiums	414	404	421	374	1 510	:	:	:
G.6.3. Total								
G.6.3.1. Gross Premiums	20 416	21 848	22 746	23 758	23 520	23 260	23 596	23 854
G.6.3.2. Ceded Premiums	3 293	3 556	3 828	3 742	3 562	3 270	3 629	3 816
G.6.3.3. Net Written Premiums	17 123	18 292	18 918	20 016	19 958	19 990	19 967	20 038
G.7. Accident, Health								
G.7.1. Direct Business								
G.7.1.1. Gross Premiums	136 025	143 340	148 969	155 222	150 002	224 648	251 156	206 108
G.7.1.2. Ceded Premiums	7 474	8 116	9 412	11 437	:	:	:	:
G.7.1.3. Net Written Premiums	128 551	135 224	139 557	143 785	150 002	:	:	:
G.7.2. Reinsurance Accepted								
G.7.2.1. Gross Premiums	1 406	1 763	2 128	2 089	11 547	11 566	17 193	10 508
G.7.2.2. Ceded Premiums	536	619	892	806	:	:	:	:
G.7.2.3. Net Written Premiums	870	1 144	1 236	1 283	11 547	:	:	:

French row labels (Assurances Directes / Réassurance Acceptée; Primes Brutes / Primes Cédées / Primes Nettes Emises) correspond to the English labels above. Section titles: G.3. Fret; G.4. Incendie, Dommages aux Biens; G.5. Pertes Pécuniaires; G.6. Responsabilité Générale; G.7. Accident, Santé.

Monetary Unit: million US dollars

Unité monétaire : million de dollars des EU

	1992	1993	1994	1995	1996	1997	1998	1999	
G.7.3. Total									G.7.3. Total
G.7.3.1. Gross Premiums	137 431	145 103	151 097	157 311	161 549	236 214	268 350	216 616	G.7.3.1. Primes Brutes
G.7.3.2. Ceded Premiums	8 010	8 735	10 304	12 243	13 999	14 893	21 419	14 127	G.7.3.2. Primes Cédées
G.7.3.3. Net Written Premiums	129 421	136 368	140 793	145 068	147 550	221 321	246 931	202 489	G.7.3.3. Primes Nettes Emises
G.8. Others									G.8. Autres
G.8.1. Direct Business									G.8.1. Assurances Directes
G.8.1.1. Gross Premiums	85 916	91 747	89 744	86 894	70 943	63 972	67 118	69 150	G.8.1.1. Primes Brutes
G.8.1.2. Ceded Premiums	17 296	17 221	16 717	15 855	::	::	::	::	G.8.1.2. Primes Cédées
G.8.1.3. Net Written Premiums	68 620	74 526	73 027	71 039	70 943	::	::	::	G.8.1.3. Primes Nettes Emises
G.8.2. Reinsurance Accepted									G.8.2. Réassurance Acceptée
G.8.2.1. Gross Premiums	4 768	3 804	4 193	4 887	18 446	17 219	17 722	19 831	G.8.2.1. Primes Brutes
G.8.2.2. Ceded Premiums	889	596	578	723	::	::	::	::	G.8.2.2. Primes Cédées
G.8.2.3. Net Written Premiums	3 879	3 208	3 615	4 164	18 446	::	::	::	G.8.2.3. Primes Nettes Emises
G.8.3. Total									G.8.3. Total
G.8.3.1. Gross Premiums	90 684	95 551	93 937	91 781	89 389	81 191	84 840	88 981	G.8.3.1. Primes Brutes
G.8.3.2. Ceded Premiums	18 185	17 817	17 295	16 578	14 813	12 311	14 840	17 907	G.8.3.2. Primes Cédées
G.8.3.3. Net Written Premiums	72 499	77 734	76 642	75 203	74 576	68 880	69 999	71 074	G.8.3.3. Primes Nettes Emises
G.10. Total									G.10. Total
G.10.1. Direct Business									G.10.1. Assurances Directes
G.10.1.1. Gross Premiums	403 847	429 219	::	458 767	433 347	509 095	544 019	507 350	G.10.1.1. Primes Brutes
G.10.1.2. Ceded Premiums	46 036	48 933	::	56 361	::	::	::	::	G.10.1.2. Primes Cédées
G.10.1.3. Net Written Premiums	357 811	380 286	::	402 406	433 347	::	::	::	G.10.1.3. Primes Nettes Emises
G.10.2. Reinsurance Accepted									G.10.2. Réassurance Acceptée
G.10.2.1. Gross Premiums	9 320	8 763	::	10 519	46 230	44 256	50 254	48 067	G.10.2.1. Primes Brutes
G.10.2.2. Ceded Premiums	2 057	1 725	::	2 306	::	::	::	::	G.10.2.2. Primes Cédées
G.10.2.3. Net Written Premiums	7 263	7 038	::	8 213	46 230	::	::	::	G.10.2.3. Primes Nettes Emises
G.10.3. Total									G.10.3. Total
G.10.3.1. Gross Premiums	413 167	437 982	453 929	469 286	479 577	553 351	594 274	555 417	G.10.3.1. Primes Brutes
G.10.3.2. Ceded Premiums	48 093	50 658	55 274	58 667	57 209	55 400	63 871	63 380	G.10.3.2. Primes Cédées
G.10.3.3. Net Written Premiums	365 074	387 324	398 655	410 619	422 368	497 951	530 403	492 037	G.10.3.3. Primes Nettes Emises

Monetary Unit: million Singaporean dollars   Unité monétaire : million de dollars de Singapour

	1992	1993	1994	1995	1996	1997	1998	1999
A. NUMBER OF COMPANIES IN THE REPORTING COUNTRY — **A. NOMBRE D'ENTREPRISES DANS LE PAYS DECLARANT**								
A.1. Life — **A.1. Vie**								
A.1.1. Domestic Companies — A.1.1. Entreprises Nationales								9
A.1.2. (Foreign Controlled Companies) — A.1.2. (Entreprises Sous Contrôle Etranger)								6
A.1. All Companies — A.1. Ensemble des Entreprises								9
A.2. Non-Life — **A.2. Non-Vie**								
A.2.1. Domestic Companies — A.2.1. Entreprises Nationales								25
A.2.2. (Foreign Controlled Companies) — A.2.2. (Entreprises Sous Contrôle Etranger)								17
A.2.3. Branches & Agencies of Foreign Cies — A.2.3. Succursales et Agences d'Ent. Etrangères								17
A.2. All Companies — A.2. Ensemble des Entreprises								42
A.3. Composite — **A.3. Mixte**								
A.3.1. Domestic Companies — A.3.1. Entreprises Nationales								5
A.3.3. Branches & Agencies of Foreign Cies — A.3.3. Succursales et Agences d'Ent. Etrangères								1
A.3. All Companies — A.3. Ensemble des Entreprises								6
A.4. Reinsurance — **A.4. Réassurance**								
A.4.1. Domestic Companies — A.4.1. Entreprises Nationales								9
A.4.2. (Foreign Controlled Companies) — A.4.2. (Entreprises Sous Contrôle Etranger)								5
A.4.3. Branches & Agencies of Foreign Cies — A.4.3. Succursales et Agences d'Ent. Etrangères								38
A.4. All Companies — A.4. Ensemble des Entreprises								47
A.5. Total — **A.5. Total**								
A.5.1. Domestic Companies — A.5.1. Entreprises Nationales								48
A.5.2. (Foreign Controlled Companies) — A.5.2. (Entreprises Sous Contrôle Etranger)								28
A.5.3. Branches & Agencies of Foreign Cies — A.5.3. Succursales et Agences d'Ent. Etrangères								56
A.5. All Insurance Companies — A.5. Ensemble des Entreprises d'Assurances								104
B. NUMBER OF EMPLOYEES — **B. NOMBRE D'EMPLOYES**								
B.1. Insurance Companies — B.1. Entreprises d'Assurances								6 617
B.2. Intermediaries — B.2. Intermediaires								145
B. Total — B. Total								6 762
C. BUSINESS WRITTEN IN THE REPORTING COUNTRY — **C. OPERATIONS CONCLUES DANS LE PAYS DECLARANT**								
C.1. Life — **C.1. Vie**								
C.1.1. Gross Premiums — C.1.1. Primes Brutes								
C.1.1.1. Direct Business — C.1.1.1. Assurances Directes								
C.1.1.1.1. Domestic Companies — C.1.1.1.1. Entreprises Nationales								4 726
C.1.1.1.2. (Foreign Controlled Companies) — C.1.1.1.2. (Entreprises Sous Contrôle Etranger)								1 339
C.1.1.1.3. Branches & Agencies of Foreign Cies — C.1.1.1.3. Succursales et Agences d'Ent. Etrangères								1 915
C.1.1.1. Total — C.1.1.1. Total								6 641
C.1.1.2. Reinsurance Accepted — C.1.1.2. Réassurance Acceptée								
C.1.1.2.3. Branches & Agencies of Foreign Cies — C.1.1.2.3. Succursales et Agences d'Ent. Etrangères								150
C.1.1.2. Total — C.1.1.2. Total								150
C.1.1.3. Total — C.1.1.3. Total								
C.1.1.3.1. Domestic Companies — C.1.1.3.1. Entreprises Nationales								4 726
C.1.1.3.2. (Foreign Controlled Companies) — C.1.1.3.2. (Entreprises Sous Contrôle Etranger)								1 339
C.1.1.3.3. Branches & Agencies of Foreign Cies — C.1.1.3.3. Succursales et Agences d'Ent. Etrangères								2 064
C.1.1.3. Total Gross Premiums — C.1.1.3. Total des Primes Brutes								6 790

Monetary Unit: million Singaporean dollars   Unité monétaire : million de dollars de Singapour

C.2. Non-Life / C.2. Non-Vie

	1992	1993	1994	1995	1996	1997	1998	1999
C.2.1. Gross premiums / C.2.1. Primes Brutes								
C.2.1.1. Direct Business / C.2.1.1. Assurances Directes								
C.2.1.1.1. Domestic Companies / C.2.1.1.1. Entreprises Nationales								1 024
C.2.1.1.2. (Foreign Controlled Companies) / C.2.1.1.2. (Entreprises Sous Contrôle Etranger)								447
C.2.1.1.3. Branches & Agencies of Foreign Cies / C.2.1.1.3. Succursales et Agences d'Ent. Etrangères								488
C.2.1.1. Total								1 512
C.2.1.2. Reinsurance Accepted / C.2.1.2. Réassurance Acceptée								
C.2.1.2.1. Domestic Companies / C.2.1.2.1. Entreprises Nationales								267
C.2.1.2.2. (Foreign Controlled Companies) / C.2.1.2.2. (Entreprises Sous Contrôle Etranger)								159
C.2.1.2.3. Branches & Agencies of Foreign Cies / C.2.1.2.3. Succursales et Agences d'Ent. Etrangères								1 095
C.2.1.2. Total								1 362
C.2.1.3. Total								
C.2.1.3.1. Domestic Companies / C.2.1.3.1. Entreprises Nationales								1 291
C.2.1.3.2. (Foreign Controlled Companies) / C.2.1.3.2. (Entreprises Sous Contrôle Etranger)								605
C.2.1.3.3. Branches & Agencies of Foreign Cies / C.2.1.3.3. Succursales et Agences d'Ent. Etrangères								1 583
C.2.1.3. Total Gross Premiums / C.2.1.3. Total des Primes Brutes								2 874
C.2.2. Ceded Premiums / C.2.2. Primes Cédées								
C.2.2.1. Domestic Companies / C.2.2.1. Entreprises Nationales								479
C.2.2.2. (Foreign Controlled Companies) / C.2.2.2. (Entreprises Sous Contrôle Etranger)								247
C.2.2.3. Branches & Agencies of Foreign Cies / C.2.2.3. Succursales et Agences d'Ent. Etrangères								244
C.2.2. Total								723
C.2.3. Net Written Premiums / C.2.3. Primes Nettes Emises								
C.2.3.1. Domestic Companies / C.2.3.1. Entreprises Nationales								812
C.2.3.2. (Foreign Controlled Companies) / C.2.3.2. (Entreprises Sous Contrôle Etranger)								359
C.2.3.3. Branches & Agencies of Foreign Cies / C.2.3.3. Succursales et Agences d'Ent. Etrangères								1 339
C.2.3. Total								2 151

C.3. Total

	1992	1993	1994	1995	1996	1997	1998	1999
C.3.1. Gross Premiums / C.3.1. Primes Brutes								
C.3.1.1. Direct Business / C.3.1.1. Assurances Directes								
C.3.1.1.1. Domestic Companies / C.3.1.1.1. Entreprises Nationales								5 750
C.3.1.1.2. (Foreign Controlled Companies) / C.3.1.1.2. (Entreprises Sous Contrôle Etranger)								1 786
C.3.1.1.3. Branches & Agencies of Foreign Cies / C.3.1.1.3. Succursales et Agences d'Ent. Etrangères								2 403
C.3.1.1. Total								8 153
C.3.1.2. Reinsurance Accepted / C.3.1.2. Réassurance Accepté								
C.3.1.2.1. Domestic Companies / C.3.1.2.1. Entreprises Nationales								267
C.3.1.2.2. (Foreign Controlled Companies) / C.3.1.2.2. (Entreprises Sous Contrôle Etranger)								159
C.3.1.2.3. Branches & Agencies of Foreign Cies / C.3.1.2.3. Succursales et Agences d'Ent. Etrangères								1 244
C.3.1.2. Total								1 511
C.3.1.3. Total								
C.3.1.3.1. Domestic Companies / C.3.1.3.1. Entreprises Nationales								6 017
C.3.1.3.2. (Foreign Controlled Companies) / C.3.1.3.2. (Entreprises Sous Contrôle Etranger)								1 944
C.3.1.3.3. Branches & Agencies of Foreign Cies / C.3.1.3.3. Succursales et Agences d'Ent. Etrangères								3 647
C.3.1.3. Total Gross Premiums / C.3.1.3. Total des Primes Brutes								9 664

D. NET WRITTEN PREMIUMS IN THE REPORTING COUNTRY IN TERMS OF DOMESTIC AND FOREIGN RISKS

D. PRIMES NETTES EMISES DANS LE PAYS DECLARANT EN RISQUES NATIONAUX ET ETRANGERS

D.2. Non-Life / D.2. Non-Vie

	1992	1993	1994	1995	1996	1997	1998	1999
D.2.1. Domestic Risks / D.2.1. Risques Nationaux								
D.2.1.1. Domestic Companies / D.2.1.1. Entreprises Nationales								718
D.2.1.2. (Foreign Controlled Companies) / D.2.1.2. (Entreprises Sous Contrôle Etranger)								278
D.2.1.3. Branches & Agencies of Foreign Cies / D.2.1.3. Succursales et Agences d'Ent. Etrangères								490
D.2.1. Total / D.2.1. Total des Primes Nettes Vie								1 208

Monetary Unit: million Singaporean dollars

Unité monétaire : million de dollars de Singapour

	1992	1993	1994	1995	1996	1997	1998	1999
D.2.2. Foreign Risks — D.2.2. Risques Etrangers								
D.2.2.1. Domestic Companies — D.2.2.1. Entreprises Nationales								94
D.2.2.2. Foreign Controlled Companies — D.2.2.2. (Entreprises Sous Contrôle Etranger)								80
D.2.2.3. Branches & Agencies of Foreign Cies — D.2.2.3. Succursales et Agences d'Ent. Etrangères								849
D.2.2 Total — D.2.2. Total des Primes Nettes Vie								943
D.2.3. Total — D.2.3. Total								
D.2.3.1. Domestic Companies — D.2.3.1. Entreprises Nationales								812
D.2.3.2. (Foreign Controlled Companies) — D.2.3.2. (Entreprises Sous Contrôle Etranger)								359
D.2.3.3. Branches & Agencies of Foreign Cies — D.2.3.3. Succursales et Agences d'Ent. Etrangères								1 339
D.2.3. Total — D.2.3. Total des Primes Nettes Vie								2 151
F. OUTSTANDING INVESTMENT BY DIRECT INSURANCE COMPANIES — **F. ENCOURS DES PLACEMENTS DES ENTREPRISES D'ASSURANCES DIRECTES**								
F.1. Life — **F.1. Vie**								
F.1. Life — **F.1. Vie**								
F.1.1. Real Estate — F.1.1. Immobilier								
F.1.1.1. Domestic Companies — F.1.1.1. Entreprises Nationales								1 508
F.1.1.2. (Foreign Controlled Companies) — F.1.1.2. (Entreprises Sous Contrôle Etranger)								200
F.1.1.3. Branches & Agencies of Foreign Cies — F.1.1.3. Succursales et Agences d'Ent. Etrangères								342
F.1.1.4. Domestic Investment — F.1.1.4. Placement dans le Pays								1 850
F.1.1. Total — F.1.1. Total								1 850
F.1.2. Mortgage Loans — F.1.2. Prêts Hypothécaires								
F.1.2.1. Domestic Companies — F.1.2.1. Entreprises Nationales								1 249
F.1.2.2. (Foreign Controlled Companies) — F.1.2.2. (Entreprises Sous Contrôle Etranger)								3
F.1.2.3. Branches & Agencies of Foreign Cies — F.1.2.3. Succursales et Agences d'Ent. Etrangères								292
F.1.2.4. Domestic Investment — F.1.2.4. Placement dans le Pays								1 542
F.1.2. Total — F.2.1. Total								1 542
F.1.3. Shares — F.1.3. Actions								
F.1.3.1. Domestic Companies — F.1.3.1. Entreprises Nationales								6 686
F.1.3.2. (Foreign Controlled Companies) — F.1.3.2. (Entreprises Sous Contrôle Etranger)								2 196
F.1.3.3. Branches & Agencies of Foreign Cies — F.1.3.3. Succursales et Agences d'Ent. Etrangères								1 032
F.1.3.4. Domestic Investment — F.1.3.4. Placement dans le Pays								7 715
F.1.3.5. Foreign Investment — F.1.3.5. Placement à l' Etranger								2
F.1.3. Total — F.1.3. Total								7 717
F.1.4. Bonds with Fixed Revenue — F.1.4. Obligations								
F.1.4.1. Domestic Companies — F.1.4.1. Entreprises Nationales								6 284
F.1.4.2. (Foreign Controlled Companies) — F.1.4.2. (Entreprises Sous Contrôle Etranger)								1 788
F.1.4.3. Branches & Agencies of Foreign Cies — F.1.4.3. Succursales et Agences d'Ent. Etrangères								3 401
F.1.4.4. Domestic Investment — F.1.4.4. Placement dans le Pays								9 666
F.1.4.5. Foreign Investment — F.1.4.5. Placement à l' Etranger								19
F.1.4. Total — F.1.4. Total								9 684
F.1.5. Loans other than Mortgage Loans — F.1.5. Prêts Autres qu'Hypothécaires								
F.1.5.1. Domestic Companies — F.1.5.1. Entreprises Nationales								2 036
F.1.5.2. (Foreign Controlled Companies) — F.1.5.2. (Entreprises Sous Contrôle Etranger)								316
F.1.5.3. Branches & Agencies of Foreign Cies — F.1.5.3. Succursales et Agences d'Ent. Etrangères								440
F.1.5.4. Domestic Investment — F.1.5.4. Placement dans le Pays								2 475
F.1.5. Total — F.1.5. Total								2 475
F.1.6. Other Investments — F.1.6. Autres Placements								
F.1.6.1. Domestic Companies — F.1.6.1. Entreprises Nationales								3 236
F.1.6.2. (Foreign Controlled Companies) — F.1.6.2. (Entreprises Sous Contrôle Etranger)								603
F.1.6.3. Branches & Agencies of Foreign Cies — F.1.6.3. Succursales et Agences d'Ent. Etrangères								1 801
F.1.6.4. Domestic Investment — F.1.6.4. Placement dans le Pays								5 037
F.1.6.5. Foreign Investment — F.1.6.5. Placement à l' Etranger								1
F.1.6. Total — F.1.6. Total								5 038
F.1.7. Total — F.1.7. Total								
F.1.7.1. Domestic Companies — F.1.7.1. Entreprises Nationales								20 999
F.1.7.2. (Foreign Controlled Companies) — F.1.7.2. (Entreprises Sous Contrôle Etranger)								5 106
F.1.7.3. Branches & Agencies of Foreign Cies — F.1.7.3. Succursales et Agences d'Ent. Etrangères								7 308
F.1.7.4. Domestic Investment — F.1.7.4. Placement dans le Pays								28 285
F.1.7.5. Foreign Investment — F.1.7.5. Placement à l' Etranger								22
F.1.7. Total of Life Investments — F.1.7. Total des Placements Vie								28 307

Monetary Unit : million Singaporean dollars

Unité monétaire : million de dollars de Singapour

F.2. Non-Life / F.2. Non-Vie

English	Français	1992	1993	1994	1995	1996	1997	1998	1999
F.2.1. Real Estate	**F.2.1. Immobilier**								
F.2.1.1. Domestic Companies	F.2.1.1. Entreprises Nationales								146
F.2.1.2. (Foreign Controlled Companies)	F.2.1.2. (Entreprises Sous Contrôle Etranger)								49
F.2.1.3. Branches & Agencies of Foreign Cies	F.2.1.3. Succursales et Agences d'Ent. Etrangères								79
F.2.1.4. Domestic Investment	F.2.1.4. Placement dans le Pays								221
F.2.1.5. Foreign Investment	F.2.1.5. Placement à l' Etranger								4
F.2.1. Total	F.2.1. Total								225
F.2.2. Mortgage Loans	**F.2.2. Prêts Hypothécaires**								
F.2.2.1. Domestic Companies	F.2.2.1. Entreprises Nationales								65
F.2.2.2. (Foreign Controlled Companies)	F.2.2.2. (Entreprises Sous Contrôle Etranger)								62
F.2.2.3. Branches & Agencies of Foreign Cies	F.2.2.3. Succursales et Agences d'Ent. Etrangères								5
F.2.2.4. Domestic Investment	F.2.2.4. Placement dans le Pays								59
F.2.2.5. Foreign Investment	F.2.2.5. Placement à l' Etranger								11
F.2.2. Total	F.2.2. Total								70
F.2.3. Shares	**F.2.3. Actions**								
F.2.3.1. Domestic Companies	F.2.3.1. Entreprises Nationales								625
F.2.3.2. (Foreign Controlled Companies)	F.2.3.2. (Entreprises Sous Contrôle Etranger)								95
F.2.3.3. Branches & Agencies of Foreign Cies	F.2.3.3. Succursales et Agences d'Ent. Etrangères								85
F.2.3.4. Domestic Investment	F.2.3.4. Placement dans le Pays								588
F.2.3.5. Foreign Investment	F.2.3.5. Placement à l' Etranger								122
F.2.3. Total	F.2.3. Total								710
F.2.4. Bonds with Fixed Revenue	**F.2.4. Obligations**								
F.2.4.1. Domestic Companies	F.2.4.1. Entreprises Nationales								836
F.2.4.2. (Foreign Controlled Companies)	F.2.4.2. (Entreprises Sous Contrôle Etranger)								497
F.2.4.3. Branches & Agencies of Foreign Cies	F.2.4.3. Succursales et Agences d'Ent. Etrangères								257
F.2.4.4. Domestic Investment	F.2.4.4. Placement dans le Pays								933
F.2.4.5. Foreign Investment	F.2.4.5. Placement à l' Etranger								160
F.2.4. Total	F.2.4. Total								1 093
F.2.5. Loans other than Mortgage Loans	**F.2.5. Prêts Autres qu'Hypothécaires**								
F.2.5.1. Domestic Companies	F.2.5.1. Entreprises Nationales								47
F.2.5.2. (Foreign Controlled Companies)	F.2.5.2. (Entreprises Sous Contrôle Etranger)								14
F.2.5.3. Branches & Agencies of Foreign Cies	F.2.5.3. Succursales et Agences d'Ent. Etrangères								2
F.2.5.4. Domestic Investment	F.2.5.4. Placement dans le Pays								44
F.2.5.5. Foreign Investment	F.2.5.5. Placement à l' Etranger								5
F.2.5. Total	F.2.5. Total								49
F.2.6. Other Investments	**F.2.6. Autres Placements**								
F.2.6.1. Domestic Companies	F.2.6.1. Entreprises Nationales								1 200
F.2.6.2. (Foreign Controlled Companies)	F.2.6.2. (Entreprises Sous Contrôle Etranger)								626
F.2.6.3. Branches & Agencies of Foreign Cies	F.2.6.3. Succursales et Agences d'Ent. Etrangères								616
F.2.6.4. Domestic Investment	F.2.6.4. Placement dans le Pays								1 486
F.2.6.5. Foreign Investment	F.2.6.5. Placement à l' Etranger								330
F.2.6. Total	F.2.6. Total								1 816
F.2.7. Total	**F.2.7. Total**								
F.2.7.1. Domestic Companies	F.2.7.1. Entreprises Nationales								2 919
F.2.7.2. (Foreign Controlled Companies)	F.2.7.2. (Entreprises Sous Contrôle Etranger)								1 343
F.2.7.3. Branches & Agencies of Foreign Cies	F.2.7.3. Succursales et Agences d'Ent. Etrangères								1 044
F.2.7.4. Domestic Investment	F.2.7.4. Placement dans le Pays								3 331
F.2.7.5. Foreign Investment	F.2.7.5. Placement à l' Etranger								632
F.2.7. Total of Non-Life Investments	F.2.7. Total des Placements Non-Vie								3 964

G. BREAKDOWN OF NON-LIFE PREMIUMS / G. VENTILATIONS DES PRIMES NON-VIE

English	Français	1992	1993	1994	1995	1996	1997	1998	1999
G.1. Motor vehicle	**G.1. Assurance Automobile**								
G.1.1. Direct Business	G.1.1. Assurances Directes								
G.1.1.1. Gross Premiums	G.1.1.1. Primes Brutes								437
G.1.2. Reinsurance Accepted	G.1.2. Réassurance Acceptée								
G.1.2.1. Gross Premiums	G.1.2.1. Primes Brutes								41
G.1.3. Total	G.1.3. Total								
G.1.3.1. Gross Premiums	G.1.3.1. Primes Brutes								478
G.1.3.2. Ceded Premiums	G.1.3.2. Primes Cédées								64
G.1.3.3. Net Written Premiums	G.1.3.3. Primes Nettes Emises								413

	1992	1993	1994	1995	1996	1997	1998	1999
G.2. Marine, Aviation — G.2. Marine, Aviation								
G.2.1. Direct Business — G.2.1. Assurances Directes								
G.2.1.1. Gross Premiums — G.2.1.1. Primes Brutes								218
G.2.2. Reinsurance Accepted — G.2.2. Réassurance Acceptée								
G.2.2.1. Gross Premiums — G.2.2.1. Primes Brutes								163
G.2.3. Total — G.2.3. Total								
G.2.3.1. Gross Premiums — G.2.3.1. Primes Brutes								381
G.2.3.2. Ceded Premiums — G.2.3.2. Primes Cédées								145
G.2.3.3. Net Written Premiums — G.2.3.3. Primes Nettes Emises								236
G.4. Fire, Property Damages — G.4. Incendie, Dommages aux Biens								
G.4.1. Direct Business — G.4.1. Assurances Directes								
G.4.1.1. Gross Premiums — G.4.1.1. Primes Brutes								203
G.4.2. Reinsurance Accepted — G.4.2. Réassurance Acceptée								
G.4.2.1. Gross Premiums — G.4.2.1. Primes Brutes								719
G.4.3. Total — G.4.3. Total								
G.4.3.1. Gross Premiums — G.4.3.1. Primes Brutes								922
G.4.3.2. Ceded Premiums — G.4.3.2. Primes Cédées								243
G.4.3.3. Net Written Premiums — G.4.3.3. Primes Nettes Emises								679
G.8. Others — G.8. Autres								
G.8.1. Direct Business — G.8.1. Assurances Directes								
G.8.1.1. Gross Premiums — G.8.1.1. Primes Brutes								655
G.8.2. Reinsurance Accepted — G.8.2. Réassurance Acceptée								
G.8.2.1. Gross Premiums — G.8.2.1. Primes Brutes								439
G.8.3. Total — G.8.3. Total								
G.8.3.1. Gross Premiums — G.8.3.1. Primes Brutes								1 094
G.8.3.2. Ceded Premiums — G.8.3.2. Primes Cédées								271
G.8.3.3. Net Written Premiums — G.8.3.3. Primes Nettes Emises								823
G.10. Total — G.10. Total								
G.10.1. Direct Business — G.10.1. Assurances Directes								
G.10.1.1. Gross Premiums — G.10.1.1. Primes Brutes								1 512
G.10.2. Reinsurance Accepted — G.10.2. Réassurance Acceptée								
G.10.2.1. Gross Premiums — G.10.2.1. Primes Brutes								1 362
G.10.3. Total — G.10.3. Total								
G.10.3.1. Gross Premiums — G.10.3.1. Primes Brutes								2 874
G.10.3.2. Ceded Premiums — G.10.3.2. Primes Cédées								723
G.10.3.3. Net Written Premiums — G.10.3.3. Primes Nettes Emises								2 151
H. GROSS CLAIMS PAYMENTS — H. PAIEMENTS BRUTS DES SINISTRES								
H.1. Life — H.1. Vie								
H.1.1. Domestic Companies — H.1.1. Entreprises Nationales								1 360
H.1.2. (Foreign Controlled Companies) — H.1.2. (Entreprises Sous Contrôle Etranger)								351
H.1.3. Branches & Agencies of Foreign Cies — H.1.3. Succursales et Agences d'Ent. Etrangères								633
H.1. Total — H.1. Total								1 993
H.2. Non-Life — H.2. Non-Vie								
H.2.1. Domestic Companies — H.2.1. Entreprises Nationales								772
H.2.2. (Foreign Controlled Companies) — H.2.2. (Entreprises Sous Contrôle Etranger)								371
H.2.3. Branches & Agencies of Foreign Cies — H.2.3. Succursales et Agences d'Ent. Etrangères								689
H.2. Total — H.2. Total								1 461

251

Monetary Unit: million Singaporean dollars · Unité monétaire : million de dollars de Singapour

	1992	1993	1994	1995	1996	1997	1998	1999
I. GROSS OPERATING EXPENSES / **I. DEPENSES BRUITES D'EXPLOITATION**								
I.1. Life / **I.1. Vie**								
I.1.1. Domestic Companies / I.1.1. Entreprises Nationales								236
I.1.2. (Foreign Controlled Companies) / I.1.2. (Entreprises Sous Contrôle Etranger)								76
I.1.3. Branches & Agencies of Foreign Cies / I.1.3. Succursales et Agences d'Ent. Etrangères								122
I.1. Total / I.1. Total des Primes Nettes Vie								358
I.2. Non-Life / **I.2. Non-Vie**								
I.2.1. Domestic Companies / I.2.1. Entreprises Nationales								196
I.2.2. (Foreign Controlled Companies) / I.2.2. (Entreprises Sous Contrôle Etranger)								100
I.2.3. Branches & Agencies of Foreign Cies / I.2.3. Succursales et Agences d'Ent. Etrangères								207
I.2. Total / I.2. Total								404
J. COMMISSIONS / **J. COMMISSIONS**								
J.1. Life / **J.1. Vie**								
J.1.1. Direct Business / J.1.1. Assurance directe								
J.1.1.1. Domestic Companies / J.1.1.1. Entreprises Nationales								410
J.1.1.2. (Foreign Controlled Companies) / J.1.1.2. (Entreprises Sous Contrôle Etranger)								165
J.1.1.3. Branches & Agencies of Foreign Cies / J.1.1.3. Succursales et Agences d'Ent. Etrangères								273
J.1.1. Total / J.1.1. Total								683
J.1.2. Reinsurance Accepted / J.1.2. Réassurances acceptées								
J.1.2.3. Branches & Agencies of Foreign Cies / J.1.2.3. Succursales et Agences d'Ent. Etrangères								24
J.1.2. Total / J.1.2. Total								24
J.1.3. Total								
J.1.3.1. Domestic Companies / J.1.3.1. Entreprises Nationales								410
J.1.3.2. (Foreign Controlled Companies) / J.1.3.2. (Entreprises Sous Contrôle Etranger)								165
J.1.3.3. Branches & Agencies of Foreign Cies / J.1.3.3. Succursales et Agences d'Ent. Etrangères								297
J.1.3. Total of Life Net Premiums / J.1.3. Total								707
J.2. Non-Life / **J.2. Non-Vie**								
J.2.1. Direct Business / J.2.1. Assurance directe								
J.2.1.1. Domestic Companies / J.2.1.1. Entreprises Nationales								211
J.2.1.2. (Foreign Controlled Companies) / J.2.1.2. (Entreprises Sous Contrôle Etranger)								109
J.2.1.3. Branches & Agencies of Foreign Cies / J.2.1.3. Succursales et Agences d'Ent. Etrangères								407
J.2.1. Total / J.2.1. Total des Primes Nettes Vie								618
J.2.2. Reinsurance Accepted / J.2.2. Réassurances acceptées								
J.2.2.1. Domestic Companies / J.2.2.1. Entreprises Nationales								112
J.2.2.2. (Foreign Controlled Companies) / J.2.2.2. (Entreprises Sous Contrôle Etranger)								50
J.2.2.3. Branches & Agencies of Foreign Cies / J.2.2.3. Succursales et Agences d'Ent. Etrangères								63
J.2.2. Total / J.2.2. Total								175
J.2.3. Total								
J.2.3.1. Domestic Companies / J.2.3.1. Entreprises Nationales								324
J.2.3.2. (Foreign Controlled Companies) / J.2.3.2. (Entreprises Sous Contrôle Etranger)								159
J.2.3.3. Branches & Agencies of Foreign Cies / J.2.3.3. Succursales et Agences d'Ent. Etrangères								469
J.2.3. Total / J.2.3. Total								793

PART III

PARTIE III

DEFINITIONS AND NOTES

DÉFINITIONS ET NOTES

I. COMMON DEFINITIONS AND NOTES

GENERAL

a) Life and Non-life categories follow the definitions used in national law. However, the premiums for accident and sickness insurances underwritten by Life companies should be included in Non-life figures;

b) Figures provided for the number of companies and for insurance premiums should include all insurance companies licensed or authorised in the reporting country, *including* professional reinsurers, whether or not these are controlled, but *excluding* any statutory system of social security administered by the State;

c) *Domestic companies* means those companies incorporated under national law, together with those companies in the reporting country which are unincorporated, but excluding the branches and agencies of foreign companies;

d) *Foreign-controlled companies* means those domestic companies controlled by foreign interests, such "control" being defined according to national law (see the definition of foreign controlled companies in notes by country). The data of *foreign-controlled companies* are part of those of *Domestic companies*;

e) *Foreign companies* means companies incorporated outside the reporting country.

A. NUMBER OF COMPANIES IN THE REPORTING COUNTRIES

a) *Composite*: Company which deals with both life and non-life business.

B. NUMBER OF EMPLOYEES

a) *Insurance companies*: Staff (full-time or part-time) employed in the insurance industry.

b) *Intermediaries*; Number of persons (brokers or agents and their staffs), excluding intermediaries who may sell insurance but are not directly involved in the insurance industry (e.g. bank managers, solicitors, garage owners) or those included under a) above.

C. BUSINESS WRITTEN IN THE REPORTING COUNTRY

a) *Business written in the reporting country* should include all business written in the reporting country, whether in respect of domestic or foreign (world-wide) risks, and analysed according to the guidelines in "General" above.

b) *"Net written premiums"* are total retention in the reporting country. There should be no double-counting in these figures, even though double-counting may exist in the gross figures.

c) *"Gross premiums"* are total premiums written, excluding any premium taxes or other charges, but before deduction of commission or reinsurance outwards. It is acknowledged that the inclusion of reinsurance will mean that there is some element of double-counting in the figures provided.

"Gross premiums" are the sum of *"premiums of direct business"* and *"premiums of reinsurance accepted"*.

d)   Facultative reinsurance may be included under "Direct business" or "Reinsurance accepted" according to practice in the reporting country.

e)   *Premiums ceded* include all premiums (reinsurance and retrocessions) ceded.

f)   Normally *"Net written premiums"* should equal total *"Gross premiums"* less *"Premiums ceded"*. If there are special problems in the reporting country which prevent this relationship an appropriate compensatory element should be then included under "Premiums ceded".

D. NET WRITTEN PREMIUMS IN THE REPORTING COUNTRY IN TERMS OF DOMESTIC AND FOREIGN RISKS

Same notes as a) and b) of Section C above.

a)   This part breaks down business between domestic and foreign risks and is an amplification of the "Net written premiums" lines of Section C ("Business Written in the Reporting Country").

b)   *"Domestic risks"* include all business in the reporting country on domestic risks.

c)   *"Foreign risks"* include all business written in the reporting country on risks situated outside the reporting country (it does not include business written outside the reporting country by national companies).

E. BUSINESS WRITTEN ABROAD

Same notes as c), d), e) and f) of Section C above.

a)   *Business written abroad* should include all business written outside the reporting country (in both OECD and non-OECD countries) by subsidiaries, branches and agencies established abroad of domestic companies.

F. OUTSTANDING INVESTMENT BY DIRECT INSURANCE COMPANIES

a)   These data include only outstanding investment by all direct insurance companies in the reporting country; investments by reinsurance companies are not included.

b)   The evaluation method for investment is defined by each country; some of them are mentioned in the notes by country.

c)   Investment has been classified by category, by companies' nationality (domestic companies, foreign controlled companies or branches and agencies of foreign companies) and by destination (inside or outside of the country).

G. BREAKDOWN OF NON-LIFE PREMIUMS

Same notes as c), d), e) and f) of Section C above,

a)   This part shows *premiums written by classes of non-life insurance* for the business written in the reporting country and breaks down figures shown on the non-life "Net written premiums" of Section C ("Business Written in the Reporting Country").

b)   For the precise definitions used for the classification, see in part III". Definitions of classes of non-life insurance".

c)   The line "Treaty Reinsurance" is used by countries having difficulty in breaking down "Reinsurance Accepted" by classes.

H. GROSS CLAIMS PAYMENTS

a)   *"Gross claims payments",* covering all gross payments on claims made during the financial year, are to be used in the calculation of gross claims incurred.

**I.	GROSS OPERATING EXPENSES**

a)	*"Gross operating expenses"* should normally mean the sum of acquisition costs, change in deferred acquisition costs and administrative expenses.

**J.	COMMISSIONS**

a)	This part shows the total of commissions and breaks down commissions for direct business and those for reinsurance accepted.

II. DEFINITIONS AND NOTES BY COUNTRY

General remarks for the EU/EEA member countries: Following regulatory changes introduced by the EU Third Insurance Directives, since 1995, data of EU/EEA countries do not include data on branches and agencies of foreign companies whose head offices are situated in other EU/EEA countries. The Working Group on insurance statistics is currently considering the way to solve this issue, in co-operation with EUROSTAT. It is hoped that at least some of these data could be added at a later stage (see section V of Part III, which provides preliminary information on this issue).

AUSTRALIA

General remarks: For 1994, all figures on life insurance data are based on the fiscal year (July 1993 to June 1994).

Definition of foreign-controlled companies: Predominant control exercised from abroad (either through share ownership or control of votes).

C. *Business written in the reporting country:* In non-life direct business, figures include inward facultative reinsurance premiums but exclude statutory charges. The figures include private sector data only.

F. *Outstanding investment by direct insurance companies:* Investment figures are mostly recorded at their market value.

G. *Breakdown of non-life premiums:*
   a) Freight Insurance is included in Marine and Aviation Insurance;
   b) Pecuniary Loss Insurance and Accident and Sickness Insurances are included in "Others".
   c) Premiums for accident and sickness insurance underwritten by life companies are not included. They are included in life figures.

AUSTRIA

General remarks: For technical reasons, the data of small mutuals are not included in the statistics. However, the premium income of those mutuals amounts to a total of 145 mio ATS only in 1996.

Definition of foreign-controlled companies: Participation of foreign companies exceeding 50 per cent of the share capital.

G.   *Breakdown of non-life premiums*:   Premiums ceded recorded in the category "Others" include retrocession premiums (other than those related to Marine and Freight Insurance) which cannot be broken down.

BELGIUM

General remarks: Concerning the number of companies and premiums, data do not include branches of foreign companies whose head offices are situated in the EEA, since 1994. Concerning the number of companies and premiums, data do not include professional reinsurers which do not need a license and are not supervised, so that no information on them is available.

B.   *Number of employees:* The figures for intermediaries represent the approximate number of brokers and non-salaried agents, including agents who occasionally write insurance contracts although this is not their main activity.

C.   *Business written in the reporting country:* Since 1996, the data on direct insurance include domestic risks only. "Reinsurance accepted" includes business written abroad through branches.

D.   *Net written premiums in the reporting country in terms of domestic and foreign risks*: No distinction can be made between domestic and foreign business, since the item "Reinsurance Accepted" cannot be broken down into these two categories of operations.

E.   *Business written abroad:*
        a) No figures on Belgian subsidiaries abroad are available;
        b) No breakdown of gross premiums into direct business and reinsurance accepted is available for the activities abroad of branches and agencies of Belgian companies.

G.   *Breakdown of non-life premiums:*
        a) Figures refer to business written on domestic risks only;
        b) Freight insurance is included in Marine and Aviation Insurance;
        c) Accident and Health Insurance includes Workmen's Compensation Insurance.

CANADA

General remarks: Provincially-regulated companies are not included. Life companies include fraternal benefit societies.

Definition of foreign-controlled companies: Insurer incorporated under the laws of Canada (Federal) where majority control of the voting stock of the insurer is held directly or indirectly by an entity or entities incorporated or established outside Canada.

A.   *Number of companies in the reporting country:* Before 1994 the number of composite reinsurance companies, which transact both life reinsurance business and property and casualty reinsurance business, is included in Composite. Since 1994, the number of these companies (7, 1994 and 1995 data) is included in Reinsurance.

C.   *Business written in the reporting country:* In principle, the accident and sickness business of life companies is shown under non-life business. However, for 1994 and 1995 the accident and sickness business of life companies is exceptionally shown under life business.

F.   *Outstanding investment by direct insurance companies*: Investment of domestic enterprises and of foreign-controlled companies refers to assets invested world-wide. Investment of branches and agencies of foreign companies, however, refers only to assets invested in Canada. Figures for life business exclude asset in segregated funds. Assets are valued in accordance with Canadian generally accepted accounting principles (GAAP) as outlined in the Canadian Institute of Chartered Accountants (CICA) Handbook. Very generally, for property and casualty insurance companies: real estate is valued at depreciated cost, mortgage loans are valued at amortised cost, shares are valued at cost unless there is a permanent decline in the market in which case market is used, and bonds are valued at amortised cost. Very generally, for life insurance companies: real estate is valued according to the moving average market method (cost amortised toward market at 10 per cent), mortgage loans are valued at amortised cost, shares are valued according to the moving average market method (cost amortised toward market at 15 per cent), and bonds are valued at amortised cost. Insurance companies and fraternals are required to adhere to investment and lending policies, standards and procedures that a reasonable and prudent person would apply in respect of a portfolio of investments and loans to avoid undue risk of loss and obtain a reasonable return. In addition, each insurance company and fraternal must comply with a few statutory investment limits as set out in the legislation.

CZECH REPUBLIC

Definition of foreign-controlled companies: Company incorporated under the law of the Czech Republic with more than 50 per cent of the share capital foreign-owned.

F.   *Outstanding investment by direct insurance companies:* Due to the change of the legislative framework in 1994, returns of insurance companies for 1993 are not comparable in many items with those on investments received in the later years.

DENMARK

General remarks: Since 1994, figures for pension funds under the Danish Insurance Business Act are included in life figures.

Definition of foreign-controlled companies: Companies of which more than 50 per cent of the share capital is foreign-owned.

B.   *Number of employees:* Numbers of employees are estimates for full-time employees.

D.   *Net written premiums in the reporting country in terms of domestic and foreign risks:* Non-life figures in this part are earned premiums, whereas the figures in Section C are written premiums.

F. *Outstanding investment by direct insurance companies:* Domestic shares includes shares in subsidiaries established abroad and shares in foreign associated companies.

FINLAND

General remarks: Since 1993, public pension is not included in data on life insurance.

Definition of foreign-controlled companies: Company in which a foreigner owns at least 50 per cent of the shares or can use at least 50 per cent of the voting rights.

A. *Number of companies in the reporting country:* Since 1994, non-life figures include small insurance associations which mainly operate in rural districts.

B. *Number of Employees:* Since 1995, the number of intermediaries include brokers only.

F. *Outstanding investment by direct insurance companies*: Investment figures are valued at book values. Since 1994, "Bonds" are included in "Loans other than Mortgage Loans".

G. *Breakdown of non-life premiums*: "Others" includes compulsory motor third party insurance.

FRANCE

Definition of foreign-controlled companies: Companies of which more than 20 per cent of the capital is held by a non-resident (legal or physical person) or by a French company under foreign control.

A. *Number of companies in the reporting country:* Composite insurers can write only life insurance and the accident and sickness classes of non-life insurance.

F. *Outstanding investment by direct insurance companies*: In general, assets are valued at historical cost. Investment of domestic companies and of branches and agencies of foreign companies refers only to domestic investment.

G. *Breakdown of non-life premiums:* All categories of Freight Insurance are included in Marine and Aviation Insurance. Treaty Reinsurance concerns companies operating in direct insurance and specialised professional reinsurers. Since 1994, Pecuniary Losses Insurance is included in "Others".

GERMANY

Definition of foreign-controlled companies: Foreign direct or indirect majority interests over 50 per cent.

A. *Number of companies in the reporting country:*
  a) The figures of the small mutual societies supervised by the Länder are excluded. Number of the small mutual societies supervised by the Länder: 1358 (1997), 1306

(1998), 1258 (1999). The market share of these small mutual societies is about 0,04 per cent;

b) In life companies, pension and death benefit schemes are included;

c) In non-life companies, specialised health insurance companies are included. Number of health insurance companies: 56 (1997), 57 (1998), 56 (1999).

C. *Business written in the reporting country:* Figures for 1992 for the first time include data from professional reinsurers. Before 1995, for premiums ceded, a distinction between business written in the reporting country and business written abroad is not available. Therefore figures in Section C and Section G show total business (domestic and abroad) for these years.

E. *Business written abroad:* Same note as Section C above. Before 1995, for reinsurance accepted, a distinction between life and non-life is not available, e.g. non-life includes life reinsurance. For reinsurance accepted, business written abroad is business accepted from an insurance enterprise located abroad. The location of the insured risk is not available.

F. *Outstanding investment by direct insurance companies:* The evaluation method for investment is historic valuation. Since 1995, a distinction between domestic companies and branches and agencies of foreign undertakings is not available, neither are separate figures for foreign controlled companies. No distinction for domestic and foreign investment is available.

G. *Breakdown of non-life premiums:* Same note as Section C above.
a) Freight Insurance is included in Marine and Aviation Insurance;
b) "Others" is the data of insurance for legal protections.

GREECE

Definition of foreign-controlled companies: In accordance with articles 1 and 41 of the Seventh Directive 349/83/EEC and articles 9 and 25 of the Fourth Directive 660/78/EEC.

A. *Number of companies in the reporting country*: Lloyd's brokers [number of Lloyd's brokers; 38 (1991)] are not included in "branches and agencies of foreign companies".

G. *Breakdown of non-life premiums*: "Others" refers only to judicial protection insurance.

HUNGARY

General remarks: Since 1996, the data of insurance associations are included. Because there are 23 insurance associations, 1996 data on the number of insurance companies are no longer comparable with previous data. As far as the data of premium income, investments, costs are concerned, however, this inclusion does not have obvious effect, because their turnover is modest.

Definition of foreign-controlled companies: More than half of shares are owned by foreign shareholders.

E.   *Business written abroad:* Insurance companies do not have subsidiaries or branches abroad.

F.   *Outstanding investment by direct insurance companies:*
   a) Only the investments of the insurance technical reserves are included. Investments of subscribed capital, capital reserve and provisions for the general operation of the company are not shown.
   b) Evaluation of investments is based on cost price. After minimum one year permanent loss of value, investments are revaluated. In Hungary only depreciation is possible.

G.   *Breakdown of non-life premiums:*
   a) Marine, aviation and other transport insurance are included in "Others".
   b) Before 1994, flat insurance was classified into "Fire and other property". Since 1995, flat insurance belongs to "Others".

ICELAND

Definition of foreign-controlled companies : More than 50% of shares controlled by foreigners.

B.   *Number of employees:* The figure is full-time equivalent, i.e., one person working 50 per cent is counted as a half employee.

F.   *Outstanding investment by direct insurance companies :* Investment figures are mostly valued at market values. There is no authorised limits of investment by categories but the safety of the technical reserves must be secured.

IRELAND

General remarks: Health insurance premiums are not included. Concerning the number of companies and premiums, data do not include professional reinsurers which do not need a license and are not supervised, so that no information on them is available.

D.   *Net written premiums in the reporting country in terms of domestic and foreign risks:* Life-business, of which risks are situated outside the reporting country, is not reported but understood to be minuscule.

E.   *Business written abroad*: Reinsurance figures are included in direct business.

F.   *Outstanding investment by direct insurance companies*: As no breakdown of linked assets (assets representing investments in linked funds/unit trusts) was available, they are included in "other investments". Foreign investment in life insurance refers only to the non-linked assets representing the life insurance business amount which are not localised in Ireland. Non-life investment comprise of cash with building societies, banks and other financial institutions. Investment figures are evaluated at market value. Due to technical reasons, since 1995, non-life figures are based on historic valuation. Other investments of life insurance include the following items; Variable Interest Securities, Deposit and Current Accounts, Unit Trusts, Cash, Mortgage Loans (on land) etc. Since 1994, the data on branches and agencies of foreign undertakings only include third country branches established in Ireland. Investments of EU branches are no longer available.

G.   *Breakdown of non-life premiums*:
a) Freight insurance is included in Marine and Aviation insurance;
b) Since 1996, Pecuniary losses insurance is included in Others.

ITALY

Definition of foreign-controlled companies: A company, over 50 per cent of whose capital is held, even indirectly, by foreign shareholders.

B.   *Number of employees:* The number of intermediaries is an estimation and includes independent agents.

F.   *Outstanding investment by direct insurance companies:* In general, investment figures are valued at historic value.

JAPAN

General remarks: Figures are for the fiscal year (1 April of the corresponding year to 31 March of the following year).

Definition of foreign-controlled companies: Companies owned for 50 per cent or more by foreign shareholders.

B.   *Number of employees*:
a) Employees of insurance companies do not include part-time employees;
b) Intermediaries include agents whose main activities are not insurance.

C.   *Business written in the reporting country*:
a) The statistics for life insurance companies are before deduction of refund premiums;
b) Gross premiums for non-life insurance are before deduction of the savings-portion of maturity-refund-type insurance. Before 1998, this is not the case with net written premiums. Therefore, before 1998, non-life net written premiums do not correspond to "gross premiums less premiums ceded".

E.   *Business written abroad*: In the non-life category, some subsidiaries are unable to supply separate figures for "Direct Business" and "Reinsurance Premiums Accepted".

F.   *Outstanding investment by direct insurance companies*:
a) Acquisition cost valuation method is applied in general. Depreciation of real estate other than land for investment is done by fixed percentage based on the reducing balance method. Listed securities are valued on a cost or market basis, whichever is lower;
b) Since 1996, "Mortgage Loans" is included in "Loans other than Mortgage Loans";
c) "Other Investments" include deposits, call loans, monetary receivables bought, commodity securities, money, trusts, etc. Since 1998, "Foreign Shares and Bonds" are included in "Other Investments".

G.   *Breakdown of non-life premiums*: Premiums for fire and property damage insurance and for accident and health insurance are before deduction of the savings-portion of maturity-refund-type insurance.

The following services and entities are not included in statistical data:

1.   Postal Life Insurance

This non-profit service operated by the government provides life insurance which is made available to the people nation-wide, thereby ensuring the economic stability of the people and promoting their well-being. It is operated by the Ministry of Posts and Telecommunications under the provisions of the Postal Life Insurance Law. Its budget and accounts are subject to deliberation by the Diet.

Insurance premiums   13,638,813 million yen   of FY 1996
Total assets   100,772,008 million yen   as of the end of FY 1996

2.   Environmental Sanitation Trade Association Mutual Aid

The environmental sanitation associations are entities whose purposes are to improve the sanitation standard through ensuring the soundness of the businesses related to environmental sanitation, thereby securing the interests of the consumers as well. They are established in accordance with the relevant law. The associations provide, as part of their operations, non-profit services similar to life and fire insurance to their members.

Premium income in direct business   NOT AVAILABLE
Total assets   NOT AVAILABLE

3.   Shopping District Promotion Association Mutual Aid

Non-profit services similar to fire insurance are provided by shopping district promotion associations to their members, based on the unique nature of the shopping districts in which many shops are clustered close together in a relatively small area. Most of the associations are small, of which minimal or very small number actually conduct mutual aid services.

Premium income in direct business   NOT AVAILABLE
Total assets   NOT AVAILABLE

4.   Consumers' Co-operation Association Mutual Aid

The consumer's co-operative associations are entities established in accordance with the relevant law whose purpose is to promote the spontaneous developments of the people's communal associations, thereby securing the stability of the people's life and promoting their living culture. Consumers' co-operative associations and their federation provide non-profit mutual aid services including life and automobile mutual aid to their members.

Premium income in direct business   669,011 million yen   according to a survey for
                                                              FY 1995

Total assets   NOT AVAILABLE

5.   Forest Co-operative Association Mutual Aid for Forest Disaster

This system is established in accordance with the relevant law which aims at improving the economic and social status of forest owners and securing sustained yield from the forests as well as increasing its potential output, thereby contributing to the development of the national economy. The National Federation of Forest Owners' Co-operative Associations operates this system for forest owners, which is similar to the non-life insurance for forests, on non-profits basis.

Premium income in   2,625 million yen   FY 1996
Total assets   NOT AVAILABLE

6.   Fishery Co-operative Association Mutual Aid

This system is established in accordance with the relevant law whose purpose is to promote the development of the fishermen's and fishery processors' communal associations, thereby promoting their economic and social status and improving the potential output of fishery, as well as developing the national economy. Fishery co-operative associations provide non-profit services similar to life and non-life insurance to their members.

Premium income in direct business   79,031 million yen   FY 1996
Total assets   404,455 million yen   as of the end of FY 1996

7.   Small and Medium Enterprise Co-operative Association Mutual Aid

Co-operative association composed of small and medium enterprises in a certain area provide non-profit services similar to life and non-life insurance to their members. The total number of such co-operative associations amounts to approximately 49,000 throughout Japan. While there is no detailed statistics, the typical types of services are as follow :

i)   Fire mutual aid provided by Fire Insurance Co-operative

These associations composed of small and medium enterprises provide, on the principle of mutual aid, non-profit services similar to fire insurance to insure their members against loss caused by fire.

Premium income in direct business   20,041 million yen   FY 1996
Total assets   66,087 million yen   as of the end of FY 1996

ii)   Automobile mutual aid provided by Motor Insurance Co-operative

These associations composed of small and medium enterprises provide, on the principle of mutual aid, non-profit services similar to automobile insurance to insure their members against accidents associated with the possession, use and control of privately-owned cars.

Premium income in direct business   24,575 million yen   FY 1996
Total assets   16,900 million yen   as of the end of FY 1996

8. Agricultural co-operative Association Mutual Aid

This system is established in accordance with the relevant law whose purpose is to promote the development of the farmer's communal associations, thereby improving the potential output of agriculture and promoting their economic and social status, as well as developing the national economy. Agricultural co-operative associations and their federation provide, as one body, non-profit services similar to life and non-life insurance to their members.

Premium income in direct business	4,713,500 million yen	FY 1996, approximate figure
Total assets	30,141,400 million yen	as of the end of FY 1996, approximate figure

9. Labour's mutual aid

Labour unions and the national federation of labour union mutual aid, which are voluntarily organised by labour with the main purpose of promoting their economic status, maintaining and providing the labour standard in particular, provide non-profit services similar to life and non-life insurance to their members.

Premium income in direct business	NOT AVAILABLE
Total assets	NOT AVAILABLE

KOREA

Definition of foreign-controlled companies: Foreign subsidiary.

F. *Outstanding investment by direct insurance companies:* The investment is evaluated on the historical cost basis other than listed stocks. The listed stocks are evaluated on the average market value (ref. Article 18-2 of the Enforcement Decree of the Insurance Business Law).

LUXEMBOURG

Definition of foreign-controlled companies: Principal shareholders are not of Luxembourg's nationality.

C. *Business written in the reporting country:* Data concern insurance products commercialised (flow).

F. *Outstanding investment by direct insurance companies:* Only data on investments in flow are available.

G. *Breakdown of non-life premiums:* Same note as Section C above.

MEXICO

Definition of foreign-controlled companies: Those undertakings which capital is mostly contributed by foreigners, that is 51 per cent and above.

G.   *Breakdown of non-life premiums:*
       a) "Marine, aviation and other transport insurance" includes "Freight Insurance";
       b) "Other non-life insurance" includes agricultural and miscellaneous insurances.

NETHERLANDS

General remarks:

       a) Before 1995, the number and the premium income of professional reinsurance companies are estimated since these companies are exempt from governmental control. Since 1995, they are no longer included. In 1995, there are 9 professional reinsures which generate premium income of about 751 millions guilders (517 millions in non-life, 234 millions in life);
       b) The number and the premium income of foreign-controlled companies are estimated since the figures provided refer to supervised companies only;

Definition of foreign-controlled companies: Locally-incorporated domestic insurance companies with a share-capital of which over 50 per cent belongs to one or more companies with (a) head office(s) located o outside the Netherlands.

A.   *Number of companies in the reporting country*:
       a) Before 1995, the number of non-life companies includes the so-called exempted small local mutuals (1995, 239). Their market share is no more than 0.2 per cent (1995).
       b) Since 1995, the number of branches of foreign insurers with a head office within the EU/EEA is no longer included. The number of these branches is 115 (1995, life= 3, non-life= 112).

B.   *Number of employees*: Numbers of insurance employees and intermediaries (carrying out business on a professional basis) are estimated.

C.   *Business written in the reporting country*: Since there is no obligation for life insurance companies in the Netherlands to disclose reinsurance business, it is to be noted that the separation of gross premiums into direct business and reinsurance accepted is not possible.

E.   *Business written abroad*: Before 1994, the figures provided are estimates related to the three major Netherlands insurance companies carrying insurance business on an international scale. Since 1994, no estimation is available.

F.   *Outstanding investment by direct insurance companies :* The following valuation methods are commonly applied :
       - real estate : market value/estimated value
       - (mortgage) loans :

life:	amortisation value or face value
non-life:	face value
- shares:	
quoted:	market value
unquoted	estimated value
- bonds:	
life:	amortisation value or market value
non-life:	market value

Before the implementation of the third EU Directives, there were no rules limiting the percentage of the investments of the total assets to be invested by an insurance company.

G.   *Breakdown of non-life premiums*:
a) Freight Insurance is included in Marine and Aviation Insurance;
b) Pecuniary Loss Insurance and General Liability Insurance are included in other non-life insurance.

NEW ZEALAND

Definition of foreign-controlled companies: 50 per cent or more overseas ownership.

C.   *Business written in the reporting country*: Gross premiums of direct life insurance by domestic companies include net premiums of life reinsurance.

G.   *Breakdown of non-life premiums:* "Other" means medical insurance.

NORWAY

General remarks: For 1994 and 1995, without data on branches and agencies of foreign undertakings for non-life insurance.

Definition of foreign-controlled companies: Companies where the voting majority is held by foreign interests. Since 1997, all undertakings belonging to the same insurance group are classified in an identical manner.

C.   *Business written in the reporting country*: As reinsurance accepted are residually calculated, i.e. total gross premiums minus direct Norwegian business, reinsurance accepted might include direct foreign business.

F.   *Outstanding investment by direct insurance companies:*
Total amount of investment placed by non-life insurance companies do not include branches and agencies of foreign companies.

POLAND

General remarks: The establishment of branches and agencies of foreign undertakings has been allowed since 1 January 1999.

Definition of foreign-controlled companies: At least 51 per cent share of foreign capital. Since 1998, companies in which the direct share of foreign undertakings in their subscribed capital exceeds 50%.

A.   *Number of companies in the reporting country:* The total number of insurance companies includes 6 mutual insurance societies and 57 stock companies (2 public insurance companies and 61 private insurers).

B.   *Number of employees:* The number of insurance employees is estimated. For 1996 - 1999, the State Office for Insurance Supervision issued 201347 permissions for conducting insurance intermediary (together permissions for agents and brokers).

F.   *Outstanding investment by direct insurance companies:* Investment figures are generally valued at historic value.

I.   *Gross operating expenses:* This item includes acquisition costs, administrative expenses and other technical expenses.

PORTUGAL

Definition of foreign-controlled companies: Proportion of foreign capital is more than 50 per cent.

C.   *Business written in the reporting country:* Total gross premiums represents total premiums and accessory charges.

F.   *Outstanding investment by direct insurance companies:*
        a) Before 1995, only assets representing technical provisions are taken into consideration. Since 1995, non-engaged investments are also included;
        b) Government securities, government bonds, credits to the public investment, bonds, shares, shares and units of shares to the investment funds are included in data on shares.
        c) "Loans other than Mortgage Loans" includes loans against policies and loans against securities;
        d) "Other Investments" includes deposits and certificates of deposits.

G.   *Breakdown of non-life premiums:* "Accident and Health Insurance" includes workmen's compensation insurance.

SLOVAK REPUBLIC

Definition of foreign-controlled companies: Share of foreign shareholders is more than 50%.

SPAIN

Definition of foreign-controlled companies: Participation in social capital equal to or more than 50 per cent.

F.   *Outstanding investment by direct insurance companies:* Acquisition cost valuation method is applied in general.

271

G.   *Breakdown of non-life premiums*: Medical insurance is included in "Accident and Health insurance".

SWEDEN

Definition of foreign-controlled companies: At least 50 per cent of the shares are under foreign control.

A.   *Number of companies in the reporting country*: The non-life figures exclude approximately 300 small local mutual insurers, whose estimated share of the non-life market is below 0.1 per cent (1999 data). Since 1994, there are no statistics available concerning branches of insurance undertakings with their head office in another EEA Member State. There are 22 such non-life branches and their share of the direct insurance premiums written is estimated to be a few per cent of the non-life premiums (1999 data). There are also two EEA life branches with a small share.

B.   *Number of employees*:
The number of employees of insurance undertakings includes employed agents, of which approximately 20,000 are working on a part-time basis (1993 data). Since 1994, the number of employees of insurance undertakings excludes agents working on part-time or franchise basis. The corresponding number for 1993 should be approximately the same as the number for 1994, i.e. 19,000. The number of intermediaries includes insurance brokers only.

C.   *Business written in the reporting country*: No reliable information is available as regards branches and agencies of foreign <u>reinsurance</u> undertakings. They are, however, believed to concentrate on non-life reinsurance, so their life reinsurance premiums written have been approximated by 0.

D.   *Net written premiums in the reporting country in terms of domestic and foreign risks:* No reliable information is available on the breakdown between domestic and foreign risks. It is probable, however, that only a minor share of the non-life direct business is written on foreign risks and that almost no direct life business is written on such risks.

E.   *Business written abroad:* There is only some information on direct business and premiums ceded for non-life branches and agencies of domestic insurers. There is no corresponding information on the subsidiaries.

F.   *Outstanding investment by direct insurance companies*:
        a) Before 1996, Investments are valued, in general, at purchase price or market value, whichever is lower. Since 1996, the market value method is used.
        b) Fixed income assets corresponding to technical provisions of life insurance may be valued at cost, even if it exceeds the market value.
        c) Before 1996, mortgage loans cannot be separated from loans other than mortgage loans. The latter has been taken to include all loans.
        d) There were no authorised limits of investments by categories, although there were restrictions on the choice of assets corresponding to technical provisions. At least 80 per

cent of the technical provisions for life insurance (other than unit-linked) must be covered by certain types of assets. The remaining 20 per cent may not be invested in shares. The holding of shares is indirectly restricted in that the voting power of shares in a single company may not in general exceed 5 per cent. On 1 July 1995 the EU rules on investments were implemented. In particular, none of the categories "shares" or "property" may exceed 25 per cent of the technical provisions net of reinsurance.

e) As regards agencies of non-EEA undertakings, only legal deposits are included. Deposits are reported under the heading of "Other investments". Since 1994, branches and agencies of EEA undertakings are no longer covered.

f) Although no reliable information is available on distribution on investment on domestic and foreign placements, foreign real estate, shares and bonds do indeed play a certain role.

G. *Breakdown of non-life premiums*:

a) As regards treaty reinsurance accepted, premiums written by branches or agencies of foreign reinsurers have not been included;

b) General liability cannot be reported as a separate class, since it is in general a component of several mixed products such as house-owner's and house-owner's comprehensive insurance;

c) Accident and health insurance includes employers' no-fault insurance.

SWITZERLAND

Definition of foreign-controlled companies: Companies with more than 50 per cent of foreign participation. Since 1993, companies with directly or indirectly more than 50 per cent of foreign participation.

B. *Number of employees*: The concept "Intermediary" means the insurance agents linked to an insurance company by a contract, excluding brokers and general independent agents whose number in Switzerland is around 400 (in 1992) and 400-500 (in 1993 and 1994).

D. *Net written premiums in the reporting country in terms of domestic and foreign risks:* Premiums from Foreign reinsurance are included.

E. *Business written abroad:* The figures of reinsurance accepted in this section are also included in the column corresponding to Section C.

F. *Outstanding investment by direct insurance companies*: Mortgages: total mortgages, since those granted for the acquisition of private accommodation are not mentioned separately. Other investments: - Life: including term deposits and money market claims, loans and advances on policies; - Life and non-life: liquid and other assets are included. These are among others the assets with agents, insurance proposers, insurers and reinsurers and deposits for reinsurance accepted.

G. *Breakdown of non-life premiums*: Gross premiums of reinsurance accepted and gross premiums of Total are estimates.

Insurance entities not included in statistical data
(activities on Swiss market only, in 1996)

Insurance entities	Number	Direct gross premiums (million SF)
Recognised Health Funds subject to the supervisory authority of the Federal Social Insurance Office	159	16,420
Swiss National Accident Insurance Organisation (SUVA)	1	3,281
Swiss Public Fire Insurances (SPFI)	19	818
Total	**179**	**20,519**

TURKEY

Definition of foreign-controlled companies: Companies, in which a foreign shareholder owns more than 50 per cent share of the capital.

B.   *Number of employees*: Number of employees for intermediaries covers only that of agents excluding banks operating as an agent.

F.   *Outstanding investment by direct insurance companies*: Real estate is re-evaluated to take inflation into account. Real estate, shares and other investments are evaluated by purchase value.

G.   *Others : Breakdown of non-life premiums:* Data by reinsurance companies are excluded in the premiums written by classes of non-life insurance. Marine and Aviation insurance includes Freight insurance.

UNITED KINGDOM

A.   *Number of companies in the reporting country:*
       a) For 1993, the number of "Domestic Companies" should be read as that of "EU companies with head office in UK", the number of "Foreign Controlled Companies" should be read as that of "EU companies with head office outside UK", and the number of "Branches and Agencies of Foreign Companies" should be read as that of "External companies". The number of "EU companies with head office outside UK" is not included in that of "EU companies with head office in UK". For 1994 and 1995, the number of "Domestic Companies" should be read as that of "EEA companies with head

office in UK", the number of "Foreign Controlled Companies" should be read as that of "EEA companies with head office outside UK", and the number of "Branches and Agencies of Foreign Companies" should be read as that of "External companies". The number of "EEA companies with head office outside UK" is not included in that of "EEA companies with head office in UK";

b) Lloyd's is counted as one domestic non-life company although, strictly speaking, it is not a corporate body. The number of companies does not include Friendly Societies; there are thousands of these but their income (included in the premium data) is very small;

c) Reinsurance companies are included in the numbers for non-life companies.

B. *Number of employees:* Since 1994, the data on the number of employees in insurance companies are based on the Standard Industrial Classification (SIC) 1992. The previous figures are based on the SIC 1980. The following figures indicate updated estimates for previous years: June 1992 - 237,280 June 1993 - 225,066.

G. *Breakdown of non-life premiums:* Marine and Aviation Insurance includes freight insurance.

UNITED STATES

General remarks: US data are based upon information provided by the National Association of Insurance Commissioners (NAIC).

Definition of foreign-controlled companies: Before 1994, foreign (non-US) person or entity owning directly or indirectly through a holding company system 10 per cent or more of the company. Farmers group, a foreign owned insurance exchange, is also defined as a foreign controlled company. Since 1994, foreign (non-US) person or entity owns directly or indirectly through a holding company system 50 per cent or more of the company.

A. *Number of companies in the reporting country:*
a) "Number of companies" refers to companies filing annual reports with the NAIC. There are several hundreds of small companies that do not file with the NAIC. The premiums of these companies are estimated at less than two per cent of all premiums;
b) The number of life insurance companies includes those whose predominant business is accident and health insurance. Insurers licensed only for accident and health are in non-life companies.

B. *Number of employees:* The number of employees is those on payroll only, which are compiled by the Bureau of Labour Statistics, US Department of Labour.

C. *Business written in the reporting country:*
Reinsurance accepted and ceded premiums reflect only business with unaffiliated companies. In general, unaffiliated business represents the market for reinsurance in the United States, while affiliated business represents reinsurance retained within an insurance group to take advantage of available surplus.

E. *Business written abroad:* Data are sales of foreign insurance affiliates of the United States entities. Sales equal premium plus investment income plus other income. These data are compiled by the United States Department of Commerce.

F. *Outstanding investment by direct insurance companies:*
    a) The NAIC recommends the method of assets valuation; it is followed in every state. Bonds are reported at amortised cost or, when not amortizable, at market value. Common stocks are reported at market value. Preferred stocks are reported at cost by life insurers and at market value by property/casualty insurers. Mortgage loans are reported at unpaid principal balance. All other invested assets are reported at cost or market value, whichever is less;
    b) Some double counting of assets is expected.

G. *Breakdown of non-life premiums:* Reinsurance accepted and ceded includes unaffiliated business only. Accident/Health insurance includes life insurance companies activities.

SINGAPORE

Definition of foreign-controlled companies: Incorporated in Singapore but foreign owned.

III. DEFINITIONS OF CLASSES OF NON-LIFE INSURANCE

(Definitions are based on OECD common classification of the classes of insurance)

CLASSES

DEFINITIONS

1. MOTOR VEHICLE

3. LAND VEHICLES (other than railway rolling stock)
   All damage to or loss of:
   -- Land motor vehicles,
   -- Land vehicles other than motor vehicles.

10. MOTOR VEHICLE LIABILITY
    All liability arising out of the use of motor vehicles operating on land (including carrier's liability).

2. TRANSPORT (including MARINE, AVIATION

4. RAILWAY ROLLING STOCK AND OTHERTRANSPORT
   All damage to or loss of railway rolling stock.

5. AIRCRAFT
   All damage to or loss of aircraft.

6. SHIPS (sea, lake, and river and canal vessels) All damage to or loss of:
   -- River and canal vessels,
   -- Lake vessels,
   -- Sea vessels.

11. AIRCRAFT LIABILITY
    All liability arising out of the use of aircraft (including carrier's liability).

12. LIABILITY FOR SHIPS (sea, lake, and river and canal vessels) All liability arising out of the use of ships, vessels or boats on the sea, lakes, rivers or canals (including carrier's liability).

3. FREIGHT

7. GOODS IN TRANSIT (including merchandise, baggage and all other goods). All damage to or loss of goods in transit or baggage, irrespective of the form of transport.

4. FIRE AND OTHER PROPERTY DAMAGE

8. FIRE AND NATURAL FORCES All damage or loss of property (other than property included in classes 3, 4, 5, 6 and 7) due to:
-- Fire
-- Explosion
-- Storm
-- Natural forces other than storm
-- Nuclear energy
-- Land subsidence

9. OTHER DAMAGE TO PROPERTY All damage to or loss of property (other than property included in classes 3, 4, 5, 6 and 7) due to hail or frost, and any event such as theft, other than those mentioned under 8.

5. PECUNIARY LOSS

14. CREDIT
-- Insolvency (general)
-- Export credit
-- Instalment credit
-- Mortgages
-- Agricultural credit

15. SURETYSHIP
-- Suretyship (direct)
-- Suretyship (indirect)

16. MISCELLANEOUS FINANCIAL LOSS
-- Employment risks
-- Insufficiency of income (general)
-- Bad weather
-- Loss of benefits
-- Continuing general expenses
-- Unforeseen trading expenses
-- Loss of market value
-- Loss of rent or revenue
-- Indirect trading losses other than those mentioned above
-- Other financial loss (non-trading)
-- Other forms of financial loss

6. GENERAL LIABILITY	13. GENERAL LIABILITY All liability other than those forms mentioned under 10, 11 and 12.
7. ACCIDENT AND SICKNESS	1. ACCIDENT (including industrial injury and occupational diseases) -- Fixed pecuniary benefits -- Benefits in the nature of indemnity -- Combinations of the two -- Injury to passengers 2. SICKNESS -- Fixed pecuniary benefits -- Benefits in the nature of indemnity -- Combinations of the two
8. OTHER NON-LIFE INSURANCE	17. LEGAL EXPENSES Legal expenses and costs of litigation. 18. ASSISTANCE 19. MISCELLANEOUS
9. TREATY REINSURANCE	

I. DEFINITIONS ET NOTES COMMUNES

REMARQUES GENERALES

a)   Les définitions des opérations "vie" et "non-vie" sont celles de la législation nationale. Les primes d'assurances-accident et maladie souscrites par des compagnies vie doivent cependant être incluses dans les chiffres d'assurances non-vie.

b)   Les chiffres fournis sur le nombre d'entreprises et le montant des primes d'assurance incluent toutes les entreprises d'assurances agréées dans le pays déclarant, *y compris* les réassureurs professionnels, qu'ils fassent ou non l'objet d'un contrôle, mais *à l'exclusion* de tout régime légal de sécurité sociale administré par l'État.

c)   Par "*entreprises nationales*" il faut entendre les entreprises constituées selon la législation nationale ainsi que les entreprises du pays déclarant qui ne sont pas constituées en sociétés; les succursales et agences d'entreprises étrangères sont exclues.

d)   Par "*entreprises sous contrôle étranger*" il faut entendre les entreprises nationales (selon la définition) qui sont contrôlées par des intérêts étrangers, le "contrôle" étant défini conformément à la législation nationale (voir la définition des entreprises sous contrôle étranger). Les données sur les "*Entreprises sous contrôle étranger*" sont incluses dans les données sur les "*Entreprises nationales*".

e)   Par "*entreprises étrangères*", il faut entendre les entreprises constituées dans un pays autre que le pays déclarant.

A.   NOMBRE D'ENTREPRISES DANS LE PAYS DECLARANT

a)   *Mixtes* : Les entreprises opérant dans le secteur de l'assurance-vie et non-vie.

B.   NOMBRE D'EMPLOYES

a)   *Entreprises d'assurances* : Effectifs employés (à plein temps ou à temps partiel) dans les entreprises d'assurances.

b)   *Intermédiaires* : Nombre des personnes se livrant à ce type d'activité (courtiers ou agents et leur personnel), à l'exclusion des intermédiaires qui peuvent vendre des contrats d'assurance mais ne se rattachent pas directement à la branche des assurances (par exemple, gestionnaires de banques, notaires, garagistes) ou de ceux qui ont été inclus en a) ci-dessus.

C.   OPERATIONS CONCLUES DANS LE PAYS DECLARANT

a)   Les *opérations conclues dans le pays déclarant* incluent toutes les opérations conclues dans le pays déclarant, qu'il s'agisse de risques nationaux ou situés à l'étranger (dans le monde entier), analysés comme indiqué dans les Remarques générales ci-dessus.

b)   Le montant des "*primes nettes émises*" représente les primes retenues dans le pays déclarant. Ces doubles comptabilisations, parfois rencontrées dans les chiffres bruts, devraient être évitées ici.

c)   Le montant des *"primes brutes"* représente le total des primes émises, sans les taxes sur les primes ou autres charges, et avant déduction des commissions ou frais de réassurances cédées. L'inclusion de la réassurance peut entraîner des doubles comptabilisations dans les chiffres fournis.

Le montant des *"primes brutes"* est la somme des *"assurances directes"* et des *"réassurances acceptées"*.

d)   La réassurance facultative peut être incluse soit sous la rubrique "assurance directe", soit sous la rubrique "réassurances acceptées", selon la pratique du pays déclarant.

e)   Les *primes cédées* incluent toutes les primes cédées (réassurances et rétrocession).

f)   En principe, le montant des *"primes nettes émises"* doit être égal au total des *"primes brutes"*, déduction faite des *"primes cédées"*. En cas d'inadéquation, un élément compensateur approprié peut être ajouté dans la rubrique "primes cédées".

D.   PRIMES NETTES EMISES DANS LE PAYS DECLARANT :
RISQUES NATIONAUX ET ETRANGERS
Mêmes notes que a) et b) de la section C ci-dessus.

a)   Cette partie traite, en les distinguant, des opérations portant sur des risques intérieurs et sur des risques situés à l'étranger, et détaille la ligne "primes nettes émises" de C "opérations conclues dans le pays déclarant".

b)   Les *"risques dans le pays"* incluent toutes les opérations conclues dans le pays déclarant qui portent sur des risques intérieurs.

c)   Les *"risques à l'étranger"* incluent toutes les opérations conclues dans le pays déclarant qui portent sur des risques situés en dehors du pays déclarant. (Ne sont pas incluses les opérations conclues en dehors du pays déclarant par des entreprises nationales.)

E.   OPERATIONS CONCLUES À L'ETRANGER
Mêmes notes que c), d), e) et f) de la Section C ci-dessus.

a)   Les *opérations à l'étranger* incluent tous les contrats conclus en dehors du pays déclarant (à la fois dans les pays Membres) de l'OCDE et dans les pays non Membres, ventilés par filiales, succursales et agences d'établir à l'étranger d'entreprises nationales.

F.   ENCOURS DES PLACEMENTS DES ENTREPRISES D'ASSURANCES DIRECTES
a)   Ces données incluent seulement les encours des placements de toutes les entreprises d'assurances directes dans le pays déclarant, mais non les placements par les entreprises de réassurance.

b)   La méthode d'évaluation des placements est définie par chaque pays ; elle est parfois mentionnée dans les notes sur ces pays.

c)   Les placements sont classés par catégorie, par nationalité des entreprises (entreprises nationales, entreprises sous contrôle étranger ou succursales et agences d'entreprises étrangères), aussi que par destination (dans le pays ou à l'étranger).

G.   VENTILATIONS DES PRIMES NON-VIE
Mêmes notes que c), d), e) et f) de la Section C ci-dessus.

a)   Cette Partie recense les *Primes émises par catégories d'assurances non-vie* pour les opérations conclues dans le pays déclarant, et donne une ventilation des "primes nettes émises" de C "Opérations conclues dans le pays déclarant".

b)   Concernant les définitions précises de la classification, voir dans la partie III : "III. Définitions relatives aux branches des assurances non-vie".

c) La ligne "Réassurance obligatoire" est utilisée par les pays Membres ayant des difficultés à ventiler le poste "Réassurances acceptées" par branches.

H. PAIEMENTS BRUTS DES SINISTRES

a) *"Les paiements bruts des sinistres"* qui couvrent tous les paiements bruts pour les sinistres au titre de l'exercice financier, doivent être utilisés dans le calcul des paiements bruts des sinistres survenus.

I. DEPENSES BRUTES D'EXPLOITATION

a) *"Les Dépenses brutes d'exploitation"*, correspondent normalement à la somme des frais d'acquisition, de la variation du montant des frais d'acquisition reportés et des frais d'administration.

J. COMMISSIONS

a) Cette partie correspond au total des commissions et ventile également celles-ci entre les commissions relatives à l'assurance directe et celles relatives à la réassurance acceptée.

II. DEFINITIONS ET NOTES PAR PAYS

Remarques générales pour les pays membres de l'Union Européenne/Espace Economique Européen (UE/EEE): Suite aux changements réglementaires introduits par les Troisièmes Directives d'assurance de l'UE, depuis 1995, les données pour les pays de l'UE/EEE n'incluent pas les succursales et agences d'entreprises étrangères dont le siège social est situé dans un autre pays de l'UE/EEE. Le Groupe de travail sur les statistiques d'assurance est actuellement en train de considérer la façon de résoudre cette question, en coopération avec EUROSTAT. Il est espéré qu'au moins certaines de ces données pourront être ajoutées dans un stade ultérieur (voir la section V de la partie III, qui fournit des informations préliminaires sur cette question).

AUSTRALIE

Remarques générales : Pour l'année 1994 toutes les données relatives à l'assurance vie sont fondées sur l'année fiscale (juillet 1993 à juin 1994).

Définition des entreprises sous contrôle étranger : Contrôle prédominant exercé de l'étranger (via la propriété de titres ou le contrôle des votes)

C.   *Opérations conclues dans le pays déclarant :* Les opérations directes non-vie incluent les primes de réassurance facultative interne, mais excluent les charges légales. Les chiffres ne prennent en compte que les données du secteur privé.

F.   *Encours des placements des entreprises d'assurances directes* : La plupart des chiffres concernant l'investissement sont établis sur base de la valeur du marché.

G.   *Ventilation des primes non-vie* :
   a) L'assurance frets est comprise dans l'assurance maritime/aviation ;
   b) L'assurance pertes pécuniaires, l'assurance-accident et l'assurance-maladie sont comptabilisées dans "Autres".
   c) Les primes pour l'assurance accident et l'assurance maladie souscrites par des compagnies d'assurance-vie ne sont pas incluses. Elles figurent dans les chiffres "vie".

AUTRICHE

Remarques générales: Pour des raisons techniques, les données relatives aux petites Mutuelles ne sont pas incluses. Cependant, les primes de ces Mutuelles se chiffraient à un total de 145 millions d'ATS seulement en 1996.

Définition des entreprises sous contrôle étranger : Participation des compagnies étrangères à hauteur de plus de 50 pour cent des actions.

G.   *Ventilation des primes non-vie :* Les primes cédées comptabilisées dans "Autres" incluent les primes de rétrocession (indépendantes de l'assurance maritime et aviation) qui ne peuvent pas être ventilées.

BELGIQUE

Remarques générales : Depuis 1994, les données relatives au nombre d'entreprises et aux primes ne comprennent pas les succursales d'entreprises étrangères dont le siège social est situé dans l'EEE. Les données relatives au nombre d'entreprises et aux primes ne comprennent pas les réassureurs professionnels qui ne sont ni soumis à l'agrément ni contrôlés, et pour lesquels il n'existe donc pas de données disponibles.

B.   *Nombre d'employés* : Le nombre d'intermédiaires représente le nombre approximatif de courtiers et d'agents non salariés, y compris les agents qui vendent occasionnellement des contrats d'assurance mais dont ce n'est pas l'activité principale.

C.   *Opérations conclues dans le pays déclarant:* Depuis 1996, les données relatives à "l'assurance directe" incluent seulement les risques dans le pays. Les données relatives à la réassurance acceptée concernent toutes les opérations en Belgique et à l'étranger, par succursale ou en libre prestation de services.

D.   *Primes nettes émises dans le pays déclarant : risques nationaux et étrangers :* Il n'est pas possible d'opérer une distinction entre les risques dans le pays et les risques à l'étranger, étant donné que le poste "Réassurances acceptées" ne peut être ventilé entre ces deux catégories d'opérations.

E.   *Opérations conclues à l'étranger* :
  a) On ne dispose pas de données relatives aux filiales d'entreprises belges établies à l'étranger ;
  b) La ventilation des primes brutes entre assurances directes et réassurances acceptées n'est pas disponible en ce qui concerne l'activité à l'étranger des succursales et agences d'entreprises belges.

G.   *Ventilation des primes non-vie :*
  a) Les chiffres reflètent exclusivement les opérations conclues quant aux risques nationaux ;
  b) L'assurance fret est incluse dans l'assurance maritime et aviation ;
  c) L'assurance-accident et maladie inclut l'assurance-accident du travail.

CANADA

Remarques générales : Les données sur des compagnies d'assurances à charte provinciale ne sont pas incluses. Les compagnies vie incluent les "fraternal benefit societies".

Définition des entreprises sous contrôle étranger : Assureur agréé selon les lois (fédérales) du Canada et dont la majorité des actions donnant le droit de vote est contrôlée directement ou indirectement par une/des entité(s) incorporée(s) ou établie(s) hors du Canada.

A. *Nombre d'entreprises dans le pays déclarant :* Avant 1994, les données sur les entreprises de réassurance mixtes (entreprises exerçant à la fois dans le domaine de la réassurance vie et non vie étaient répertoriées sous la rubrique "mixte". Depuis 1994, le nombre de ces compagnies (7 en 1994 et 1995) est inclus sous la rubrique "Réassurance".

C *Primes nettes émises dans le pays déclarant :* En principe les activités accident et maladie des compagnies d'assurance vie sont intégrées dans les chiffres d'assurance non vie. Cependant, en 1994 et 1995, ces activités sont exceptionnellement incluses dans les chiffres d'assurance vie.

F. *Encours des placements des entreprises d'assurances directes* : Les investissements des entreprises domestiques et ceux des entreprises sous contrôle étranger correspondent à des actifs placés dans le monde entier. En revanche, ne sont comptabilisés parmi les investissements des succursales et agences d'entreprises étrangères que ceux réalisés au Canada. Les données sur l'assurance vie excluent les actifs des fonds cantonnés. Au Canada, les actifs sont évalués en fonction des principes comptables généralement reconnus (PCGR), comme il l'est indiqué dans le Manuel de l'Institut Canadien des Comptables Agréés (ICCA). En résumé, pour les compagnies d'assurance non-vie, l'immobilier est évalué au prix déprécié, les prêts hypothécaires : sur la base du coût d'amortissement, les actions : au prix d'achat sauf si le marché est en baisse permanente, auquel cas on retient le prix du marché et les obligations : en fonction du coût d'amortissement. Pour les compagnies d'assurance-vie, l'immobilier est évalué en fonction de la méthode du cours moyen du marché (le coût d'amortissement par rapport au marché étant de 10 pour cent), les prêts hypothécaires : en fonction du coût d'amortissement, les actions : en fonction de la méthode du cours moyen du marché (le coût d'amortissement par rapport au marché étant de 15 pour cent), et les obligations : en fonction du coût d'amortissement. Les compagnies d'assurance et les sociétés de secours mutuel doivent se plier aux politiques de prêts et d'investissements, aux normes et procédures qu'une personne sensée et prudente appliquerait vis-à-vis d'un portefeuille d'investissements et de prêts, et ce, afin d'éviter des risques et pertes injustifiables et d'obtenir le meilleur rendement. De plus, chaque compagnie d'assurance et société de secours mutuel doit se conformer à quelques limites statutaires sur les investissements, comme l'indique la législation.

REPUBLIQUE TCHEQUE

Définition des entreprises sous contrôle étranger : Compagnies agréées selon la loi Tchèque et qui ont plus de 50 pour cent de leur capital détenu par des étrangers.

F. *Encours des placements des entreprises d'assurance directes:* Suite au changement législatif de 1994, les rapports relatifs aux investissements des compagnies d'assurance en 1993, ne sont pas comparables à plusieurs égards à ceux transmis les années précédentes.

DANEMARK

Remarques générales : Depuis 1994, les chiffres sur les fonds de pensions couverts par la loi danoise sur les activités d'assurances sont compris dans la rubrique "Vie".

Définition des entreprises sous contrôle étranger : Entreprises dont plus de 50 pour cent du capital est détenu par des étrangers.

B.   *Nombre d'employés* : L'estimation du nombre d'employés ne se rapporte qu'aux employés à plein temps.

D.   *Primes nettes émises dans le pays déclarant : risques nationaux et étrangers* : Les chiffres de la branche non-vie de cette Section sont des primes acquises, tandis que les chiffres de la Section C sont des primes émises.

F.   *Encours des placements des entreprises d'assurances directes :* Les actions dans le pays incluent les actions détenues dans les filiales établis à l'étranger et les actions détenues dans des entreprises liées étrangères.

FINLANDE

Remarques générales : Depuis 1993, les fonds de pension publics ne sont pas inclus dans les données sur l'assurance-vie.

Définition des entreprises sous contrôle étranger : Entreprises dans lesquelles un étranger détient au moins 50 pour cent des actions ou peut disposer d'au moins 50 pour cent des droits de vote.

A.   *Nombre d'entreprises dans le pays déclarant :* Depuis 1994, les données "non-vie" comprennent les petites associations d'assurance opérant principalement dans les zones rurales.

B.   *Nombre d'employés :* Depuis 1995, le nombre des intermédiaires n'inclut que les courtiers.

F.   *Encours des placements des entreprises d'assurances directes* : Les investissements sont comptabilisés à leur coût d'acquisition. Depuis 1994, les "obligations" sont incluses dans "prêts autres qu'hypothécaires".

G.   *Ventilation des primes non-vie* : "Autres" inclut l'assurance RC automobile obligatoire.

FRANCE

Définition des entreprises sous contrôle étranger : Entreprises dont 20 pour cent au moins du capital est détenu par un non-résident (personne physique ou morale) ou par une société française elle-même sous contrôle étranger.

A.   *Nombre d'entreprises dans le pays déclarant:* Les sociétés "mixtes" ne peuvent pratiquer que l'assurance vie et les branches d'assurance non-vie "accidents" et "maladie".

F. *Encours des placements des entreprises d'assurances directes* : D'une manière générale, les actifs sont évalués à leur valeur historique. Les investissements des entreprises nationales et des succursales et agences d'entreprises étrangères correspondent seulement aux placements dans le pays.

G. *Ventilation des primes non-vie :* Toutes les catégories d'assurance fret sont incluses dans l'assurance maritime et aviation. La réassurance obligatoire concerne les sociétés opérant en assurance directe et les réassureurs professionnels spécialisés. Depuis 1994, les données sur l'assurance des pertes pécuniaires sont répertoriées sous l'intitulé "Autres".

ALLEMAGNE

Définition des entreprises sous contrôle étranger : Intérêts étrangers, directs ou indirects, supérieurs à 50 pour cent.

A. *Nombre d'entreprises dans le pays déclarant* :
   a) Les données relatives aux petites sociétés mutuelles soumises au contrôle des Länder sont exclues. Nombre des petites sociétés mutuelles soumises au contrôle des Länder ; 1358 (1997), 1306 (1998), 1258 (1999). La part de marché de ces sociétés est de plus ou moins 0,04 pour cent;
   b) S'agissant des entreprises d'assurance-vie, les régimes de pension et d'indemnités en cas de décès sont inclus ;
   c) Dans le cas des entreprises d'assurance non-vie, les entreprises d'assurance-maladie spécialisées sont incluses. Nombre des entreprises d'assurance-maladie : 56 (1997), 57 (1998), 56 (1999).

C. *Opérations conclues dans le pays déclarant:* Les chiffres pour 1992 incluent pour la première fois ceux concernant les réassureurs professionnels. Avant 1995, pour les primes cédées, on ne dispose pas de ventilation entre les opérations souscrites dans le pays déclarant et celles souscrites à l'étranger. Par conséquent, les chiffres de la section C et la section G concernent les opérations totales (nationales et étrangères) pour ces années .

E. *Opérations conclues à l'étranger* : Même remarque que sous le point C. Avant 1995, pour les opérations de réassurance acceptées, on ne dispose pas de ventilation entre les branches vie et non-vie ; par conséquent la réassurance vie comprend la réassurance non-vie. Les opérations de réassurance acceptées souscrites à l'étranger sont celles acceptées d'une entreprise d'assurance située à l'étranger. On ne dispose pas de données concernant la localisation du risque assuré.

F. *Encours des placements des entreprises d'assurances directes* : La méthode d'évaluation des placements est la méthode du coût historique. Depuis 1995, une distinction entre entreprises nationales et succursales et agences d'entreprises étrangères n'est pas disponible; Il n'y a de même pas de données séparées pour les entreprises sous contrôle étranger. Les placements nationaux et étrangers ne sont pas ventilés.

G. *Ventilations des primes non-vie :* Même note que la Section C ci-dessus.
   a) L'assurance fret est incluse dans l'assurance maritime et aviation.

b) La rubrique "Divers " correspond aux données sur l'assurance "protection juridique".

GRECE

Définition des entreprises sous contrôle étranger : Définitions conformes aux articles 1 et 41 de la Septième Directive 349/83 de la CEE et aux articles 9 et 25 de la Quatrième Directive 660/78 de la CEE.

A.   *Nombre d'entreprises dans le pays déclarant :* Les représentants des courtiers d'assurance Lloyds [nombre des courtiers d'assurance Lloyds : 38 (1991)] ne sont pas inclus dans "les succursales et agences d'entreprises étrangères".

G.   *Ventilation des primes non-vie :* "Autres" renvoie uniquement à l'assurance protection juridique.

HONGRIE

Remarques générales : Depuis 1996, les données des associations d'assurance sont incluses. Comme il y a 23 associations d'assurance, les données de 1996 sur le nombre des compagnies d'assurance ne sont plus comparables avec les données antérieures. En ce qui concerne les données sur les primes, les investissements, les coûts, cette addition n'a pas d'effet évident parce que le chiffre d'affaires de ces associations est modeste.

Définition des entreprises sous contrôle étranger : Plus de la moitié du capital est détenu par des actionnaires étrangers.

E.   *Opérations conclues à l'étranger :* Aucune compagnie d'assurance n'a de filiale ou de succursale à l'étranger.

F.   *Encours des placements des entreprises d'assurances directes :*
     a) Seuls les investissements relatifs aux provisions techniques sont inclus. Les investissements du capital souscrit, du capital réservé et des provisions pour les opérations générales de la compagnie ne sont pas indiqués.
     b) L'évaluation des placements se fait au prix coûtant. Après un minimum d'un an de perte de valeurs, les investissements sont réévalués. En Hongrie, seule la dépréciation est admise.

G.   *Ventilation des primes non-vie.*
     a) Les données sur "marine, aviation et autres transports" sont répertoriés sous l'intitulé "Autres";
     b) Avant 1994, l'assurance habitation était classée dans la rubrique "incendie et autres". Depuis 1995, elle est classée dans la rubrique "Autres".

ISLANDE

Définition des entreprises sous contrôle étranger : Plus de 50% des actions détenues par des entreprises étrangères.

B.   *Nombre d'employés :* Le chiffre correspond à des emplois à plein temps. Ainsi, une personne travaillant à mi-temps est considérée comme représentant la moitié d'un employé.

F.   *Encours des placements des entreprises d'assurances directes :* L'évaluation s'effectue essentiellement sur base de la valeur de marché. Il n'existe aucune limite autorisée de placement par catégorie, mais la sécurité des réserves techniques doit être assurée.

IRLANDE

Remarques générales : Les primes d'assurance-maladie sont exclues. Les données sur le nombre d'entreprises et les primes excluent les réassureurs professionnels qui ne sont pas soumis à agrément, et qui ne sont pas supervisés. Aucune information n'est donc disponible à leur sujet.

D.   *Primes nettes émises dans le pays déclarant :* risques nationaux et étrangers : Les chiffres concernant l'assurance-vie de risques situés à l'étranger, ne sont pas disponibles. Cependant, ils sont estimés négligeables.

E.   *Opérations conclues à l'étranger :* Les chiffres concernant la réassurance sont compris dans les assurances directes.

F.   *Encours des placements des entreprises d'assurances directes :* Comme la ventilation des actifs liés (actifs représentant des placements dans des fonds d'investissements ou des OPCVM) n'est pas disponible, ils sont comptabilisés dans "autres placements". L'investissement à l'étranger dans la branche assurance vie correspond seulement aux actifs non liés représentant l'activité de l'assurance vie qui n'est pas localisée en Irlande. L'investissement dans la branche non-vie inclut les liquidités placées dans des sociétés immobilières, banques et autres institutions financières. Les chiffres sur les placements sont évalués à leur valeur de marché. Suite à des raisons techniques, depuis 1995, les données non-vie sont basées sur la valeur historique. Autres placements de l'assurance-vie incluant les postes ci-après ; Titres à intérêt variable, Comptes de dépôt et comptes ordinaires, Fonds de placement, Espèces et Prêts hypothécaires (immobilier), etc. Depuis 1994, les données sur les succursales et agences d'entreprises étrangères comprennent seulement les succursales d'un pays tiers (hors Union Européenne) établies en Irlande. Les investissements de succursales d'entreprises UE ne sont plus disponibles.

G.   *Ventilation des primes non-vie :*
     a) L'assurance fret est incluse dans l'assurance maritime et aviation ;
     b) Depuis 1996, l'assurance des pertes pécuniaires est incluse dans la rubrique "Autres".

ITALIE

Définition des entreprises sous contrôle étranger : Toute entreprise dont plus de 50 pour cent du capital appartient, même indirectement, à des actionnaires étrangers.

B.   *Nombre d'employés :* Le chiffre des intermédiaires est une estimation et comprend les producteurs indépendants.

F.   *Encours des placements des entreprises d'assurances directes* : En général, les chiffres sur les placements sont enregistrés à leur valeur historique.

JAPON

Remarques générales: Les chiffres sont ceux de l'année fiscale (1 avril de l'année examinée au 31 mars de l'année suivante).

Définition des entreprises sous contrôle étranger : Compagnies détenues par des actionnaires étrangers à hauteur de 50 pour cent au moins du capital.

B.   *Nombre d'employés :*
    a) Les effectifs employés à temps partiel ne sont pas inclus dans "Effectifs employés" ;
    b) Les agents dont l'assurance n'est pas l'activité principale figurent dans les "intermédiaires"

C.   *Opérations conclues dans le pays déclarant :*
    a) Les chiffres concernant les entreprises d'assurance-vie s'entendent avant déduction des primes de remboursement ;
    b) Les primes brutes pour l'assurance non-vie comprennent l'élément épargne des "assurances avec remboursement à l'échéance". Avant 1998, ce n'est pas le cas des primes nettes émises. Dès lors, avant 1998, les primes nettes émises de l'assurance non-vie ne correspondent pas aux "primes brutes moins primes cédées".

E.   *Opérations conclues à l'étranger :* Dans la partie non-vie, certaines filiales ne sont pas en mesure de fournir des chiffres distincts pour les "assurance directes" et les "réassurances acceptées".

F.   *Encours des placements des entreprises d'assurances directes :*
    a) La méthode de l'évaluation au coût d'acquisition est généralement appliquée. L'amortissement de l'immobilier (autre que les terrains) à des fins de placement s'effectue par application d'un pourcentage fixe sur la base de la méthode de l'amortissement dégressif. L'évaluation des valeurs cotées s'effectue sur la base du coût d'acquisition ou du prix du marché (en choisissant le chiffre le plus bas) ;
    b) Depuis 1996, les prêts hypothécaires sont inclus dans les "Prêts autres qu'hypothécaires".
    c) Autres investissements : inclut les dépôts, prêts au jour le jour, "Monetary Receivables Bought", "Commodity Securities", fonds de gestion de patrimoine, etc. Depuis 1998, les actions et obligations étrangères sont inclues dans les "autres investissements".

G.	*Ventilation des primes non-vie :* Les primes d'assurance incendie et dommages aux biens, ainsi que celles d'assurance-accident et maladie, sont calculées avant déduction de la composante épargne des "assurances avec remboursement à l'échéance".

Les services et entités suivants ne sont pas inclus dans les données statistiques :

## 1.	Assurance vie de la Poste

Ce service à but non lucratif administré par l'Etat distribue des assurances vie auprès de la population dans tout le pays, ce qui contribue à la stabilité économique de la population et à son bien-être. Il est administré par le ministère de la Poste et des Télécommunications conformément aux dispositions de la Loi sur l'assurance vie de la poste. Son budget et sa comptabilité font l'objet de délibérations à la Diète.

Revenu de primes d'assurance directe	13 638.813 milliards de yen	Exercice 1996
Total des actifs	100 772.008 milliards de yen	fin de l'exercice 1996

## 2.	Assistance mutuelle des associations d'entreprises soumises aux normes d'hygiène et de conditions sanitaires

Les associations d'entreprises soumises aux normes d'hygiène et de conditions sanitaires sont des entités dont le but est d'améliorer les normes d'hygiène et de conditions sanitaires en veillant au bon état sanitaire des entreprises concernées, ce qui va dans le sens des intérêts des consommateurs. Ces associations sont établies conformément à la loi correspondante. Les associations fournissent, dans le cadre de leur exploitation, des services sans but lucratif assimilables à des assurances vie ou assurance incendie à leurs adhérents.

Revenu de primes d'assurance directe	NON DISPONIBLE
Total des actifs	NON DISPONIBLE

## 3.	Assistance mutuelle des associations de promotion des centres commerciaux

Ces services sans but lucratif assimilables à des assurances incendie sont fournis par les associations de promotion des centres commerciaux à leurs adhérents, en raison des caractéristiques spécifiques des centres commerciaux dans lesquels de nombreuses boutiques sont concentrées sur une surface relativement petite. La plupart des associations sont petites et elles sont très peu nombreuses à fournir effectivement des services d'assistance mutuelle.

Revenu de primes d'assurance directe	NON DISPONIBLE
Total des actifs	NON DISPONIBLE

4.   Assistance mutuelle des coopératives de consommateurs

Les coopératives de consommateurs sont des associations établies conformément à la Loi et dont l'objet est de promouvoir le développement spontané des associations locales, ce qui contribue à la stabilité économique de la population et à la mise en valeur de son mode de vie. Les coopératives de consommateurs et leur fédération fournissent à leurs adhérents des services sans but lucratif d'assistance mutuelle, notamment dans le domaine de l'assurance vie ou de l'assurance automobile.

Revenu de primes d'assurance directe	669.011 milliards de yen	d'après une enquête pour l'exercice 1995
Total des actifs	NON DISPONIBLE	

5.   Assistance mutuelle des coopératives sylvicoles au titre des calamités

Ce dispositif a été mis en place conformément à la Loi et vise à améliorer le statut économique et social des propriétaires d'exploitations sylvicoles, à garantir un rendement durable des forêts ainsi qu'à accroître leur production potentielle, ce qui contribue au développement de l'économie nationale. La Fédération nationale des coopératives de propriétaires d'exploitations sylvicoles administre ce dispositif sans but lucratif qui est analogue à une assurance non-vie pour les exploitations sylvicoles.

Revenu de primes d'assurance directe	2.625 milliards de yen	exercice 1996
Total des actifs	NON DISPONIBLE	

6.   Assistance mutuelle des coopératives de pêche

Ce dispositif a été mis en place conformément à la Loi et vise à promouvoir le développement des associations locales de pêcheurs et d'intervenants de la transformation du produit de la pêche, ce qui favorise leur statut économique et social, améliore la production potentielle des pêcheries et contribue par là-même au développement de l'économie nationale. Les coopératives de pêche fournissent à leurs adhérents des services sans but lucratif assimilables à des assurances vie et non-vie.

Revenu de primes d'assurance directe	79.031 milliards de yen	exercice 1996
Total des actifs	404.455 milliards de yen	fin de l'exercice 1996

7.   Assistance mutuelle des coopératives de PME

Ces associations composées de petites et moyennes entreprises de certaines zones fournissent à leurs adhérents des services sans but lucratif assimilables à des assurances vie et non-vie. Le nombre total de ces coopératives s'élève approximativement à 49 000 dans tout le Japon. Même si l'on ne dispose pas de statistiques précises, leurs services habituels sont les suivants :

i)   Assistance mutuelle incendie des coopératives d'assurance incendie

Ces coopératives composées de PME fournissent, selon le principe de l'assistance mutuelle, des services sans but lucratif assimilables à des assurances incendie afin de couvrir les adhérents contre les sinistres provoqués par le feu.

Revenu de primes d'assurance directe	20.041 milliards de yen	exercice 1996
Total des actifs	66.087 milliards de yen	fin de l'exercice 1996

ii)   Assistance mutuelle automobile des coopératives d'assurance des véhicules à moteur

Ces coopératives composées de PME fournissent, selon le principe de l'assistance mutuelle, des services sans but lucratif assimilables à des assurances automobile afin de couvrir les adhérents contre les accidents liés à la possession, à l'utilisation et au contrôle de véhicules personnels.

Revenu de primes d'assurance directe	24.575 milliards de yen	exercice 1996
Total des actifs	16.900 milliards de yen	fin de l'exercice 1996

8.   Assistance mutuelle des coopératives agricoles

Ce dispositif a été mis en place conformément à la Loi et vise à promouvoir le développement des associations collectives d'agriculteurs, ce qui améliore la production potentielle de l'agriculture, favorise leur statut économique et social et contribue au développement de l'économie nationale. Les coopératives agricoles et leur fédération fournissent à leurs adhérents, en tant qu'organisme unique, des services sans but lucratif assimilables à des assurances vie et non-vie.

Revenu de primes d'assurance directe	4 713.500 milliards de yen	chiffre approximatif en fin d'exercice 1996
Total des actifs	30 141.400 milliards de yen	chiffre approximatif en fin d'exercice 1996

9.   Assistance mutuelle des syndicats de salariés

Les syndicats de salariés et la fédération nationale d'assistance mutuelle des syndicats, qui sont organisées volontairement par les salariés avec pour principal objectif de promouvoir leur statut économique, et plus particulièrement de maintenir et améliorer les normes du travail, fournissent à leurs adhérents des services sans but lucratif assimilables à des assurances vie et non-vie.

Revenu de primes d'assurance directe	NON DISPONIBLE
Total des actifs	NON DISPONIBLE

CORÉE

Définition des entreprises sous contrôle étranger : filiale d'une entreprise étrangère.

F.   *Encours des placements des entreprises d'assurances directes :* Les investissements se mesurent sur la base du coût historique, à l'exception des titres cotés, pour lesquels on retient le cours moyen du marché (cf. Article 18-2 du décret mettant en oeuvre la loi sur les activités d'assurance.

LUXEMBOURG

Définition des entreprises sous contrôle étranger : L'actionnaire principal n'est pas de nationalité luxembourgeoise.

C.   *Opérations conclues dans le pays déclarant:* Les chiffres concernent les produits d'assurance commercialisés (flux).

F.   *Encours des placements des entreprises d'assurances directes :* Seuls les données sur les placements en flux sont disponibles.

G.   *Ventilation des primes non-vie :* Même note que la Section C ci-dessus.

MEXIQUE

Définition des entreprises sous contrôle étranger : Entreprises dont 51 pour cent ou plus du capital est détenu par des étrangers.

G.   *Ventilation des primes non-vie :*
       a) "Assurances transport maritime, aviation et autres transports" inclut l'assurance fret.
       b) Les autres assurances non-vie incluent l'assurance des risques agricoles et divers.

PAYS-BAS

Remarques générales :

       a) Avant 1995, le nombre, ainsi que les primes encaissées par les réassureurs professionnels, sont des estimations puisque ces entreprises sont exemptées du contrôle gouvernemental ; Depuis 1995, ces entreprises ne sont plus incluses. En 1995, il y avait 9 réassureurs professionnels qui ont généré des primes de près de 751 millions de florins (517 millions en non-vie et 234 millions en vie).
       b) Le nombre, ainsi que les primes encaissées par les entreprises sous contrôle étranger, sont des estimations, les chiffres fournis ne concernant que les entreprises soumises au contrôle ;

Définition des entreprises sous contrôle étranger : Compagnies d'assurance agréées dans le pays, dont au moins 50 pour cent du capital est détenu par une ou plusieurs compagnies, dont les sièges sociaux sont situés hors des Pays-Bas.

A. *Nombre d'entreprises dans le pays déclarant* :
    a) Avant 1995, le nombre des entreprises d'assurance non-vie inclut de petites compagnies mutuelles qui ne sont pas soumises au contrôle (1995, 239). Leur part du marché n'a pas excédé 0,2 pour cent(1995).
    b) Depuis 1995, le nombre de succursales d'entreprises étrangères avec un siège social au sein de l'UE/EEE n'est plus inclus. Le nombre de ces succursales est de 115 (en 1995, soit 3 en vie et 112 en non-vie).

B. *Nombre d'employés :* Les chiffres sur les effectifs employés et les intermédiaires (réalisant des affaires sur une base professionnelle) sont des estimations ;

C. *Opérations conclues dans le pays déclarant* : Les compagnies d'assurance-vie aux Pays-Bas n'étant pas tenues de déclarer leurs activités de réassurance, on ne peut distinguer, dans les primes brutes, les assurances directes des réassurances acceptées.

E. *Opérations conclues à l'étranger :* Avant 1995 les données disponibles sont des approximations relatives aux trois plus grandes compagnies d'assurances hollandaises opérant à l'échelle internationale. Depuis 1994, aucune estimation n'est disponible.

F. *Encours des placements des entreprises d'assurances directes* : Les techniques d'évaluation en vigueur sont généralement les suivantes :
    - immobilier : valeur du marché/valeur estimée
    - prêts (hypothécaires) :
        vie: valeur d'amortissement ou valeur nominale
        non-vie: valeur nominale
    - actions :
        côtées :   valeur du marché
        non-côtées :   valeur estimée
    - obligations
        vie :   valeur d'amortissement ou valeur du marché
        non-vie :   valeur du marché
    Avant la mise en oeuvre des Troisièmes Directives de L'UE, il n'y avait aucune limite réglementaire quant au pourcentage des placements des actifs totaux par une entreprise d'assurance.

G. *Ventilation des primes non-vie :*
    a) L'assurance fret est incluse dans l'assurance maritime/aviation ;
    b) Les assurances pertes pécuniaires et responsabilité générale sont incluses dans les autres assurances non-vie.

NOUVELLE-ZELANDE

Définition des entreprises sous contrôle étranger : 50 pour cent ou plus d'intérêts étrangers.

C. *Opérations conclues dans le pays déclarant* : Les primes brutes d'assurance-vie directe par les entreprises nationales incluent les primes nettes de réassurance-vie.

G. *Ventilation des primes non-vie* : "Autres" correspond à l'assurance médicale.

NORVEGE

Remarques générales : Pour 1994 et 1995, sans les données concernant les succursales et agences d'entreprises étrangères de l'assurance non-vie.

Définition des entreprises sous contrôle étranger : Entreprises où la majorité des droits de vote est détenue par des étrangers. Depuis 1997, toutes les compagnies appartenant au même groupe d'assurance sont classées de façon identique.

C. *Opérations conclues dans le pays déclarant :* Les réassurances acceptées sont calculées par soustraction, c'est-à-dire le montant total des primes brutes diminué des primes correspondant à des assurances directes en Norvège. Cela signifie que les réassurances acceptées peuvent englober des assurances directes souscrites à l'étranger.

F. *Encours des placements des entreprises d'assurances directes* : Le total des placements effectués par les sociétés de la branche non-vie ne comprend pas les placements des succursales et agences de sociétés étrangères.

POLOGNE

Remarques générales: L'établissement des succursales et agences d'entreprises étrangères est autorisé depuis 1er janvier 1999.

Définition des entreprises sous contrôle étranger : 51 pour cent au moins du capital sous contrôle étranger. Depuis 1998: les entreprises dans lesquelles la part directe des entreprises étrangères dans le capital souscrit dépasse 50%.

A. *Nombre d'entreprises dans le pays déclarant :* Le nombre total d'entreprises d'assurance inclut 6 mutuelles d'assurance et 57 sociétés par action (2 entreprises publiques et 61 entreprises privées).

B. *Nombre d'employés :* Le nombre d'employés d'assurance est estimé. En 1996 et 1999, l'organe étatique en charge du contrôle de l'assurance a donné approximativement 201347 autorisations de mener une activité d'intermédiation (les autorisations concernaient tant des agents que des courtiers).

F. *Encours des placements des entreprises d'assurances directes* : Les chiffres sur les placements sont généralement enregistrés à leur valeur historique.

I.   *Dépenses brutes d'exploitation :* Cette rubrique inclut les coûts d'acquisition, les dépenses administratives et les autres dépenses techniques.

PORTUGAL

Définition des entreprises sous contrôle étranger : Proportion du capital détenu par des étrangers supérieure à 50 pour cent.

C.   *Opérations conclues dans le pays déclarant :* Le montant des primes brutes représente le total des primes et accessoires.

F.   *Encours des placements des entreprises d'assurances directes :*
a) Avant 1995, seuls les actifs représentatifs des provisions techniques sont considérés ; Depuis 1995, les actifs libres sont aussi inclus.
b) Parmi les valeurs mobilières sont inclus : titres du trésor, bons du trésor, titres de créance pour l'investissement public, obligations, actions, titres de participation et parts de fonds communs de placement.
c) "Prêts autres qu'hypothécaires" comprennent les emprunts sur les polices et les emprunts sur les titres ;
d) "Autres placements" incluent les dépôts et les certificats de dépôts.

G.   *Ventilation des primes non-vie :* Les assurances-maladie et accident incluent l'assurance contre les accidents du travail.

REPUBLIQUE SLOVAQUE

Définition des entreprises sous contrôle étranger : celles où la part des actionnaires étrangers excède 50%.

ESPAGNE

Définition des entreprises sous contrôle étranger : Participation dans le capital social égale ou supérieure à 50 pour cent.

F.   *Encours des placements des entreprises d'assurances directes :* En général, la méthode d'estimation du coût d'acquisition est appliquée.

G.   *Ventilation des primes non-vie :* L'assurance médicale est incluse dans l'assurance-accident et santé.

SUEDE

Définition des entreprises sous contrôle étranger : 50 pour cent des titres au moins est sous contrôle étranger.

A. *Nombre d'entreprises dans le pays déclarant* : Les données "non-vie" excluent environ 300 petites mutuelles d'assurance locales dont la part estimée de marché "non-vie" est inférieure à 0,1 pour cent (données 1999). Depuis 1994, il n'existe aucun chiffre pour les succursales d'assurances non-vie dont le siège social est situé dans un pays membre de l'EEE. Il en existe 22 ; et le chiffre de leurs primes directes est estimé à un pourcentage réduit des primes non-vie (données 1999). Il y a également deux branches d'assurance vie appartenant à l'EEE et représentant une faible proportion.

B. *Nombre d'employés :*
Le nombre d'employés de compagnies d'assurance inclut les agents employés, dont approximativement 20 000 travaillent à temps partiel (données de 1993). Depuis 1994, les données des employés des compagnies d'assurance excluent les agents à temps partiel ou travaillant en franchise. Les données de 1993 correspondantes devraient être du même ordre de grandeur qu'en 1994 soit, 19 000. Le nombre des intermédiaires inclut seulement les courtiers d'assurance.

C. *Opérations conclues dans le pays déclarant* : Aucune information fiable n'est disponible concernant les succursales et les agences des entreprises de réassurance étrangères. Cependant, comme on considère qu'elles se concentrent sur la réassurance non-vie, leurs primes de réassurance vie sont estimées à 0 (zéro).

D. *Primes nettes émises dans le pays déclarant : risques nationaux et étrangers* : Aucune information fiable n'est disponible sur la ventilation entre les risques nationaux et les risques étrangers. Cependant, il est probable que seulement une part de marché mineure de l'assurance non-vie directe est émise sur les risques étrangers et qu'il n'y a pratiquement aucune activité d'assurance vie directe sur cette catégorie de risques.

E. *Opérations conclues à l'étranger :* On ne dispose que de certaines informations pour les assurances directes et les primes cédées dans le cas des succursales et agences non-vie des assureurs nationaux. Il n'existe pas d'information correspondante sur les filiales.

F. *Encours des placements des entreprises d'assurances directes* :
  a) Avant 1996, l'évaluation s'effectue, en général, sur la base de la valeur d'achat ou de la valeur du marché (en choisissant le chiffre le plus bas). Depuis 1996, la méthode de la valeur du marché est utilisée ;
  b) L'évaluation des actifs à revenu fixe correspondant aux provisions techniques de l'assurance vie peut être faite en fonction du coût, même si la valeur obtenue est supérieure à la valeur du marché.
  c) Avant 1996, les prêts hypothécaires ne peuvent être séparés des prêts autres qu'hypothécaires ; ces derniers incluent donc tous les prêts.
  d) Il n'y avait aucune limite autorisée du placement par catégorie, cependant il y avait des restrictions sur le choix des actifs correspondant aux provisions techniques. Au moins 80 pour cent des provisions techniques en assurance-vie (autre qu'à capital variable) doit être couverts par certains types d'actifs. Les 80 pour cent restant ne peuvent être investis en actions. La détention d'actions est limitée indirectement du fait que les droits de vote détenus dans une même société ne peuvent en général dépasser 5 pour cent. Le 1er juillet 1995, les règles de l'UE sur les investissements ont été mises ne vigueur. En particulier, aucune des catégories "actions" ou "immobilier" ne peuvent excéder 25 pour cent des provisions techniques nets de réassurance.

e) Les données sur les agences d'entreprises non EEE n'incluent que les dépôts juridiquement reconnus. Les dépôts sont comptabilisés sous la rubrique "Autres Placements". Depuis 1994, les données ne couvrent plus celles des pays membres de l'EEE.

f) Quoi qu'aucune information fiable ne soit disponible concernant la distribution des placements dans le pays et à l'étranger, les placements en immobilier, actions et obligations à l'étranger ont certainement une influence.

G. *Ventilation des primes non-vie* :

a) En ce qui concerne les réassurances obligatoires acceptées, les primes émises par les succursales ou agences de réassureurs étrangers n'ont pas été prises en compte ;

b) L'assurance de responsabilité générale ne peut être comptabilisée comme une catégorie séparée puisque, en général, elle fait partie d'un ensemble de produits variés tels que l'assurance risques habitation et "tous risques" habitation ;

c) L'assurance-accident et santé inclut l'assurance sans faute des employeurs ;

SUISSE

Définition des entreprises sous contrôle étranger : Entreprises avec une participation étrangère de plus de 50 pour cent. Depuis 1993, entreprises dont plus de 50 pour cent du capital est détenu pas des étrangers, directement ou en cascade.

B. *Nombre d'employés* : La notion d'"intermédiaire" signifie les agents d'assurance liés à une société d'assurances par un contrat de travail, à l'exclusion des courtiers et des agents généraux indépendants dont le nombre s'élève à 400 en 1992 et 400-500 en 1993 et 1994.

D. *Primes nettes émises dans le pays déclarant : risques nationaux et étrangers :* Les primes de réassurance étrangères sont incluses.

E. *Opérations conclues à l'étranger* : Les chiffres des réassurances acceptées dans cette Section sont également inclus dans les colonnes correspondantes des tableaux de la Section C.

F. *Encours des placements des entreprises d'assurances directes* : Hypothèques : ensemble des hypothèques, celles accordées pour l'acquisition d'un logement privé n'étant pas mentionnées séparément. Autres placements : - Vie : ils incluent les dépôts à terme et créances sur le marché monétaire, prêts et avances sur polices. - Vie et non-vie : les avoirs liquides et autres actifs sont inclus, il s'agit entre autres d'avoirs auprès d'agents, de preneurs d'assurances, d'assureurs et réassureurs, et de dépôts pour réassurances acceptées.

G. *Ventilation des primes non-vie :* Les primes brutes de réassurances acceptées ainsi que le total des primes brutes sont des estimations.

Entités d'assurance ne figurant pas dans les statistiques
(Activités sur le marché suisse seulement, en 1996)

Entités d'assurance	Nombre des entités	Primes brutes assurances directe en million de CHF
Caisses maladie reconnues soumises à la surveillance de l'Office fédéral des assurances sociales	159	16,420
Caisse nationale suisse d'assurance en cas d'accidents (CNA)	1	3,281
Etablissements cantonaux d'assurance incendie	19	818
Total	**179**	**20,519**

TURQUIE

Définition des entreprises sous contrôle étranger : Entreprises dont plus de 50 pour cent du capital sont détenus par un actionnaire étranger.

B.	*Nombre d'employés :* Le nombre d'employés des intermédiaires ne représente que celui des agents, et exclut les banques agissant en tant qu'agents.

D.	*Primes nettes émises dans le pays déclarant :* risques nationaux et étrangers : Tous les chiffres sont établis sur la base des primes brutes avant 1990.

F.	*Encours des placements des entreprises d'assurances directes :* Les immeubles sont réévalués pour tenir compte de l'inflation. Les immeubles, actions et autres placements sont évalués sur base de la valeur d'acquisition.

G	*Ventilation des primes non-vie :* Les données relatives aux sociétés de réassurance ne sont pas comprises dans les primes ventilées par catégories d'assurance non vie. L'assurance maritime et aviation inclut l'assurance fret.

ROYAUME-UNI

A.	*Nombre d'entreprises dans le pays déclarant :*
	a) Pour l'année 1993, les données concernant l'intitulé "Entreprises Nationales" se réfèrent aux "Entreprises UE dont le siège social est au Royaume-Uni". L'intitulé "Entreprises

Sous Contrôle Etranger" porte sur les "Entreprises UE dont le siège social est situé en dehors du Royaume-Uni" et l'intitulé "Succursales et Agences d'Entreprises Etrangères" correspond aux "Entreprises Externes". Le nombre d'"Entreprise UE dont le siège social est situé en dehors du Royaume-Uni" ne tient pas compte des "Entreprises UE dont le siège est au Royaume-Uni". Pour les années 1994 et 1995, les données pour les "Entreprises Nationales" se réfèrent aux "Entreprises de l'EEE dont le siège est au Royaume-Uni", "Entreprises Sous Contrôle Etranger" aux "Entreprises de l'EEE dont le siège est situé en dehors du Royaume-Uni" et Succursales et Agences d'Entreprises Etrangères" aux "Entreprises Externes". Le nombre d'"Entreprises EEE dont le siège est au Royaume-Uni" exclut les "Entreprises EEE dont le siège social est situé en dehors du Royaume-Uni".

b) Le Lloyds est comptabilisé comme une seule entreprise nationale non-vie même si ce n'est pas, à proprement parler, une personne morale. Le nombre d'entreprises ne comprend pas les sociétés de secours mutuel ; il en existe des milliers mais leurs recettes (qui figurent dans les données relatives aux primes) sont très faibles.

c) Les entreprises de réassurance sont comprises dans le nombre d'entreprises non-vie.

B.   *Nombre d'employés :* Depuis 1994, les informations sur le nombre d'employés dans les entreprises d'assurance est basé sur la CITI de 1992. Les données pour les années antérieures sont basées sur celles de 1980. Les chiffres suivants mettent à jour ceux publiés pour les années précédentes : juin 1992 - 237 280, juin 1993 - 225 066.

G.   *Ventilation des primes non-vie :* Les assurances maritimes/aviation comprennent l'assurance fret.

ETATS-UNIS

Remarques générales : Les données sont fondées sur les informations fournies par "the National Association of Insurance Commissioners" (NAIC).

Définition des entreprises sous contrôle étranger : Avant 1994, personne ou entité étrangère détenant directement ou indirectement par le biais d'un holding, au moins 10 pour cent du capital de la société. Le "Farmers group", bourses d'assurance détenues par des intérêts étrangers, est également considéré comme une société étrangère. Depuis 1994, une personne ou entité étrangère détenant directement ou indirectement par le biais d'un holding, au moins 50 pour cent du capital de la compagnie. Le "Farmer's Group" est également considéré comme une entité étrangère.

A.   *Nombre d'entreprises dans le pays déclarant :*
a) Les entreprises dénombrées sont celles dont les rapports annuels sont enregistrés auprès de la NAIC. Il existe cependant plusieurs centaines de petites entreprises qui ne sont pas enregistrées à la NAIC. Les primes de ces compagnies sont estimées à moins de 2 pour cent du total des primes de la profession ;
b) Les chiffres concernant l'assurance-vie incluent les compagnies d'assurance-vie dont l'activité principale est l'assurance-accident et maladie. Les assureurs agréés seulement pour les accidents et la maladie sont classés parmi les entreprises d'assurance non-vie.

B.   *Nombre d'employés :* Le nombre d'employés comprend les salariés seulement. Chiffres recueillis par le "Bureau of Labour Statistics, US Department of Labour".

C.	*Opérations conclues dans le pays déclarant* :
Les primes de réassurances acceptées et cédées ne reflètent que des affaires avec des entreprises non liées. En général, aux Etats-Unis, les affaires avec des entreprises non liées représentent le marché de la réassurance, tandis que les affaires avec des entreprises liées représentent, en fait, la réassurance retenue à l'intérieur d'un groupe d'assurances pour mieux utiliser les excédents ;

E.	*Opérations conclues à l'étranger* : Les données correspondent aux ventes des filiales étrangères des compagnies américaines. Ces ventes sont égales à la somme des primes, des revenus d'investissement et d'autres revenus. Ces données sont fournies par le "Department of Commerce" des Etats-Unis.

F.	*Encours des placements des entreprises d'assurances directes* :
a) La NAIC recommande la méthode d'évaluation des actifs qui est employée dans tous les états. Les obligations sont déclarées à leur coût après amortissement ou, lorsqu'elles ne sont pas amortissables, au prix du marché. Les actions ordinaires sont comptabilisées à leur cours sur le marché. Pour les actions à droit de vote préférentiel, les assureurs-vie indiquent le coût d'acquisition et les assureurs-dommages le prix du marché. Les prêts hypothécaires figurent pour le capital restant dû. Tous les autres actifs de placement figurent à leur prix le plus bas (coût ou prix du marché) ;
b) Il faut s'attendre à ce que certains actifs soient comptabilisés deux fois.

G.	*Ventilation des primes non-vie* : Les réassurances acceptées et cédées incluent seulement les affaires non affiliées. L'assurance "Accident et maladie" inclut les activités des compagnies d'assurance-vie.

SINGPOUR

Définition des entreprises sous contrôle étranger : exerçant légalement des activités à Singapour mais détenues par l'étranger.

III. DEFINITIONS RELATIVES AUX BRANCHES DES ASSURANCES NON-VIE

(Les définitions sont fondées sur la classification des branches d'assurances
commune aux pays Membres de l'OCDE)

BRANCHES   *DÉFINITIONS*

1. AUTOMOBILE

3. CORPS DE VÉHICULES
TERRESTRES (autres que
ferroviaires)Tout dommage subi par :
-- véhicules terrestres automoteurs,
-- véhicules terrestres non automoteurs.

10. RC VÉHICULES TERRESTRES
AUTOMOTEURS
Toute responsabilité résultant de
l'emploi de véhicules terrestres
automoteurs (y compris la
responsabilité du transporteur).

2. TRANSPORTS (y compris
MARITIME ET AVIATION

4. CORPS DE VÉHICULES
FERROVIAIRES
Tout dommage subi par les véhicules
ferroviaires.

5. CORPS DE VÉHICULES AÉRIENS
Tout dommage subi par les véhicules
aériens.

6. CORPS DE VÉHICULES
MARITIMES, LACUSTRES ET
FLUVIAUX
Tout dommage subi par :
-- véhicules fluviaux,
-- véhicules lacustres,
-- véhicules maritimes.

11. RC VÉHICULES AÉRIENS
Toute responsabilité résultant de
l'emploi de véhicules aériens (y compris
la responsabilité transporteur).

12. RC VÉHICULES MARITIMES,
LACUSTRES ET FLUVIAUX
Toute responsabilité résultant de
l'emploi de véhicules fluviaux, lacustres

et maritimes (y compris la responsabilité du transporteur).

3. FRET

7. MARCHANDISES TRANSPORTÉES
(y compris les marchandises, bagages et tous autres biens)
Tout dommage subi par les marchandises transportées ou bagages, quel que soit le moyen de transport.

4. INCENDIE ET DOMMAGES AUX BIENS

8. INCENDIE ET ÉLÉMENTS NATURELS
Tout dommage subi par les biens (autres que les biens compris dans les branches 3, 4, 5, 6 et 7) lorsqu'il est causé par :
-- incendie,
-- explosion,
-- tempête,
-- éléments naturels autres que la tempête,
-- énergie nucléaire,
-- affaissement de terrain.

9. AUTRES DOMMAGES AUX BIENS
Tout dommage subi par les biens (autres que les biens compris dans les branches 3, 4, 5, 6 et 7) lorsque ce dommage est causé par la grêle ou la gelée, ainsi que par tout événement, tel le vol, autre que ceux compris sous 8.

5. PERTES PÉCUNIAIRES

14. CRÉDIT
-- insolvabilité générale
-- crédit à l'exportation
-- vente à tempérament
-- crédit hypothécaire
-- crédit agricole

15. CAUTION
-- caution directe
-- caution indirecte

16. PERTES PÉCUNIAIRES DIVERSES
-- risques liés à l'emploi
-- insuffisance de recettes (générale)
-- mauvais temps
-- perte de bénéfices
-- persistance de frais généraux
-- dépenses commerciales imprévues
-- perte de la valeur vénale
-- pertes de loyers ou de revenus
-- pertes commerciales indirectes autres que celles mentionnées précédemment
-- pertes pécuniaires non commerciales
-- autres pertes pécuniaires

6. RESPONSABILITÉ CIVILE GÉNÉRALE

13. RC GÉNÉRALE
Toute responsabilité autre que celles mentionnées sous les numéros 10, 11 et 12.

7. ACCIDENTS ET MALADIE

1. ACCIDENTS (y compris les accidents du travail et les maladies professionnelles)
-- prestations forfaitaires
-- prestations indemnitaires
-- personnes transportées

2. MALADIE
-- prestations forfaitaires
-- prestations indemnitaires
-- combinaisons

8. AUTRES ASSURANCES NON-VIE

17. PROTECTION JURIDIQUE
Protection juridique et coûts des litiges

18. ASSISTANCE

19. ASSURANCES DIVERSES

9. RÉASSURANCES OBLIGATOIRES

A. NUMBER OF COMPANIES IN THE REPORTING COUNTRY

A.1. Life
    A.1.1. Domestic Companies
      A.1.2. (Foreign Controlled Companies)
    A.1.3. Branches & Agencies of Foreign Cies
    A.1. All Companies
A.2. Non-Life
    A.2.1. Domestic Companies
      A.2.2. (Foreign Controlled Companies)
    A.2.3. Branches & Agencies of Foreign Cies
    A.2. All Companies
A.3. Composite
    A.3.1. Domestic Companies
      A.3.2. (Foreign Controlled Companies)
    A.3.3. Branches & Agencies of Foreign Cies
    A.3. All Companies
A.4. Reinsurance
    A.4.1. Domestic Companies
      A.4.2. (Foreign Controlled Companies)
    A.4.3. Branches & Agencies of Foreign Cies
    A.4. All Companies
A.5. Total
    A.5.1. Domestic Companies
      A.5.2. (Foreign Controlled Companies)
    A.5.3. Branches & Agencies of Foreign Cies
    A.5. All Insurance Companies

B. NUMBER OF EMPLOYEES

B.1. Insurance Companies
B.2. Intermediaries
B. Total

C. BUSINESS WRITTEN IN THE REPORTING COUNTRY

C.1. Life

C.1.1. Gross Premiums
    C.1.1.1. Direct Business
      C.1.1.1.1. Domestic Companies
        C.1.1.1.2. (Foreign Controlled Companies)
      C.1.1.1.3. Branches & Agencies of Foreign Cies
      C.1.1.1. Total
    C.1.1.2. Reinsurance Accepted
      C.1.1.2.1. Domestic Companies
        C.1.1.2.2. (Foreign Controlled Companies)
      C.1.1.2.3. Branches & Agencies of Foreign Cies
      C.1.1.2. Total
    C.1.1.3. Total
      C.1.1.3.1. Domestic Companies
        C.1.1.3.2. (Foreign Controlled Companies)
      C.1.1.3.3. Branches & Agencies of Foreign Cies
      C.1.1.3. Total Gross Premiums
C.1.2. Ceded Premiums
    C.1.2.1. Domestic Companies
      C.1.2.2. (Foreign Controlled Companies)
    C.1.2.3. Branches & Agencies of Foreign Cies
    C.1.2. Total
C.1.3. Net Written Premiums
    C.1.3.1. Domestic Companies
      C.1.3.2. (Foreign Controlled Companies)
    C.1.3.3. Branches & Agencies of Foreign Cies
    C.1.3. Total

C.2. Non-Life

C.2.1. Gross premiums
    C.2.1.1. Direct Business
      C.2.1.1.1. Domestic Companies
        C.2.1.1.2. (Foreign Controlled Companies)
      C.2.1.1.3. Branches & Agencies of Foreign Cies
      C.2.1.1. Total

A. NOMBRE D'ENTREPRISES DANS LE PAYS DECLARANT

A.1. Vie
    A.1.1. Entreprises nationales
      A.1.2. (Entreprises sous contrôle étranger)
    A.1.3. Succursales et agences d'ent. étrangères
    A.1. Ensemble des entreprises
A.2. Non-vie
    A.2.1. Entreprises nationales
      A.2.2. (Entreprises sous contrôle étranger)
    A.2.3. Succursales et agences d'ent. étrangères
    A.2. Ensemble des entreprises
A.3. Mixte
    A.3.1. Entreprises nationales
      A.3.2. (Entreprises sous contrôle étranger)
    A.3.3. Succursales et agences d'ent. étrangères
    A.3. Ensemble des entreprises
A.4. Réassurance
    A.4.1. Entreprises nationales
      A.4.2. (Entreprises sous contrôle étranger)
    A.4.3. Succursales et agences d'ent. étrangères
    A.4. Ensemble des entreprises
A.5. Total
    A.5.1. Entreprises nationales
      A.5.2. (Entreprises sous contrôle étranger)
    A.5.3. Succursales et agences d'ent. étrangères
    A.5. Ensemble des entreprises d'assurances

B. NOMBRE D'EMPLOYES

B.1. Entreprises d'assurances
B.2. Intermédiaires
B. Total

C. OPERATIONS CONCLUES DANS LE PAYS DECLARANT

C.1. Vie

C.1.1. Primes brutes
    C.1.1.1. Assurances directes
      C.1.1.1.1. Entreprises nationales
        C.1.1.1.2. (Entreprises sous contrôle étranger)
      C.1.1.1.3. Succursales et agences d'ent. étrangères
      C.1.1.1. Total
    C.1.1.2. Réassurance acceptée
      C.1.1.2.1. Entreprises nationales
        C.1.1.2.2. (Entreprises sous contrôle étranger)
      C.1.1.2.3. Succursales et agences d'ent. étrangères
      C.1.1.2. Total
    C.1.1.3. Total
      C.1.1.3.1. Entreprises nationales
        C.1.1.3.2. (Entreprises sous contrôle étranger)
      C.1.1.3.3. Succursales et agences d'ent. étrangères
      C.1.1.3. Total des primes brutes
C.1.2. Primes cédées
    C.1.2.1. Entreprises nationales
      C.1.2.2. (Entreprises sous contrôle étranger)
    C.1.2.3. Succursales et agences d'ent. étrangères
    C.1.2. Total
C.1.3. Primes nettes émises
    C.1.3.1. Entreprises nationales
      C.1.3.2. (Entreprises sous contrôle étranger)
    C.1.3.3. Succursales et agences d'ent. étrangères
    C.1.3. Total

C.2. Non-vie

C.2.1. Primes brutes
    C.2.1.1. Assurances directes
      C.2.1.1.1. Entreprises nationales
        C.2.1.1.2. (Entreprises sous contrôle étranger)
      C.2.1.1.3. Succursales et agences d'ent. étrangères
      C.2.1.1. Total

C.2.1.2. *Reinsurance Accepted*
    C.2.1.2.1. Domestic Companies
      C.2.1.2.2. (Foreign Controlled Companies)
    C.2.1.2.3. Branches & Agencies of Foreign Cies
    C.2.1.2. Total
C.2.1.3. *Total*
    C.2.1.3.1. Domestic Companies
      C.2.1.3.2. (Foreign Controlled Companies)
    C.2.1.3.3. Branches & Agencies of Foreign Cies
    C.2.1.3. Total Gross Premiums

C.2.2. Ceded Premiums
    C.2.2.1. Domestic Companies
      C.2.2.2. (Foreign Controlled Companies)
    C.2.2.3. Branches & Agencies of Foreign Cies
    C.2.2. Total
C.2.3. Net Written Premiums
    C.2.3.1. Domestic Companies
      C.2.3.2. (Foreign Controlled Companies)
    C.2.3.3. Branches & Agencies of Foreign Cies
    C.2.3. Total

C.3. Total

C.3.1. Gross Premiums
    C.3.1.1. *Direct Business*
      C.3.1.1.1. Domestic Companies
        C.3.1.1.2. (Foreign Controlled Companies)
      C.3.1.1.3. Branches & Agencies of Foreign Cies
      C.3.1.1. Total
    C.3.1.2. *Reinsurance Accepted*
      C.3.1.2.1. Domestic Companies
        C.3.1.2.2. (Foreign Controlled Companies)
      C.3.1.2.3. Branches & Agencies of Foreign Cies
      C.3.1.2. Total
    C.3.1.3. *Total*
      C.3.1.3.1. Domestic Companies
        C.3.1.3.2. (Foreign Controlled Companies)
      C.3.1.3.3. Branches & Agencies of Foreign Cies
      C.3.1.3. Total Gross Premiums
C.3.2. Ceded Premiums
    C.3.2.1. Domestic Companies
      C.3.2.2. (Foreign Controlled Companies)
    C.3.2.3. Branches & Agencies of Foreign Cies
    C.3.2. Total
C.3.3. Net Written Premiums
    C.3.3.1. Domestic Companies
      C.3.3.2. (Foreign Controlled Companies)
    C.3.3.3. Branches & Agencies of Foreign Cies
    C.3.3. Total

D. NET WRITTEN PREMIUMS IN THE REPORTING COUNTRY IN TERMS OF DOMESTIC AND FOREIGN RISKS

D.1. Life

D.1.1. Domestic Risks
    D.1.1.1. Domestic Companies
      D.1.1.2. (Foreign Controlled Companies)
    D.1.1.3. Branches & Agencies of Foreign Cies
    D.1.1. Total
D.1.2. Foreign Risks
    D.1.2.1. Domestic Companies
      D.1.2.2. (Foreign Controlled Companies)
    D.1.2.3. Branches & Agencies of Foreign Cies
    D.1.2. Total
D.1.3. Total
    D.1.3.1. Domestic Companies
      D.1.3.2. (Foreign Controlled Companies)
    D.1.3.3. Branches & Agencies of Foreign Cies
    D.1.3. Total of Life Net Premiums

D.2. Non-Life

D.2.1. Domestic Risks
    D.2.1.1. Domestic Companies
      D.2.1.2. (Foreign Controlled Companies)
    D.2.1.3. Branches & Agencies of Foreign Cies
    D.2.1. Total

C.2.1.2. *Réassurance acceptée*
    C.2.1.2.1. Entreprises nationales
      C.2.1.2.2. (Entreprises sous contrôle étranger)
    C.2.1.2.3. Succursales et agences d'ent. étrangères
    C.2.1.2. Total
C.2.1.3. *Total*
    C.2.1.3.1. Entreprises nationales
      C.2.1.3.2. (Entreprises sous contrôle étranger)
    C.2.1.3.3. Succursales et agences d'ent. étrangères
    C.2.1.3. Total des primes brutes

C.2.2. Primes cédées
    C.2.2.1. Entreprises nationales
      C.2.2.2. (Entreprises sous contrôle étranger)
    C.2.2.3. Succursales et agences d'ent. étrangères
    C.2.2. Total
C.2.3. Primes nettes émises
    C.2.3.1. Entreprises nationales
      C.2.3.2. (Entreprises sous contrôle étranger)
    C.2.3.3. Succursales et agences d'ent. étrangères
    C.2.3. Total

C.3. Total

C.3.1. Primes brutes
    C.3.1.1. *Assurances directes*
      C.3.1.1.1. Entreprises nationales
        C.3.1.1.2. (Entreprises sous contrôle étranger)
      C.3.1.1.3. Succursales et agences d'ent. étrangères
      C.3.1.1. Total
    C.3.1.2. *Réassurance acceptée*
      C.3.1.2.1. Entreprises nationales
        C.3.1.2.2. (Entreprises sous contrôle étranger)
      C.3.1.2.3. Succursales et agences d'ent. étrangères
      C.3.1.2. Total
    C.3.1.3. *Total*
      C.3.1.3.1. Entreprises nationales
        C.3.1.3.2. (Entreprises sous contrôle étranger)
      C.3.1.3.3. Succursales et agences d'ent. étrangères
      C.3.1.3. Total des primes brutes
C.3.2. Primes cédées
    C.3.2.1. Entreprises nationales
    C.3.2.2. (Entreprises sous contrôle étranger)
    C.3.2.3. Succursales et agences d'ent. étrangères
    C.3.2. Total
C.3.3. Primes nettes émises
    C.3.3.1. Entreprises nationales
      C.3.3.2. (Entreprises sous contrôle étranger)
    C.3.3.3. Succursales et agences d'ent. étrangères
    C.3.3. Total

D. Primes nettes émises DANS LE PAYS DECLARANT : RISQUES NATIONAUX ET ETRANGERS

D.1. Vie

D.1.1. Risques nationaux
    D.1.1.1. Entreprises nationales
      D.1.1.2. (Entreprises sous contrôle étranger)
    D.1.1.3. Succursales et agences d'ent. étrangères
    D.1.1. Total
D.1.2. Risques étrangers
    D.1.2.1. Entreprises nationales
      D.1.2.2. (Entreprises sous contrôle étranger)
    D.1.2.3. Succursales et agences d'ent. étrangères
    D.1.2. Total
D.1.3. Total
    D.1.3.1. Entreprises nationales
      D.1.3.2. (Entreprises sous contrôle étranger)
    D.1.3.3. Succursales et agences d'ent. étrangères
    D.1.3. Total des primes nettes vie

D.2. Non-vie

D.2.1. Risques nationaux
    D.2.1.1. Entreprises nationales
      D.2.1.2. (Entreprises sous contrôle étranger)
    D.2.1.3. Succursales et agences d'ent. étrangères
    D.2.1. Total

D.2.2. Foreign Risks	D.2.2. Risques étrangers
D.2.2.1. Domestic Companies	D.2.2.1. Entreprises nationales
D.2.2.2. (Foreign Controlled Companies)	D.2.2.2. (Entreprises sous contrôle étranger)
D.2.2.3. Branches & Agencies of Foreign Cies	D.2.2.3. Succursales et agences d'ent. étrangères
D.2.2. Total	D.2.2. Total
D.2.3. Total	D.2.3. Total
D.2.3.1. Domestic Companies	D.2.3.1. Entreprises nationales
D.2.3.2. (Foreign Controlled Companies)	D.2.3.2. (Entreprises sous contrôle étranger)
D.2.3.3. Branches & Agencies of Foreign Cies	D.2.3.3. Succursales et agences d'ent. étrangères
D.2.3. Total of Non-Life Net Premiums	D.2.3. Total des primes nettes non-vie

E. BUSINESS WRITTEN ABROAD — **E. OPERATIONS A L'ETRANGER**

E.1. Life — **E.1. Vie**

E.1.1. Gross Premiums	E.1.1. Primes brutes
E.1.1.1. Direct Business	*E.1.1.1. Assurance directe*
E.1.1.1.1. Branches & Agencies	E.1.1.1.1. Succursales & agences
E.1.1.1.2. Subsidiaries	E.1.1.1.2. Filiales
E.1.1.1. Total	E.1.1.1. Total
E.1.1.2. Reinsurance Accepted	*E.1.1.2. Réassurance acceptée*
E.1.1.2.1. Branches & Agencies	E.1.1.2.1. Succursales & agences
E.1.1.2.2. Subsidiaries	E.1.1.2.2. Filiales
E.1.1.2. Total	E.1.1.2. Total
E.1.1.3. Total	*E.1.1.3. Total*
E.1.1.3.1. Branches & Agencies	E.1.1.3.1. Succursales & agences
E.1.1.3.2. Subsidiaries	E.1.1.3.2. Filiales
E.1.1.3. Total Gross Premiums	E.1.1.3. Total des primes brutes
E.1.2. Ceded Premiums	E.1.2. Primes cédées
E.1.2.1. Branches & Agencies	E.1.2.1. Succursales & agences
E.1.2.2. Subsidiaries	E.1.2.2. Filiales
E.1.2. Total	E.1.2. Total
E.1.3. Net Written Premiums	E.1.3. Primes nettes émises
E.1.3.1. Branches & Agencies	E.1.3.1. Succursales & agences
E.1.3.2. Subsidiaries	E.1.3.2. Filiales
E.1.3. Total	E.1.3. Total

E.2. Non-Life — **E.2. Non-vie**

E.2.1. Gross Premiums	E.2.1. Primes brutes
E.2.1.1. Direct Business	*E.2.1.1. Assurance directe*
E.2.1.1.1. Branches & Agencies	E.2.1.1.1. Succursales & agences
E.2.1.1.2. Subsidiaries	E.2.1.1.2. Filiales
E.2.1.1. Total	E.2.1.1. Total
E.2.1.2. Reinsurance Accepted	*E.2.1.2. Réassurance acceptée*
E.2.1.2.1. Branches & Agencies	E.2.1.2.1. Succursales & agences
E.2.1.2.2. Subsidiaries	E.2.1.2.2. Filiales
E.2.1.2. Total	E.2.1.2. Total
E.2.1.3. Total	*E.2.1.3. Total*
E.2.1.3.1. Branches & Agencies	E.2.1.3.1. Succursales & agences
E.2.1.3.2. Subsidiaries	E.2.1.3.2. Filiales
E.2.1.3. Total Gross Premiums	E.2.1.3. Total des primes brutes
E.2.2. Ceded Premiums	E.2.2. Primes cédées
E.2.2.1. Branches & Agencies	E.2.2.1. Succursales & agences
E.2.2.2. Subsidiaries	E.2.2.2. Filiales
E.2.2. Total	E.2.2. Total
E.2.3. Net Written Premiums	E.2.3. Primes nettes émises
E.2.3.1. Branches & Agencies	E.2.3.1. Succursales & agences
E.2.3.2. Subsidiaries	E.2.3.2. Filiales
E.2.3. Total	E.2.3. Total

F. OUTSTANDING INVESTMENT BY DIRECT INSURANCE COMPANIES — **F. ENCOURS DES PLACEMENTS DES ENTREPRISES D'Assurances directes**

F.1. Life — **F.1. Vie**

F.1.1. Real Estate	F.1.1. Immobilier
F.1.1.1. Domestic Companies	F.1.1.1. Entreprises nationales
F.1.1.2. (Foreign Controlled Companies)	F.1.1.2. (Entreprises sous contrôle étranger)
F.1.1.3. Branches & Agencies of Foreign Cies	F.1.1.3. Succursales et agences d'ent. étrangères
F.1.1.4. Domestic Investment	F.1.1.4. Placement dans le pays
F.1.1.5. Foreign Investment	F.1.1.5. Placement à l'étranger
F.1.1. Total	F.1.1. Total
F.1.2. Mortgage Loans	F.1.2. Prêts hypothécaires
F.1.2.1. Domestic Companies	F.1.2.1. Entreprises nationales
F.1.2.2. (Foreign Controlled Companies)	F.1.2.2. (Entreprises sous contrôle étranger)
F.1.2.3. Branches & Agencies of Foreign Cies	F.1.2.3. Succursales et agences d'ent. étrangères
F.1.2.4. Domestic Investment	F.1.2.4. Placement dans le pays
F.1.2.5. Foreign Investment	F.1.2.5. Placement à l'étranger
F.1.2. Total	F.1.2. Total

F.1.3. Shares
    F.1.3.1. Domestic Companies
      F.1.3.2. (Foreign Controlled Companies)
    F.1.3.3. Branches & Agencies of Foreign Cies
    F.1.3.4. Domestic Investment
    F.1.3.5. Foreign Investment
    F.1.3.   Total
F.1.4. Bonds with Fixed Revenue
    F.1.4.1. Domestic Companies
      F.1.4.2. (Foreign Controlled Companies)
    F.1.4.3. Branches & Agencies of Foreign Cies
    F.1.4.4. Domestic Investment
    F.1.4.5. Foreign Investment
    F.1.4.   Total
F.1.5. Loans other than Mortgage Loans
    F.1.5.1. Domestic Companies
      F.1.5.2. (Foreign Controlled Companies)
    F.1.5.3. Branches & Agencies of Foreign Cies
    F.1.5.4. Domestic Investment
    F.1.5.5. Foreign Investment
    F.1.5.   Total
F.1.6. Other Investments
    F.1.6.1. Domestic Companies
      F.1.6.2. (Foreign Controlled Companies)
    F.1.6.3. Branches & Agencies of Foreign Cies
    F.1.6.4. Domestic Investment
    F.1.6.5. Foreign Investment
    F.1.6.   Total
F.1.7. Total
    F.1.7.1. Domestic Companies
      F.1.7.2. (Foreign Controlled Companies)
    F.1.7.3. Branches & Agencies of Foreign Cies
    F.1.7.4. Domestic Investment
    F.1.7.5. Foreign Investment
    F.1.7.   Total of Life Investments

F.2. Non-Life

F.2.1. Real Estate
    F.2.1.1. Domestic Companies
      F.2.1.2. (Foreign Controlled Companies)
    F.2.1.3. Branches & Agencies of Foreign Cies
    F.2.1.4. Domestic Investment
    F.2.1.5. Foreign Investment
    F.2.1.   Total
F.2.2. Mortgage Loans
    F.2.2.1. Domestic Companies
      F.2.2.2. (Foreign Controlled Companies)
    F.2.2.3. Branches & Agencies of Foreign Cies
    F.2.2.4. Domestic Investment
    F.2.2.5. Foreign Investment
    F.2.2.   Total
F.2.3. Shares
    F.2.3.1. Domestic Companies
      F.2.3.2. (Foreign Controlled Companies)
    F.2.3.3. Branches & Agencies of Foreign Cies
    F.2.3.4. Domestic Investment
    F.2.3.5. Foreign Investment
    F.2.3.   Total
F.2.4. Bonds with Fixed Revenue
    F.2.4.1. Domestic Companies
      F.2.4.2. (Foreign Controlled Companies)
    F.2.4.3. Branches & Agencies of Foreign Cies
    F.2.4.4. Domestic Investment
    F.2.4.5. Foreign Investment
    F.2.4.   Total
F.2.5. Loans other than Mortgage Loans
    F.2.5.1. Domestic Companies
      F.2.5.2. (Foreign Controlled Companies)
    F.2.5.3. Branches & Agencies of Foreign Cies
    F.2.5.4. Domestic Investment
    F.2.5.5. Foreign Investment
    F.2.5.   Total
F.2.6. Other Investments
    F.2.6.1. Domestic Companies
      F.2.6.2. (Foreign Controlled Companies)
    F.2.6.3. Branches & Agencies of Foreign Cies
    F.2.6.4. Domestic Investment
    F.2.6.5. Foreign Investment
    F.2.6.   Total

F.1.3. Actions
    F.1.3.1. Entreprises nationales
      F.1.3.2. (Entreprises sous contrôle étranger)
    F.1.3.3. Succursales et agences d'ent. étrangères
    F.1.3.4. Placement dans le pays
    F.1.3.5. Placement à l'étranger
    F.1.3.   Total
F.1.4. Obligations
    F.1.4.1. Entreprises nationales
      F.1.4.2. (Entreprises sous contrôle étranger)
    F.1.4.3. Succursales et agences d'ent. étrangères
    F.1.4.4. Placement dans le pays
    F.1.4.5. Placement à l'étranger
    F.1.4.   Total
F.1.5. Prêts autres qu'hypothécaires
    F.1.5.1. Entreprises nationales
      F.1.5.2. (Entreprises sous contrôle étranger)
    F.1.5.3. Succursales et agences d'ent. étrangères
    F.1.5.4. Placement dans le pays
    F.1.5.5. Placement à l'étranger
    F.1.5.   Total
F.1.6. Autres Placements
    F.1.6.1. Entreprises nationales
      F.1.6.2. (Entreprises sous contrôle étranger)
    F.1.6.3. Succursales et agences d'ent. étrangères
    F.1.6.4. Placement dans le pays
    F.1.6.5. Placement à l'étranger
    F.1.6.   Total
F.1.7. Total
    F.1.7.1. Entreprises nationales
      F.1.7.2. (Entreprises sous contrôle étranger)
    F.1.7.3. Succursales et agences d'ent. étrangères
    F.1.7.4. Placement dans le pays
    F.1.7.5. Placement à l'étranger
    F.1.7.   Total des placements vie

F.2. Non-vie

F.2.1. Immobilier
    F.2.1.1. Entreprises nationales
      F.2.1.2. (Entreprises sous contrôle étranger)
    F.2.1.3. Succursales et agences d'ent. étrangères
    F.2.1.4. Placement dans le pays
    F.2.1.5. Placement à l'étranger
    F.2.1.   Total
F.2.2. Prêts hypothécaires
    F.2.2.1. Entreprises nationales
      F.2.2.2. (Entreprises sous contrôle étranger)
    F.2.2.3. Succursales et agences d'ent. étrangères
    F.2.2.4. Placement dans le pays
    F.2.2.5. Placement à l'étranger
    F.2.2.   Total
F.2.3. Actions
    F.2.3.1. Entreprises nationales
      F.2.3.2. (Entreprises sous contrôle étranger)
    F.2.3.3. Succursales et agences d'ent. étrangères
    F.2.3.4. Placement dans le pays
    F.2.3.5. Placement à l'étranger
    F.2.3.   Total
F.2.4. Obligations
    F.2.4.1. Entreprises nationales
      F.2.4.2. (Entreprises sous contrôle étranger)
    F.2.4.3. Succursales et agences d'ent. étrangères
    F.2.4.4. Placement dans le pays
    F.2.4.5. Placement à l'étranger
    F.2.4.   Total
F.2.5. Prêts Autres qu'hypothécaires
    F.2.5.1. Entreprises nationales
      F.2.5.2. (Entreprises sous contrôle étranger)
    F.2.5.3. Succursales et agences d'ent. étrangères
    F.2.5.4. Placement dans le pays
    F.2.5.5. Placement à l'étranger
    F.2.5.   Total
F.2.6. Autres Placements
    F.2.6.1. Entreprises nationales
      F.2.6.2. (Entreprises sous contrôle étranger)
    F.2.6.3. Succursales et agences d'ent. étrangères
    F.2.6.4. Placement dans le pays
    F.2.6.5. Placement à l'étranger
    F.2.6.   Total

F.2.7. Total
- F.2.7.1. Domestic Companies
  - F.2.7.2. (Foreign Controlled Companies)
- F.2.7.3. Branches & Agencies of Foreign Cies
- F.2.7.4. Domestic Investment
- F.2.7.5. Foreign Investment
- F.2.7. Total of Non-Life Investments

G. BREAKDOWN OF NON-LIFE PREMIUMS

G.1. Motor vehicle
- G.1.1. Direct Business
  - G.1.1.1. Gross Premiums
  - G.1.1.2. Ceded Premiums
  - G.1.1.3. Net Written Premiums
- G.1.2. Reinsurance Accepted
  - G.1.2.1. Gross Premiums
  - G.1.2.2. Ceded Premiums
  - G.1.2.3. Net Written Premiums
- G.1.3. Total
  - G.1.3.1. Gross Premiums
  - G.1.3.2. Ceded Premiums
  - G.1.3.3. Net Written Premiums

G.2. Marine, Aviation
- G.2.1. Direct Business
  - G.2.1.1. Gross Premiums
  - G.2.1.2. Ceded Premiums
  - G.2.1.3. Net Written Premiums
- G.2.2. Reinsurance Accepted
  - G.2.2.1. Gross Premiums
  - G.2.2.2. Ceded Premiums
  - G.2.2.3. Net Written Premiums
- G.2.3. Total
  - G.2.3.1. Gross Premiums
  - G.2.3.2. Ceded Premiums
  - G.2.3.3. Net Written Premiums

G.3. Freight
- G.3.1. Direct Business
  - G.3.1.1. Gross Premiums
  - G.3.1.2. Ceded Premiums
  - G.3.1.3. Net Written Premiums
- G.3.2. Reinsurance Accepted
  - G.3.2.1. Gross Premiums
  - G.3.2.2. Ceded Premiums
  - G.3.2.3. Net Written Premiums
- G.3.3. Total
  - G.3.3.1. Gross Premiums
  - G.3.3.2. Ceded Premiums
  - G.3.3.3. Net Written Premiums

G.4. Fire, Property Damages
- G.4.1. Direct Business
  - G.4.1.1. Gross Premiums
  - G.4.1.2. Ceded Premiums
  - G.4.1.3. Net Written Premiums
- G.4.2. Reinsurance Accepted
  - G.4.2.1. Gross Premiums
  - G.4.2.2. Ceded Premiums
  - G.4.2.3. Net Written Premiums
- G.4.3. Total
  - G.4.3.1. Gross Premiums
  - G.4.3.2. Ceded Premiums
  - G.4.3.3. Net Written Premiums

G.5. Pecuniary Losses
- G.5.1. Direct Business
  - G.5.1.1. Gross Premiums
  - G.5.1.2. Ceded Premiums
  - G.5.1.3. Net Written Premiums
- G.5.2. Reinsurance Accepted
  - G.5.2.1. Gross Premiums
  - G.5.2.2. Ceded Premiums
  - G.5.2.3. Net Written Premiums
- G.5.3. Total
  - G.5.3.1. Gross Premiums
  - G.5.3.2. Ceded Premiums
  - G.5.3.3. Net Written Premiums

G.6. General Liability
- G.6.1. Direct Business
  - G.6.1.1. Gross Premiums
  - G.6.1.2. Ceded Premiums
  - G.6.1.3. Net Written Premiums

F.2.7. Total
- F.2.7.1. Entreprises nationales
  - F.2.7.2. (Entreprises sous contrôle étranger)
- F.2.7.3. Succursales et agences d'ent. étrangères
- F.2.7.4. Placement dans le pays
- F.2.7.5. Placement à l'étranger
- F.2.7. Total des placements non-vie

G. VENTILATIONS DES PRIMES Non-vie

G.1. Assurance automobile
- G.1.1. Assurances directes
  - G.1.1.1. Primes brutes
  - G.1.1.2. Primes cédées
  - G.1.1.3. Primes nettes émises
- G.1.2. Réassurance acceptée
  - G.1.2.1. Primes brutes
  - G.1.2.2. Primes cédées
  - G.1.2.3. Primes nettes émises
- G.1.3. Total
  - G.1.3.1. Primes brutes
  - G.1.3.2. Primes cédées
  - G.1.3.3. Primes nettes émises

G.2. Marine, aviation
- G.2.1. Assurances directes
  - G.2.1.1. Primes brutes
  - G.2.1.2. Primes cédées
  - G.2.1.3. Primes nettes émises
- G.2.2. Réassurance acceptée
  - G.2.2.1. Primes brutes
  - G.2.2.2. Primes cédées
  - G.2.2.3. Primes nettes émises
- G.2.3. Total
  - G.2.3.1. Primes brutes
  - G.2.3.2. Primes cédées
  - G.2.3.3. Primes nettes émises

G.3. Fret
- G.3.1. Assurances directes
  - G.3.1.1. Primes brutes
  - G.3.1.2. Primes cédées
  - G.3.1.3. Primes nettes émises
- G.3.2. Réassurance acceptée
  - G.3.2.1. Primes brutes
  - G.3.2.2. Primes cédées
  - G.3.2.3. Primes nettes émises
- G.3.3. Total
  - G.3.3.1. Primes brutes
  - G.3.3.2. Primes cédées
  - G.3.3.3. Primes nettes émises

G.4. Incendie, dommages aux biens
- G.4.1. Assurances directes
  - G.4.1.1. Primes brutes
  - G.4.1.2. Primes cédées
  - G.4.1.3. Primes nettes émises
- G.4.2. Réassurance acceptée
  - G.4.2.1. Primes brutes
  - G.4.2.2. Primes cédées
  - G.4.2.3. Primes nettes émises
- G.4.3. Total
  - G.4.3.1. Primes brutes
  - G.4.3.2. Primes cédées
  - G.4.3.3. Primes nettes émises

G.5. Pertes pécunières
- G.5.1. Assurances directes
  - G.5.1.1. Primes brutes
  - G.5.1.2. Primes cédées
  - G.5.1.3. Primes nettes émises
- G.5.2. Réassurance acceptée
  - G.5.2.1. Primes brutes
  - G.5.2.2. Primes cédées
  - G.5.2.3. Primes nettes émises
- G.5.3. Total
  - G.5.3.1. Primes brutes
  - G.5.3.2. Primes cédées
  - G.5.3.3. Primes nettes émises

G.6. Responsabilité générale
- G.6.1. Assurances directes
  - G.6.1.1. Primes brutes
  - G.6.1.2. Primes cédées
  - G.6.1.3. Primes nettes émises

G.6.2. Reinsurance Accepted
    G.6.2.1. Gross Premiums
    G.6.2.2. Ceded Premiums
    G.6.2.3. Net Written Premiums
G.6.3. Total
    G.6.3.1. Gross Premiums
    G.6.3.2. Ceded Premiums
    G.6.3.3. Net Written Premiums

G.7. Accident, Health
  G.7.1. Direct Business
    G.7.1.1. Gross Premiums
    G.7.1.2. Ceded Premiums
    G.7.1.3. Net Written Premiums
  G.7.2. Reinsurance Accepted
    G.7.2.1. Gross Premiums
    G.7.2.2. Ceded Premiums
    G.7.2.3. Net Written Premiums
  G.7.3. Total
    G.7.3.1. Gross Premiums
    G.7.3.2. Ceded Premiums
    G.7.3.3. Net Written Premiums

G.8. Others
  G.8.1. Direct Business
    G.8.1.1. Gross Premiums
    G.8.1.2. Ceded Premiums
    G.8.1.3. Net Written Premiums
  G.8.2. Reinsurance Accepted
    G.8.2.1. Gross Premiums
    G.8.2.2. Ceded Premiums
    G.8.2.3. Net Written Premiums
  G.8.3. Total
    G.8.3.1. Gross Premiums
    G.8.3.2. Ceded Premiums
    G.8.3.3. Net Written Premiums

G.9. Treaty Reinsurance
  G.9.1. Direct Business
    G.9.1.1. Gross Premiums
    G.9.1.2. Ceded Premiums
    G.9.1.3. Net Written Premiums
  G.9.2. Reinsurance Accepted
    G.9.2.1. Gross Premiums
    G.9.2.2. Ceded Premiums
    G.9.2.3. Net Written Premiums
  G.9.3. Total
    G.9.3.1. Gross Premiums
    G.9.3.2. Ceded Premiums
    G.9.3.3. Net Written Premiums

G.10. Total
  G.10.1. Direct Business
    G.10.1.1. Gross Premiums
    G.10.1.2. Ceded Premiums
    G.10.1.3. Net Written Premiums
  G.10.2. Reinsurance Accepted
    G.10.2.1. Gross Premiums
    G.10.2.2. Ceded Premiums
    G.10.2.3. Net Written Premiums
  G.10.3. Total
    G.10.3.1. Gross Premiums
    G.10.3.2. Ceded Premiums
    G.10.3.3. Net Written Premiums

H. GROSS CLAIMS PAYMENTS

H.1. Life
  H.1.1. Domestic Companies
  H.1.2. (Foreign Controlled Companies)
  H.1.3. Branches & Agencies of Foreign Cies
  H.1. Total
H.2. Non-Life
  H.2.1. Domestic Companies
  H.2.2. (Foreign Controlled Companies)
  H.2.3. Branches & Agencies Cies
  H.2. Total

G.6.2. Réassurance acceptée
    G.6.2.1. Primes brutes
    G.6.2.2. Primes cédées
    G.6.2.3. Primes nettes émises
G.6.3. Total
    G.6.3.1. Primes brutes
    G.6.3.2. Primes cédées
    G.6.3.3. Primes nettes émises

G.7. Accident, santé
  G.7.1. Assurances directes
    G.7.1.1. Primes brutes
    G.7.1.2. Primes cédées
    G.7.1.3. Primes nettes émises
  G.7.2. Réassurance acceptée
    G.7.2.1. Primes brutes
    G.7.2.2. Primes cédées
    G.7.2.3. Primes nettes émises
  G.7.3. Total
    G.7.3.1. Primes brutes
    G.7.3.2. Primes cédées
    G.7.3.3. Primes nettes émises

G.8. Autres
  G.8.1. Assurances directes
    G.8.1.1. Primes brutes
    G.8.1.2. Primes cédées
    G.8.1.3. Primes nettes émises
  G.8.2. Réassurance acceptée
    G.8.2.1. Primes brutes
    G.8.2.2. Primes cédées
    G.8.2.3. Primes nettes émises
  G.8.3. Total
    G.8.3.1. Primes brutes
    G.8.3.2. Primes cédées
    G.8.3.3. Primes nettes émises

G.9. Réassurance obligatoire
  G.9.1. Assurances directes
    G.9.1.1. Primes brutes
    G.9.1.2. Primes cédées
    G.9.1.3. Primes nettes émises
  G.9.2. Réassurance acceptée
    G.9.2.1. Primes brutes
    G.9.2.2. Primes cédées
    G.9.2.3. Primes nettes émises
  G.9.3. Total
    G.9.3.1. Primes brutes
    G.9.3.2. Primes cédées
    G.9.3.3. Primes nettes émises

G.10. Total
  G.10.1. Assurances directes
    G.10.1.1. Primes brutes
    G.10.1.2. Primes cédées
    G.10.1.3. Primes nettes émises
  G.10.2. Réassurance acceptée
    G.10.2.1. Primes brutes
    G.10.2.2. Primes cédées
    G.10.2.3. Primes nettes émises
  G.10.3. Total
    G.10.3.1. Primes brutes
    G.10.3.2. Primes cédées
    G.10.3.3. Primes nettes émises

H. SINISTRES BRUTS

H.1. Vie
  H.1.1. Entreprises nationales
  H.1.2. (Entreprises sous contrôle étranger)
  H.1.3. Succursales et agences d'ent. étrangère
  H.1. Total
H.2. Non-vie
  H.2.1. Entreprises nationales
  H.2.2. (Entreprises sous contrôle étranger)
  H.2.3. Succursales et agences d'ent. étrangère
  H.2. Total

I. GROSS OPERATING EXPENSES

I.1. Life
    I.1.1. Domestic Companies
      I.1.2. (Foreign Controlled Companies)
    I.1.3. Branches & Agencies of Foreign Cies
    I.1.   Total

I.2. Non-Life
    I.2.1. Domestic Companies
      I.2.2. (Foreign Controlled Companies)
    I.2.3. Branches & Agencies of Foreign Cies
    I.2.   Total

J. COMMISSIONS

J.1. Life
    J.1.1. Direct Business
        J.1.1.1. Domestic Companies
          J.1.1.2. (Foreign Controlled Companies)
        J.1.1.3. Branches & Agencies of Foreign Cies
        J.1.1.   Total
    J.1.2. Reinsurance Accepted
        J.1.2.1. Domestic Companies
          J.1.2.2. (Foreign Controlled Companies)
        J.1.2.3. Branches & Agencies of Foreign Cies
        J.1.2.   Total
    J.1.3. Total
        J.1.3.1. Domestic Companies
          J.1.3.2. (Foreign Controlled Companies)
        J.1.3.3. Branches & Agencies of Foreign Cies
        J.1.3.   Total
J.2. Non-Life
    J.2.1. Direct Business
        J.2.1.1. Domestic Companies
          J.2.1.2. (Foreign Controlled Companies)
        J.2.1.3. Branches & Agencies of Foreign Cies
        J.2.1.   Total
    J.2.2. Reinsurance Accepted
        J.2.2.1. Domestic Companies
          J.2.2.2. (Foreign Controlled Companies)
        J.2.2.3. Branches & Agencies of Foreign Cies
        J.2.2.   Total
    J.2.3. Total
        J.2.3.1. Domestic Companies
          J.2.3.2. (Foreign Controlled Companies)
        J.2.3.3. Branches & Agencies of Foreign Cies
        J.2.3.   Total

I. DEPENSES BRUTES

I.1. Vie
    I.1.1. Entreprises nationales
      I.1.2. (Entreprises sous contrôle étranger)
    I.1.3. Succursales et agences d'ent. étrangère
    I.1.   Total

I.2. Non-vie
    I.2.1. Entreprises nationales
      I.2.2. (Entreprises sous contrôle étranger)
    I.2.3. Succursales et agences d'ent. étrangère
    I.2.   Total

J. COMMISSIONS

J.1. Vie
    J.1.1. Assurance directe
        J.1.1.1. Entreprises nationales
          J.1.1.2. (Entreprises sous contrôle étranger)
        J.1.1.3. Succursales et agences d'ent. étrangère
        J.1.1.   Total
    J.1.2. Réassurances acceptées
        J.1.2.1. Entreprises nationales
          J.1.2.2. (Entreprises sous contrôle étranger)
        J.1.2.3. Succursales et agences d'ent. étrangère
        J.1.2.   Total
    J.1.3. Total
        J.1.3.1. Entreprises nationales
          J.1.3.2. (Entreprises sous contrôle étranger)
        J.1.3.3. Succursales et agences d'ent. étrangère
        J.1.3.   Total
J.2. Non-Life
    J.2.1. Assurance directe
        J.2.1.1. Entreprises nationales
          J.2.1.2. (Entreprises sous contrôle étranger)
        J.2.1.3. Succursales et agences d'ent. étrangère
        J.2.1.   Total
    J.2.2. Réassurances acceptées
        J.2.2.1. Entreprises nationales
          J.2.2.2. (Entreprises sous contrôle étranger)
        J.2.2.3. Succursales et agences d'ent. étrangère
        J.2.2.   Total
    J.2.3. Total
        J.2.3.1. Entreprises nationales
          J.2.3.2. (Entreprises sous contrôle étranger)
        J.2.3.3. Succursales et agences d'ent. étrangère
        J.2.3.   Total

V. BUSINESS WRITTEN ABROAD BY EU/EEA INSURERS THROUGH BRANCHES AND AGENCIES
V. OPERATIONS DES ASSUREURS DE L'UE/EEE A L'ETRANGER PAR DES AGENCES ET SUCCURSALES

LIFE INSURANCE / ASSURANCE VIE (1999)

Direct Gross Premiums / Primes brutes directes

Monetary Unit = million of the local currency of each home country / Unité monétaire: en millions de monnaie nationale

HOME COUNTRY / PAYS D'ACCUEIL \ PAYS D'ORIGINE	Austria / Autriche (S)	Belgium / Belgique (BFr)	Denmark / Danemark (DKr)	Finland / Finlande (Fmk)	France / France (FF)	Germany / Allemagne (DM)	Greece / Grèce[1] (Dr)	Iceland / Islande (ISK)	Ireland / Irlande (I£)	Italy / Italie (Lit)	Luxembourg / Luxembourg (LuxF)	Netherlands / Pays-Bas (Fl)	Norway / Norvège (NKr)	Portugal / Portugal (Esc)	Spain / Espagne (Ptas)	Sweden / Suède (SKr)	United Kingdom / Royaume-Uni (£)
Austria / Autriche						65	1										--
Belgium / Belgique					7							--					--
Denmark / Danemark						17						--					--
Finland / Finlande			30														--
France / France		90							8					5 525		1	--
Germany / Allemagne		62					14 749							10			--
Greece / Grèce						4											--
Iceland / Islande																	--
Ireland / Irlande		51															--
Italy / Italie		12			13				72		--			2 028			--
Luxembourg / Luxembourg		709									--						--
Netherlands / Pays-Bas		280			79	1						--					--
Norway / Norvège		29	131						1		--					22	--
Portugal / Portugal		1			112										16 383		--
Spain / Espagne		7			13												--
Sweden / Suède		27		2 430			743							454			--
United Kingdom / Royaume-Uni		1 150							6	87 146							
EU 15 + EEA Total / Total de l'UE 15 + EEE	0	2 417	161	2 430	223	87	15 493	0	87	87 146	11788	--	0	8 017	16 383	23	--
Total Other OECD countries / Total autres pays OCDE	0	--	0	--	--	--	--	0	--	--	0	--	0	--	0	0	--
Total Outside OECD countries / Total des pays hors de l'OCDE	0	--	0	--	--	--	--	0	--	40 077	0	--	0	--	461	0	--
TOTAL	0	2 424	161	2 430	243	87	15 493	0	87	127 223	11788	--	0	8 017	16 844	23	--

[1] Total gross premiums / Primes brutes totales

NON-LIFE INSURANCE / ASSURANCE NON-VIE (1999)

Direct Gross Premiums / Primes brutes directes

Monetary Unit = million of the local currency of each home country / Unité monétaire: en millions de monnaie nationale

HOME COUNTRY / PAYS D'ORIGINE (columns) — **HOST COUNTRY / PAYS D'ACCUEIL** (rows)

HOST COUNTRY / PAYS D'ACCUEIL	Austria / Autriche (S)	Belgium / Belgique (BFr)	Denmark / Danemark (DKr)	Finland / Finlande (Fmk)	France / France (FF)	Germany / Allemagne (DM)	Greece / Grèce (Dr)	Iceland / Islande (ISK)	Ireland / Irlande (IE)	Italy / Italie (Lit)	Luxembourg / Luxembourg (LuxF)	Netherlands / Pays-Bas (Fl)	Norway / Norvège (NKr)	Portugal / Portugal¹ (Esc)	Spain / Espagne (Ptas)	Sweden / Suède (SKr)	United Kingdom / Royaume-Uni (£)
Austria / Autriche		227			20	73	--					--					--
Belgium / Belgique				1	741	112	--			8 604		--			1		--
Denmark / Danemark		1 174			144	29	--			3 237		--	382			1 443	--
Finland / Finlande		148	3		52		--					--				13	--
France / France		13 413	4	4		300	--			13 270		--		512	156	59	--
Germany / Allemagne		5 238	10		833		--			11 581		--		399		71	--
Greece / Grèce		49			46	45						--		3 186	27		--
Iceland / Islande		5					--					--					--
Ireland / Irlande		1 685				9	--			47 646		--			77		--
Italy / Italie		4 480			932	84	--		1			--					--
Luxembourg / Luxembourg		1 969			59	4	--					--		14			--
Netherlands / Pays-Bas		3 474	- 1	- 8	276	92	--			6 465				- 1	40	27	--
Norway / Norvège		609	36		98	24	--					--				6 675	--
Portugal / Portugal		65			92	10	--			82 985		--			6 065		--
Spain / Espagne		2 341	2		479	65	--			32		--		1 559			--
Sweden / Suède		1 473	73	33	138	3	--					--	179		1 043		--
United Kingdom / Royaume-Uni		28 481	3	1	1 476	258	--		76	267 093		--		10		75	
EU 15 + EEA Total / Total de l'UE 15 + EEE	0	64 830	130	31	5 386	1 108	--	0	77	440 913	271	--	561	5 679	7 409	8 363	--
Total Other OECD countries / Total autres pays OCDE	0	..	..	..	--	225	..	0	..	283 347	..	..	..	--	126	..	..
Total Outside OECD countries / Total des pays hors de l'OCDE	0	..	..	..	--	23	..	0	..	51 506	..	..	..	--	2 130	..	..
TOTAL	0	67 802	159	31	5 904	1 356	--	0	77	775 766	271	--	..	5 679	9 665	9 483	--

¹ Total gross premiums / Primes brutes totales

317

OECD PUBLICATIONS, 2, rue André-Pascal, 75775 PARIS CEDEX 16
PRINTED IN FRANCE
(21 2001 07 3 P) ISBN 92-64-08663-3 – No. 51992 2001